AFRICA

AFRICA

A Social, Economic, and Political Geography of its Major Regions

Walter Fitzgerald

Tenth edition revised by

W. C. BRICE

*Lecturer in Geography
in the University of Manchester*

METHUEN & CO LTD
11 NEW FETTER LANE LONDON EC4

First Published July 19th 1934
Second Edition February 1936
Third Edition, Revised, July 1940
Fourth Edition June 1943
Fifth Edition January 1946
Sixth Edition, Revised, January 1949
Seventh Edition, Revised, September 1950
Reprinted July 1952
Eighth Edition, Revised, October 1955
Reprinted (with minor corrections) 1957
Ninth Edition 1961
Reprinted 1964
Tenth Edition 1967
Reprinted 1968

S.B.N. 416 30080 4

10.2

PRINTED AND BOUND IN GREAT BRITAIN BY
BUTLER AND TANNER LTD, FROME AND LONDON

TO
PERCY MAUDE ROXBY

PREFACE TO THE TENTH EDITION

THE most notable changes during the last few years have been in the realm of political geography. As more territories become independent, three main factors appear to be shaping the political map of the continent: the ethnic ties, of which Africans seem to be becoming increasingly conscious, and which often, as with the Somali, the Bakongo, and the Lunda, are felt across existing frontiers; the old links of culture and loyalty which continue to bind members of the French Community and of the British Commonwealth, for example; and the practical arguments of economic advantage which have inspired various plans for federal association. This revision has attempted to show how these motives, which sometimes work in opposition, may influence the evolution of the map of Africa. In addition, special note has been made of the new industries which are being set up in various parts of the continent; of the schemes of river control to which these industries are often connected; and of the new discoveries of oil, in Algeria, in Nigeria, and possibly also in Angola. There is no doubt that the Sahara, with its oil, iron and artesian water, will very soon become much more significant in the economic geography of Africa.

W. C. B.

Manchester
April, 1966

CONTENTS

MAPS

AFRICA

PART I

THE PHYSICAL ENVIRONMENT

CHAPTER I

STRUCTURE AND CONFIGURATION

STAGES IN THE EVOLUTION OF THE AFRICAN PLATEAU

IN its structure as in its relief Africa is the continent of simplest form and provides a marked contrast with the complexity of Eurasia. By far the greater part consists of a plateau of marked geological stability, whose foundation of ancient (Archaean) rocks has resisted compressional and tensional movements of the earth's crust. Within the limits of the Plateau there is an absence of recent, folded mountain systems such as result from the compression of crustal strata. Flanking the Plateau on its extreme north-western and southern margins, however, such folded mountain systems occur, in the Atlas and Cape regions respectively, and the mountain-building of these marginal lands has greatly complicated their geology and physical geography.

The Archaean base or platform is actually exposed at the surface over areas which, in the aggregate, equal about one-third of the superficies of Africa. Such intermittent outcroppings of the continental core have been mapped from the Guinea region as far east as Somaliland and from the Union of South Africa to Southern Egypt.

The primitive rocks of Africa have been investigated most thoroughly where they outcrop in South Africa and there a detailed geological sequence has been worked out. These pre-Palaeozoic rocks are classified together by the local geologists as the ' Pre-Cape Systems '. The oldest, the Swaziland system consisting of gneisses and schists, are believed to provide the

greater part of the continental core : in character and age they
may be compared with the Laurentian Shield series of Canada.
Other pre-Palaeozoic rocks include the Witwatersrand and
Transvaal systems which are composed of quartzites, limestones and schists. No fossils have been discovered in these
ancient systems. They have great mineral-bearing importance,
for they supply the rich copper-fields of Katanga (Belgian Congo)
and Northern Rhodesia, together with the gold fields of the
Gold Coast and, greatest of all, of the Transvaal, where the
gold is a constituent of quartzitic conglomerates belonging
to the Witwatersrand system of sedimentary rocks. Another
Archaean system which includes, as a prominent member, the
Waterberg sandstone—investigated most thoroughly in the
Northern Transvaal—is comparable in age with the well-known
Torridonian sandstone of North Scotland.

Most of the African Plateau has stood above sea-level since
Archaean times, but intermittently from the Devonian Age onwards the sea has advanced over the continental margins,
occasionally extending gulfs into the northern interior from
the present site of the Mediterranean Sea. On the floor of the
submerged margins limestones were deposited and now, un-
submerged and exposed, they bear witness to the marine invasion.

Palaeozoic rocks older than Devonian are rare in Africa,
and the system which corresponds to the Devonian of Europe
is the earliest which includes extensive fossiliferous beds. Such
sediments occur in the Cape Province of South Africa as well as
widely in the Sahara and the Western Sudan. Continuing the
geological sequence, the Carboniferous system contains very
extensive land deposits, especially notable of which are those
of the lower Karroo beds in the Union of South Africa : these
are Upper Carboniferous in age and, like the corresponding
series of Europe, include very valuable coal-seams. Outside the
Union similar coal-bearing beds occur in Tanganyika Territory,
Nyasaland and Southern Rhodesia. At times in the Carboniferous epoch the sea invaded the extremities of the continent,
notably in parts of Egypt and the Cape Province, where marine
limestones of this age are found.

At the close of Triassic times the sea reached the East African
littoral, as indicated by the occurrence of Jurassic marine beds
on the coasts of Tanganyika, Kenya and Somaliland ; and at
this time a sea-gulf intervened between the mainland and Madagascar which, like the parent continent, consists fundamentally
of Archaean gneisses and schists. On the western side of the
island, as on the opposite mainland shore, marine Jurassic deposits
indicate the existence of an ancient Mozambique Channel.

During the Cretaceous Age (late Mesozoic) a sea-strait extended from the present site of the Mediterranean across the Central Sahara to Southern Nigeria, the Camerouns and Angola.

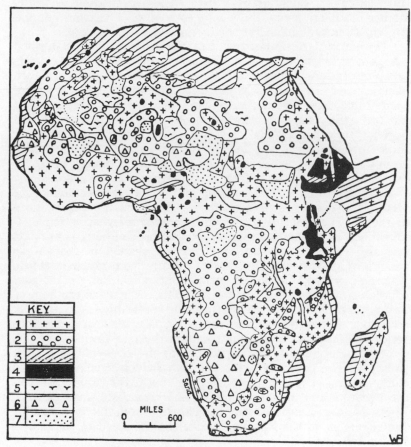

FIG. 1.—The surface rocks of Africa

1. Archaean, including the Pre-Cape Systems of South Africa.
2. Palaeozoic and Early Mesozoic rocks, with sandstones very prominent.
3. Rocks of marine origin, from the Jurassic to the Tertiary.
4. Volcanic rocks of different ages.
5. Drifted sand.
6. Sands, outside the desert, that are fixed by vegetation. (Sudan and Kalahari.)
7. Alluvium.
   (For areas where no symbols are shown there is lack of information.)

Marine rocks of this phase are well developed in the Atlas region, much of which was then occupied by sea. At the south-eastern extremity of the continent, near or on the coasts of Portuguese East Africa, Natal and the Cape Province, marine Cretaceous rocks are again found.

Subsequent marine invasions, in Tertiary times, were mainly confined to the continental area north of the Equator, and in the Eocene period limestones were laid down in a sea which, at one time, extended widely across North Africa from lower Egypt to Morocco, whilst, as in the Cretaceous Age, a marine channel stretched across the Sahara to Nigeria and the Camerouns.

Throughout the Palaeozoic Era the African Plateau formed a large interior fragment of a vast continent, known to geologists as Gondwanaland, which included—on the west—much of South America (e.g. the Brazilian Plateau) and—on the east—Peninsular India (the Deccan) and the greater part of Australia.[1] By the early phases of the Mesozoic Era Gondwanaland had begun to undergo gradual disruption and thus there ultimately came into existence the Atlantic and Indian Oceans, which occupy the wide intervals between the great fragments of Gondwanaland that appear on the map of the modern world.

In order to explain the disintegration of Gondwanaland the views of two schools of geological theory will be briefly summarized. The differing hypotheses provide alternative explanations, not only for the separation of the southern continents but also for the existence of the great system of trough-like valleys which traverse East Africa mainly from north to south. Although remarkably stable throughout much the greater part of geological time the African Plateau, in its eastern region, has undergone extensive faulting and fissuring comparatively recently. There has been formed in consequence a continuous series of deep narrow troughs to which the late Professor J. W. Gregory applied the useful and graphic term—'Great Rift Valley'. The generally orthodox view held by geologists, until thirty years or so ago, concerning both the origin of this great feature and the disruption of Gondwanaland was published in its most persuasive form by Gregory and, after describing the alignment of the Rift Valley, we shall proceed to summarize his conclusions.[2]

The Great Rift Valley : Gregory's Hypothesis

This major feature of the physical geography and geology of East Africa can be traced from north to south over one-sixth of the earth's circumference and may be taken as beginning in Northern Syria. The Dead Sea, Jordan Valley and the Gulf of Akaba lie along its course, whilst the trough of the Red Sea

---

[1] Antarctica was also included.

[2] Gregory's views were summarized in *The Rift Valleys and Geology of East Africa*, London, 1921. More recent work on the causative factors in African geography and geology is admirably condensed by du Toit. (See p. 27.)

may be considered to form the connecting link between the northern, or Asiatic, section of the Great Rift and its southern continuation in East Africa. Although the Red Sea narrows to 14 miles at the Straits of Bab-el-Mandeb the depression between the Arabian and Abyssinian Plateaux, of which the southern waters of the Red Sea fill only a part, continues its south-eastward trend with approximately the same width as that of the northern Red Sea basin : its western wall which is the eastern scarp of Abyssinia is parallel to the Arabian and not to the African coast. Between Abyssinia and the ancient *horst* of Somaliland opens the northern gateway to the African section of the Great Rift Valley.

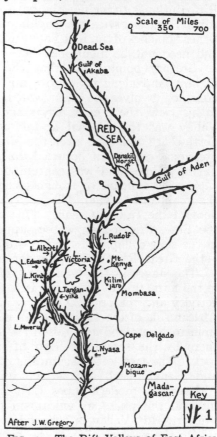

Following its course southwards past the southern end of Lake Rudolf we find that in Kenya Colony the Rift Valley forms a deep, steeply-walled trench whose course is indicated by a chain of small lakes including Naivasha. Southwards again, in Tanganyika Territory, the definition of the walls is not so clear, partly owing to the processes of erosion, but along the borders of Lake Nyasa the sharply-cut outline of the trough is repeated. This great lake, very deep and fjord-like, with a length of

FIG. 2.—The Rift Valleys of East Africa
1. Boundaries of the rift valleys.

360 miles and a width of only 15–20 miles, is due to the collapse of a crustal block along parallel north-south faults whose lines are easily perceptible even on a small-scale map. The normal outlet of the Lake—the Shiré River—flows southwards along the continuation of the Rift Valley, which has been traced to the coast in the neighbourhood of Beira (Portuguese East Africa).

The principal line of the Rift Valley, whose course has been followed, is joined near the northern end of Lake Nyasa by a long and continuous branch usually known as the Western Rift Valley. Within this subsidiary system of troughs lies Lake Tanganyika, the greatest of the natural reservoirs of the Rift Valley and, after Lake Baikal, the deepest lake of the world, with a sounding of more than 4700 feet. Northwards the Western Rift continues to include the basins of Lakes Kivu, Edward and Albert, together with the neighbouring section of the Nile Valley. Other branches of the Rift Valley are of only secondary importance and need not be mentioned here.

Gregory pointed out that the Rift Valley cuts across the highest land along its course, and his explanation of this phenomenon involves the theory which is outlined below. According to his view, the preparatory stage of the evolution of the Rift Valley was the gradual up-folding of a crustal arch along a north-south axis and over the site of East Africa. This compressional movement occurred during Cretaceous and very early Tertiary times and was contemporary with the formation of a submerged syncline or trough which separated Madagascar from the mainland.[1] Then followed the gradual foundering of the floor of the Indian Ocean. This vast dislocation reacted upon the East African arch whose supports were weakened, resulting in the slow collapse of the key-stone. Thus—in Gregory's view —the Great Rift Valley was formed.

The stages in the foundering of the Indian Ocean floor and in the formation of the Great Rift were accompanied by volcanic activity and the pouring forth of lava on a vast scale. On the African side of the Indian Ocean eruptions extended from Abyssinia to Nyasaland and raised the level of the Plateau here and there by the superimposition of successive outflows of molten rock. The two loftiest summits of Africa, Mounts Kilimanjaro and Kenya—each an old volcano—were similarly built up. Although in modern times East Africa is experiencing a quiet interval the phase of vulcanism in the neighbourhood of the Western Rift Valley is believed to have not yet terminated.

On the western side of the continent along lines of fracture associated with the formation of the Atlantic Ocean volcanic activity raised the still active crater of the Camerouns Mountain and the chain of islands in the Gulf of Biafra, viz. Fernando Po, São Thomé, Principe and Annobon.

Contemporary with the crustal disturbances in East Africa there were similar events in India, where great lava outpourings produced the ' Deccan Traps ' that cover about 250,000 square

[1] In the Oligocene (Tertiary) period Madagascar was temporarily re-united to the continent.

miles of peninsular India. Yet another great episode, contemporary with the evolution of the Great Rift Valley, was the mountain-building of Eurasia which raised the massive Alpine and Himalayan chains. Africa was affected on its north-western margin, for the Atlas ranges belong to the Alpine system which encloses the western basin of the Mediterranean.

Before leaving Gregory's hypothesis which is based on the events that have been described, his view concerning the causes of continental destruction in the case of Gondwanaland is to be noted. Gregory postulates that during the great part of the Jurassic and Cretaceous Ages, when the earth was comparatively quiescent, the slow shrinkage of the crust proceeded, so as ultimately to produce a condition of instability of which the colossal fracturing and foundering already indicated were the outcome.

Wegener's Theory of Continental Displacement as applied to Africa

After investigating the same set of geological events that have been described the late Professor Wegener reached a very different conclusion regarding their origins from that of Gregory, and his hypothesis of ' Continental Displacement ', or ' Continental Drift '—as it is more popularly known—requires our attention in so far as it relates to the origin of the African continent and of the Rift Valley.

Wegener concluded that the oceanic basins and the continental masses do not form, respectively, temporary inundations and elevations of the earth's crust, but that they correspond to fundamental differences in the composition and density of the rocks of the continents and of the ocean floor. The continental rocks as a whole are comparatively low in density and consist mainly of granite and gneiss, for the sedimentary strata that are exposed so widely on the earth's surface are superficial only. On the other hand the rocks underlying the ocean basins are of higher density, being more basic in character, and rocks or magma of this type are believed to underlie the acid rocks of the continents, which float and drift like icebergs in the denser substratum.

The inspiration for this theory came partly from a consideration of the outlines of the South Atlantic coasts of Africa and South America. Wegener noted that the great right-angled bulge of Brazil which has Cape San Roque at its apex would fit closely into the West African indentation of the Biafra Bight, if the two continents were contiguous ; furthermore, that southwards from these latitudes every promontory on the coast of one continent has its counterpart in a bay of similar outline on the opposite shore.

This strange correspondence is explained by the view that
South America, Africa, Antarctica, India and Australia were at
one time attached in a single continent which, during Jurassic
times, began to split into parts corresponding to the above-mentioned land masses; and that these drifted away from each
other, leaving gradually-widening oceanic gaps. It will be
remembered that Gregory explains the existence of the oceanic
basins not by the drifting apart of continental fragments but by
the foundering of vast earth-blocks.

Assuming that the South Atlantic represents a gradually-widening rift caused by the westward floating-away of South
America it should be possible not only to find analogies in the

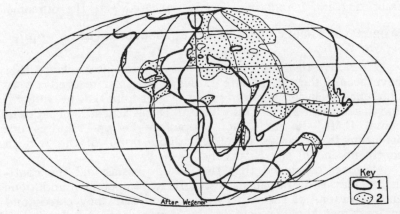

FIG. 3.—Wegener's re-construction of the Map of the World for early Tertiary
times

(Note that S. America, Africa and Arabia are contiguous and that South Africa and peninsular India are
but narrowly separated from each other)

1. Continental boundaries.
2. Shallow seas.

configuration of the coasts of South America and Africa, but
also to trace the continuation of the same structural and orographical features across the dividing ocean. Wegener supplies
evidence of this kind : in the Cape Province, for example, there
is a folded mountain range—the Zwartebergen—whose axial line
runs east-west ; and in the Sierras of the Province of Buenos
Aires Wegener indicates the presence of a closely similar folded
system of related strata. Again, the vast and stable Archaean
plateau of Africa resembles in all important geological respects
the Brazilian Plateau. Furthermore, biologists who have compared the plant forms of South America and Africa believe that

certain close resemblances between them are best explained by a theory that admits the former contiguity of the two continents.

Certain critics of Wegener challenged his fitting the masses of Africa and South America together by their coast-lines rather than by the submerged margins of their continental shelves. Wegener accepted his error in this, though in any case the validity of his argument was not affected fundamentally.

According to Wegener, therefore, tensional forces have produced the great ocean rifts and the present isolation of the southern continents. He explains the African Rift Valley by the tearing apart of the East African Plateau, and believes that the enormous fissure is likely to increase in width so as to complete the disruption of Eastern Africa. The up-turning of the margins of the Great Rift which Gregory explains, it will be remembered, by faulting and collapse along the summit of an arch is considered by Wegener to be due to isostatic compensation which has left the deceptive impression that the trench passes longitudinally through an anticline.

In 1921, E. J. Wayland, after investigating the Lake Albert region, put forward a different hypothesis, according to which neither arching nor tension were responsible for the rift ; the cause was compression, which produced crustal fractures and forced upwards the margins of the rift valleys. In 1930, Bailey Willis produced further evidence to support Wayland's theory. Bullard in 1936 investigated gravity anomalies in East Africa and found an excess of light matter under the rift, which suggested that horizontal compression of the margins was holding down the floor of the valley. A number of regional studies all indicate that the present system is the result of a complex series of movements extending from a very early epoch.

CONFIGURATION AND DRAINAGE

The following survey of the surface form and drainage systems of Africa is intended to be general and introductory only : more detailed consideration is left for the separate regional studies that follow.

The African Plateau extends uninterruptedly from the Guinea Coast to Somaliland and from the northern margins of the Sahara to the central districts of the Cape Province. It has no modern fold mountains, for the Atlas ranges lie beyond, pressed against its north-western flanks ; and the only important folded system of greater antiquity which is still prominent in relief is that— in the extreme south—which includes the east-west trending

Zwartebergen and Langebergen of the southern districts of the
Cape.

Much of the highest land of the Plateau—apart from isolated
and comparatively rare peaks—owes its present eminence to the
reduction of the surrounding country by the processes of erosion

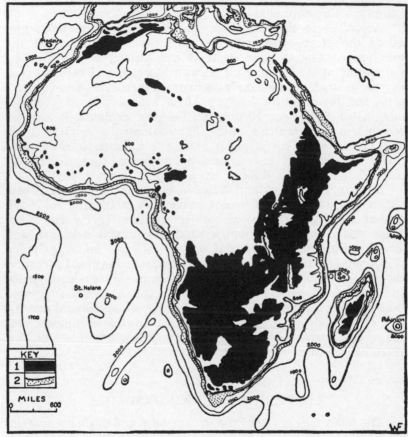

FIG. 4.—The African plateau and neighbouring oceanic depths

1. Land more than 3,000 feet above sea-level.
2. Continental shelf, as far as the isobath of 100 fathoms. The contour of 600 feet and the isobaths
of 1,000, 2,000 and 3,000 fathoms are also shown.

and to its own greater resistance ; while in certain elevated
districts, such as Abyssinia and the East African Plateau, the
pouring out of lava in recent geological time has raised the surface
level over wide areas. Within the limits of the Plateau the
loftiest summits are almost invariably volcanic masses piled up
on the surface of an already high plateau : such are the craters

of Kilimanjaro, Kenya, Elgon and Ras Dashan (Abyssinia), all of which are in East Africa.[1] Mount Ruwenzori (16,790 ft.), also rising from the East African Plateau, is of different origin and represents a block of the ancient land surface which has been left in lofty isolation. Apart from East Africa and the Atlas region the only peak which exceeds 12,000 feet is the volcano of the Camerouns Mountain (13,350 ft.).

Another land form which is notably rare in the build of Africa is that of extensive alluvial lowland, and in no other continent does the area of plain below 600 feet represent so small a proportion of the total area. Great flood-plains opening freely to the sea and of high agricultural value, such as are common in the Americas and South-eastern Asia, do not appear in Africa. Usually the plateau edge is very close to the sea-board—a distance of 20 miles is not a too conservative average figure—and the great rivers of the interior—the Nile, Congo, Niger and Zambezi—in making their ways to the sea drop in successive stages over the ledges of the tableland so that the navigability of their lower or lower middle courses is greatly impeded. The term ' coastal plain ' when applied to Africa should be used only in a relative sense, as, very commonly, a line of cliffs rises to the plateau behind from the limits of high tide.

The absence of deeply-penetrating indentations of the coast and the rarity both of well-defined peninsulas and of neighbouring islands are readily remarked on the map of Africa. Madagascar is unique by reason of its great size, though the part this island has played in the life of modern Africa has not been nearly so considerable as that of Zanzibar. The latter, from the standpoint of human affairs, must be classed as the most notable African island. As a rule, the neighbouring Mediterranean islands—Sicily, Malta and Crete—are not included in an enumeration of the maritime outposts of the continent because of their political connexion with Europe and their intimate association with Mediterranean civilization.

The usually straight shore is not well-endowed with natural harbours and on nearly every margin of the continent there are to be found coastal stretches—each exceeding 1000 miles—which are virtually harbourless. Lack of adequate protection and of inshore anchorage for shipping, together with the difficulties involved in navigating the lower courses of the principal rivers, have delayed the commercial development of the African interior, and these negative influences are still apparent even to-day when the science of transport is able to provide in some measure the facilities which Nature has withheld. It is frequently difficult

[1] Their altitudes are respectively 19,590, 17,040, 14,140, 15,000 feet.

for ships to approach the coast on account of the existence of sand-bars deposited by currents flowing parallel to the shore and by rivers in their lower courses. These hindrances to shipping are emphasized on the Guinea Coast which has no first-class natural harbour between Freetown (Sierra Leone) and the Niger Delta. Only one of the great rivers of Africa—namely the Congo —has an estuary of deep water ; in the cases of the Nile, Niger and Zambezi each has a delta providing difficulties for navigation. One of the most obvious exceptions to the rule of coasts inadequately supplied with good harbourage is provided by the Barbary littoral of North-west Africa, especially where it cuts across the ends of the Atlas ranges. It was in eastern Tunisia that the great Phoenician trading station of Carthage was founded.

Off all coasts except the Mediterranean and the extreme southern—in the Cape Province—the descent to oceanic depths is comparatively abrupt, so that on the Atlantic side, for example, the 1000 fathoms sub-marine contour is rarely more than 50 miles off-shore. This lack of an extensive ' continental shelf ' means that there is little feeding ground for fish, so that ' the harvest of the sea ' is of comparatively small account in the life of the people. The widest sub-marine extension of the mainland, submerged not more than 100 fathoms, is a triangular ' shelf ', known as the Agulhas Bank, whose base lies between the Cape of Good Hope and Port Elizabeth, with the apex more than 100 miles south of Cape Agulhas, the southernmost point of the continent. Fishing activities off-shore from the Cape are important in consequence, more important indeed than elsewhere in Africa.

The most notable general feature of the plateau surface is the remarkable uniformity of level between 2000 and 4000 feet over vast areas. Sharp contrasts in altitude, such as are common in the neighbourhood of the great folded-mountain systems of the Americas and Eurasia, are not a usual feature of Africa, and, within the limits of the Plateau proper, are almost entirely confined to the vicinity of the East African Rift Valleys.

The Southern Sub-Continent

It is within the sub-continental peninsula lying to the south of the Equator that the high tableland shows maximum development. Apart from narrow coastal districts—10 to 20 miles in width—the average altitude approaches 3500 feet and the land under 1000 feet is negligible. The region of central Mozambique is the only instance in Southern Africa of a coastal lowland stretching widely for 200 miles into the interior : such a wide breach in the plateau's margin is only repeated throughout the continent as a whole in the region of the lower Niger basin.

An important feature of the southern tableland is the series of shallow plateau basins whose floors are usually considerably more than 1000 feet above sea-level and which are practically encircled by higher plateau exceeding 3000 feet. Such are the basins of the Congo, upper Zambezi and Orange Rivers. Each lies mainly within the western half of the sub-continent and is succeeded eastwards—this is most apparent in the cases of the Congo and Orange depressions—by massive platforms, from

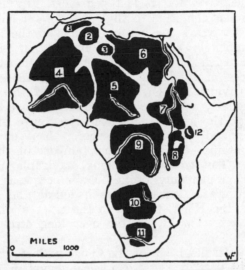

FIG. 5.—Principal basins of inland drainage or of very restricted outlet to the sea

1. Shotts Plateau.	7. White Nile.
2. Igharghar Basin.	8. Basin of East Africa.
3. Basin of Fezzan.	9. Congo.
4. Basin of Western Sahara and Middle Niger.	10. Northern Kalahari.
5. Chad Basin.	11. Southern Kalahari.
6. Libyan Basin.	12. Lake Rudolf.

4000 to 8000 feet in height. The first of these great tabular masses is the deeply-entrenched plateau within the territories of Uganda, Kenya and Tanganyika, while the most southerly includes the High Veld of the Orange Free State and the Transvaal at 4000–6000 feet and culminates farther to the east in the lofty 'massif' of Basutoland, whose eastern wall is the mountainous edge of the Drakensbergen.[1]

In each of the three broad interior depressions mentioned the drainage is provided by an arterial river which trenches through the outer ledges of the Plateau in a well-defined groove

[1] The term 'Mountains' applied to the Drakensbergen is liable to be misleading as this feature is merely the plateau escarpment, here at its loftiest (9000–10,000 ft.).

before escaping to the coast. Yet their drainage systems are not really comparable owing to the great differences in their rainfall régimes. Abundant precipitation over the Congo Basin is contrasted with desert or semi-desert conditions within the middle and lower districts of the Orange Basin. This notable distinction is reflected, on the one hand, in the complicated system of tributary streams which reach the Congo throughout the greater part of its course and, on the other, in the solitary flow of the Orange River for its last 500 miles. In the latter case there is a similar condition to that of the lower Nile.

In very dry years the winter volume of the lower Orange may be completely absorbed by evaporation or percolation before it can reach the sea ; and this desiccation together with the occurrence of sand-flats and waterfalls renders the river useless for navigation. On the other hand the Congo main stream is regularly navigable for 1000 miles above Stanley Pool, from which to the estuary, however, the course of the river is narrowly confined and broken where it has cut through the Crystal Mountains—as the western rampart of the Plateau is here known. This feature of a long, navigable middle course succeeded by a generally broken lower course is repeated by certain other great African rivers including the Nile and, to some extent, the Niger, though in the cases of the two rivers mentioned navigation is possible over long stretches of their lower courses.

The great circular basin of the Congo with its narrow-necked outlet may be described as the nuclear region of Africa, which helps to explain the rivalry that prevented any one of the leading European Powers with imperial ambitions from acquiring sovereignty over it. Very probably this vast but shallow depression represents the bed of a former inland sea or lake which was drained to the ocean with the evolution of the lower Congo. Its average altitude is about 1000 feet, so that it differs from the other great equatorial basin to which it is sometimes compared, namely that of the Amazon—a true lowland. As it lies athwart the equatorial zone there is no season in which rain does not fall heavily in some part of the Congo Basin and consequently the level of water in the main stream is well maintained by tributaries of large volume, such as the Kasai and Ubangi Rivers, which flow towards the centre from all parts of the periphery. No African river carries annually to the sea so great a volume of water : yet on account of the wide extent of level tracts in the heart of the depression much of it is ill-drained by sluggish rivers ; and lakes, such as that known as Lake Leopold II, have remained from a former inland sea.

The structural framework of the Orange Basin [1] though smaller is not markedly dissimilar from that of the Congo. Much of the precipitation over the central districts does not reach the main river but collects in shallow lakes known locally as ' vleis ' and ' pans ', and undergoes evaporation, with the result that in the dry season (winter) a salt-encrusted surface is exposed. Farther north, in the northern Kalahari, which was formerly a basin of inland drainage, some surface water is drained away by the Zambezi head-streams ; but much of the precipitation collects so that vleis are common. There is Ngami—still recorded in atlases as a lake though it is no longer a permanently flooded depression—as well as the many salt-pans of Makarikari lying farther east which record the former existence of an early nineteenth-century lake.

To the east of the basin-depressions described above the East African Plateau and the Plateau of South-East Africa require further if brief attention. The outstanding feature of the former is the great trench of the Rift Valley whose trend and origins have been discussed on an earlier page. Average altitude is difficult to estimate on account of the sharp contrasts that rifting and vulcanism have produced, but it is between 3000 and 6000 feet, whilst the land most favoured by European settlers is above this average. Subsidence along the great rifts has been followed by lake accumulations in this generally well-watered country, as we have seen in the cases of Tanganyika and Nyasa. The greatest lake of Africa—Victoria—is not, however, within a rift valley ; its basin is shallow with a maximum depth of about 270 feet, and it possesses low shores of very irregular configuration. As one of the great reservoirs of the Nile its level is determined by the outlet of that river over the Ripon Falls. Victoria Nile water occupies the shallow swamp-filled depression of Lake Kioga with which the Victoria Nyanza was formerly continuous. In the neighbourhood of Lake Albert the river descends over another ledge of the Plateau by the Murchison Falls, above which its course is only a few yards wide. Drainage on the East-African Plateau is complicated, for apart from small districts of internal drainage the river courses are the head-streams of three systems—the Nile with its northerly flow ; the Congo with its westerly outlet ; and the eastward-flowing rivers which reach the Indian Ocean independently of each other.

Farther south the Plateau remains moderately high, though it has been extensively eroded, vertically and laterally, by the

[1] The term ' Orange Basin ' is here made to include the greater part of the southern Kalahari which, under heavier rainfall, would have perennial drainage to the middle Orange River.

Zambezi and Limpopo river-systems. It culminates, so far as South Africa is concerned, in the ' massif ' of Basutoland whose level sedimentary beds clearly show that folding has had nothing to do with their lofty elevation of 5000–10,000 feet. This high platform, protected by a resistant rock-capping, stands prominently above the surrounding country—including the High Veld—which has been degraded by the processes of denudation. Seen from the east the Drakensberg escarpment rising to over 10,000 feet appears not only imposing but wellnigh impregnable.

Limiting the South African Plateau on its southern side is the escarpment of the Stormbergen and the Nieuwveld Range which together, as viewed from the southern side, have the appearance of a lofty, serrated mountain range. To the south is the shallow depression of the Great Karroo (1500–3000 ft.) which represents a lower terrace in front of the Plateau proper. The arid Karroo extends east and west between the Nieuwveld Range and the Zwartebergen and there is evidence, in the gentle buckling of its strata, of the ground-swell from the folding movements which raised the Zwartebergen and Langebergen. These, the best-developed of the Cape Ranges, enclose the Little Karroo, an elongated depression about 1000 feet above sea-level which may be described as the foreland country of the Great Karroo. The Cape Ranges which are cut off by the north-eastward trend of the coast in the Eastern Cape Province are derived from older mountain-building than that of the Atlas system and have undergone weathering since the close of the Palaeozoic Age.

The origin of Madagascar has already received some attention and it has been shown that this great island, whose area is twice that of the British Isles, was united in comparatively recent geological times to the parent continent and that it consists essentially of pre-Palaeozoic rocks, including schists and granites, similar to those of the mainland. Its western side has been affected by a series of marine intrusions, so that the primitive platform is here concealed by Mesozoic and more recent sediments. An abrupt descent from the interior plateau, which rises over 6000 feet, to the very straight eastern coast and beyond, to the ocean floor, bears witness to fracturing and, according to Gregory, to the deep foundering of land immediately east of Madagascar.

During Oligocene (Tertiary) times Madagascar was reunited to Africa and was entered by the primitive lemurs whose descendants are now the characteristic members of the Malagasy fauna. With the re-advance of the sea in early Pleistocene times the Malagasy mammals were isolated from the main group of the similar species which formerly ranged throughout South America and Africa. The island has not shared in the comparatively recent interchange of fauna between Eurasia and Africa, although during the Pliocene (late Tertiary), when the remnants of a land-bridge were only partly submerged, the hippopotamus was able to cross from Africa by way of a channel provided, as it were, with stepping-stones. East of Madagascar lie the small but commercially important islands of Mauritius and Réunion which are mainly of volcanic origin.

Northern Africa

Here we are concerned with Africa north of the Congo Basin and of the East African Plateau. The parallel of 5° N. closely approaches the approximate border and, continuing westwards, remains a convenient boundary, keeping close to the Guinea Coast, so that practically the whole of the great westerly bulge of the continent lies on its northern side. Any boundary chosen to demarcate regions within a continent where sharp contrasts of configuration and structure are comparatively rare has the disadvantage of being rather arbitrary ; but for the purposes of convenience in classification and description the use of a boundary is legitimate, so long as it is accepted not as a line but rather as indicating a zone of transition between clearly distinguished regions.

The Saharan Plateau, with an average elevation of 1000 feet, dominates the geography of Northern Africa to which it is, so to speak, the general background. The geographical monotony—involving relief, climate and vegetation—of vast Saharan areas encourages a tendency to bestow a greater degree of attention on the border lands where contrasts of physical characteristics, together with the human significance of these regions, present more of interest to the geographer ; but such regions should not be considered in isolation or without a full appreciation of the Saharan Plateau background.

The varying character of the desert surface—especially the distinctions between sandy, rocky and pebble wastes—is considered in a later chapter, and there it is shown that Saharan vegetation, though always meagre, reflects local differences in topography.

Modern physical maps of North Africa emphasize the prominence of the high ridge, widening in places to a broad plateau, which crosses the Central Sahara diagonally from ESE. to WNW. The wide Ahaggar Plateau and the more ridge-like highland of Tibesti attain altitudes of over 9000 feet in places, and these rocky lands which owe their eminence to a hard, resistant capping are linked by a narrow but elevated saddle (over 3000 ft.), situated to the south of Fezzan. Geological inquiry has established that the Central Saharan highlands represent the greatly reduced, but hard-compressed, core of an ancient mountain-system whose trend is still to be perceived in the diagonal line of the Ahaggar-Tibesti country.

North-west of Ahaggar the land gradually descends across the oasis country of Tuat and Gurara towards the depression, formerly occupied by a river-system draining from Ahaggar, which extends along the base of the Saharan Atlas like a dry moat. This feature may be followed along the Wadi Draa from the Atlantic coast between Cape Juby and Cape Nun ; its widest and lowest levels are reached in Southern Algeria and Tunisia where occur the

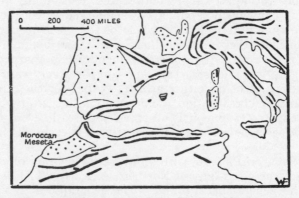

FIG. 6.—The mountain systems of the Western Mediterranean lands
(Showing the relationship of the Atlas folds to the Apennine and Iberian systems)
N.B.—Old residual plateaus shown by stippling.

salt-lakes, known locally as ' shotts ', of which the Shott Jerid in Southern Tunisia is the most extensive. Farther to the east the depression is submerged by the Gulf of Gabes, an arm of the Mediterranean. To the south-east of Biskra the basin of the Shotts is lower than sea-level and provides a system of internal drainage situated remarkably close to the Mediterranean sea-board.

The Atlas ranges do not form a complete and isolated mountain group but rather an African extension of an ' Alpine ' system which is most extensively developed in Europe and encloses the western basin of the Mediterranean. From the ' Alpine ' Sierra Nevada of south-eastern Spain a range—the Riff Atlas (6000 ft.) —enters Africa, if we ignore the recently-formed hiatus occupied by the Straits of Gibraltar, and curves to the east across northern Barbary as the Mediterranean branch of the

Atlas system. The folds are cut off abruptly on the eastern coast of Tunisia, but were in a former age continuous across the straits to Sicily and the Apennines of Italy. In addition to this close physical connexion with Mediterranean Europe the lands of the Atlas form a biological province of Europe as is shown by their characteristic flora and fauna. The large mammals which are representative of the fauna of tropical Africa, such as the elephant, rhinoceros and giraffe, are completely absent.

The Great Atlas of Morocco not only possesses the loftiest peaks of the system, with one summit of 14,500 feet, but also is the only range providing a complete barrier between north and south. With the neighbouring and lower fold of the Anti-Atlas (5000–10,000 ft.) to the south, the Moroccan ranges extend into Algeria and are transformed into a broad high plateau—about 100 miles across—which is well defined by northern and southern ramparts known respectively as the Tell Atlas and the Saharan Atlas. This is the Plateau of the Shotts (3000–3500 ft.), a region of internal drainage with numerous salt-lakes ('shotts'). The fertile terraces on the coastward side of the Tell Atlas, which mark the irregular descent to the sea-board, form the Tell, renowned as one of the richest agricultural zones of the Mediterranean Basin.

Involved in the mountain-building which produced the Atlas ranges were rocks of the primitive base of Africa : they form the Archaean core of the Great Atlas of Morocco, where overlying Mesozoic sediments, mainly limestones, are gently folded and widely appear at the surface, though erosion is steadily reducing their thickness so as ultimately to expose the core of ancient rocks. Offshore from the western end of the Moroccan Atlas the Canary Islands, though superficially volcanic, may represent in their foundations a former continuation of the mountain-system with which they are in line.

The western district of the Sahara which includes Mauritania [1] is of monotonous relief, and only at one or two isolated points does the level exceed 1500 feet. Within it and the neighbouring Senegal Colony is the largest area (250,000 sq. miles) of Northern Africa with an average altitude of less than 600 ft. ; though in the Eastern Sahara—or Libyan Desert—there is a region comparable in area and surface form which extends up to the lower Nile.

Throughout the Sudan the prominent features of relief are provided by isolated masses of the primitive tableland of the continent which rise above the general level of the Sudan, itself

---

[1] ' Mauritania '—the land of the Mauri, from which comes the modern term ' Moors '—was, in ancient times, the land of the Western Sahara. The French Colony between the Senegal Colony and Morocco provides a political revival of the name.

a plateau averaging rather less than 1500 feet. They include the Futa Jallon Highland of the Western Sudan and the much smaller Bauchi Plateau of Northern Nigeria, each of which exceeds 5000 feet in places, though such altitudes are comparatively rare.[1] Their prominence is due not to up-raising along lines of fault but to weathering and stream-erosion which have degraded the country around their more resistant slopes. Rivers engaged in this work of erosion include the Senegal and upper Niger of the Western Sudan, the lower Niger and Benue and in the Eastern Sudan, the Bahr-el-Ghazal of the Nile system.

The Futa Jallon Plateau though very close to the Atlantic sea-board in French Guinea, Sierra Leone and Liberia is easily the most important hydrographic 'divide' of West Africa. Down its much-dissected inward facing slope flow head-streams of the Senegal and Niger which, merging into the two main streams of these systems, meander circuitously to the Atlantic, though in directly opposite directions to each other. More abrupt is the Atlantic slope of Futa Jallon and on this side numerous short but vigorous streams, fed by torrential summer rains, are steadily cutting back the escarpment and are likely to capture head-streams of the Niger.

There is little doubt that the upper Niger as far down-stream as the vicinity of Timbuktu was formerly the principal artery of a vast inland drainage system whose lake focus was in the region of the present great bend of the middle Niger. The remnants of the lake into which the upper Niger once flowed are still visible to the west and south of Timbuktu, and these depressions are filled each summer during the flooding of the sluggish middle Niger.

The Benue, easily the greatest tributary of the Niger, is likely to complete the capture of certain head-streams of the Shari river-system (draining to Lake Chad) that it has already begun. At present, however, the Shari is the longest African river without an outlet to the sea ; it rises on a low plateau ridge, averaging 2000–3000 feet, dividing the Chad and Bahr-el-Ghazal drainage from that of the Ubangi (Congo system), and its main stream flows for 700 miles in a north-westerly direction to the swamps around the shallow Lake Chad.

More prominent in relief than Futa Jallon is the highland of the Camerouns. A high ridge trending NE-SW. and culminating in the Camerouns Mountain of over 13,000 feet represents a greatly denuded stump of an ancient mountain range. It has gained in elevation, however, by comparatively recent lava

[1] The culminating summit of West Africa is Mt. Loma (6390 ft.) in Sierra Leone.

outflow, as the craters of the Camerouns Mountain impressively indicate.

In the Sudanese and Egyptian sections of its valley the Nile occupies part of an ancient depression which, during Cretaceous and later times, was a gulf of the Mediterranean. The existing Nile evolved through the union of a series of rivers which flowed into the north-south trending depression after the retreat of the sea. Below Khartoum the Nile is re-excavating an older river valley that has been filled with sandstone. At Abu Hamed (approximately 19° Lat. N.) the river bends back and flows to the south-west for 150 miles or so, and this deflection of course Gregory has explained by the river's utilization of a line of fault extending at right angles to the direction of its previous course.

From the point of its confluence with the Sobat the Nile flows—throughout the greater part of its course to the sea—in a narrow trench cut into the desert plateau which, in these parts, is 1000–1500 feet above sea-level. The great river in its lower course has had only a very local effect on the topography of its region, and in this respect the Nile is unique among the major rivers of the world. Its very restricted influence on the physical geography is largely a consequence of a complete lack of tributary streams throughout the last thousand miles of flow to the sea : so that it is rather inaccurate to apply the hydrographic term ' basin ' to the drainage area of the lower Nile.

The frontier of Abyssinia corresponds fairly closely, especially on the west, to the boundary of an immense ' massif ' whose mean elevation of 5000–6000 feet over an area exceeding 300,000 square miles distinguishes it as one of the most clearly-defined natural regions of the continent. A line of fracture coincides with each of the escarpments that bounds the Plateau on its eastern and western side respectively ; and it is the sinking of the crust to form the depressed areas of the White Nile Basin and the Plains of Afar,[1] together with uplift of the Plateau in Jurassic time, that has granted to Abyssinia its present lofty isolation.

It has already been noted that the eastern escarpment is also part of the western wall of the Great Rift Valley and that the submerged basin of the Red Sea formerly extended across the Plains of Afar to the edge of the Plateau, leaving the detached plateau of Danakil as an island.

The plateau surface is deeply dissected, partly as a result of fracturing and partly owing to the action of erosive agents, including the head-streams of the great eastern tributaries of

[1] Afar lies to the east of Northern Abyssinia

3

the Nile. Extensive areas of level upland plain are not uncommon, however, and are often surmounted by flat-topped hills. In the numerous and often deep hollows of the surface lakes have collected, some of them, like Tana, forming natural reservoirs of Nile tributaries. Volcanic action has built up, above the Archaean platform, cratered cones including some of the highest summits, such as Ras Dashan (15,000 ft.)—the loftiest of all—in the north of the country. Widespread lava has weathered into a generally rich soil : consequently Abyssinia is not only a natural fortress but also a region of economic attractiveness that is practically encircled by poor grass or scrub-land, and these two factors of geography have determined some of the main events of Abyssinian history.

To the east, across the threshold of the East African Rift Valley is the ' Eastern Horn '—Somaliland—whose structure is that of an up-tilted horst of ancient rocks dipping to the southeast and broken off abruptly along the coast of the Gulf of Aden, beyond which the island of Socotra represents a detached projection of the mainland plateau.

THE SOILS OF AFRICA

Despite their obvious significance in the development of the agricultural resources of Africa the soils of the continent have begun to receive only very recently the attention which they deserve. The geological survey departments of the various European Administrations in Africa have been mainly concerned with the solid sub-structure and its mineral wealth. More is known of the soils of the Union of South Africa than of those of any other territory, and in the following statement it is therefore excusable that the Union should receive more than the proportion of attention that would be due to it were the soils of other regions known as fully. But even in South Africa a classification of soils and their accurate mapping provide a vast field of inquiry which is practically unworked.

Mr. C. F. Marbut of the U.S. Department of Agriculture was one of the first to attempt, in spite of very inadequate evidence, to suggest the distribution of the main classes of African soils. A summary of his conclusions has been published [1] and much of the following discussion is derived therefrom. Marbut has been adversely criticized for hastily drawing conclusions regarding soil distributions in the absence of the necessary data, but such criticism is unduly severe and his published

[1] Shantz and Marbut, *The Vegetation and Soils of Africa*, New York, 1923.

work on the soils of Africa should be regarded as that of a pioneer investigator readily willing to admit the paucity of knowledge available. In the case of East Africa the late Professor Gregory, E. Krenkel and others have given some attention to the soils of particular districts, but a soil survey of the region as a whole has yet to be undertaken. The Government of the Belgian Congo has provided in the *Atlas du Katanga* maps of soil distributions as well as of other surface features, and so has pointed the way for the extension of similar surveys to the whole of inter-tropical Africa.

Before passing to outline the geographical occurrence of some of the soil groups, as far as the very limited evidence permits, the reader is reminded that in Africa as in other continents the characteristics of mature soils are largely determined by the weathering agency of climate and by the influence of the vegetation covering, but that ' young ' or immature soils formed *in situ* usually represent the only slightly modified detritus of the parent rock. As to be expected, the soils of the desert and semi-desert areas, which make up one-half of the continent, contain very little humus.

Soils of Humid Regions in Inter-Tropical Africa

African explorers of the early and middle periods of the nineteenth century frequently referred in their records to the red colouring of the soils of the tropical zone, and it was a common practice until the close of the century to classify all such soils as ' laterite '.

It is widely accepted to-day that true laterite is the mature soil product of chemical changes that are peculiar to tropical or equatorial latitudes where crystalline rocks are found and where the annual rainfall tends to be heavy. Laterite includes in its composition a very high percentage of the oxides of aluminum, iron and manganese, and where it is known or thought to occur in the Tropics of the world it seems to be associated, more often than not, with the occurrence of iron concretions.

Over the central zone of Africa from the Southern Sudan to the savanna of Angola, Southern Congo and Northern Rhodesia, the soils as a whole are more uniform in character than in the case of any region of similar size, with the possible exception of the Sahara. They tend to be light in texture—often sandy —and reddish in colour, whilst the sub-soil is usually of a much heavier—frequently clayey—nature. Under the prevailing humid conditions the soils tend to be partially or even wholly leached ; this is particularly true of the mature soils, including laterite, and such leaching has resulted in the removal of agriculturally valuable lime carbonate.

(a) Laterite

Fully-developed laterite is believed to have a very limited range and is probably most abundant in regions where precipitation attains or exceeds 80 inches. One region where laterite almost certainly extends widely is the Atlantic slope of the Futa Jallon Plateau from French Guinea south-eastwards to Sierra Leone and Liberia.

(b) Lateritic Red Loams

An intermediate stage in the full development of mature laterite is represented by certain of the red loams of Central Africa. They contain a much smaller percentage of aluminum hydroxide than does the soil class just considered, but more than in the case of very ' young ' soils, from which this compound is practically absent. Where agriculture is practised the lateritic red loams appear to be very productive, but their distribution may be only very tentatively suggested as a fairly widespread occurrence in the Belgian Congo and the neighbouring districts of French Equatorial Africa.

(c) Red Loams

These soils represent an earlier stage of evolution than do the lateritic red loams, and aluminum hydroxide is almost entirely absent. They are found overlying a variety of rocks, including gneiss and sandstone, and show, despite their comparative immaturity, the effects of considerable weathering. As a rule, the amount of leaching they have suffered is less than in the cases of the soils already mentioned, and generally the conditions for successful agriculture are very favourable. The red loams seem to be associated with park savanna country and rainfall of moderate quantity, and it is claimed that they occupy large parts of those districts of Northern Rhodesia, Southern Congo and Angola where precipitation does not exceed 50 inches.

(d) Upland Red Loams of very immature age

Soils of this class are distributed fairly commonly on hillsides within inter-tropical Africa where erosion is considerable and where the rock detritus is kept fresh by constant renewal. They are not leached to any considerable extent. Although they have been examined in very few and small localities only, they probably provide much of the hill-slope covering of the East African Plateau (e.g. the flanks of Mounts Kenya and Kilimanjaro) as well as of the Camerouns Highland. Frequently they are well cultivated both by Native and by European farmers.

Soils of the Hot Deserts

The humus content is low and soils of this class tend to be of light colouring. As they are unleached and contain an abundance of carbonates they prove highly fertile where irrigation can be introduced, as in the Saharan oases. In places where there is very intermittent surface drainage the accumulation of alkali at the surface is a prominent feature.

Soils of Moderate Rainfall Areas in Tropical and Extra-tropical Latitudes

(a) Chernozems

On the Low Veld of the Transvaal, north of the latitude of Pretoria, and in neighbouring parts of Southern Rhodesia black, heavy soils extend widely. Their dark colour is associated with the accumulation of organic material and in their general characteristics such soils resemble the chernozems of Southern Russia and of the cotton lands of Texas. Of all the African soils they are richest in nitrogen and lime, whilst the percentage of phosphorus, though low, is higher than in most of the other soils of the continent : yet they are often difficult to work, for they remain sticky and wet during the period of rains (summer) and in the dry season they become brittle and crack, so that the sub-soil moisture is evaporated.

The physical conditions which seem to favour the development of the Transvaal chernozem are low relief, such as is found on the Springbok Flats of the Northern Transvaal, with precipitation in the form of intense, thunderstorm rainfall. Marbut considers it likely that a similar belt of chernozems extends across Africa in the northern and middle latitudes of the Sudan, and that a corresponding though smaller zone in Southern Africa stretches westwards or north-westwards from the Northern Transvaal and Southern Rhodesia towards the Atlantic coast. He admits, however, that his actual evidence is very meagre and argues mainly from the similarity of physical conditions in these regions to those in the Low Veld where chernozem has been recognized.

Similar soils occurring in a hilly environment and of grey or brown colour are known in parts of East Africa and in the Transvaal. They contain much less organic material, for the rapid run-off discourages vegetation and therein the light colouring is explained ; but they also are rich in lime and, in addition, are notable for their potash content. In texture they vary from light sandy loams to heavy clay and are found covering a wide variety of rocks from sandstones to igneous types. Usually they are distinctly fertile when irrigated.

(b) *Prairie Soils of the High Veld*

In eastern districts of the Orange Free State and in neighbouring parts of the Transvaal, where altitude exceeds 4000 feet but where topography may be described as smooth, fertile dark-brown soils are common and have been likened to those of the prairies of the ' Corn Belt ' of the U.S.A., in Illinois, Iowa and adjacent States. The rainfall on the High Veld of South Africa is over 25 inches but not very much more, and the soils appear to be mature, though they are not excessively leached. As in the U.S.A.—if the soil analogy holds—they provide very good maize land, the best in South Africa. Without actual evidence to support a too-positive assertion it is possible that similar soils occupy large parts of the Sudan.

Brown Soils of the Cape and Atlas Regions

These soils have been analysed most thoroughly in the region of considerable winter rainfall and summer drought that occupies a small part of the Western Cape Province. No comprehensive information concerning the soils of the Atlas lands in North-West Africa has yet been published, but there, under similar physical conditions, the brown soils of the Cape district may be repeated. They are deficient in carbonates through much leaching and also are rather low in phosphoric acid, potash and nitrogen, whilst in texture they may be described as loams or sandy loams. In consequence of the deficiency of the chemical constituents mentioned these soils tend to restrict the progress of agriculture in one of the best-watered districts of South Africa, and cultivation requires the re-fertilization of the leached soil. Although they occur in one of the coolest districts of Africa they have not the protection in winter of either a frozen surface or a snow covering.

The Red Loams of Natal

Soils of this class extend widely both in Natal and on the seaward slopes of the Plateau in the Eastern Cape Province. Throughout this terraced country there is active erosion, for the rainfall is considerable, usually over 30 inches, and much of it is in the form of thunder showers. Consequently, on level patches there is much accumulation of detritus derived from crystalline rocks as well as from sandstone and shales ; but on the slopes the soil is thin. When not constantly renewed the loams tend to be deficient in lime and often the content of potash and phosphorus is also low. Like the Cape soils they require—for successful and permanent agriculture—frequent re-fertilization.

From these notes on the soils of the southern districts of the Union of South Africa it is obvious that they are far from rich, and we may expect to find that farming in this region is confronted with a considerable soil problem.

REFERENCES

The official year-books and hand-books of various countries (e.g. Union of South Africa, Tanganyika Territory, &c.) should not be overlooked as they contain valuable information on the physical as well as on the human side. For maps the reader is recommended to the African sheets of the International Map of the World (Scale = 1/million) and to *The Times* Atlas (Bartholomew).

Bernard, A., *Afrique Septentrionale et Occidentale Tome XI*, Géographie Universelle, Paris, 1938.
Bullard, E. C., ' Gravity measurements in East Africa ', *Phil. Trans. Roy. Soc.*, 235A (1936), pp. 445–531.
du Toit, A. L., *Our Wandering Continents*, London, 1937.
The Geology of South Africa, 2nd ed., London, 1939.
Gregory J. W., *The Rift Valleys and Geology of East Africa*, London, 1921.
Herbertson, A. J., and Howarth, O. J. R. (Editors), *The Oxford Survey of the British Empire*, Vol. III, Oxford, 1914.
Hurst, H. E., and Phillips, P., *The Nile Basin*, Vol. 8, I (General Description, &c.), Cairo, 1931.
Jaeger, F., *Afrika*, Leipzig, 1928.
King, L. C., ' On the Ages of African Land Surfaces ', *Quart. Journ. Geol. Soc.*, Vol. CIV (1948), pp. 439–59.
Krenkel, E., *Die Geologie Afrikas*, 1925. (Especially useful for East Africa).
Reed, F. R. C., *The Geology of the British Empire*, London, 1921.
Shackleton, R. M., ' A Contribution to the Geology of the Kavirondo Rift Valley ', *Quart. Journ. Geol. Soc.*, Vol. CVI (1951), pp. 345–92.
Shantz, H. L., and Marbut, C. F., *The Vegetation and Soils of Africa*, New York, 1923.
Suess, E., *The Face of the Earth*, English edit., trans. Sollas, H. B. C., 5 vols., Oxford, 1904–24.
Wayland, E. J., ' Some account of the Geology of the Lake Albert Rift Valley ', *Geog. Journ.*, Vol. LVIII (1921), pp. 344–59.
Wegener, A., *The Origin of Continents and Oceans* (trans. Skerl), London, 1922.
Willis, Bailey, *East African Plateaus and Rift Valleys* (Carnegie Institution), Washington, 1936.
Worthington, E. B., *Science in Africa*, Oxford, 1938.
Worthington, E. B. and S., *Inland Waters of Africa*, London, 1933.

CHAPTER II

CLIMATE AND VEGETATION

SO closely dependent are the characteristics of vegetation upon climatic conditions, not only in Africa but throughout the world, that it is permissible here to associate closely these two aspects of the physical environment of man in Africa, rather than to separate them in distinct chapters. The reader will be aware that although variations in forms of plant life frequently correspond to differences in classes of soils, it is climate, acting mainly through temperature and rainfall, that determines the major regional differences in vegetation : so that the distribution of desert, grass-land and forest types throughout the continents may be explained in terms of climate. Later in this chapter the procedure will be to describe in relation to each of the principal climatic regions of Africa the corresponding vegetational environment, but first it is necessary to summarize briefly the origins and characteristics of the climates of the continent.

The tropical climates of Africa are generally unsuited to White settlement and it is only near the north-western and southern extremities of the continent that more genial conditions have attracted European colonists in considerable numbers. This factor of generally unfavourable climate helps to explain the long delay before the penetration of the continental interior : moreover, it is always likely to place a limit to the extent and effectiveness of European enterprise in Africa. North and South America and Australia—all three continents of White colonization—provided extensive virgin lands where climatic conditions were not fundamentally different from those of the homeland of the settler : but the intending colonist, coming to Africa from a northern environment, discovered that the continent does not offer, except in the sub-tropical north-west and south—both very limited in area—climatic attractions comparable to those of the New World.

No part of Africa duplicates the climates of Western and North-Western Europe, from which by far the largest proportion of the colonists of ' new ' lands have come during the past three centuries. On the contrary, the most widespread climates of Africa are associated with great if not extreme heat, at least in the summer half-year, whilst in the vast equatorial zone the added factor of a high degree of atmospheric humidity is a complete bar to the continued health and vitality of the unacclimated immigrants.

Africa, indeed, is the most tropical of the continents : its latitudinal extent is traversed approximately midway by the Equator, so that the northern and southern extremities, in Tunisia and the Cape Province respectively, are between 2400 and 2600 miles from the equatorial line. These extremities are not sufficiently far removed from the Tropics to experience climates of cool temperate type, and elsewhere, with the exception of two or three isolated East African peaks, including Kenya and Kilimanjaro Mountains, highland altitudes do not compensate sufficiently for low latitude to produce cool temperate conditions.

Climates with varying amounts of rainfall, from over 100 inches on the one hand to continuous drought on the other, but with great heat as the common factor of all, determine the three most characteristic vegetation zones of Africa, namely tropical rain forest, tropical grass-land or savanna and hot desert. The symmetrical arrangement of the climatic belts and their associated vegetations is a notable feature. With the exception of the middle or equatorial zone the climates are duplicated, so that going polewards a similar distribution is found in North and South Africa. The symmetry is not, however, complete, although on the western side of the continent it is very noticeable : it is disturbed by the very much greater extent of desert in North than in South Africa, for whilst the Sahara is prolonged right up to the eastern shores of North Africa its counterpart in the southern hemisphere is limited to the western half of South Africa.

It cannot be too strongly emphasized when considering the distribution of either the climatic or the vegetation belts of Africa that very rarely are they sharply divided one from another. In this continent where relief is not strongly accentuated and where there is an absence of great mountain barriers comparable to those of Eurasia there is a general tendency for the gradual, almost imperceptible, mergence of the climatic or vegetational characteristics of one zone into those of its neighbour.

In a study of North African climates we are reminded of the proximity of the great land-mass of Eurasia by the extension into Africa of pressure and wind systems which have formed over the most spacious land-surface of the world. So is explained the similarity of climatic and vegetational conditions between

North-East Africa and South-West Asia, each with its hot desert as the dominating feature. The intervening narrow trough of the Red Sea, on account of its very restricted area, modifies but slightly the climates of the African and Arabian regions in its vicinity.

In contrast to the great continental area of North Africa, whose interior is but little affected by oceanic influences, Africa south of lat. 5° N., projecting as a narrowing peninsula between two oceans each of much greater extent than itself, shows more pronouncedly in its climate the influence of winds of maritime origin.

January   July

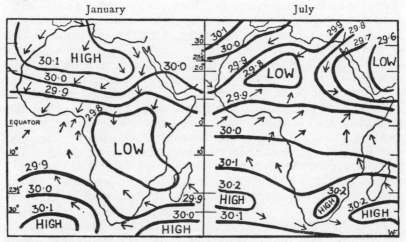

FIG. 7.—Mean pressure distribution and directions of predominant winds
(Isobars shown at intervals of 0·1 inch)

Pressure and Wind régimes of January

During the winter of the northern hemisphere the great atmospheric system of high pressure set up over the cold heart of Eurasia extends westwards as a narrowing wedge to dominate the climate of West-Central Europe. At the same time the permanent high-pressure system over the southern part of the North Atlantic—the Azores ' High '—extends far eastwards over North Africa to meet and merge with a prolongation of the Asiatic ' High '. Atmospheric pressure is then comparatively high over Central Europe and North Africa, whilst between lies the Mediterranean Sea with warm air for its latitude and lower pressure than is to be found over the European and North African continents, respectively north and south of it.

The ' winter lake ' of low pressure which is associated with the Mediterranean provides a southern path of ingress for

Atlantic cyclones and, in so far as they affect the shores of North Africa, the cyclonic winds are frequently westerlies and rain-bearing.

In the Saharan region of winter high pressure the atmosphere is usually calm and when winds occur they are variable rather than regular. Farther south the belt of North-East Trades has taken up its southern or winter position over the Southern Sahara and the Sudan. These regular winds blow towards the vast low-pressure system which lies athwart the equatorial zone and which is characterized by calms—the ' Doldrums '. Even during the northern winter the equatorial ' Low ' extends approximately as far as lat. 5° N. The strength of the North-East Trades is maintained almost as far as the Guinea Coast on the west, while farther east, in Central Africa, they are felt as northerly winds a little to the south of the Equator.

As the zenithal sun at this season is over the southern Tropic it might be expected that the doldrum belt, which swings seasonally in the wake of the apparent northward and southward movement of the sun, would lie wholly within the southern hemisphere. The reason for its prolongation to the north of the Equator is to be found in the intensive heating of the Guinea and Sudan lands which occurs even during the winter months : thus pressure is lower than over the neighbouring middle Atlantic, and the South-East Trades whose normal régime is confined to the southern hemisphere are drawn across the Equator in the Gulf of Guinea. As deflected winds blowing from the south-west they reach the Guinea Coast from Sierra Leone eastwards.

During the summer of Southern Africa there is a long southward extension of the equatorial low-pressure system. Thereby is formed an infrabaric wedge breaking the continuity of the sub-tropical high-pressure system which, in consequence, is represented by the two separate anticyclones of the South Atlantic and South Indian Oceans, respectively. It follows that ocean winds—especially the South-East Trades—are drawn into the sub-continent, and their penetration as rain-bearing currents of air is most pronounced in South-East Africa (Mozambique and Natal).

At one point only does the broken belt of the sub-tropical ' High ' invade Southern Africa and that is where the South Atlantic anticyclone covers the south-western district of the Cape Province and gives to a comparatively small area the fine calm weather that is associated with high atmospheric pressure. Apart from the South African desert, popularly but incorrectly known as the Kalahari, the Cape district alone in the sub-continent is without summer rainfall.

Pressure and Wind régimes of July

During the northern spring the Saharan ' High ' completely disappears and gives place to the establishment of a summer low-pressure system which is a consequence of the extreme insolation over the great North African land-mass. Pressure is lowest over a district to the north-west of Lake Chad and also to the east of the middle Nile, but the latter zone of the ' Low ' is virtually a western prolongation of the even more extensive Asiatic low-pressure system the centre of which lies between the Indus plains and South-East Arabia. It is the extreme summer heating of North Africa, therefore, which attracts the vortex of lowest pressure away from its ' normal ' position athwart the equatorial zone and towards the Sahara. Nevertheless pressure remains low at least as far south as the Equator. In the neighbourhood of the Saharan ' Low ' winds tend to be indrawn and they reach the continental interior of North Africa from three widely-separated coasts.

The air over the Mediterranean is cooler and denser than that over either Central Europe to the north or North Africa to the south so that the inland sea is associated with comparatively high pressures. From the Mediterranean ' High ', northerly and north-easterly winds, which are the Trades, blow to the interior of the Sahara. In their Saharan passage their temperature is steadily raised and their moisture-bearing capacity is correspondingly increased, so that they bring no rain to North Africa.[1] The Etesian winds, known to the early Greek navigators of the Eastern Mediterranean, are the northerly winds which cross the sea to the North African shore as regular air currents during summer. At night they are weak and their day-time strength is a consequence of intense daily insolation over the Sahara which temporarily increases the pressure gradient, especially during the afternoon. In contrast to the winter régime, Atlantic rain-bearing cyclones are repelled by the Mediterranean ' High ' and are limited to a path much farther north over the maritime lands of North-West Europe.

On its southern side the great North African ' Low ' draws in moisture-laden air both from the Indian Ocean and from the Gulf of Guinea : so that we find on comparing the winter and summer régimes of the Sudan from the Atlantic to Abyssinia that a monsoonal condition is produced by the alternating high and low pressures over North Africa. Part, probably a small part, of the rainfall of Abyssinia is supplied by the monsoon

[1] The Trades which blow over the Ahaggar Plateau deposit small, infrequent showers of rain.

drawn in from the Indian Ocean, but farther west over the Central and Western Sudan the summer rain-bearing winds are almost entirely derived from the Gulf of Guinea and from the ocean farther south, and blow over the land as a south-west monsoon. Within the two monsoonal currents rainfall may be either convectional or orographical (as it is on the western flanks of the Abyssinian Plateau). The Indian Ocean rain-bearing winds which reach Abyssinia are to be regarded as forming a branch of the great monsoon which approaches and penetrates Western India in the same season.

At this time, when winter conditions prevail in Southern Africa, the air lying over the sub-continent is cooler than that over the neighbouring oceans, to the west and east respectively; and a system of high pressure which reaches its maximum intensity to the south of the Tropic of Capricorn forms over the plateau. The South African winter anticyclone with its still, unclouded atmosphere produces brilliant sunshine and drought over the greater part of the sub-continent. In the extreme south-west, however, there is an outstanding exception to this climatic condition, for at this season the district of Cape Town is directly affected by the northward swing of the belt of stormy westerly winds. Alone in South Africa this district receives practically all of its rainfall in the winter season. From the sub-tropical ' Highs ', over the southern parts of the South Atlantic and Indian Oceans respectively, and from the South African anticyclone the Trades blow as south-easters as far as equatorial latitudes and are then deflected, as we have seen, towards the North African ' Low ' as a south-westerly or southerly monsoon.

With this general statement of the distribution of atmospheric pressure and winds over the continent before us we may proceed to discuss briefly the characteristics of the most important climatic regions of Africa.

I. EQUATORIAL CLIMATES

The equatorial lands of Africa,[1] excepting the ' Eastern Horn ', are characterized by one or other of the following régimes :

(a) Constant heat, well-distributed rainfall and high atmospheric humidity. Territories with this type of climate include the northern half of the Congo Basin. Luxuriant tropical forest is the dominant form of vegetation accompanying this régime.

(b) Constant heat with heavy summer (monsoon) rainfall and high atmospheric humidity throughout much the greater part of the year ; a marked, but brief, period of low rainfall or actual

[1] The limits may be taken about as far as lat. 7° N. and lat. 5° S.

drought.   The region mainly concerned is the Guinea Coast and its immediate hinterland, where the characteristic vegetation is similar to that of (a).

(c) Moderately high day temperatures throughout the year, relieved, however, by much cooler nights ; moderate, but well-distributed rainfall.   This type is confined to the equatorial highlands of East Africa, where the vegetation is of park savanna character.

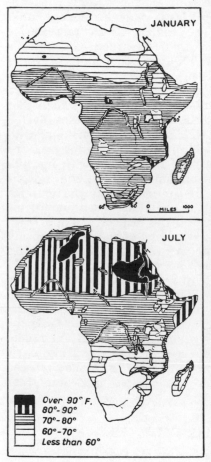

FIG. 8.—Actual mean temperatures for January and July

I (a). EQUATORIAL CLIMATE : CENTRAL AFRICAN TYPE

The Congo Basin, north of lat. 5° S., is the typical region. Temperatures throughout the year are high and always close to 80° F.   From the standpoint of the European's health the constant heat added to very high humidity is a most unfavourable condition.   Rainfall which is convectional and occurs mainly in afternoon thunderstorms is associated with the permanent low pressure of the equatorial neighbourhood.   It is a feature of every season, but reaches a maximum at a given station shortly after the apparent northward and southward passage of the overhead sun.   In the extreme north (Ubangi Basin) and in the south there is a tendency towards a period of low rainfall in midwinter [1]—if such a term may be used in regard to a region of almost uniform temperature.

Districts on the Equator usually receive their heaviest precipitation in April, shortly after the sun has passed the zenith in its northward progress, and again in October, which is sub-

[1] In December and June respectively.

sequent to the return of the sun to the overhead position at the Equator. Thus two maxima are a normal feature of the rainfall régime.

Generally it is found that the rainfall of the northern part of the Basin exceeds that of the southern. The most typical equatorial climate occurs two or three degrees north of the Equator, which is a consequence of the contrast in the dis-

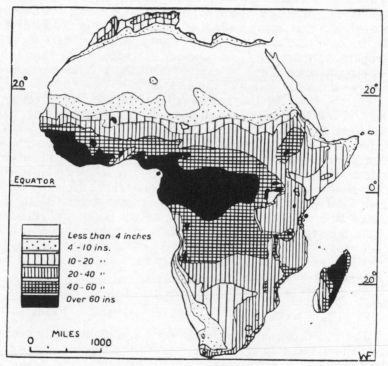

FIG. 9.—Average Annual Rainfall

tribution of land and water between Africa north and Africa south of the Equator. The most intense heating of the continent, on the average of the year, takes place in the northern hemisphere where Africa is widest ; and the occurrence of both the lowest pressure and the zone of meeting of the North-East and South-East Trades is, therefore, to the north of the Equator throughout the greater part, if not the whole, of the year.

The mean annual rainfall of Central Africa is not as high as that of equatorial South America, especially the Amazon

Basin, with which the Congo lands provide a useful geographical comparison. Whilst in the Amazon lowlands precipitation of 80–100 inches is normal, in the Congo the average is between 50 and 60 inches. The lower rainfall of the African region is partly due to the obstruction to the South-East Trades provided by the East African Plateau which traps much of the rain that otherwise would reach Central Africa. Nevertheless, the Congo system of rivers receives an adequate contribution of rainfall at all seasons. When the northern tributaries are lowest—in December—those of the southern half of the Basin are in flood ; while the floods of the northern streams in July compensate for the comparatively low water of the southern affluents at that time —a circumstance which is favourable to the permanent navigability of the main stream of the Congo.

On the coast in the neighbourhood of the Congo estuary there is a much lower rainfall than is usually associated with equatorial position. Banana, for example, has rather less than 30 inches.[1] Blowing offshore as the regular winds are the South-East Trades, which carry away from the coast the warm surface water. Upwelling of cold water from below follows, and so the daily sea-breezes which blow over the littoral are cooled. When these local winds pass from the cold coastal waters on to the heated land the possibility of precipitation is diminished.

As the vegetation of Central Africa resembles that which is associated with equatorial climatic type (b), which is now to be described, we shall postpone reference to it until the end of the following section :

I (b). EQUATORIAL CLIMATE : GUINEA TYPE

The region concerned extends along and immediately behind the Guinea Coast from Sierra Leone to the western district of the Camerouns : northwards its limits may be taken as far as lat. 7° or 8° N.

We have already briefly considered the origin of the monsoonal régime which affects a large part of the Guinea Coast. Certain districts towards the east, however, experience a climate similar to that of Central Africa, both in regard to range of temperature and distribution of rainfall, the latter being marked by a double maximum corresponding in time to the northward and southward swing of the equatorial low-pressure trough in the wake of the zenithal sun. The coast of Southern Nigeria is the outstanding instance, and here there is little evidence of

[1] Climatic data for typical stations will be found at the end of this chapter.

the reversal of winds associated with a monsoonal régime. The south-west wind from off the Gulf blows almost constantly throughout the year, though occasionally in late winter land-winds from the Sahara reach the littoral.

On the other hand, in western districts of the Guinea Coast the régime is definitely monsoonal and there is a short but well-marked winter period when dry north-east winds replace the more normal rain-bearing inflow from the south-west. Precipitation reaches its maximum in middle or late summer, after which there is a regular and rapid decline to winter. The highest rainfall occurs where the coast is approximately at right angles to the path of the south-westerlies and where the hinterland is of elevated relief, as in the cases of the Camerouns Mountain, overlooking the Bight of Biafra, and the Futa Jallon Plateau, behind the coasts of Sierra Leone and Liberia. On the western flanks of the Camerouns Peak (13,400 ft.) the mean annual precipitation is not less than 400 inches, which recalls the comparably heavy rainfall, in similar climatic circumstances, of Cherrapunji, on the southern slopes of the Assam Hills, India. That stations whose records show a single rainfall maximum usually have little precipitation in winter is a rule exemplified by Freetown (Sierra Leone) which has a measurement of over 170 inches, of which less than 3 inches falls between December and February inclusive. On the other hand, despite the tendency to short winter drought the annual aggregate is often as high as, and sometimes exceeds, that of stations with a double maximum : Freetown illustrates this position.

The lowest rainfall on the Guinea Coast eastwards from Sierra Leone, so far as available records give evidence,[1] occurs in the Gold Coast Colony, to the east of its southernmost promontory of Cape Three Points. West of the Cape the precipitation usually exceeds 40 inches, but to the east there is a steady diminution, so that Accra receives 27 inches and Christiansborg about 20 inches only. This narrow strip of low rainfall fringeing the coast provides a meteorological problem, the solution of which probably depends on the following two factors : (1) the change in direction of the trend of the coastline to the east of Cape Three Points, so that the south-west winds tend to blow parallel to the shore rather than to penetrate the land ; (2) the influence of the Guinea Current which flows eastwards along-shore towards the Cameroons coast before swinging equatorwards. After passing Cape Three Points the trend of the coast leaves

[1] It must be remembered that for vast areas of Africa there are no meteorological stations and that the lack of long-period climatic records is most marked in the equatorial lands.

4

the current farther out to sea and it is believed that the ' Guinea stream ' ' pulls ' warm surface water away from the coast to the east of the Cape, thereby causing an upwelling of cold water in these parts. Winds blowing onshore are consequently chilled and their moisture-bearing capacity reduced before they reach land.

Temperature distribution on the Guinea Coast throughout the year resembles that of Central Africa, so that no month has a lower mean than 75° F.[1] Accompanying the constant heat there is usually a high degree of humidity. In the higher latitudes of ' the Coast,' however, as in the case of Sierra Leone, the normal south-west wind régime is frequently interrupted in winter, when an outblowing wind—a north-easter—from the Sahara tends to predominate. This is the *Harmattan*, a rainless wind of low humidity, hot withal, as is to be expected considering its place of origin. Its dryness is favourable to health and it is actually invigorating after a long spell of humid sea winds : it has a cooling effect on the human body by assisting evaporation.

STATIONS SHOWING DOUBLE MAXIMUM OF RAINFALL

Station	Location	Alt. (Feet)	Jan.	Feb.	Mar.	Apr.	May	June	July	Aug.	Sept.	Oct.	Nov.	Dec.	Total (Ins.)
Akassa	Niger Delta	Sea-level	2·6	6·5	10	8·6	17·0	18·6	10·1	9·3	19·3	24·7	10·6	6·5	143·8
Lulua-burg	Upper Kasai Basin in Southern Congo	2000	7·2	5·4	7·9	6·1	3·1	0·2	0·1	2·5	6·5	6·6	9·1	6·6	60·8
Banana	Congo estuary	Sea-level	2·1	2·3	3·7	6·1	1·9	Nil	Nil	0·1	0·1	1·6	5·9	4·7	28·6
Mobaie	Middle Ubangi R., Northern Congo	1300	0·2	1·7	3·9	5·7	5·8	9·6	4·7	9·1	10·5	8·3	4·8	0·9	65·2

STATIONS SHOWING THE SINGLE RAINFALL MAXIMUM OF THE MONSOON RÉGIME

Station	Location	Alt.	Jan.	Feb.	Mar.	Apr.	May	June	July	Aug.	Sept.	Oct.	Nov.	Dec.	Total (Ins.)
Duala	Coast, French Camerouns	Sea-level	1·9	3·7	8·0	8·9	12·0	21·5	29·3	27·2	20·7	16·9	6·3	2·6	159·0
Free-town	Sierra Leone	Sea-level	0·6	0·5	1·1	5·4	14·8	21·3	36·8	39·6	32·5	15·2	5·3	1·3	174·4

[1] Fahrenheit readings are used throughout.

The beneficial influence of the north-easter has earned it the name of 'the doctor', though farther north, in the Sudan, its association with sand-storms earns for it a less complimentary title. The prevailing humid and hot conditions of the Guinea Coast are, without doubt, inimicable to the virility of the White immigrant, but the introduction of modern hygiene and sanitation has greatly changed the conditions of life, especially in the towns, such as Freetown and Lagos, where European influence is strongest ; and the formerly dreaded coasts of Southern Nigeria and Sierra Leone are no longer feared by the White administrator or trader.

In the tables on page 38 are included rainfall records for stations in Central Africa and the Guinea region whose climates have been outlined. On account of (a) the general uniformity of temperature conditions throughout the two regions, (b) the very small annual range of temperature at any station, it has not been considered necessary to include temperature readings. It may be remembered that nowhere is a monthly mean lower than 70° F.

The Vegetation of Central Africa and the Guinea Region

Steaming conditions of torrid heat and high humidity are reflected in the luxuriant growth of plant life. The densest type of tropical rain-forest, similar to that known as selva in the Amazon Basin of South America, is the dominant vegetation covering : but there are considerable areas in the regions under consideration where comparatively low rainfall—less than 50 inches—produces a non-forested growth of grass-and-tree savanna. The distribution of the African selva is briefly as follows :

In Central Africa rain-forest is practically continuous from the southern half of the Camerouns, southwards across French Equatorial Africa and Rio Muni, as far as the Equator. The lower Congo Basin which drains to the sea south of the Equator is characterized by park savanna rather than by forest : an exception is, however, provided in the vicinity of the main stream and its tributaries where there are moister conditions due to annual flooding and where dense tree growth is usual. A lack of equatorial conditions of rainfall in the neighbourhood of the Congo estuary has been indicated and the absence of dense forest is thereby explained. In the Belgian Congo the proportion of land heavily forested is probably between 50 and 60 per cent. and is practically confined to the most central and easterly districts. Its approximate west-east extent is from the junction of the Sanga with the main river as far as a longitudinal line about 50 miles to the west of the chain of lakes—Albert,

Edward and Kivu : while from north to south it lies between
lat. 4° N., which is to the south of the Ubangi River, and lat. 4° S.,
or fairly close to the course of the Kasai-Sankuru Rivers.

Turning now to West Africa—the Guinea region—we find
that the highlands of the Camerouns-Nigeria border country
narrowly confine the extent of selva to a coastal strip between
Duala and Buea. Beyond this ' strait ' between the two great
expanses of equatorial forest, in Central Africa and the Guinea
lands respectively, the selva widens considerably in Southern
Nigeria. In the eastern district of this Province, i.e. to the
east of the Niger Delta, the rain forest stretches in a belt 100
miles wide behind the coast, but west of the Delta there is
considerable narrowing once again, which is emphasized in the
hinterland of Lagos.

On the outer side of the Delta and on the coast immediately
to the east—especially the neighbourhood of Calabar—there is
one of the most extensive mangrove forests of the world. The
mangrove is a coastal swamp forest which is partly inundated
during the tidal flow. The tree-trunks stand above the limits
of high tide with their roots deep in saline mud and reach an
average height of 50 feet. It is estimated that about three-fifths
of the area of the Niger Delta is covered with rank mangrove
growth. Farther west on the Guinea Coast mangrove forest
and swamp is of frequent occurrence and the following sequence
is normal—sandy shore backed by lagoons, the habitat of the
mangrove, then inland on firmer soil the belt of the selva proper.

West of the district of Lagos, into Dahomey, the occurrence
of the rain-forest is but intermittent, and behind the lagoon
coast of Togoland as also in the eastern district of the Gold
Coast Colony it is entirely replaced by savanna. This coastal
zone of grass-land corresponds in its limits to the area of very
low rainfall to the east of Cape Three Points which was mentioned earlier. Over southern parts of the Ivory Coast and in
Liberia extends the most westerly belt of the African selva :
it is both widespread and continuous and attains a width
of considerably more than 100 miles, from the coast inland. The
coastal and southern districts of Sierra Leone provide a small
outpost of the rain-forest, but much of the northern interior is
savanna. Such is the extent of the selva of Africa.

A lighter form of tropical forest is found in the highlands
of the Western Cameroons which rise to over 6000 feet. The
selva reaches a level between 1000 and 2000 feet, but higher as
far as 5000–6000 feet it is replaced by less dense forest, above
which there is mergence into bush and grass-land.

Even later than the time of Stanley's explorations the Congo

Basin was thought to be clothed with rain-forest throughout, but it is now known that a very large part, especially the south-western and southern districts, has too low a rainfall to support dense tree growth. Late nineteenth-century explorers rarely

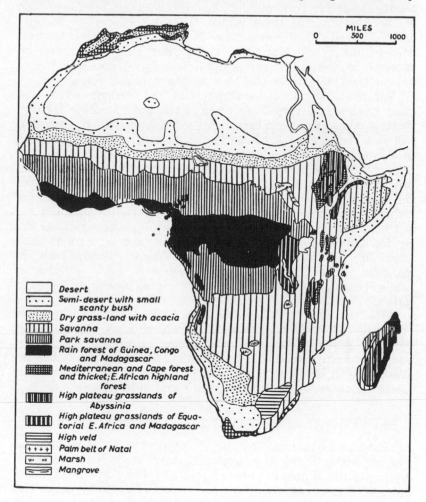

MILES
0   500   1000

Desert
Semi-desert with small
    scanty bush
Dry grass-land with acacia
Savanna
Park savanna
Rain forest of Guinea, Congo
    and Madagascar
Mediterranean and Cape forest
    and thicket; E.African highland
        forest
High plateau grasslands of
        Abyssinia
High plateau grasslands of Equa-
    torial E.Africa and Madagascar
High veld
Palm belt of Natal
Marsh
Mangrove

FIG. 10.—The vegetation of Africa

penetrated far from the rivers which they used for transport over long stages of their Congo travels. The tree growth of the river banks is luxuriant enough, but on the inter-riverine tracts, especially towards the south of the Congo Basin, park savanna

tends to predominate over forest. In this connexion it should
be borne in mind that the Congo drainage area is a plateau basin,
not a true lowland as is the Amazon Basin. The valleys of the
Congo tributaries and of the main stream are generally more
clearly defined in their middle and lower sections than are those
of the Amazon and there is not the same extent of flooding
and of alluvial deposition at times of high water that is characteristic of the South American river. For this reason, and on
account of the only moderate rainfall, forest and swamp are
not so predominant as they are in the Amazon region.

Summarizing the characteristics of the African selva—the
close grouping of very lofty trees is the most notable feature.
Beneath these giant timbers rising on an average to over 100
feet is a dense growth of smaller trees which add their foliage
to a canopy that excludes the sunlight. Then there is matted
undergrowth whose luxuriance distinguishes the selva from all
other forests of the world. From the point of view of species
the rain-forest is of heterogeneous membership, and the scattered,
rather than closely grouped, occurrence of certain valuable trees
is a hindrance to their commerical exploitation, especially as the
natural difficulties in the way of land transport are here at their
maximum. Hard woods, including cabinet woods such as
mahogany, the oil palm (*Elaeis guineensis*) and varieties of
rubber-bearing plants, such as the Landolphia vine and *Funtumia
elastica*, are characteristic of the forest.

Where the agricultural Negroes have made clearings for
cultivation the banana, manioc (known also as cassava) and
yams are probably the commonest crops. European plantation-
owning companies and the skilled native agriculturists of certain
West African lands, including the Gold Coast, are successful in
forest clearings with oil-palm, cacao and rubber.

I (c). EQUATORIAL CLIMATE: EAST AFRICAN TYPE

The third equatorial régime is confined to the East African
Plateau within limits from approximately lat. 3° N. to lat. 5° S.
Average altitude does not exceed 4000 feet, but there are elevated
areas with levels of over 6000 feet, from which lofty peaks rise
above the snow-line. Widely separated from each other, these
areas are : (1) the high western flanks of the Plateau which
overlook the Eastern Congo lands, from Mount Ruwenzori
southwards to the northern end of Lake Tanganyika, (2) the
Kenya Highlands, well within the western half of that Colony,
(3) the much-restricted mountain area around Kilimanjaro
(19,300 ft.), in the north-east of Tanganyika Territory

The benefit of altitude is readily perceived in the very moderate temperatures. As usual in equatorial lands the annual range is small, but the mean monthly figures are usually at least 10° lower than those for Central and West Africa. Nairobi (5500 ft.), the principal centre of White settlement in equatorial Africa and therefore a useful station to select for the purpose of showing the moderate temperatures of the Plateau, has no higher monthly record than 66°, which is the temperature for March, although on the other hand no month shows a lower figure than 58°. This range is general throughout the Kenya Highlands.

The climate has been described as one of perpetual spring and it recalls the régime on the Andean Plateau of Colombia and Ecuador at a similar elevation. But, for the health of the unacclimatized European immigrant there is the unfavourable feature of absence of well-marked seasonal rhythm, so that there is no resting period such as that to which the peoples of northern temperate climates are accustomed. Indeed, serious consequences to the mental and physical health of the majority are likely, should residence in these equatorial highlands be prolonged. It is true, however, that a considerable diurnal range permits of cool nights during much of the year, and the relaxation that is possible after sundown is greatly welcomed by the white colonist.

Annual rainfall shows usually the characteristic double maximum of equatorial latitude, and the periods of most intense precipitation usually occur a few weeks after the equinoxes of March and September. In addition to convectional rainfall of the doldrum belt, the south-east winds, in-drawn as a consequence of the development of the North African ' Low ' in the spring of the northern hemisphere, usually bring fairly abundant rain at this season.

The mean precipitation for the Plateau as a whole does not reach 45 inches. One of the wettest districts is in the vicinity of the western and northern shores of Lake Victoria, where stations show records of 60–70 inches.[1] A contrast is provided by the eastern and southern shores of the Victoria Nyanza where the precipitation is at least 20 inches lower ; and it is conclusive that the south-east winds in crossing the Lake draw up moisture which later is deposited when they strike the farther shores. The generally humid condition of the Uganda climate renders this country one of the least attractive of East Africa from the standpoint of White health.

Within the bounds of the high plateau one of the low rainfall areas is the sheltered trench of the Eastern Rift Valley of Western

[1] Entebbe, on the Uganda shore of the Lake, has about 60 inches and Bukoba, farther south, has over 70 inches.

Kenya which is little affected by the rain-bearing south-east winds whose moisture is trapped farther east. A little more than 30 inches is the mean annual rainfall for several stations of the Eastern Rift.

On the East African littoral from the neighbourhood of Mombasa southwards to Cape Delgado temperature conditions conform to normal equatorial lowland type. Mombasa has no month with a lower mean than 73° ; the same is true for Dar-es-Salaam, and these stations are typical of the range on the coast. Much of the coastal rain is brought by the in-drawn South-East Trade or monsoon which develops strongly in April and May, the months of highest precipitation on the coast of Tanganyika and Southern Kenya. Farther north than Mombasa the summer monsoon is deflected to the north-east and is drawn towards the ' Low ' of South-Western Asia. A corresponding change in the trend of the coast results in parallel-to-shore summer winds that deposit very little moisture on the north-east coast of Kenya and over Italian Somaliland. In the northern winter the same shores are under the influence of the North-East Trades which blow parallel to the coast-line and are practically rainless. Behind the southern littoral of Kenya is the dry area (less than 30 inches) of the Nyika, where the very gradual rise in altitude from the coast does not tend to promote heavy precipitation from winds drawn inland.

The summer monsoon is part of the great monsoonal flow of air from the Indian Ocean which affects India and East Africa alike. From year to year this current fluctuates in strength and the amount of precipitation dependent on it varies correspondingly. Years of excessive drought or of abnormal rains in India usually coincide with years of low or high Nile floods.

So vital is the rainfall of April–October to the life of these regions—to which Egypt should be added as it is fed largely by Abyssinian water—that much research has already been undertaken into the causes of the fluctuation of the monsoon current year by year, and attempts are made to forecast the rainfall of the Nile head-streams and of India from the evidence provided by the distribution of barometric pressure in the early months of the year over the Indian Ocean and its peripheral lands. One occurrence that has been noticed is that heavy convectional rainfall in the neighbourhood of Zanzibar during April often precedes a poor monsoon developing in May. Heavy convectional rainfall in this equatorial zone accompanies abnormally low pressure, and if at the time when the south-east monsoon should be developing there is a low pressure gradient from eastern equatorial Africa to North-East Africa and South-West

EAST AFRICA : TYPICAL CLIMATIC STATIONS

Station	Location	Alt. (Feet)		Jan.	Feb.	Mar.	Apr.	May	June	July	Aug.	Sept.	Oct.	Nov.	Dec.	
(a) Nairobi.	Kenya Highlands	5500	Temp.	63·8	64·7	65·2	63·9	63·4	61·6	58·5	59·3	61·6	64·8	64·0	62·3	Range 6·7
			Rainfall (Inches)	1·9	4·2	3·7	8·3	5·2	2·0	0·8	0·9	0·9	2·0	5·8	3·5	Total 39·2
(b) Dar-es-Salaam	Coast	—	Temp.	81·9	81·7	80·8	78·4	76·6	74·3	73·8	73·6	74·7	76·6	79·3	81·1	Range 8·3
			Rainfall	3·7	2·1	5·2	12·3	8·1	1·1	1·6	1·1	1·3	1·3	3·1	4·4	Total 45·3
Mombasa	Coast	—	Temp.	79·9	80·3	81·8	80·6	78·4	76·5	75·3	75·7	77·0	78·4	79·4	79·9	Range 6·5
			Rainfall	0·8	0·9	2·3	7·8	13·7	3·6	3·5	2·2	1·9	3·4	5·0	2·2	Total 47·3
(c) Naivasha	Kenya, E. Rift Valley	6300	Temp.	64·8	64·7	63·8	62·7	63·3	61·4	60·5	61·5	62·1	63·6	63·0	62·8	Range 4·3
			Rainfall	1·1	1·4	3·0	6·4	2·3	4·0	2·2	2·7	2·0	2·2	3·1	1·8	Total 32·2
(d) Entebbe	North-West Shore of L. Victoria	3900	Temp.	72·7	72·4	71·8	70·2	71·2	70·9	70·0	70·5	71·8	72·5	72·2	71·5	Range 2·7
			Rainfall	3·2	2·9	6·2	10·2	8·3	4·9	3·0	3·3	2·6	3·2	5·4	5·8	Total 59·0
Mwanza	South-East Shore of L. Victoria	3900	Temp.	72·1	71·4	72·1	71·8	72·1	68·4	71·8	71·2	72·5	70·5	70·9	70·5	Range 4·1
			Rainfall	2·5	3·2	6·5	8·7	3·3	1·9	0·1	1·5	1·8	3·1	5·1	4·9	Total 42·6

45

Asia it follows that the consequent winds will be weak and variable rather than strong and regular and that their rainfall will be below normal. Again, as Colonel H. G. Lyons first showed, comparatively poor rains in the region of the Nile head-streams are sometimes a consequence of higher barometric pressure than the normal over North-East Africa in summer when, as a rule, pressure is here lowest over the continent.

On the previous page are given climatic records for typical stations in the following regions of East Africa—(a) Kenya Highlands, (b) the Coast, (c) Eastern Rift Valley, (d) the coast of Lake Victoria.

The Vegetation of the East African Plateau

Lowered temperatures, resulting from high altitude, and very moderate rainfall are factors which determine the absence of selva from this equatorial region. Diversity of relief is marked, and there are wide contrasts in altitude which are reflected in contrasts of rainfall and temperature ; so that vegetation is likely to be varied. Indeed, in respect of its range of plant life the region is almost unique in Africa.

Savanna, with rank, coarse grasses sometimes as high as 12 feet, is usually dominant. At its richest it partakes of the character of tropical park-land : at its poorest it is arid grass-land with much thorn bush, as in the drier parts of the Eastern Rift Valley and on the Nyika. Southern and eastern slopes that face the summer monsoon are usually more luxuriant in plant life than those which have a northerly or westerly aspect.

The savanna is usually continuous between the levels of 4000 and 6000 feet. Then up to 8000–9000 feet, that is to say between levels which are much higher than the average for the Plateau and where the rains are abundant, there is tall, dense forest on whose upper side bamboo thickets, still the home of the elephant, are common. Much of the temperate rain forest has been des-troyed by Natives in their endeavour to provide clearings for agriculture. Bananas and yams are typical of the crops native-grown in the clearings, and, where the European has introduced his agriculture, temperate cereals such as wheat and oats succeed on these highland levels. Beyond the limits of the bamboo thickets the vegetation gradually changes to grass-land of steppe-like character which is found in the few districts rising above 8000–9000 feet.

The East African savanna provides the critical connecting link between the two vast belts of tropical grass-land that border the equatorial forest on its northern and southern sides respec-tively. Not only has it provided a home for pastoral peoples ;

it has also offered the only easy route which migrating pastoral tribes, moving north or south, might follow so as to skirt the barrier of the selva, which is inimical to the traditional life of the stock-rearing nomad. On the eastern side of the Plateau the herdsmen and agriculturists have tended to avoid the immediate hinterland of the coast, where thorn bush and meagre grass provide poorer sustenance for animals than does the highland savanna of the Plateau proper. Long settlement and

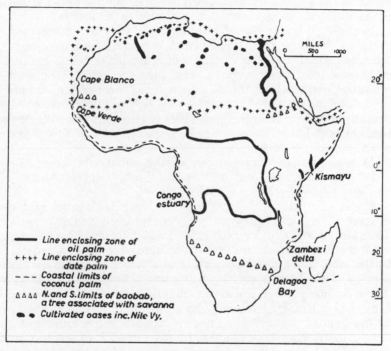

FIG. II.—Geographical limits of growth of the Date-, Oil- and Coconut-palms

extended agricultural practice have obliterated most of the tropical rain forest which formerly occupied the moistest tracts of the East African coast.

In a region of so considerable a range of vegetation a wide variety of pastoral and agricultural activities is to be expected. Nomad stock-rearers live in close proximity to sedentary agriculturists and, unless checked by European intervention, the pastoralists tend to act aggressively towards their neighbours, by reason of their greater virility and war-like propensities. One of the greatest hindrances to the success and extension of stock-rearing in East Africa is the presence of the almost ubiquitous tsetse fly, whose ravages frequently decimate the herds of the pastoral tribes.[1]

II. TROPICAL CLIMATES: THE 'SUDAN' TYPE

This climatic type is associated with two vast zones respectively to the north and south of equatorial latitudes ; they represent climatic and vegetational transition from the equatorial conditions of great heat and humidity with dense forest growth to the dry heat of the northern and southern deserts.

Because Africa north of the Equator is much more continental in character than Southern Africa the ' Sudan ' climate, which is ' continental ' as distinguished from ' oceanic,' is found in its most ideal form in north- and west-central regions, whilst in South-Central Africa there is a modified form of the ' Sudan ' régime which is affected somewhat by oceanic influence and by plateau elevation greater than that of the Sudan. We may, therefore, subdivide the zones and characteristics of this climate into :

(A) the ' Sudan ' type, north of the equatorial zone ;
(B) the modified ' Sudan ' type of South-Central Africa.

(A) A characteristic feature is the very high level of temperature throughout the year. The extreme is usually reached in late spring when, under clear skies, insolation is at its maximum, and the mean temperature of May at many stations exceeds 90°. A little later in the year the coming of the rains and the development of cloud have a cooling influence, though the diminution of heat is not perceptible to the inhabitants as the accompaniment of high humidity renders the atmosphere less tolerable than the dry heat of the spring. There is a considerable annual range of 15–20°, as may be expected in the interior of a great and compact land-mass whose extent from Senegal to the Abyssinian border is not less than 3600 miles. It is rare, however, to find a mean monthly temperature as low as 70°. The diurnal range is very considerable and night frosts sometimes occur in the coolest season.

During the months October to early March inclusive, when pressure is comparatively high over the Northern Sahara, the North-East Trade or monsoon blows with fair regularity across the Sudan towards the equatorial trough of low pressure. This regular winter wind, the *Harmattan*, has already been mentioned as occasionally carrying invigorating dry air to the normally humid Guinea Coast. As a Sudan wind the *Harmattan* is extremely desiccating in its effects on plant, animal and human

[1] *v.* Fig. 46. Distribution of the Tsetse Fly, p. 239.

life, and its relative humidity is frequently lower than 25 per cent. Great heat and the load of fine sand particles which it carries from the desert render it very unwelcome to the inhabitants of the Sudan.

In summer the south-west monsoon is drawn towards the North African ' Low ' and crosses the Guinea Coast to penetrate the Sudan as a rain-bearing current ; so is provided a large part of the rainfall. From the northern limit of the equatorial forest to the border of the Sahara—a distance of approximately 600 miles—there is usually a steady diminution in precipitation wherever a south-to-north section of the Sudan is taken. From 40–50 inches to 8–10 inches on the desert fringe is the normal distribution. Furthermore, the duration of the rainy season decreases towards the north and in the same direction precipitation becomes less reliable in its occurrence. The rain-bearing south-westerlies reach their limit of effectiveness on the Saharan border which lies approximately east-west across the continent from the Atlantic coast to the Abyssinian frontier, though with slight southward dipping towards the east.

Examination of the few available rainfall records for stations in the Southern Sudan reveals a double maximum : this is a consequence of the passage northward and again southward of the equatorial convectional rain-belt in the wake of the apparent seasonal movement of the sun. Such rainfall is additional to the contribution of the south-west monsoon. The sun is near its overhead position throughout the greater part of the Sudan in May and again in July, so that allowing for a considerable ' lag ' and remembering the occurrence of the south-westerlies one may expect that June–July and August–September will be periods of heavy rainfall. Makurdi, near the southern border of the Sudan in Nigeria, shows such an occurrence of the double maximum.[1]

It is claimed by certain observers that a season of particularly heavy rainfall on the Guinea Coast coincides with deficient rains over the Western and Central Sudan ; and that over the Eastern Sudan and Abyssinia sub-normal precipitation usually occurs at the same time that there are abundant rains on the East African littoral, south of the Equator.[2]

There are wide areas of the Sudan where the amount of precipitation, measured by the rain-gauge, seems to be adequate for agriculture and yet where cultivation is out of the question without the aid of irrigation. This is explained by the intensity of evaporation as a result of which the value of the rainfall to

[1] See climatic data at the end of this section.
[2] See article by Renner in *Geog. Review*, Vol. XVI, pp. 583–96.

man is very much reduced. Lands with the 'Sudan' climate are at a marked disadvantage in this respect when compared with regions of the 'Mediterranean' régime—of which there are two in Africa—where rainfall is confined to winter, the season of minimum evaporation.

The view is widely held that aridity is increasing over the Sudan and that desert conditions are spreading southwards. In support of this view, so far as evidence over a considerable period is available, there is no doubt that peoples of the Northern Sudan are tending to migrate in consequence of the desiccation of their pasture lands. It is doubtful, however, in consideration of the complete absence of long-period rainfall records in the Sudan, if decreasing rainfall rather than destruction of vegetation by the Natives, or the drift of sand by the Harmattan, is the principal agent of desiccation. There is good evidence that the gradual filling of the Lake Chad basin by the drift of the Saharan sand is proceeding at the present time.

The climatic régime of Abyssinia is associated with that of the Sudan and would resemble it closely but for the great difference of altitude. Abyssinia is a lofty plateau rising in peaks to over 12,000 feet and with an average level not less than 6000 feet above the sea. Particular mention must be made of the distribution of its rains which are of vital importance not only to the pastoralists of the high Plateau but also and more particularly to the sedentary agriculturists of Egypt who use water carried by the Nile across more than 1000 miles of desert.

The rain-bearing agent is the summer monsoon which is fed by both the Gulf of Guinea and Indian Ocean wind currents. The southern and south-western flanks of the great 'massif' receive the heaviest fall which exceeds 60 inches, practically all occurring between April and October. Farther into the interior there is a marked diminution in the annual precipitation, so that the northern and eastern borders approach desert conditions.

Tabulated below are rainfall records (mean monthly) for representative stations in (a) Northern Sudan, with its single maximum, (b) Southern Sudan where a double maximum is developed, (c) Abyssinia, for which a temperature record is included on account of special conditions due to high altitude.

Consideration of the character and distribution of vegetation in the region will follow a statement of the modified 'Sudan' climate of South-Central Africa to which we now proceed.

(B) The lands concerned have no rigid delimitation but may be defined as extending approximately from the southern districts of the Congo Basin and from southern parts of Tanganyika Territory southwards to the Tropic of Capricorn, but excluding

Station	Location	Alt. (feet)	Jan.	Feb.	Mar.	Apr.	May	June	July	Aug.	Sept.	Oct.	Nov.	Dec.	Total Inches
(a) El Obeid	Kordofan .	1870	0	0	0·1	0	0·4	1·2	3·6	4·5	3·4	0·7	0	0	13·9
Kano .	N. Nigeria	1570	0·1	0·1	0·3	0·7	2·5	4·5	8·0	12·0	5·6	0·5	0	0·5	34·8
Timbuktu	Northern bend of Niger .	850	0	0	0·1	0	0·3	0·9	3·5	2·8	1·1	0·4	0	0	9·1
(b) Makurdi	Benue River, Nigeria .	340	0·8	0	0·5	1·2	5·3	6·7	4·8	8·7	15·2	6·1	0·9	0	50·7
Gondo-koro	Southern part A— Egypt: Sudan .	1600	0·1	0·8	2·0	3·5	6·5	3·9	5·0	4·9	4·4	4·7	1·9	0·4	38·1

		Alt. 8000 ft.													(Range)
(c) Addis Ababa	Central Abyssinia	Temp.	61·9	59·4	64·0	61·2	63·2	59·2	56·7	58·9	58·0	60·0	61·4	60·0	7·3
		R'fall Inches	0·6	1·9	2·8	3·4	3·0	5·7	11·0	12·1	7·6	0·8	0·6	0·2	Total 49·7

the Bechuanaland Protectorate and South-West Africa over which desert or semi-desert conditions prevail : and so defined this climatic region lies practically wholly to the north of the Union of South Africa.

The sub-continental peninsula between the Indian and South Atlantic Oceans is narrow from east to west when compared with North Africa, unlike which, moreover, its poleward coast opens to a wide ocean. We may expect, therefore, the penetration of oceanic influences serving to moderate temperatures and to introduce moisture-bearing winds to the interior. High plateau altitude, another factor distinguishing the sub-continent from its northern and much more spacious counterpart, is on the average not less than 3000 feet.

Temperatures are high throughout the year though rarely excessive, and it is unusual for the mean of the hottest month, which immediately precedes the summer rains, to exceed 82°. On the other hand, the mid-winter mean rarely descends as low as 60° at any station. Exceptions to the normal temperature range occur in depressions of the Plateau such as the Rift Valley of Lake Nyasa, where intense heat is experienced before the coming of the rains.

The rainfall régime is marked by monsoonal influence. During the southern winter—June to August—the anticyclonic system over the sub-continent prevents the penetration of the South-East Trades whose influence is limited to the coast-lands of South-East Africa. Uninterrupted sunshine together with comparatively low atmospheric humidity distinguish winter as the pleasant season. Six months later when the anticyclone is replaced by low pressure there is convectional rainfall which is reinforced especially in the eastern half of the sub-continent, by orographical rains borne by the south-east winds from the Indian Ocean. From equatorial latitudes towards the southern tropic and from the eastern flanks of the Plateau towards the Atlantic coast there tends to be a steady diminution of rainfall up to the borders of the Kalahari and neighbouring desert.

On the western coast, in Angola, a low rainfall of 10–20 inches is partly explained by the occurrence of cold surface water offshore. This is a condition for which the cool Benguella Current, flowing northwards close to the coast, is in part responsible. South-west winds pass from the South Atlantic ' High ' over cool surface water to the heated continent, and condensation tends to be deficient as a result. Beyond the coastal plain, going inland, where the altitude of the Plateau is 3000–5000 feet, precipitation is considerably higher, though the meteorological records for this very inadequately known land of Portuguese West Africa are too meagre to permit certainty of statement with regard to rainfall occurrence over tens of thousands of square miles.

Rather more is known of the rainfall régime of Northern Rhodesia and Nyasaland over which extends the modified ' Sudan ' climate that is characteristic of interior Angola. Their latitudes, almost entirely on the poleward side of the parallel of 10° South, are beyond the reach of the equatorial low-pressure rain-belt, but the south-east winds of summer bring abundant rain, especially in Nyasaland, where altitude is higher and relief more accentuated and where 50 inches may be taken as the average. The southern highlands of Nyasaland, to the south of the Lake, experience a cooler climate than the normal for the region : this has encouraged European settlement, and Southern Nyasaland is to be associated from the standpoint of climate and habitability with the higher parts of the Plateau in Kenya and Tanganyika.

Farther east and south-east on the littoral belt of Portuguese East Africa and in the lower valley of the Zambezi temperatures are generally higher. The climate is unhealthy—particularly for the European—and diseases, such as malaria, which are associated with low altitudes in the wet Tropics are a very unfavourable feature of the environment. Rainfall seems to be similar in seasonal occurrence to that of the Plateau but less in total amount and the average does not appear to reach 40 inches. Meteorological records are, however, inadequate and any statement concerning the climate of Portuguese East Africa must be considered with reserve. A factor in the coastal climate is the warm

Mozambique Current, which flows southwards, close to the coast, from equatorial latitudes and is responsible for raising the temperature and humidity of the prevalent onshore winds.

Temperature and rainfall records are included below and refer to stations distributed as follows :

(a) at comparatively low altitude on the shore of Lake Nyasa ;
(b) at moderately high altitude in Southern Nyasaland ;
(c) on the coast of Mozambique.

Station	Alt. (feet)	(1) Temp. (2) R'fall	Jan.	Feb.	Mar.	Apr.	May	June	July	Aug.	Sept.	Oct.	Nov.	Dec.	(1) Range (2) Total
(a) Nkata Bay	1400	(1)	77·2	75·6	76·6	75·0	72·0	67·7	66·9	68·6	73·6	77·1	80·0	78·0	(1) 13·1
		(2)	8·1	12·4	13·2	11·6	3·3	2·4	2·2	1·1	0·3	0·4	0·9	8·6	(2) 64·5
(b) Zomba	3200	(1)	71·8	70·7	69·8	68·5	64·8	61·9	60·6	64·0	68·9	74·5	74·5	71·8	(1) 13·9
		(2)	11·3	11·0	8·5	3·8	0·7	0·4	0·3	0·1	0·3	1·7	5·4	10·7	(2) 54·2
(c) Mozambique	Near sea-level	(1)	81·9	81·5	82·8	81·0	77·7	73·9	73·8	74·5	77·2	80·1	82·8	83·3	(1) 9·5
		(2)	7·9	8·7	7·4	4·4	2·3	1·0	0·5	1·1	0·5	0·1	0·3	4·9	(2) 39·1

The Vegetation associated with the ' Sudan ' Climate

Luxuriant growth of tall grasses, attaining a height of 5–12 feet by the close of summer, is characteristic not only of the Sudan and the plateau of South-Central Africa, but also, as we have seen, of certain parts of the East African Plateau in equatorial latitudes. Passing from the savanna there is gradual transition on the poleward side to semi-desert and scrub-land, and, on the equator-ward border, to park savanna followed by transition to forest.

On the savanna the long period—3–5 months—of very low rainfall or actual drought is opposed to the growth of forest trees, though tall thorn-bushes including varieties of acacia and mimosa are common. Trees must be capable of storing water, as in the case of the massive baobab—the ' sentinel of the savanna '—or of reducing transpiration to a minimum during the period of drought. The life of the grasses is short and limited to the period of the rains, after which they die, withered and scorched, exposing the hard-baked soil.

Not very satisfactory pasturage is provided for domesticated animals by the tall, rank grasses, though wild game such as the elephant, rhinoceros and many types of buck, find on the savanna very favourable conditions. Stock-rearing is, however, more important than cultivation throughout the tropical grass-lands of Africa as a whole, and cattle are especially important within the zone which is transitional to the true savanna and the semi-

5

desert : elsewhere stock consists mainly of sheep and goats. Prior to the days of European occupation the pastoralists, especially the nomads of the lands bordering the desert, tended to appropriate the holdings of the agriculturists, and in the ensuing struggles much of the history of the savannas of Africa was unrolled.

Native-grown foodstuffs usually include root crops such as yams, manioc and sweet potatoes, and cereals of which maize, sorghum and rice are typical. There are almost limitless prospects for agricultural and pastoral development along modern lines which will, however, involve, on the drier parts of the savanna, costly schemes of irrigation for the purpose of counteracting the naturally waterless condition of the surface soil during the rainless months. Amongst the commercial crops the future of which is assured are ground-nuts (or pea-nuts)—valuable for their oil content and already a staple of commerce in the Western Sudan —cotton, maize and tobacco. In addition to ground-nut the shea tree is also valuable for its oil, best known as shea butter, and grows near or within the border zone intermediate to the Sahara and Sudan.

The transition from savanna to desert, so far as North Africa is concerned, occurs throughout a belt varying in width from 200 to 300 miles and extending from north of the Senegal River almost to the Red Sea coast of the Anglo-Egyptian Sudan. This intermediate zone has been termed the acacia—desert grass savanna.[1] In its wells and holes it possesses considerable water supplies despite deficient rainfall, and this advantage, added to the absence of densely-growing vegetation which hinders movement on the more luxuriant savanna, assists the nomadism which is determined by the sparseness of pasturage. It has been from early human times an avenue of migration used by sheep and cattle herdsmen. Within historic times the camel has been introduced and has proved to be the most useful animal for transport purposes in this semi-desert environment.

Rather exceptional in their vegetation character are the Chad Basin, the Sudan section of the Nile Basin, the Abyssinian Plateau and the low plateau of Portuguese East Africa.

The depression of which the waters of Lake Chad occupy but a small part is situated in the zone of transition from acacia— desert grass to richer savanna. Marshes covering vast areas are formed or augmented during the summer rains and the delta of the Shari River is typical of this vegetation. Not dissimilar is the swamp or marsh land with tall reed growth which is characteristic

[1] See Shantz and Marbut, *The Vegetation and Soils of Africa*, pp. 63 et seq.

of the districts near the confluence of the Bahr-el-Ghazal and Bahr-el-Jebel in the Sudan.

On the Abyssinian Plateau the regional differences of rainfall, especially marked between the south-west and the north, and the considerable range of temperature between altitude zones, together produce great contrasts in vegetation. Indeed, all forms of African vegetation except the selva are represented in this country. The plateau levels of the interior at an average of 6000 feet are usually treeless steppe rather than tropical savanna. On the south-western flanks and on other well-watered tracts between 6000 and 9000 feet there is abundant forest growth which includes the quite typical juniper tree. In some other fairly moist parts of the Plateau at elevations higher than 6000 feet park savanna is discovered. Abyssinia supports a pastoral economy mainly, though primitive agriculture is present in most parts. An indigenous coffee shrub bears well, though production is small compared with that of Yemen in *Arabia Felix*, where physical conditions show resemblance to those of Abyssinia. Various types of gum-bearing shrubs are characteristic of the drier parts of the Plateau and of neighbouring Eritrea, and here again there is correspondence in vegetation with the near-by strip of Arabia.[1]

The low plateau foreland in Portuguese East Africa supports rather poor grass-and-acacia savanna in response to a meagre or uncertain rainfall. There are considerable areas in the lower valleys of the Zambezi and Limpopo Rivers, however, where the moist land is capable of supporting richer savanna with occasional tracts of tropical rain forest.

Although in the above paragraphs the Sudan is more particularly mentioned, it is to be remembered that the savanna of South-Central Africa bears a close resemblance to that which extends north of the equatorial forest. The same sequence from park-savanna to acacia semi-desert is present, though in the eastern half of the sub-continent there is not a southward transition to desert, but a continuance of the grass-land environment, under cooler conditions, as far as the extreme south.

III. TROPICAL CLIMATES: THE 'HOT DESERT' TYPE

The hot arid lands of Africa may be described as the 'trade wind' deserts, for the prevalence of the North-East or South-East Trades—according to the hemisphere—is marked throughout the greater part of the year and, failing these winds, there

[1] Certain types of acacia produce the ' gum arabic ' of commerce.

are calm, anticyclonic conditions due to the setting up of high pressure over the land during the coolest season.

The Sahara is a desert on a continental scale.[1] If we omit local names, such as Libyan Desert, it extends uninterruptedly from the Atlantic coast over to the Red Sea with an average north-south span of not less than 800 miles. Very approximately we may place the southern limit close to the parallel of 18° N. In addition there is the desert of the ' Eastern Horn ', a partially-detached outpost of the Sahara, as well as the arid land of the south-west, traversed by the Tropic of Capricorn. Both of the latter are definitely marginal in position, and it is only in the Sahara that desert conditions are carried far into the interior of the continent.

As the deserts meet the sea along four coasts of Africa [2] one may expect a rather different climatic régime on these margins from that which is typical of the Saharan interior. Such is indeed the case and the desert climates may be classified as :
(a) interior continental, or true Saharan,
(b) coastal.

(a) The southern interior districts of the Sahara experience the highest summer temperatures of the continent, if not of the world, and it is not unusual in the hottest season for the afternoon temperature (at 2 p.m.) to exceed 120°. Winter offers considerable relief from this excessive heat and in December–January the mean is, in most districts for which there are records, below 60°. A very wide diurnal range, especially in winter, has, however, to be taken into account : the intensity of insolation under cloudless skies is balanced by the rapid loss of heat through radiation which follows sunset. A diurnal range of over 50° is common throughout the year and in mid-winter night frosts are not unusual.

There is practically no precipitation : in addition, the relative humidity of the atmosphere is low, usually varying from 30 to 50 per cent. We recall that the prevalent North-East Trades are blowing over land where mean temperature increases towards the south so that they are warmed in their passage. Thus the possibility of precipitation diminishes and, especially in the Southern and Central Sahara, rainfall is rendered more unlikely by reason of the long land passage of the Trades. As more becomes known of the high central plateaux of Ahaggar and Tibesti it seems evident that these altitudes, in some places

[1] ' Sahara ' is an Arabic word—Sahrā signifying ' wilderness '.
[2] Including the Mediterranean coast in Libya and Egypt (west of the Delta).

exceeding 8000 feet, receive a meagre rainfall which is quickly re-absorbed by the atmosphere under the conditions of intense evaporation. This precipitation indicates that although the relative humidity of Saharan winds is low their absolute humidity is still considerable.

The lack of rainfall in Egypt, even in those parts close to the Mediterranean sea-board, is not always fully realized, for we are accustomed to the association of densely-populated agricultural lands with plentiful rainfall. Egypt is climatically a desert. Cairo, the largest city of Africa, has a rainfall of 2 inches ; and no other city of the world which compares in size and consequence with Cairo has anything approaching such meagre precipitation. Farther up the Nile Valley the readings descend to zero, as in the case of the important centre of Aswan.

One of the least desirable features of a climate which is generally favourable to health is the frequency of sandstorms, local swirls set up by convection currents. The dreaded 'simoon', of scorching breath, belongs to this type.

(b) Immediately offshore from the Western Sahara cold surface water has an important modifying influence on the normal desert climate. The cold Canary Current flowing equator-wards reduces the temperature of the surface waters and of the lower layers of the atmosphere in the vicinity. Moreover, the upwelling of cold water close to the shore has to be taken into account : this occurs when the Trades cause a drift of surface water away from the coast. Although the western margin of the Sahara is well within the zone of the North-East Trades the alternate heating and cooling of the land-mass each day and night produces land and sea breezes which, especially in the summer, have sometimes more local importance than the Trades. The onshore breezes of the day are cooled when passing over the cold coastal waters and they tend to reduce shore temperatures very considerably during the summer, so that the high levels of the thermometer in the interior are never approached. Usually, the mean of each month of the year is lower than 70°.

The moderating influence of the sea-breezes prevents the great diurnal range that is generally characteristic of the Sahara, while yet another important distinguishing feature of the coastal climate is the frequent occurrence of fogs which are formed when the localized onshore winds blow over the cold waters of the littoral. A considerable degree of atmospheric humidity provides a climatic paradox, for there is practically no precipitation in the form of rain. At Cape Juby, a typical station, the mean relative humidity for the year exceeds 80 per cent., yet the rainfall is less than 5 inches.

On the desert coast of South-West Africa are repeated the climatic conditions of the extreme Western Sahara. Unlike the regular winds of North Africa, the South-East Trades are responsible for abundant rainfall which is, however, limited to the eastern half of the sub-continent and is largely precipitated on the high eastern flanks of the South African Plateau. From the eastern escarpment—the Drakensberg—to the Atlantic coast there is a steady diminution of rainfall, until on the shore it is almost completely lacking.

The description of desert should not be applied to the Kalahari, for the greater part of this arid grass-land, which occupies an interior position mainly within the Bechuanaland Protectorate, has a not inconsiderable rainfall varying from 5 to 10 inches. True desert in South Africa is limited to a coastal strip extending approximately from the neighbourhood of Port Nolloth in the Western Cape Province to the lower course of the Cunene River. The cold Benguella Current helps to produce on this land margin the lowered temperatures of summer and the humid atmosphere which, as we have seen, are also characteristic of the Atlantic coast of the Sahara. Onshore winds, usually local sea-breezes, are a common feature of the littoral and, especially in summer, interrupt the normal Trade Wind régime which is associated with offshore winds and the upwelling of cold water close to the shore. The Trades are fairly regular and strong in winter when high pressure is established over the southern part of the sub-continent. As they approach the Atlantic coast in the process of a comparatively abrupt descent from the western edge of the Plateau —in these parts not less than 3000 feet in altitude—they are warmed by compression (cf. Foehn winds) and the shore temperatures in winter are high in consequence and about equal to those of summer.

The Somaliland coast facing the Indian Ocean and the Gulf of Aden is sufficiently arid to be classed as desert, for there are very few districts where the rainfall exceeds 5 inches. On the plateau behind the littoral belt the high altitudes rising to over 6000 feet catch rain—sometimes as much as 20 inches in a year— drawn from the summer monsoon which also waters the Abyssinian Plateau. In addition, the northern slope of the Somaliland Plateau overlooking the Gulf of Aden receives meagre rains from the North-East Trade or winter monsoon. The aridity of the coast of Italian Somaliland is due to the regularity with which the north-east and south-west monsoons, of winter and summer respectively, blow parallel to the shore, thus offering little opportunity for the precipitation of 'orographical' rains.

As we are concerned with regions whose annual rainfall is

less than 5 inches a statement of the distribution of precipitation from month to month at selected stations is unnecessary. In the cases of the following desert stations there is a distinction between (a) continental interior or true Saharan, and (b) marginal or coastal. The annual temperature range is shown, but the important factor of diurnal range, which should not be overlooked, is not indicated here. (Mean monthly temperatures are estimated to the nearest degree, Fahrenheit.)

Station	Location	Alt. (ft.)	Rainfall (inches)	Mean Temperature												
				Jan.	Feb.	Mar.	Apr.	May	June	July	Aug.	Sept.	Oct.	Nov.	Dec.	Range
(a) In Salah	Tidikelt	1100	Nil	54	57	66	77	85	94	98	95	90	80	68	57	44
Aswan	Upper Egypt	400	Nil	59	63	70	78	85	90	91	90	88	82	72	62	32
(b) Cape Juby	Rio de Oro	Near sea-level	4·5	61	61	63	64	65	67	68	68	69	68	65	62	8
Walvis Bay	South-West Africa	do.	Nil	65	66	66	65	62	60	59	57	58	60	61	64	9
Port Nolloth	Western Cape Province	do.	2·5	60	60	59	58	57	55	55	54	55	58	59	60	6

The Vegetation of the Tropical Deserts

Though practically rainless the deserts are not altogether without subterranean water which may usually be brought to the surface by the sinking of deep wells, as practised in the great oases of the Sahara, e.g. those of the Tuat group (North-Central Sahara). The palm groves and intensive garden cultivation of these oases are not repeated in the desert of South-West Africa. Agricultural wealth together with nodal position on lines of trans-Saharan communication bestow on the northern oases very considerable economic and commercial significance : on the other hand, the desert of South-West Africa is a zone of extreme isolation which is avoided, except by the primitive Bushmen who have taken refuge on its arid borders.

One very important resource of the Saharan oases is the abundant date-palm which is numbered in millions and provides a most important article in the food supply of the desert peoples. It seems to flourish only in almost rainless districts where there is subterranean water which its roots may reach, and it has not become successfully acclimatized in those parts of the Mediterranean fringe where the winter rainfall is considerable.

Saharan scenery is of wide variety, as determined by the geological character of the surface rocks and the action of erosive

agents which include wind and frost. Usually there is a very
meagre vegetation of stunted shrubs, occurring sporadically;
but this plant life is not perceptible at a distance, so that the
landscape appears to be uniformly barren.

Sandy wastes, composed largely of drifting dunes, are the
Saharan type known as the ' erg '. Here and there occur small
shrubs, including the Saharan broom, and tufts of very harsh
grass, though it is true that vast stretches are devoid of all vegetation. One of the great areas of sandy desert includes the ' Great
Erg ' and extends from the Saharan border of Tunisia and
Algeria southwards towards the Ahaggar Plateau, with a south-
eastward prolongation to the north of the Tibesti Plateau.
Probably the most spacious area of unmitigated sandy waste is
provided by the Libyan Desert, stretching southwards for 800
miles from the neighbourhood of the Siwa group of oases. Naturally, the ' erg ' is avoided by caravans which keep as far as possible
to the rocky and pebble or gravel desert, where the movement of
transport is easier and where subterranean water and camel
pasture are more abundant, though still very rare.

Rocky wastes with the bare exposure of fissured rocks as
dominant features of the scene, form the ' hamada ' type of the
Sahara. Much of the central plateaux of Ahaggar and Tibesti
is of this nature, though the ' hamada ' is found also at lower
altitudes as, for example, in parts of Rio de Oro and its hinterland. In the cracks of the rocks that result from the alternate
and intense insolation and radiation of the day and night, respectively, numerous shrubs of different varieties take shelter and
provide rough camel pasture which is not ignored by the desert
nomads.

An intermediate stage between rocky and sandy desert is
represented by the gravel and pebble wastes that are the detritus
of the eroded ' hamada '. This type is the ' areg ' or ' reg '.
Though dwarf bushes such as the ' cushion plant ' (bot. : *anabasis*)
occur much of the ' reg ' is without plant life.

In the driest districts of Somaliland there is much sand and
stony ground. A distinguishing feature of the scanty vegetation
is the very occasional occurrence of acacia and other thorn
bush. Grass is absent almost everywhere and in its rare occurrence is of little value for pasture by reason of its harshness.
In the south of Italian Somaliland streams fed by Abyssinian
snows and rains meander across the coastal desert, and their
courses are marked by much richer vegetation than that which is
characteristic of the normal desert landscape. The utilization
of these intermittent streams for extensive irrigation was intended
by the former Italian Government which hoped to emulate,

though on a smaller scale, the magnificent irrigation achievements of the Nile Valley.

The littoral desert of South-West Africa is most arid close to the sea, where there is a wide belt of almost continuous sand-dunes from the Cunene to the Orange River. Farther inland a meagre increase in the vegetation is represented by the occasional appearance of acacia and euphorbia.

IV. SUB-TROPICAL CLIMATES: (A) " MEDITERRANEAN " TYPE

North-West Africa

The northernmost littoral of Africa in Barbary, Cyrenaica and Egypt experiences a climate of similar régime to that of the coastlands throughout the greater part of the Mediterranean Basin ; though, as we may readily suppose, the southern position of the African shores is associated with higher temperatures than those measured on the northern, or European border.

The distinctive feature is the virtual limitation of rainfall to the winter half-year, and a station is rarely found where the three-months' period, June to August, receives as much as 2 inches. This highly-emphasized rhythm in rainfall occurrence suggests comparison with the ' Sudan ' climate, but the coincidence of the periods of highest rainfall and minimum evaporation is, from the agricultural standpoint, a very favourable circumstance not shared by the tropical climate. ' Mediterranean ' rainfall is light in annual aggregate when compared with the precipitation of equatorial Africa ; and the normals for North African stations whose latitudes exceed 34° range from 18 to 30 inches, though orographical rainfall on the slopes of the Atlas reaches higher figures in specially favoured places.

It is suggestive in a study of the climate and vegetation of North Africa to compare the latitude position of the western and eastern basins of the Mediterranean. We note that the Barbary coast is almost entirely to the north of the parallel of 34° and that the coast of Tunisia actually extends farther north than the southern coast of Spain in the provinces of Malaga and Cadiz : and, looking east, that the southernmost isles of Greece together with the extremity of Sicily are farther south than is Northern Tunisia. On the other hand, no part of the Egyptian littoral is as high in latitude as 33°, and a similar position is true for the eastern coast of Libya, excepting Cyrenaica.

It is not surprising, therefore, that the winter rainfall belt of Barbary should be much wider and more continuous than that of Libya and Egypt ; and that northernmost Barbary, stretching as a peninsula into the Mediterranean Basin, should receive much heavier rains than any other part of North Africa. Moreover, in Southern Barbary the Atlas system of plateaux and folded ranges provides, as it were, a northern containing wall for the Saharan climate, while farther east the low Saharan plateau extends uninterruptedly to the sea in Libya and Egypt.

Summers of Mediterranean Africa are usually excessively hot, indeed almost Saharan in this respect as also in their aridity. The mean temperature for midsummer everywhere exceeds 70° and is usually well above 75°, while the winters are warm with a mean that is higher, in most places considerably higher, than 45°. Increase of summer temperature along the sea-board from west to east is to be expected as a consequence of a weakening of moderating oceanic influences in the same direction. So we note that at Mogador (Atlantic coast) the July mean is 68°, at Algiers 77°, at Tripoli 79° and at Alexandria 80°.

The factors which explain the unique rainfall régime termed ' Mediterranean ' have been briefly mentioned in early paragraphs of this chapter. We saw that the winter precipitation is associated with cyclones passing generally from west to east across the Mediterranean Basin. Not all the winds belonging to the cyclonic systems and affecting North Africa are, however, rain-bearing. Indeed the *sirocco*, a winter wind on the Algerian and Libyan coasts, is ill-famed for its heat and desiccating influence : it is southerly, i.e. Saharan, in origin and blows as the front wind of advancing cyclones. The *khamsin* of Egypt is of similar type. The heat and aridity of the *sirocco* as it reaches the Algerian coast are intensified by its descent from the high Atlas Plateau as a ' foehn ' wind.

Winter cyclones passing from the Atlantic to the Mediterranean by way of the straits between the converging folded ranges of Spain and Morocco affect the climate of the western coast of Morocco about as far south as Mogador, whose rainfall measures 13 inches. There are, however, in the ' Mediterranean ' climate of this coast important temperature modifications to be taken into account. The effect on shore temperatures produced partly by the cold water of the Canary Current is evident, particularly in the summer whose heat is much tempered by sea-breezes ; and we know that the comparatively cool summers of the Saharan coast farther south have a similar explanation. July mean temperatures are rarely in excess of 70°, as compared with an average of 75° for the Mediterranean coast of Barbary which is in higher latitudes. Reduced summer temperature is also found on the Atlas plateaux and folded ranges, and at 4000 feet above sea-level the mean is approximately 10° lower than in the case of low-altitude, interior stations of similar latitude. (Compare Biskra and Géryville in the table provided at the end of the section on ' Mediterranean ' climate.)

The Cape District of South Africa

In the introductory paragraphs of this chapter brief indication was given of the repetition of a climate such as we have just described within the south-western corner of South Africa. Climatic data for the Union of South Africa are very abundant by contrast with most other regions of the continent, and much study has already been devoted to the climatology of the sub-continent.[1] For these reasons it is considered advisable to postpone fuller treatment of the climate to a later chapter devoted exclusively to the geography of the Union of South Africa.

The northerly swing of the stormy and rainy westerly wind belt during winter is sufficient only to affect land about as far north from Cape Town as the outlet of the Olifants River, about 150 miles from Table Bay : in this direction the ' Mediterranean ' régime gradually merges with that of the hot desert. To the east of Cape Town, along the coast, winter rains and summer drought persist some distance beyond Cape Agulhas, but towards Port Elizabeth there is an increasing proportion of summer rainfall in the annual aggregate : indeed, at the station mentioned the distribution of precipitation throughout the year is comparatively close to uniformity. Directly inland from Cape Town, i.e. towards the north-east, the ' Mediterranean ' fringe is limited, less than 100 miles away, by the border ranges, immediately beyond which extends the first step of the South African Plateau, the semi-desert of the Karroo.[2]

As on the Atlantic coast of Morocco so on the western shore of the Cape Province a cold equator-ward current—the ' Benguella '—has the effect of lowering summer temperatures through the medium of local onshore breezes : and another factor in the production of cold coastal water is associated with the South-East Trades of summer which exert a seaward drag on the surface water, so that there is upwelling from the colder depths. Referring to Cape Town temperature we note the effect of local sea-breezes : the midsummer (January) mean is lower than 70° which is subnormal for a ' Mediterranean ' station. Winters at Cape Town almost attain the ideal of mildness—the July mean is 55°—and mention may be made of the warming influence of a ' foehn ' wind, known locally as the ' Berg wind ', which blows

---

[1] Notably by Mr. C. Stewart, late Chief Meteorologist of the Union.
[2] Hottentot word meaning ' waterless '.

off the Plateau, where pressure is high, during 'breaks' in the normal westerly wind régime of the Cape district.

By reason of its genial climate, without excessively heated summers and without the disadvantage of high altitude at which the majority of South African colonists live, the Cape region may fairly be described as the most favourable region for European settlement within the sub-continent. In summer and winter alike it provides a resort for the nerve-strained settler whose working days are spent in the high altitudes that rule throughout the interior.

Included below are mean temperature and rainfall records in inches for 'Mediterranean' stations, grouped as follows—(a) North Atlantic and Mediterranean coasts, (b) interior Barbary, (c) Cape District.

	Station	Alt. (feet)	(1) Temp. / (2) R'nfall	Jan.	Feb.	Mar.	Apr.	May	June	July	Aug.	Sept.	Oct.	Nov.	Dec.	(1) Range / (2) Total
(a)	Mogador .	Sea-level	(1)	57	59	60	63	65	68	68	68	68	67	63	59	(1) 11
			(2)	2·2	1·5	2·2	0·7	0·6	0·1	—	—	0·2	1·3	2·4	2·0	(2) 13·2
	Algiers .	Sea-level	(1)	53	55	58	61	66	71	77	78	75	69	62	56	(1) 25
			(2)	4·2	3·5	3·5	2·3	1·3	0·6	0·1	0·3	1·1	3·1	4·6	5·4	(2) 30·0
	Alexandria	Sea-level	(1)	58	60	63	67	72	76	79	81	79	75	68	61	(1) 23
			(2)	2·2	0·9	0·5	0·2	—	—	—	—	—	0·3	1·4	2·6	(2) 8·1
(b)	Biskra .	400	(1)	51	55	60	67	75	84	89	88	82	70	59	52	(1) 38
			(2)	0·5	0·7	0·8	1·2	0·6	0·4	0·2	0·1	0·6	0·8	0·4	0·6	(2) 6·9
	Géryville	4300	(1)	39	42	46	52	60	70	78	77	68	56	46	40	(1) 39
			(2)	0·9	1·2	2·4	1·7	2·2	0·7	0·2	0·5	1·2	1·5	1·3	1·5	(2) 15·3
(c)	Cape Town	Sea-level	(1)	69	69	68	63	59	56	55	56	57	61	64	67	(1) 14
			(2)	0·7	0·6	0·9	1·8	3·9	4·4	3·5	3·3	2·2	1·6	1·1	0·8	(2) 24·8

The 'Mediterranean' Vegetation of Barbary and the Cape District

The long drought which is characteristic of the Mediterranean summer hinders vigorous plant growth at this season: on the other hand, growing activity is usually maintained during the winter when rains accompany mild temperature. Temperate cereals including wheat, barley and oats, as well as early vegetables for European markets, are grown successfully as winter crops. In summer the attention of agriculturists is largely devoted to deeply-rooted plants such as the vine, olive and fig which are able to withstand long drought. The variety of crops within the Mediterranean region is therefore extensive and the basis of agriculture is broad, with farming activity of one form or another throughout the year.

In order to endure through the rainless period when evaporation is at its highest, vegetation needs to be adapted in its structure, so as to be able to minimize transpiration. Xerophytic adaptations of plants are shown by the bearing of thorns and spiny leaves, or by the thick cuticle of shrub foliage.

On the north-facing slopes of the Maritime Atlas where precipitation usually exceeds 25 inches there is, still remaining, fairly extensive woodland and open forest. At altitudes below 1500 feet the evergreen-oak and cork-oak, together with certain types of pine, are characteristic members of the forest, while above this level cedars are commonly found. The highest forest stretching above 5000 feet is in a zone of cold winter, and here deciduous trees are acclimatized.

In early historic times certain regions of Barbary, now treeless though with rainfall exceeding 20 inches, supported forest which was subsequently cut down. After such destruction it is rare for tree growth to reappear ; its place is taken by thickets of evergreen shrubs, including the laurel, myrtle and strawberry tree. Vegetation of this kind is common throughout the Mediterranean Basin and is known to the residents of Southern France as ' maquis ', a term which has come into general use. Maquis deteriorates to poor scrub and heath—known in Mediterranean France as ' garigue '—where rainfall is deficient or where permeable limestone is the underlying rock.

The rarity of meadow-land is characteristic of the Mediterranean Basin and explains the insignificance of the dairying industry in this region. The hardy goat which is able to subsist even on the scanty vegetation of the garique makes an important contribution to milk supply, but butter is a very rare food, and its place is taken in the diet of Mediterranean peoples by vegetable oils, especially that of the olive. This tree, one of the most typical and, commercially, one of the most valuable members of Mediterranean flora, is practically confined to regions where the ' Mediterranean ' characteristics of climate are strongly emphasized.

Similar climatic conditions within the mountainous Cape district support vegetation which is closely akin to that of the Mediterranean Basin, and this despite the space interval of 5000 miles separating the two regions. The formerly existing forests on the highlands of abundant winter rain have been completely destroyed, if we except the almost insignificant remnant on the Cedarbergen (Cedar Mountains), whose name is suggestive of earlier wood-land on this, as well as on neighbouring, Cape ranges. Their slopes were clothed with cedars and cypresses similar to those of the Syrian Lebanon and of the Maritime Atlas, until a period of wasteful felling which began in the late seventeenth century.[1] The only considerable extent of forest now standing in sub-tropical South Africa is found in a narrow coastal belt of well-distributed rainfall, to the west of Port Elizabeth and on the southern slopes of the Outeniqua and Zitzikamma Mountains. This remnant, usually known as the Knysna Forest, consists largely of broad-leaved evergreens, though the yellow-wood, formerly the most representative tree, is not of this type.   Wholesale destruction of the yellow-woods has proceeded during the period of European settlement.

Thicket growth, similar to the ' maquis ' of the Mediterranean, represents the typical vegetation of the Cape, and the variety of shrubs is shown most abundantly within the narrow, well-watered

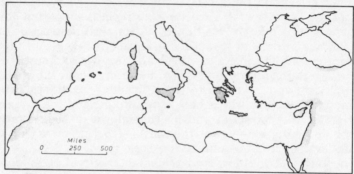

FIG. 12.—Olive-growing Districts of the Mediterranean Basin
(Shown by stipple)

highland of the Cape Peninsula.   Evergreen and hard-leaved bush and shrub attain a height usually not more than 6 feet, and many varieties of protea, including the ' sugar bushes ' well known to Cape Town citizens, are very characteristic.

SUB-TROPICAL CLIMATES : (B) SUMMER RAINS TYPE

Finally, we turn to consider the general features of climate within the region which occupies the eastern half of South Africa from the Limpopo River (approximately) to the southernmost coast.   In view of the strong contrast in physical geography, especially marked in respect of altitude, between, on the one hand, the high plateau (High Veld) of over 4000 feet within the eastern districts of the Transvaal and the Orange Free State, and on the other, the narrow littoral belt of Natal and the Eastern

[1] The Cape cedar is known as the Clanwilliam cedar (*Widdringtonia juniperoides*).

Cape Province, we may expect a considerable climatic divergence between the two regions. Their climates are, however, related by reason of a common dependence on summer rainfall which is associated with the indrawn South-East Trades, although on the eastern coast the rainy season is usually two to three months longer than in the interior.

On the High Veld there is reversal of winds seasonally in response to the alternate low pressure and anticyclonic systems that are established over the sub-continent in summer and winter respectively. Summer day temperatures on the plateau are high—as indicated by the January mean of 72° at Pretoria—but in winter when skies are cloudless the loss of heat through radiation after sunset exceeds the insolation of the day and there is a tendency to frost at night. The diurnal range of midwinter is as much as 35° at Pretoria. Farther south than the Transvaal, though still on the High Veld, there is, from the standpoint of agriculture, a danger of night frost in every month of the year, so that the range of cultivated crops requiring a considerable frost-free period is strictly limited in these parts. Although the winter of the High Veld is famed for health, a serious disadvantage results from aridity, for winds are dust-laden and the lungs tend to be adversely affected in consequence. More than three-quarters of the rainfall is confined to the summer half-year, and precipitation diminishes in amount westwards from the crest of the Drakensbergen, where it exceeds 40 inches, to less than 20 inches near the western boundary of the Transvaal and the Orange Free State. The lower the mean annual rainfall the more precarious is the occurrence of precipitation. Concerning the uncertainty of rainfall in the interior of South Africa more will be included in a later chapter, for it is a matter of serious consequence to agriculture.

Although the entire eastern coast of the Union of South Africa lies to the south of lat. 26° S. the temperatures common to all coastal stations are higher, during the winter especially, than their extra-tropical positions would suggest. Taking Durban as typifying Natal coastal conditions, we find that the mean for the coldest month (July) is as high as 65°. There is a marked tendency for winds to blow onshore throughout the year : the South-East Trades of the long summer are actually maintained, with reduced strength and regularity, during the winter, but their influence is not carried far into the interior on account of the anticyclonic conditions which prevail over the High Veld in winter. The supremacy of ' maritime ' as opposed to ' continental ' influence is indicated by the equability of temperature ; so, turning again to Durban, we note an annual range of only

12° as compared with about 26° at Kimberley, a town of similar latitude position.

South-westwards from Durban along the coast to beyond Port Elizabeth comparatively high winter temperatures are maintained, and for this the warm Mozambique Current, flowing close to the coast from equatorial latitudes, is largely responsible. An interesting contrast is afforded by the winter records of the Namaqualand and Natal coasts, respectively, and is explained by the presence of cold water offshore in the case of the first, as previously noted, and of a warm coastal current in the case of the second, the prevalent local winds in each instance being off the sea. On the same parallel of latitude the difference is as much as 12°. Despite the fairly high latitude of the south coast of the Cape Province, frosts are practically unknown, though the temperatures of the winter half-year are not adequate, as they are in the case of the Natal coast, for essentially tropical crops such as sugar-cane.

The Natal coast experiences a rainy season of nine months, from August to April, and the total annual precipitation is usually from 5 to 10 inches more than on the coast of the ' winter rains ' zone. On the littoral of the Eastern Cape Province, especially in the neighbourhood of Port Elizabeth, rainfall is still more balanced in its seasonal distribution, so that there is no month without considerable measurement. As close to the Cape as Knysna the lowest monthly mean is almost 2 inches. Summer is, however, the rainiest period for the greater part of the east coast of the Union, and during this season atmospheric humidity also is high. For these reasons the South Natal coast is not a

	Station	Alt. (ft.)	(1) Temp. (2) R'fall (inches)	Jan.	Feb.	Mar.	April	May	June	July	Aug.	Sept.	Oct.	Nov.	Dec.	(1) Range (2) Total
(a)	Johannesburg	6000	(1)	65	64	62	59	55	50	50	55	59	61	63	65	(1) 15
			(2)	5·6	5·0	3·8	1·3	0·7	0·1	0·3	0·6	0·9	2·7	5·1	4·8	(2) 30·9
	Bloemfontein	4500	(1)	73	71	67	60	53	47	48	52	59	63	68	72	(1) 26
			(2)	3·8	3·3	3·6	1·8	1·1	0·4	0·4	0·5	0·9	1·7	2·1	2·3	(2) 21·9
(b)	Durban	Near sea-level	(1)	77	77	76	72	68	65	65	66	68	71	73	75	(1) 12
			(2)	4·4	4·7	5·1	3·6	1·9	1·2	1·2	1·6	3·1	4·9	5·0	4·9	(2) 41·6
	Stanger	do.	(1)	77	77	74	72	67	64	64	65	67	69	71	75	(1) 13
			(2)	5·3	4·5	4·8	2·8	1·9	1·0	1·1	1·3	3·2	5·5	5·3	6·1	(2) 42·8
(c)	East London	do.	(1)	70	70	69	66	62	60	60	61	62	64	66	69	(1) 10
			(2)	3·2	3·3	3·6	2·7	2·3	1·4	1·2	2·0	3·1	3·6	3·1	3·2	(2) 32·7
	Port Elizabeth	do.	(1)	70	70	69	66	62	59	59	59	60	62	65	68	(1) 11
			(2)	1·2	1·3	1·8	1·9	2·4	1·7	1·9	2·1	2·3	2·2	2·0	1·6	(2) 22·4

favoured resort during the hottest months, though the conditions are enervating, rather than actually unhealthy. During summer there is considerable risk of malaria on the north coast of Natal (in Zululand).

In order to illustrate the climatic differences within the eastern half of the Union of South Africa there are given on page 68 mean records for stations, grouped as follows—(a) High Veld, (b) Natal Coast, (c) Coast of Eastern Cape Province.

The Vegetation of the Sub-Tropical Region of Summer Rains

The climatic distinctions we noted when comparing the High Veld and the coastal plain of Natal are reflected in the vegetation of these regions : particularly notable is the greater luxuriance of the flora of the littoral, due to more equable conditions of temperature and to a heavier, more evenly-distributed annual rainfall.

On the littoral belt to the east of the Drakensberg the wild-growing vegetation consists primarily of thickets and woods, attaining a height of 20–30 feet. Varieties of palm tree, euphorbias and aloes, and the wild banana, are characteristic of the flora. Where the land has been cleared for cultivation the eastern littoral belt produces an abundant variety of tropical and sub-tropical crops, including one or two, such as sugar-cane and banana, which do not succeed elsewhere in the Union.

Between the tropical palm-and-bush vegetation of the Natal coast and the High Veld grass there extends a zone of grass-and-thorn veld which is continuous at levels between 1500 and 4000 feet from the hinterland of Port Elizabeth to northern Natal and beyond. This vegetation belt is associated with the terraces which mark the descent of the eastern slope of the South African Plateau. Grasses, such as rooi-grass and blue grass, are dominant, but thorn bushes (acacias) and succulent plants, particularly tall aloes, appear fairly regularly both in scattered, sentry-like isolation and, occasionally, in ' plantation ' formation.

The High Veld is true plateau grass-land ascending to levels between 4000 and 6000 feet. It provides a generally monotonous landscape, particularly in winter when the bare earth shows reddish brown. The grasses, of which rooi-grass is typical, as on the eastern veld just described, are scorched by the long period of hot summer days, despite the rainfall of this period. There is no tree growth, though occasional acacias on rocky ground relieve the otherwise continuous extent of grass, which is green only in spring and early summer.

6

Before closing this chapter attention is drawn to the importance of the study of climatic changes in Africa. It is a phase
of African geography that offers an extensive field of research
for numerous investigators. At present there is little evidence
available, even for comparatively modern decades.

The theory of oscillatory or pulsatory [1] changes of climate
is generally accepted by climatologists to-day. It supposes
periods of comparative warmth and aridity alternating with
epochs of comparative coolness and moisture, although it is
claimed that over a long era there is not any marked tendency
either towards desiccation or towards increasing precipitation.
It is suggested that an eleven-year periodicity is observable in
climatic oscillations over certain parts of Africa, including the
Eastern Plateau, and that the changing levels of the Great Lakes
offer evidence in support of this hypothesis. Unfortunately,
climatic records over a long period for any part of Africa are
extremely rare, so that generalization, however cautious, is
always liable to serious modification in the light of new sources
of evidence.

African Climates in Pleistocene Times

Of recent years there has been much inquiry into the subject
of African climates during times contemporaneous with the
Quaternary Ice Age of Northern Europe. The extent of our
knowledge is briefly summarized below, and the reader is advised
to refer to the authorities included in the short bibliography at
the end of this chapter.

During the four great glacial periods of Pleistocene Europe—
named by geologists the Gunz, Mindel, Riss and Wurm—in
Africa, by reason of its low latitudes, there was glaciation only
on the folded ranges of the Atlas and Cape systems, and on the
highest peaks (15,000–20,000 ft.) of the East African Plateau.

The sequence of climatic episodes during the glacial epoch
is known more fully for Mediterranean Africa than for any other
region of the continent. During the very extensive Mindel
glaciation of Northern Europe this region, together with other
lands of the Mediterranean Basin, stood higher in relation to the
sea than now. The elevation was sufficient to expose a land-
bridge, in the form of a sill, across the Straits of Gibraltar and,
in addition, Tunisia was united to Italy by way of Sicily. This
was a period of cold humid conditions in the Mediterranean,
when glaciers on the Atlas Mountains, fed by heavy snowfall,
descended to within 2000 feet of sea-level, as the remnants of
their moraines clearly show.

[1] To use the term of the late Professor Ellsworth Huntington.

The comparatively warm inter-glacial period which preceded the Riss glaciation of Northern Europe was marked by the lowering of the Mediterranean lands in relation to the Atlantic, so that oceanic waters re-entered the inland sea. Contemporaneously with the Riss glaciation, however, the oscillation was renewed with the re-elevation of the land, and this period, like the Mindelian, was characterized by heavy precipitation and comparatively low temperatures over northernmost Africa.

Mediterranean pluvial periods of the Pleistocene were a consequence of the southerly position of the North Atlantic cyclonic belt, with its stormy Westerlies, which was thus situated on account of the southward extension of a great anti-cyclone from the ice-cap of Northern Europe. Between this high-pressure system and equatorial latitudes the climatic belts were compressed to narrower limits than those of modern, post-glacial times. As for the Mediterranean cyclonic climate, it was not restricted to the winter season as now, but continued throughout the year.

During the main phases of the Ice Age the vast anticyclone that was strongly developed as far south as the centre of Eurasia prevented the full development of the monsoonal régime which is now characteristic of India and Eastern Africa, so that regular north-easterly winds tended to prevail throughout the year. In consequence, the head-streams of the Nile received little accumulated precipitation from the Abyssinian Plateau, and the main river was therefore unable to reach the Mediterranean coast. The present hydrographic régime of North-East Africa was not inaugurated until the close of the last great glaciation of Northern Europe, probably about 12,000 B.C.

Important evidence of climatic change since the beginning of the Pleistocene is found in the African deserts. The former comparatively abundant precipitation over the Sahara is indicated by river-beds, now unoccupied by streams, which are easily distinguished in form from the 'wadis' that carry the rare storm waters of modern times. In the Shari Basin to the south-east of Lake Chad there are accumulations of water-borne pebbles which were transported southwards by perennial rivers from the Tibesti Highlands during Pleistocene times. Much farther west, north of the Senegal River, alluvial soils are found underlying deep deposits of blown sand, and are a witness to river action during an early pluvial phase. The Kalahari appears to have experienced two pluvial periods during the Pleistocene, and throughout at least one of these moist phases there was a great enlargement of Lake Ngami.

In equatorial latitudes of Africa permanent snow-and-ice caps were confined to the higher altitudes of the great volcanic cones, though the snow-line and the limit of the glaciers were lower by several thousand feet than they are to-day. From the summits of Kilimanjaro (over 19,000 ft.) glaciers descended to about 5000 feet above sea-level, and on Mount Kenya the snow-line of certain phases of the Pleistocene was 3000 feet lower than the 15,000 feet level of to-day.

The Great Lakes of East Africa are known to have extended more widely than in modern times during the Pleistocene pluvial periods. Evidence provided by ancient beach gravels on the borders of Victoria Nyanza indicates the occurrence of two very moist phases, and the former of these probably coincided approximately with the Mindel glaciation of Northern Europe and with the heavy snowfall and enlargement of glaciers on the high equatorial summits. Victoria Nyanza extended to twice its present area and to it was united Lake Kioga. Victoria and certain of the other Great Lakes have diminished in area during historic times, but, apart from probable changes in precipitation, the diversion of drainage has also been a contributory cause.

REFERENCES

CLIMATE

Knox, A., *The Climates of the Continent of Africa*, Cambridge, 1911.
Kendrew, W. G., *The Climates of the Continents*, 2nd ed., Oxford, 1927.
Miller, A. A., *Climatology* (Methuen), London, 1931.
Worthington, E. B., *Science in Africa*, Oxford, 1938.
Hann, J., *Handbuch de Klimatologie*, Stuttgart, 1910–11.
Lyons, H. G., ' Meteorology and Climatology of German East Africa ', *Quart. Journ. R. Meteor. Soc.*, 1917.
Hurst, H. E., and Phillips, P., *The Nile Basin*, Vol. I (Meteorology, etc.), Cairo, 1931.
Craig, J., *Rainfall of the Nile Basin*, Cairo, 1913.
Robertson, C. L., and Sellick, N. P., *The Climate of Rhodesia, etc.* (Handbuch der Klimatologie, Band V), Berlin, 1933.
Brooks, C. E. P., ' The Rainfall of Nyasaland ', *Quart. Journ. R. Meteor. Soc.*, 1919.
' The Rainfall of Nigeria and the Gold Coast ', *Quart. Journ. R. Meteor. Soc.*, 1916.
' The Distribution of Rainfall over Uganda ', *Quart. Journ. R. Meteor. Soc.*, 1924.
Brooks, C. E. P., and Mirrlees, S. T. A., *A Study of the Atmospheric Circulation over Tropical Africa*, Meteor. Office, London, 1932.
Chamney, N. P., *Climatology of the Gold Coast*, Bull. 15, Dept. of Agric.. Accra, 1928.
Notes on the Climates of the Eastern Mediterranean and Adjacent Countries, I.D. 1117, H.M. Stationery Office.
Goetz, E., ' The Rainfall of Rhodesia ', *Proc. Sci. Assoc.*, Rhodesia, 1909.
Plummer, F., and Leppan, H. D., *Rainfall and Farming in the Transvaal*, Pretoria, 1927.
' Report of the Drought Investigation Commission ', Union Govt., Cape Town, 1923.
Various official year-books and hand-books, including those of Union of South Africa, Southern Rhodesia, Gold Coast, Tanganyika, &c.

The following atlases are especially useful for the representation of climatological data :

Atlas of Egypt, Survey of Egypt, Giza, 1928.
Atlas de l'Algérie, Gouvernement Générale de l'Algérie, Alger et Paris, 1923 (onwards).
Atlas of the Gold Coast, Accra, c. 1923.

CLIMATIC CHANGES IN AFRICA

Bovill, E. W., ' The Dessication of North Africa in Historic Times ', *Antiquity*, 1929.
Brooks, C. E. P., *Evolution of Climate*, 2nd ed., London, 1925.
Hobley, C. W., ' The Alleged Dessication of East Africa ', *Geog. Journal*, 1914.
Hume, W., and Craig, J., ' The Glacial Period and Climatic Change in North-East Africa ', Rep. Brit. Assoc, 1911.
Leakey, L. S. B., *The Stone Age Cultures of Kenya Colony*, Cambridge, 1931.
Murray, G. W., ' The Egyptian Climate, an Historical Outline ', *Geog. Journ.*, Vol. CXVII (1951), p. 422.
Variations in the Levels of the Central African Lakes (Geophysical Memoirs, No. 20), Meteorological Office, London.

VEGETATION

Shantz, H. L., and Marbut, C. F., *The Vegetation and Soils of Africa*, New York, 1923. ' Agricultural Regions of Africa ', *Economic Geography*, Worcester, Mass., Vol. 16, 1940.
Campbell, D. H., *An Outline of Plant Geography*, London, 1926.
Hardy, M. E., *The Geography of Plants*, Oxford, 1920.
Engler, A., *Die Pflanzenwelt Africas—Die Vegetation der Erde*, Vol. IX, 1910.
Bews, J. W., *The Grasses and Grasslands of South Africa*, Maritzburg, 1918.
Pole Evans, I. B., *The Plant Geography of South Africa*, Reprint from Year Book, Pretoria, 1918.
Sim, T. R., ' The Flora of Portuguese East Africa ', Rept. S. African Assoc. for Advancement of Science, No. 7, 1910.
Chipp, T. F., ' The Vegetation of the Central Sahara ', *Geog. Journ.*, August, 1930.
Brunhes, J., ' Les Oasis du Souf et du M'Zab ', *La Géographie*, Vol. V, 1902.
Dudgeon, G. C., *The Agricultural and Forest Products of British West Africa*, London, 1911.
Unwin, A. H., *West African Forests and Forestry*, London, 1920.
Hutchins, D. E., ' Rept. on the Forests of British East Africa ', Cd. 4723, H.M. Stationery Office, 1909.

PART II

THE PEOPLE—IMMIGRANT AND NATIVE

CHAPTER I

DISCOVERY AND PARTITION

IN ancient times Africa [1] was thought of as including only the Barbary coasts and their immediate hinterland, together with Egypt and the Red Sea littoral. Bridging the great gulf of time down to the early years of the nineteenth century, we find that during the accumulated centuries there was surprisingly little added to the store of geographical knowledge relating to the continent. The vast inter-tropical regions, apart from their coasts which had long been known and fairly accurately mapped, were still *terra incognita*. North Africa was viewed solely from the standpoint of its significance as the southern rim of the Mediterranean World, and there was some justification for this conception ; though with equal reason the Barbary lands, Islamic in culture, might have been considered a western prolongation of Semitic Asia. East Africa, so far as it received attention in the early nineteenth century, was counted as part of the Moslem world on account of its Arabian and Persian associations.

The Phoenicians, a Semitic people, are credited with the first systematic exploration of the North African coasts, but their discoveries were forgotten and did not inaugurate a period of further exploration. From their Levantine bases, including Sidon and Tyre, they traded in the Mediterranean long before 1000 B.C., and ultimately their head-quarters were removed from the Syrian to the Barbary coast. They established their first African trading post at Utica on the north coast of Tunisia (as it now is called) about 1100 B.C., and Carthage was founded near-by

[1] The term ' Africa ' may have been derived from the Berber community known as ' Afriga ' which occupied a district to the south of Carthage in Roman imperial times. The Roman 'province of Africa' generally corresponded in extent to the modern Tunisia.

some three centuries later. For a considerable period after 550 B.C. Carthage controlled the northern littoral from Tripoli to Tangier, and about the same time Phoenician merchants were organizing regular sea-borne commerce between the head of the Red Sea and the southern coasts of Persia and Arabia. It was recorded by Herodotus that about the year 600 B.C. certain Phoenician adventurers completed the circumnavigation of Africa, starting from the Red Sea and two years later passing the Pillars of Hercules on their way to the Levant : but the extent of Phoenician exploration on the African coasts does not depend solely on this very doubtful record. Passing beyond the Mediterranean they established trade depôts on the coast of Rio de Oro (c. 500 B.C.), and from this advance-base undertook at least one voyage southward beyond the desert to the neighbourhood of the Senegal and Gambia rivers. It is even probable that they visited the Sierra Leone coast. Through the medium of such West African enterprises, and by virtue of their ability to tap the trans-Saharan caravan trade, the Carthaginians were able to offer in Mediterranean port-markets tropical products similar to those—namely, ivory, gold, and Negro slaves—which were sought two thousand years later by European adventurers on the West African coast.

Greek cultural influence reached the shores of North Africa as early as 1000 B.C., but the only firmly established Hellenic colony on the continent was not founded until c. 630 B.C., when the city of Cyrene (cf. Cyrenaica) together with several neighbouring Greek settlements came into existence. About the same time Greek merchants acquired important trade connexions in the lower Nile Valley. Heredotus (fifth century B.C.) was one of the Greek travellers who journeyed as far up-stream as the First Cataract (Aswan). He learned of a vast river system occupying much of West Africa south of the Sahara, but the Niger [1] of Heredotus's conjecture was extended to include the Senegal and rivers of the Chad Basin. This same fancy was retained as late as the seventeenth century of our era, as witness the map of Visscher (A.D. 1652). The lower Nile region was added to Alexander's empire about 332 B.C., and the city which bears his name and which was to remain for nine centuries the capital of Egypt was then founded.

It was one of the colonial achievements of Rome to be the first Power to incorporate within a single empire the whole of the Mediterranean littoral, including that portion of Africa which was fairly accurately known at the time. Yet at its

---

[1] The name ' Niger ' was first mentioned by Claudius Ptolemaeus, the Alexandrian geographer of the first century A.D.

greatest extent Roman Africa did not penetrate the Negro domain. Moreover, the Roman period did not bring any important increase of geographical knowledge concerning Africa. The Roman ' province of Africa ' was founded in 145 B.C. with the destruction of Carthage, but a contemporary event of greater significance for North Africa was the introduction of the camel to Barbary and Mauritania by way of Egypt. By the close of the first half-century of the Christian era Roman Africa extended from Mauritania to the Red Sea and up-stream in the Nile

FIG. 13.—Africa—as mapped in A.D. 1652

The Coasts, River Systems and Lake Basins of Africa, according to the map prepared by Nicolas Visscher.

Note the great westward-flowing river shown in the Sudan ; the source of the Nile in two lakes of South Central Africa; and the vast area represented as Abyssinia.

Valley as far as the Second Cataract (Wady Halfa). Outside these limits the most ambitious project of African exploration undertaken by Rome was the attempted discovery of the Nile source—this by command of the Emperor Nero (A.D. 66) ; but beyond Fashoda the marshy lands of the Bahr-el-Jebel neighbourhood offered too serious an obstacle to advance, and the expedition failed. About this time Greek traders were well versed in the geography of the coasts of East Africa as far south as Zanzibar : so much is indicated by the work published in

A.D. 77 by the Alexandrian Greek whose 'Periplus of the Erythraean Sea' (Red Sea) consists of a compilation of sailing directions intended for mariners.

Roman authority in North-West Africa, often precarious over the turbulent Berbers of the Atlas, was for a time completely obliterated with the incursions of the Vandals early in the fifth century; but in the following century Byzantine emperors re-established the Roman tradition, and something of the former Roman authority and these influences persisted until the arrival of the Mahomedan Arabs. It is to be remembered that in the Imperial economy the Roman domain of North Africa represented a store-house of agricultural wealth in which wheat, the olive and various fruits were characteristic products. Many parts of North Africa which, during the Roman era, were able to support fairly intensive cultivation of typical 'Mediterranean' crops were later gradually absorbed by the desert, and so remain to-day.

Of much more lasting importance to Africa than Phoenician, Greek or Roman penetration was the series of Moslem incursions which began in Egypt in the seventh century. The Arabs not only swept across and conquered with great rapidity the whole of North Africa,[1] but also completely obliterated the cultural influence introduced by Greek and Roman. Moreover, they succeeded as no previous Power had done in drawing the North African peoples into closer cultural and political relations one with another. The East African littoral became equally early a Moslem domain.

From these limits Islam has not receded [2] : indeed, it may be said that, with the exception of Abyssinia and the Christian groups of Egypt, Africa as far south as lat. 10° or 11° N. is Moslem in faith, whilst on the eastern side of the continent the zone of allegiance to Islam is carried much farther south so as to include the coast of Kenya and the island of Zanzibar.[3] By the twelfth century the colonization of the East African coast by Arabs and Persians at points of trading vantage extended as far south as the Zambezi outlets, and Sofala, near the modern port of Beira, was founded as a Moslem town about this time.

[1] The tidal wave of Moslem conquest failed to override the fortress of Septa (the modern Ceuta in Morocco) held by a Count of the Roman Empire.
[2] The Mahomedan population of the world has been calculated very approximately as 240 millions, of whom more than 60 millions are in Africa.
[3] Islam has many adherents on the coast of Tanganyika Territory, Portuguese East Africa and Natal. The most southerly community of Moslems in Africa is that of the Malays of Cape Town and district.

The Arab trade on the East African shores included the capture of Bantu Negro slaves and their transport to Southern Arabia and Persia. From these early contacts with the Bantu zone of Africa has come the much-abused term, ' Kafir '—which in the Arabic signifies ' Unbeliever '. A more creditable Arab influence was the introduction of rice and the sugar-cane to tropical Africa from India. The Arabian and Persian colonies on the eastern littoral attained their highest prosperity in the period between 1100 and 1300, and their wealth and activity are recorded by the Arabian geographer, Ibn Batuta, who visited East Africa in 1328. One result of a revival and extension of Islam in North Africa during the tenth and eleventh centuries was that many of the Sudanic peoples of negroid stock accepted Moslem faith and culture. Such conversion affected the Hausa, Mandingan and Songhai and the peoples of Darfur and Wadai, and through its means they were brought indirectly into commercial contact with the Mahomedan world of South-West Asia.[1]

Subsequent to the discovery and colonization of the Caribbean region of the Americas the demand for Negro slaves offered an inducement, not only to the Arab traders who supplied European dealers, but also to the occupation—temporary or permanent—of the west coasts of Africa by adventurers from the maritime countries of Europe. Earlier, however, the search for the sea-road to India and to other countries of spice production had led to the rounding of Southern Africa and, incidentally, to the systematic exploration of West African coasts by Portuguese seamen.

The liberation of the western districts of the Iberian Peninsula from Moorish invaders occurred before 1300, but it was not until 1415 that the Portuguese proceeded to invade Africa by way of Tangier and Ceuta, in order to carry the war into the Moslem territory of the African mainland. Directed by Prince Henry of Portugal (known as ' the Navigator '), who had learned from Moorish merchants of the wealth of tropical African forests, Portuguese mariners inaugurated a splendid phase of exploration, so that in the brief period of about half a century 5000 miles of African coastal waters were navigated and charted as never before. Cape Bojador—the head-land which ' bulges ' or ' juts out '—provided an early difficulty on account of the adverse currents of its neighbourhood, but it was successfully passed in 1434. The following fifty years of Portuguese maritime activity led to the re-discovery of the Senegal River,

[1] The use of chain mail in the Sudan, particularly Bornu, was an innovation introduced from the parts of Syria visited by the Crusaders.

to the doubling of Cape Verde—Africa's most westerly point —to a thorough investigation of the Guinea Coast and to the sighting of the Congo estuary. The main promontories of the comparatively straight West African coast still bear witness in their names to Portuguese discovery : Bojador, Blanco, Verde, Palmas—these were the main milestones in the southward spread of exploration.

Coastal discovery was not succeeded by any serious penetration of the West African hinterland [1] : all the Portuguese posts were intended for trade and were not to be the bases for colonization. Benin, a native kingdom (in modern South-West Nigeria), offered considerable opportunities for trade in spices,[2] ivory and slaves, and its ancient bronze-casting industry—already well developed—was a further indication of commercial possibilities. On the Guinea Coast [3] the Portuguese seem to have established their most important trading posts at Arguin, at the mouth of the River Gambia, and at Elmina on the Gold Coast, and from the second of these depôts they tapped a rich trade in gold.

As suggested by the geographical disposition and extent of their existing colonies,[4] the Portuguese were more thorough in their penetration of Africa south of the Equator, and in one or two districts, notably the lower Zambezi Basin, they undertook considerable exploration at a very early period of their settlement ; but generally with them, as also with the Dutch at a later time, the monsoon lands of south-eastern Asia proved more attractive than Africa as a region for colonial expansion.

The achievement of passing the Cape of Good Hope was first accomplished in 1487 by Bartolomeu Diaz, who also sighted Algoa Bay where Port Elizabeth now stands. A few years later his countryman, Vasco da Gama, proceeded farther, passed Cape Agulhas and the coast of Natal—the name was of Da Gama's choosing—and later gained contact with Arab traders at their southern trading post of Sofala. From here his ventures on the East African shore carried him to Zanzibar, Mombasa

---

[1] The largest Portuguese expedition into the interior of the Guinea lands was associated with an unsuccessful attempt to reach Timbuktu which, by A.D. 1150, had become a vigorous trading centre, where Sudanese and Saharan caravan routes converged.

[2] Spices included Guinea pepper or malaguetta pepper, known sometimes as ' Grain ' ; hence the term ' Grain Coast ' which, though now out of use, formerly referred to what is now the coast of Liberia.

[3] Its limits may be accepted as extending from the Senegal River to the Niger Delta.

[4] The area of Angola is 486,000 sq. miles ; of Portuguese East Africa, 288,000 sq. miles.

and Malindi. Then under Arab guidance he learned to utilize the Indian Ocean monsoons on a voyage to and from Western India, his real objective.

The trading settlements which da Gama discovered on the East African coast, though largely Arab in population, were independent of any political tie with Arabia. They soon fell to their Portuguese conquerors, who thus added a far-flung chain of trade depôts on the western border of the Indian Ocean to the imperial responsibilities of the small European Power. Chief among the Arab ports commandeered by the Portuguese were Malindi, Mombasa, Zanzibar, Mozambique and Sofala,[1] in addition to Aden and the Isle of Socotra whose function it was to control the critical and narrow passage between the Red Sea and the Indian Ocean. In view of their extensive littoral conquests it was a remarkable oversight on the part of the Portuguese to fail to establish trade depôts on the coast of South Africa between the two spheres of their commerce—the Eastern Atlantic and the Indian Ocean. Especially is it difficult to appreciate why Table Bay, the recognized base for later European penetration of South Africa, was not selected for regular occupation, at least for the purpose of the watering and revictualling of ships bound between Portugal and the Indies ; certainly it was not fear of the primitive Hottentots which caused the Portuguese to avoid the southern shores of the continent.

The Arabs of Oman (South-Eastern Arabia) succeeded in ejecting the Portuguese from their territory in 1650, after which they proceeded also to oust the Europeans from East Africa ; and so began the political connexion between Oman and Zanzibar, together with the neighbouring shore of the mainland, which was a prominent feature of the political geography of the Arab world as late as the nineteenth century. By the beginning of the eighteenth century the Portuguese had lost all their possessions north of Cape Delgado (lat. 10° 23 S.). We look in vain for many surviving traces of the Portuguese Empire in East Africa north of this point ; an important one, however, is to be found in those Goanese inhabitants of Zanzibar and the neighbouring mainland coast who are descended from colonists introduced by the Portuguese from the colony of South-Western India which still belongs to them. Control of the East African coast, as far south as Delgado, by Oman sultans who operated mainly from their base at Muscat, was relaxed after the retreat of the Portuguese to South-east Africa, though they continued

---

[1] The Portuguese did not establish a post on Delagoa Bay until the eighteenth century. This was their most southerly African settlement.

to exert their spiritual authority over the East African Moslem population. The tradition of this Arabian-East African connexion was long maintained and was vigorously revived after 1832, when the reigning sultan of Oman transferred his court to Zanzibar, from which he extended his authority over the coast-lands now politically included within the Protectorate of Kenya and Tanganyika Territory.

In the later part of the sixteenth century Portugal was impoverished in man-power and wealth, a consequence of the vast imperial commitments undertaken by this small nation-state of not more than two million inhabitants. Spain temporarily destroyed the separate state-hood of Portugal and the way lay open for the Dutch, English and French to dispute the Portuguese claims both on the African littoral and in the Far East of Asia.[1] As early as 1650 the Portuguese were expelled from the entire West African coast-line north of the Equator, with the exception of a small holding to the south of the Gambia River, a colony which still survives as Portuguese Guinea. The Gold Coast became the principal stage in Africa for the commercial rivalries which arose between the various claimants for the rôle Portugal had formerly occupied ; yet this strip of the Guinea Coast had then, as now, no good natural harbour, and in this respect was much inferior to Sierra Leone, with its natural port of Freetown, and to the lands about the Gambia estuary. Gold-dust and easily-acquired slaves were the special inducements to trade on the Gold Coast which outweighed the difficulties of harbourage. For two centuries ' the Coast '[2] was the main objective of English adventurers who traded with Africa, though the easily navigable Gambia gained early an estimation that was almost as high. It is worthy of note that despite early attention from English merchants trading with West Africa, the Gambia dependency—officially the Gambia Protectorate—has remained a small British enclave isolated within a vast French West African domain. Throughout the three centuries during which the French have established and extended their tropical empire in Africa the district about the lower Senegal River has persisted as the primary base for their imperial operations, and in this connexion is to be noted the

---

[1] At the close of the fifteenth century a division of the colonial ' spheres of influence '—to use a modern term—of Spain and Portugal was arranged whereby Spain was debarred from expansion in Africa, though her special claims in Morocco and the Canary Islands (acquired in the thirteenth century) were exempted from this exclusion.

[2] By which in British circles of West Africa the Gold Coast is always understood.

recent choice of Dakar—a seaport half-way between the Senegal and the Gambia—as the capital of French West Africa.[1]

The European settlements on the Guinea Coast which were established after the withdrawal of the Portuguese were not intended to provide bases for the ultimate penetration of the hinterland : they were considered to be merely depôts suitably placed for tapping West African trade, and their advantages as the starting-points of territorial conquest were not appreciated until the nineteenth century was well advanced.

Slaves were the first important export from West Africa, and the development of this traffic in human bodies must be considered in relation to the economic exploitation of the Caribbean lands, especially the islands, where the Spaniards, who already realized the agricultural and mining possibilities of such possessions as Haiti,[2] were faced with a shortage of suitable labour. Certain of the West Indian Islands—Barbados is an instance—whose considerable population to-day is largely African in origin, were in the sixteenth century virtually without inhabitants. At the height of their maritime power the Portuguese supplied Spain, practically excluded from tropical Africa, with West African slaves, and Lisbon rose to special prominence in the commerce of the world as the greatest entrepôt of the Negro slave traffic. This was at a time before direct slave trade between West African and Caribbean ports was established by the English and French. Many of the slaves remained in Portugal to provide agricultural labour, especially in the southern half of the country, and so are explained the traces of Negro blood which are found in the Iberian Peninsula to-day.

It was not until about 1660 that English merchantmen entered fully into the slave trade, and the rapid growth of Liverpool as a great Atlantic port began with the participation of Mersey-owned ships in the carrying of slave cargoes at the commencement of the eighteenth century. The ' trade triangle ' of ports such as Bristol and Liverpool provided very lucrative cargoes on each side of the ' triangle ' except the outward voyage to West African slave depôts, such as Bonny and Calabar, when cheap trinkets, fire-arms and similar objects intended as barter for Negroes were carried. The return voyages to the home ports were usually made with full cargoes of such characteristic Caribbean products as cotton, sugar, molasses and rum, tobacco and various tropical fruits ; some of these still provide

[1] See later section devoted to the progress of colonization in French West Africa.

[2] Haiti, known then and sometimes to-day as Hispaniola, was the main Spanish base in the West Indies.

the raw materials for important industries in the neighbourhoods of the two English ports mentioned. Towards the close
of the eighteenth century the aggregate of slaves exported
from West Africa in ships of all nations concerned reached an
average figure of 100,000 per annum, and of this drain on the
native population, England—mainly Liverpool—was responsible
for one half.

In an effort to make reparation for this discreditable enterprise and in order to foster the repatriation of liberated slaves,
Great Britain created the Crown Colony of Sierra Leone in 1807.[1]
This was the first instance on the Guinea Coast of a European
possession which claimed to be more than a trading post. Several
years later certain philanthropic Americans, with a similar purpose, founded colonies [2] on the Grain Coast, and from them has
developed the State of Liberia.

Vigorous as was the trading activity on the West African
sea-board during the seventeenth and eighteenth centuries the
resultant increase of geographical knowledge was comparatively
meagre. Unlike the Arabs of East Africa the English and other
Western European slave-traders did not explore the hinterland
in order to establish routes for the transport of Negroes to the
coast ; they depended entirely on the raids of the ' slave kings '
—themselves natives of West Africa—to provide cargoes at
times when ships called at the various forts on ' the Coast '
between the Senegal River and the Bight of Biafra. Until the
series of great explorations which began towards the close of
the eighteenth century there were very few important additions
to the published knowledge of inter-tropical Africa, although
valuable exploratory work was done, first by the Dutch and
later by the French, on the coasts of the islands—easily the
largest of which is Madagascar—to the east of the continent.
From the middle of the seventeenth century onwards the special
interests of France in Madagascar were recognized, although it
was not until the nineteenth century that French settlement was
effected.

In the period preceding the momentous discoveries of the
late eighteenth and nineteenth centuries the only permanent
and really important settlement of European colonists was con-

[1] An English settlement at Freetown, as it was later known, had been
established twenty years earlier.

[2] Except for these instances of Liberia and Sierra Leone, the term
' colony ' applied to West Africa—e.g. Gold Coast Colony—is inappropriate, for there never has been any serious attempt at colonization by
nationals of the sovereign European Powers. The use of the term is due
to the nineteenth-century conception, common in Europe, that the Tropics
were colonizable by the White race.

fined to the extra-tropical South, where the Dutch founded a calling station, on the shores of Table Bay, in 1652. Their intention was to provide the ships of the Netherlands East India Company, on their way to and from the East, with food and water ; and Table Bay proved to be a much more convenient intermediate port of call than St. Helens, which the Dutch had formerly used. No ambitions of territorial annexation were contemplated ; but when, after the first few years, it was realized that the re-victualling station was menaced by a failure of supplies, the directors of the Company at Amsterdam agreed to the extension of agricultural settlement beyond the narrow limits of the Cape Peninsula. The distribution of rainfall and the orographical trend lines encouraged an eastward rather than northward movement of colonists away from the neighbourhood of the Cape, and gradually the settlers of the outposts abandoned their traditions as the descendants of a maritime people. By the later years of the eighteenth century the semi-desert of the Great Karroo had been skirted on its southern and eastern flanks, so that the way lay open to the Boer (i.e. ' Farmer ') migration on to the high grassy plateau—the High Veld [1]—which began in the fourth decade of the nineteenth century.

Although British control of the Cape station was not interrupted after 1814, the first purely British colony established in South Africa grew from settlement on the shores of Algoa Bay, where Port Elizabeth was founded in 1820. The eastward and north-eastward penetration of the Boers and the establishment of British control and settlement in the coastal lands of Cape Colony were contemporaneous with the steady onward move ment of the Bantu Negroes south-westwards across the high eastern plateau of what we now term the Union of South Africa. South Africa became then, as it has remained, an arena of struggle for land between Black and White settlers. Armed with their superior weapons and military science the Europeans were able to place a limit to the western advance of the Bantu, and this ' racial frontier ' is still perceptible in the Eastern Cape Province approximately along the line of the Great Fish River, which descends to the sea between Port Elizabeth and East London.[2]

The modern period of exploration in the African Tropics was at the outset associated with the discovery of the upper courses of the Niger and Blue Nile. It began with the expedition of

[1] It extends across the east of the Orange Free State and the south of the Transvaal.

[2] See map (in the later chapter devoted to South Africa) which shows the low density of Bantu population in the Western Cape Province and the high density in the Eastern Cape Province.

7

James Bruce, who visited Abyssinia in 1770–72, and after discovering the source of the Blue Nile, was able to trace the river to its meeting with the White Nile at Khartoum. As early as the sixteenth century a Portuguese party had entered Abyssinia from the east Coast and, it is believed, had reached the source of the Blue Nile, but this and other features of Abyssinian geography were soon forgotten. There is no accurate cartographical record of this Portuguese investigation, and Europeans continued for long to credit Abyssinia with an extent reaching as far south as the region of the Zambezi.

In 1788 the African Association of London was formed for the encouragement of African exploration, and this body remained distinct for about forty years until merged with the Royal Geographical Society. Under its auspices Mungo Park—one of the greatest names in African exploration—visited the Gambia River in 1795 and made his way overland to the Niger at Segou (in modern French Sudan). With the intention of following the Niger to its coastal outlet Park returned to the upper Niger in 1805, but his expedition was unsuccessful. Prior to his travels it was generally believed that the lower Senegal and Gambia rivers, together with the Rio Grande (Portuguese Guinea), were the outlets of a westward-flowing Niger, but Mungo Park learned sufficient to disprove this theory, though at the time of his death he probably believed that the Niger entered the sea by the Congo estuary.

From the time of Park until the middle of the nineteenth century exploration in tropical Africa was mainly limited to the Guinea lands and to the Western Sudan. To an objective in the latter region from Western Europe the easiest route was certainly via a base on either the Gambia or Senegal, but several southward passages of the Sahara from the Mediterranean coast, for the purpose of exploring the Sudan, were also characteristic of this period of discovery.

In 1823 Clapperton, Oudney and Denham were members of an expedition that crossed the Sahara from Tripoli to Lake Chad, the neighbourhood of which was then for the first time explored. As a result important information concerning the powerful Sultanates of Sokoto and Bornu was brought to Europe, while a few years later the brothers Lander fulfilled the intention of Mungo Park and traced the course of the lower Niger, to prove that the Oil Rivers, long known to slave-traders, were the distributaries of the Niger Delta. Onwards from the twelfth century, the time of its establishment as a great market of the Sudan, Timbuktu, the focus of desert and savanna routes, was vaguely known to Europe, and it was natural that the great emporium should attract the attention of early nineteenth-century travellers. To it by different routes came Laing and the Frenchman Caillé in 1825 and 1826 respectively, but it remained to a German—Dr. Barth—to make the first thorough geographical investigation of the vast tract which extends between Lake Chad and the neighbourhood of Timbuktu. His long and valuable investigations in the Sudan were carried out in the period 1851–55, and at about the same time David Livingstone was at the beginning of his career in South-Central Africa.

The establishment by European Powers of spheres of influence [1] in the region between the Sahara and the Guinea Coast followed close upon the work of exploration that has been outlined and represented the first steps towards the annexation of ' colonies '. The ' scramble ' for territory which, in the latter part of the nineteenth century, dominated the attitude of certain of the European Powers towards Africa and brought about the steady disruption of the institutions of native life must be considered in relation to the domestic circumstances of each of the interested Powers. As late as 1880 Great Britain still retained its foremost position in the organization and technique of large-scale manufacturing industry. At that time Germany had just entered the phase of industrial and commercial expansion which ultimately enabled her to exert a close rivalry with Great Britain in the application of science to industry. These were the outstanding instances of great industrial States whose expanding industries and congested urban populations were in urgent need of the resources—raw materials and foodstuffs—which the tropical lands, especially those of Africa, seemed able to supply.

Africa offered special inducements to the commercialism of Western Europe not only by reason of its vast tropical extent [2] but also on account of the comparative proximity of its luxuriantly rich forest and park savanna belts. [3] Industrialists were quick to measure the resources of the continent in oil-palms, rubber and other wild-growing vegetation of industrial value, and to estimate the enormous possibilities for the cultivation of a wide variety of commercial crops amongst which cotton, cacao, hemp,

[1] The term—' sphere of influence '—was not actually brought into use, in connexion with the partition of Africa by European Powers, until the end of the nineteenth century. Introduced by the British Foreign Office, it was intended to designate regions over which a right to exclusive political influence was claimed, though over which no legal powers of sovereignty could yet be exercised.

[2] Africa possesses a greater tropical area than any continent.

[3] For the West European industrial States the African forest and savanna are much more conveniently situated than the corresponding zones of Central and South America or of South-Eastern Asia.

coffee and sugar were numbered. It was believed that such products could be gathered cheaply through the bounty of Nature and the seeming abundance of native labour ; while it was not overlooked that such organization as the Negroes possessed would be powerless to resist the establishment of a commercial régime, dependent at least to some degree on forced, possibly wageless, labour. There were, of course, honourable exceptions to this attitude in every one of the European States which had dealings with Africa. Further, it was recognized by the leaders of European industry that the many million Africans, black and brown, would provide an extensive market for the cheap products of mill and factory.

Such a conception of an industrial and commercial régime to be applied to an unopened continent was not confined to Africa. A great part of the Far Eastern margins of Asia was at the same time equally exposed to the aggressive commercialism of Western Powers and was passing through a phase similar to that experienced by Africa. In the seventy years which preceded the Great War the islands, peninsulas and ports of China and her dependencies were selected by one or other of the Powers either for the purpose of extending commerce, irrespective of the wishes of the indigenous population, or for the establishment of an exclusive sphere of interest.

The rather sinister record of the penetration and partition of Africa during the last twenty years of the nineteenth and first decade of the twentieth century is relieved by occasional instances where the policy of ruthless exploitation for commercial gain was rejected in favour of an enlightened interest in the economic welfare of native peoples. Such a policy, whilst recognizing the natural aspirations and rights of Africans, was directed towards assisting them in their most difficult and even painful adjustment to the all-pervading influences of Western civilization. In West Africa the outstanding case of enlightened administration which had strict regard both for native well-being and for the progressive development of natural resources was the régime established in Nigeria by Sir Frederick (later Lord) Lugard. Again, in South Africa the praiseworthy administration of the lands and people of the Trans-Keian Territories is one bright feature to be detached from a generally unfavourable record in the sub-continent as a whole. Uganda offers yet a further instance where modern and very successful economic development has been made possible without the spoliation of indigenous society. The aims of the ' dual mandate ' [1] set

---

[1] The policy is discussed in *The Dual Mandate in British Tropical Africa*, by Sir F. D. (later Lord) Lugard, 3rd ed., London, 1926.

forth by Lugard attempted to associate and harmonize two aspects of policy—first, the utilization of the material resources of Africa for the advancement of civilization in Africa and in the world as a whole ; and, secondly, though not subordinately, the cultural, social, economic and political advancement of Native life so that it might increasingly contribute to human progress. Such motives as those of Lugard tended to be obscured prior to the First World War by the widespread and wasteful exploitation of land and Natives for European gain, and no colonial Power in Africa was free from such criticism. Thus was injury done to Africa. Moreover, the competing Powers, distrustful and envious of each other, were ready to foster the baser imperial motives which made war inevitable.

In West Africa the establishment of spheres of interest by Western European States began as early as the middle of the nineteenth century. By means of an agreement of 1857 France and Great Britain defined their zones of special privilege, France consenting to recognize a British régime on the banks of the Gambia, Great Britain agreeing to relinquish her claims in the neighbourhood of the Senegal in favour of France. As an avenue for political and commercial penetration into the interior of the Sudan the Gambia offers superior facilities to those of any other natural highway of the western Guinea lands, and, until the age of the steamship, it was navigable for nearly 200 miles by sea-going vessels. With a greater and longer-assured depth of water than the Senegal it had the additional advantage over that river in that it traversed a richer savanna belt with greater agricultural possibilities. Yet it was the Senegal, not the Gambia, that provided the base for the vast imperial projects from which the French West African federation of colonies has grown.

The inaugural step towards the foundation of the French African Empire, the greatest undivided area possessed by one Power on the continent, was taken when a French military force entered Algeria in 1830. The motive of this expedition arose from the need to suppress the Barbary corsairs who for two centuries had levied tribute on Mediterranean shipping which used the passage between Spain and Africa. On the Algerian and Moroccan coasts Turkey had lost all semblance of authority and, shortly after the Napoleonic Wars, the maritime Powers of Europe agreed that the chaotic state of affairs in Barbary required undelayed attention. By 1847 the French had pacified the immediate hinterland of the Algerian littoral, and a phase which opened with a punitive expedition developed into occupation for an indefinite period.

In West Africa there was no important forward movement of French conquest inwards from the Senegal coast until the arrival of General Faidherbe in 1854. He selected the Senegal River as the first line of advance, but also chose several *points d'appui* along the Guinea Coast in what are now the French colonies of Dahomey and Ivory Coast. Employing these bases Faidherbe evolved a plan by which French military forces were to converge upon the West-Central Sudan from three or four different directions : and associated with this idea was one for the effective linking of the French empires of the Sudan and the Coi.go, in which project the Chad-Shari district was already seen to be of vital importance.

Thus very early the French had formulated an imperial scheme on a continental scale, whilst, in contrast, Great Britain continued to regard her West African dependencies as separate colonial units. At a time (1860–70) when the representatives of France in Africa planned the acquisition of the entire Sudan west of Lake Chad the colonial authority of Great Britain in West Africa reached its *nadir*, and it was possible for a Select Committee of Parliament to recommend the withdrawal from all possessions other than Sierra Leone. This Crown Colony was excepted because Great Britain had there undertaken special responsibilities to liberated and repatriated slaves ; and a second reason was provided by the natural harbour of Freetown, a naval port half-way along the extended chain of communications between Great Britain and the western sea-board of Africa, as far south as the Cape of Good Hope.

Before another twenty years had elapsed, however, the competition for West African territory between Great Britain, France and Germany was in full vigour. The conflicting claims of these Powers were in evidence especially in the neighbourhood of Lake Chad where their possessions or protectorates converged.[1] Great Britain claimed a necessity to extend inland from the littoral of Sierra Leone, the Gold Coast and Nigeria in order to protect the effective hinterland of her coastal trading stations from the aggressive ambitions of the other two Powers. France was especially feared because of her great sweep across the Sudan : this, together with the rapid northward expansion of the French interests from the Guinea littoral at several points, threatened to confine narrowly the English ' colonies ' on every land frontier. It was not difficult, however, for each of the three Powers to justify, at least to its own satisfaction, the case for territorial aggrandisement.

[1] Great Britain from Northern Nigeria, Germany from the Cameroons and France from the district of the middle Niger.

The only serious opposition to European penetration of the Guinea forest belt offered by Native peoples was that organized by the Ashanti of the Gold Coast hinterland. In military organization they were unrivalled by any Negro community throughout the Guinea lands, so that British tenure of the Gold Coast was insecure until the capture of Kumasi, the Ashanti headquarters, in 1873.[1]

Germany did not obtain its first foothold in Africa until 1884, when, from a coastal base at Lome, the Protectorate [2] of Togoland was proclaimed and the German eagle was carried to represent sovereignty along a comparatively narrow strip stretching across the Guinea forest on to the savanna of the Sudan. Thus was placed an effective barrier to the eastward expansion of the British Gold Coast Colony, and the move was typical of the manner in which each of the three Powers attempted to frustrate the designs of its rivals.

Passing to the central and eastern regions of the continent, we begin the period of modern exploration with the name of David Livingstone. He and others of similar humane sympathy believed that the slave trade carried on by the Arabs throughout a large part of East Africa would not be exterminated until the region was fully opened up to legitimate trade. More than any other man Livingstone brought to the world enlightenment regarding physical and human conditions in the most inaccessible districts of ' the dark continent '. Each step in his exploration is associated with the discovery of one or more of the Great Lakes which form so prominent a feature of East African geography ; and ultimately he and others whom he inspired by his example were able to show the relationship between the Lakes and the principal rivers of the region—Nile, Congo and Zambezi.

Livingstone began to travel in unknown country shortly after reaching Bechuanaland, and a journey across the Kalahari [3] to Lake Ngami in 1849 was his first big achievement. After investigating the region of the upper Zambezi he determined to

---

[1] The Ashanti capital was occupied by British troops again in 1896, when King Prempeh was sent into exile from which he was not allowed to return until 1925.

[2] At first the term ' Protectorate ', as understood by Great Britain, France and Germany, implied the rights of external but not internal sovereignty. Later its scope was widened to include internal sovereignty also, and in Africa there is little to distinguish a ' Protectorate ' from a ' Colony '. The only difference of importance is that the inhabitants of a ' Protectorate ' are not classed as ' subjects ' of the ' protecting ' Power.

[3] Called ' Desert ', but including large areas of poor grassland which afford sheep pasture in certain years.

discover a practicable route to the Atlantic coast, and traversed Portuguese West Africa as far as the port of Loanda (in 1854). From there he journeyed back right across the continent, by way of the Zambezi valley, to the Indian Ocean, and on the way discovered the most spectacular natural feature of Africa —the Victoria Falls—which he named. Livingstone's second series of travels began in 1858, when he was commissioned by the British Government to explore Central Africa. From a starting-point on the lower Zambezi he passed on to the Shiré River and to Lake Nyasa. Hereabouts two well-known place-names commemorate the explorer's visit—Blantyre, the head-quarters of European settlement in the Shiré Highlands; and the Livingstone Mountains which fringe the north-eastern coast of Lake Nyasa.

Contemporaneous exploration was carried out much farther north by John Speke and Richard Burton when, from the shore of the Indian Ocean, they crossed the East African Plateau, partly for the purpose of determining beyond doubt the source of the Nile. Together they discovered Lake Tanganyika, and Speke continued the journey without his companion to Victoria Nyanza,[1] though it was not until a later visit that he discovered the Nile outlet from the great Lake. Aided by Speke's knowledge Sir Samuel Baker followed the Nile up-stream to discover Albert Nyanza and to show that this lake came within the course of the Nile. It was still not known, however, whether or not the Nile could be traced up-stream beyond Victoria Nyanza, and there seemed to be a possibility of Lake Tanganyika proving to be the ultimate source of the great river.

Livingstone participated in the last stage of the determination of the Nile problem. In 1865 he went, unaccompanied by European, to the southern end of Lake Nyasa and from there carried out careful and important investigations in the district which we know as North-Eastern Rhodesia. He discovered Lakes Mweru and Bangweolu, and held the theory that the Congo head-stream (the Luvua River), which provides a northern outlet for Mweru, flowed to the upper Nile. After his meeting with Stanley in 1871 the two explorers ventured to the northern shore of Lake Tanganyika and proved that there was no outlet to the Nile. Then, subsequent to Livingstone's death, Stanley finally elucidated the Congo problem by showing that the rivers west of Lake Tanganyika were tributary to the Congo and that

---

[1] Tanganyika is the longest fresh-water lake in the world (length— 400 miles) and it is of great depth. Victoria Nyanza, with an area of 26,000 sq. miles, is the largest lake of Africa and is rather smaller than Scotland.

the Lualaba and the main stream with which it merges could be traced to the Atlantic. So that mainly to Speke, Livingstone and Stanley is due the definition of the main outlines of Central and East African geography, and this great achievement was accomplished in the short space of thirty years. The work of amplifying the geographical detail was left to their successors.

Just as in West Africa exploration prepared the way for the imperial ambitions of great Powers, so in Central and Eastern Africa a ' scramble ' for territory was the immediate sequel to the achievements of the pioneers who have been mentioned. One of the most creditable aspects of European penetration was the suppression of the slave traffic, which trade was largely organized by the Arabs, yet it is unfortunately true that the forced labour instituted by several Western Powers has had little to recommend it in comparison with slavery.

Subsequent to a meeting of geographers and others interested in the future of Central Africa which was convened by Leopold II, King of the Belgians, there came into existence, in 1876, the International Association of the Congo. This society, which was dominated increasingly by the Belgian king, carried on, through the medium of Stanley, work of exploration mainly in the lower Congo region. Not far away at about the same time a French traveller, De Brazza, was preparing the way for the realization of French imperial ambitions in equatorial Africa. From the Gabun coast in 1880 he journeyed up-stream by way of the Ogowe River, reached and crossed the watershed which separates the Ogowe Basin from the lower Congo, and proceeded to the neighbourhood of Stanley Pool which is a lacustrine expansion of the latter river. At Stanley Pool, De Brazza came into contact with the régime of the ' Association of the Congo ' which had assumed political claims over territory bounded on its western side by the left bank of the Ubangi and of the lower Congo.

Farther west, on the Atlantic coast, the Portuguese were able to claim, with some show of justice, their priority of interest in territory immediately north and south of the Congo estuary. Alarmed by the activities of the Congo Association and by the enlargement of the French sphere of interest in the Gabun, the Portuguese attempted to obtain formal international recognition of their claims on the littoral of West-Central Africa ; for the Lisbon Government was not slow to realize the future significance of the only natural oceanic outlet for the vast potential resources of the Congo Basin. In answer to the Portuguese claim a compromise was effected, and this occurred at about the same time that the Independent State of the Congo, successor to the

Association of the Congo, was founded. The States represented at the International Congress of Berlin, 1884-5, agreed to the Portuguese possession of the left bank of the estuary of the great Central African river, but with their sanction the north bank passed to the new State of the Congo, which became the personal possession of Leopold, King of the Belgians. Immediately north of the estuary Portugal retained a small coastal tract around Kabinda [1] which, by the new partition of territory, was cut off from the vast colony of Angola.

In 1886 Germany and France—Powers rarely in agreement on questions of African partition—sanctioned the annexation by Portugal of all territory lying between Angola and Portuguese East Africa. Such a development would have proved fatal to the conception, already taking shape, of a continuous British sphere of influence throughout the region which we now know as Northern and Southern Rhodesia, Nyasaland and the northern part of the Bechuanaland Protectorate. The only territory in this region to which Great Britain had strong claim was the Bechuanaland Protectorate—proclaimed in 1885—whose limits extended as far north as Lat. 22° S. (which is also the latitude of the northern border of the Transvaal Province). In face of British hostility the Portuguese were forced to abandon in South-Central Africa ambitions which, if realized, would have meant continuous empire from the South Atlantic to the Indian Ocean. There was, in fact, no effective opposition to the annexation by Great Britain of the territory which the much smaller Power had been pressed to relinquish. In this episode we have a fairly typical instance of the methods by which the partition of Central Africa was accomplished : each of the Powers concerned sought to acquire for itself the greatest possible area of territory and, without much scruple, to obstruct its rivals, while the welfare of the native inhabitants was not even considered.

The General Act of the International Congress of Berlin (1884-5) included a quite unsuccessful attempt to apply a system to the partition of Africa and to place to some extent the new colonial administrations under international supervision. This introduction of the principles of international co-operation to the sphere of colonial government in Africa provided a precedent for the modern experiment known as the Mandates system, which is concerned with the international administration of territories ceded by Germany in the Peace Treaty of 1919. The General Act enjoined freedom of trade within the Congo Basin to all nations, whose representatives were to be afforded

[1] The claim of Portugal to the Kabinda Enclave rests on the establishment of a ' fort ' at Kabinda in 1783.

unrestricted navigation of the main river and its affluents ; and similar provisions were extended to the lower Niger Basin. Further, the Powers signatory to the General Act agreed not to lay claim in future to protectorates or ' colonies ' unless they were able to prove to international satisfaction that their occupation was effective. ' Effective occupation ' was intended to signify complete penetration of the territory concerned, but within this definition a wide range of interpretation was possible : before the close of the nineteenth century, however, it must have been obvious that widespread European settlement was out of the question in the tropical lowlands of Africa.

Throughout the entire phase of partition there was nothing more remarkable than the rapidity with which Germany acquired a great colonial empire. At the Berlin Congress this Power took the initiative in the discussion of African affairs, and by that time her territorial responsibilities on the continent had given her some qualification for such leadership : yet less than a year before the opening of the Congress the German flag had not been unfurled anywhere in Africa. In one year, 1884, the German Protectorates [1] of Togoland, the Cameroons and South-West Africa [2] were proclaimed.

It is difficult to refer to the European penetration of East Africa in the later part of the nineteenth century without including a statement of the geographical disposition and movements of important Native communities, such as the Baganda, Kikuyu and Masai ; but in order to avoid repetition the reader is here referred to the chapter specially devoted to African societies. There has been brief indication of the main phase of Arab influence on the East African littoral and of the decline of Portuguese authority on this coast. The cultural and commercial links between Oman and Zanzibar were strengthened when, in 1832, the reigning sultan at Muscat transferred his court to the East African island ; but not many years later—in 1861—the political connexion with South-Eastern Arabia was severed, while both Great Britain and France agreed to recognize Zanzibar as an independent State. Considerable economic development of the island was associated with the régime of the Oman Arabs, and the successful clove industry of the early twentieth century is one instance of their commercial energy and initiative.

By the middle years of the nineteenth century Arab traders, many of them financed by Indians residing on the East African

[1] In these cases Protectorate signified complete annexation.
[2] Germany annexed the entire desert coastline between the Angola frontier and the Orange River with the exception of the small British enclave of Walvis Bay.

coast or in Zanzibar, had acquired in the course of their ivory and slave trade an adequate geographical knowledge of the East African Plateau as far west as Lakes Victoria and Tanganyika ; moreover, they had established regularly-followed caravan routes between the Great Lakes and the nearest ports of the east coast. But the systematic mapping of the East African Plateau did not begin until the journey of Burton and Speke in 1856. It was Speke who brought to the world the first account of the civilization of the Baganda (in modern Uganda) who, from a cultural standpoint, represent one of the most advanced Negro communities in Africa.

Early British interests in East Africa were mainly confined to the commerce of Zanzibar and to the attempted suppression of the slave trade for which traffic Zanzibar was the principal entrepôt. This island gained greatly in commercial importance as a result of the opening of the Suez Canal in 1869, when it acquired connexions with the maritime trade carried on between the Mediterranean and India. At this time the Sultan of Zanzibar claimed sovereignty over the littoral now included in Tanganyika Territory and the Kenya Protectorate. The claim was allowed both by Great Britain and by Germany who had developed rival interests in East Africa, although almost at the same time they shared equally a lease of this coastal belt to a width of about 10 miles. In Kenya to-day the littoral is still, nominally at least, a part of the Protected State of Zanzibar. Behind the coastal margin the plateau was divided into two spheres of interest—one German ; the other, and more northerly, British—and the line of separation was drawn immediately to the north of Mount Kilimanjaro, from which it extended direct to the eastern shore of Victoria Nyanza in lat. 1° S.

It was soon obvious to the British East Africa Company, which in 1888 received its charter giving rights of administration, that, in relation to the probable development of trade between the coast and the interior, the Kingdom of Buganda was likely to occupy a controlling position. Consequently the Uganda Railway constructed between Kisumu, on Lake Victoria, and Mombasa, and completed in 1903, was projected primarily for the purpose of bringing the densely-populated agricultural lands close to the western shores of Victoria Nyanza within the effective reach of world markets.[1] The Plateau lands nearer the coast and traversed by the railway were not considered to be so favourable for economic development owing to unsuitable con-

[1] The railway did not enter Uganda, though the rail-head at Kisumu was easily reached from the Uganda coast of the Lake by means of a fleet of steamers which worked in conjunction with the railway.

ditions of climate, soil and labour. The administrative functions of the Chartered Company within the territories which we now know as Kenya and Uganda were discontinued very soon and the British sphere of interest came directly under the control of the Colonial Office. Unlike the other two great chartered companies of British Africa—the Royal Niger Company which operated in the basin of the lower Niger and the British South Africa Company whose main domain lay in Northern and Southern Rhodesia—the B.E.A.C. was not intended mainly as an organization for the commercial development of its territory, nor did it obtain possession of vast mineral and agricultural resources as the British South Africa Company was able to do. Indeed, it was frequently in financial difficulties owing to heavy administrative expenditure, as at the time of the construction of the Uganda Railway.

Very early in the twentieth century it was proposed to test the suitability of the Kenya and Kilimanjaro Highlands as areas for European settlement, the colonists to be British or German according to the political division of East Africa. It was not until after the First World War, however, that White colonization attained considerable proportions : then for the first time the European population of the Kenya Plateau exceeded 10,000 persons. During their short colonial experience in East Africa the Germans were remarkable for the energy of their concentration upon commercial development : so, for example, they constructed in the short period between 1904 and 1914 a trunk line of railway, about 800 miles in length, across the Plateau from Dar-es-Salaam, their leading port, to Kigoma, on the eastern shore of Lake Tanganyika, and were proceeding with the projection and construction of branches leading from or to the central line when war came to Africa. The German railway was intended to compete for the increasing commerce of Central Africa with the Uganda Railway and with a Belgian line—the Lukuga Railway—which reached the western shore of Lake Tanganyika from the upper Congo.

As noted earlier the first organized attempt to colonize the interior of South Africa occurred in the period 1830–40 when the pioneering Dutch stock-farmers advanced slowly in the face of almost overwhelming Bantu opposition on to the High Veld of the Transvaal.[1] Much of the country they traversed had been denuded of population by the ravages of the ruthless Zulu and their Matabele kinsmen against whom the small bands of Boers were forced to maintain a desperate struggle. Much later—

[1] The pioneer Boers—the Voor-trekkers—did not number more than 8000.

about 1870—diamonds were discovered in dry grass-land districts formerly traversed by the Voor-trekkers in their colonizing progress. The Kimberley district, with its massive diamond 'pipes', became the first great mining centre, but was very soon overshadowed in importance when the most valuable gold-field in the world was discovered and opened in the Southern Transvaal. The vigorous and extensive exploitation of mineral wealth introduced to the up-country parts of South Africa new types of settler—the mining prospector and the mining camp storekeeper—whose interests were immediately at variance with those of the conservatively-minded Boer pastoralists. Mining development also provided a powerful inducement to railway construction along the most accessible routes between the coast ports and the new towns of Kimberley and Johannesburg, so that by 1885 the diamond centre was linked by rail to Cape Town, Port Elizabeth and East London.

Between 1886—when Johannesburg was founded—and the years immediately preceding the First World War there continued, except for the short period of the Anglo-Boer struggle, a considerable immigration of European settlers—mainly British. They congregated mainly in close proximity to the auriferous Reef which was, until the opening of this century, within the independent Dutch State known as the South African Republic. Fortunately for the gold industry, which for sixty years has borne the financial burden of South Africa, coal was discovered close at hand in 1887 and on such a considerable scale as to meet the probable fuel needs of the future.

The Anglo-Boer War at the end of the century, the memories of which unfortunately still influence the relations of the two European stocks in South Africa, was primarily a struggle for territory between two societies with very different conceptions of land development. The political subordination of the Dutch after their military defeat was of brief duration. They represent to-day the more numerous and widespread of the two European nationalities which are still distinct within the Union of South Africa, and, because of their numerical strength, they are in a position to determine the political future of the Union. Since 1910 South Africa as far north as the Limpopo River, but omitting the Native Territories of Basutoland, Bechuanaland and Swaziland, has held the status of a self-governing Dominion of the British Commonwealth and amongst the Dominions is unique in that the large majority of its citizens are not of European origin but of dark skin. Nevertheless, the White settlement of South Africa is by far the most important instance of widespread European colonization on the continent ; there is nothing comparable except the settlement of Southern Europeans— Italians, French and Spaniards—within the littoral belt of Algeria and Tunisia. In the case of North-West Africa the climatic similarity to Southern Europe and, secondly, the proximity of the colonists to their home-lands were advantages which made the possibility of successful acclimatization much less doubtful than in the case of sub-tropical South Africa, most of whose immigrants belonged to the cool temperate lands of North-Western Europe.

The wealth acquired at Kimberley by diamond prospectors, of whom Cecil Rhodes was the most far-seeing, furnished the capital for mineral prospecting in districts closer to Central Africa, e.g. Northern and Southern Rhodesia. Until about three decades ago the Rhodesias were administered by the British South Africa Chartered Company which was incorporated in 1889. With its enormous resources of land for mining and agricultural production,[1] that are still retained even though administrative powers have ceased, the Company has proved commercially to be by far the most successful of the three British chartered companies which have operated in Africa. Since 1923 the British Colonial Office has been directly concerned in the administration of the two Rhodesias. Southern Rhodesia with a much larger European population than its northern neighbour across the Zambezi[2] was granted responsible government. Northern Rhodesia received a status similar to that of a Crown Colony, in which a majority of the members of the Legislative Assembly are appointed not by popular franchise but by the Governor who represents the Colonial Office.

So far in this brief record of the partition of Africa reference to the northern or Mediterranean region has been postponed. Outside the old Spanish holdings on the coast of Morocco[3] and, secondly, the Algerian coast to which the French despatched a punitive expedition in 1830, it may be said that Africa north of the Sahara remained outside the range of imperial ambitions of European nations until half a century ago. The advantage of proximity so far as the Mediterranean Powers, France and later Italy, were concerned was counterbalanced by an early recognition, first, of the narrow limits of the fertile Mediterranean fringe imposed by the sterile, inhospitable Sahara, and, secondly,

---

[1] The Company is estimated to possess about 10,000,000 acres of land.

[2] In the early years of the British régime the two Rhodesias were known respectively as Northern and Southern Zambezia.

[3] The Riff of Northern Morocco and the Ifni enclave of the south-west.

of the inability of North Africa even in its most luxuriant tracts to offer in an abundance equal to that of inter-tropical Africa the variety of foodstuffs and raw materials which were urgently needed in industrial Europe. A third factor which tended to delay French penetration was the considerable military resistance exerted by numerous and virile groups of native peoples—including the Berbers, Arabs and Abyssinians—very tenacious of their ancestral lands and rights and with much greater capacity for defending them than was possessed by the more primitive Negro communities.

From the coast, at starting-points such as Tripoli and Alexandria, expeditions set out fairly frequently for the exploration of the Central and Eastern Sudan (including the region of the upper Nile) from the third decade of the nineteenth century onwards. The travellers tended to follow well-recognized caravan routes and acquired considerable knowledge concerning the life of the desert communities. We have noted that by the middle of the century French colonial pioneers had entertained the ambition of incorporating within one empire the entire Sudan from the upper Nile to the Atlantic coast. The plan grew to involve four lines of simultaneous advance—eastwards from the well-consolidated French bases in Senegal and the middle Niger region ; north-eastwards from the Ubangi district of the Congo Basin which was destined to become the heart of French Equatorial Africa; south-eastwards from the Barbary lands, mainly after 1880 ; and westwards, also after 1880, from a Somaliland base at Obok which, since 1883, has been included in the small but strategically-significant Protectorate of French Somaliland.[1]

This formidable French ambition inevitably menaced the authority which Egypt claimed over the neighbouring Sudan lands as well as over much of the Somaliland coast separated from the Egyptian Sudan by the independent State of Abyssinia. The nominal status of Egypt as late as the early years of the twentieth century was that of an autonomous but tributary State of the Ottoman Empire, though Turkish control had long been feeble. During the régime of the great Albanian soldier and statesman, Mehemet Ali, who was Turkish Viceroy in Egypt from 1805 to 1848, the foundations were prepared for the modern economic prosperity of the land of the lower Nile, but the political chaos which followed the death of Mehemet threatened to destroy his good work. The anarchy which was

---

[1] Jibuti is the modern head-quarters of French authority on the Somaliland coast and as a port holds an important position in relation to the critical sea-passage of Bab-el-Mandeb.

especially aggravated after 1880 gave Great Britain excuse and opportunity for military intervention, not only in Egypt but also in the nominal Egyptian dependencies of the Eastern Sudan and the Somaliland littoral. On the coast to the east of French Somaliland a British Protectorate was established in 1887 and, with Aden on the opposite, i.e. Arabian, shore was thereafter administered by the India Office. Kitchener's campaign of 1898 in the neighbourhood of Khartoum enabled Egypt to regain nominal authority over much of the Eastern Sudan although the region was henceforth to be virtually a British Protectorate and, officially, the condominium of the Anglo-Egyptian Sudan.

The British penetration southwards from Egypt imposed an abrupt check on French territorial ambitions in the Eastern Sudan and, in 1899 under pressure, the French withdrew entirely from the Nile Basin. Throughout the lands drained by the greatest African river—excepting Abyssinia, independent until 1935—Great Britain was henceforth in practical control, so that in her plans for the economic restoration of the potentially-rich Basin she was not disturbed by rival claims for Nile water on the part of other ambitious imperial Powers. The British proceeded to project schemes of irrigation which were to recognize the economic claims of the several sub-regions of the Nile Basin. Germany alone, represented by her East African Protectorate,[1] interrupted a British zone otherwise extending continuously from the Mediterranean coast of Egypt to the southernmost point of Africa.

Frustrated in the Eastern Sudan French ambitions turned to the strengthening of the links of an empire, vast and continuous, pivoting on Lake Chad and extending from Barbary and Senegal to the Congo. From the middle years of the nineteenth century onwards Algeria was the head-quarters of French influence and colonization in North-West Africa, and it was administered as if it formed a southern prolongation of France.[2] Tunisia was not involved in French ambitions until much later and a Protectorate was proclaimed in 1881, when Italy was awakening to a realization of her needs for colonial expansion in the same region. In 1904 a considerable improvement in the diplomatic relations of France and Great Britain permitted an agreement whereby each ceased to obstruct the ambitions of the other in North Africa ; so that France accepted British military domination in Egypt in return for British acknowledge-

---

[1] Renamed Tanganyika Territory after the First World War.
[2] Algeria has never been counted a French colony and is a responsibility of the Minister of the Interior.

8

ment of her special interests in Morocco. This *rapprochement* of the two Powers appeared from the German standpoint to be a sinister move for the isolation of Germany in the African field, and it is known to have contributed to the causes of the First World War. German ambitions were, however, somewhat appeased a few years later, in 1911, as a result of a territorial deal with France, by which the French Protectorate in Morocco was freed from German surveillance in return for a vast extension of the area of the German Camerouns as far as the Congo River. Germany was thus in a position to isolate the Gabun and its neighbourhood from the remainder of French Africa.

In 1912 the Sultan of Morocco was forced to accept French suzerainty, but the thorough conquest of the country was delayed until the period of General Lyautey's régime during the First World War. In the definition of the limits of the French Protectorate it was necessary to recognize the long-standing territorial claims of Spain both on the Atlantic and on the Mediterranean coasts. France agreed to a northward extension of the Spanish colony of Rio de Oro, a vast tract (109,000 sq. miles) of almost unmitigated desert, as far as the Wad Draa which extends parallel to, and to the south of, the Anti-Atlas. In addition, within Morocco as newly defined, two Spanish enclaves were left intact, namely Ifni and the territory of the Riff. The latter includes the coastal towns of Ceuta and Melilla, two long-recognized gateways into Barbary from Europe, which in powerful hands might dominate the Atlantic-Mediterranean passage from the African side. Closer than Ceuta in its relation to the ocean approaches to the Straits, Tangier is of significance to all nations interested in Mediterranean traffic; it remains politically distinct both from French and from Spanish Morocco and, with its environs, constitutes a zone under international supervision.

Almost contemporaneously with the founding of the German tropical empire Italy entered Africa as a colonial aspirant. As in the case of Germany, territorial ambitions abroad followed closely upon the unification of the State and were associated with the infancy of its modern industrial career. Italian projects of colonization in Africa have been, by necessity, restricted to the northern half of the continent and particularly to regions where the proportion of arid and generally useless land is very high. The penalty for late arrival was exclusion by more fortunate and powerful competitors from all the attractive districts with assured agricultural resources; so that, until the recent conquest of Abyssinia, the Italian empire in Africa was little better than a group of detached desert territories which were of little account alike in their contribution to the national wealth and in their assistance to a solution of the pressing problem of over-population at home.

Four years before the close of the nineteenth century Italian plans for a Protectorate over Abyssinia were scotched by complete military defeat at Adowa, an event providing the only instance of an indigenous African community successfully defending itself against the aggression of a Western Power. Italian claims in East Africa were consequently limited to little more than arid coastal strips in the neighbourhood of the ' Horn ', where triangular competition for territory involving Great Britain, France and Italy was a feature of the latter part of the century. Shortly after 1880 Italy acquired port bases on the Red Sea coast at Massowah and Assab Bay ; she thereby showed appreciation of the strategic significance of Assab in relation to the Straits of Bab-el-Mandeb, where the sea passage between Africa and Arabia is shortest and where communications linking the Mediterranean and the Indian Ocean might easily be menaced in time of war. From these coastal bases the Italian Protectorate of Eritrea was established immediately before the abortive attempt to annex Abyssinia. About the same time the very extensive strip of eastern Somaliland acquired Italian sovereignty and the limits of this Protectorate were extended to equatorial latitudes. After the First World War Great Britain voluntarily ceded a district of North-Eastern Kenya, west and south-west of the Juba River, and thereby greatly augmented the area and economic resources of Italian Somaliland.

On the North African shore Italian ambitions were necessarily limited to the territory intermediate to the British and French spheres of influence, in Egypt and Tunisia respectively. It has long been a sore point with Italy that she was forestalled by France in Tunisia and yet has provided the Protectorate with more colonists than her western rival has contributed. The littoral of Tripolitania and Cyrenaica together with the desert hinterland—all comprising the former Italian colony of Libya—was a Turkish province until 1911, in which year Italy deprived the Porte of its last African holding.[1] Altogether the area of Italian possessions in Africa by 1912 had expanded to a formidable area, but deficiency of rain was characteristic throughout. Indeed, much the greater part was unrelieved desert whose poverty of economic resources and vulnerability to attack from turbulent desert nomads involved a liability which might have been relinquished with advantage to Italy, but for the demands of national prestige. During the war of 1914–18

[1] The formal declaration of a British Protectorate over Egypt was not issued till 1914 though the substance of power has been in British hands since the closing years of the nineteenth century.

the insurrection of the desert men went near to forcing the evacuation by Italy of the Libyan coast, and in this counter-move to Italian penetration the Arab fraternity known as the Senussi, operating from their base in the Kufara oases, played an important rôle. More recently Italian colonial enterprise undertook both the settlement of Libya by Italian peasantry and, shortly before the Second World War, the conquest and economic development of Abyssinia.

An inevitable consequence of the European penetration of Africa has been the introduction to the continent of both bene-ficial and sinister aspects of Western civilization. Undoubtedly, Africa has gained by the European gift of scientific technique, especially in its application to tropical agriculture. It is also to our credit that the widespread decimation of native com-munities by inter-tribal warfare has generally ceased with the establishment of European authority. Against such gain must be placed the disruption of native institutions and the unscrupu-lous expropriation of tribal lands by European settlers and syndicates—processes which have been especially prominent in Central, Eastern and Southern Africa. Further, one cannot overlook the baneful effects on the native African derived from his contact with European vice, of which alcoholism has proved the most obvious, if not the most deadly, instance.

It is claimed that a new principle in colonial government was introduced by the statesmen of the Allied Powers at the Paris Peace Conference and thereafter applied to the confiscated lands of the dismembered German and Turkish Empires. The case for depriving Germany of every vestige of her colonial domain, which was mainly located in Africa, rested on the traditional usage of penalizing the loser in war and on the argu-ment that Germany had proved herself to be unfitted for the rôle of colonial administrator.

Instead, however, of a division of the spoils of war—mainly tropical lands—between the victorious Powers a system of international guardianship and control of the confiscated terri-tories was devised. All member States of the League of Nations were to co-operate in the new enterprise, though for the sake of convenience a particular member State was to be selected, by reason of its special opportunities or experience, for the actual work of administration, it being understood that the League should always retain the right of surveillance.[1] It was agreed, moreover, that administration by the Mandatory Power should terminate when the indigenous community, having bene-fited by the training in self-government which the Mandatory

[1] Such surveillance was undertaken, in theory, by the Permanent Man-dates Commission of the League.

Power was expected to confer, showed capacity to accept, without danger to itself, the gift of independent statehood. A Mandatory Power was thus in the position of the trustee of an estate, whose heir had not yet come of age.

This experiment in international co-operation was not without precedent, for it will be remembered that the Congress of Berlin (1884–5) had initiated the principle of international supervision in respect of the newly-discovered regions of tropical Africa, though it is also true that very little had resulted from the attempted application of the principle.

Great Britain, the Union of South Africa, France and Belgium thus received separately mandates to administer, on behalf of the League, the several ex-German colonies of Africa. Italy, though very willing to accept the responsibilities and privileges of a Mandatory Power in either Africa or the former Turkish Empire of Asia, was overlooked in the distribution of territory and later complained strongly against her exclusion. The Mandatory States agreed to permit freedom of trade, within the territories they administered, to member States of the League,[1] and they were expected very definitely to observe certain guarantees relating to the integrity of native society and tribal lands. As from time to time one or other of the Mandatory Powers has been known in its own interests to violate one or more terms of its charter of government there were critics who claimed, with considerable evidence in support, that ' mandated territory ' was synonymous with ' annexed territory '. On the other hand, there have been instances of adherence to the mandate which have encouraged hopes for the success of the international experiment in colonial government.

The allocation of the mandates in Africa has added to the overseas responsibilities of France and Great Britain, especially. In East Africa the greater part of the former German Protectorate, now Tanganyika Territory, is entrusted to Great Britain ; the remaining part, comprising the districts of Ruanda and Urundi, which are situated on the high eastern rim of the Congo Basin, has been allotted to Belgium in response to her claim for these elevated and comparatively healthy grass-lands which are in marked contrast with the general geographical character of the Belgian Congo. The natives of Ruanda-Urundi have not been properly considered in the new political division, for they have been divorced from their natural association with the grass-land peoples of the East African Plateau who are of similar culture and traditions to themselves.

[1] This is not applicable in the case of the mandate for South-West Africa

Former German South-West Africa was administered by the Union of South Africa first under Class C Mandate, the terms of which enabled the Union virtually to annex the territory as a fifth province of the federation.[1] The ex-German ' colonies ' of West-Central Africa, namely the Camerouns[2] and Togoland, were allotted mainly to France, although in each case a strip of territory of considerable significance was added to the British ' colonies ' of Nigeria and the Gold Coast respectively.

The Second World War destroyed the League of Nations, but after it the United Nations Organization claimed responsibility for all Mandated Territories. Great Britain, France and Belgium have undertaken the international trusteeship, with responsibility to the U.N.O., of the ex-German territories of Africa, of which they formerly held the mandates. The Union of South Africa continues to administer South-West Africa, with all the responsibilities of international mandate, as confirmed by the International Court of Justice at the Hague in 1950. Of the former Italian colonies, Somalia will remain until 1960 under Italian authority, Eritrea, after being administered by Great Britain from the end of the War, was federated with Ethiopia in September, 1952, while Libya became an independent kingdom in the previous year.

REFERENCES

Beer, G. L., *African Questions at the Paris Peace Conference*, New York, 1923.
Church, R. J. H., *Modern Colonization*, London, 1951.
Colonial Government : Annotated reading list on British Colonial Government, with an introduction by Margery Perham, London ; (O.U.P. for Nuffield College), 1950.
Coupland, R., *East Africa and its Invaders*, Oxford, 1938.
Evans, I. L., *The British in Tropical Africa*, Cambridge, 1929.
Hailey, Lord, *An African Survey*, 2nd ed., Oxford, 1945.
Native Administration in the British Territories in Africa, 4 vols., London; H.M.S.O., 1951.
Hertslet, Sir E., *The Map of Africa by Treaty*, 3 vols., London, 1909.
Johnston, Sir H. H., *A History of the Colonization of Africa by Alien Races*, 2nd ed., Cambridge, 1913.
The Opening-up of Africa, London, 1911.
Keltie, Sir J. S., *The Partition of Africa*, London, 1895.
Laure, René, *Le Continent africain au Milieu du Siècle*, Paris, 1952.
Lucas, Sir C. P., *The Partition and Colonization of Africa*, Oxford, 1922.
The Historical Geography of the Colonies (Africa volume), Oxford, 1913.
Perham, M., and Simmons, J., *African Discovery*, London, 1942.

---

[1] The four provinces of the Union are the Cape of Good Hope, the Transvaal, Natal and the Orange Free State.

[2] ' Camerouns ' is derived from the Portuguese—' Camarões '—that refers to the ' prawns ' which occur in abundance on the coast.

CHAPTER II

THE SOCIETIES OF AFRICA : THEIR CHARACTERISTICS AND GEOGRAPHICAL DISTRIBUTION

OUR purpose in this chapter is to provide a general survey of the principal communities of Africa, to place them in their geographical setting and to note the extent to which geographical conditions have shaped the ways of life of the different societies. Attention will be confined almost entirely to the peoples who have inhabited Africa for several hundred years at least, that is to say, to those to whom the term ' Natives ' is usually applied by the European settlers. The British and Dutch populations of South Africa, the Mediterranean peoples —French, Italians and Spaniards—in Barbary and the Indian groups of East and South-East Africa will be treated when we come later to a statement of the conditions of life in the principal regions of the continent.

The Distribution of Population Density

Apart from the Egyptian section of the Nile valley, where the average density has been estimated at 1,500 persons to the square mile, even the most attractive agricultural lands of Africa possess a generally low density. The total population of the continent in 1959 was 225 millions, which may be compared with about 253 millions for North (including Central) America, a continent of smaller area.[1] With the exception of Australia, where the proportion of desert to total area is higher than in any continent, Africa has the lowest density of the great land masses. This is a consequence of the enormous extent of arid and unused land. The area of the Sahara Desert alone is two and a half million square miles, which is approximately the extent of the United States of America without Alaska and is equal to more than one-fifth of the area of Africa : again, in Southern Africa desert and poor scrub-land cover more than one-third of the sub-continent.

[1] The respective areas (approximate) are—Africa, 11½ million sq. miles ; N. America, 9⅜ million sq. miles.

Only in the region of the lower Nile—the ribbon-like agricultural strip of Egypt—is the density comparable to figures which are typical of the great river plains of monsoonal Asia.[1] Elsewhere in Africa close concentration of population is not geographically associated with the more important rivers. Forest, jungle and swamp are generally hostile to dense settlement in the regions of the Congo rivers and of the lower Niger, while difficulties of navigation and irrigation associated with a prolonged season of aridity, during which the rivers are greatly

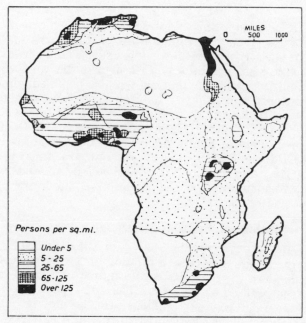

FIG. 14.—Density of Population

reduced in volume, are equally negative factors in such cases as the Orange and Upper Zambezi rivers of Southern Africa.

Omitting, first, Egypt where the relationships of social and economic life to physical environment are quite unique and, secondly, the mining areas recently settled in Southern and South-Central Africa, one may say that there is a fairly close correspondence between the distribution of population density and the distribution of mean annual rainfall. In a continent where modern large-scale irrigation projects are still compara-

[1] In the Nile Delta the density is approximately 1,500 per square mile.

tively rare—Egypt is quite exceptional—climatic aridity remains the principal barrier to the expansion of settlement.

Indicated below are the main regions where the population density is considerably higher than the average for Africa and where livelihood is dependent on a mean annual rainfall of not less than 25 inches : they are :

(1) the Guinea lands from the Gambia to the Niger, together with a littoral extension southwards to the Congo estuary and a hinterland extension in the Sudan which is especially wide in the basin of the lower-middle Niger :

(2) the Great Lakes region of the East African Plateau, particularly the near neighbourhood of Victoria Nyanza :

(3) the littoral belt of Eastern and Southern Africa from the neighbourhood of Mombasa (Kenya) as far as Cape Town. High density is not continuous throughout, and a wide tract in Portuguese East Africa between the lower Limpopo and the district of Beira does not show a higher density than the low average for the continent :

(4) the Mediterranean fringe of Barbary from the eastern coast of Tunisia westwards, and certain parts of Western Morocco ;

(5) the Plateau of Abyssinia.[1]

Cities of vast populations—characteristic expressions of modern ' Western ' civilization—are rare in Africa. Although commerce and industry on ' Western ' lines are steadily, indeed quickly, pervading the continent it is still only within the Mediterranean strip of the north, especially lower Egypt, and in the south—where the recent exploitation of precious minerals has produced embryo townships, as it were, overnight—that cities of European style are to be found. Cairo, exceeding two million inhabitants, is the largest urban concentration in Africa, and Alexandria, the main port of the Nile Delta, has approximately half this total. With the exception of Johannesburg, the metropolis of South Africa, no other African city exceeds the figure of one million inhabitants. Most other towns which exceed 100,000 persons and resemble European centres in their plan and organization are seaports. The Negro peoples of Africa rarely show a disposition for urban concentration, but a very notable exception occurs in Southern Nigeria where it is estimated that half of the thirteen million inhabitants live in very large villages or in towns. Of these Ibadan is the greatest with

[1] With an estimated population of 18 millions Abyssinia (including Eritrea) has a density of about 42 per square mile.

about 500,000 inhabitants, and, if the number of Natives who enter the town daily from farm suburbs be added, the day-time population is raised considerably higher. Ibadan is within the territory of the Yoruba, a Negro people who are remarkable for the complex form of their social organization.

Such towns as Ibadan and Kano (Northern Nigeria) are not constructed of durable material such as stone, and it is a remarkable fact that the African Negro has never discovered the arts of building in stone and of road construction. Apart from the Hamitic zone of North Africa there were no roads in the continent prior to European penetration. The Rhodesian stone buildings such as Zimbabwe, concerning whose origins much · dispute still lingers, were almost certainly raised by Bantu Negro labour, but it is also likely that Arab or other Asiatic influence was concerned in their erection, and in any case the art of the stone-mason entirely disappeared from Bantu Africa.

Very little relationship is found to exist between the territorial limits of the more prominent ethnic groups and the political units into which the continent has been divided by the colonizing Powers. Where the acquisition of territory and of industrial raw materials was the initial motive for European penetration it was unlikely that the traditional limits of tribal lands would be respected in the process of re-dividing the continent. Less culpable though not less serious in effect was European ignorance of the ethnological facts concerning African societies which frequently led, though unintentionally, to the destruction of the integrity of tribal groups. Egypt and, to a less extent, Abyssinia are indigenous states, whose nationalism has intensified in recent years, and in Egypt the great majority of the inhabitants recognize common bonds of traditional culture, of language and religion.

When distinguishing the principal human groups of Africa we employ the criteria of race as well as those of culture, language and social organization. Physical traits offer the most stable, and therefore most satisfactory, basis for the classification of races because they represent the characters that are least subject to change and cannot be borrowed, whilst language and culture may be passed from one group to another. But the intermixture of races is a continual process, especially on the borders of racial zones, so that in Africa as elsewhere racial purity is very rare and confined to regions of isolation which are unattractive or characterized by economic hardship. The widespread movement of peoples is the most potent agency of race mingling, and, in company with the other continents, Africa throughout history and prehistory has experienced migrations on a big scale. Usually their progress across the continent has

been slow, occupying several or even many centuries and has
represented a gradual infiltration of peoples from one zone into
another rather than organized conquest ; yet military conquest
as a means of population displacement has also been important,
as, for example, in the case of the Arab conquest of North Africa.

There is a general tendency for a migrating people to confine
their movement to regions where conditions of life, as determined
by climate and vegetation, are similar to those of the earlier
home-land. So the Moslem conquerors of North Africa with
their traditions of desert or dry grass-land life and their dependence for transport on horse and camel were repelled, beyond
the Sudan, by the southward spreading forests which were
hostile to pastoralism and concealed new terrors of disease both
to man and to domesticated animals.[1] The southward advance
of Islam on the western side of the continent has usually been
limited to the northern edges of the tropical forest.

Physical barriers to migration in the form of lofty and continuous mountain systems are rare in Africa. The plateau structure
of the continent is widespread and, considering the vastness of the
area, the land surface is remarkably uniform. Only on the extreme
north-western and southern margins are there folded mountain
systems which could check and, in fact, have actually hindered
movement on to the plateau from the coast. More potent as
a barrier to migration than the minor difficulties of relief is the
unsuitability of the vegetation and climate in certain regions of
the continent. The dense, trackless forests have generally been
avoided by pastoral peoples in their migrations, but have served
as refuges for less virile communities that, under pressure, have
evacuated the savanna. The tropical forests of Guinea and the
Congo now shelter primitive peoples who, in that struggle for
land which is a concomitant of migrations, were forced to leave
the Sudanese or East African grass-lands for the protection of
dense tree-growth. Similarly, in Southern Africa the hot deserts
on the western side of the sub-continent became the refuge of
primitive aboriginal stocks expelled from the veld by successive
waves of more virile negroid peoples : these aborigines have
obtained refuge but little else, and their inhospitable lands that
offer no scope for economic advance explain their miserable and
dying condition. As the more aggressive stocks in Africa, before
the arrival of the Europeans, were almost entirely pastoral in
mode of life they tended, when on the move, to follow the zones
of open grass-land. Many of the conquering peoples of tropical
Africa have entered the continent in the neighbourhood of the

[1] The ravages of the tsetse fly to which cattle are easy victims has
been one of the main deterrents to the advance of Islam in tropical Africa.
See Fig. 46.

' Eastern Horn ' : thence their routes have been mainly two, one
diverging westwards to the grass-lands of the Eastern Sudan, the
other southwards or south-westwards on to the park savanna of
the East African Plateau.

African peoples may first be broadly classified according to
their negroid or non-negroid characters. The southern border
of the Sahara may be taken in a general way to mark the northern
boundary of Negro Africa. More precisely this ethnic frontier

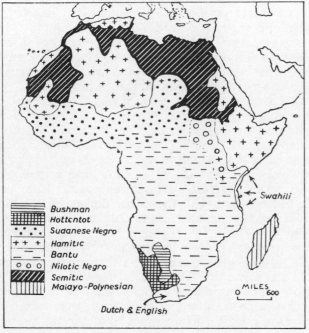

FIG. 15.—Africa : distribution of principal ethnic groups

line is followed from the lower Senegal River eastwards by way
of Timbuktu to the Nile at Khartoum, whence it loops southwards
and eastwards to the Juba River of Italian Somaliland—Abyssinia
being left to the north of the line. The Sahara, middle and
lower Nile region and the Mediterranean fringe together form
the domain of peoples who are closer to the inhabitants of the
southern peninsulas of Europe than they are to the Sudanese
Negroes. These dominant people of North Africa are racially
akin to the Arabs and Jews, known collectively to the ethnol-

ogist as Semites. No satisfactory group-name has been assigned
to them, though ' Hamites ' is the usual ethnological term. It
must not be supposed that the ethnic division between the
Negroes and the Hamites is clear cut. Some of the most
important African stocks show in their physical characters and
in their culture a blend of Negro and Hamitic strains, and there
are innumerable gradations intermediate to the two basic races.
We shall give a distinct place to the Hamito-Negroid stocks
in our survey, bearing in mind at the same time that many of
the types which we class as Negro or Hamite usually show some
proportion of foreign traits.

THE NEGROID PEOPLES

(a) Bushmen, Negrillos and Hottentots

Three of the most primitive and interesting of African communities—the Bushmen, Pygmy Negrillos and Hottentots—have
comparatively little geographical significance and will be considered very briefly. The Bushmen at present are mainly confined to the central and northern districts of the Kalahari and
to the northern part of South-West Africa. In much earlier
times they roamed freely over South Africa and their ancestors
probably reached the sub-continent from an earlier home on the
East African Plateau, for there are found in this region and
farther south traces of their former occupation, including their
artistic rock-paintings. In build the Bushman is short, averaging
5 feet. The hair of the head is arranged in small separate tufts,
while the skin is wrinkled and of yellowish brown colour. They
are essentially hunters and, although for centuries in contact
with other civilizations, have not assimilated any appreciable
amount of foreign culture. Agriculture is unknown to them
and on their own initiative they do not undertake stock-rearing.
A Bushman hunting band is of about 50 persons, representing
a number of family groups, and wanders over hunting grounds the
limits of which are settled by tradition. Habitations are usually
for temporary occupation only and consist of crude shelters of
branches. The Bushmen are a people without a future and their
decreasing numbers point to ultimate extinction. It was probably
in the seventeenth century that they were pressed desertwards
by the Hottentots, and later the more numerous and powerful
Bantu Negroes in addition to the European colonists—especially
the Dutch farmers—carried on the process of expulsion.

Like the Bushmen the Pygmy Negrillos of Central Africa
are hunters, but their domains are in the densest tropical forest
found within the limits of 6° N. and 6° S. of the Equator. It

is probable that formerly they had a much wider extension. They are shorter in stature than the Bushmen and average from 4 feet 4 inches to 4 feet 9 inches. Their negroid features include broad nose together with prognathism. Although they are in friendly contact with Negro peoples who barter agricultural stores for the products of the Pygmy chase, they remain hunters armed with the bow and poisoned arrow.

Sharing the fate of the Bushmen, with whom they are in contact, the Hottentots have been driven from the richer veld of South Africa by the oncoming Bantu Negroes and are now confined to the fringes of the desert, where they are steadily losing their virility and their numbers. Their tribal organization has been destroyed except amongst those, about 15,000 in number, who occupy the districts of South-West Africa which lie just to the north of the Orange River. Farther south, in the Western Cape Province, the Hottentot territory formerly extended widely and they, not the Bantu Negroes, were the Natives whom the early Dutch settlers met in the neighbourhood of Table Bay. It is the general view among ethnologists that the Hottentots are the result of a crossing between the Bushmen and an early Hamitic stock which took place possibly on the East African Plateau. They entered South Africa subsequent to the Bushmen and their route led to the south-west by way of the upper basin of the Zambezi. In the Western Cape Province the ' Cape Coloured ' population, as it is officially designated in the census returns, represents a half-caste stock (numbering about three-quarters of a million), in which the Hottentot strain is strongly preserved in association with European, mainly Dutch characteristics. Nomadic pastoralism is the art of the Hottentots and their wealth is in cattle and sheep. They show ability in the smelting of iron and in the weaving of mats and baskets, and, in recent years, a few have turned to a primitive agriculture. Less nomadic than the Bushmen, their habitations are of a more permanent nature and resemble the kraals of the Bantu Negroes. An encampment is usually enclosed by a fence of thorn, and is composed of bee-hive huts and a cattle-fold. Stature is taller than among the Bushmen, by an average of 3 inches, but negroid features are nearly as prominent as among the hunting people.

(b) The Guinea and Sudanese Negroes

The West African Negro, sometimes known as the Sudanese Negro—though the purest types are found usually within the Guinea forests—is the closest approximation in Africa to the true Negro unmixed with foreign blood. Characteristic features are fairly tall stature, averaging 5 feet 8 inches in the male adult, black or very dark brown skin, woolly hair—a trait that usually survives cross-breeding with non-negroid types—broad nose and wide nostrils, prognathism, in addition to thick, everted lips. The head-form is usually long (dolichocephalic) though not markedly so, as indicated by a cephalic index of about 75. There are relatively few Negroes who possess all the above-mentioned characteristics which are, of course, associated only with the ideal type. The West African Negro who has been unaffected by foreign culture is a cultivator and not a pastoralist, and typical of the foodstuffs grown are bananas, beans and millet.[1] From the West African forest across the Sudan [2] towards the edges of the Sahara there is evidence of diminishing purity amongst the Negroes, and of an increasing proportion of Hamitic features including lighter skin colour, more aquiline nose and narrower nostrils. The influence of the Hamitic invasions from the Sahara is also shown in the culture and religion of many negroid groups of the Sudan, as, for example, in the common practice of stock-rearing and in the—at least nominal—adherence to the Mahomedan faith and social code. On the other hand, certain Negro communities retreated forest-wards in front of the Hamitic advance, and within the coastal belt of Guinea are preserved some of the purest representatives of their race.

The Wolof, amongst the blackest of African peoples, are distributed between the latitude of Cape Verde and the left bank of the lower Senegal, which river provides an approximate boundary to the Negro zone over against the westernmost group of Saharan Hamites. Inland the Wolof extend over much of the French Colony of Senegal, and the old Wolof kingdom of Cayor has not been entirely obliterated under the French régime. Other important Negro groups of Senegal are the Serer, a tall people, the Tukolor (Fr.—Toucouleurs) and the Mandingans. The majority of these tribesmen have been converted to Islam, though, like so many of the negroid Mahomedans of West Africa, they bear the acquired religion very lightly. The Mandingans are the most numerous and important group of negroid tribes in the Western Sudan and they claim an almost national tradition. Natives with Mandingan pretensions are found throughout an enormous area, and from the coast between the Senegal River and northern Sierra Leone they extend eastwards as the dominant

---

[1] The hoe, not the plough, is the farm implement of the negro African.

[2] The term ' Sudan ' is derived from ' Bilad es Sudán ' (' Land of the Blacks '), which was applied by medieval Arab writers to Africa south of the Sahara.

people of the northern part of the Futa Jallon Plateau and of the upper basin of the Niger. But they are by no means uniform in ethnic features, and those Mandingans who are nearest in position to the Sahara possess certain Hamitic traits and are usually Mahomedans.

The Mandingans look back to a notable history of over 1000 years. In pre-Moslem times they founded the State of Guiné whose name is preserved in the geographical expression—'Guinea'.[1]

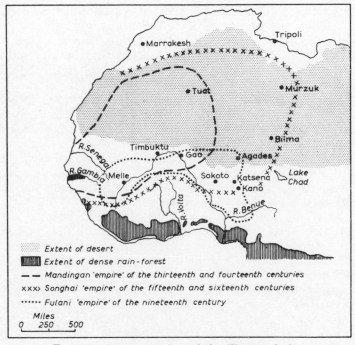

FIG. 16.—Former empires of the Western Sudan
(Approximate limits)

(N.B.—The southern limit of the Fulani power corresponds fairly closely to the southern limit of horse-rearing in the Western Sudan at the present day.)

The greatest of their empires was organized from the district of Manding, within the territory now known as French Guinea. Of the Mandingans one of the best-known groups is the Bambara, an agricultural people from whom the French Administration expects much in its ambitious schemes for the cultivation of large tracts of the upper Niger basin.

Along the coast of Guinea from the Gambia River southeastwards to Cape Palmas there is a number of fairly typical Negro groups including the Felup of Portuguese Guinea, the

[1] The guinea took its name from the coin struck in the seventeenth century by the Company of Royal Adventurers of England trading in Africa.

Timne (or Temne [1]) of Sierra Leone and, most important of all so far as European interests are concerned, the Kru of the Liberian coast. The Kru are distributed in small independent communities around the port townships of the Liberian coast and they provide crews for many merchant vessels plying in West African waters. They are usually of fine physique and many are almost typical Negroes. Farther east the best-known Guinea Negroes include the Fanti and Ashanti of the Gold Coast and the Yoruba of South-West Nigeria. In this region of Eastern Guinea there was, prior to European conquest, a very considerable degree of cultural and political development. A number of well-organized negro states existed, such as Benin, Ashanti, Yoruba and Dahomey. The Ashanti, numbering about half a million, are forest dwellers of the South-Central Gold Coast and their long seclusion in forest strongholds has preserved them from Hamitic intrusion. With a formidable military organization centralized at their capital, Kumasi, they strongly opposed the northward spread of British conquest. Though differing little in physique from other Guinea Negroes, the Yoruba exhibit higher qualities of mind and culture than the majority of their race. They are keen traders and agriculturists, while, as has been mentioned, their large towns such as Ibadan and Abeokuta are almost exceptional in Negro Africa.

Now to continue our survey of the Negroes in the Sudan hinterland from the Mandingan domain eastwards. The Songhai, about two millions in number, have a strong military tradition.. Their territory stretches from the neighbourhood of Timbuktu southwards across the great bend of the Niger. About the year 1500 they destroyed the Mandingan empire, and their military domination of the Western Sudan lasted until the French captured the Songhai capital of Timbuktu. Though classed as Negroes the Songhai offer an instance where clear-cut classification is most difficult ; for many of them show strong traces of intermixture with Hamites of Saharan origin, although the woolly hair, characteristic of Negroes, is widespread amongst them. To the south of the Songhai and in the French Colony of Upper Volta, which includes much of the upper basin of the Volta, a prominent people are the Mossi who have their main centre at Wagaduga. They are mainly agriculturists, millet growers, but sometimes turn to pastoralism as breeders of horses and cattle. Unlike the Songhai they have successfully resisted the spread of Islam in their domain.

[1] The majority of African tribes possess names for the spelling of which there are alternatives. I have tried to select the spelling which is the best known to English students.

9

East of the Mossi country and in the Central Sudan it is true as a general rule that the negroid peoples have been more permeated by Hamitic blood and culture than is the case in the Western Sudan. The region includes important Hamitic groups concerning whom discussion is postponed to a later section of this chapter. Islam has played an all-important part in the political organization of the negroid peoples of the Central Sudan and, until comparatively recent times, important Negro principalities or emirates were in existence. In the region between the Songhai domain and Lake Chad the Hausa are easily the foremost Negroes, though there is little approximation to ethnic unity amongst those whose claim to be Hausa rests mainly on their use of a language which is the *lingua franca* for large parts of the Central Sudan.[1] The heart of Hausa-land has as its northern limits a line drawn between the important North Nigerian towns of Katsina and Sokoto, and it extends southwards to the latitude of the town of Zaria (N. Nigeria). The purest Negroes among the Hausa are distributed throughout the Moslem emirates which are still ruled, under British supervision, by the Fulani (i.e. Hamitic) aristocracy of North Nigeria : the more important of these principalities are those of Kano, Sokoto, Katsina and Zaria. As traders, artisans and farmers the Hausa rival the most advanced of the Mandingans and they are especially notable for their industrial skill in textile and leather processes. Until the early years of the nineteenth century the Hausa were organized in a confederation of states which, though weak from a military or political standpoint, steadily increased in its cultural and commercial influence over much of the Central Sudan, to be subsequently reduced by the non-negroid Fulani conquerors. In Hausa-land to-day the social unit has a territorial rather than a tribal basis and represents a group of villages united by common allegiance to a chief. Apart from the Hausa and Fulani of Northern Nigeria there are numerous pagan groups of more primitive characteristics who are very little known though they are estimated at several million tribesmen.

Around Lake Chad are several Moslem emirates each with its Hamitic or Arab aristocracy, but with a negroid population basis. The majority are in French territory, the main exception being Bornu [2] (N.E. Nigeria) whose people are the negroid Kanuri, and they include Kanem to the north of

[1] The population of true Hausa in Northern Nigeria and the immediate neighbourhood is estimated at five to six millions.

[2] Bornu gained commercial supremacy in the Central Sudan after the tenth century and owed this importance to its position controlling the southern terminus of the Saharan trade-route from Tripoli.

Chad and Baghirmi which occupies the country to the north and east of the swampy basin of the lower Shari, a river which is the greatest tributary of the Chad Basin. Farther east the negroid domain extends to the Anglo-Egyptian Sudan, though it is rare for the true Negro to be found. The Hamitic infusion is strong everywhere even though the ethnic basis remains negroid. In the Anglo-Egyptian Sudan the Nuba of Southern Kordofan are one of the most prominent groups and, farther west in Dar Fur and in Wadai of the French Sudan, there are people akin to the Nuba and who, like the Nuba, have to some extent preserved their ethnic individuality by retreating to the hills before the Hamitic and Arab invaders. Also related to the Sudanese Negroes are a number of communities who extend across the Nile-Congo divide into the basin of the Ubangi-Welle rivers. These groups (including the tribes of the Azande) live in close proximity to peoples of Hamito-Negroid character but are clearly marked off from the latter not only by racial traits but also by their life as tillers of the soil. As has been indicated, the infusion of Hamite blood among the Sudanese populations has produced a Hamito-Negroid type which is commonly associated with the Hamitic pastoral tradition.

(c) The Bantu Negroes

The name ' Bantu ' or ' Aba-ntu ' is the plural of a word meaning ' human being ' and is used in reference to the largest group of related negroid communities in Africa. Bantu Negroes, numbering about 50 millions, occupy at least one-third of the continent, including much the greater part of the area south of the Equator. They speak various dialects of a common language and, although the term ' Bantu ' is most suitably employed in its philological sense, it is true that over the great tract of the continent which the Bantu-speaking peoples occupy one dominant race type is observed and that with it is associated a definite set of social and cultural traits.

As in the case of many Sudanese peoples, there is a varying proportion of Hamitic strain in the Bantu stocks, and this non-negroid element is particularly strong in East and South-East Africa. The map on page 112 indicates approximately the division between the Bantu and their northern neighbours who are Sudanese Negroes, Hamites and Hamito-Negroid stocks. From the west coast at the boundary of Nigeria and the Cameroons the line passes eastwards so as to leave the Southern Cameroons in the Bantu domain. Extreme northern districts of the Belgian Congo lie to the north of the ' Bantu line ' which is followed south of the Welle River to the neighbourhood of Lake Albert.

Thence the boundary crosses Uganda by way of Lake Kioga, skirts Victoria Nyanza, leaving the entire lake littoral to the Bantu, and cuts across Northern Tanganyika Territory towards the coast near Mombasa. In this eastern region the line should be extended north-westwards from Mombasa to the neighbourhood of Mount Kenya, then eastwards across the River Tana to the lower Juba River in Italian Somaliland, so as to include the greater part of the southern half of Kenya Colony within the Bantu domain.

Before European penetration into South and East Africa the Bantu in these parts might have been classified either as 'military and pastoral' or as 'agricultural and industrial'. Amongst the military tribes—for example, the Zulu—the power of the chief was absolute and his principal kraal or village resembled an armed camp arranged with a view to the defence of the soldiery and their dependants and of the cattle which were the main source of livelihood. Very little attention was paid to land cultivation which was considered a servile occupation to be left to subject tribes. This prejudice against tillage still persists in parts of East and South Africa, especially where the Hamitic strain in the population is most marked. The military tribes usually seized the most fertile lands for cattle pasture and, in so doing, deprived the weaker agricultural tribes of tracts well suited to cultivation : this explains why those groups of the South African Bantu who were, until recently, very aggressive are found dwelling in the eastern districts of the subcontinent where rainfall and vegetation are most abundant. Amongst the agricultural and industrial tribes, during the pre-European era, the power of the paramount chief was limited by the *Pitso* or parliament of the tribesmen, which is still found as a working institution in Basutoland. These tribes cultivated permanently the lands in the neighbourhood of their kraals which were usually left unfenced and undefended, and their industries included the weaving of cloth and metal-working.

So vast is their domain that it is convenient to group the Bantu regionally, and we shall refer to (1) Eastern Bantu, distributed between Uganda and the Zambezi River, (2) Southern Bantu, mainly in British South Africa, (3) Bantu of Central and West-Central Africa.

(1) *The Eastern Bantu* cluster with a particularly high density in the close neighbourhood of all coasts of Lake Victoria, where the littoral is comparatively low-lying. Contrast is marked with the steep margins of the Rift Valley lakes—e.g. Tanganyika and Nyasa—where both extensive and dense settlement are rarely

possible. A fairly high concentration of population is continued north-west and south-west of Victoria towards Lakes Albert and Tanganyika respectively. These thickly-populated areas are occupied by the most advanced peoples of East Africa and several communities have almost attained the dignity of nations, as in the cases of the kingdom of Buganda,[1] situated in southern districts of the Uganda Protectorate, and of Bunyoro, whose position is between Buganda and the neighbourhood of Lake Albert. As previously indicated, the proportion of Hamitic blood amongst the East African Bantu is comparatively high ; it is due to infusions both in the distant past and in relatively modern times. Sometimes the fusion has not been complete, as in the case of Bunyoro where two groups co-exist, the Hamito-Negroid Bahima who are stock-rearers and the negroid Bahera, agriculturists, who are regarded rather contemptuously by the Bahima. Of all African negroid peoples the Baganda, numbering about one million, have shown the quickest aptitude in deriving benefit from the introduction of Western civilization. They are becoming almost European in their tastes in dress and domestic accommodation, and have been eager to develop their country in order to compete in the markets of the world. This is shown by the remarkable initiative and energy which they have devoted to cotton cultivation. Long prior to the British occupation they had evolved a highly-organized society and a political system resembling a constitutional monarchy.

To the east of the Uganda Protectorate in the territory now known as Kenya Colony the most notable of the Bantu are the Kikuyu, who occupy a considerable district in the neighbourhood of Mount Kenya, and their neighbours the Akamba, who are situated between Mount Kilimanjaro and the Tana River. Both peoples are agriculturists and traditional enemies of the Masai, a pastoral and nomadic tribe of Hamito-Negroid origin who, earlier, were accustomed to trespass on the farms of the agricultural Bantu. Methods of cultivation among the Akamba are very primitive and the hoe and digging stick are employed. They are not exclusively agriculturists, however, and keep cattle as well as sheep and goats. Closely related by race, culture and language to the Akamba the Kikuyu occupy a fertile country, much encroached upon by White settlers, which they claim to have brought to its present well-cultivated condition from a state of wild forest. They are careful growers of the manioc and banana and the more affluent among them take pride in cattle-rearing, as the possession of cattle, with them

[1] Bantu prefixes referring to people, land and state are Ba or Wa = People, Bu = Kingdom or State.

as with the Bantu generally, is an indication of wealth. Other agricultural Bantu close at hand include the Wachagga, who cultivate banana groves on the lower slopes of Mount Kilimanjaro. They are also cattle-rearers, but have difficulty in finding pasture for their herds on account of the extensiveness of banana cultivation. Their method of surmounting this difficulty is rarely employed in Negro Africa : quite frequently their cattle are stall-fed with grass carried to the kraals from the bottoms of the valleys.

From the other fairly representative groups of the East African Bantu may be chosen for mention the Wa Yao and Anyanja. The former occupied in comparatively recent times a wide area in the north of Portuguese East Africa between Lake Nyasa and the coast, but they are now settled within narrower limits and are particularly prominent in the Shiré Highlands of Southern Nyasaland, the agricultural development of which is largely due to their co-operation. The Anyanja are in contact with the Yao people and a considerable degree of intermarriage has occurred. Under different tribal names they have an extensive range and are found in eastern districts of Northern Rhodesia, as well as in the southern and central districts of Nyasaland.

An East Coast Bantu group known as Swahili [1] are especially notable because their language has been borrowed by a great variety of peoples in East Africa and is spoken in the great ports such as Zanzibar, Mombasa and Dar-es-Salaam as well as in many interior districts of the East African Plateau, at least as far west as the borders of the Belgian Congo. It is important, therefore, to distinguish the Bantu Swahili from those peoples of various racial origins who have adopted the language and who are loosely classed as Swahili. The Swahili proper are distributed in detached groups throughout the littoral of Kenya and Tanganyika Territory and in the islands of Zanzibar and neighbouring Pemba. Swahili as the dominant language of Zanzibar followed the trade-routes which radiated from or converged on the island when, until little more than half a century ago, it was the greatest slave market within the circle of the Indian Ocean. Outside the African coasts Swahili is known and spoken in North-West Madagascar and in Southern Arabia. It has been called the *lingua franca* of East Africa, by which is meant that in nearly every part of this region there are to be found individuals who speak it : and so the traveller speaking Swahili may count on finding in almost every village some one who can understand him. On account of its extensive range it must be classed

[1] Swahili signifies ' coastmen '.

amongst the great languages of the world, and to some extent there is rivalry between English and Swahili for priority as the most used commercial language of East Africa. It ranks as a Bantu language, but its vocabulary has been enriched by words drawn chiefly from Arabic and, to a smaller extent, from Hindustani, Persian, Portuguese and English.

(2) *The Southern Bantu*, who occupy that part of Africa which is most favoured by European settlers, have been induced to play a laborious part in the industrial development of the sub-continent. As a result tribal life has been more dislocated in South Africa than in any other part of the continent where the European has intruded. The acquisition by White settlers of the greater part of the most fertile land formerly owned by the Southern Bantu has assisted tribal disintegration, and nowhere else in Africa, save perhaps Kenya where the scale of operations is smaller, has the impact of European civilization upon the Negro been so disturbing.

In the Union of South Africa the two great groups of the Bantu are, first, the Suto-Chuana who include, amongst many tribes, the Bechuana and the Basuto and who inhabit the high plateau to the north of the Orange River in the Orange Free State, Basutoland and the Transvaal. Secondly, there are the Zulu-Xosa who occupy wide districts of the Eastern Cape Province, Natal (with Zululand) and Swaziland. Groups of the Zulu-Xosa found farther north are the Matabele of Southern Rhodesia and the Angoni, kinsmen of the Zulu, who live north of the Zambezi River, in Nyasaland and Northern Rhodesia. Between these tribes there are no fundamental differences of race. One of the chief variations is in skin colour, though chocolate brown is dominant. The Negro basis has received Hamitic infusions and, in the case of the Bechuana, in western districts of the Union and in the Bechuanaland Protectorate, the skin frequently takes on a yellowish-brown tinge, indicating contact with Bushmen or Hottentots. Amongst the Zulu are found a number of individuals of taller stature and finer facial features than the average, and the Zulu seem to have suffered less in physical degeneration from the poverty and industrial conditions which European civilization has introduced to Native life than have the majority of the Southern Bantu.

In the Suto-Chuana group the Basuto are the most numerous and, possibly, the most interesting people. Their tribal life has been less disturbed by the European penetration of South Africa than that of any other large Native community : this is certainly not unrelated to the formidable natural defence which the high plateau and higher mountains of Basutoland afford to this hardy stock. The Basuto nation or federation, which has now a population of over half a million, was brought into being about one hundred years ago by the genius of the paramount chief, Moshesh, the greatest Bantu statesman of South Africa who has yet arisen.

There is a tendency for the Bechuana and the Basuto to group themselves in village communities. In Basutoland the villages are usually small, with a maximum of about 50 households, but in Bechuanaland the aggregations are often large, and one sub-group of the Bechuana known as the Bamangwato, who occupy an eastern district of the Protectorate, possess a 'town'—Serowe, their 'capital'—which has a population of about 30,000 out of a total tribal membership of approximately 110,000. The Bechuana, occupying the land which bears their tribal name as well as the Western Transvaal, are not a federation of tribes under a paramount chief as are the Basuto : yet the various sub-groups, such as the Bamangwato and the Bakwena, are closely interrelated from the standpoint of race and culture.

In the other great group of Southern Bantu, the Zulu-Xosa, which occupies districts mainly to the east and south of the Drakensberg Escarpment, the Zulu federation was formerly paramount. Less fortunate than the Basuto, the Zulu ' nation ' has suffered almost complete disintegration, a consequence of the penetration of White settlement and of economic pressure, which has forced many to seek employment in mine or town far from their homes. About the early nineteenth century the various tribes of the district which is now the Province of Natal were welded into one great tribal unit by the Zulu warrior Chaka ; but through war and massacre much of Chaka's work was destructive and several of his successors maintained a warlike aggression which was their undoing when they encountered European arms. A break-away from the Zulu federation occurred in Chaka's time and resulted in, first, the penetration of the Matabele into Southern Rhodesia (as it now is) where the tradition of Zulu warfare and massacre was employed against the more peaceful Mashona until the time of the British occupation ; and, secondly, in the settlement of the Angoni north of the Zambezi River, especially in Portuguese territory to the east of Lake Nyasa.

Ethnically allied to the Zulu and settled in eastern districts of the Cape Province are the Bantu tribes including the important Tembu, Pondo, Pondomisi and Fingo. Here in the Transkei [1] and neighbouring parts they have been to some extent preserved, by Acts of Parliament dating from 1894 on-

[1] ' Across the Kei ', that is the territory to the east of the Great Kei River.

wards, from the tribal disintegration to which so many of the Southern Bantu have been exposed. As a rule, the Zulu-Xosa do not congregate in villages and the unit of settlement is the kraal or homestead, complete with huts, cattle-fold and, especially in the case of the Zulu, with an encircling fence. In a recent tour of the Transkei and Natal the author studied the types of habitation amongst the Zulu-Xosa and found a usual distinction between the bee-hive dwellings of the Zulu and the circular huts, walled strongly with hardened clay or dung, which, with their cone-shaped roofs of thatch, are characteristic of the Transkei. The latter type of hut is not uncommon amongst the Basuto also, and in their land a large rectangular hut with inverted V-shaped roof is frequently seen and suggests a simple imitation of the European house. Amongst the Transkei Bantu the arrangement of huts in the kraal is often quite haphazard, and here again there is contrast with the Zulu. Pastoralism is characteristic of the Zulu-Xosa and usually when they turn to agriculture, especially the cultivation of maize (' mealies ') and millet, they are less successful than are the Basuto.

We need also to include mention, however brief, of the scattered and generally disorganized Bantu tribes who occupy the dry grass-lands of South-West Africa and Southern Angola. The principal groups in these parts are the Ova-Herero, who extend into the semi-desert of South-West Africa, and the Ovambo of Ovamboland (northern S.W. Africa) and Southern Angola. Altogether these and related groups probably barely exceed a quarter of a million.

(3) The Bantu of Central and West-Central Africa

On the whole very little is known of the life, characteristics and environment of these Negroes. Much of their vast territory is forest-clothed, for it extends from the centre of the Cameroons southwards to Central Angola and from the Atlantic coast across the Congo Basin into Northern Rhodesia. The Congo Basin is the heart of this great domain, and, on account of its very recent exploration and of its climatic and other natural obstacles to European penetration, it still remains one of the least-known regions of Africa.

At the time of the Portuguese discovery of the West African coast—Diego Çao reached the Congo estuary in 1484—there were in existence in Central Africa a number of Negro ' empires ' or confederations of which there is only a vague knowledge remaining. The forested or jungle condition of much of the land, with its tendency to foster isolated settlements in clearings, was a very formidable hindrance to the maintenance of cohesion

between the numerous tribal communities of which these so-called
' empires ' were composed : so that strong, centralized government over a long period of time was rendered wellnigh impossible
by the geographical conditions.

During the sixteenth century and later the tribes of the lower
Congo were grouped under a ' king ' or paramount chief whose
territory became known in Europe as the kingdom of Kongo.
About the same time a Negro ' empire ' is thought to have existed
in much of the region now included in the southern part of the
Belgian Congo and in neighbouring districts of Angola. A Negro
potentate—the Great Jumbo—claimed a similar extent of territory even as late as 1890, when the greater part of the Congo
Basin was already marked out as a Belgian sphere of influence.

Probably the most important group of the Congo Bantu,
all of whom are definitely Negro in character, are the Bakuba,
better known as the Bushongo, who occupy part of the Kasai
Basin, especially the section between the Sankuru and Lulua
Rivers. At the time of European penetration they were observed
to have evolved a complex and efficient system of government.
The Fang are a Bantu community fairly well known to French
students of ethnology.[1] They are the most important people
of the Gabun, one of the constituent colonies of French Equatorial Africa, and are believed to have reached their present position after migration across the northern part of the Congo Basin.
They practise shifting cultivation in clearings of the forest and
may be described as primitive nomadic agriculturists whose average domicile in a district is not longer than five years.

Other Bantu of Central Africa worthy of particular mention
are the Bateke, who occupy a great area to the north of the lower
Congo. The Balunda in the upper basin of the Kasai extend
across the boundary between the Belgian Congo and Angola and;
under Baluba leadership, founded an important confederation,
referred to as the Lunda ' empire ', which is believed to have
flourished in the eighteenth century. As previously mentioned,
the centre of the Cameroons marks the north-western limit of the
Bantu domain. In the south of the Cameroons forest abounds,
but to the north the country is more open park savanna and there
the Sudanese Negro is dominant. Between the two types of
Negro, however, there is very little difference of physical traits.

(d) The Hamito-Negroid Peoples of East Central Africa

Before referring to the non-negroid population of North
Africa we shall devote some space to a number of important

[1] v. ' Nomadisme des Fang ', by L. Martrou. in *Revue de Géographie*,
Vol. III, 1909.

secondary race types, partly Negro and partly Hamite, who are found in many parts of the upper Nile Basin (Anglo-Egyptian Sudan) and, farther south-east, on the East African Plateau. The relative proportions of Hamitic and Negro features vary considerably as between the various groups, so that it is frequently difficult to determine which of the two is dominant in a particular stock ; but generally it may be said that they have adopted Hamitic culture and have acquired the lighter complexion and finer facial features of the Hamite, though they retain certain marked negroid features, including woolly hair. The majority are exclusively pastoral in their life.

We may regard the region in which the Hamito-Negroid peoples are found geographically associated with more or less pure Negroes to have been at some very early time entirely negroid in its population. From a distant period there has been a southward penetration of Hamites into East Africa and through their tendency to marriage with the sedentary agricultural Negroes has evolved the virile type to which we now refer. Apart from the introduction of pastoralism—early Hamites are credited with the bringing of the ox and fat-tailed sheep to East Africa—the Hamites taught the Negroes the art of iron-working and in many other ways have affected their culture.

Certain of the Hamito-Negroid groups are assigned the name ' Nilotes ' by ethnologists and are geographically associated with the Sudanese section of the Nile Valley. Their most typical representatives are the Shilluk and the Dinka. Each of these is a tall, dark-skinned stock characterized by pride of race which is indicated by their lack of desire for intercourse with Europeans or for imitation of Western dress and customs. In such social tendencies they are in striking contrast with the Baganda whom we have noted. They live chiefly by the products of stock-rearing, and milk is a staple of diet. The Dinka, the more numerous of the two groups, are found in the Sudd region of the Nile (here known as the Bahr-el-Jebel) and also farther west, in the basin of the Bahr-el-Ghazal. The Shilluk, numbering about 50,000, are a more united people than the Dinka and are ruled by a paramount chief or ' king ' whose head-quarters are at Fashoda, a few miles from Kodok (on the Nile below the incoming of the Sobat River).

Farther south than the range of the Nilotes and from Northern Uganda to North-Central Tanganyika Territory there are scattered groups of Hamito-Negroid stock in a region where Bantu Negroes form the dominant race. Probably the best known are the Masai and the Nandi. The former are typical pastoral nomads, tall, virile and war-like with a remarkable attachment

to, and dependence on, their cattle. Their military aggression
has long been the dread of the agricultural Kikuyu, Akamba and
Wachagga. Not many years ago the Masai roamed freely over
great stretches of grass country in the south of Kenya and
north of Tanganyika (to use modern political terms), but
European settlement has been accompanied by a considerable
encroachment on to the best grazing lands of the Masai. Their
numbers are not much more than 50,000 and, in spite of their
tradition of conquest, they have never established permanent
empire over the tribes they have from time to time subordinated.
The Nandi occupy territory in Kenya to the north of the Masai
and, although by tradition a nomadic pastoral people, they have
become sedentary and have adopted agriculture whilst still
remaining cattle-owners.

(e) The Non-Negroid Peoples of Northern Africa
(1) *The Hamites*

Before the Arab-Mahomedan expansion over North Africa
Hamitic languages predominated throughout the Sahara and the
Mediterranean border ; and although Arab culture and religion
have been freely borrowed in recent centuries invasions from
Arabia have had comparatively slight effect on the ethnic composition of the main mass of the North African population which
is predominantly Hamitic in race.

The theory is authoritatively held that the Saharan and
Arabian regions provided the cradle for one of the primary races
of the world whose branches include the Hamites as well as the
similarly brunet, long-headed peoples of Southern Europe to
whom the ethnologist, Sergi, applied the term ' Mediterranean
Race '. Geographical conditions in the Sahara during Quaternary times were more hospitable to human life than they are
now, while land connexions across the Mediterranean at two
or three points, notably between the southernmost shore of Spain
and the northern peninsula of Morocco and between North-
Eastern Tunisia, Sicily and Calabria, made possible the passage
of Man and fauna between the two continents. It has been
estimated that in Pleistocene times the Sahara, whose mean
altitude to-day is about 1000 feet above sea-level, was an elevated
plateau of 2000 feet. During this epoch when glacial conditions
generally prevailed, if intermittently, over Northern Europe
there was, compared to their present position, a general southward
shift of the climatic belts of the northern hemisphere : so that
in place of the present desert régime over the Sahara that region
experienced a ' Mediterranean ' condition of climate, characterized by cyclonic rainfall during the winter season. Evidence

of the former well-watered condition of the Sahara is afforded by the dry river-beds whose graded courses can be traced sometimes for several hundred miles. One instance is that of the Igharghar, whose desiccated channels are to be traced in places from the northern slopes of the Ahaggar Plateau (Central Sahara) across the lowlands of South-Eastern Algeria towards the Mediterranean Sea in the neighbourhood of the Gulf of Gabes. In the opposite direction a formerly-existing river, the Massarawa, crossed the South-Central Sahara to the Niger during Pleistocene times. In response to comparatively abundant rainfall the vegetation took on the character of rich steppe, with park savanna in more favoured tracts of tropical latitudes. In such an environment lived many of the larger mammals, e.g. the elephant, rhinoceros and hippopotamus, which were able to move across the Mediterranean land-bridges into Southern Europe. Wide spaces, abundance of water and food supplies for Man and his domesticated animals were suitable conditions for the free development of one of the principal branches of the human race. Sergi's view [1] that the Neolithic inhabitants of Southern Europe were of North African origin and that their type, short, long-headed and brunet, still persists in both regions, is generally accepted by the main body of anthropologists. As late as Roman Imperial times certain northerly districts of the Sahara, at present quite arid, were capable of fairly dense agricultural settlement, and, because of abundant wheat and other cereal production, Mediterranean Africa from Barbary to Lower Egypt has been referred to as 'the granary of the Roman Empire'.

The principal physical traits of the Hamites may be summarized as : fairly tall stature, light-brown skin colour, frizzly or wavy hair of dark-brown or black, orthognathism in contrast to the prognathism of the majority of negroid peoples, straight thin nose and non-everted lips.

For purpose of convenience we may group the Hamites in eastern, central and western zones. The Eastern Hamites include the people of the lower and middle Nile Valley, together with the inhabitants of districts farther east up to the Red Sea and Indian Ocean coasts.

During the fourth millennium B.C. and even earlier the population of Egypt was, as indicated by skeletal remains, of Hamitic stock and the main body of modern Egyptians resemble, in most important features of race, their ancestors of pre-Dynastic times. In the modern Egyptian population the old social and economic division between the majority of Fellahin who are Moslem peasants and the minority of Christian Copts—formerly

[1] v. G. Sergi, *The Mediterranean Race*, London, 1901.

the commercial and official class—is breaking down fairly quickly. The process of national consolidation is assisted also by the practically homogeneous racial character of the Egyptians. The desert oases which lie fairly close to the lower Nile, including the Oasis of Kharga, are inhabited by Egyptians, but those of Western Egypt, including the Oasis of Siwa, are occupied by peoples of very different traditions and their political inclusion in Egypt is a purely arbitrary arrangement.

In early Dynastic times Egypt did not extend south of the First Cataract (near Aswan). Nubia, its southern neighbour, was then regarded as the zone which marked the transition from Egyptian civilization to the Negro world of Africa, though ultimately a considerable part of Nubia in the vicinity of the Nile was settled with Egyptian colonists who intermarried with the Natives, including some of negroid origin. The modern boundary delimitation of Egypt extends that country to include the northern part of the historic Nubia as far south as Wadi Halfa, near the Second Cataract. The Nubians, sometimes known as Barabra, are predominantly Hamitic, but there are those who show the ethnic crossing to which we have referred, and numbers of these negriticized Nubians are found north of the Egyptian frontier. Pastoralism is forced on the people on account of scantiness of rainfall, but wherever possible they turn to agriculture. In the Arabian [1] and Nubian Deserts, east of the Nile, and farther south in Northern Eritrea, the Beja represent one of the most important groups of the Eastern Hamites. On account of their proximity to the lower Nile many of the northern Beja have absorbed much of Egyptian culture, while the southern Beja are nomadic herdsmen who use the camel (introduced to N.E. Africa 2000 years ago) : yet all alike are true Hamites, so far as ethnic characters are concerned, and generally they are staunch Mahomedans.

Farther south the ethnic unity of the Hamitic population is preserved across the Abyssinian and Somaliland frontiers into Northern Kenya. The Abyssinians are more complex in composition than any other large group of East Africa, but, except in south-western districts, their Hamitic basis is always evident. The south-western ramparts of Abyssinia, unlike the greater part of the Plateau which is grass-land, are clothed with forest—a response to the heavy monsoonal rainfall of summer—and in this environment are found the Shangalla negroid tribes who form the north-eastern outpost of Negro Africa. Semitic influence in Abyssinia is strongly emphasized in culture, language and tradition and, to a minor degree, is shown in the ethnic

[1] The Arabian Desert of Egypt should not be confused with the deserts east of the Red Sea.

composition of the people ; though the similarity of Semites to Hamites frequently renders differentiation very difficult. The royal house, claiming descent from the Queen of Sheba, is strong in its support of the Semitic tradition. Abyssinian languages are mainly Semitic and the three great religions of Semitic origin—Christianity, Islam and Judaism—are all represented. Of them Christianity may be described as the ' official ' faith.

Near the northern limits of the Plateau the Beja type predominates, while on the eastern slopes descending towards the Somaliland coast the most notable Hamites are the Galla who, during the last five centuries, have tended to penetrate westwards from the littoral belt. They are a virile group undertaking both agriculture and cattle-rearing, and Galla horsemen form the nucleus of the Abyssinian army. Almost alone amongst the Eastern Hamites they have remained pagan. Their eastern neighbours in the peninsula of Somaliland—the ' Horn of Africa ' —are the Somali who have similar characteristics and are believed to have succeeded the Galla in the occupation of the coastal lands. The Somali are generally impoverished in their environment of poor grass-and-scrub land and the dominant social type is the nomadic herdsman, though many have entered the military service of the Italian, French and British colonial governments as cavalrymen.

The Central Hamites include two or three widespread and notable communities of the Sahara and Northern Sudan and we may specially mention the Fulani and the Tuareg. The latter, whose chief reputation is as ' the People of the Veil ', have their geographical centre on the Ahaggar Plateau, widest area of the highland which crosses the Sahara diagonally from north-west to south-east : but their outposts are widely extended, north-west as far as the Tuat oases, north-east to the Fezzan district of Italian Libya, south-west to the neighbourhood of Timbuktu and south to Zinder, west of Lake Chad. Throughout this vast area, estimated in hundreds of thousands of square miles, the Tuareg, though approximately uniform so far as racial and social characteristics are concerned, are not in any sense politically united, except in so far as they have been forced, very recently, to accept the suzerainty of France. They represent a series of independent confederations of tribes. Each tribe has its ' noble ' class who wear black veils and who are tall Hamites of very fine physique and handsome appearance. The White Tuareg, so called because of their white veils, form the ' vassal ' class of the tribes, and in their case there is generally an admixture of Negro blood which is especially perceptible in the texture of the hair. Below these two social classes are the slaves who are usually of Sudanese Negro origin and who have been taken into captivity along the trans-Saharan caravan routes. The life of the Tuareg is that of pastoral nomads who use the camel for transport. Strong military organization, mobility and the occupation of the Central Saharan oases gave them an almost complete command of several trans-desert routes prior to the extension of French control a few years ago.

The Tibesti Plateau, to the south-east of Ahaggar, is the home of the Tibu [1] who are akin to the Tuareg in race, social life and martial characteristics. Until their expulsion at the hands of the Islamic fraternity of the Senussi who, during the nineteenth century, extended their domination over the greater part of modern Libya, the Tibu acquired considerable economic prosperity from their occupation of the Kufara group of oases.

In the section devoted to the Negro population of the Central Sudan, particularly Northern Nigeria, incidental reference was made to the overlordship exerted by the Fulani emirs. The Fulani [2] have their main centre of distribution in Northern Nigeria where their numbers are estimated at more than two millions. They are specially prominent in the Provinces of Kano, Sokoto and Adamawa where their aristocratic class still retains much of the semblance of power, though supervised by the British Colonial Government. Some centuries ago the Fulani began gradually to penetrate the Central Sudan from the direction of the Sahara, but it was not until the early years of last century that they carried out the conquest of the Hausa States and established in their stead a series of Moslem principalities or emirates. In addition to the Nigerian Fulani the type is represented in scattered groups much farther west, across the great bend of the Niger, where they are found as semi-nomadic cattlemen who have no pretensions to overlordship. Long contact with the Sudanese Negroes has brought about a dilution of the Hamitic strain amongst the Fulani generally. In Northern Nigeria they have become almost sedentary and it is believed that here they are evolving more and more into a negroid type through intermarriage with the Hausa.

The Berbers of Barbary, the lands of the Atlas, constitute the last of the more important Hamitic groups that merit special attention. In a territory which is as much a region from the standpoint of the physical geographer as it is from that of the ethnologist the threefold political division represented by Morocco, Algeria and Tunisia has very little scientific justification ; but

[1] The name ' Ti-bu ' means ' rock people ' and is derived from their inhospitable environment.
[2] Also variously known as Fulah and Fula.

we have seen elsewhere that the partition of Africa has had little regard for geographical or ethnological facts. The Berber type. though always Hamitic at basis, varies somewhat throughout its range between Morocco and Western Libya. Variation in stature and the cephalic index is considerable, but a fairly representative type is tall, lithe and brunet in hair and eyes. The difference between this type and that of the true Arab is not considerable.[1] There is some difficulty in distinguishing the ethnic groups of North-West Africa on account of the all-pervading influence of Islamic culture and religion which Berber society has freely borrowed. In North-West Africa a majority of those who are popularly termed ' Arabs ' are really Moslem Hamites, and the true Arab of Semitic stock with ancestors of Arabian origin is comparatively rare. To add to the confusion in attempting to use the term ' Arab ' for ethnic definition, many of the negroid peoples of the Sudan are so called because they have adopted a veneer of Arab civilization.

The Berber is the prevalent type of the Atlas ranges and of the fertile zone of the Tell. The environment varies from well-watered, cultivated valleys and well-timbered hill-sides of the Mediterranean slope to the poor steppe of the Plateau of the Shotts ; and there is a corresponding variation in economic life, for although the most characteristic of the Berbers are agriculturists there are many who are forced by arid conditions to undertake stock-rearing and to migrate seasonally in search of pasture.

Among the sedentary and agricultural Berbers the social and political organization is strongly contrasted with that of the nomadic pastoral Arab who, from the desert margins, for centuries has been prone to raid the attractive cultivated lands behind the Mediterranean littoral. The contrast is mainly a consequence of the very different geographical conditions under which the two types have long existed. The Arab, predominantly a tent-dweller, is unaccustomed to permanent village life and of agriculture he is usually contemptuous. His propensities for raiding have fostered the antagonism between himself and the agricultural Berber which the difference in their social outlook does not diminish. Berber society consists at basis of a large number of small, autonomous and democratic village communities whose organization is well suited to the needs of sedentary agriculturists. So far as there are ' tribes ' among the Berbers they merely represent confederations of villages formed for administrative con-

[1] Certain ethnologists claim ethnic evidence from a minority of the Berber population of the very early settlement of a tall blond stock associated with the Nordic race of Northern Europe.

venience in such joint services as education, religion and road-construction. Village government is controlled by a parliament of adult male citizens known as the jemâa and, before the extension of French law, this assembly provided the judicial court for both civil and criminal cases. Executive control is theoretically in the hands of the ' chief ' (amin) of the village who is appointed by the jemâa, but in practice he is unable to act independently of the village assembly. There is a considerable degree of communal life in the Berber village ; one aspect of it is the assistance which any citizen may claim of his fellows at the more critical agricultural seasons, such as that of harvesting.

(2) *The Semites of North Africa*

In contrast to the democratic Berber organization outlined above Arab society is under despotic control and the sheikh is regarded as the agent of theocratic government. It must be remembered, however, that nearly all the Berbers are at least nominally Mahomedans. On the other hand there are, particularly in Eastern Barbary, a large number of Arabs who, having assimilated Berber culture, form a part of Berber society. The number of Berberized Arabs in Tunisia is given as three-quarters of a million, out of a total Mahomedan population of about three millions. Farther west, in Algeria, the proportion of Berberized Arabs is much smaller, whilst in Morocco it is estimated that not more than 10 per cent. of the inhabitants are Arabs and Berberized Arabs. Eastwards from Barbary across Libya the purity of the Arab stock increases and civilization changes from a Hamitic to a Semitic basis. The inhabitants of the region, like the true Arabs of Barbary, are mainly descended from the Arabian nomads who re-conquered and partially colonized North Africa during the eleventh century.

Arabs of the Eastern Sahara and Nile neighbourhood may be classified in the following three social groups—(1) true nomads or ' camel men ', (2) semi-nomadic ' cattle men ' who are less migratory than the ' camel men ', and occupy a better-watered country, (3) settled agriculturists of the oases and of the Nile Valley. Of these the closest to the Arab ethnic type is the first group, and, as a general rule, with a decrease in the degree of nomadism there is an increase in the proportion of alien blood. The distribution of the ' cattle men ' is to the south of the ' camel men ' and the zone of division is where the Libyan Desert gives place to the grass-lands of the Anglo-Egyptian Sudan. In the latter region—Dar Fur and Southern Kordofan—the Baqqara roam widely, and with this people cattle provide the means of transport as well as of food and clothing. Their migrations are to some extent restricted by the ravages of the tsetse fly. Of the camel-owning tribes the Kababish of North-western Kordofan represent perhaps the most important group. In Egypt the western desert districts include a number of nomadic Arab groups some of whom extend info uncultivated parts of the Nile Delta.

One of the most striking manifestations of the modern politico-religious organization of the North African Arabs [1] is offered by the 'orders', of which the fraternity of the Senussi is easily the best known. The 'orders' had originally a religious basis and represented distinctive cults of Islam, but in time their political power evolved, mainly in consequence of their control of trans-desert routes. Caravans crossing the desert were forced to accept, in return for heavy dues, the protection which the fraternities, with their centres in the various oases along the more important routes, were alone able to afford. The Senussi 'order', which is associated with the Wahabi movement of Central Arabia, was established in the early nineteenth century, its head-quarters being first in Arabia and later at the Jaghbub oases (recently ceded to Italian Libya by Egypt). The authority of the Senussi Sheikh was extended ultimately from the Mediterranean coast in Cyrenaica southwards across the Libyan Desert as far as Wadai and Dar Fur of the Eastern Sudan. The north-south caravan route from the Cyrenaican coast to the Eastern Sudan was the principal highway crossing the country of the Senussi, and its stages were marked by a chain of widely-separated oases of the Libyan Desert, including Siwa and Kufara. The head-quarters of the 'order' are at Kufara, but its power was greatly reduced in consequence of Italian re-conquest after the First World War.

It is appropriate to introduce into this chapter brief reference to the revolutionary changes which have been brought about in the social, political and economic order of native African life as a result of the impact of Western civilization. Particularly have these changes affected the Negro population. The Hamitic and Semitic peoples occupy a zone which is for the greater part poor grass-land or desert and economically unattractive. Moreover, these non-negroid groups have been much longer in contact with the peoples of Europe and Western Asia, and in particular became familiar with imperial administration while North Africa was under Ottoman rule. There are two aspects to consider : first, the disruption of native civilizations, with their

[1] The term—' Arabs '—is here used mainly in a cultural and religious sense.

distinctive traditions, customs and institutions, and the intrusion of a transplanted civilization which although it has not grown out of the African environment, has profoundly influenced the African economy; secondly, there is the aspect of the extensive reservation of land for the purpose either of European settlement or, more usually, of large-scale industrial enterprise, including plantation agriculture and mineral exploitation. In addition to brief mention here these aspects will receive further attention later in the geographical analysis of the principal regions of the continent.

Taking into account the extent of European penetration in Africa south of the Sahara a classification of the social groups of negroid Africans may be summarized on the following basis:

(1) Primitive peoples, usually hunters, such as the Bushmen, who are comparatively few in number and possess no tribal life.

(2) Tribalized Natives, still the majority of the population of Negro Africa, though steady de-tribalization—generally encouraged by the Europeans—is reducing their numbers year by year. Their political and social organization is generally suited to a pastoral life, and an aristocratic hierarchy of government headed by a paramount chief is a normal characteristic. The Zulu-Xosa peoples of South-East Africa afford a good example.

(3) Advanced Negro groups approaching the status of nations, usually with an agricultural basis of economic life. Their social and political systems show a greater tendency towards democracy than in the case of the more backward, pastoral tribes; and the individual's right of exclusive occupation of an agricultural plot is frequently recognized. The Baganda are perhaps the best instance, and the Yoruba and Hausa of West Africa may also be mentioned.

(4) ' Westernized ' Natives who have lost their place in indigenous society owing to tribal disentegration. They are mainly town-dwellers and industrial workers, yet their ' Western ' culture is largely a veneer covering the fundamental African, whose primitive ideas and native philosophy exist alongside outward forms and usages which imitate the European. The attempt to make Europeans of black Africans has been, from time to time, a definite policy in French West Africa, especially Senegal, although the wisest of French colonial administrators realize that the learning of a European language and the adoption of a body of European customs are not accompanied by a corresponding change of physical and mental traits.

In the Union of South Africa where the ' Westernized ' Negroes number about four millions—by far the largest aggregate for any region of the continent—a system of administration obtains by the name of 'apartheid', the aim of which is to allow the Bantu and the White inhabitants to develop their distinct economics and cultures in separate parts of the country. In certain other parts of Negro Africa where European influence has spread extensively the Native is able to rise to higher economic status than is possible in the Union. Such regions are, however, generally unsuited to White colonization because of unfavourable climate so that most of the manual work, skilled as well as unskilled, can only be supplied by the indigenous population. Lands where the Negro's opportunity for economic progress is most satisfactory include British West Africa, parts of French West Africa (particularly Senegal) and Uganda.

Many of these territories, which contain no large resident populations of European origin, are already self-governing or are about to become so (see Figure 102). But at this stage their internal stability is often threatened by ethnic rivalries within their own boundaries. This is notably the case in the erstwhile Belgian Congo, in Ruanda-Urundi, and in Nigeria, where a federal association of its four subdivisions has been adopted in preference to a more centralized form of government. Sierra Leone presents a special case, for there the contrast is between the sophisticated creole population of Freetown and the more numerous pagan tribes of the remoter districts of the territory.

The ethnic problems which have followed the withdrawal of European administration are often aggravated by the division of tribal groups by political frontiers. Thus the Sanwi tribes are split by the boundary between Ghana and the Ivory Coast, while the Ewe peoples, who form almost three-quarters of the population of Togoland, also live in considerable numbers in the adjacent parts of Ghana. In each of these instances, Ghana has suggested that the frontier should be readjusted to unite the racial group, but her neighbours are opposed to any change which would be made at the expense of their territory.

In East Africa, and particularly in the case of Kenya, the withdrawal of the colonial administration would be complicated by the need to protect the rights of the established minorities of European and Asian origin. These elements have been responsible in Kenya for pacifying the country and for developing the modern agriculture and commerce on which its economy now depends. Great advances have been made recently in introducing improved methods of farming, especially of saleable crops, to the native reserves; and the Highlands, the formerly unoccupied zone which was developed by European settlers, may now be leased to able farmers of any community. Nevertheless, the stability and prosperity of Kenya is still largely dependent

on the immigrant elements in its population. The problem here
is clearly to formulate such a constitution as will make tolerable
the status of the minorities.

In Central Africa there is a manifest difference between the
Rhodesias and Nyasaland, the European proportion of the population being considerably smaller in the case of the last territory.
All economic considerations would argue in favour of the continued federation of these three territories; but the differences
between their ethnic and political constitutions have already imposed a strain on their loose but highly beneficial economic association so great as to bring about its disruption.

The abruptness of the transition has been greatly softened in
those parts where European authority is most enlightened, by
liberal grants of land for the establishment of native reserves,
from which the European is excluded, and by the introduction of
' indirect rule', the principles of which were defined and put into
practice, most notably in Nigeria, by Sir George Goldie and Sir
Frederick (later Lord) Lugard.[1] This system of government is
based on the preservation of those native institutions and laws
which make for social and economic welfare and, secondly, on
the acknowledgment and support of the traditional authority of
the chiefs. So does the indigenous machinery of government
survive with a minimum of British supervision. ' Indirect rule '
is in contrast with the usual practice in French West and Equatorial Africa where the native chiefs were encouraged to become
Europeanized officials, deriving authority and sanction not from
native tradition and custom, but from the highly centralized
French administration which has been generally averse to the
maintenance of indigenous political organizations.

Lugard's system has been applied to other parts of British
West Africa, notably the Gold Coast, but there are other territories
of British Africa in which similar policies were tried with immediate and enduring success, as early as, in some cases earlier than,
Lugard's régime in Northern Nigeria. The Glen Grey Act of
1894 which concerned a native reserve in the eastern district
of Cape Colony permitted the principle of native self-government,
and its model has been used and extended within the Native
Territories of the Transkei which have their ' parliament ' at
Umtata. Sir Theophilus Shepstone, one of the greatest administrators of Native affairs that Africa has known, established
reserves for the Zulu-Xosa peoples of Natal with the similar
aim of preserving the integrity of Bantu society, while among
other instances which may be mentioned are the Native Terri-

[1] v. *The Dual Mandate in British Tropical Africa*, by Lugard, which
is virtually the complete thesis of ' indirect rule '.

tories of Basutoland, Swaziland and Bechuanaland and the Protectorate of Uganda, in all of which the principle of ' indirect rule ' has long been applied.

Where indigenous government was already strongly organized at the time of British intervention the task of instituting ' indirect rule ' was comparatively simple, as the foundations were already laid : but where tribal disintegration had proceeded far before British occupation, as in the case of the mandated Territory of Tanganyika, the arduous work of re-constructing society had to be the preliminary undertaking. Scattered units are first drawn together under the administration of a chief, after which the object is to organize representative councils of chiefs to whom, with administrative experience, an increasing measure of self-government may be entrusted. It should be remembered that, even in British Africa, advanced tribal communities form a very small proportion of the Negro population and that for the greater part, as in the case of Tropical Africa as a whole, the old order of tribal civilization has already passed away or is in process of rapid disintegration ; so that social and political reconstruction on the lines indicated is a very urgent need.

Indirect rule was the form of administration sanctioned by the League of Nations in its mandates to Great Britain, France and Belgium for the government of the ex-German possessions in Africa, and it was hopefully anticipated by those who had a regard for the welfare of Negro Africa that similar principles would ultimately extend throughout the African ' colonies ' and protectorates of European Powers.

Lastly, there remain to be briefly considered the consequences to native life of European demands for land, which has been or is to be reserved either for White settlement or for large-scale commercial agriculture and mineral exploitation. With regard to White settlement it may be stated confidently that West Africa and Central Africa offer no prospects on account of their very unfavourable climate of great, unrelieved heat and high humidity. South Africa, especially the Union and Southern Rhodesia, and the most fertile tracts of the East African Plateau in Kenya and Tanganyika, are the parts of Negro Africa most desired by European colonists, though it has yet to be proved that permanent residence of successive generations of White settlers anywhere in Tropical Africa north of the Limpopo River is possible without physical and mental degeneration.

Within the Union, Southern Rhodesia and Kenya Colony in which, taken together, more than 90 per cent of the European settlers south of the Sahara reside, the greater part of the good agricultural and pastoral land has been made so by European ownership : furthermore, excepting the case of Southern Rhodesia, where the Native policy of the Administration is generally enlightened, the areas reserved for Native occupation have suffered from inefficient and improvident farming. British West Africa shows a strongly contrasted position : there White settlement is out of the question and, owing to the strict policy of land control adopted by the Administrations, it was not possible for the Natives of the Gold Coast or Nigeria to lose their lands to mining or land development syndicates. The Belgian and French Administrations have not been so watchful in regard to the land interests of Native subjects, though the position in their ' colonies ' has somewhat improved during the last two decades.

When considering the extensive allocation of land to European settlers and land companies, which has occasioned much economic advance in Africa, it has to be borne in mind that to the Negro African the principle of individual title to land is a totally foreign conception. According to his age-long tradition, all land occupied by a tribe belongs to that community as a whole, in perpetuity, and no part can be alienated by sale. Tenure, as distinct from ownership, of land by individual members of agricultural tribes is not, however, unknown, and where individual tenure is not the rule every tribesman has a right to a share of the communal use of the land. Usually it is found that ideas of individual ownership entered with the European, though in the very important instance of Uganda Hamitic invaders are believed to have introduced the principle long before British occupation. Apart from the active encouragement which the European has given to the abandonment of communal ownership the new conception of land holding is spreading to Native society, in consequence of the over-pressure of population on the available land and of the replacement of annual by permanent crops such as oil-palm, cocoa and rubber.

Three widely separated areas of Africa where individual ownership has been implanted or encouraged to extend by the British régime, with general economic benefit to the Natives, are : the state of. Ghana whose great cocoa crop is grown without direct European participation : Uganda, the success of whose cotton crop is one of the most striking features of the economic geography of Tropical Africa : and the Cis-Kei and Trans-Kei Territories of the Eastern Cape Province. In the latter case the substitution of individual for tribal tenure began very early ; indeed, it was initiated by the Native policy of Sir George Grey in the period 1854–62, and thirty years after his time Rhodes sought to achieve Grey's object in the Glen Grey Act of 1894, to which reference has been made.

In African conditions, the intensity of population which the land will support varies widely according to the type of farming which is pursued thereon. In certain forested parts of Northern Rhodesia, where a wasteful system of shifting cultivation is universal, it has been calculated that the -maximum possible density of population is 4 to the square mile. Any occupation denser than this would result in famine or other distress. Again, in Kenya the contrast between the poor state of the land in the Reserves, and its healthy condition in the Highlands, is due less to any inherent superiority in the soils or climate of the Highlands —indeed, the Reserves are frequently better provided in these respects—than to differences in methods of cultivation. The remedy for pressure of population in the Reserves will be found not in re-allocation of land but in improving by encouragement and force of example the standard of farming on the Reserves, by enclosure, by fertilization, and by the conservation of soil and water.

REFERENCES

Our knowledge of African peoples is unevenly distributed, for on the one hand there are vast areas the inhabitants of which have not so far been studied, whilst on the other, excellent monographs on particular communities have been contributed. The ethnology of two regions in particular has now been very fully explored, the Anglo-Egyptian Sudan, where *Sudan Notes and Records* have been published since 1918, and British Central Africa, where the Rhodes-Livingstone Institute has sponsored wide research. The following two important publications of the International Institute of African Languages and Cultures co-ordinate ethnographic work from different parts of the continent :

Fortes, M., and Evans-Pritchard, E. E. (editors), *African Political Systems*, London (O.U.P.), 1940.
Radcliffe-Brown, A.R., and Forde, D., *African Systems of Kinship and Marriage*, London (O.U.P.), 1951.

On the subject of the relations of the Natives and Immigrants in Africa the outstanding works in English are :

Buell, R. L., *The Native Problem in Africa*, 2 vols., New York, 1928.
Lugard, Sir F. D., *The Dual Mandate in British Tropical Africa*, 3rd ed., London, 1926.

Works which are of value to the geographer and to the ethnologist include the following small selection :

Bartlett, V., *Struggle for Africa*, London, 1953.
Batten, T. R., *Problems of African Development. Part I : Land and Labour* London (O.U.P.), 1947.
De Préville, A., *Les Sociétés Africaines*, Paris, 1894.
Hailey, Lord, *An African Survey*, Revised ed., Oxford, 1957.
Hambly, W. D., *Ethnology of Africa*. Field Museum of Natural Hist., Chicago, 1930.
Hellman, E., *Rooiyard, a Sociological Survey of an Urban Native Slum*, Rhodes-Livingstone Papers (13), Cape Town, 1948.

Hollis, A. C., *The Masai*, Oxford, 1905.
The Nandi, Oxford, 1909.
Junod, H. A., *The Life of a South African Tribe*, 2 vols., 1927.
Keane, A. H., *Man, Past and Present*. Revised by Haddon and Quiggin, Cambridge, 1920.
Kuper, Dr. H., *The Uniform of Colour. A study of White-Black Relationships in Swaziland*, Johannesburg, 1947.
MacMichael, H. A., *History of the Arabs in the Sudan*, 2 vols., Cambridge, 1922.
Mair, L. P., *Native Policies in Africa*, London, 1936.
' Modern developments in African Land Tenure : an aspect of culture change', *Africa*, Vol. XVIII, no. 3 (July, 1948), pp. 184–89.
Meek, C. K., *Northern Tribes of Nigeria*, 2 vols., Oxford, 1925.
Land Law and Custom in the Colonies, London, 1946.
Orde Browne, G. St. J., *The African Labourer*, Oxford, 1933.
Post, L. van der, *Venture to the Interior*, London, 1952.
Rattray, R. S., *Ashanti*, Oxford, 1923.
Review of Economic Conditions in Africa (Supplement to World Economic Report, 1949–50), U.N. Dept. of Economic Affairs, New York, 1951.
Rodd, F. R., *The People of the Veil*, 1926.
Roome, W. J. W., *Ethnographic Map of Africa*, London, 1925.
Roscoe, G., *The Baganda*, Cambridge, 1911.
The Banyoro, Cambridge, 1923.
Seligman, C. G., *Races of Africa*, 2nd ed., London, 1939.
Sergi, G., *The Mediterranean Race*, London, 1901.
Talbot, P. A., *Peoples of Southern Nigeria*, 4 vols., Oxford, 1926.
Torday, E., *Descriptive Sociology—African Races*, London, 1930.
Wellington, J. H., *Possibilities of Settlement in Africa*, in *Limits of Land Settlement*, Paris, 1937.

PART III

REGIONAL STUDIES

FOREWORD

OUR main purpose in the study of each of the bigger units of Africa is to elucidate its distinctive geographical features, characteristics that in combination grant 'individuality' to the region. In the case of a continent where, as a rule, the geographical conditions that are characteristic of one region give place gradually through an often wide zone of transition to those of a neighbouring region any attempt at regional classification should avoid, except where contrasts are obviously sharply defined, the error of claiming exactitude for boundary lines that may be brought into use for convenience in study. We should think of boundaries as belts or zones of transition rather than as lines. As already noticed, political frontiers in Africa usually bear little relationship to geographical realities, and for this reason political units generally provide very unsatisfactory bases for geographical division, though they cannot be ignored.

In the case of each of the major regions of Africa there are to be found local differences so considerable as to warrant division of the region into what we may call 'sub-regions'[1]; and attention will be devoted to the contributions of these minor geographical units to the life of the bigger entities, of which they form parts, as well as to the life of the continent as a whole.

[1] We have no suitable term in English corresponding to 'pays' which is employed by the French school of regional geography.

CHAPTER I

SOUTH AFRICA

WE are concerned with the sub-continental peninsula of South Africa where are grouped a number of contiguous political units owing allegiance to the British Commonwealth of Nations. An exception is provided by Portuguese East Africa whose economic welfare, however, is so closely bound up with the progress of the remainder of South Africa that there is strong justification for its inclusion in our region.

High plateau levels and, for the greater part, sub-tropical latitude help to determine a climate that is more favourable than any other in Africa to the health of the European colonist. For this reason and also on account of its economic attractiveness South Africa is the region of the continent most influenced by 'Western' civilization, and this despite its distant isolation from Europe. In contrast to the political, social and commercial institutions of the European settler Bantu civilization, with little science and no commercialism, is simpler but still thriving. Obviously, the geography of European settlement must receive considerable attention, but its importance should not overshadow that of Bantu settlement, for the latter people are the great majority of the total population and are likely to remain so, as far as we can foresee. Where commercial geography is concerned, South Africa is the only major region where the wealth derived from mineral output exceeds that from agriculture.

The foregoing are some of the distinguishing features of South Africa which justify separate and considerable treatment of its geography.

On its northern side the approximate limits of our region may be taken along the southern border of the Zambezi valley so as to include the plateau of Southern Rhodesia. The Zambezi valley and all land to the north are, by reason of their climate and vegetation—always foremost factors in a geographical division of Africa—more closely associated with essentially tropical East Africa than with the sub-tropical zone of South

Africa. Farther to the west the northern boundary extends across upper Zambezi, in the north of Bechuanaland Protectorate, and then due westwards to the Atlantic, so as to include the Kalahari as well as the desert land of South-West Africa. Our northern boundary has the advantage of following, nearly throughout, a belt of low population density.

The following political units are included :

(a) the Republic (in 1961 the Union) of South Africa (472,347 sq. miles)—a federation comprising the four Provinces of the Cape of Good Hope, The Transvaal, Orange Free State and Natal : to which should be added the Mandated Territory of South-West Africa (332,767 sq. miles), formerly under German administration and now to be considered an integral part of the Union,

(b) the self-governing Colony of Southern Rhodesia (152,344 sq. miles),

(c) the Native Territories (British Protectorates) of Bechuanaland (275,000 sq. miles), Basutoland (11,700 sq. miles) and Swaziland (6,700 sq. miles),

(d) the southern district of Portuguese East Africa,[1] from the lower Zambezi valley southwards to the Natal frontier (c. 140,000 sq. miles).

PHYSICAL GEOGRAPHY OF SOUTH AFRICA

Very broadly, the big physical regions of South Africa may be classified as :

(1) the high plateau of the Union of South Africa and its coastal borderlands, including that of Portuguese East Africa. By virtue of its desert-like aridity and its very moderate elevation the northern district of the Cape Province, within the basin of the Orange River, should be considered along with—

(2) the desert and dry grass-land plateaux and basins of South-West Africa and the Kalahari,

(3) the plateau of Southern Rhodesia.

The Structural Basis

Two geological ' provinces' are recognized in the build of South Africa—

(a) a northern plateau, without folded mountain ranges, where the Archaean platform of the continent is widely

---

[1] Total area of Portuguese East Africa is 287,760 sq. miles.

exposed : it comprises Southern Rhodesia, the northern and central districts of the Transvaal, Bechuanaland and neighbouring parts of the Cape Province, together with much of South-West Africa ;

(b) a southern plateau of greater elevation than (a), together with a marginal belt of folded mountain ranges, occupying the southern district of the Transvaal, Natal, Basutoland, Orange Free State and the greater part of the Cape Province. Palaeozoic sediments here are very extensive.

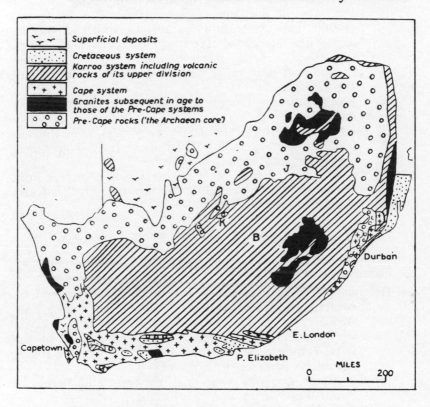

Superficial deposits

Cretaceous system

Karroo system including volcanic rocks of its upper division

Cape system

Granites subsequent in age to those of the Pre-Cape systems

Pre-Cape rocks ('the Archaean core')

FIG. 17.—Geological map of the Union of South Africa

There is no evidence that either 'province' has been submerged by sea, except along a usually narrow littoral belt, since Palaeozoic times. On the other hand, vertical movements on a great scale have affected the entire sub-continent, and it is to these uplifts of Mesozoic and later time that the high elevation of the South African Plateau is at present due.

The Pre-Cape (Archaean) rocks which, as noted, are widely represented at the surface of the northern ' province ', consist of quartzites, schists, sandstones and shales. Where, as in the southern ' province ' particularly, they are concealed by Palaeozoic sediments the latter include the little disturbed Karroo beds of sandstones, shales and coal-measures that are comparable in age to European rocks laid down between late Devonian and Triassic times. The Karroo beds are thickest in the south and east ; farther north, as for example in Southern Rhodesia, they are thinner or have been entirely worn off the underlying and now exposed Archaean core. Easily the greatest unbroken exposure of Karroo rocks extends from the western limit of the Great Karroo, in the Ceres district of the Cape Province, to the southern district of the Transvaal, and from the neighbourhood of Kimberley southwards to well within the Eastern Cape Province. Although these beds have an average depth estimated at 17,000 feet, no marine fossils have been found throughout the greater part of their range. Of later date than the Karroo formation there are no beds in the interior, other than very superficial deposits.

Towards the close of the deposition of the Karroo series in early Triassic times, crustal folding directed mainly from the south but also, in the south-west of the Cape Province, from the west, produced the Cape Ranges of which the Zwartebergen and Langebergen are the most prominent remnants. After this period of folding igneous activity was widespread over the plateau and lava floods poured out over large areas in the eastern and east-central districts of the Union as well as in Southern Rhodesia and the northern parts of South-West Africa.

During the latter part of Cretaceous times faulting occurred in the extreme south, but was preceded by the deposition of marine sediments over the greatly denuded folds. of the Cape Ranges so that the folding of the older strata was masked. As a result of the faulting of late Cretaceous date, which gradually brought about down-throw of several thousands of feet on the southern sides of the Zwartebergen and Langebergen, there came into existence longitudinal troughs over the sites of synclines produced by the folding of late Palaeozoic times. Prior to the development of the longitudinal troughs and with the emergence of the southern margin of the continent from the Cretaceous Sea, a river system was born and included a number of parallel streams flowing south-eastwards across the Cretaceous land surface that concealed the worn-down Cape Ranges. By the time that longitudinal faulting occurred these ' consequent ' streams were well established and retained their south-eastward courses as steadily as their tributaries, working back along the longitudinal troughs, excavated, through soft Cretaceous rocks, the stumps of the Palaeozoic Cape Ranges. So, for example, a ' consequent ' river, the Gouritz, which enters the sea west of Mossel Bay, has kept pace with the excavation of the Lange-bergen and Zwartebergen by cutting through in steep-walled gaps known as ' poorts '.[1]

The most spectacular structural feature of South Africa is the Great Escarpment which encloses the interior Plateau at distances between 50 and 250 miles from the coast. Viewed from the seaward side it has the appearance of a continuous, lofty and serrated range ; but actually throughout its 1200 miles it is free from folds and faults. The Escarpment is highest in the Quathlamba Range, or Drakensberg, of Natal where are the maximum levels—over 10,000 feet—in Africa south of the Zambezi. This part of the Plateau edge is formed of rocks of Upper Karroo age, though there is an igneous capping in places. From the south-western end of the Drakensberg the Escarpment has a westerly trend for about 400 miles and is known under a succession of local names—Stormberg, Sneeuw-berg, Nieuwveld Range, and Komsberg. From the latter it swings sharply to the north-west nearly parallel to the western coast of the Cape Province, and one of its local names here is the Roggeveld Range. Farther north, in Namaqualand and South-West Africa, the edge of the Plateau approaches to within 50 miles of the Atlantic shore. Generally the altitude of the Escarpment on the east exceeds that on the western side of the sub-continent by 3000 feet.

The even coast-line of South Africa has been explained by faulting, but although this may be the most likely theory little actual evidence in support is yet available. The poverty of the coast in secluded bays and sheltering head-lands is a serious disadvantage to shipping. River estuaries are useless as harbours, for they are, in almost every case, completely blocked by sand-bars : farther up-stream, in the case of the eastern rivers of plentiful water, the courses are made un-navigable for long dis-tances by the presence of rock-ledges, whilst western rivers, such as the Orange and the Olifants, are little more than empty channels by the end of the dry season. First-class coastal har-bours are separated by many hundreds of miles of inhospitable shore ; thus between Table Bay and Port Natal (Durban)— a distance of over 800 miles—there are no natural facilities for shipping.

[1] ' Poort ' is the South African equivalent of a river-gap in a range of hills that extend at right angles to the course of the river.

NATURAL REGIONS OF SOUTH AFRICA

Included first are those on the seaward side of the Great Escarpment.

The Cape Ranges

These prominent folds within the Western Cape Province are arranged in two series of wide arcs, concave to the coast, which converge and meet in the mountain node of the Worcester–Ceres district. From this locality one system, including the

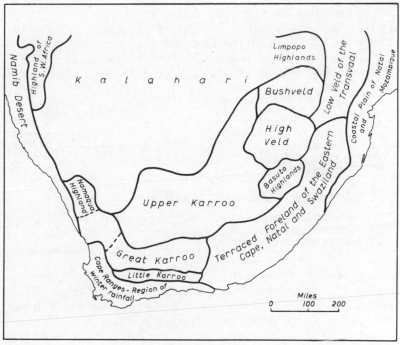

FIG. 18.—Natural Regions of South Africa (south of the Limpopo)

Cedarberg and Olifants Mountains, leads NNW. and approaches the coast in the vicinity of the lower Olifants River : the other system which embraces the east–west trending Zwartebergen and Langebergen finally dips to the south-east and is cut off sharply by the coast between Knysna and Port Elizabeth. The line of the Cedarberg, a broad and regular anticline, is continued south of the Tulbagh Kloof,[1] which divides the drainage of the Great Berg and Breede Rivers, by the Drakenstein and Hottentots

[1] ' Kloof ', a Dutch word, signifies ' cleft ' or ' pass '.

Holland Mountains. These ranges reach the sea in the sentry-peak of Cape Hangklip and overlook from the east the sterile land known as the Cape Flats and its submerged continuation in False Bay.

The second system, much more extensive and prominent, has a general east–west trend and includes two parallel series of folds and over-folds—the Zwartebergen and Langebergen, with summits over 7000 feet—and these under local names, such as the Zitzikamma Mountains, gradually curve to the south-east and are cut off sharply at the coast between Knysna and Port Elizabeth.

Between the Zwartebergen and Langebergen is the Little Karroo, the most important of the longitudinal troughs that occupy the synclines of the Cape folds and are partly due to faulting that occurred in late Cretaceous times. This groove-like depression, about 40 miles wide between the bordering

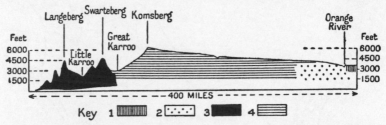

FIG. 19.—Section across the Cape folded ranges and the Upper Karroo
(Longitude is approximately that of Laingsburg, viz. 21° E.)

1. Pre-Cape rocks (Transvaal System).
2. Granites.   3. Cape System.   4. Karroo System.

ranges, extends from east to west for about 200 miles and throughout is traversed by longitudinal tributaries of the Gouritz River which reach the main stream before it breaks through the Langebergen in a typical ' poort '.

Between the Langebergen Range—together with its extension, the Zitzikamma Mountains—and the sea the land rises rather steeply, in terraces, to about 1000 feet; but to the north-west of Cape Agulhas there are occasional areas of low country, such as the plains behind St. Helena, Table and False Bays. Northwards to the Orange River and beyond the rise inland to the Great Escarpment is comparatively steep and regular.

Characteristic of the climate throughout the Cape Ranges, at least as far east as the longitude of Mossel Bay, is winter rainfall—with snow only on the high summits—and summer drought. Much of the rain is in the form of steady drizzle that saturates the ground without producing excessive run-off and soil erosion. From Cape Agulhas to Port Elizabeth, near which the eastern folds reach the sea, there is an increasing proportion of summer rainfall, though the winter supply remains the more important. Districts receiving abundant moisture up to 70 inches include the seaward slopes of the Drakenstein, Hottentots Holland and Langebergen Ranges, as well as the highlands of the Cape Peninsula : but readings as high as 70

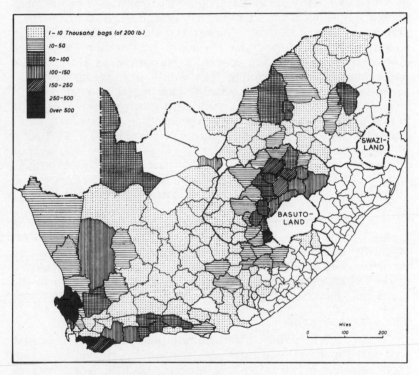

	1 – 10 Thousand bags (of 200 lb.)
	10 – 50
	50 – 100
	100 – 150
	150 – 250
	250 – 500
	Over 500

Fig. 20.—Wheat Production in the Union, by districts (Census year 1947–48)

inches occur in few and confined mountainous areas only. The best-watered plains and lower hill-slopes receive not more than 30 inches, and 15–25 inches may be taken as a fair average. For cultivation without the aid of irrigation the minimum precipitation is usually 15 inches.

Parts where the rainfall is precarious and generally insufficient for agriculture include the Little Karroo and the district to the west of the lower Olifants River : usually not more than 10 inches are received and pastoral activities, particularly sheep-farming become inevitable. The Little Karroo is good sheep country and formerly, when feminine fashions in Europe demanded feather display, ostrich farming was a very profitable industry with its centre at Oudtshoorn (rainfall 9·6 inches). The lowlands around the westernmost ranges have been continuously farmed by European colonists for nearly three centuries. It is the country of the oldest agricultural colony in Africa and many of the farmers, apart from the Cape Coloured population which is considerable, are descended from the earliest Dutch and French settlers. Wheat and the grape are the staples of agriculture as, during the period of colonization, they have always been. Cultivation is not as intensive as it might be under more scientific farming that would pay greater attention to re-fertilization. Unfortunately, the region is deficient in stock animals and manure is generally costly ; moreover, soils are usually impoverished owing to the leaching of their carbonates and nitrates, while potash and phosphorus are other constituents found in very deficient proportions. Consequently, the output per acre is low—in the case of wheat little more than 12 bushels only. But for the protection of a high tariff that restricts the import of foreign wheat it is almost certain that wheat-farming in South Africa would disappear.

Two of the most fertile and productive districts are (a) the lowland to the west and north-west of the Drakenstein Mountains, especially the neighbourhood of Malmesbury ; this is known to the Dutch farmer as the ' Zwartland ', (b) Caledon and Bredasdorp in the extreme south, the best wheat country, and known to the Dutch as the ' ruens ' or ' ridge-lands '.

The Great Karroo

This is the foreland of the interior plateau ; it extends east and west for about 250 miles as a dissected platform, averaging 1500–2500 feet between the Zwartebergen and the Great Escarpment (known here as the Nieuwveld Range).[1] Geologically, the region covers the southern margin of the Karroo beds of sandstones and shales that occupy a large part of the ' southern province ' of the sub-continent. Usually, the strata are gently inclined, but towards the Zwartebergen they have been mildly affected by the folding which produced the Cape Ranges.

Especially towards the west, flat-topped hills and plateaux standing above a level floor indicate the former elevation of the Karroo platform before erosion was far advanced. In this western district where the Karroo is narrower and higher than

[1] The breadth of the Karroo from north to south is about 80 miles, on the average.

in the east the mean annual rainfall is only about 5 inches, and the region merits the Hottentot description 'waterless', which is the translation of ' Karroo '. Stream channels are dry for much the greater part of the year, but subterranean water is reached at moderate depths. Much of the ground is bare, though lowly scrub, thinly scattered, is usually found. Eastwards the rainfall increases steadily to 15 inches,[1] but even so, grass is usually absent : the low Karroo bush becomes more plentiful and provides sustenance for the merino sheep, accustomed to arid conditions, that supply a big share of the wool output of the Union. The sheep farms are very extensive, usually more than 5000 acres, as compared with an average of 1000–2000 acres for farms in the ' winter rainfall ' region.

The head-stream channels of the Gouritz River, including the Gamka and Dwyka, unite and lead across the Karroo to a great ' poort ' in the Zwartebergen. It is only occasionally, however, that they contain water and the poort which marks their exit from the region is the product of a moister epoch. Immediately below the Great Escarpment small streams which reach the Karroo level are utilized in a narrow ribbon of cultivation with wheat and lucerne, a valuable fodder, as typical crops. More important is the irrigated belt of the Sundays River whose north-south course from Graaff Reinet marks the approximate eastern limit of the Karroo. Here the cultivation of citrus fruits is a flourishing industry and the local irrigation works represent one of the greatest achievements of the kind in South Africa.

The Terraced Foreland of the Eastern Cape Province and Natal

The region includes the belt of country between the foot of the Great Escarpment and the narrow coast-lands ; it extends from the eastern limits of the Great Karroo, with which it merges, across the Eastern Cape Province, Natal and Swaziland at altitudes—varying usually according to distance from the coast —of 1000 to 4000 feet. In the Cape section there is very little development of coastal plain and, from a cliff-bound shore, the rise across complicated terraces continues to the foot of the Stormbergen and the Quathlamba. On the other hand, in North-Eastern Natal (Zululand) and Portuguese East Africa the littoral plain is a much more pronounced feature and requires separate consideration. Seen from a point of vantage on the

---

[1] Going from west to east on the Karroo the following rainfall stations are typical—Laingsburg 4·6 inches, Beaufort West 10·6 inches, Graaff Reinet 13·8 inches.

Drakensberg the typical landscape is that of a confused, tumbled array of hummocks, grass-covered and with thickets of bush scattered in the innumerable hollows ; but viewed from the coast the scene is more rugged, with the escarpments standing out in tiers boldly.

Over much of the country, especially within the Cape Province, the strata are nearly horizontal Karroo beds and the Cape Ranges do not enter the region, save in the hinterland of Port Elizabeth where the folds die out. In Natal, however, there is

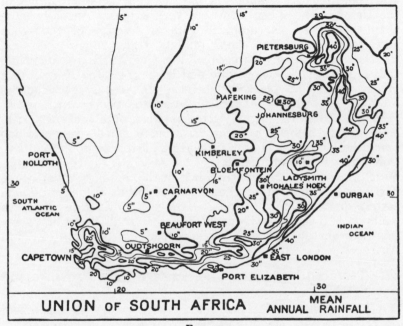

UNION OF SOUTH AFRICA ANNUAL MEAN RAINFALL

FIG. 21

evidence of crustal disturbance in post-Karroo times. Although the soils are varied they are not usually fertile, except in a few favoured valleys, and the thinly-covered, often steep, slopes are difficult for cultivation.

Rainfall, mainly confined to the summer half-year, is plentiful, in no place less than 20 inches and usually rather more than 30 inches.[1] Grass is abundant for the greater part of the year, while there are scattered thorn-bush (especially acacia) and succulents, of which tall aloes are characteristic. Streams are perennial in flow and very numerous : their courses are south-

[1] Representative rainfall stations are King William's Town 21 inches, Maclear 33·2 inches, Pietermaritzburg 36·9 inches.

eastwards, and, in addition to many independent rivers, there are the tributaries of the big systems of the Tugela (in Natal) and of the Kei and Great Fish Rivers of the Eastern Cape. All are useless for serious navigation and their steeply-graded courses are much interrupted by rapids and falls over resistant outcrops—often sills of dolerite.

Mainly on account of the social traditions of the native inhabitants whose settlement is denser than elsewhere in rural South Africa, the region has remained mainly pastoral. This is particularly true of the Eastern Cape Province, much of which is in Native Reserves devoted to cattle pasture. Maize ('mealies') is produced as a subsistence crop and not for export. Physical conditions are suited to maize, but the output, because of primitive methods of agriculture, is small compared with that on the High Veld of the Transvaal and Orange Free State.

In Natal the zone—sometimes known as the Middle Veld —between 2000 feet and 4000 feet has recently become important for the production of wattle bark, the extract from which is used in tanning. The tree is native to Australia, but it thrives well in its South African habitat, particularly on the Natal Uplands where the greater part of the wattle is planted. Although native labour is used for this 'forest industry' the plantations are almost entirely on European-owned farms.

The Coastal Lowlands of Natal and Southern Mozambique

In Natal the littoral belt below 600 feet is confined to a 10-mile strip about as far north as Stanger. Over Zululand, however, the lowland widens, and this part of Natal lying between the shore and the terraced plateau of Swaziland extends northwards with a width of 50 miles and provides the only considerable area of low plain to be found throughout the Union of South Africa.

Across the Natal-Mozambique frontier, which is quite arbitrary in the sense that it does not correspond to a geographical division, the hinterland of Delagoa Bay resembles in its physical features the plain of Zululand. On the north-western shore of the wide but sheltered inner bay stands the port of Lourenço Marques, naturally the finest harbour in Southern Africa and one of the best-equipped for the reception of shipping. A deep channel—25 feet of water at low water of spring tides—leads to its spacious quays. On account of its comparative proximity to the industrial region of the Southern Transvaal the port of Delagoa Bay competes strenuously for up-country traffic with the Natal port of Durban which is more distant—by about 100 miles—from Johannesburg.

Beyond Delagoa Bay going northwards, the lowland of Mozambique widens as the coast trends sharply to the northeast and away from the edge of the Plateau ; and, as far as the Zambezi River, lowland and low plateau (not exceeding 1500 feet) form a littoral belt about 150 miles wide. Included is the low, limestone platform of Gazaland. As a whole the region is one where submergence in comparatively late geological time (Cretaceous and Tertiary) was more extensive than elsewhere in South Africa.

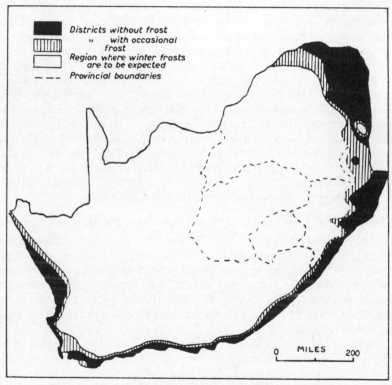

Districts without frost
„ with occasional frost
Region where winter frosts are to be expected
— — — Provincial boundaries

FIG. 22.—Union of South Africa : Occurrence of Frost

For part of its length the Transvaal–Mozambique frontier follows the crest of the Lebombo Range—a monocline upraised in Mesozoic times—and immediately to the west is the Low Veld of the Transvaal whose characteristics are repeated across the Southern Rhodesian border. This belt may be incorporated in the region of the eastern littoral which it closely resembles in climate and vegetation, though its elevation is rather more —about 1500 feet on the average. Within the Union there is no district so unhealthy as the Low Veld during summer,[1] but winter is attractive to those whose visit includes a tour of the Kruger National Park, the greatest wild game reserve in Southern Africa with an area comparable to that of Yorkshire.

Conditions of climate are essentially tropical throughout, even though, in Natal, the region extends well to the south of lat. 30° S. Never is there risk of frost, and lowland crops, requiring constantly high temperature and fairly abundant summer rainfall of not less than 30 inches, thrive well. Precipitation up to this amount is usual, but areas of lower rainfall occur ; for example, in the rain-shadow immediately west of the Lebombo Range where less than 25 inches is registered and on the low shore around Lourenço Marques where there is little opportunity for ' orographical ' rainfall.[2]

Vegetation, both wild and cultivated, is more luxuriant than is to be found on the Plateau of South Africa, and rather exceptional are a number of semi-arid tracts due to deficient rains or to the exposure of limestone at the surface (e.g. Gazaland). Usually thorn-bush savanna prevails. The Natal plain is often described by South African botanists as ' the palm belt ', for the raphia and other varieties of palm are well represented, though there is also much thorn-bush as elsewhere throughout the region. The coast of Zululand and Southern Mozambique is generally sandy, whilst around lagoons grows mangrove forest, which is especially extensive near the outlets of the principal rivers—Zambezi and Limpopo.

Cultivation is intensive on the Natal lowland (including southern districts of Zululand) where sugar-cane is by far the most important crop. Apart from Zululand there is practically no more land in Natal available for this lowland and essentially tropical plant. In 1939 sugar plantations in Natal (without Zululand) covered 340,000 acres, of which over one-third were in Zululand. The acreage in the latter territory could be increased —though not without hardship to the present native occupants— especially in the vicinity of the Mozambique border and behind St. Lucia Bay, where are the rich alluvial soils of the Pongola and Umfolozi Rivers. The clash of interests is likely to be violent as between the Natives, quite naturally desirous of preserving the sanctity of their reserves, and the industrialists confronted with a dearth of good sugar land.[3]

[1] There is risk of malaria almost everywhere in the region.

[2] Representative rainfall stations on the Mozambique littoral are Lourenço Marques 28 inches, Beira 57 inches, Quelimane 56·3 inches, Tete 21·2 inches.

[3] On a later page will be found reference to the evolution of the sugar industry of South-East Africa.

Settlement of European farmers in Zululand is restricted not only by the Reserves but also by the widespread danger of malaria, and it is unfortunate that some of the most fertile land in the Union should have this disadvantage. Serious also is the menace of the tsetse fly to both man and stock.

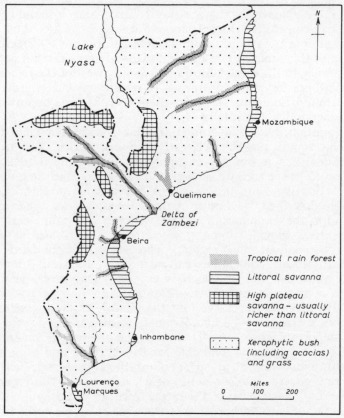

FIG. 23.—Mozambique : Generalized Map of Vegetation
(Partly based on map by C. de Melo Vicira)

As the trend of economic development in Mozambique has been very different from that in British South Africa it requires a separate place in our attention. In the territory as a whole [1] there is general stagnation in farming and industry, relieved

[1] Where ' Mozambique ' is used for convenience the entire area of Portuguese East Africa is included. It is necessary to distinguish between (a) the Colony of Mozambique, (b) the territory of the Mozambique Company, (c) the island and town of Mozambique. For this reason ' Portuguese East Africa ' is preferable though cumbrous.

only by the activities of one or two ports, especially Lourenço Marques and Beira, whose business is largely furnished by transit trade to and from the commercially-developed hinterland of the Transvaal and Southern Rhodesia.

The colonial policy of Portugal has long been governed by the principle that administrative commitments should be reduced to a bare minimum. There has been practically no European colonization of the interior, large parts of which are still unsurveyed : and the traditional conception of enterprise confined to port depôts still considerably influences official policy. During her most prosperous colonial days Portugal planned the control of the entire trade of the Indian Ocean borderlands, which was to be effected by means of two fleets operating from a chain of ports along the shores of East Africa, Southern Arabia and Western India ; in this period Mozambique formed part of the ' State of India ' and was controlled from Goa.

Portugal has attempted to restrict colonial trade to her own shipping and markets, partly through fear of losing not only trade but even the colonies themselves to her great rivals in African enterprise, until recently Germany as well as Britain. Down to the time of the First World War the Lisbon Government would not consider the suggestion of extending some degree of freedom of trade and autonomy to her colonies. During the modern republican régime rather more sympathy has been shown to the aspirations of the colonists and reforms have been promised, including the institution of geological and topographical surveys—very necessary undertakings in an undeveloped, little known but potentially rich territory.

Unity of administration has been achieved only recently with the winding-up of chartered companies. The district south of lat. 22° S., including Lourenço Marques, has long been directly administered by the Governor-General ; but until the expiration of its Charter in 1941 the Mozambique Company [1] had powers of both government and economic development in the district north of this parallel as far as the lower Zambezi. Outside our region but still within the political limits of Portuguese East Africa a similar corporation—the Nyasa Company—held administrative powers between the south-eastern shore of Lake Nyasa and the Indian Ocean until 1929, when the Governor-General took over.

The white population in Mozambique Colony as a whole was small in numbers until the end of the Second World War, when it totalled about 31,000. Since the War it has increased rapidly, largely as a consequence of immigration from Portugal, to an estimated 101,000 in 1960. About one-fifth of those classed as

[1] Companhia de Moçambique—whose land exceeded 52,000 sq. miles.

' civilized ' are similar to the Cape Coloured of the Republic of
South Africa ; they are of mixed parentage—Portuguese with
Bantu or Asiatics. The civilized element is concentrated in the few
important ports : official returns (1960) show 163,000, of whom
nearly 62,000 are in the district of Lourenço Marques, which includes the capital and chief port of that name. The only other
town of size is Beira, where there are about 21,000 civilized
residents in addition to 38,500 classified as non-civilized. In
the entire Colony there are only some 20,000 Asiatics, chiefly
Indians, the overwhelming proportion of the inhabitants are
Bantu who, in 1960, numbered about 6,430,000.

Two separate aspects of the commercial geography of Mozambique merit attention, namely, (a) agricultural production for
export, (b) port development in response to the commercial needs
of the Transvaal and Rhodesia, for which Lourenço Marques and
Beira respectively are the ocean gateways.

The soil and climate of the greater part of the Colony are
well suited to the cultivation of a wide variety of tropical crops
including sugar-cane, cotton, maize, sisal, coco-nut (on the sandy
coast-lands) and rubber. But there is not enough rainfall for some
tropical plants of high commercial value: for example, the Hevea
(rubber) tree will not thrive, as it needs at least 60–80 inches of
rain. The Manihot tree, suited to more arid conditions, should do
well, though rubber production from it is at present insignificant.

Sugar is the outstanding crop intended mainly for export and,
although the output is small when compared with that of Natal,[1]
it has shown a steady increase except during the several years
of world-wide trade depression.[2] The most spectacular achievement of the second Six Year Plan (1959–64) has been the irrigation and reclamation of a large area of the Limpopo valley. The
low barrage which carries the railway from Lourenço Marques
across the river to Rhodesia has been used to deflect water into a
natural digression to the south, whence it is led to irrigate 30,000
hectares of reclaimed land. The new territory has been carefully
cleared of malaria, and settled in small holdings by peasant
farmers brought in from metropolitan Portugal, and by selected
African farmers. By the end of 1960 some 560 families had been
settled. Long-staple Egyptian cotton and potatoes have both
done well in this region, and there is a ready market for fresh
vegetables in Bulawayo.

There are also plans to reclaim and settle the Maputo, In-
comati and Zambezi valleys, and to tap the subterranean waters
of the arid south-west, to serve a cattle industry. One of the
most promising regions for future settlement is the northern district of Niassa which stands at about 4,000 feet and

[1] 130,000 tons as against 994,000 tons for Natal (1958).
[2] Two British firms are well established and lead in production.

has a fertile soil, but which, as Fig. 24 shows, still has a very thin population and has suffered from the handicap of poor communications. With the completion of the railway to Vila Cabral, it is hoped to attract many more farmers to this area, where the pyrethrum crop in particular is expected to thrive.

The Administration has encouraged sugar production up to the requirements of the Lisbon market, which are about 40,000 tons. An additional outlet for Mozambique sugar has until recently been open in the Transvaal where, by the terms of the Transvaal–Mozambique Convention of 1909, Portuguese sugar was permitted to compete on favourable terms with the product of Natal. This treaty provided for the free interchange of agricultural commodities between the two colonies

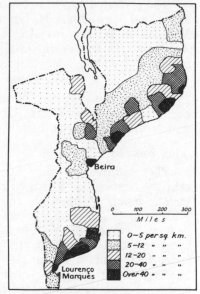

FIG. 24.—Mozambique :
Density of Population (1960)

and for the recruitment of native labour in Mozambique, south of lat. 22° S., for the Transvaal mines. In 1923 the Convention lapsed, but a few years later it was renewed in a modified form. Nowadays emigration is regulated by international agreements and internal legislation, so as to protect the interests of the natives and guarantee them good conditions of employment. This type of controlled emigration, though in some ways to be deplored, helps to ease the natives' living conditions and to develop the frontier regions through which it passes.

Sugar was for long the only important commercial crop of Mozambique, but rapid strides have recently been made in the cultivation of copra, sisal, ground-nuts and cotton.

The high place amongst African ports occupied by Lourenço Marques and Beira is almost entirely due to the enterprise of the Administrations of the Transvaal and Southern Rhodesia which encouraged the Portuguese to permit the inland railway systems to be linked to their natural outlets on the Mozambique coast.[1] Port facilities at Lourenço Marques are especially good, partly in consequence of the initiative of the South African Railways Administration, the state-owned system of the Union which has running powers over the Delagoa Bay line. Indeed, for all practical purposes the port is within the economic system of the Union.[2] By a twenty-year convention on the development of the port of Beira, signed in June, 1950, the Portuguese government undertook to carry out the works necessary to make the port and railway adequate to handle traffic from the Rhodesias and Nyasaland.

The principal exports of Mozambique are cotton, copra, sisal, sugar and vegetable oils, but the outflowing trade of Lourenço Marques is largely in coal, copper ore[3] and maize from the Transvaal. Much of the coal goes to ports of Western India, including Bombay, where it is used for bunkering.

Continuing the survey of the natural regions of South Africa, our attention is now directed towards those that are situated within the Plateau, as defined by the Great Escarpment.

The Basuto Highland

The country of the Basutos formerly—early nineteenth century—extended westwards beyond its present limits to include much of the High Veld of what is now the Orange Free State. The Voor-trekkers who, going northwards in search of new land, crossed the Vaal in the decade 1830–40, later encroached upon the best farming country of the Basutos and drove the latter to mountain fastnesses west of the Drakensberg.

Basutoland, roughly equal to Belgium in area, lies wholly within the upper reaches of the Orange River basin and as a region of bold relief almost throughout marks the culmination of the South African Plateau. A narrow western strip in the neighbourhood of the Caledon River belongs to the High Veld, but the remainder of the country is as distinct from the Orange Free State as it is from the Eastern Terraces of Natal and the Cape Province.

[1] The line from Delagoa Bay to the Transvaal is only 57 miles in length : the lines from Beira and Lourenço Marques to the Rhodesian border are respectively about 200 miles and 350 miles long.
[2] Both Great Britain and the Union have, unsuccessfully, on different occasions offered to purchase Lourenço Marques.
[3] Chiefly from the Messina mine in the Northern Transvaal.

Here is a great 'massif' of undisturbed rocks, chiefly sandstones of Upper Karroo (Triassic) age, above which rise a series of mountainous ridges formed of dark basalt that have been carved out by erosive action. Altitude ranges from 5000 feet (High Veld) to over 10,000 feet on the Drakensberg; but gradual rise to the east is interrupted by the south-westward trending ridges—the Malutis—which appear on the orographical map as spurs of the Drakensberg and separate the head-streams of the Orange. In the eastern half of the country, where the dark soils are volcanic and fertile and where rainfall exceeds 30 inches, grass is abundant in summer and, in favoured localities, wheat grows with comparatively big yields. On the western and lower belt of sandstones, however, the rainfall is under 30 inches (e.g. at Mafeteng, 26·7 inches), soils are permeable and there is little surface water; so that in winter the ground has a very parched appearance.

Since the forced evacuation of lands west of the Caledon River the Basutos have tended to migrate farther towards the east into the volcanic highlands which until about half a century ago were practically uninhabited; but still the greater part of the Basuto nation (about 600,000) occupies the western districts.[1]

There are many parts where—owing to excessive altitude, as in the east, or to rather deficient rains and sterile sandy soil, as in the west—agriculture cannot compete with sheep-rearing: but although the Basutos retain their partial dependence on stock, they possess an agricultural tradition that is stronger than that of any group of the Southern Bantu. In a sub-continent of very primitive agriculture, so far as Natives are concerned, it is notable that many Basuto farmers have exchanged the simple hoe for the more efficient ox-drawn plough.

Although the conception of individual farm-holdings is gradually penetrating, land is still considered to be vested in the nation as a whole and to be unsaleable. During the farming season, however, where land is sown, the sub-chieftains with the authority of the Paramount Chief allot temporary holdings to farmers who grow chiefly kaffir-corn[2] and maize. After harvest-time all land reverts to commonage for pastoral purposes.

Maize does not succeed at the high altitudes of eastern districts where frost may be expected in most months of the year, but grows well in the west between 5000 feet and 6000 feet. On the other hand, wheat, a hardier crop, has become the staple of the eastern lands. The districts of most successful farming practice (for kaffir corn and maize) are in the north-west,

---

[1] From north to south—Leribe, Berea, Maseru, Mafeteng, Mohale's Hoek.
[2] Also known as 'great millet' and 'guinea-corn' and probably the most widespread crop in Africa.

especially Leribe and Berea, which usually have a considerable surplus for export to the poorer parts of the Protectorate. Taking the country as a whole, it is estimated that less than 7 per cent of the land is cultivated and that little more is cultivable without the aid of expensive irrigation.

Stock animals, chiefly sheep of about 1½ million head, remain the principal source of wealth, and wool is the only product of the country that plays an important part in external trade. But the country is overstocked, which is a matter of serious consequence to the maintenance of pasture and the soil covering. The horse or mountain pony is in common use as a mount, and the Basutos are expert riders though they keep their animals in extremely poor condition.[1]

Each year a very high proportion of the adult male population of Basutoland leaves the country and enters the South African Republic for work in the Rand mines or as houseboys and farmhands. As it happens their own country is not greatly coveted for European settlement and, under the direct protection of the Crown, the Basuto nation enjoys a greater degree of tribal solidarity and cultural independence than any Native group in Africa south of the Equator. No White man may purchase land, and European traders are carefully restricted in numbers and in the scope of their commerce with the Basutos.

There are no towns, nor are there villages of considerable size, and settlement is rarely of a nucleated character. Maseru, the head-quarters of the British administrative staff which co-operates with the Paramount Chief, is known locally as a ' camp '. Here also is the site of the *Pitso* or parliament of the Basuto which is held annually, so that in spite of its marginal position, and though without municipal government, Maseru fulfils the functions of a capital. It is within a mile of the Orange Free State frontier and this distance is covered by the terminus of a railway connecting Maseru with Bloemfontein. Apart from a main road, or rather track, extending along the western border and linking a number of administrative posts, there are many by-roads, and a mountain road of 80 miles.

Basutoland has been a Protectorate since 1884, but along with the other ' Native Territories ' of Bechuanaland and Swaziland its future status is uncertain. A clause in the Act of 1909 which brought the Union of South Africa into being foreshadows the ultimate incorporation of these Protectorates within the Republic. The chief wealth of Basutoland is in its cattle, and its

---

[1] The Bantu as a whole are harsh and ignorant in their treatment of farm animals.

main exports are livestock, hides and skins, sent mainly to the Republic and to Rhodesia. Crops are dependent on rainfall and the flow from artesian boreholes, but drought is a continual risk, and it struck heavily in 1965.

The High Veld

On an earlier page brief reference was made to the climate and vegetation of this region whose elevation varies from 4000 to 6000 feet throughout the Southern Transvaal and the greater part of the Orange Free State. The northern border follows the low divide of the Limpopo and Vaal systems which crosses the Transvaal westwards from the neighbourhood of Carolina by way of the ridge of the Witwatersrand. Johannesburg (alt. 5990 ft.) is thus at the northern extreme, while Pretoria, 40 miles farther north, is 1000 feet lower and experiences a more tropical régime of climate. On its southern side the High Veld is approximately bounded by the line of the Orange River from where it leaves Basutoland to near its junction with the Vaal.

Temperate climatic conditions and comparatively abundant rains, with plentiful summer pasture in consequence, were attractive to the Voor-trekkers who, having crossed arid lands such as the Great Karroo, found on the High Veld better farming land than Dutch colonists had ever met since the early days when began migration from the ' winter rainfall ' region of the Cape. Onwards from the middle of the nineteenth century the High Veld has steadily increased its importance in both cereal and stock farming, and to-day, for general agriculture, it is the outstanding region of the Union.

Of even more immediate consequence in the commercial geography of the High Veld is the occurrence within its borders of the greatest gold-field yet discovered : so that in addition to a greater density of European farming population than the average for the cultivated lands of the Union there is the largest urban concentration to be found in Africa outside the delta of the Nile.

Usually the surface is level or gently undulating and provides fewer difficulties for transport than any region within the continent. The uppermost strata towards the east are undisturbed Lower Karroo beds, some of which contain valuable coal seams. In more westerly parts occur low but often boldly-scarped ridges and isolated hills (' kopjes ') where outcrop Pre-Cape (Archaean) rocks, including the quartzites and gold-bearing conglomerates of the Witwatersrand (' White Waters Ridge ') or Rand, as it is simply called.

Although the rains of the High Veld are described above as comparatively abundant—and this is true if mean annual precipitation, varying, according to district, from 20 to 35 inches, alone be taken into account—their variability, especially on the Western High Veld, is a serious disadvantage to agriculture and imposes strict limitations on the range of possible crops. F. Plummer and H. D. Leppan [1] have together investigated the variability of Transvaal rainfall and its relationship to local farming ; and for this purpose compare western and eastern stations, taking Bloemhof and Zeerust as representative of the one and Bethal as typical of the other. In the east, where mean annual rainfall is heavier than elsewhere, it is fairly reliable year by year ; while, from 1903 to 1925, in the case of the Western Transvaal the range in particular years was from 11 to 32 inches at Bloemhof and from 16 to 41 inches at Zeerust. The staple crop of the High Veld—maize—requires for success at least 20 inches, and it follows that the western lands cannot be relied upon for steady production of the cereal and must turn to crops which offer greater resistance to drought, such as sorghums, including kaffir corn, and cotton. For the latter crop the Rustenburg district of the Western Transvaal has become one of the most notable in British South Africa. [2]

Apart from unreliability of rainfall in western parts serious climatic disadvantages shared by all districts of the inner Plateau of South Africa are the short duration and the high intensity of the rains, together with excessive evaporation. Over both the Transvaal and the Free State more than 80 per cent. of the precipitation occurs during the six months of maximum evaporation : it is mainly of thunderstorm character occurring in violent showers which promote excessive run-off and soil erosion. The conservation of storm-water is recognized as of vital importance, and vast reservoirs have been constructed or are projected. The Hartebeestpoort Dam, on the Crocodile River, was completed early this century. With a storage capacity of 5400 million cu. ft., its reservoir is greatly surpassed by the Vaal River Development project with a capacity of 38,000 million cu. ft. The latter, whose great reservoir is the Vaalbank Dam, benefits parts of three Provinces ; but, in aggregate, from all schemes only a small proportion of the High Veld is irrigated. [3]

[1] *Rainfall and Farming in the Transvaal*, Pretoria, 1927.

[2] Rustenburg is on the north-western edge of the High Veld, beyond which lower altitude is accompanied by more unhealthy conditions.

[3] On the subject of irrigation in South Africa the reader is advised to consult the ' Report of the Drought Investigation Commission ', Union Government, Cape Town, 1923.

Although soils are by no means uniformly fertile over the
High Veld there is a compact area of fairly rich loams in the
east-centre of the region within the ' maize triangle ', where the
largest crops of this cereal are produced.[1] In the ' triangle '
the parts of specially good soil and rain (over 25 inches) include
in the Transvaal the district to the east and south-east of
Johannesburg, and in the Free State the district north of the
latitude of Bloemfontein, but east of the main line of railway
from Bloemfontein to Kroonstad and Johannesburg. Although
comparatively well farmed the ' maize triangle ' has less than
15 per cent. of its area under cultivation, but a winter crop
of wheat adds considerably to the total cereal production. It
is also true that the output per acre is very low compared with
that of the great maize lands of the world, such as the ' Corn
Belt ' of the U.S.A. and the Pampas of the Argentine.[2]

The importance of arable farming does not overshadow the
basic agricultural enterprise of stock-rearing—cattle for beef
and dairy produce, and sheep for wool and mutton. Concerning these and other features of the geography of the Transvaal
more will be added later.

The Bushveld

From the latitude of Pretoria the surface falls gradually
towards the north-central depression of the Transvaal. This
is the region of the Bushveld whose vegetation consists of thorn-
bush and savanna grasses (in summer). It is drained by head-
streams of the Limpopo, namely the Crocodile, Olifants and
Nyl,[3] which differ remarkably in their directions of flow—the
Crocodile leading towards the north-west and to the Bechuanaland frontier, the Olifants flowing eastwards to meet the main
river in Portuguese territory, and the Nyl taking a northerly
course across the low Waterberg upland which encloses the
Bush Veld on the north and marks it off from the Low Veld
of the Limpopo valley. In the vicinity of Pretoria the Crocodile
and Olifants are almost in contact, yet their respective outlets
into the Limpopo are 400 miles apart, or 600 miles by way of
the wide sweep of the river. Eastwards along the course of the
Olifants the Bushveld merges with the Low Veld of the Eastern
Transvaal and Mozambique.

---

[1] The apices of the ' triangle ' are Carolina in the east, Mafeking in
the west, and Ladybrand in the south.

[2] On the maize lands of the Americas the output is over 20 bags (each
of 200 lb.) per acre, against 4–5 bags on the High Veld.

[3] It is recorded that the Voor-trekkers who entered the Transvaal
believed they had reached (at the ' Nyl stroom ') the source of the Nile.

The surface is generally even and indeed almost flat over wide expanses, such as the Springbok Flats which extend for 100 miles well to the north-east of Pretoria. Elevation is normally 1000–2000 feet lower than that of the High Veld, i.e. approximately 3000 feet above sea-level. Igneous rocks belonging to the system known as the ' Bushveld Complex ' are widely distributed at the surface in consequence of the removal by erosion of the overlying sediments. Pre-Cape rocks are exposed, especially on the margins. There are also outliers of the Karroo system (sandstones and shales), including those that occupy the Springbok Flats. The Limpopo Highlands of the Waterberg and Zoutpansberg form part of the ancient core of the continent : they are greatly worn down, yet stand in comparatively bold relief above the low veld of the Zambezi.

The very moderate altitude of the Bushveld taken into conjunction with the low, almost tropical, latitude results in a summer climate that is not conducive to the health of the European, so that there are few permanent settlers. Much of the region is in Native Reserves, though these lands have been and are being encroached upon by mining companies intent upon exploiting the gold, platinum, tin and other resources of one of the most remarkable mineral-bearing areas of the world.

The invasion of native land rights is likely to proceed further with the establishment of plantations for crops—such as cotton— that obtain on the Bushveld a sufficiently long frost-free season. But the production of commercial crops is still on a very small scale and began only about the time of the First World War. In a region where the mean annual rainfall varies, according to district, from 15 to 25 inches and where evaporation is excessive, agriculture is dependent on irrigation. So far the conservation of water for agriculture has received insufficient attention, the most notable exception being the Hartebeestpoort reservoir, by means of which good crops of cotton, maize and tobacco are grown in the neighbourhood of the Magaliesberg.

The Upper Karroo

Intermediate to the Great Karroo and to the High Veld of the Free State, and bounded southwards by the Great Escarpment (as represented by the Nieuwveld Range and the Sneeuwbergen), is the region suitably named Upper Karroo, higher than the Great Karroo and with an average of 3000 to 4000 feet. Along with the Upper Karroo it is permissible to include the country of the Middle Veld, north of the Orange and situated between the Western High Veld, of the Free State and Transvaal, and the Kalahari [1]: elevation, climate and vegetation are similar.

For the greater part the region is occupied by horizontal Karroo beds : this is especially true of the Upper Karroo where, however, intrusions of dolerite are numerous and stand out as ridges above the plain. In the South-Western Transvaal the Karroo sediments have been largely removed by denudation and the Pre-Cape horizon is exposed : here in the neighbourhood of the Vaal [2] the ' river diggings ' have given rich yields of alluvial diamonds.

Unreliability of rainfall and its occurrence in violent showers of short duration, together with a low annual mean of 10 to 15 inches, impose strict limits on agricultural enterprise. The railway from the Cape to Mafeking traverses the Upper Karroo and Middle Veld after leaving the Great Karroo, and the rainfall of stations at regular intervals along it indicates a gradual and regular increase from south-west to north-east ; so we have the following figures—Victoria West, 10·5 inches ; De Aar, 12·7 inches ; Kimberley, 15·7 inches. Droughts are frequent and of long duration and it is claimed to be a region of increasing desiccation, due not necessarily to a diminishing rainfall, but rather to the removal of the plant covering by veld fires [3] and overstocking, with consequent soil erosion. As on the Great Karroo, the ' wind pump ' drawing water to the surface is to be seen wherever there is habitation. In the west and south-west the country is scrub-land, but vegetation improves towards the north-east and there is an increase of grass as the High Veld is approached.

A sparse population engages mainly in the rearing of sheep and goats (including the Angora variety introduced from Asia Minor about one hundred years ago), so that wool and mohair are the farm products of commercial value. There is no town of size except Kimberley which has about 80,000 inhabitants and is diminishing in importance with the decline of the town's only industry—diamond mining.[4] Apart from the mine Natives at Kimberley there are very few Bantu in the region, and farm labour is provided partly by European, partly by Cape Coloured.

[1] The Middle Veld includes eastern districts of Griqualand West (including Kimberley), together with the South-Western Transvaal.

[2] The name ' Vaal ' signifies ' muddy ', a description that might be applied to any South African river.

[3] Before the summer rains it is a common practice amongst the more backward Dutch farmers to burn the grass or scrub covering that remains.

[4] In 1926 the European population was 17,000. By 1936 it had diminished to 15,750, but rose to 79,000 in 1960.

The Kalahari and its Neighbourhood

Between the Upper Karroo and the central plateau of South-West Africa lies the vast area which, though going under a series of local names, may be classed as the Kalahari semi-desert. Rainfall, which is the criterion of supreme importance in deciding the limits of the region, is always deficient—between 5 and 10 inches.[1] Politically, it comprises the north-west of the Cape Province, the southern half of the Bechuanaland Protectorate and the south-eastern district of South-West Africa. Passing northwards from the Kalahari into the northern parts of the Bechuanaland Protectorate and westwards on to the high plateau in the interior of South-West Africa, rainfall increases to about 29 inches. There is a corresponding improvement in the quality and quantity of the grasses, with which is to be associated increase of stock and of population, as well as transition from sheep- to cattle-farming.

The Kalahari has no surface drainage, and even though the Orange has cut its way westwards across the region it receives no tributaries except an occasional storm torrent. Formerly the Southern Kalahari drained to the Orange and there were perennial streams where none exist to-day. The basin-like character of the Kalahari is apparent from the orographical map, and it is seen to have an elevation of 2000–3000 feet and to be enclosed on all sides except the northern by a borderland rising to 5000 feet.

Horizontal Karroo beds overlaid with accumulations of sand occupy the greater part, but here and there, especially in the south, are bare hills of the ' inselberg ' type. Yet the Kalahari is not a wilderness of sand, for there is a partial covering of grass. Furthermore, underground water is reached at no great depth, and here is found one of the most valuable springs in South Africa —that of Kuruman, which supplies over four million gallons a day. Shallow depressions—' pans '—are numerous ; their surfaces are often impervious to rain, so that the storm waters that occasionally collect give them the temporary appearance of lakes, until evaporation restores their arid condition.[2]

Bordering the Kalahari on the south-east is the escarpment of the Kaap Plateau at approximately 4000 feet, while farther into the interior of the Kalahari are the ancient folds of the Korannaberg and Langeberg (up to 6000 ft.). To the south-west, Namaqualand is to be associated with the Kalahari. Here is an

[1] Typical stations are Kenhardt (Cape)—5·8 inches ; Keetmanshoop (South-West Africa)—5·1 inches.
[2] Such is the Haakschien Vlei, 80 sq. miles in extent.

ancient (Pre-Cape) and rugged highland of gneiss rising to over 5000 feet. Namaqualand is of interest to the climatologist, as it provides a rather abrupt transition from meagre winter rains on the Atlantic slope to deficient summer showers on the Bushmanland side.

In its course across the Southern Kalahari the Orange is usually sharply and narrowly confined by steep banks, and even where the valley is more open the strips of alluvium on either side are very narrow. Below the junction of the channel which carries the occasional storm waters of the Hartebeest River the Orange drops more than 400 feet over the Aughrabies Falls, close to the frontier of South-West Africa ; and below, for many miles, the river flows in a gorge. It passes through desert country to the sea which it reaches over a sand-bar. The great Orange River Scheme, announced in 1962, will control the river for irrigation and water power, supply water to revivify irrigation works on the Sunday and Fish rivers and be linked with an extensive plan of soil conservation (Fig. 26).

Life within the Kalahari is necessarily semi-nomadic. Apart from Hottentots and Griquas—half-caste people whose rôle in South African affairs is an interesting one and who date from the early nineteenth century—Dutch sheep-farmers regularly visit the Southern Kalahari, and their extensive movement is necessitated by the inability of the pasture to support a higher density than one sheep to every 15–20 acres.

Only the southern half of the Bechuanaland Protectorate belongs to the Kalahari. Part of the northern district is drained by the intermittent tributaries of the Zambezi and the remainder is a region of inland drainage, including the system of ' Lake ' Ngami which in winter is no more than a swamp. The northern half of the Protectorate should, for purposes of strict regional classification, be grouped along with the neighbouring grass-land —much richer than the Kalahari—on the borders of the four territories whose boundaries here converge, namely, Southern and Northern Rhodesia, Angola and South-West Africa.

The Bantu population of the Protectorate (534,000 in 1964) is mainly found to the east of the Kalahari and near the borders of the Transvaal and Southern Rhodesia. The most populous Native Reserves are within 100 miles of the trunk line of railway that links Southern Rhodesia with the Cape and traverses 400 miles of Eastern Bechuanaland. Mafeking—on this railway— though within the Cape Province, is chosen for reasons of convenience and accessibility as the head-quarters of the British staff of the Protectorate Government, while the principal native centre —Serowe—is west of the railway-station of Palapye Road. Of the various Bantu groups, all independent of each other, the Bamangwato are the most influential and numerous.[1] A small European community is settled at stations along the railway, and trades with those Bechuana who have cattle for export.

Cattle-rearing is the decisive factor in the economy of eastern and northern districts of the Protectorate. Agriculture is rendered very precarious on account of the short duration and unreliability of the rainfall, whose comparatively high mean of 15–18 inches may give a misleading impression regarding its usefulness. The Bechuana have recently succeeded in re-stocking their farms after a terrible period of rinderpest which at the close of the last century destroyed nearly every animal they possessed.[2] Apart from the rearing of cattle for beef the only industry which has a promising future is dairying. Unfortunately in Southern Rhodesia and South-West Africa there is a complete embargo on Bechuanaland cattle, and export to the Union is strictly limited : on the other hand, Angola and the Belgian Congo welcome supplies of stock.

As a country of recurrent drought Bechuanaland tends to export population, and the number of men who are temporarily absent working in the Union, Southern Rhodesia and South-West Africa has been put as high as 50 per cent. of the total adult male population. The Protectorate has played a big part in the mining of gold on the Rand and of diamonds at Kimberley, through its contribution of labour. It is rather paradoxical that the Protectorate Government should have, at one and the same time, encouraged labour migration and striven to preserve the integrity of the tribes and of their social order. Rather than encourage emigration which inevitably tends towards de-tribalization the Government should promote the re-distribution of population within the better-watered districts of the Territory. At present population is not properly distributed in relation to water supply : villages should be more numerous and smaller, for it is largely the crowding of settlement into large units that has rendered the water problem acute.

The north-eastern district of South-West Africa, which includes Ovamboland, is similar in characteristics of climate and vegetation to Northern Bechuanaland with which, as with South-Eastern Angola, it merges. It is the rainiest part of the Mandated Territory and annual precipitation goes up to 20 inches and over.[3] The prevalent vegetation is mixed bush and grass savanna, with

[1] Estimated at 200,000 in 1964.

[2] The cattle of the Protectorate were estimated at 1,350,000 in 1963.

[3] Typical stations are Tsumeb and Grootfontein with 22 inches and 21·7 inches respectively.

the former growing very dense in places. One of the most notable
features of a region where streams are usually intermittent is the
Etosha Pan, which is entered occasionally by flood waters of the
Cunene and has, during a summer of good rains, a shallow water
area of 1300 square miles. The natural facilities for large-scale
irrigation seem to be very favourable in the country between

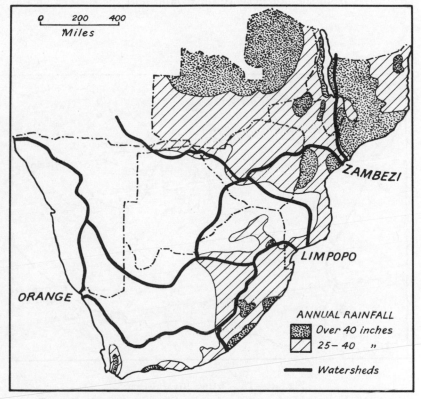

FIG. 25.—Southern Africa : Drainage, Basins and Annual Rainfall

the Cunene and the great Pan. At the same time it is an unhealthy country for stock, as is shown by the comparative
scarcity of cattle, despite the abundance of grass.[1] Malaria is
prevalent and White settlement is at present impracticable. Yet
it is the most densely populated district of South-West Africa,
and the Ovambo number about one-half of the total Native
population (for South-West Africa) of 452,000 (1960). Agricul-

[1] See accompanying map.

ture largely displaces pastoralism, and kaffir-corn and maize are the staple crops. At Tsumeb to the south-east of the Etosha Pan the richest copper ores of the Territory are worked. Under German rule Ovamboland was allowed to retain its tribal organization, and to-day it is the only part of ' South-West ' where this organization can be utilized for the purpose of indirect rule. Elsewhere tribal disintegration is complete.

Apart from the northern tropical land and the eastern (Kala-

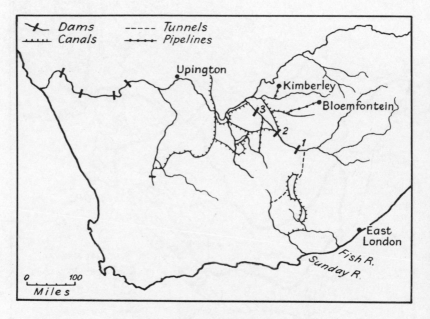

Fig. 26.—The Orange River Scheme
1.—Verwoerd Dam   2. Van der Kloof Dam   3. Torquay Dam

hari) district of South-West Africa two other natural regions of the Mandated Territory merit special attention.

The first may be described as the interior highland of Damaraland and Northern Namaqualand, with the district around Windhoek marking the culmination of altitude, 6000–8000 feet. This is a region of very adequate grass pastures and is indeed the finest ranching country in South Africa, west of the

High Veld. Long droughts are by no means uncommon, but the normally considerable rainfall of 12–15 inches, together with abundant underground water and a comparatively healthy climate, is in favour of prosperous ranching. The Hereros who, of the Bantu groups, follow the Ovambo in importance lived until recently as semi-nomadic cattlemen ; but in the last half-century their numbers have diminished and they have been forced into a sedentary life. Towards the south of Namaqualand the rainfall lessens rapidly and the pasture, like that of the neighbouring Kalahari, becomes inadequate for cattle, though it supports the greatest flocks of sheep in the Territory.

Much the greater part of the European population of South-West Africa is settled on the interior highland at altitudes from 4000 to 5500 feet, and the community includes a group of about 2000 Angola Boers whose request for settlement on the highlands of the Territory in order to rejoin Dutch South Africa was recently granted by the Union Government. After 1918 German settlers were allowed to remain, and, together with immigrants from the Union, have brought the European population up to 73,500 (1960).

Windhoek, the capital, at 5600 feet possesses a comparatively cool climate (there are 7 months each with a mean below 70° F.) which is reminiscent of the High Veld, though rainfall (14·4 inches) is meagre. One-fifth of the Europeans of the Territory live in this well-planned town through which passes the central line of railway. To the south the railway bifurcates, to Luderitz, the southern port, and to the Cape Province by way of Upington and De Aar Junction. Northwards the central line loops round to Usakos and Walvis Bay.

The Namib or coastal desert of South-West Africa extends for 850 miles between the Cunene and the Orange, with a width varying from 30 to 80 miles. As earlier mentioned, it is practically bare of vegetation. Yet for the reception of shipping it is by no means an altogether inhospitable coast, and possesses two of the finest natural harbours in the subcontinent—Walvis Bay and Luderitz. The former, now incorporated in South-West Africa, was formerly a British enclave of over 400 sq. miles within the German Protectorate. Its harbour, facing north, is well sheltered and deep enough to allow large vessels to go alongside. Very probably its importance will increase, in spite of the decline of its whale industry. A project of a railway from Southern Rhodesia across the northern part of Bechuanaland to link with the Walvis-Usakos line has been seriously contemplated and would, if realized, offer the advantage of a four days' shorter journey than at present between England and Southern Rhodesia. The successful inauguration in 1931 of the Benguella Railway (between Lobito Bay and the Katanga Province of the Belgian Congo) and the world-wide depression in trade have caused a re-consideration of the project.[1]

The settlement at Luderitz, formerly known to the Portuguese as Angra Pequena, has grown in importance by the discovery of diamonds in its neighbourhood. This district of the Namib is known to be one of the richest alluvial sources of diamonds in Africa, and in 1962 the output of precious stones in the coastal belt was 943,000 carats.

In 1949, wide changes were made in the constitutional position of the Territory, which now elects its own Legislative Assembly and sends representatives to the Union House of Assembly. Since then, requests from South Africa for the incorporation of the Territory within the Union have been refused by the United Nations Organization. In 1950 the International Court of Justice at the Hague confirmed that international obligations resulting from the mandate were still incumbent on the Union, and that South Africa was not competent to modify the international status of the Territory without the consent of the United Nations.

The Plateau of Southern Rhodesia

The region, corresponding approximately in its limits to the Colony of Southern Rhodesia, is essentially an ' island ' of High Veld, generally from 4000 to 5000 feet above sea-level, enclosed by the Low Veld of the Zambezi and Limpopo valleys to the north and south respectively, and of Mozambique on the eastern flank. Combined, the areas below 4000 feet occupy the greater part of the Colony—a factor notably important in determining the range of White settlement : and even below 3000 feet, where conditions are tropical and unhealthy both for settlers and their stock-animals,[2] the area is considerable, probably not less than 30 per cent. of the total surface.

From the neighbourhood of Bulawayo to that of Salisbury the High Veld continues uninterruptedly, though in a belt usually not more than 50 miles wide. Then, from the environs of Salisbury there are two narrow extensions each exceeding 5000 feet— the lesser in area continues north-eastwards before sinking to the Low Veld of the Zambezi ; the other leads eastwards to the Portuguese border near which (district of Inyanga) the relief is mountainous with altitudes exceeding 8000 feet.

---

[1] The Protectorate Government of Bechuanaland has already provided a preliminary survey of possible routes that the line might follow across its Territory.

[2] The tsetse fly is prevalent in the Low Veld of the north.

River drainage is well distributed and determined by the transverse 'ridge' of the High Veld which forms an unbroken divide. To the north are the roughly parallel courses of a series of Zambezi tributaries, while southwards streams flow to the Sabi and Limpopo. The border of the High Veld appears abruptly in places as a scarp slope overlooking the Middle Veld (3000–4000 ft.) : this feature is a consequence of stream erosion and represents a stage in the cutting back of the Plateau towards its axis.

A former covering of Karroo beds has been almost entirely stripped off the higher lands, and over much the greater part of the High Veld the underlying core of Archaean schists, gneisses and granite is exposed : indeed, granite occupies nearly 50 per cent of the area of the Colony and is especially well developed towards the east. The Karroo system is best represented on the Low Veld near to the Zambezi, Limpopo and Sabi. One other important series, viz. unconsolidated sands of late Cretaceous or early Tertiary age, is widely exposed in the extreme west of the Colony.

Contrary to the views of Marbut (set forth on an earlier page), the Geological Survey officers of Southern Rhodesia believe geological character to be of primary consequence in determining the type of soil in a given locality, and both climate and vegetation of secondary account only in this respect. They admit, however, that fertile 'black vlei' soils, belonging to the same group as the chernozem of the Transvaal Low Veld, are discovered overlying practically every geological formation represented in the Colony.

Overlying much of the granite is a sandy detritus, developed *in silu*, and the most representative soil of the Colony. As it receives an adequate rainfall it is agriculturally important and much of the maize crop is produced from it. The ancient schists occupying much of the High Veld supply dark-red loams whose fertility is indicated by their very large contribution to the maize production of the Colony. Between Bulawayo and Salisbury the main line of railway traverses the loams for much the greater part of the way, so that with this advantage of transport it is not surprising that the districts of Bulawayo, Gwelo, Gatooma, Hartley and Salisbury are prominent in agricultural output. On the Karroo beds of the Low Veld soils vary greatly, both in texture and fertility, but the districts concerned have the serious disadvantage of unhealthy conditions in summer, together with isolation from modern means of transport, although the extension of motor services is steadily improving the position ; so that the Low Veld plays an almost insignificant part in the production of commercial crops and is mainly reserved to the subsistence agriculture of Natives. The unconsolidated sands of the western district (within the basin of the Gwai River and westwards to the frontier) are generally sterile, and as, in addition, their porosity promotes surface aridity, they are left uncultivated : the region, though on the Middle Veld, is outside the zone of White settlement.[1] There is, however, considerable bush and tree growth, especially towards the Gwai River where the rainfall exceeds 25 inches.

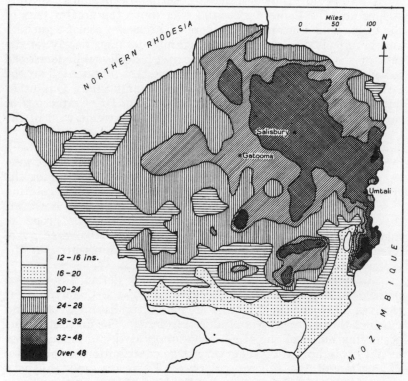

FIG. 27.—Southern Rhodesia : Average Annual Rainfall

On the High Veld, where European settlement is concentrated and where agricultural practice is most advanced, rainfall is usually reliable and adequate for a variety of tropical and warm temperate crops, without the necessity for irrigation ; so that the region has a marked advantage over the High Veld of the

[1] European settlement occurs only at small stations along the railway to Wankie and the Victoria Falls.

Transvaal, though it must be remembered that the days on which rain occurs are together less than one quarter of the year (e.g. Salisbury, 87 days). Irrigation on a really large scale is lacking, so that crops, such as citrus fruits, that require water during Rhodesia's long, dry season, are produced only on a small scale. An important irrigation achievement is the reservoir (with its distributing canals) on the Mazoe River, about 30 miles north of Salisbury.

The High Veld of Matabeleland is not so well endowed with rains as is Mashonaland,[1] and the south-west of the colony is even drier. Yet here there are good prospects for producing grain, dairy produce and beef with the diverted waters of the Sabi River. It is hoped to double the country's output of crops when this region enters full production.

The emphasis on particular phases of agriculture changes from one district to another in correspondence with the rainfall trend (Fig. 27), so that around Bulawayo (Matabeleland), where the rainfall is not only lower but also more precarious than on the High Veld, ranching displaces cropping in first importance. Usually only areas with 25 inches or more are arable. Away from the High Veld there is a falling off in precipitation both towards the Limpopo and towards the Zambezi, especially towards the former, in the vicinity of which there is less than 15 inches. Much of the southern Low Veld is free from tsetse fly, and ranching has been justified by profitable results.[2]

Commercial development in Southern Rhodesia is a very recent phase that began in the decade 1880–90 with the grant by the ' king ' of the Matabele—whose kraal lay close to the site of the future Bulawayo—of a mining concession to a group of gold prospectors. Almost immediately afterwards, in 1889, the British South Africa Company received its Charter for land development and administration in both Northern and Southern Rhodesia, and it remained in effect until 1923.

The attraction of farming on land richer than the High Veld of the Transvaal encouraged parties of Boers to cross the Limpopo,[3] but the earliest immigrants down to 1900 were mainly intent on mineral prospecting. Railway construction was an

[1] The terms ' Matabeleland ' and ' Mashonaland ' are passing out of use. They were the two ' native provinces ' incorporated in the Colony at the close of last century and, respectively, its western and eastern districts. The Mashonas are not a homogeneous group and include most of the Bantu of Southern Rhodesia who are not of Matabele (i.e. Zulu) stock.

[2] There are 150,000 head of cattle in two European-owned ranches of the Limpopo and Sabi Low Veld.

[3] The Dutch immigrants settled mainly in the Melsetter district.

obvious necessity and was quickly undertaken, so that as early as
1893 the extension of the line from Mafeking to Buluwayo and
of that from Salisbury—the earliest European settlement—to the
coast at Beira were proceeding energetically, thereby assuring
for the Territory outlets to the coast in two directions.[1]

The extraction of gold, though easily the most important
mining industry, has no local concentration as in the Transvaal :
moreover, the Colony is losing, relatively to other gold-producing
countries, in its output of the precious metal. Occurrences of
the ore are associated with the ancient schists and granites and
are widespread throughout the central zone, production being
greatest on the High Veld, where main line rail transport is near
at hand. The output has fallen recently, from 790,000 fine oz.
in 1939 to 566,000 fine oz. in 1963, and tobacco has now replaced
gold as the chief export. Of a wide variety of other minerals
chrome ore, asbestos and coal have attained real significance in
the life of the country. The coal seams are contained in the
Karroo beds of the Low Veld—of Northern Matabeleland particularly—so that they are not easily accessible from the main
centres of European settlement. Actually, the only coal mine that
produces is at Wankie, on the railway between Bulawayo and
Livingstone (N. Rhodesia), but its present output, little more
than a million tons annually, could be increased in the event of
an expansion of industry.

Agriculture now dominates the economic life of the Colony;
but although a wide variety of tropical and sub-tropical crops find
here favourable conditions of soil and climate, abundant output
is limited to two commodities— maize and tobacco—which succeed on the High Veld where the majority of the European
farm-steads are to be found. It was inevitable in the case of a
'young' territory that attention should first be confined to crops
requiring little skilled labour and small capital outlay ; so maize
became the pioneer crop—and is still the essential staple of
agriculture. This cereal produces well even on indifferent soils
where the conditions of temperature and rainfall are satisfactory, as they are in Mashonaland. No attention to the plant
is necessary during the growing season, which is one of the
reasons for its popularity with the Natives, not only of the Colony
but of South and East Africa generally.

Neither the Matabele nor the Mashona could be expected to
show, in early colonial days, farming skill comparable, shall we
say, to that of the Negro population of the Southern States
of the U.S.A. The Mashona have, however, acquired in very

[1] By rail Buluwayo is 2032 miles from Cape Town ; Salisbury is 374
miles from Beira.

short time reasonable aptitude in tending the tobacco plants on European farms. It should be realized that in Southern Rhodesia, as in other parts of South Africa, the Native plays an essential, if little acknowledged, part in the production of both agricultural and mineral wealth. He is not encouraged to compete with the European farmer-settler, but there would be no farming or mining without him, for it is he, and he exclusively, who provides manual labour. In 1964, there were over 630,000 Natives in European employment, although one-half originated outside the Colony, and came in from Nyasaland, Northern Rhodesia, and Portuguese territory.

Southern Rhodesia now imports maize, although until recently there was a regular surplus for export. This change is partly due to the rapid expansion of the local industries, partly to the increase in immigration, and above all to the change in the last decade from monoculture to mixed farming. Efforts are now being made to increase maize production. It is the staple diet for the majority of Natives, whilst as a fodder crop it has great significance. Production per acre is low on the average, even in the case of European farms, but at least as high as in the 'maize triangle' of the High Veld of the Union.[1]

Very few European farmers depend entirely on maize. Mixed farming is general and tobacco is the usual companion crop, and there are cattle on most farms. Tobacco is mainly of Virginian variety and in recent years the export of the leaf has increased rapidly, so that Southern Rhodesia is now one of the world's principal producers. The industry was long hampered by the lack of an organized system of sale, and growers often found the market glutted. This was remedied by the constitution, in 1936, of the Southern Rhodesian Tobacco Marketing Board, which controls production, grading, sale and marketing, and the spectacular prosperity of the industry dates from then.[2] Cotton, for long an experimental crop, is now an important product. Sufficient is grown to supply local factories, and a little is exported. It fits with great advantage into rotations with maize and tobacco. Cotton output from the farms of Africans, which was insignificant as late as 1946–47, was double that from European farms in 1949–50.

The size of individual farms is tending to diminish below the former unwieldy acreage of the average European holding. Farms of 6000 acres and over—apart altogether from ranches— were common before 1914, but the modern settler of the small

---

[1] In Southern Rhodesia, on European farms the average is 5 bags (each of 200 lb.) to the acre.

[2] The tobacco production of Southern Rhodesia grew from 26·7 million lb. in 1937–38 to 181·0 million lb. in 1962–63.

13

capitalist class [1] finds that a holding of 1000 acres or less is best suited to his capacity and to his range of production.

Matabeleland is the cattle country of the Colony, though stock is also of big, if secondary, importance in Mashonaland. Rather more than half the total cattle is owned by the Bantu who number more than 3,600,000, and their stock is entirely native and unimproved. European and especially English breeds[2] have been introduced by the White settlers, mainly for crossing with the hardy native cattle of rather indifferent quality that still forms the basis of their herds.

Of critical importance in the affairs of Rhodesia is the apportionment of land between the Natives and the settlers, and in 1964, over 20 million acres of Tribal Trust Land were set aside entirely for African occupation.

Apart from the distribution of lands under European ownership or lease, it is important to note the occupational character of the White population and the comparative importance of the main centres of urban life. The number of Europeans in 1964 was about 217,000, ten times the number in the period prior to the First World War.[3] In the case of a Colony mainly dependent upon agriculture it is rather surprising to find that only about one-quarter of the White residents are farmers and the dependents of farmers ; on the other hand, a large proportion of the total European population represents temporary residents, notably officials and merchants. The large proportion of urban population is to be noted. Despite the fact that no centre is larger in number of inhabitants than an English market town of average size,[4] Bulawayo and Salisbury have between them over one-half of the total White population of the Colony.[5]

The Mineral Wealth of the Union of South Africa

As the Union supplies more than 50 per cent of the world's annual output of gold, this metal is of primary consequence in

[1] The normal initial capital of a Rhodesian settler is not less than £2000.

[2] For beef, Herefords and Shorthorns are most in favour, whilst Frieslands are the chief dairy breed introduced.

[3] Of the Europeans about 96 per cent are of British origin.

[4] South and East African towns established by Europeans tend to be very extensive in area having regard to their populations. When land was cheap urban settlement, while taking into account the need for a focus, was able to proceed with generous town-planning ; and the extensive use of motor transport overcomes the disadvantage of outlying suburban residence.

[5] In 1962 the estimated populations of these towns were—Bulawayo, total 211,000 (Europeans 50,000) ; Salisbury (the capital), total 313,000 (Europeans 91,000).

the commercial life of the leading State of South Africa and temporarily overshadows a wide variety of minerals, some of them of great potential significance.

The resources are mainly concentrated in the east-central districts of the Union, with the entire production of gold and tin coming from the Transvaal, the diamond output mainly from the Transvaal and Griqualand West, and workable coal seams confined to the Transvaal and Natal. The obvious eminence of the Transvaal is increased by its rich stores of platinum and iron. The rural character of the Free State is likely to be transformed since the discovery (1946) of gold at Odendaalsrust, where eight companies are prospecting.

The Witwatersrand Gold-Field

Of the gold-bearing conglomerates that are associated with sediments of the Witwatersrand (Pre-Cape) series by far the most

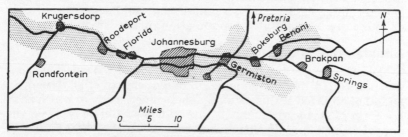

FIG. 28.—The Rand Industrial Zone
(The principal areas of gold-mining are shown by stippling. Railways also are shown)

lucrative are those of the Main Reef group, popularly known as the 'banket'.[1] The latter is from 3 to 10 feet in thickness and is overlaid by quartzites which, in the central part of the Rand, are about 3000 feet deep. Mining occurs throughout an almost continuous zone 70 miles in extent, east and west of Johannesburg, at depths varying greatly and reaching 7700 feet in the Village Deep Mine [2] south of the City.

The peak of gold production in the Rand was reached in 1941–42. After that a steady decline set in.[3] This has been arrested, however, since 1949, when devaluation of South African currency increased the sterling value of gold, thus bringing large

[1] A Dutch name given to an almond sweet-meat that the conglomerate is supposed to resemble.
[2] Claimed to be the world's deepest mine.
[3] There is great hope that the opening of new mines on the Far East Rand, especially near Springs, will counterbalance the exhaustion of old mines on the West and Central Rand.

quantities of low grade ore back into the payable reserves. Economic exploitation of these ores of the banket series has also been aided by improved mechanical methods and labour organization, the proximity of coal deposits, absence of heavy pumping charges, and a good water supply.[1]

So far the economic structure of the Union has been supported on gold mainly, and the falling-off in output that is anticipated suggests an insecurity of basis. New supports to the structure—both agricultural and industrial—are being slowly built, but they may not be sufficiently strong to bear the weight of the edifice in the event of an early exhaustion of the precious metal. That is the critical economic problem confronting the Union to-day.

In the early days of mining the industry was developed entirely by European capital and was manned by European technicians and miners,[2] many of them Cornishmen : so that by the Dutch agricultural community it was inevitably regarded as an alien influence in their simple national life. This attitude has almost entirely disappeared as it is realized that gold supports directly or indirectly one-half of the population of the Union.

Alluvial and Mine Diamonds

During late Cretaceous times the plateau of the sub-continent was penetrated by basaltic pipes, a consequence of crustal disturbance that occurred at this period. These pipes, many of which have the form of steep-sided funnels, are widely scattered between the Cape Province and the northern part of Tanganyika Territory, and some are diamond-bearing. The Union includes the richest, notably those of Kimberley and the Premier Mine near Pretoria, though the best-known pipe of Kimberley, by far the most lucrative ever discovered, was worked out and abandoned in 1921.

Until two decades ago mine diamonds provided the bulk of the output, but since 1927 the production from alluvial sources has risen in a phenomenal way with the discovery and opening of new ' fields ' in Namaqualand (Cape) where the State is owner, and in the Lichtenburg District of the South-Western Transvaal. Within a year of the discovery of the alluvial deposits in the valleys of the Vaal and Harts Rivers there were 140,000 Europeans and Natives engaged in the search for treasure. When, in 1928, exploitation of the Lichtenburg field was at its height the total

---

[1] It is thought that in the next few years a rise in working costs will hamper the output from low-grade ores, but the production of the new Orange Free State and Western Transvaal fields may counterbalance this.

[2] A White miner in South Africa is, irrespective of the nature of the mine, an overseer of Native labour and has a social and economic status superior to that of a miner in Europe.

production of diamonds for that year from all sources in the Union reached the enormous sum of 17 million sterling, a figure that had never been approached in any previous year or in any other country. The competition of the more easily-won alluvial supplies, and their over-production in relation to world demand, have hit both Kimberley and the Premier Mine at Pretoria severely. When, ultimately, mining at Kimberley is abandoned it seems as if the town is bound to decline to relative insignificance, for it has not acquired any alternative function during its brief history. Founded in 1870, it had by 1911 risen to the rank of sixth city in South Africa, but, after many fluctuations, its population was less than 56,000 in 1946. Of late the Belgian Congo and Angola have displaced South Africa from first place in diamond output. The Chikapa district is now the centre of alluvial mining in Africa, but Kimberley remains the organizing centre of the diamond industry, not of the Union only but of Africa as a whole.

Coal

Although there is little available space to allot to other minerals of actual or potential importance, such as copper, platinum, iron and tin, an exception must be made in the case of coal as it is the source of heat and power.[1]

Taking into account actual consumption and prospective requirements the Union is amply supplied, the estimates of the reserves reaching almost astronomical figures. The coal measures of the Karroo system lie nearly horizontally and easily accessible to mining. Most of the coal is bituminous, though the Natal fields contain some anthracite as well.

Coal-Fields of the High Veld

The Transvaal is known to possess vast resources in three or four different regions,[2] but the only seams at present worked are those of the south, i.e. of the High Veld, where coal extends beyond the provincial boundary into the Free State. About 40 per cent. of the annual output of the Union, which exceeds 49 million tons, is obtained from the Witbank field close to—within 80 miles—and to the east-north-east of Johannesburg. The Witbank product is good steam coal but is not suitable for coking purposes. The seams with an average aggregate thickness

[1] Petroleum and sources of abundant hydro-electric power are absent from South Africa.

[2] In addition to the High Veld—the Bush Veld, Low Veld (Lebombo and Limpopo neighbourhoods) and Northern Waterberg.

of 57 feet have played an all-important part in the industrial life of the Union, and it is difficult to believe that gold production would have reached its present enormous proportions without the fortunate occurrence near by of cheap, abundant and suitable coal.[1]   Other fields of the Southern Transvaal that together make a valuable contribution to the total output of the Province are those of Ermelo, Carolina, Heidelberg and Vereeniging, the latter extending beyond the Vaal into the Free State where, however, the quality is uniformly low.

Natal Coal-Fields

In Natal the seams are usually thinner than those of the best Transvaal fields though the quality of the product is at least as high.   Four coal-bearing tracts occur within the northern half of Natal, but only two are of present consequence.   The Vryheid field produces more than half of Natal's output.   In the extreme north-west and close to the main line of railway, where it traverses the Natal terraces between Newcastle and Ladysmith, is the most extensive field, covering more than 1000 sq. miles and producing the high-grade steam coal that is transported to Durban for the bunkering of ships.   Much of Southern Zululand is underlaid by coal measures, but exploitation has hardly yet begun.

In view of the comparative rarity of accessible coal-fields in the Southern Hemisphere the output of Natal has been much stimulated by demands for bunker coal as well as by orders from southern countries with little or no supply.   The export of coal overseas really began during the First World War when European supplies were cut off and Argentina, East Africa and Madagascar had to depend increasingly upon South African coal. The very low pit-head price of the Natal product—much less than half that of Welsh coal—has given it a big advantage in competition, and Durban is much used for coaling.   At Cape Town, which is about 1000 miles from the nearest up-country field, the price is high, for South African standards, and Table Bay is not so commonly used for bunkering as Port Natal (Durban).   It must be noted, however, that even in Natal there is no coal-mining less than 200 miles from the coast and that the costs of railage are high.

Other Minerals of Considerable Output

Copper is the metal longest mined on a large scale in South Africa.   Two districts—Little Namaqualand and Zoutpansberg

---

[1] At the pit-head the price, before 1939, was about 5s. per ton, a low figure only made possible by very cheap native labour.

(Messina Mine) of the Northern Transvaal—have been most productive, though the mines of the former have been almost exhausted. Of iron the Union has considerable reserves of high-grade and a vast resource of medium-quality ore. Both occur mainly in the Transvaal, and are being increasingly worked by the Iron and Steel Industrial Corporation which has its headquarters at Pretoria. Recently also the magnitude of the platinum resources of the Union, particularly of the Transvaal, has been proved, and South Africa is the world's leading producer of osmiridium : whilst the discovery of manganese at Postmasburg in 1922 led to a considerable new mining industry (1,491,000 tons in 1963).

AGRICULTURE IN THE UNION OF SOUTH AFRICA

The Expansion of Farming Settlement

(a) ' Mediterranean ' Husbandry at the Cape

The earliest agriculture practised by the Dutch outside the gardens of Cape Town was on the eastern slopes of the Cape Peninsula. At Rondebosch the first wheat was grown, and near by the vine was planted at Wynberg. By 1680 adventurous farmers had crossed the sterile Cape Flats and were tilling the land around Stellenbosch, on the western side of the Drakenstein Mountains, from which wheat and vine farming spread northwards down the valley of the Great Berg River towards Tulbagh. More production was harvested than the re-victualling station of the Netherlands East India Company required, so that, even earlier than 1690, wine and wheat were exported to Batavia, the principal depôt of the Company. Of the 700 Europeans at the Cape in 1682—thirty years after the first settlement—more than half lived outside Cape Town and represented the pioneers of the farming colony. Before the close of the century Huguenots, some two or three hundred in number, were granted land on the western side of the Drakenstein Mountains, particularly at Fransche Hoek (the ' French Corner '), but they were quickly absorbed into the Dutch community and lost even their identity of language.

Although the vine was introduced from France before the arrival of the Huguenots, the latter, by virtue of their special skill in viticulture, were mainly responsible for fostering this side of farming. To-day the vine is the feature of Cape agriculture that distinguishes the region from every other in South Africa. Wheat and tobacco, also staples at the Cape, are grown with considerable success in other parts also, but the vine is strictly limited to the occurrence of ' winter rainfall '. The manufacture of brandy was included in the arts of the Huguenots, for many of these settlers came from the Charente region of France which still produces the brandies of highest reputation. In the Paarl and Stellenbosch Districts the vine dominated agriculture from the beginning, as it does to-day, whilst other parts which have retained a similar specialization include Worcester and Malmesbury,[1] as well as the Cape Peninsula itself.

Viticulture developed normally, though without contributing very seriously to the export trade of South Africa, until 1886,

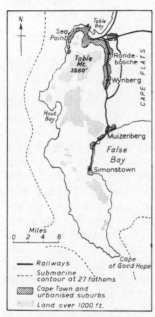

when the phylloxera pest invaded the Cape, after ravaging the vineyards of the Mediterranean, and completely destroyed grape cultivation. The industry revived, however, a few years later when immune American vines were imported. Within recent time the exports of Cape wines have strengthened, but the quite groundless prejudice against all but European vintages still remains in Great Britain, the chief market for South African products, in spite of the commercial campaign for the stimulation of trade within the Empire. Wine production is measured in many millions of gallons, but, large as the output is, it has not increased greatly in the last 20 years, indicating that all available land suited to the vine is being utilized.

When, simultaneously with the beginnings of farming, slaves, chiefly from the East Indies, were imported for the heavy field work, the evil tradition that the White man in South Africa is exempt from laborious work was permitted to take root : it has increased in strength, so that to-day the settler whether he be Dutch or British does not fulfil one of the main tests of colonization—wherein he differs from the Australian or Canadian who is independent of labour provided by an alien race.

FIG. 29.—The Cape Peninsula

(b) The Pastoral Phase

From the neighbourhood of Tulbagh settlement proceeded mainly down the Breede River valley, towards the south-east, for it was obvious to the Boers that, north of Tulbagh as well

[1] Only in certain parts of Malmesbury where, as a whole, wheat predominates.

as eastwards on the Karroo, rainfall quickly diminished, becoming too small for farming. As it was, the Breede valley was found to be drier than the land west of the Drakenstein Mountains [1] : indeed, the change in the basis of farming, from fairly intensive cultivation to stock-rearing, that became pronounced, away from the district of Cape Town, in the eighteenth century, had its origin in the climatic environment of the Breede valley.

By 1746 Swellendam, more than 120 miles from Cape Town, was recognized by the Cape Governor as the centre of a local government area that stretched as far as the farming outposts near Mossel Bay. As the colonists increased their distance from the port which was the only market for their agricultural produce the difficulties of transport, so far as marketing were concerned, became insuperable. Consequently, increasing attention to stock, both cattle and sheep, which provided their own transport, was inevitable even in districts where cultivation was rendered possible by the inherent physical conditions. So grew up a semi-nomadic society in response to the seasonal movement of herds from the pasture grounds to the main centres of European settlement at the Cape, where cattle pasture was rare. Stock farms of the widely scattered Trek-Boers, the typical colonists of eighteenth-century South Africa, were of vast extent—usually from 6000 to 10,000 acres—and the attraction of large individual holdings persisted after the Great Trek when the comparatively rich grass-lands of the High Veld were occupied, though in this region such extensive farms were unnecessary.

An English traveller who was at the Cape in 1801 classified the colonists as (a) burghers of Cape Town, (b) vine growers, (c) grain farmers, (d) pastoralists. Even as late as this there was practically no cultivation north of Malmesbury and east of a line drawn southwards from Tulbagh along the crest of the Drakenstein and Hottentots Holland Mountains.

About the beginning of the nineteenth century, just before English and Scottish immigration began, the Great Fish River which flows to the sea between Port Elizabeth and East London was the eastern limit of the Dutch colony. On the north no frontier was drawn and from the neighbourhood of Graaff Reinet Boers occasionally trekked across the Great Escarpment (Sneeuwbergen) having outflanked the Great Karroo on its eastern side ; though there was no systematic settlement of the High Veld until the Great Trek of 1836. No doubt the Dutch would have pushed on across the Great Fish River—for the promise of richer

---

[1] The mean annual rainfall at representative stations in the Breede valley is shown by Worcester, 12·3 inches; and Robertson, 12·5 inches.

cattle pasture was very attractive—but for the south-westward advance of the Bantu, with whom for the first time the Dutch came into contact in 1778.

A convenient point has been reached at which to introduce brief reference to the two main pastoral industries of the Union.

Native sheep acquired by barter from Hottentots in the early Dutch phase were poor in wool and meat, and the Netherlands Company from 1654 onwards introduced ewes and rams from Holland for crossing with the African stock. At the beginning of the nineteenth century the Spanish merino was proved to be well adapted to South African conditions, and, from about 1810 onwards, the export of merino wool, chiefly to England, advanced rapidly. When the Great Trek opened up the High Veld to pastoral farming the merino was introduced there; and the Southern Transvaal and Free State have important crops of wool to-day, though surpassed in output by the Cape Province [1] whose western district, apart from the Cape 'corner', is suited to little more than sheep and goat farms. With the increasing competition of great wool-exporting countries,[2] such as Australia and the Argentine, an improvement in the quality of the South African product has been needed in order to satisfy the requirements of manufacturing interests in Western Europe.

'Afrikander' cattle, the basis of practically all beef and dairy stock in the Union and Southern Rhodesia to-day, is a distinct breed which evolved from the native variety in the eighteenth century as a result of selection—primarily for draught purposes—undertaken by the colonists. Frieslands were imported during the same century especially for the purpose of improving the milking qualities of the 'Afrikanders', whilst throughout the British colonial phase Ayrshires, Jerseys and other valuable breeds were introduced.[3] So long has the process of improvement continued in the Western Cape Province that nowadays the 'Afrikander' characteristics are largely eliminated in this area. On the other hand, in the Eastern Cape Province and Natal, where the Bantu population is denser than elsewhere in the Union, the cattle are largely unimproved, though on European farms the crossing of the 'Afrikanders' with Shorthorns is common. In a recent year the number of cattle in the Union exceeded eleven millions, and their distribution showed the

---

[1] The wool output of the Cape Province is approximately equal to that of the other three Provinces combined.

[2] In 1928 the output of wool was about equal to that of New Zealand, though by 1964 it was only half as great.

[3] Under the Ocean Mail Contract of 1912 pedigree cattle are conveyed to South Africa free of freight charges : the number imported as a result of this agreement was, down to the end of 1923, about 3400.

prominence of the richer grass-lands of the High Veld and Middle Veld, in the Transvaal and Natal respectively.

Down to the time of the First World War South Africa was unable to supply sufficient beef of satisfactory quality for the demands of the home market ; but during the war period, forced to rely more on its own resources, the country became and has remained self-sufficient in this respect, as also in dairy production. The dearth of grass during winter is common throughout the Provinces and has necessitated considerable attention to fodder crops, amongst which maize and lucerne are prominent.

(c) The Modern Agricultural Phase

During the nineteenth century two crops of outstanding importance—as later proved to be the case—were introduced to South Africa, namely maize and sugar-cane. The planting of these crops, production of which was not considerable until the last quarter of the century, may be taken to mark the passing of the essentially pastoral phase, in which wool supplied the only important export, and its replacement by an agricultural system based on a wide variety of crops. Some crops were new, like those above-mentioned; others were of old interest, such as wheat and the vine, production of which proceeded on a scale never before attained. The trend of agriculture from 1870 down to the time of the First World War was almost entirely obscured by the overwhelming significance attached to the mining of gold and diamonds ; but nowadays, as the menace to economic security of too great a dependence on precious minerals —already threatened with exhaustion—is being realized, the scientific fostering of agriculture is widely believed to be a sheer national necessity.[1]

Factors that are likely to continue for long to hinder the expansion of agriculture in the Union may be summarized as :

(a) the aridity of the West ;

(b) the generally poor quality of soils, though there are notable exceptions that have been mentioned ;

(c) the backward state of farming in the ' back-veld ' areas— which applies not only to the Natives and Cape Coloured but also to many of the Dutch who are out of touch with modern ideas ;

(d) the slow but steady drift of rural population to the towns;

(e) the great distance separating South African produce from its chief markets, which are in Europe (especially Great

[1] At present only about 5 or 6 per cent of the farm-land of the Union is cultivated.

Britain) ; a disadvantage that is, however, partly offset by the early appearance of South African fruit in
Europe before Mediterranean production has ripened.

In very recent years only has it been possible to begin to
estimate the resources of the country as a whole and to proceed
with development on an ordered plan, by means of which each
region will be able to make its distinctive contribution to the
national wealth, through specialization in those forms of agricul-

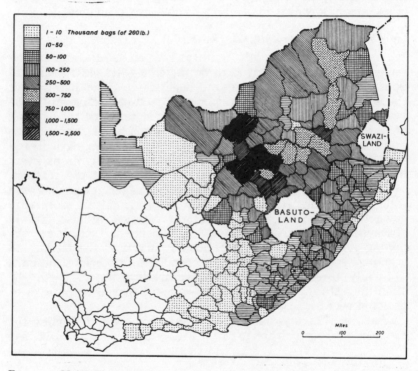

FIG. 30.—Maize Production in the Union, by districts (Census year 1947–48).

ture, mining or manufacturing industry for which it is best fitted
in view of both local and external geographical conditions.

Prior to the arrival of the British settlers at Algoa Bay in
1820, maize—known always in South Africa as 'mealies'— was
practically unknown in Cape Colony,[1] and it was not until after

[1] Maize or Indian corn is a native of America. In the U.S.A., the
land of greatest output, it is known simply as 'corn'.

1880 that production was undertaken on an appreciable scale. The principal maize lands are, as we have seen, those that were occupied in the Great Trek of 1836, namely the High Veld, and the limits of most intensive farming within the ' maize triangle ' have been indicated. ' Mealies ' is essentially a summer-rainfall crop, and in consequence it does not succeed in the South-Western Cape where the Dutch farmers have, after unfortunate experience, come to realize the unsuitability of the local climate.

At first the cereal was grown for human food and became, as it remains, the staple of the Natives' diet : on the other hand, it is a minor item of the Europeans' diet, except in cases of poverty when it is preferred to wheat on account of its cheapness. There is a constant increase in the amount of maize used as cattle food, but there remains for export a large annual surplus of which Britain takes the greater part. Wool and maize, the staples of South African farming, continue to dominate the list of agricultural exports, and as they are mainly the products of Dutch farming it follows that the Boers tend to give their political support to the party whose economic policy promises an expansion in the export trade of these commodities.

In the ' maize triangle ', responsible for about 60 per cent of total production, the crop is almost entirely confined to European farms and much of it is intended for export : in contrast, of the remainder of the Union's output about one-half is grown in the Native Reserves of the Transkei and Zululand, where there is no appreciable surplus for export.

Before maize was introduced into South Africa the Bantu subsisted largely on ' kaffir corn ', a type of grain sorghum that is indigenous to Africa. Very little attention to it has been paid by European cultivators, but its capacity for withstanding long drought renders it much more suited than maize to the environment of the western half of the Union where the rainfall is less than 20 inches. As maize is derived ultimately from America it was fitting that kaffir corn should provide the ' exchange crop ' : it has been introduced into the arid south-western States of the U.S.A., where production now exceeds that of South Africa.

Sugar-cane—a grass of Southern Asiatic origin requiring tropical conditions of temperature and a well-distributed rainfall of not less than 35 inches—was tried, about the middle of last century, on the Natal coastal plain, the only part of British South Africa where suitable conditions prevail. After 1860 cultivation expanded fairly regularly and rapidly, the first districts concerned being close to Durban. The labour in the early years was provided by Indians (chiefly Tamils) many of whom, after their period of indentured service, elected to stay in Natal, though not as plantation labour. From 1911 onwards restrictions on Indian immigration have been rigidly maintained and, in consequence, there are to-day very few Asiatics employed on the plantations and in the sugar mills. They have been replaced by Bantu labour drawn both from Natal and from the neighbouring Provinces and Protectorates. This has not been so, however, in the case of the Natal tea industry whose progress has been completely arrested since the ban on Indian immigrants.

In the early phase of the sugar industry the chief stimulus to production was provided by the phenomenal growth of European population in the mining towns of the Rand. By means of tariffs the expanding Union market has been reserved to the Natal product in recent times, except for a brief period when, as a result of the Transvaal-Mozambique Convention of 1909, Portuguese East African sugar was admitted freely to the Transvaal. The annual output—about 1,000,000 tons of sugar in 1962—is greater than consumption within the Union ; and it is necessary to export much of the crop at world prices. There is not much possibility of considerably extending the area under cultivation except within the confined limits of Zululand, where planting began early this century.

POPULATION DISTRIBUTION IN ITS RELATION TO INDUSTRIAL AND COMMERCIAL DEVELOPMENT

Of the two principal White stocks in the population of the Union the Dutch have a slight preponderance of numbers, representing about 52 per cent of the European total. The distribution of British colonists includes one feature that has persisted since the early part of the nineteenth century, namely a concentration at the ports of Cape Town, Port Elizabeth, East London and Durban.

Of the ports only Cape Town has a large proportion of Dutch. This city, the second in the Union and the legislative capital, with 305,000 Europeans, is the principal passenger port through which pass travellers between Europe and all parts of the subcontinent south of the Zambezi. The Benguella Railway, which connects the Katanga Province of the Congo with the Portuguese port of Lobito Bay, is likely to divert to the latter much of the Northern and Southern Rhodesian traffic that formerly passed through Cape Town ; and the possibility of a railway between

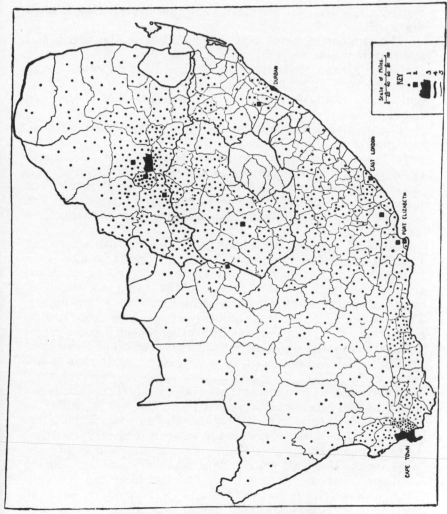

Fig. 31.—Distribution of White Population in the Union of South Africa, Basutoland, and Swaziland (By Districts)

1. 1000 persons.
2. Towns of over 7200 White inhabitants. The districts in which these towns are situated show a density of White population of less than 15 to the square mile outside the indicated towns.
3. Districts (with towns) of Johannesburg, Benoni, Germiston, Boksburg, and Springs, where the average density of White population for the districts as a whole is over 350 to the square mile. (In the district of Durban—including the town—the average density is over 500 to the square mile, and in the Cape Town districts of Cape Town, Wynberg, and Simonstown as a whole the average density is over 190 to the square mile.)

4. Provincial boundaries.
5. District boundaries.

195

Southern Rhodesia (or the Transvaal) and Walvis Bay is often discussed.

The harbour of Table Bay opens widely to the north, and shipping requires the protection of a sea-wall. In addition to its South African trade the port is visited by shipping, bound between Europe and Australia or India, which is making a leisurely and circuitous voyage and avoiding the heavy dues of the Suez Canal.

For general cargo, both landed and shipped, and for coal, bunkered or exported, Durban, more than 800 miles by sea from Cape Town, is much more important than the latter, whose agricultural and industrial hinterland is small and confined by arid lands of little commercial value and sparse population.[1] The distance from Durban to the main centres of agricultural and mining activity is little more than half that which isolates Cape Town.

Durban is situated on a land-locked lagoon, with a deep but narrow entrance, which accepts the largest vessels (of more than 27,000 tons) on the South African service. Miscellaneous industries are spreading around the shores of the lagoon, and the town, in manufacturing importance, is second only to Johannesburg. The European inhabitants, numbering 196,000 in 1960, include a majority who are intensely British in sentiment ; and a recent political movement whose object was the secession of Natal from the Union had its head-quarters at Port Natal, as Durban is still occasionally known.

Among the other seaports that of Algoa Bay (Port Elizabeth), about half-way between Cape Town and Durban, is easily the most considerable, though its natural facilities for shipping are poor. Until recently it was merely an open roadstead, like East London, but harbour construction is proceeding and will enable large vessels to go alongside. Port Elizabeth has been chosen as the principal centre of the Union for assembling and distributing motor vehicles imported from Europe and North America : for this undertaking it was preferred to Cape Town because of its closer proximity to the ' centre of gravity ' of European population in the Union.

The big urban concentration of the Rand,[2] including Johannesburg and its satellite towns (extending from Krugersdorp to

---

[1] Apart from coal the total cargoes handled at Durban and Cape Town respectively were, in 1928–9, 5,222,000 tons and 1,697,000 tons. Coal bunkered and coal exported at Durban totalled 2,600,000 metric tons ; at Cape Town, 267,000 metric tons.

[2] In 1960 the European populations of the largest Rand towns were—Johannesburg, 413,000 ; Germiston, 86,000 ; Benoni, 42,000 ; Boksburg, 27,000 ; Krugersdorp, 30,000 ; Roodepoort, 41,000.

Springs), contains one-sixth of the Europeans of the Union,[1] or one-half of those of the Transvaal. Except in the years immediately succeeding the Second World War, immigration from Great Britain has practically ceased, and the proportion of Dutch in the population of Johannesburg, as of most towns, has steadily increased and is likely to continue to do so.[2]

The ' City of the Rand ' seems destined to develop as an industrial centre and great market even after the exhaustion of the local gold ore. It lies just within the ' maize triangle ' and is a convenient collecting and distributing centre for the varied agricultural and pastoral production of the High Veld. Near at hand, towards the north-east, is the largest production of coal in the entire continent, whilst the extensiveness of iron resources from which the city will benefit has been proved not more than 50 miles to the north. Johannesburg is much more fitted by geographical position and general importance to be the administrative capital of the Union than Pretoria, 40 miles farther north, whose claim to metropolitan rank depends largely on sentiment and tradition that recall its status as capital of the former South African Republic (now the Transvaal).

Johannesburg is the great railway node of South Africa—a result of the planning of the transport system in the last quarter of the nineteenth century, when every consideration was subordinated to the exploitation of gold. Until 1886 all railway construction was dominated by the need to reach the diamond centre of Kimberley from the coast. A line was pushed north-east from Cape Town, but there was also a competing route opened from Port Elizabeth which met the first line at De Aar Junction in 1884. Immediately the Rand was opened to mining, just two years later, strong rivalry arose as to which of two lines should first reach Johannesburg—the continuation of the Cape, De Aar, Kimberley line, or that from Port Elizabeth which left the line to De Aar, crossed the Orange River at Norvals Pont and was permitted by the Dutch Government to traverse the entire length of the Orange Free State by way of Bloemfontein, the capital. Both were completed in very short time. Before the difficult and costly line from Durban to Johannesburg, via Glencoe, was finished the Transvaal Government, desiring an outlet to the coast that should be independent of British territory, gained its objective by laying a track from Pretoria to the Mozambique border, where junction was made with the line from Delagoa Bay.

[1] The White population of the Union was (1964) 3,335,000.
[2] One reason for this is that a comparatively large family unit still represents an ideal of Dutch domestic life.

14

Engineering difficulties in railway construction were mainly limited to the zone on the seaward side of the Great Escarpment, especially the crossing of the Cape Ranges and the ascent of the Natal terraces east of the Drakensberg. Once the Upper Karroo or High Veld was reached the gradients were easy.

The lines mentioned form the main arteries of the South African Railways, and from them branch lines and motor services —more thoroughly and widely developed than in any part of Africa—have opened up new farming and mining areas or have

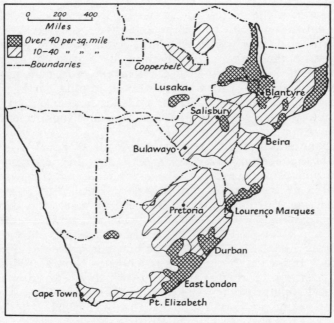

Fig. 32.—Southern Africa : Density of Population (1960)

provided necessary access to the main routes from already settled districts. There are, however, two or three gaps in the system to bridge which costs of railway construction would be heavier than the resultant traffic would be likely to justify. The relief of the coastal zone has prevented a direct link between Durban and East London : there is very roundabout communication by rail between Cape Town and Port Elizabeth, whilst Durban is isolated from the central districts of the Cape Province, except in so far as there is communication by the extremely circuitous line which swings round the north of Basutoland. Travellers between Durban and Cape Town prefer a sea voyage to the land journey.

In spite of its importance as a railway centre in relation to the South African system Johannesburg is not yet on a direct line to Central Africa : for north of Kimberley the Rhodesian and Transvaal routes bifurcate, and whilst the former is extended to the Belgian Congo, the latter ends immediately north of the Limpopo, where the Beit Bridge was completed in 1929. Within a very few years, however, it is expected that the Transvaal line north from Johannesburg and Pretoria will be connected by way of West Nicholson with Bulawayo and so with the trunk line to the north.

The Dutch population has its strength outside the largest towns. Apart from the Rand the Transvaal is almost entirely rural and of Dutch stock, whilst the Free State and the central districts of the Cape Province are other strongholds of the Boer. Natal, the most British of the Provinces in race and sentiment, has been experiencing for the last decade or so a steady penetration of Dutch stock from the Free State and the Transvaal which is likely to be more permanent than the quickly evacuated settlement that took place during the Great Trek.

The gradual migration of Dutch from certain ' back-veld ' areas to the towns, and especially to the Rand, where high rates of wages and amenities of town life are very attractive, is a significant trend. Steady depopulation of central districts of the Cape Province was noticed in the decade 1911–21 [1] and continues both there and in the Free State, providing the Union with one of its most serious socio-economic problems. Rural depopulation is a menacing tendency in a country that hopes to establish its prosperity on a secure agricultural basis.

Many of those who drift into the towns are of the ' bywoner ' class, i.e. landless Whites who, in the rural areas, are permitted to live on land owned by other Europeans though without any clearly defined rights or duties. Especially on the industrial Rand, they tend to swell the population of the slums and to deteriorate in physical and mental calibre so as to be classed as ' Poor Whites '. Although South Africans point with justifiable pride to the physical fitness of the flower of the White stock, they are perturbed by the increasing number of Poor Whites, whose existence was not generally realized before 1910 though they now represent one-tenth of the Europeans of the

---

[1] The farming land of the Cape Midlands is considered to be deteriorating, not through climatic desiccation, but as a result of erosion for which careless methods of land utilization are partly responsible (v. ' Report of Drought Investigation Commission ' Union Government, 1923).

Union, according to the findings of the Carnegie Commission which reported in 1932. In the view of the writer some factor in addition to indigency is partly responsible for their condition, which may be found to be symptomatic of the imperfect acclimatization of a North European people in a sub-tropical environment.

The ' Poor Whites ' should be clearly distinguished from the ' Cape Coloured ', a half-caste people to whom reference was made in an earlier chapter. The latter number close on one million and are mainly confined to the Western Cape Province, especially the ' winter rainfall ' region. In Cape Town they represent about 40 per cent of the inhabitants. In the Western Cape Province there are very few Bantu, and the unskilled and semi-skilled labour is largely supplied by the Cape Coloured whose opportunities for social, economic and political advancement are little better than those afforded the Bantu in the other Provinces.

The ' colour ' problem of the Union—perhaps the most conplex and critical in the world—is much aggravated by the presence of Indians, chiefly in Natal, where they number 395,000 (1960) and are occupied in market-gardening and retail trade. It was a matter for alarm to Europeans when it was discovered early this century that the Asiatics of Natal were as numerous as the Europeans ; and from 1911 onwards the White community has not ceased its unavailing efforts to repatriate the descendants of indentured labourers who were introduced by European tea and sugar planters and have come to regard South Africa as their home-land. Outside the coastal plain and north-western coal-field of Natal the only considerable number of Indians— about 20,000 in scattered groups—is to be found in the mining towns of the Rand and in Pretoria where retail trade is the main occupation of the Bombay immigrants.[1]

The ready skill of the Indian, combined with his low standard of comfort, enables him to compete with the European on favourable terms to himself in a variety of trades, and this despite many disabilities. The purchase of land by Indians, in Natal and the Transvaal, is still difficult and, until recently, illegal. Moreover, they are disfranchised, whilst socially they are regarded by Europeans as definitely inferior, no matter what their degree of refinement or attainment may be. And there is little recognition of the contribution that Indian labour made in the early stages of the economic development of Natal.

[1] The Indian trader of South Africa has not been recruited so much from descendants of Madrassi plantation-workers as from commercial communities of the North-Western Deccan.

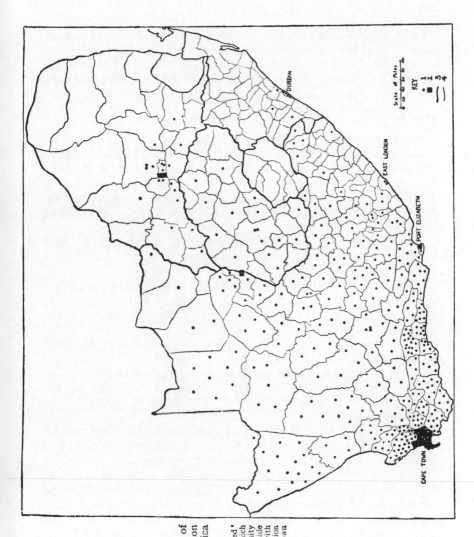

Fig. 33.—Distribution of 'Cape Coloured' Population in the Union of South Africa (By Districts)

1. 1000 persons.
2. Towns of over 7000 'Coloured' inhabitants. The districts in which these towns are situated have a density of less than 10 to the square mile outside the indicated towns. Districts (with towns) where the 'Coloured' population is over 65 to the square mile are shown in black.
3. Provincial boundaries.
4. District boundaries.

201

The Cape Malays are the only other Asiatic group of importance.   They are descended from slaves brought in by the Netherlands East India Company, and number about 12,000 in and
around Cape Town.   It is generally admitted that they represent
a valuable element in the population of the city.

The Reserves and other Native Areas

In regard to the distribution of the Bantu, who, in 1960, were
estimated to exceed 10 millions, we have to consider the situation
and extent of the Reserves and the outflow from these lands to
the areas of European settlement.   Only in one Province, namely
the Eastern Cape, is the land that is reserved exclusively for
Native occupation approximately adequate in both extent and
fertility.

The Bantu may be classified according to occupation and
condition in society, in the following way :

(1) Tribal Natives in Reserves.

(2) Those who attempt to retain their tribal allegiance but
go to the towns for brief periods of employment, in order to
obtain sufficient funds for the payment of the poll-tax and other
liabilities.

(3) Urban Natives outside tribal society and forced to adopt
a low European standard of life.

(4) Squatters or labour tenants on European farms.

The last two classes combined include a majority of the
Bantu, and the proportion that they represent is constantly on
the increase.

In the western half of the Union the Natives [1] are less numerous than the Europeans, for the eighteenth-century colonists had
expelled the Bushmen and Hottentots from the most attractive
part of the Western Cape Province and had occupied it before
the southward penetration of the Zulu-Xosa peoples.   Around
Kimberley and in the railway zone from there to the Rand the
greater density of Bantu is due to recent immigration for work
in the diamond mines and alluvial workings (of the Vaal).

In the Transvaal there is contrast between the north and
south, so far as Bantu society is concerned.   The Rand towns
have big concentrations of Natives who actually outnumber the
Europeans.   Many of the Negroes are not of local origin, and the
mine Natives include about 90,000 from Mozambique, to which
they ultimately return.   Without doubt, amongst the influences
that are working towards the disintegration of native society in
South Africa the increasing industrialization of the Rand is the
most potent.

[1] The term ' Native ' in South Africa does not include Cape Coloured.

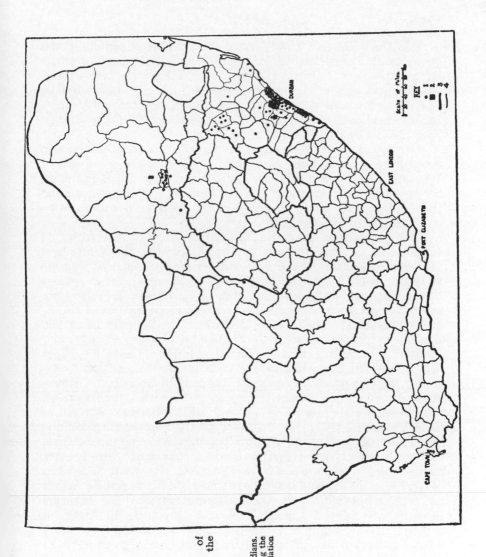

FIG. 34.—Distribution of Asiatic Population in the Union of South Africa (By Districts)

1. 1000 persons.
2. Maritzburg with 7000 Indians. In the district of Durban, including the town, the density of Indian population is 500 to the square mile.
3. Provincial boundaries.
4. District boundaries.

The Bushveld and Low Veld of the Transvaal, especially the Districts of Pietersburg, Zoutpansberg and Lydenburg, contain big groupings of Bantu. Here the Reserves are far more extensive than elsewhere in the Province, a fact that is related to climatic unsuitability from the point of view of White settlement. Land is held communally as in the small Reserves of the Orange Free State now to be mentioned.

Density of Bantu population in the Free State increases towards the east and north-east. The Reserves—those of Witzieshoek (Harrismith) and Thaba'Nchu near the Basutoland border—are together a very small proportion of the area of the Province, and the large majority of the Natives live outside as squatters or urban dwellers.[1]

The population of Natal is characterized, apart from its Indian element, by great disproportion between the White and Bantu communities, the Europeans being outnumbered by nine to one. Of over two million Natives about one-quarter occupy the twenty-one Reserves[2] of Zululand and there are also considerable native areas outside this north-eastern district of Natal. If sugar-growing is to be extended widely it can only be at the expense of the tribal areas of Zululand.

We turn to the most extensive native lands of the Union, those of the Eastern Cape Province known as the Transkeian Territories, viz. Transkei, Pondoland, Tembuland and East Griqualand, which together we shall name for convenience the Transkei. Here there are more than 75 per cent of the Bantu of the entire Cape Province. No other Province nearly approaches the Cape in the proportion of its Native population living apart from European society on reserved land. From much the greater part of the 16,000 sq. miles of the Transkei European ownership of land is excluded, and it really represents a Native State within the Union, but with a separate administration. The Transkei provides one of the comparatively rare instances in Africa of generous and enlightened treatment of the Native, a policy whose inception lies to the credit of the Cape Government in days long before Union.

Rather paradoxically, although the Transkeian system has preserved Native society from the expropriation of land and from commercial exploitation it tends to weaken the integrity of tribal groupings. The Territories are divided into twenty-seven Districts, quite irrespective of the traditional boundaries of the tribal lands of the Pondos, Tembus, Fingos and other

[1] Witzieshoek Reserve is an outpost of the lofty Basutoland Plateau and has an area of 110,000 acres.
[2] Area of the Zululand Reserves—3,882,000 acres.

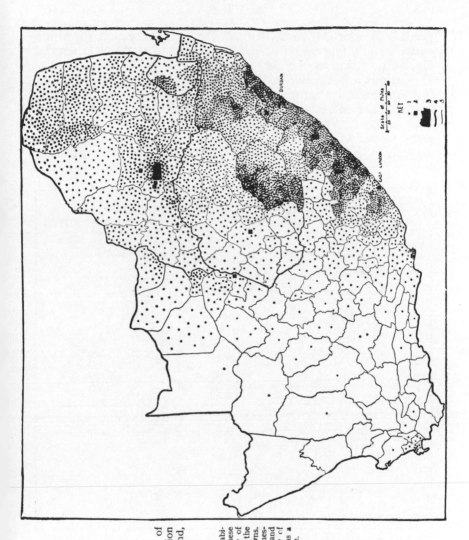

Fig. 35.—Distribution of
Bantu Population in the Union
of South Africa, Basutoland,
and Swaziland
(By Districts)

1. 1000 persons.
2. Towns of over 7000 Bantu inhabitants. The Districts in which these
towns are situated show a density of
Bantu population of less than 100 to the
square mile, outside the indicated towns.
3. Districts (with towns) of Johannesburg, Benoni, Germiston, Boksburg, and
Springs, where the average density of
Bantu population for the Districts as a
whole is over 400 to the square mile.
4. Provincial boundaries.
5. District boundaries.

groups. Herein is similarity to the French system in Africa which usually ignores tribal units and adopts artificial territorial divisions known as 'cercles'.

There is a European magistrate in each District, and Umtata, the administrative centre of the Transkei, is also the head-quarters of the Chief Magistrate. A District is divided into locations. Each of the latter divisions contains about 1000 inhabitants and a proportion of the land is set apart for individual agricultural allotments, so that the Natives are encouraged to forgo their

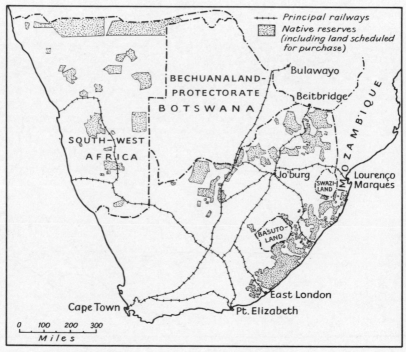

Fig. 36.—Southern Africa : Principal Railways and Native Reserves (from D. Hobart Houghton, *The South African Economy*)

allegiance to the traditional system of communal tenure. It is extremely doubtful if the Districts will serve to promote—as the former tribal units certainly did—the corporate social sense in the minds of the Natives.

Although the magistrates are responsible for administration, the more advanced Natives are encouraged to take a share in the work of government. District Councils have been set up each of which includes a small representative group of Natives with the magistrate as chairman. They are deliberative assemblies with advisory powers only, but they have considerable influence, as the Administration usually attempts to bring its policy into line with the public opinion they express. Matters relating to local government, such as public health and road construction, are their concern. Each District Council is represented on the General Council or Bunga which is a native parliament meeting annually at Umtata, though again the powers are deliberative and advisory only.

The economic prosperity of the Transkei might be assured if the Union Government would give greater care to the improvement of native husbandry. Owing to primitive methods of cultivation and to over-stocking of cattle—with its dire consequences for the condition of the pasturage—the region with its two million inhabitants is not self-supporting ; usually there is need to import maize from the High Veld. On account of their economic poverty the male Natives usually find it necessary sooner or later to leave the Transkei for temporary employment in other parts of the Union, especially the Rand whose three main sources of labour are Mozambique, the Transkei and Basutoland. Unfortunately, the steady drain on man-power tends towards the disintegration of community life.

Immediately to the west of the Kei River, in the Ciskei, there are several Native Districts interspersed amongst areas of European occupation, and for these King William's Town is the administrative centre.

Although outside the political framework of the Union so far, Basutoland and Swaziland are really two big Native Reserves whose economic—and possibly political—future, as in the case of the Transkei, is closely linked to that of the Union.

The ' Protectorate ' rule of Basutoland differs from the Transkei system mainly in its recognition and support of the traditional authority of the chiefs, who allot land according to custom and control the native courts. Furthermore, there is no enforcement of individual tenure of land in any part of the Protectorate. Neither the Basutos nor the Bechuanas desire amalgamation with the Union since it would, at best, involve the type of administration that prevails in the Transkei, with its alien institution of White officialdom.

In Swaziland rather more than one-third of the total area of 6700 sq. miles has been set aside for the exclusive use of the Natives. The greater part of the remainder is held by concession companies intent on developing the mineral (e.g. tin and gold) and agricultural (e.g. cotton) resources of the country.

On the land that is assured to them the Swazis, who are of Zulu-Xosa stock and number about 270,000 have reasonable accommodation at present, but much of their land is deteriorating rapidly, due to chronic overstocking.[1] There is very little White settlement ; the European population is about 8,000, but nearly one-half are nominal occupants only.

Land and Labour in South Africa

Competition for land between Bantu and European began in the later part of the eighteenth century when both were spreading into the virtually empty sub-continent. It is now clear that the Native Reserves are inadequate to support their present population. Almost in every case they are overcrowded, and unless the solution of the land problem is to introduce the Natives on an even larger scale than at present into the towns, some extension of the area reserved for Native occupation will be necessary. At the present time, the Native population represents about four-fifths of the Union's total, and the reserved areas only 10 per cent of its territory.

Prior to 1913 Natives in the Cape Province and Natal could acquire land by freehold or lease without any discrimination against them : but the right was withdrawn by the Natives Land Act of 1913 which applied to the Union as a whole and forbade the Bantu to purchase territory outside of existing locations and reserves, i.e. outside of 8 per cent of the area of the Union. By the terms of the Act, however, a land commission was appointed to recommend additional areas in which Natives might be permitted to purchase land to the exclusion of Europeans. The recommendation was that, in all, rather more than 13 per cent of the Union should be reserved to Native occupation with the aim of bringing about at least a partial segregation of the White and Black communities. In 1936 a more generous land policy seemed to be inaugurated by the setting up of the South African Native Trust. The latter was empowered to acquire additional land for Native settlement to bring the gross total up to 35,000,000 acres, or 75 per cent more than the area available to Natives before 1936 : but much of the additional land was already congested. It seems clear that there should be the early establishment of Native territories in at least two regions of the Union where effective White settlement is quite impracticable by reason of climatic unsuitability, viz. the

[1] Sir Alan Pim, *The Financial and Economic Situation of Swaziland,* Cmd. 4114, 1932.
    Scott, P., ' Land Policy and the Native Population of Swaziland ', *Geog. Journ.,* Vol. CXVII (1951), p. 435.

entire regions of the Low Veld and Bush Veld, of the Northern and Eastern Transvaal.

In 1949, the total number of natives employed in labour districts throughout the Union was 749,000, of whom over 100,000 came from Mozambique. The licensing of employers, execution of contracts, and inspection of working conditions are the duties of the Director of Native Labour in Johannesburg. Labour recruited from rural locations and reserves, and from territories outside the Union, is employed mostly in the mines, but also on the plantations of Natal, and in industrialized agriculture in the Transvaal.

On the farms of the Union, however, little immigrant labour is employed, and the bulk of the native workers reside on the farms. The conditions of their employment are settled by contract. For some time after 1913, the labour tenant system remained popular in large areas of the Union. Under this arrangement, a native is allowed to reside on a farm with his family, to cultivate a certain area of land, and to graze a specified number of cattle, on condition that he and such members of his family as are stated in the agreement should render service to the farmer for a specified period, either of months in the year or days in the week. This system, while well suited to the early days when land was plentiful and markets scarce, has been found recently less well adapted to modern conditions. In the Transvaal and Natal it remains fairly strong, in a modified form whereby, though he still has free time, the native receives a wage and a supply of food during his period of service. In Cape Province and the Orange Free State the system is now practically unknown. Instead, the native worker is entitled to regular cash wages and rations, and he and his family have their own dwelling on the farm, a vegetable garden, and a limited number of stock. In return, he renders continuous service throughout the year.

Although not permitted to undertake trades or professions that are classified as skilled, the Bantu have shown by rapidly-acquired proficiency that they are capable of taking a responsible part in many branches of farming and industry. As it is there is a noticeable tendency on the part of employers to engage cheap Kaffir labour for types of occupation long deemed to be the preserve of the White worker, and no legislation is able to arrest this tendency indefinitely. The increasing employment of Natives in European-controlled industry will inevitably intensify a competition from which sooner or later will arise the challenge that merit and skill—not race—should alone provide the basis of discrimination. The growing strength of such trade unions of Bantu labour as the ' African Workers' Union ' which has its head-quarters on the Rand is a very significant portent.

Though such developments are vaguely realized and their future still uncertain, it is not widely appreciated that they are the inevitable consequence of the disintegration of tribal society and of the European community's dependence on native labour.

Territorial Segregation in Southern Rhodesia

In this self-governing Colony where the beginnings of White settlement are very recent the extension of European land-ownership has not gone nearly so far as in the Union, nor are White and Black communities so much intermingled as they are farther south. Consequently, partial segregation is practicable without serious dislocation of economic interests, and it has here been carried out according to a plan that shows more apprecia-

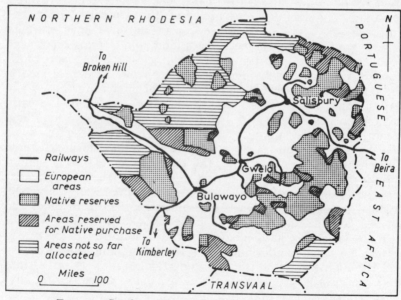

FIG. 37.—Southern Rhodesia. The Allocation of Lands
(Note that the railways keep almost entirely to the European areas.)

tion of Native requirements than any scheme of the kind yet attempted in British Africa.

Very early this century the principle was approved of reserving certain lands exclusively for Native occupation, and in these areas there was to be no interference with the Bantu system of communal tenure. Their situation was mainly confined to the Middle and Low Veld, for even as early as forty years ago practically the entire High Veld was claimed for European farming and mining. Natives already occupying the land to be reserved for Europeans became tenants of the latter ; and to-day their scattered groups, landless and with an insecure status, number about 630,000, or more than one-fifth of the Bantu of the Colony, and provide the bulk of the labour required for the various industrial and agricultural enterprises of the White community.

In order to raise the economic status of the Bantu it was decided about thirty years ago to allocate for native purchase lands, in addition to the Reserves, where the European buyers' competition would not be permitted. On the other hand, in view of the guarantees already given to European settlers the High Veld is not to be opened to native purchase. In this way territorial segregation was recommended by the Land Commission which reported in 1926. The division of territory proposed by the Commission received Government sanction and is on the following lines :

(a) There are left out of account about 18,000,000 acres considered to be generally unsuitable for human occupation at present, particularly the tsetse-infested Low Veld of the Zambezi and of the Sabi-Limpopo. Decision is postponed regarding the future of these lands.

The remainder, about 78,000,000 acres, is divided into three zones—

(b) The continuous area mainly on the High Veld already owned and partially occupied by Europeans—about 32,000,000 acres—extended to 35,600,000 acres by 1964 ;

(c) Flanking the High Veld on both sides, the discontinuous zone of the Native Reserves—established early this century—renamed Tribal Trust Land and extended to 42,000,000 acres by 1964;

(d) Attached to the Native Reserves a large number of comparatively small plots—in all about 7,500,000 acres —which are to be supplementary Reserves or ' Native Purchase Areas '. In this category but not in (c) individual tenure is introduced.

It is recommended that all Natives living, at the time of the Report, on European farms as labour tenants or squatters should be gradually moved to the ' Native Purchase Areas '. If this is to be carried out thoroughly it seems inevitable that there will be a shortage of labour available for European enterprise, as it would require a psychological revolution to induce White Rhodesia to provide field- and mine-labour from its own ranks. It will be interesting to observe how far there is Government insistence on the termination of the squatter system and on the withdrawal of all Natives to reserved lands.

Undoubtedly Southern Rhodesia is learning from the experience of the Union. The segregation scheme will certainly postpone for long the disintegration of tribal society and the consequent flooding of the European areas by a Black proletariat : and at the same time it offers opportunity for the progressive Natives to reach economic independence and to raise the standard of their agricultural production.

REFERENCES

Thanks to the University Schools of Geography in the Union geographical literature is steadily accumulating, and Professor Wellington of Johannesburg has already contributed a series of very useful papers.

Adamson, R. S., *The Vegetation of S. Africa* (Monographs of Empire Vegetation), London, 1938.

Ashton, H., *The Basuto*, London (O.U.P. for International African Institute), 1952.

Barth, P., *Suedwest-Afrika*, Leipzig, 1926.

Bennett, H. H., *Soil Erosion and Land Use in the Union*, Dept. of Agric., Pretoria, 1945.

Bews, J. W., *Grasses and Grasslands of South Africa*, Maritzburg, 1918.

Brooks, E. H., *History of Native Policy in South Africa*, Cape Town, 1924.

Buchanan, Sir G., ' Report on the Principal Harbours of the Union ', Pretoria, 1923.

Buell, R. L., *The Native Problem in Africa*, Vol. I, New York, 1928.

Camacho, B., *Moçambique : Problemas Colonias*, Lisbon, 1932.

Cambridge History of the British Empire, Vol. VIII, 1936.

Doveton, Dorothy M., *The Human Geography of Swaziland*, London, 1937.

du Toit, A. L., *The Geology of South Africa*, 2nd ed., London, 1939.

Dutton, E. A. T., *The Basuto of Basutoland*, London, 1923.

Evans, I. B. Pole-, *A Vegetation Map of S. Africa, Botanical Survey of S. Africa*, Memoir No. 15, Pretoria, 1936.

Evans, I. L., *Native Policy in Southern Africa*, Cambridge, 1934.

Evans, M., *Black and White in South-East Africa*, London, 1911.

Eveleigh, W., *South-West Africa*, London, 1915.

Fitzgerald, W., ' The Population Problem of South Africa ', *Scott. Geog. Mag.*, Vol. XLIV, 1928.

Hellmann, E. (ed.), *Handbook on Race Relations in South Africa*, London (O.U.P.), 1949.

Jennings, A. C., ' Irrigation and Water Supplies in S. Rhodesia ', *South Afr. Journ. of Sci.*, Vol. XXIV, 1927.

Junod, H. A., *The Life of a South African Tribe*, 2 vols., 1927.

King, L. C., *South African Scenery*, Edinb., 1951.

Lagden, Sir G., *The Basutos*, 2 vols., New York and London, 1909.

Leppan, H. D., *The Agricultural Development of Semi-arid Regions*, Cape Town, 1929.

The Stabilisation of South African Farming, Univ. of Pretoria, 1938.

Mackenzie, L. A., ' Report on the Kalahari Expedition, 1945 ', Pretoria, 1946.

Macmillan, W. M., *The Cape Colour Question*, London, 1927.

Complex South Africa, London, 1930.

Bantu, Boer and Briton, London, 1930.

Mair, L. P., *Native Policies in Africa*, London, 1936.
Manual of Portuguese East Africa, Naval Staff Handbook, London, 1918.
Marwick, B. A., *The Swazi*, London, 1940.
Mogg, E. H., ' The Oliphants River Irrigation Scheme ', *Africa*, Vol. XVIII, No. 3 (July, 1948), pp. 199–204.
Moolman, J. H., ' The Orange River ', *Geog. Rev.*, Vol. 36, 1946.
Plummer, F. E., and Leppan, H. D., *Rainfall and Farming in the Transvaal*, Pretoria, 1927.
' Rainfall Normals to end of 1935 ', Meteor. Office, Pretoria, 1939.
Robertson, C. L., ' The Variability of S. Rhodesian Rainfall ', *South Afr. Journ. of Sci.*, Vol. XXIV, 1927.
Rogers, A. W., *Handbook of Regional Geology* (Union of South Africa), Heidelberg, 1929.
' Report on Census of Agriculture and Pastoral Production ', Pretoria, 1917–18 et seqq.
' Report of the Drought Investigation Commission ', Union Govt., Cape Town, 1923.
' Report of the Land Commission, Southern Rhodesia ', Salisbury, 1926.
' Report on the Kalahari Reconnaissance of 1925 ', Pretoria, 1926.
' Report on the Poor White Problem in South Africa ', Carnegie Commission of Investigation, 5 Vols., 1932.
' Report, South-West Africa and its Possibilities ', Windhoek, 1925.
Sayce, R. U., ' An Ethno-Geographical Essay on Basutoland ', *Geographical Teacher*, Vol. XII.
' The Natives of Natal ', *Geog. Teacher*, Vol. XIII.
' Habitations in South Africa ', *Geog. Teacher*, Vol. XIV.
Schapera, I., *Migrant Labour and Tribal Life*, Oxford, 1947 (with reference to Bechuanaland).
Schwarz, E. H. L., *The Kalahari or Thirstland Redemption*, Cape Town, 1920.
Scott, P., ' Mineral Development in Swaziland ', *Econ. Geog.*, Vol. 26 (1950), pp. 196–213.
Stent, G. E., ' Migrancy and Urbanization in the Union of South Africa ', *Africa*, Vol. XVIII, No. 3 (July, 1948), pp. 161–83.
Teale, E., and Wilson, R., ' Physiography of Portuguese East Africa ', *Geog. Journ.*, Vols. XLV and XLVI, 1915.
Walker, E., *Historical Atlas of South Africa*, London, 1922.
Wellington, J. H., ' A new development scheme for the Okovango Delta, Northern Kalahari ', *Geog. Journ.*, Vol. CXIII, 1949.
' A physiographic regional classification of South Africa ', *South Afr. Geog. Journ.*, Vol. XXVIII, 1946.
' Land Utilization in South Africa ', *Geog. Review*, New York, 1932 (April).

Series of monographs relating to Mozambique and prepared for l'Exposition Coloniale Internationale, Paris, 1931, including ' Sol et Climat ', ' Les Indigènes ', ' L'Agriculture ', &c. (Imprimerie Nationale, Lourenço Marques, 1931).

Also the Official Year-Books of the Union and of Southern Rhodesia.

CHAPTER II

EAST AFRICA

THE Great Lakes Plateau, average elevation over 3000 feet, is a region of distinctive physique in the geography of Africa. The neighbouring ocean littoral is to be included with it, for the cultural and commercial associations with the interior highland are intimate. The political units of the region are Uganda (92,525 sq. miles), Tanzania (362,000 sq. miles) Malawi (37,596 sq. miles), Zambia (287,950 sq. miles), and the northern part of Portuguese East Africa. With the exception of the last mentioned, all these territories became self-governing between the years 1960 and 1964.

On its northern side the boundary zone of the region is clearly indicated by the existence of two basin depressions of average altitude not more than 1500–2000 feet, which, except where a narrow neck of plateau connects, detach lofty Abyssinia from the Great Lakes Plateau in Northern Uganda and South-Western Kenya. Of these depressions one is part of the broad basin of the Bahr-el-Jebel in the Sudan ; the other, culminating in Lake Rudolf, occupies the northern third of Kenya and by reason of its low elevation, aridity and sparse population is more closely associated with Eastern Somali than with the East African Plateau.

Westwards there is a comparatively abrupt contrast between the highlands of the Western Rift Valley and the Congo Basin. The delimitation of the region on this side has both geographical and ethnological justification, though such considerations were set aside by the inclusion of the Ruanda-Urundi highland within the Belgian Congo after the elimination of Germany from East Africa after the First World War.

Southwards our region marches with South Africa and goes up to the Zambezi valley. Nyasaland, in its physical character as well as in its social and commercial life, is essentially a part of the East African Plateau, but the unwieldy and very unsatisfactory unit of Zambia is not so easily allotted a

[1] Of which area 13,600 sq. miles represent lake water.

place in regional classification. The eastern lobe of Northern Rhodesia has affinities with Nyasaland and South-Western Tanganyika; but the western, with its long extension towards the heart of the continent, is Central African in situation and—in its industrial and commercial life—is more naturally grouped with the Katanga Province of the Belgian Congo. But there would be confusion to the reader if the Protectorate were to be divided in the manner suggested, and Northern Rhodesia as a whole is included in this chapter. It will not, however, be overlooked that here is a striking instance of disregard for geographical principles in frontier delimitation, which has been carried out only with the view of incorporating as much land as possible in order to forestall rival colonial Powers with similar ambitions. Once drawn, the boundary line becomes rigid and its rectification in the light of geographical and ethnic realities is likely to be increasingly opposed by vested interests.

The littoral belt with which we are concerned is mainly that of Tanganyika and Kenya, together with the neighbouring islands, especially Zanzibar. This coastal zone provides the commercial and cultural contacts between the interior Plateau and the outer world, and its alien civilization, mainly Arabian in origin, has penetrated the interior at least as far as the Great Lakes.

As a detached fragment of the East African Plateau, Madagascar is suitably included, but in respect of cultural life there is little connexion between the great island and the continent, despite its proximity—at one point not more than 200 miles distant. The civilization of Madagascar owes more to Malayan and other easterly contacts than to the Negro world near at hand.

The Lands of Trans-Zambezia

Situated far inside the inter-tropical zone and with a very small proportion of its area as high as 5000 feet, the Republic of Zambia (formerly Northern Rhodesia) has never proved as attractive to European settlement as the lands farther south. In 1939 there were still only 13,000 Europeans in the Protectorate, of whom a great many came in after the First World War. By 1962, owing to another post-war influx, the number had reached 77,000.[1] Yet there is still more land available for immigrants, without depressing the standards of native life, than in any other territory of East Africa, as indicated by the exceptionally low density of five persons to the square mile. The total population

[1] As late as 1911 there were only 1,500 Europeans resident in the Protectorate.

—about 2,577,600 (1962)—is roughly equal, numerically, to those of Rhodesia whose area is but half as great.

As in the case of neighbouring Nyasaland, agricultural progress continues to be held in check, an undoubted consequence of isolation from markets and prohibitive costs of transport. Communications are still quite inadequate, largely based as they continue to be on a single railway track, across the centre of the Protectorate, that was intended by its promoters solely as an outlet for the mineral wealth discovered at Broken Hill and Bwana Mkubwa.

The portion of the African Plateau represented by the Protectorate is a dissected platform, from 3000 to 4000 feet above sea-level, traversed by streams flowing down either side of a low divide to the Congo and Zambezi, respectively. The great Luangwa tributary of the Zambezi isolates by means of its malarious and sparsely-peopled valley, impassable during the rainy season, the extreme eastern district from the main body of the Protectorate. Eastern Luangwa—as this outlying district is known—merges with the high land of Western Nyasaland and, in respect both of its native life and of its modern economic development, is more naturally associated with Nyasaland than with the remainder of the Protectorate. Immediately to the west of the Luangwa River and parallel to its course runs the escarpment of the Muchinga Mountains, whose alignment tends to accentuate the separateness of the easternmost district.

Excepting the south-western zone bordering the Zambezi, where the rainfall is less than 30 inches and thin bush and sparse grass are characteristic, the general vegetation is savanna, merging into park savanna on the Nyasaland and Belgian Congo borders, in response to longer and heavier rains. Everywhere the winter period of drought is considerable—usually from early May to the end of October—and in the south-west where the rainfall is not only lowest but also most uncertain many tributaries of the Zambezi are intermittent in flow.[1]

The rains are most reliable in Eastern Luangwa where higher altitude than the average is also an inducement to White farming settlement. Here agriculture is normally more successful and varied than in any part of Northern Rhodesia. Fort Jameson close to the Nyasaland border is the centre of this European farming community of a few hundred settlers. It is about 400 miles from the nearest point on the Rhodesian Railway—either Lusaka or Broken Hill—and although a motor-service is maintained along this ' Great East Road ' between the

[1] At Kalomo, near Victoria Falls, the mean rainfall is 29 inches. In 1923–4 the total for the year was only 15 inches.

centre of the Protectorate and its eastern outpost, the latter looks eastwards to Nyasaland as an indirect outlet to ocean ports and overseas markets. Motor-lorry transport is in regular operation between Fort Jameson and Blantyre, 300 miles distant and the rail-head of the Nyasaland system.[1] Tobacco is the principal commercial crop and indeed the only one of importance that will bear the costs of long-distance freightage. Maize, though grown more extensively than any other crop, does not repay export, and

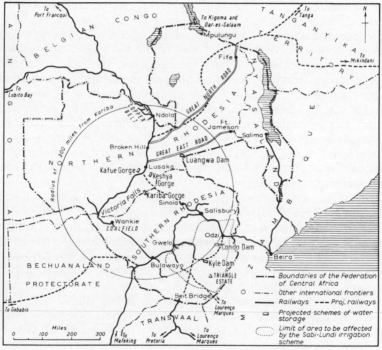

FIG. 38.—Central Africa : Communications and Development Schemes

is retained for local needs. The production of maize and tobacco, though it has recently increased, still remains low in consequence of commercial isolation that is more marked than in the case of any other European farming community of Africa with the possible exception of the small Fife-Abercorn settlement in the extreme north-east of the Protectorate. In the latter district coffee and tobacco, together with subsistence

[1] In 1951, work was proceeding on a second highway, the Great North Road, from Broken Hill to Tunduma (560 miles), which is being improved to Class II standard.

crops, are grown on a very small scale, and trading intercourse with the outer world is maintained by the navigable Lake Tanganyika as far as Kigoma, from which Dar-es-Salaam is reached by railway. It has been repeatedly proposed to construct a line from Dodoma on the Central Tanzania Railway to Fife, and such an enterprise would seem to be one of the most necessary stages in the evolution of the railway net of East Africa—unless the success of motor transport should render it superfluous.

The agricultural progress of Zambia is closely dependent on the extension of irrigation, reclamation, and resettlement. The Kariba dam will permit irrigation along the Zambian as well as the Rhodesian side of the Zambezi valley, and the other main region offering scope for irrigation is the Luangwa valley, where sugar and rice could thrive. As for reclamation, the plateau surface includes wide areas of swamps and land seasonally flooded whose potentialities are immense. The most significant work in terrain of this sort has been undertaken on the Kafue Flats, where land which has been divided into polders, drained and irrigated, has successfully grown wheat, potatoes, cotton and peanuts. In the completed scheme, 14,000 people could be settled on 20,000 acres, and the dam at Meshi Teshi would provide hydro-electric power and water for irrigation.

More limited schemes of settlement have been undertaken in the Fort Jameson district of the Eastern Province, and in the Northern and Luapula province. Prosperous rural communities have been established here after provision of wells, roads, industries and means of eradicating the tsetse fly. These and other rural areas will benefit from the nitrogenous fertilizer factory planned for Livingstone.

In the railway zone of the centre are distributed the majority of the European settlers. From a point, about 100 miles northeast of Livingstone, along the railway to within a short distance of Broken Hill, economic interests are practically confined to ranching and agriculture, with maize as the staple crop. Beyond Broken Hill, an important mining centre for zinc, as far as the Katanga (Congo—Leopoldville) border, and especially in the district of Ndola, the recent opening of the rich copper-field that is an extension of the great metalliferous belt of Katanga has introduced a population of mining supervisors and technicians. As a whole the Katanga–Zambia industrial zone possesses the greatest copper resources yet found within a single area of the world, and in Zambia annual production has exceeded 500,000 tons (since 1961). The mineral industry accounts for over 95 per cent of the total value of Zambia's exports, and reserves are inferred for another 70 years. Two outlets on the African coas⸍

now compete for the evacuation of Zambia copper. Until the 30's of the century the greater part was exported by Beira, but the opening of the Benguella Railway from Katanga to Lobito Bay offers a much shorter route to Europe, with about the same distance overland.

The farming community of the railway zone is well placed to supply maize and cattle to the mining camps both of the Republic and of Katanga. Traffic of this kind is the main commercial enterprise undertaken by the commercial farmers : indeed, the demand for cattle and dairy products has been greater than they have been able to satisfy, and each year thousands of head of stock are carried by rail across Zambia from Rhodesia and Bechuana-land to Katanga.

Economic Relations of the Central African States (Fig. 38)

After a brief life of just over a decade, the Federation of Central Africa, comprising the countries of Rhodesia (then Southern Rhodesia), Zambia (Northern Rhodesia) and Malawi (Nyasaland), was terminated at the end of 1963. However, certain public services, especially in the field of communications, had by this time become so closely co-ordinated throughout the three territories that the separate governments agreed to continue to run them on a shared basis for the benefit of all. The services concerned were Central African Airways, operating within all three territories, the hydro-electric installations at Kariba, and the Rhodesian Railways, which serve both Zambia and Rhodesia.

Altl ough political federation proved impossible, the common interests of the three countries are so strong, and their resources so complementary, that some forms of economic collaboration seem bound to continue, in addition to the sharing of services concerned with transport and the supply of power. The wealth of Malawi comes chiefly from her output of tobacco and tea ; in Zambia, on the other hand, metals, mainly copper, contribute about 95 per cent. by value of the exports. A slump in the market for its chief product would be disastrous for either country in isolation. In combination, however, their economy would be much more secure and resilient.

Rhodesia has a more diversified economy than either of her northern neighbours. Tobacco has recently replaced gold as her most valuable export, while in third place comes asbestos, fol-lowed by chrome, coal and hides. Moreover, the country has built up a thriving textile and clothing industry, the chief markets for which have for some time been found in Zambia *and* Malawi ; But the main advantage to Rhodesia of economic collaboration is that native labour for her mines, farms and factories should be able to move freely from her northern neighbours. Malawi in particular is a regular exporter of labour, and in 1961, 171,000 of her inhabitants were absent at work in other countries. A substantial proportion of this steady migration will doubtless continue to be employed for the development of her former Federal partners.

Within Central Africa it should still prove easier to plan and control the use and extension of the communications, which are already seriously congested. For example, in the federal years the present railway between Wankie and Bulawayo, and a stretch from Bulawayo to Gwelo, almost reached the limit of their capacity. A solution within the frontiers of Rhodesia alone would be to double these lines. But Zambia is also concerned, since a large part of the Wankie coal output is sent to the Copper Belt, which in turn uses the southward line for exporting its manufactures. A wiser solution to this transport problem would therefore be to plan on an international scale and complete the Sinoia–Kafue link between the two territories. This would both provide an alternative route from Wankie to Gwelo, and also cut 400 miles off the rail route between the Copper Belt and the port of Beira.

The external connections of the three countries call for as much co-ordination as do their internal links. It seems that the Portuguese port of Beira will be, at least for some time, the main seaward exit for the produce of all this area. As regards the alternatives, some of the Copper Belt trade at present goes by the long haul to Lobito Bay; but the Kafue–Sinoia link would give Beira a decided advantage over Lobito Bay for this traffic. The long line to South Africa is only of single track, and the alternative route by way of Beit Bridge has still to be completed. The tobacco growers of the northern districts of both Zambia and Malawi use the new North and East Roads to market their produce in Salisbury, rather than the long passage by lake and railway to Dar-es-Salaam; and the railways from Tanga or Mikindani in the east, and from Walvis Bay in the west are still remote projects. Thus Beira seems likely to remain the chief port for Central Africa, though some of its traffic has begun to be diverted to Lourenço Marques since the railway to that port from Salisbury, the ' Southeast Link ', was completed in August 1955.

The most ambitious project of the Federation was that for generating hydro-electric power at Kariba. This site lies near the centre of the area, and can be most usefully developed through the combined capital and to the general benefit of the three united territories. The Copper Belt drew sufficient power for its needs until 1960 from its thermal stations, using the coal of the Wankie fields, and from the Belgian Congo net. Rhodesia was until the closing phases of the federal period adequately supplied with power from its coalfield, and also drew on the Victoria Falls installation, whose capacity is to be increased to 8000 kilowatts by 1956. Subsequently, however, further extension of the copper mines, and of the industries of Rhodesia, will depend on alternative supplies of power. The coal reserves south-east of the Copper Belt in Zambia may help, but plans are centred on the potentialities for water-power of the Zambezi River.

The Kariba Gorge dam on the Zambezi began to provide power between 1961 and 1963, but will not be in full production until 1970. The project for a large dam at Kafue has been shelved ; but a smaller dam may be built for flood control and irrigation of wheat and rice. Further, the Sabi-Lundi irrigation project is also designed to produce food for the growing population. A trial scheme is already working at Triangle Estate and eventually two dams will supply water for irrigating a quarter of the total area of Rhodesia. A new railway from Odzi to Beit Bridge will serve the region. Similar development has been undertaken within the Luangwa Valley of Zambia.

Malawi

The great lake, 360 miles long and occupying part of the southern extension of the Great Rift Valley, is steeply bordered both eastwards and westwards by scarped highlands that in places exceed 8000 feet. These highland masses enclosing the lake together with the usually narrow lacustrine shore represent, within the East African Plateau, a distinct physical unit which is, however, divided between three administrations—of Malawi, Portuguese East Africa (Mozambique), and Tanzania respectively.

In respect of natural resources and density of settlement the western and southern borderlands of the Lake are of greater consequence than those of the east. The boundaries of the Malawi state are the result of hasty annexation that was considered necessary in order to forestall the claims of Portuguese and Germans. Modern European penetration, apart from the occasional visits to the lower Shiré region of Portuguese traders and gold prospectors, began with British missionary enterprise in the highlands to the east of the upper Shiré valley : this from 1876 onwards. The districts of Blantyre and neighbouring Limbe became in the later years of the nineteenth century, and have remained, the principal centres of European settlement. From these bases missionaries and traders extended their influence northwards along the margins of Lake Nyasa, and in so doing aroused the Portuguese and German Administrations to make effective their territorial claims right up to the eastern shore.

Outside the Shiré Highlands, with its centres of Blantyre, Limbe and Zomba (the head quarters of the Administration), European settlement was negligible, and in and around the townships mentioned are the majority of the 9400 (1962) members of the European community, together with a similar number of Indian traders. So far there has been no tendency for the expatriates to extend into the northern district of the country. Yet tiny as are the proportions of European colonization in Malawi, they are very much more considerable than in the neighbouring highland areas of Portuguese East Africa and the state of Tanzania. During the last few years of the British administration the then government of Tanganyika initiated the experiment of opening to European settlement the highlands of the Iringa and Songea districts in the extreme south-west of Tanzania, where over considerable areas, the indigenous population is sparse.

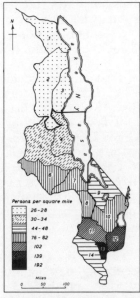

FIG. 39.—Malawi—Density of Population, by Districts (Census of 1945)

Northern Province
1. Karonga
2. Mzimba
3. Chinteche

Central Province
4. Kota Kota
5. Dowa
6. Lilongwe
7. Dedza
8. Ncheu

Southern Province
9. Fort Johnston
10. Zomba
11. Blantyre
12. Mlanje
13. Cholo
4. Lower River

Although equal to about one-seventh only of the area of Zambia, Malawi has a larger number of inhabitants—2,470,000 in 1962. According to available data it is conclusive that density is here relatively high and certainly higher than in the Portuguese districts east of the Lake, but distribution is exceedingly uneven, with the greatest concentration in the south. In parts of the Shiré Highlands (3000–7000 ft.), that extend for 90 miles from north to south, the density exceeds 200 per square mile : the district of Blantyre is a case in point.

Undoubtedly the presence of the commercial farming has attracted the villager to settle as a squatter in the southern highlands because of the opportunities for wage-labour ; but apart from this special factor, important in determining the general distribution throughout the country is the wide variation of soil fertility. Nearly all the Malawi peoples, including such important groups as the Yao and Angoni, are concerned with agriculture

FIG. 40.—Malawi : Economic Frontiers

rather than with stock, and in the country are some of the most enlightened native farmers in East Africa. Indeed, we find that village cultivation exceeds the output of commercial farms in respect not only of subsistence crops—bananas, maize, rice—but also of the chief commercial crops—tobacco and cotton—which normally are able to bear the costs of long-distance transport. This position suggests comparison with Uganda where, however, there is no possibility of considerable European settlement. It is notable that every year there are more Malawian people working in other parts of Africa than there are employed by farmers within the state. By its export of labour Malawi is playing a big part in the development of such lands as Zambia, Rhodesia, the Republic of South Africa and Tanzania.

The variations in relief, soil and climate throughout Malawi are so wide that a considerable range of tropical and sub-tropical crops is made possible. It is, as a whole, a country of reliable and abundant rainfall, with usually from 30 to 40 inches in the lowlands and from 40 to 100 inches in the highlands, though the latter figure is confined to rather exceptional areas such as the Mlanje Plateau (6000–9000 ft.) in the south-east. A savanna vegetation gives place here and there to patches of hard-wood forest, with bamboo forest at higher altitudes. European settlers avoid the lowlands where the combination of intense heat and high humidity would prove intolerable to them. In such districts, whose climatic conditions are unfavourable to European immigration, the agriculture of the villages is often very successful and includes the production of the greater part of the cotton crop of the country, for which the special region is the valley of the Shiré River. Cotton has had a hazardous history in the European areas ; the acreage planted is small as also is the output. Tobacco is the stable of the export trade—nearly £4 millions worth are exported annually—and here again it is the native cultivator who plays the most prominent part. It is regrettable, in view of the very favourable conditions for agriculture, that Malawi plays a small, almost insignificant, part in the commerce of East Africa. But its exports are expanding, especially with the increase in the tea crop, now almost as valuable as the tobacco.

Malawi began an independent existence on July 6th 1964 and promptly embarked on a five-year development plan to improve its economic foundations. During the period of the Central African Federation, the country had benefited from an expansion of social services, which was only made possible by the aid of Federal funds. The fundamental weakness of Malawi's economy is that it is overwhelmingly dependent on agriculture, and this is mainly concerned with the growing of subsistence crops. In relation to its resources as at present developed, the country cannot provide a livelihood for all its people, and there is a regular exodus of labour to neighbouring countries. According to the census of 1961, of the 298,000 Malawians in paid employment, 171,000 were engaged in work in Zambia, Rhodesia and South Africa. Their remittances amount to about £2 million annually and are a significant factor in the country's economy. Another reason why the economy of Malawi is closely dependent on the goodwill of its neighbours is that it is an inland state and its overseas trade must pass through adjacent territories.

Economists are confident that as a result of the completion of the Zambezi bridge at Sena (200 miles from Beira and on Portuguese territory), the greatly improved facilities for through traffic by the 3 ft. 6 in. gauge railway from Blantyre to the coast will greatly stimulate commerce. This is, indeed, borne out by recent trade figures. From Blantyre southwards to Port Herald on the frontier, the Shiré Highlands Railway has a length of 113 miles : then from Port Herald to the north bank of the Zambezi at

Chindio there are 61 miles of the Central Africa Railway: and from the opposite bank of the river—traversed by the new railway bridge—the Trans-Zambezi Railway leads to Beira. To the general advantage of traffic the three lines are under joint administration. The Shiré River is, unfortunately, useless for long-distance transport as, apart from the difficulties of low water in the dry season, there is a stretch of 70 miles in which rapids occur.

Another similarly outstanding transport development is the continuation of the railway from Blantyre to Chipoka on the south shore of Lake Nyasa ; whilst a proposal to continue this line in order to connect Fort Jameson with Blantyre by rail is also receiving attention. If the construction of a line from the Central Tanzania Railway, possibly at Dodoma, to the north shore of Lake Nyasa should be undertaken it will mean that the northern districts of the Protectorate—at present almost isolated—will be provided with a short route to the coast at Dar-es-Salaam. Considerable progress is being made with the improvement of routes for motor vehicles by the building of bridges and culverts. Of the two motor roads for long-distance communication that enter Malawi one, between Fort Jameson and Blantyre, has already been mentioned ; the other links Blantyre to Salisbury (Rhodesia).

A considerable part of Malawi's development plans are rightly concerned with the potentialities of Lake Nyasa and its outlet, the Lhiré River. Nyasa, meaning 'the broad water', gave the country its name prior to independence and has always dominated the geography and guided the history of the territory. The lake and its outlet have a threefold economic significance : first, as providing cheap facilities for water transport, as a supplement to the rail and road systems ; second, as a source of fish, to supplement the diet of the riparian population which is largely dependent on subsistence agriculture ; and thirdly, providing a head of water which can be controlled to generate hydro-electricity and to supply water for irrigation.

Unfortunately the lake is subject to periodic variations in level, for reasons which are obscure but which may be connected with the blocking of its outlets by vegetation. In order to stabilize the lake level, and thereby make possible the construction of safe and permanent harbours, the Liwonde Barrage has been built, between 1963 and 1966, on the Lhiré River. This is the largest single enterprise of the new state, and its expense, which was to be met largely from Federal funds, has been covered mainly from British sources.

Associated with the barrage is the long-projected Nkula Falls hydro-electric scheme, which should provide welcome help to the country's modest plans for the establishment of secondary industries. Once the flow of the Lhiré is under control, a further benefit from the barrage will be the possibility of starting irrigation works in its lower reaches. Many extensive swamps in this area, like the Elephant Marsh, now virtually useless, have soil and climatic conditions suitable for the growing of sugar, rice and cotton, and could contribute markedly to the country's economy.

Undoubtedly the first requirement of the Malawian economy is to extend its commercial agriculture, if necessary at the expense of subsistence farming. The rapid extension of the tea plantations in post-war years in the Cholo and Mlanje areas of the Southern Province and opening of tracts around Lilongwe to tobacco farming have shown what can be achieved. Groundnuts and cotton, grown largely by small farmers and marketed on co-operative systems, and tung oil, produced mainly on estates, could all be more widely grown. For the foreseeable future, Malawi is likely to remain a primarily agricultural country.

Zanzibar and the Mainland Coast

The place of Zanzibar[1] in the civilization of East Africa, prior to British and German penetration of the mainland during the last quarter of the nineteenth century, has been briefly discussed in an earlier chapter. No longer is the island the organizing centre for trade undertaken by Arabs across the East African Plateau. Indeed, with the growth of mainland ports such as Dar-es-Salaam and Mombasa, which are also the termini of continental railway systems, Zanzibar has ceased even to be an important commercial entrepôt between Southern Asia and East Africa.

Both in the larger island (640 sq. miles) and in Pemba Bantu, Arab and Indian groups are in contact. The population of the islands combined is about 317,000 (1962) of which a very large majority are native African, the Arab and Indian minorities having been considerably reduced in numbers since the revolution of 1964. The former mixture of cultures was well illustrated by the number of languages that were widely spoken throughout both islands : there were many dialects of Bantu, in addition to Swahili, as well as Arabic, Indian (Gujarati, &c.) and English.

In theory the Sultan of Zanzibar until 1963 exerted his

---

[1] The name is derived from two terms, one Persian, the other Indian, viz. Zanz- bar, which means ' Country of the Black Man '.

sovereignty over the coastal belt known as the Kenya Protectorate ; but the distinction between ' Colony ' and ' Protectorate '
in Kenya disappeared at the time of independence, before when
the European settlers of the former Colony were making strong
demands for the incorporation of the 10-mile strip. Arab influence on the mainland has been weakening since the abolition of
slavery, and many of the plantations that were Arab-owned are
now derelict or have passed under Indian or European ownership.

Reasons for associating within one region the continental
shore and the islands are not confined to racial, cultural and commercial relationships. In respect of climate there is general
similarity, with the exception of the northern part of the Kenya
Protectorate. Nowhere is there considerable altitude to temper
the excessive equatorial heat. The mean temperature of the
coolest month—July—on the islands is 73° F., which compares
with 74° and 76° at Tanga and Mombasa respectively. Rainfall over Zanzibar and Pemba is abundant and well distributed
throughout the year, the mean annual figures being 60 inches and
81 inches respectively. The latter averages are not reached
on the mainland shore, except in the immediate vicinity of
Tanga which has 59 inches, and from this port both in a northerly
direction and towards the south there is steady decrease, as
shown by means of 48 inches at Mombasa and 45 inches at
Dar-es-Salaam. From Mombasa to the Equator, i.e. along the
greater part of the coast of Kenya, precipitation diminishes to
less than 20 inches, as indicated by Kismayu—15 inches—a
station that lies within the Jubaland territory ceded to Italy
in 1924.

The heavier and more evenly distributed rainfall on the islands,
when compared with the opposite shore, is reflected in a more
luxuriant vegetation and richer tropical agriculture. Both Pemba
and Zanzibar were formerly clothed—so far as their western and
central districts were concerned—with dense forest which has
been almost entirely cleared for agriculture. On these islands
there is an assemblage not only of African plants but also of many
cultivated varieties from India, Madagascar and the East Indies
—a further indication of the trading connexions of the cosmopolitan island communities.

From the East Indies the clove tree was introduced by way
of Réunion in the early part of the nineteenth century, and the
Sultanate now controls over 80 per cent of the total crop of the
world. Two-thirds of the area under clove cultivation is in
Pemba, and both there and on Zanzibar the large plantations
were formerly Arab- or Indian-owned. The sub-division of the

large estates into small holdings owned and worked by African Negroes is steadily proceeding, and in this way the labour problem that was formerly a serious menace to the clove industry is becoming easier. Clove culture has always depended mainly on Bantu labour drawn from Tanzania. A comparatively high wage for unskilled plantation work is attractive to the mainland Native whose labour is rarely so well remunerated in other parts of East Africa.

A threat to the prosperity of the islands, whose revenues are almost entirely dependent on the clove industry, comes from Madagascar, where the French are encouraging similar production. At present in Zanzibar the coconut is the only alternative crop of any importance and there is real need for a wider agricultural basis. More should be done for the cultivation of subsistence crops and for tobacco which, it seems, would be very remunerative. A greater degree of economic security is expected to follow from the fusion of the mainland and the islands into a single state.

The continental shore is generally a zone of agricultural neglect. There is a fringe of mangrove, especially around river outlets, succeeded inland by a narrow palm-belt where the coconut is grown. Much of the remainder is savanna and tree-savanna extending about as far north as the latitude of Malindi. Going inland we find that the littoral zone of considerable possibilities for tropical agriculture gives place, especially in Kenya, to the arid steppe belt known as the Nyika (500–3000 ft.) which is widely represented in Tanaland and the eastern district of Kitui Province (Kenya).

Sisal, from whose leaves cordage and twine are manufactured, was introduced from Yucatan (Mexico) in 1893, and is now easily the most successful commercial plant of the littoral and its vicinity. It grows well even on soils of indifferent quality, and a rainfall of less than 30 inches is not too low. On or near the Tanzania coast-lands is grown the greater part of the sisal which dominates the exports of the Territory.[1] It is not a native-grown crop, but is confined to plantations of European or Indian ownership : indeed, there has been difficulty in obtaining sufficient labour, as injury is easily received from handling the sharp-pointed leaves of the plant.

Throughout, the coast-lands are avoided by North European settlers, though Indian, Arab and, more recently, Greek immigrants appear to be successfully acclimatized. Apart from

---

[1] In the vigorous development of sisal Tanzania has become (1950) a leading producer, with an output of about 35 per cent of the world's supply. The districts of Tanga, Pangani, Dar-es-Salaam, Morogoro and Lindi are important.

malaria and other diseases affecting man, the tsetse fly renders stock-rearing virtually impossible throughout the littoral. Except in Tanga Province and districts around the ports population is generally sparse and is estimated to have actually declined numerically in recent years. So far as Kenya is concerned the coast-lands have been virtually reserved for purchase or lease by Indians since 1923, but this inducement has not yet produced considerable agricultural settlement by Asiatics.

Mombasa, Dar-es-Salaam and Tanga are the ports of prominence. The first two mentioned serve a hinterland as far west as the Great Lakes—Victoria and Tanganyika. Dar-es-Salaam (' Haven of Peace '), with 140,000 inhabitants in 1961—as mixed

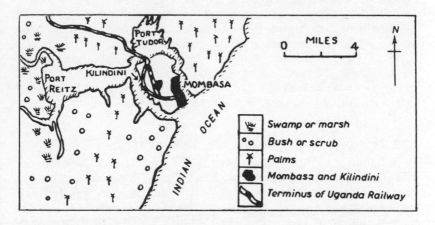

FIG. 41.—Mombasa

in race and culture as those of the port of Zanzibar—is the capital of the Territory and its principal port. Indian commercial interests are paramount and control much the greater part of the real estate of the town. Although the harbour is spacious it is, unfortunately, handicapped by a narrow and winding channel difficult for large vessels. Before the war of 1914 Dar-es-Salaam was superseded for a short time by Tanga, which was the first of the ports under German sovereignty to become the terminus of a railway penetrating the interior : but when the Central Railway from Dar-es-Salaam to Kigoma (L. Tanganyika) was completed in the year of the outbreak of the First World War it was obvious that the more southerly port, by reason of its newly-acquired access to a vast hinterland, would recover its pre-eminence in the German zone. Nowadays, more than

16

one-half of the trade of Tanzania passes through Dar-es-Salaam and less than one-quarter through Tanga.

Since the completion of the two railways that compete for up-country traffic between the Great Lakes and the coast the commercial rivalry of Dar-es-Salaam and Mombasa—the respective termini—has been enhanced. The latter is now the greatest port of the East African littoral and may be considered the twentieth-century successor to the former commercial rôle of Zanzibar. Not only is it the gateway to and from Kenya and Uganda ; also, by virtue of a railway link to the Kilimanjaro Highlands of North-Eastern Tanzania from the Uganda Railway at Voi, Mombasa is able to tap much of the traffic that otherwise would pass through Tanga. The town extends from an island, 3 miles long and within a deep sea inlet, on to the neighbouring mainland. Kilindini on the south-western side of the island is the modern port and also the original terminus of the Uganda Railway that is carried by the Salisbury Bridge on to Mombasa Island. There is an average depth of 20 fathoms in the harbour, so that the port, which has been greatly improved in its equipment of late, is able to accept the largest vessels.

The North-Eastern Highlands of Tanzania

Kilimanjaro, Meru and Usambara are here associated for consideration not only because of their distinctive physical character as mountainous areas with much heavier rainfall and more luxuriant vegetation than are found throughout the greater part of the Great Lakes Plateau, but also because of their significance to the native and immigrant civilizations of East Africa. Both from the standpoint of commercial development and from that of the relations between Bantu and European, the highlands are of critical importance in the geography of the region.

To Sir Richard Burton and Captain Speke credit. for momentous discovery in East Africa is rightly awarded, yet these travellers were not the first Europeans to view the loftiest summits of the continent—Kilimanjaro and Kenya. Two German missionaries—J. Rebmann and L. Krapf—in 1848-9 recorded their discoveries of the snow-capped domes and peaks of equatorial Africa, and though the accounts were in many quarters considered fanciful they were sufficiently authoritative to help to promote the expeditions of Burton and Speke.

The German Administration was early aware of the advantage likely to be obtained from the first railway from the coast to the densely-populated lands around the Victoria Nyanza which were believed to offer great possibilities for commercial agriculture.

Consequently, during the earliest phase of German penetration, Tanga was preferred to Dar-es-Salaam as a terminal port on the grounds of shorter distance to Lake Victoria, and railway construction proceeded vigorously along a line to the north-west. In 1903, however, forestalled by the completion of the

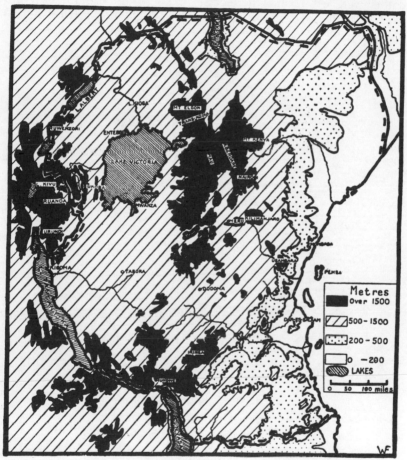

Fig. 42.—Northern and Central Districts of the East African Plateau : Orographical

Uganda Railway from Mombasa, the Germans abandoned the main part of their project and selected an alternative railway route into the hinterland, to be not only wholly within their sphere of influence, but also removed from competition. Attention was thereupon diverted to the line—Dar-es-Salaam, Tabora, Kigoma.

A secondary consideration that helped to determine railway construction from Tanga towards the north-west was the attractiveness of the Usambara and Kilimanjaro Highlands for European agricultural settlement. At altitudes between 3000 and 5000 feet in Usambara plantations of rubber—of the Ceara type—and coffee were established a decade or so before the First World War. In this district, as in the loftier highlands farther north-

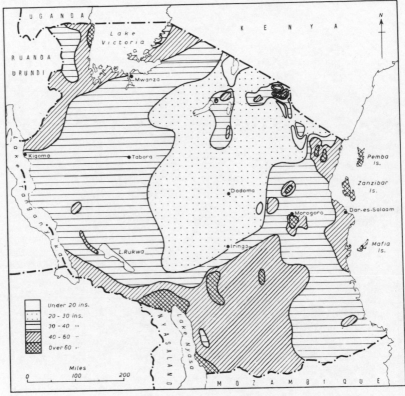

FIG. 43.—Tanganyika Territory : Average Annual Rainfall

west, conditions of soil and climate are admirable for tropical agriculture. Precipitation ranges from 40 to 80 inches and over. Its abundance is instanced by the wealth of forest that includes valuable cabinet woods as well as camphor trees, though much timber was destroyed even prior to German settlement in order to provide room for crops.[1] The rubber production of Usambara

[1] Only about 1 per cent. of the area of Tanganyika Territory is densely forested, and of this proportion much the greater part is in the North-Eastern Highlands.

would have succeeded but for the great decline in prices during the pre-war years : this led to its abandonment, and sisal, for which the commercial future seemed more secure, was planted in its stead.

One of the most notable achievements in connexion with agricultural progress in the highlands of German East Africa was the establishment in 1902 of the Amani Agricultural Research Institute in Usambara. To the credit of the German Administration, it became easily the most valuable enterprise of its kind in Africa, and served a similar purpose to that of the Buitenzorg Institute of Java whose influence on the progress of tropical agriculture in the Netherlands East Indies has been remarkable. Since the Great War the Amani Institute has been revived and the scope of its usefulness widened by the co-operation of the British East African Dependencies, all of which contribute to its upkeep. Another welcome instance of co-operation in East Africa may be mentioned. In 1926 the Egyptian Government, realizing the importance of accurate information regarding weather conditions in the Upper Nile region in connexion with the supply of water in the great river, recommended the formation of a meteorological service to which, in addition to Egypt, the Governments of the Anglo-Egyptian Sudan, Kenya, Uganda, and the Republics of Tanzania and Zambia should contribute both funds and research. It is expected that Abyssinia will shortly possess a number of well-distributed stations and so make possible a more complete climatological service for East Africa.

Influenced by an impression of Kilimanjaro as an isolated highland mass it would be inaccurate to think of it as only comparable, in the horizontal area it covers, to say, one of the Alpine peaks of Europe. Actually the circumference of the base is much more than 100 miles, giving an area larger than that of the Cumbrian Mountains of England.

By 1911 the Usambara Railway was extended as far as Moshi on the southern flanks of Kilimanjaro, and the settlement of German planters proceeded. The land alienated for their use was mainly in the zone between 5000 and 6000 feet above sea-level. Such altitudes proved to be satisfactory for ' arabica ' coffee, to the cultivation of which attention was directed. Unlike the hardier ' robusta ' variety, ' arabica ' does not endure the heat of altitudes under 5000 feet in equatorial latitudes. Moderately heavy rainfall exceeding 50 inches and good drainage were recognized as additional factors of advantage for the coffee estates, whilst the volcanic soil proved to be superior to the gneissic soils of Usambara where coffee is grown with less success. Moshi, the rail-head during the German phase, became the principal collecting centre from which the commercial crops of the Highlands were evacuated to Tanga. After the War —in 1929—the planters on the southern flanks of Mount Meru [1] were, for the first time, provided with satisfactory transport facilities as a result of the extension of the railway to Arusha, the present rail-head.

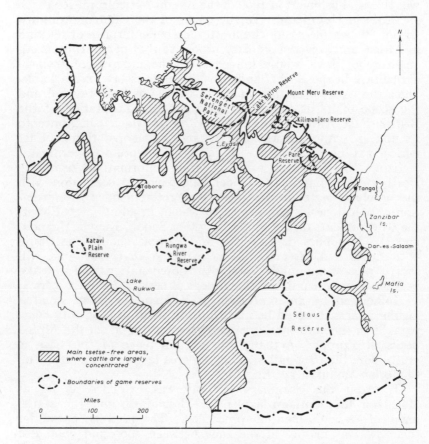

FIG. 44.—Tanzania—Chief game reserves, and regions free from the Tsetse fly

The alienation of land for European-owned plantations, carried out as it was in the midst of densely-settled native lands, resulted in much dislocation and hardship to local Bantu society. The policy of the German Administration was, however, sufficiently enlightened to prevent wholesale expropriation, and just before the Great War further immigration of Europeans

[1] Summit altitude nearly 15,000 feet.

into the highlands was definitely discouraged. According to German figures, there were in 1913 about 15,000 immigrants in the Protectorate (subsequently Mandated Territory), of whom the majority were Asiatics of the coast zone. Europeans numbered 5300, including about 900 German planters in addition to their families ; and these agriculturists were almost entirely confined to the highland areas now under review. The German estates were confiscated after the War, but by 1925 the former colonists were permitted to return and to lease land as equals with other nationals under the Mandate system. In 1935 a count of the White population of the Territory showed a total of 8455, of whom 5500 were British and South Africans (Dutch), and nearly 2700 Germans. Europeans numbered 22,700 in 1961.

The British Administration was not entirely opposed to the extension of European settlement in those parts of Tanganyika where natural conditions were favourable, so long as the inevitable alienation of land did not result in serious loss to native society. The terms of the Mandate did not expressly forbid the expropriation of native land, but it was argued that any considerable extension of the area under European or Asiatic lease would be contrary to the Mandate principle—which upheld the paramountcy of native interests—especially as it was likely to occur in districts that, by reason of their suitability for agriculture, already effectively occupied by fairly dense indigenous groups.

By an order of 1923 the densely-populated North-Eastern Highlands were closed to further White settlement. On the other hand, part of the South-Western Highlands—especially the districts of Iringa, Njombe and Songea—were at a later stage opened to immigration,[1] for it is considered, in view of the comparatively low density of Native population (Iringa Province, 1·5 persons per square mile), that a cautious scheme of land alienation need not result either in undue congestion of Natives on the remaining land or in the growth of a landless community. It is, however, doubtful if commercial agriculture based on tropical crops would be so successful in the South-West as in the North-East of the Territory. Rainfall is generally lower than in the latter region, though still considerable, and temperatures are less, altitude for altitude. In any event, immigration on a large scale will not be possible until regular and modern transport is provided, either by road or by rail.

By the end of 1929 the area of Tanganyika acquired under lease by immigrants exceeded 1,600,000 acres, including much of the most fertile soil. The British share greatly exceeded the German which was not much higher than that of the Indian

[1] As previously mentioned in the section on Nyasaland.

community.[1] With the deportation of German planters and traders immediately after the war of 1914–18, Indian immigrants had an opportunity, readily accepted, of establishing themselves. They were able to lease some of the land confiscated from German ownership and, in addition, provided a large proportion—30 per cent—of all capital invested in agriculture. The number of Indians and Pakistanis present in 1961 was 90,500 and many of

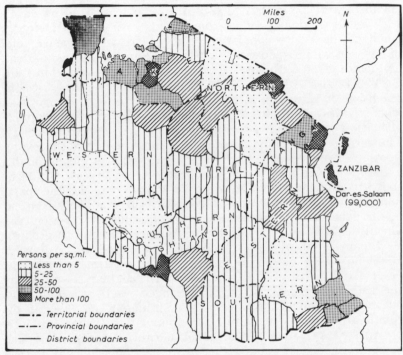

Fig. 45.—Tanganyika Territory—Density of Population, by Districts (Censuses of 1948 (for African population) and 1952 (for others))

them live in the Highlands of the North-East. During the inter-war period, the Government of the Territory was not empowered to discriminate against them, for the Mandate guaranteed equality of treatment to nationals of all member States of the League of Nations, in which India was represented. Accordingly there was as we shall note, a sharp contrast between Tanzania and Kenya

[1] The distribution of land between the principal immigrant groups was (1929)—British, 750,000 acres; Germans, 362,000; Indians, 310,000; Greeks, 230,000. The Greek element was introduced in the pre-war years especially for work on the railways of the German Protectorate.

in so far as the status of Indian immigrants was concerned. In addition to their interest in farming, the Indians controlled much the greater part of both the export and import trade of the Territory.

At the time of Independence European and Asian farmers were responsible for about one-third of Tanzania's agricultural exports, comprising for the most part sisal, coffee, tea, livestock products and seed beans. In addition, they owned the most valuable specially bred herds of stock, and produced a notable surplus of wheat and maize, which was sold and consumed within the country. It is indicative of the extreme concentration of this intensive commercial farming that it was carried on in less than one per cent of the total area of the country.

The experience and example of this intensive agriculture have been passed on to the African farmers, to the advantage of the country as a whole. In order to provide the capital and organization necessary for the prosecution of commercial cultivation, these African farmers have made notable use of the co-operative system. This movement first began during the period of the Mandate, in the early 1930's, but made its most rapid progress during the prosperous period for agriculture which followed the Second World War. At the time of Independence, there were about 750 societies throughout Tanzania, with a membership of some 300,000 farmers, and they were responsible for marketing one-third of the country's agricultural produce. In addition, the co-operative movement, in collaboration with the Ministry of Agriculture, provides services for spraying against pests and diseases, supplies selected seeds and plants, and offers services of advice. It is also becoming increasingly important in providing banking and credit facilities. The prosperous Chagga community, which grows coffee in the area of Mount Kilimanjaro, offers an outstanding example of the benefits brought by the co-operative system.

Even in this relatively densely settled corner of Tanzania, there is much room for expansion. Unlike so many African states, Tanzania has a rich surplus of cultivable land, and at a conservative estimate the population of nine million could be trebled while still remaining essentially dependent on the land for a living.

Central Tanzania

Apart from the North-Eastern and South-Western Highlands to which reference has been made, the greater part of the interior of Tanzania represents a vast undulating plateau, averaging 2000–4000 feet from sea-level, whose surface is broken by residual hills and ridges left by the lowering of the plateau through denudation. In respect of their significance to native civilization the districts bordering Lake Victoria are quite distinct from the remainder of the Territory and require—as they will later receive—separate consideration.

In view of the comparatively low altitudes White settlement is out of the question, and yet only a small proportion of the region is suited to plantation agriculture. It is true that there are many districts of assured soil fertility, but the inadequacy of rainfall is general. Precipitation rarely exceeds 35 inches and wide areas receive considerably less—for example, Tabora, the main centre of native life in Central Tanzania, has only 32 inches; Manyoni, also on the Central Railway and within 100 miles of Dodoma, has but 27 inches; while to the north-east of Dodoma the average falls to no more than 20 inches. The wet season lasts only from November to April, and during the long period of drought many streams cease to flow. Under such climatic conditions the most widespread vegetation is dry bush savanna, similar to the bushveld of the Northern Transvaal. Without irrigation the greater part of the region will remain uncultivated, unless drought-resisting crops, such as ground-nut, are introduced. Ground-nuts have long been grown in Central Tanzania by villagers, but an ambitious scheme to extend their cultivation on a commercial scale, which was devised by the Colonial Office in 1947, proved a failure. The chief lessons of this venture are the need for a close appreciation of natural conditions and for a small-scale experimental beginning.

Recently the Tanzania Department of Agriculture has done much to raise the standard of cultivation in selected areas which have suffered from severe overpopulation. This condition has resulted from a variety of causes, including encroachment of the tsetse fly, and excessive alienation of tribal land by the former German administration. One area which has benefited is the Uluguru mountain country of the Morogoro District of the Eastern Province. Over 100,000 Luguru have taken refuge in these forests from Angoni raids since the later years of the last century. Their shifting cultivation made disastrous inroads on the forest, the best remaining areas of which have now been made a reserve. On the rest of their land, the tribesfolk are being encouraged to redress the damage caused by soil erosion, and to practise a more sedentary cultivation, with the aid of terracing, tie-ridging, fruit tree planting, and the use of compost and manure.

One of the difficulties in the way of the improvement of cultivation is the native attitude to the land, which under a system of shifting agriculture is considered a resource to be exploited rather than a trust to be preserved. However, the indigenous system of land-tenure, by which territory belongs to the tribe rather than the individual, has often helped to engender, with careful teaching, a sense of communal responsibility towards the soil.

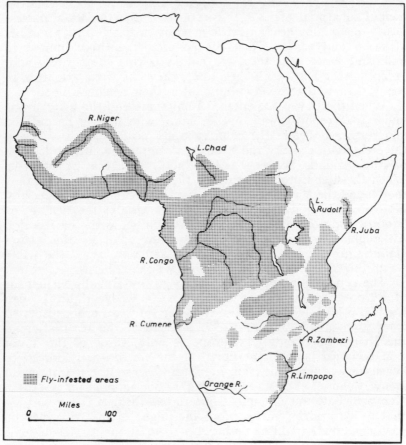

FIG. 46.—Distribution of the Tsetse Fly

The ravages of the tsetse fly are more widespread in Tanzania than in any other East African territory, and fully four-fifths of the area is affected. Although in the central zone the fly is not so serious a menace as in other parts of the Territory, its range is extending and already has resulted in the virtual depopulation of much of the Plateau between Dodoma and Tabora, including the vicinity of the Central Railway. One of the provinces that is comparatively free is the Northern which includes, in addition to the Arusha and Moshi districts, the Masai Reserve

(17,500 sq. miles), that occupies the part of the Rift Valley west and north-west of the Arusha district.

Reference to the Masai brings us to one of the most interesting communities of the region—a people who, despite their small numbers, not exceeding 100,000,[1] are among the leading cattlemen of equatorial Africa. It is estimated that the Masai possess nearly one million head of cattle in addition to twice that number of sheep and goats. Their diet is almost entirely limited to milk and blood, yet they are not as a rule meat-eaters and, excepting the lion which they hunt, they pay little attention to the wild game that is very abundant in their neighbourhood.

When the Europeans entered Kenya, most of the plateau was under the despotic sway of the Masai, who had to be pacified and restricted before the country could be developed. During the eighteenth century the tribesmen migrated southwards from pasture grounds between Lake Rudolf and the Upper Nile. When the first Europeans entered the Kenya Highlands in 1903 they found the Masai roaming freely in the Rift Valley, especially between Lake Naivasha and Molo, and also in the neighbourhood of Nairobi,[2] where they were in conflict with the Kikuyu. Although a conquering people, they differed from other semi-Hamitic groups, in that they did not attempt to rule the tribes whom they defeated but merely took away their herds.

The construction of the Uganda Railway and the settlement of Europeans close to the track drove a wedge right through the Masai domain, so dividing the tribe into two groups isolated from each other. Later, in consequence of the reservation of the Kenya Highlands for Europeans only, those of the Masai who occupied land to the north of the railway were forced to evacuate and join their kinsmen near the southern frontier of Kenya Colony. The Masai Reserve (14,600 sq. miles) of Southern Kenya includes much land—equal to one-third of the Reserve—that is too arid for cattle ; and the plight of the tribesmen on pastures, greatly reduced both in area and in quality, has become wellnigh desperate. Their condition was a little improved some years ago by the extension of the Reserve to include good grassland west of Lake Naivasha, but a much larger grant of well-watered country in both Kenya and Tanzania will be necessary if the Masai are to be saved from destitution. The division of the tribe into two reserves under separate administrations—of Kenya and Tanzania respectively—is not only opposed to Masai

[1] Of this number about 23,000 are in Tanganyika and the remainder in Kenya.

[2] A Masai word meaning ' cold ' and applied to a stream, near which is the site of the capital of Kenya.

sentiment but actually incomprehensible to them. There can be no doubt that all should be united under one administration—a proposal made twenty years ago by the ' Hilton Young ' Commission.[1]

During the phase of Arab commerce in ivory and slaves, between Central Africa and the Indian Ocean shore, Tabora and Dodoma were caravan-centres of importance. Both lay on the main route of traffic—followed closely by the present railway—from Ujiji (L. Tanganyika) to Dar-es-Salaam, and at each centre ' feeder ' tracks converged on the east–west highway. With its population of 30,000 Tabora remains prominent in the commerce of Central Tanzania, and its importance has increased since the completion of the railway that links it to the lake port of Mwanza on the southern shore of Victoria Nyanza. Its inhabitants are mainly Bantu, though there are still a few descendants of Arab merchants who made Tabora their permanent home. Not improbably Dodoma will attain greater significance than Tabora, for it lies at the crossing of the Central Railway by the ' Great North Road '—as the motor highway of the future is known—from Nairobi to Cape Town. Already there is a regular lorry service between Dodoma and Tukuyu, near the head of Lake Nyasa, and a railway along the same route has been proposed, so that the nodal character of Dodoma tends to be increasingly emphasized.

If Tanzania is to remain a separate political unit detached administratively from the other East African Dependencies—as seems likely—there is a strong case to be made for the removal of the capital from Dar-es-Salaam to a more central position : either Dodoma or Tabora would serve the interests of the Territory as a whole better than the present port-capital.

In the central and eastern districts of their Protectorate the German Government inherited and developed an administration first introduced by the Sultanate of Zanzibar. The latter did not recognize tribal entities, and under its régime native society disintegrated. In place of native chiefs, paid officials, usually of Arab or Swahili extraction and known as ' akidas ', were introduced. They were usually ignorant and regardless of native law and custom : the establishment of Islam was the only important aim in their estimation.

Since 1925 the ' akida ' system has been abolished and in its place ' indirect rule ' introduced. Where tribes have become dispersed their cohesion is being restored as far as possible :

[1] As expressed by the ' Hilton Young ' Commission in its Report of 1929 (p. 300) : ' The boundary cuts this people in two with no more concern for their ideas or for the justice or convenience of their administration than the scythe has for a blade of grass.

furthermore, the traditional authority of the chiefs is being revived in the case of those who give evidence of their heritage of leadership. The Government pledges itself ' to maintain and develop all that is best in tribal customs and institutions and to avoid everything that has a de-tribalizing tendency '. Local government bodies, known as ' Native Councils ', have been established in most, if not all, districts of Central Tanzania. Their duties are concerned with such matters as the maintenance of law and order, the collection of hut and poll taxes, and the care and improvement of local roads.

The Borderlands of Lake Victoria

This region may be defined as the vast but shallow depression, partially lake-filled by Victoria Nyanza and Kioga, that extends between the highlands of the Western Rift Valley—from Lake Albert to the northern shore of Lake Tanganyika—and the highlands of the Eastern or Main Rift Valley. By reason of high population density, the intensity and success of native agriculture —where both subsistence and commercial crops are concerned— and the advanced cultural level of the local Bantu, this region holds an almost unique position in the geography of East Africa.

Although British authority extends throughout, a comprehensive system of administration is lacking. From the standpoint of physical as well as of human geography there is an essential unity, of which the political boundaries take no account. These lake lands are divided between Uganda Protectorate, Kenya Colony and Tanzania; while to the west of the Bukoba Province that forms the south-western borderland of Lake Victoria there are, in Ruanda and Urundi, communities, including the Watusi, who have been turned away from their natural association with the lake-land peoples and are now joined politically with the forest-dwellers of different affinities and lower cultural development within the Belgian Congo.

Lake Victoria is not, as we have seen, of ' rift ' origin, and its gradually shelving shores permit extensive as well as close settlement such as is impossible throughout the greater part of the coasts of the steeply-walled lakes—Nyasa and Tanganyika. An average altitude of 3000–4000 feet is maintained, but in consideration of the equatorial situation is much too low to induce permanent White settlement. There were not in 1931 more than 2500 Europeans throughout the entire region. Moreover, it can be said that generally there has been less interference with native civilization than in any other part of East Africa where extensive and rich soils offer abundant scope to plantation agriculture and to the establishment of large European estates ; but the position seemed likely to change rapidly in 1938 after gold had been discovered over a wide area—about 6000 sq. miles it was supposed—within the north-eastern borderlands of the great lake.

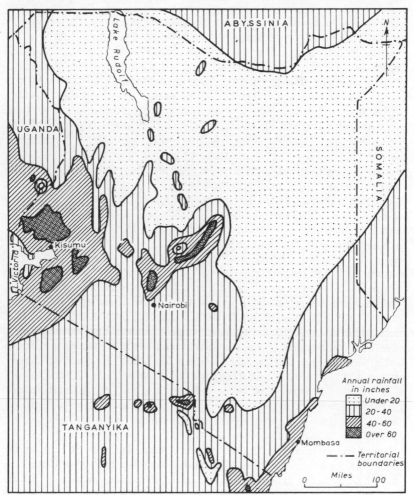

FIG. 47.—Kenya : Average Annual Rainfall

There is an opportunity at this stage for more detailed reference to the climate of the lake region than was possible in an earlier and more general chapter.

The high and equable temperatures that are associated with lands of only moderate elevation in equatorial latitudes are

prevalent throughout, though the normal south-east wind, cooled
in crossing Lake Victoria, mitigates to some extent the severity
of the heat on the western and north-western shores. This is
borne out by a comparison of temperature conditions at Entebbe
with those at Mwanza. The monthly means of the former are
from 1 to 3° lower than those of Mwanza and the difference is
most marked in the period, April–November. Yet there is no
month at Entebbe with a lower average than 69°F. It is in
respect of rainfall distribution that there is greatest variation
throughout the lake borders. On the eastern and south-eastern
shores, approximately from Kisumu round to Mwanza, precipitation varies from 27 to 48 inches, but much higher averages
are characteristic of the western and north-western coasts, as
instanced by Entebbe (59 inches) and Bukoba (75 inches).
Where the measurement exceeds 50 inches it is unusual for any
month to receive less than 1 inch, but on the eastern and south-
eastern shores July and August usually provide a dry period.
Assuming a fairly even distribution of soil fertility, it is therefore reasonable to suppose that the Uganda shore and the neighbouring part of Tanzania, viz. Bukoba Province, will offer,
in comparison with the eastern and south-eastern borderlands,
superior physical conditions for intensive agriculture covering
a fairly wide range of tropical crops.

In the districts of greatest precipitation are to be found small
remnants of an equatorial forest that formerly clothed a large
part, if not the greater part, of the Lake Victoria region. Deforestation has not been merely a recent episode, but has extended
over many centuries and has made possible the dense agricultural
settlement that now exists. Over the areas of comparatively
low precipitation savanna represents the primitive vegetation as
also where the land has been deforested but left uncultivated.
Elephant-grass, growing to 10–15 feet, is characteristic of much
of the savanna. It provides a useful fodder, and shorter edible
grasses are also abundant.

Native agriculture in Tropical Africa is seen in its most
successful phase in Southern Uganda, and especially in Buganda
and the southern half of the Eastern Province, which includes
Busoga. Inherent aptitude for the art of cultivation accompanies
advantageous conditions of soil and climate. Near the lake-
shore the Hamitic element in the population is much less than in
western and northern districts of the Uganda Protectorate where
it is associated with pastoralism. Although Buganda was invaded
by the Bahima, an Hamitic people, the latter have amalgamated
with the more numerous indigenous inhabitants (Bantu), and
even the aristocratic element in the Kingdom of Buganda that

claims descent from Bahima chiefs is as much negroid as Hamitic.

For food the Buganda and Basoka depend mainly on plantains which are cultivated in groves covering more than half a million acres in Buganda alone. Millet is an important secondary food crop, but the zone of its maximum cultivation is farther north, especially to the east and north of Lake Kioga, where conditions are too arid for the banana.[1]

Of outstanding importance in the agricultural geography of the borderlands of Lake Victoria is the cultivation of cotton in South-Eastern Uganda. Although the plant is indigenous it is not from native stocks that the present large output is derived,[2] but from American of the ' Uplands ' variety. Throughout the greater part of the lake borderlands conditions of soil and climate are satisfactory for cotton, but Eastern Uganda alone is concerned with production for export.

The entire crop is intended for overseas markets, and cultivation has, therefore, depended on the provision of adequate transport facilities to the nearest seaport—Mombasa—which is about 650 miles distant from the main centres of production. From 1903 onwards, with the completion of the Uganda Railway as far as Kisumu (at the head of the Kavirondo Gulf of Lake Victoria), the outgoing cotton was transported to rail-head by steamers that were able to negotiate the shallow waters of the Gulf, where the limit of draught is 8 feet.

In 1931 a railway bridge was opened across the Victoria Nile outlet at Jinja, so that a through route is now available from the main centre of Uganda—Kampala, the native capital —to Mombasa. As, however, transport across the Lake from Entebbe (about 25 miles from Kampala) is cheaper than rail carriage by the longer land route around the northern side of Victoria Nyanza, much of the export of cotton from Buganda continues to be handled at Kisumu.

Within Uganda the region which specializes in cotton production includes the southern and central districts of the Eastern Province and eastern parts of Buganda. Very intensively planted is an area of deep, sandy loams on the plains to the east of Lake Kioga. As the crop is essentially one of native farming, the holdings are small, mainly varying from a quarter of an acre to five acres. An important discovery in 1952 was the treatment of blackarm disease in cotton seed.

Sooner or later the vast marsh region of Lake Kioga will

---

[1] i.e. Rainfall less than 35 inches.
[2] In 1937-8 the production was 316,000 bales (of 400 lb.), compared with the lower production, after the Second World War, of 231,700 bales in 1946-7. Output had risen to 346,408 bales in 1950-1.

17

be reclaimed for cultivation, possibly of rice by Indian settlers. The *mbwa* fly, which afflicts the eyes, has deterred natives from taking work here ; but in 1952 it was eradicated in an experiment on the Victoria Nile.   Within or close to the districts of Uganda, in which cotton is the primary crop for export, the indigenous ' robusta ' coffee is planted.   This the Government has encouraged in order to widen the basis of commercial agriculture which at present is narrowly confined to one crop—with consequent economic insecurity to the Protectorate.   The ' robusta ' variety of coffee is well able to withstand the extreme heat of the Uganda plains, but is not so acceptable to the Natives as is cotton on account of the interval of a few years that must elapse between planting and the first harvest ; but more coffee has been grown recently, and cotton is no longer so preponderant an export.[1] Of the European residents, who now exceed two thousand, a small proportion are coffee planters.   On the lower slopes of Mounts Elgon and Ruwenzori small quantities of ' arabica ' are grown, for which crop the soil and climatic conditions are very satisfactory, but the few estates on the plains of Buganda are necessarily limited to the coarser and hardier variety of coffee.

In the commercial life of Uganda the Indian population, about 77,400 (1961), is of critical importance, and it is believed that they control 90 per cent of the total trade of the Protectorate. One of their special interests is the preparation of the raw cotton for export, and of 200 ginneries, the majority are Indian-owned and controlled.   Commercial contact with India is naturally very close, and practically the whole of the cotton crop is consumed in the textile industry of the Bombay Presidency.   The relations of the Indian and European communities in Uganda are more friendly than in any other part of British East Africa.   As the Indians are adequately represented on the Legislative Council there is an absence of acute political unrest, while there is no discrimination against them in regard to the leasing of land or to residence.

In explaining the agricultural and commercial pre-eminence of Eastern Uganda within the region of the Lake Victoria borderlands considerable significance should be attached to the extensive and modern motor-road system which is unrivalled in any part of tropical Africa.   The main highways of a fairly close network converge on Kampala and grant a well-emphasized nodal character to that township.   Many of the modern roads follow earlier native tracks, for in the pre-European period, as also at present,

[1] In 1952 the value of exported coffee (both ' arabica ' and ' robusta ') was £12,000,000 (cf. £229,000 in 1936).   In the same year the raw cotton exports were valued at close on £30,000,000.

the chiefs considered it necessary to have direct contact between their villages and the capital of the ' kingdom ' of Buganda. The extension of the Uganda Railway from Kampala to Kasese, which was completed in August 1956, will open up some of the best cattle country in Africa, and may attract northward some of the population of the overcrowded district of Kigezi.

Outside Uganda there are few facilities for the movement of heavy traffic—except where there is easy access to lake-steamer—and agriculture is usually for subsistence only. In Tanzania Republic, however, the Tabora–Mwanza railway has greatly stimulated cultivation for export. In addition to native varieties of cotton, grown almost entirely for local requirements, ' robusta ' coffee within the last twenty years has been extensively planted in Bukoba and to a less extent in Mwanza Province. The greater part of the coffee output of Tanzania is not ' arabica ' from the North-Eastern Highlands, but the coarser ' robusta ' produced in the borderlands of Lake Victoria.[1] The Bantu, who include the Sukuma tribe, the largest community in Tanzania, with a membership of over 880,000, grow a variety of food crops, including rice—some of which is exported to lake-shore ports in Kenya and Uganda—plantains, millet and maize ; and generally the standard of farming is more advanced in Bukoba and Mwanza than in other native areas of the Territory.

Bukoba Province was, when under German administration, one of the three Residencies in which ' indirect rule ' was permitted, in contrast to the remainder of the Protectorate where, on account of the disintegration of tribal society, the Administration considered it impossible to depart from the ' akida system ' which already has been mentioned. Rwanda and Burundi, the countries formerly associated with Bukova, are now politically divorced from their natural union with the people of the plateau lands west of Lake Victoria. Under Belgian administration, the traditional authority of the paramount chiefs (or ' sultans ') of Tuanda and Urundi was recognized. They became independent states on July 1, 1962.

The north-western districts of Tanzania Republic are the most closely-settled of the entire country. Similarly high densities of population are true also for Rwanda and Burundi, for which the combined figure in 1961 was 240 per sq. mile. This is a very high average when it is remembered that large areas are retained in pasture. Out of a total population of 7,600,000 in the former German Protectorate nearly one-half were

[1] In 1946 the exports of all grades of coffee from the Territory totalled 31,416 tons, of which a large proportion was from Bukoba.

inhabitants of the two Residencies that were later administered as part of the Belgian Congo. One of the motives that inspired the Belgian claim to ex-German territory was the desire to add to the sparsely-populated Congo domain a vast reserve of potential labour for big mining and land development schemes. On the other hand, the European planters of the Kilimanjaro and Usambara Highlands complain that they are inadequately supplied with native labour largely as a result of the closing of Ruanda-Urundi to recruiting for the requirements of Tanzania.

The high density of native settlement that is characteristic practically throughout the borderlands of Lake Victoria is not entirely explained by the favourable conditions of soil and climate for intensive cultivation, potent though these factors certainly have been. The stability of government in native ' kingdoms ' such as Buganda and Bukoba prior to European penetration was the outcome of strong tribal discipline that rendered inter-tribal warfare, with its depopulating tendencies, a comparatively rare occurrence. In Bukoba, Ruanda and Urundi, as in Buganda and other ' kingdoms ' now merged in the Uganda Protectorate, the ruling class claims descent from Hamitic incomers with a tradition of leadership and of pastoralism. In this connexion we may mention the Watusi of Ruanda-Urundi who, like the Bahima of Buganda, are now little different from the indigenous Bantu with whom they have inter-married.

It is in these naturally favoured districts, which were already densely settled before the days of British rule, that the recent increase of population has been most marked. This increase, which in parts amounts to 2 per cent each year, has been due partly to improved standards of health, but principally to the removal of the checks, such as warfare and famine, which formerly kept down numbers.

The result has been that in certain areas of East Africa the population has become too numerous for the land to support under the existing economy,[1] In Kenya this is the case notably in the Kikuyu and Machakos Districts of the Central Province, the Maragoli-Bunyore-Kakamega area of North Nyanza, the Teita Hills and the Kisii Highlands ; while the same is true of the Districts of Tukuyu, Morogoro, the Usambaras, Pares, Kilimanjaro and Meru and parts of the Lake Victoria region in Tanzania and of parts of Kigezi and Bugishu and the region around Kampala in Uganda.

Not only are these districts overpopulated, but in many cases they are attempting to support an excessive number of cattle,

[1] See Sir Philip Mitchell's despatch in *Land and Population in East Africa*, Colonial No. 290. H.M.S.O. for the Colonial Office, London, 1952.

sheep and goats. The native farmer is often reluctant to sell his surplus animals, which in many districts are regarded as an index of wealth and status, and even when this prejudice is overcome, there is the additional difficulty of transporting them to market. This overstocking naturally results in soil erosion, loss of fertility, and a fall in the carrying capacity of the land.

There are two possible solutions to this problem of over-population and overstocking. The first is to add more land to the reserves. This, however could only be done at the expense of barren lands like the Northern Frontier Province of Kenya, which would be of little agricultural value ; or by encroachment on the reserved forests, which form one of the most valuable natural resources of these territories ; or again by settlement of former European farmland, a policy which by 1965 had led to the establishment of 19,000 African families in ' high-density ' schemes on one million acres of former European farms. But there were signs that the standard of farming had declined in the process and some of the remaining 2,000,000 acres may be left in large units, as State farms, individual large-holdings or co-operatives. These would naturally absorb fewer settlers. The second pos-sibility, which has so far been tried out mainly in Kenya, is by research, financial help, and education, to raise the whole standard of farming within the existing reserves.

The latter policy has now been generally adopted by the Government, as the wiser and more far-sighted solution. Im-proved techniques of agriculture are being taught, and barren country reclaimed within the limits of the reserves. The Chepa-lungu and Lambwe Valley development areas of the Nyanza Province, for example, have been opened for stock-breeding as a result of road building, well sinking, and bush clearance to eradicate the tsetse fly and dangerous game.

Some of the best results have been achieved in the Machakos District, where hillsides made barren by overgrazing have been brought back into use through replanting, terracing, and dam construction, carried out partly by local communal effort.

Research work is helping native subsistence farming by developing grasses and legumes, suitable for leys, by experimenting with locally available fertilizers, and by selecting drought-resistant varieties of maize and millet and virus-free stocks of cassava. At the same time, the African farmer is being helped to grow cash crops—cotton, coffee, pyrethrum and sugar—and to invest the resulting income in improvement of his land.

The topography and climate of Kenya do not favour large-scale schemes of irrigation and reclamation. Of its rivers, only the Tana seems to lend itself to undertakings of this sort, but in 1948

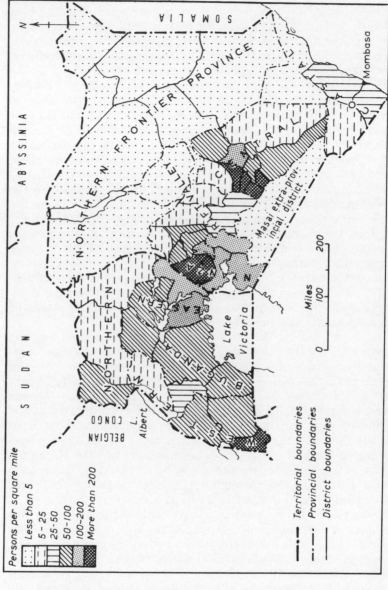

Fig. 48.—Kenya and Uganda—Density of Population, by Districts
(Census of 1948)

the Public Works Department, after a close examination of water, soils and markets, advised against a project for irrigating this valley. However, under the ten-year scheme begun in 1946, the cumulative effect of the many small enterprises of land development throughout the native territories has been decisive in relieving pressure on the soil, and a grant of £5 millions by the United Kingdom Government in December 1953 made it possible to intensify this work over the succeeding five years.

While the main wealth of Kenya is agricultural, it has also an appreciable output of certain special minerals, notably soda from Lake Magadi, an important ingredient in the manufacture of glass, copper, diatomite, graphite and gypsum. Gold, which was at one time expected to become an important export, is now only obtained in small quantities as a by-product of the Macalder-Nyanza copper mine.

A more recent discovery of precious mineral wealth in East Africa was largely concealed at the time from public attention in Europe by the events of the Second World War. It was that of diamonds at Shinyanga, north-east of Tabora, in Tanzania Republic. The mine, possibly richer than the famous Kimberley mine in its day, in 1962 exported diamonds valued at over five million sterling, and Tanzania is now permitted a quota of 10 per cent of world diamond sales.

The Protectorate of Uganda had a creditable record in native administration, uncomplicated by land alienation on a considerable scale to immigrants, whether from Europe or Asia. Although Asian and European immigrants have played a notable part in the development of Uganda, the state has retained its status as an African country. In 1962, the population of 7,016,000 included only 77,400 Asians and 11,600 Europeans.

Although, on account of its major share in the production of cotton and of its large proportion—more than one-third—of the total population, the Eastern Province ranks high in the commercial life of the Protectorate, from the standpoint of social and political geography Buganda is pre-eminent. It corresponds in area to one of the five provinces of Uganda, but the other ' kingdoms '—including Bunyoro in the Northern Province, Ankole and Toro in the Western Province, and Busoga in the Eastern Province—are sub-provincial units or ' districts ' for administrative purposes. The political entities of Buganda, Bunyoro, Toro and Ankole have a long history, and are as fully accepted by the people as are the emirates of Northern Nigeria by their inhabitants.

' Indirect rule' with its emphasis upon the authority of native leadership has met with signal success in Buganda since it was

first introduced by Sir H. H. Johnston at the beginning of this
century. Before that time the Baganda had already evolved
the most advanced political system in Bantu Africa. At the
head of the Baganda nation is the ' king ' (*kabaka*), assisted and
controlled by an assembly of the chiefs—the *lukiko*—whose
powers include the initiation of legislative measures. Under
the *kabaka* the chiefs acquire their privileges and authority not
through heredity but through personal qualification, and to this
extent may be regarded as salaried civil servants selected and
promoted by merit.

Under the Uganda Agreement of 1900, provision was made
for the freehold tenure of estates which were claimed as belonging
to various ' chiefs and private landowners '. These estates, the
' mailo ' lands, comprised about half of the total area of Buganda,
and the rest of its territory was vested in the Crown.

As the British administration extended its control beyond the
kingdom of Buganda, the settlement which had been effected
there was taken as a model. The result has been that the styles
of administration and of land tenure characteristic of the Buganda
have had a powerful influence on the system of land settlement
which has been applied throughout the whole of present-day
Uganda.

Outside Buganda, however, freeholdings of the ' mailo ' type
were not so widely claimed or granted. In the Ankole and Toro
agreements, for example, only 6 per cent of the land area was
eventually recognized as private estates. The bulk of the territory
of the Protectorate, therefore, is now Crown land, which it is the
Government's policy to hold in trust for the indigenous population.

Although legally the Africans occupying Crown land are
tenants-at-will, it is the declared policy of the Government to
respect African customary rights of tenure. In effect these
rights usually involve communal obligations and excessive frag-
mentation, and often severely restrict the enterprise of any native
farmer who wishes to improve his land by consolidation, fencing,
manuring or mechanization. If the standard of native farming
is to improve, and in particular if it is to become more diversified,
these systems of customary land tenure will have to be replaced
by a more formal and secure individual kind of title.[1]

Although the economy of the Protectorate is overwhelmingly
dependent on agriculture, Uganda has rich resources for basic
industries, for in addition to a steady output of raw cotton, the
territory possesses large reserves of limestone, magnetite, copper,
iron pyrites, salt and phosphate rock. Until recently the country

---

[1] *East Africa Royal Commission 1953–1955 Report*, Cmd. 9475, H.M.S.O.
London, 1955, Part V. The whole document is of the first importance.

has been handicapped by its poverty in resources of power, but the opening of the Owen Falls Dam on the Nile (1954) has vastly improved the prospects for industrial expansion. An electric smelter at Jinja will treat copper ore brought from the Kilembe mine over the extension of the Uganda Railway which was opened in November, 1956. The Uganda Development Corporation has also begun work on a textile factory at Jinja, and on a cement works at Tororo, in a district rich in minerals where it is hoped soon to set up chemical industries.

The Kenya Highlands

This region has marked physical individuality and, from the standpoint of human relations—especially the contacts of native and immigrant societies—is the most critical land in East Africa. It represents but a small fraction—about one-fifth—of the total area of Kenya Colony, and yet, excepting the lofty and vast plateau of Abyssinia, it is the most considerable tract of highland, exceeding 5000 feet, in tropical Africa.

In respect of physical geography the Highlands are clearly divided into two main zones separated by the section of the Great Rift Valley lying between Lakes Baringo and Magadi.

The eastern zone, extending from north to south for over 200 miles, is comprised of the plateau lands of Laikipia, Aberdare and Kikuyu ; and with these ' massifs ' that are largely overlaid with lava flows there is, in close proximity, the great volcanic mass of Mount Kenya—a giant outpost on the eastern margin of the Highlands.

It is on the Aberdare Plateau that the eastern escarpment of the Rift Valley attains its greatest altitude within the Colony : there are considerable areas over 10,000 feet, with one or two eminences nearly 2000 feet higher. Between these mountainous levels and Mount Kenya extend the Nyeri Plains that form a northerly continuation of the Kikuyu Plateau and maintain an average elevation of 6000–7000 feet.

The heart of the Kenya Highlands, which may be conveniently called the Kikuyu Plateau, stretches from the neighbourhood of Nairobi to the southern slopes of Mount Kenya. There is very little level ground, and a succession of alternating ridges and river valleys is typical of the landscape : yet the Kikuyu Plateau, ranging in altitude from 5000 feet—as around Nairobi—to 8000 feet, at the edge of the Rift Valley, is one of the most densely peopled parts of East Africa and is characterized by extensive and very successful farming, both European and Native. Much of the soil, usually deep and rich, is derived from soft volcanic tuffs that supported dense forest down to the time of the incoming of the Kikuyu people. It is very retentive of moisture on account of its fine-grained texture, and remains moist even in time of drought : moreover, it is very light to work and is, therefore, suited to the hoe-labour of the Natives.

Farther north-west on the Aberdare Plateau, where again volcanic soils are abundant, there are extensive tracts of virgin forest. Before the Kikuyu settlement of the Nyeri Plains woodland was continuous from the Aberdare Plateau to the western flanks of Mount Kenya, where to-day dense tree growth still forms an almost continuous fringe, 8–15 miles in width, on the lower slopes and around the mountain's circumference of not less than 120 miles. The Laikipia Plateau shows the transition from savanna—the most characteristic vegetation of the Kenya Highlands as a whole—to the dry grass- and scrub-land that is to be found south of Lake Rudolf. In contrast to the northern districts of Laikipia where rainfall is deficient—that is, less than 28 inches—the southern parts provide excellent pasture and have attracted the European immigrant.

The floor of the Rift Valley declines in level both northwards and southwards of the ' saddle ' of Gilgil, near Lake Naivasha, where it is 6581 feet above sea-level. Between Lakes Nakuru and Naivasha the scenery of East Africa attains its most lovely if not its grandest phase : vegetation is more luxuriant than elsewhere in the Rift in consequence of the assured and plentiful rainfall of over 30 inches. The surface of Lake Naivasha, one of the twenty lakes that stud the Rift Valley in Kenya, is about 6000 feet above sea-level. Northwards, after passing Gilgil, there is a fairly steady fall of level, accompanied by increasing aridity, to Lake Rudolf whose surface is nearly 5000 feet lower than that of Lake Naivasha. Southwards from Naivasha the descent is like that of a great staircase, and at the foot is Lake Magadi—a vast and increasing deposit of carbonate of soda, rather than a lake. In this district on the southern border of Kenya the Rift Valley passes through the Masai Reserve and is as arid and inhospitable as the section between Lakes Baringo and Rudolf.

One of the most remarkable features of the Rift is the large number of denuded cones and ' necks ' of dormant or extinct volcanoes scattered on the floor. Especially prominent is Longonot, which rises 3000 feet, not far from the southern end of Lake Naivasha.

Where the Uganda Railway crosses the great trough the walls of the Kikuyu and Mau Plateaux respectively are 40 miles apart, with their summits reaching over 8000 feet from sea-level.

After descending the Kikuyu Escarpment on a gradient of 1 in 50, the line leads diagonally across the valley between Lakes Naivasha and Nakuru, and then the difficult ascent of the gigantic Mau Escarpment is begun. Here the Uganda Railway reaches the highest altitude scaled by any permanent way in Africa, namely 8321 feet. Nakuru village is now the junction of the two branches of the Uganda Railway that reach the summit of the Mau Plateau within 9 miles of each other—one, the more southerly, is the original line, opened in 1903, to the Victoria Nyanza at Kisumu : the other extends to the north-west and enters Uganda, ultimately crossing the Victoria Nile.

The western section of the Kenya Highlands is generally more lofty than its eastern counterpart. A heavy rainfall, in places far exceeding 60 inches, is reflected in more widespread forest than is to be found to the east of the Rift Valley. The Mau Plateau is the outstanding physical unit. This ' massif ' attains 10,000 feet and is for the most part forested, though there are treeless grassy downs at the highest altitudes. North-west of the Mau country the level declines to 7000 feet on the Nandi Plateau. Here is the home of the Nandi tribe, a people who resemble the Masai rather than the Kikuyu in their Hamito-Negroid characteristics. Beyond, going northwards, the plateau bears the name of Uasin Gishu and is excellent pasture land, whilst away to the north-west, across the low plateau of Trans-Nzoia,[1] large parts of which are below 5000 feet, rises lofty Mount Elgon whose crater-summit is traversed by the Uganda–Kenya boundary.

The foregoing brief description will help to indicate the desirability of the Kenya Highlands from the standpoint of European colonization. In this equatorial region the altitude zone, 6000–7000 feet, is the most satisfactory to the health as well as to the agricultural enterprise of the White immigrants, although the main centre of their civilization—Nairobi—is considerably lower (5400 ft.). In an earlier chapter it was noted that the equable equatorial climate, opposed to prolonged maintenance of vigour, is relieved of its most trying feature—excessive temperature—by high altitude ; so that at Nairobi, for example, there is no monthly mean higher than 66°F., whilst most districts of European occupation experience even more temperate conditions.

The rich red volcanic soil, highly suited to mixed farming, and particularly, in some districts, to 'arabica' coffee, covers a large proportion of the plateau highlands and adds a strong inducement

[1] i.e. land across the Nzoia, one of the principal tributaries of Lake Victoria and fed by the heavy rains on Mount Elgon.

to the farmer settler, so that here—more especially in the districts to the east of the Rift Valley—is the largest colony of Europeans established on the African Plateau north of the Zambezi River. From its beginnings in 1903, the European population has grown slowly to the number of about 65,000.

Before European colonization, the Kenya plateau was occupied by peoples with a wide variety of cultures, among whom the predominant folk were the Masai, who ranged with their herds over a large section of the southern and western highlands. They were accustomed to plunder their neighbours, in particular the Kikuyu, who were restricted to a wedge of country, east of the Aberdare range and south of Mount Kenya, where they lived by cultivating clearings in the forest.

From the start of European settlement, the British Government took great care to assign to the colonists only uninhabited land, and of the 16,000 square miles included in the ' Highlands ', or region set aside for European colonization, 4,000 square miles are reserved forest, and of the rest 9,000 square miles were unoccupied except for intermittent grazing by the predatory Masai, before they were moved to their present reservation in southern Kenya, and the remaining 3,000 square miles were uninhabited. The irregular boundaries of the alienated areas or ' Highlands ', as shown in Fig. 49, are due therefore simply to the accidents of tribal distribution at the time of colonization. Naturally, there were cases of doubt where districts which were vacant at the time of colonization were assumed to be ownerless, but were later claimed by certain tribes as territory which they occupied from time to time as they moved in search of fresh grazing grounds or of areas of forest to be cleared for cultivation. All these cases were carefully considered by the Carter Land Commission of 1933, and every genuine claim was settled, usually by the grant of compensation in money and land elsewhere.

It was as an outcome of the recommendations of the Carter Land Commission that the territory of the Colony was divided by two Orders in Council into two divisions, the ' Highlands ', or areas reserved for the European farmers, and the ' Native Areas ', set aside for the various tribes. Despite the use of the term ' Highlands ' to describe the areas of European farming, this division clearly involves no discrimination as to elevation, climate or fertility, but simply reflects the rights of tribal land ownership as finally settled by the Carter Commission. In fact, nearly 90 per cent of the total population of the Colony, including practically all of the Kamba, Kikuyu, Kavirondo, Nandi, Kipsigis, Elgeyo, Meru and Embu, live above 3,750 feet, the level of Lake Victoria.

In 1952 the land of Kenya was divided in the following areas :

	sq. miles.
Native areas	52,021
Alienated land	13,347
Crown forests and Royal National Parks. . . .	11,894
Townships and government reserves	984
Northern Frontier, and unclassified Crown Land . .	141,487
Total land area, Kenya Colony . .	219,733

No part of the alienated lands is allowed to lie idle, and they not only support the European population of the colony, but also provide work for most of the 439,000 Africans who in 1952 were calculated to be in paid employment in Kenya.

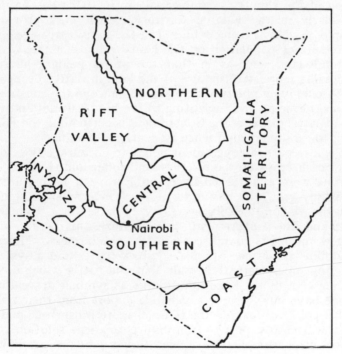

FIG. 49.—Kenya : Provincial Boundaries (1963)

The restriction of grants of such lands to settlers from Europe has ceased, for in October, 1959, the Government of Kenya presented a proposal whereby leases of alienated land may be granted to Asian and African as well as European farmers of proved competence. It has been calculated that, if all the alienated arable land in Kenya were to be distributed between the

Africans at present employed thereon and those occupying arable land in the reserves, the average size of holdings would only increase by 8·4 per cent, from 15·5 to 16·8 acres ; while if Africans employed in industry and the public service were also to be given land, the average size of holdings would fall to 11·5 acres.[1] For such doubtful benefits, it would clearly be disastrous to incorporate the alienated lands in the reserves.

Some of the most important recent economic developments in the Colony have taken place not in the districts of European farming but in the Native Areas. As the population of these areas has grown, it has become clear that subsistence farming alone will not be sufficient to support the inhabitants, and they have therefore been encouraged to produce a substantial proportion of the country's commercial crops. This has happened particularly in the Kikuyu territory, which may provide an example of what is being achieved in the native areas generally.

Pressure of population on the land is almost as heavy as in Kavirondo-land and, as in that reserve, is being relieved by encouraging more scientific use of the land in native occupation. Apart from giving practical help and guidance in the construction of dams, terracing and replanting of the bare hillsides and treatment of cattle diseases, the Government is persuading the Kikuyu farmer to consolidate and fence his scattered holdings.

It is also part of government policy to encourage the cultivation of cash crops on the reserves, and coffee and sisal, which at one time were raised exclusively on European farms, are now successfully grown on native territory. Government instructors teach the elaborate skills necessary to raise these commercial crops, and the Government also organizes marketing of the produce, and offers guaranteed prices to the farmers. Moreover, the administration has established stock-routes and a system of marketing hides, with the result that the cattle which were at one time kept by the Kikuyu primarily as symbols of wealth and prestige have now become a valuable export from their reserve.

This policy of making the reserves more prosperous and self-reliant will clearly provide the only permanent solution to the problem of over-population. Such Crown lands as are now left unallocated (Fig. 49) are in the dry and barren districts of the north and east, and the detachment of alienated land to enlarge the reserves would be at best only a palliative.

Hence the native territories are no longer to be regarded primarily as areas of subsistence agriculture and convenient reservoirs of labour for the commercial farms on alienated land.

[1] B. R. Davidson and R. J. Yates, ' Relations between population and potential arable land . . . ,' *East African Economics Review*, December, 1959.

Instead they are becoming increasingly important in the production, alongside the European farms, of the cash crops on which the welfare of the colony depends.

Intensive efforts to improve native cultivation, however, have only been made since 1946, and there is still much to be done. In 1953 the urgency of the problem of overcrowding in some native areas was increased when many Kikuyu in European employ were sent back to their reserves. Consequently it is intended to spend in the Kikuyu Reserve almost half of the special grant made in that year by the United Kingdom Government for the improvement of African agriculture in the colony. At present the expenditure involved is heavy, but the dams, wells, and terraces which are the outcome of this policy will be lasting improvements, while the skills disseminated among the African farmers should yield even richer dividends for the prosperity of the country.

On the Kenya Highlands, the commercial cultivation which is being encouraged in the native areas is more varied than that which has become traditional on the European farms. Thus tea, pineapples, tobacco and pyrethrum are often grown in the reserves along with coffee and sisal, while commercial stock-rearing is based on traditional customs. In shaping this policy, a moral has been drawn from the experience of the European farmers of the dangers, through the uncertainties of weather and markets, of excessive specialization, especially in maize and wheat.

It was not until about 1910 that the colonists were in a position to export their products on a considerable scale, but already hopes, largely fulfilled, were being entertained for the two crops, coffee and sisal, that now virtually monopolize the export trade. Sisal is, as noted previously, a hardy crop that succeeds under a variety of tropical climates and on soils of indifferent quality. Consequently, its cultivation in East Africa is widespread wherever transport and labour (for decortication) are available. In Kenya cultivation is not confined to the Highlands—though here it is at its maximum—but also extends intermittently throughout the railway zone between Nairobi and Mombasa.

' Arabica ' coffee, which is exacting in its requirements of temperature, rainfall and soil, grows most successfully on the fine-grained volcanic soils of the Highlands, between 5000 and 6000 feet above sea-level, but its cultivation is still largely confined to the eastern zone and reaches its greatest intensity in the southern districts of the Kikuyu Plateau, where the output of sisal is also most considerable for Kenya Colony.[1]

[1] For commercial agriculture, where both coffee and sisal are concerned, the Fort Hall district is outstanding.

Since the year 1918 maize and wheat have been widely planted, especially in the western zone of the Highlands, including the Trans-Nzoia, Uasin Gishu and Mau Plateaux. The long haul to the coast via the Uganda Railway renders the export of these low-priced crops unprofitable. They have, however, a considerable market at hand, and especially is this true of maize which has become increasingly popular as an item of native diet. In addition to a very large area under maize on European farms, the cereal is grown throughout the Kikuyu Reserve along with millet and pulses. An interesting development of recent years in the Kenya Highlands has been the cultivation of tea, whose exports increased from 1 ton to 4,279 tons between 1927 and 1947, and to nearly 10,900 tons in 1962.[1]

Land Reclamation in Kenya

The Government of Kenya, in its policy of forestalling the threatened pressure on the land in the native areas, as the population continues to grow, is naturally concentrating its efforts on the most immediate and practicable solution, the improvement of the standard of agriculture on land already occupied, and the diversification of this farming, in particular by the introduction of more cash crops.

At the same time, experiments are being carried out to explore the possibilities of reclamation in certain drier regions and areas of special conditions, which until now have never been tilled. Such reclamation would be slow, arduous and expensive, and in the absence of large rivers suitable for diversion for purposes of irrigation, results are unlikely to be immediate and spectacular. But there is reason to hope that selected districts within the large areas of unoccupied country in the Coast districts and Northern Frontier Province could be made to support at least a light population, and thus relieve pressure in the more densely settled parts of the country.

The most instructive experiment of this sort has been that undertaken by the African Land Utilization and Settlement Organization using Development and Reconstruction Authority funds, in the Makueni Settlement Area in Machakos District. Until 1946 this was waste country, abandoned to rhinoceros, elephants and buffaloes, and of course the tsetse fly. After the first essential step of controlling this wild life, a suitable economy had to be found for the immigrant settlers. The soils were light and of low fertility, and the rainfall, which averages only 25 to 30 inches a year and falls in two brief seasons, was not reliable

[1] The acreage under tea on village farms was, in 1959, 1541, but this cultivation had extended to 6400 acres by 1962.

enough for continuous agriculture. Hence stock ranching was
adopted as the chief economy, and the arable land retired regularly
under leys. Although a few water boreholes have been successfully harnessed and some small dams constructed, such crops as are
grown have to rely for the most part on direct rainfall. It has
been found that the efficacy of this rainfall can be increased by
tie-ridging ; while yields have also been greatly improved following mulching with grass and the application of phosphate.
Moderate dressings of farmyard manure have been shown to
raise production by an average of over 50 per cent for several
seasons, and also to assist in the establishment of leys. In 1950,
there began an initial 5-year plan to settle 1250 landless Wakamba
families in this area. During 1953, 317 new farms covering an
area of 15,000 acres were surveyed and occupied, and by the end
of that year settlement was well ahead of schedule. 908 families,
with a total population of 5800, had been settled, the entire
occupied area being 40,000 acres, of which 4750 acres were under
cultivation. During the famine of 1953, a few basic rules of good
husbandry were insisted upon, with the result that the settlers
were preserved from the shortages suffered by the rest of the
Machakos Akamba.

A rather different problem is presented by certain ' special
areas ', such as the ' bracken zone ' of Kikuyuland where the task
is to eradicate the existing useless vegetation cover and to produce
instead ploughable land or pasture. The bracken zone covers
300 square miles in the Kikuyu Reserve. The rainfall is good,
but the soil is very acid and light-textured. The very steep
slopes limit the area which might be turned into arable land, so
the chief aim of the experiments has been to convert the bracken
country into pasture. After clearance it is essential to apply
lime and phosphate to correct the natural deficiences of the soil.
After this it has been found that seeding is necessary, as a satisfactory grass cover takes too long to establish itself naturally.
Unfortunately, the local Kikuyu grass is not very productive
even when manured, but molasses or guinea grass, if given farmyard manure and phosphate, are producing better yields, while
under the same conditions potatoes, millets and silage oats have
proved very successful. The outcome of this experiment and its
value for wider application will largely depend on how frequently
and heavily fertilizers have to be applied to the land in order to
keep it in good condition, and this is not yet certain.

Administration

' Indirect rule ' on the Nigerian model was never possible
in Kenya, since there were here no large autonomous kingdoms
18

through which administration could function. But ethnic considerations were taken into account in dividing the administrative districts into locations, based on clan groupings. Within these locations, elders administer justice on traditional lines, and speak for their people on matters of common concern.

The population of Kenya included, in 1962, 39,000 Arabs and 178,000 Indians and Pakistanis. The Arabs, who have long been established as sea-traders, live mainly in the coastal protectorate ; while the Indian community largely dates from 1895, when many came over to help in the construction of the Uganda Railway. They perform numerous valuable services in the life of the country, particularly by extending commerce into even the remotest districts.

In 1963, for the purpose of organizing elections under the constitution of the independent state, Kenya was divided into seven regions, including one carved from the eastern extremity of the former Northern Frontier District, where the population was largely composed of Somali and kindred peoples. The 10-mile deep Kenya Coastal Strip, which was leased by Britain from the Sultan of Zanzibar 68 years previously, was to continue to be administered as part of Kenya.

Kenya has lately seen both expansion of primary production, and also the extension of towns and factories. For already the manufacture of cement and margarine, the processing of sisal, and the tinning of garden crops have been started on a small scale, and the port of Mombasa is beginning to take on the functions of an industrial city.

The Proposed Closer Union of the East African Dependencies

Official proposals for greater co-operation between the Territories of British East Africa were vigorously renewed immediately after the Second World War, and discussion was very active in 1947. By that time the official view firmly favoured a grouping of Territories in which Nyasaland, Northern Rhodesia and Southern Rhodesia would be associated, as would also be Tanganyika, Kenya and Uganda in a separate, northern group. For the southern group the Central African Federation provides unified administration in matters such as railway and road communications, labour, agriculture and economic relations.

The East African High Commission, consisting of the Governors of Kenya, Tanganyika and Uganda, was constituted by an Order in Council in 1947, and came into operation in 1948. The East African Central Legislative Assembly was established by the same Order in Council, and lasted until the end of 1955. In contained delegates from each of the British East African territories, including African and Indian members and one Arab representative. The High Commission had power to legislate, with the advice and consent of the Assembly, on affairs of common interest to the three territories, including civil aviation, customs, defence, railways, harbours and inter-territorial research. It also administered certain inter-territorial services.

The three independent East African states, Kenya, Tanzania and Uganda, have continued to work for co-operation in the economic field, through the East African Common Services Organization.

REFERENCES

In English alone the literature is very voluminous. The following list of works will provide, it is hoped, a useful guide to further reading :

Allan, W., *Studies in African Land Usage in Northern Rhodesia* (Rhodes-Livingstone Papers, No. 15), Cape Town, 1949.

Baker, S. J. K., ' Distribution of Native Population over East Africa ', *Africa*, Vol. X, 1937.

Baker, S. J. K., and White, R. T., ' The Distribution of Native Population over S.E. Central Africa ', *Geog. Journ.*, Vol. CVIII (pp. 198–210), 1946.

Brooks, C. E. P., ' The Distribution of Rainfall over Uganda ', *Quart. Jour. R. Meteor. Soc.*, 1924.

Brown, G. St. O., *The Vanishing Tribes of Kenya*, Philadelphia, 1925.

Buell, R. L., *The Native Problem in Africa* (Vol. I), New York, 1928.

Buxton, C. R., *The Race Problem in Africa*, London, 1931.

Coupland, R., *The Exploitation of East Africa, 1856–1899*, London, 1939.

Davies, Merle, *Modern Industry and the African*, London, 1934.

Debenham, F., *Report on the Water Resources of the Bechuanaland Protectorate, Northern Rhodesia, the Nyasaland Protectorate, Tanganyika Territory, Kenya and the Uganda Protectorate*, Colonial Research Publications, No. 2, London, 1948.

Dilley, M. R., *British Policy in Kenya Colony*, New York, 1937.

Gillman, C., ' A Population Map of Tanganyika ', *Geog. Review* (New York), Vol. 26, 1936.

' A Vegetation-Types Map of Tanganyika Territory ', *Geog. Rev.*, Vol. XXXIX, No. 1, 1949.

Gluckman, M., and Colson, E. (editors), *Seven Tribes of British Central Africa*, London (O.U.P. for Rhodes-Livingstone Institute), 1951.

Gouldsbury, C., *The Great Plateau of Northern Rhodesia*, London, 1911.

Gregory, J. W., *The Rift Valleys and Geology of East Africa*, London, 1921.

Hailey, Lord, *An African Survey*, Oxford, 1938.

Hall, Sir John, ' Some Aspects of Economic Development in Uganda ', *African Affairs*, Vol. 51 (1952), pp. 124–34.

Handbook of Nyasaland, Crown Agents for Colonies, London, 1932.

Hollis, A. C., *The Masai*, Oxford, 1905.

Huxley, E., *White Man's Country* (2 vols.), London, 1935.

The Sorcerer's Apprentice ; a Journey through East Africa, London, 1948.

Huxley, E., and Perham, M., *Race and Politics in Kenya*, London, 1944.

Johnston, Sir H. H., *The Uganda Protectorate*, 2 vols., London, 1902.

Koeppen, W., and Geiger, R., *Handbuch der Klimatologie*, Bd. V, Teil X; *The Climate of Rhodesia, Nyasaland and Mozambique* (C. L. Robertson and W. D. Sellick), 1933.

Lambert, H. E., *The Use of Indigenous Authorities in Tribal Administration: Studies of the Meru in Kenya Colony*, School of African Studies, University of Cape Town, 1947.

Leys, N. M., *Kenya*, London, 1924.

Lugard, Sir F. (later Lord), *The Dual Mandate in British Tropical Africa*, 3rd ed., London, 1926.

Lyons, H. G., ' Meteorology and Climatology of German East Africa ', *Quart. Jour. R. Meteor. Soc.*, 1917.

Mair, L. P., *Native Policies in Africa*, London, 1936.

Matheson, J. K., and Bovill, E. W. (editors), *East African Agriculture*, Oxford, 1950.

Maurette, F., *Afrique Equatoriale, Orientale et Australe*, Géographie Universelle, Vol. 2, Tome XII, Paris, 1938.

Olivier, Lord, *White Capital and Coloured Labour*, London, 1929.

Rosco, G., *The Baganda*, Cambridge, 1911.

The Banyoro, Cambridge, 1923.

Ross McGregor, W., *Kenya from Within*, London, 1927.

Roux, L., *L'Est Africain Britannique*, Soc. d'Editions Géog., Marit. et Colon., Paris, 1950.

Sayers, G. F. (ed.), *The Handbook of Tanganyika*, London, 1930.

Thomas, H. B., and Scott, R., *Uganda—A Handbook*, Oxford Univ. Press, 1935.

Tothill, J. D. (Editor), *Agriculture in Uganda*, London, 1940.

Twining, Sir E., ' The Situation in Tanganyika ', *African Affairs*, Vol. 50 (1951), pp. 297–310.

' U.N. Mission's Report on Tanganyika Territory ', Nov. 1948.

Wakefield, A. J., *The East and Central African Groundnut Project*, Royal Society of Arts, London, 1948.

Worthington, E. B., *A Development Plan for Uganda*, Entebbe, 1946. (This Report is particularly important : it is a recommendation to the Uganda Government of a method of experimental land utilization involving what Dr. Worthington knows as ' Pilot Schemes '.)

' Zanzibar, Report of the Commission on Agriculture ', Zanzibar, 1923.

Reference should also be made to the Colonial Reports (annual) and to the reports on the censuses of population and agriculture in the various Dependencies.

CHAPTER III

MADAGASCAR

L A GRANDE ÎLE', as it is known to the French, is one of the four greatest islands of the world, to be compared in area with Borneo.[1] All through the Portuguese and Dutch periods of maritime enterprise in the Indian Ocean it remained outside the ken of Europe ; in fact it was not until 1865-70 that Madagascar was systematically explored. This scientific investigation was undertaken in the years mentioned by Alfred Grandidier whose massive work remains the standard treatise on the island and its peoples.[2]

In 1885 France, whose claims—however vague—to special interest go back to the time of Louis XIII, proclaimed a Protectorate throughout the island but agreed not to interfere in its internal government. At that time only the natural harbour of Diego-Suarez in the extreme north was annexed. The Protectorate was first really exerted in 1895 and in the following year, with the formal annexation of Madagascar, General Galliéni, perhaps the greatest figure in French colonial history, was sent out as first Governor.

Physical Character

The great ' horst ' of Madagascar is, as noted in an early chapter, composed chiefly of pre-Palaeozoic rocks (schists, granites, &c.) similar to those of the East African Plateau with which it was formerly continuous ; whilst over large parts of the ancient platform vulcanism has resulted in the extensive flow of lava. Near the western coast there is a fairly complete sequence of beds from early Mesozoic to middle Tertiary, and it is these sediments whose weathering has produced some of the most fertile, though little used, soils of the island. About two-thirds of the total area, including the greater part of the interior, is covered with lateritic soils that rest directly upon the Archaean

[1] Each is over 230,000 sq. miles in extent, or about twice the area of the British Isles.
[2] See bibliography at end of chapter.

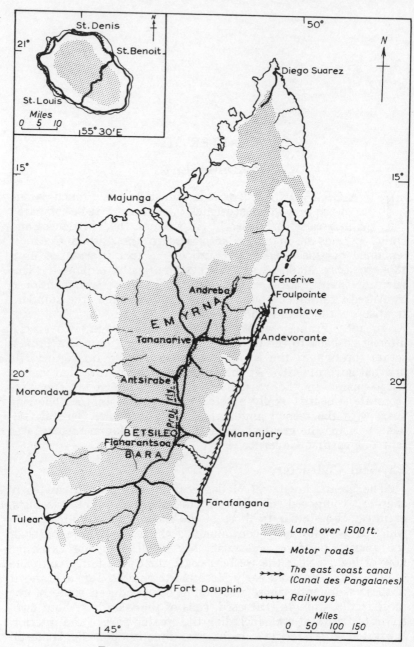

FIG. 50.—Communications in Madagascar
(Réunion inset)

266

platform and are usually of indifferent quality as well as heavy to work.

As late as the Oligocene phase of the Tertiary there was land connexion with Africa which permitted the passage of the many species of lemurs—' half apes ' as they have been called—that are the most distinctive feature of the island's fauna. The eastern coast, much of it remarkably straight, was determined not earlier than the Upper Cretaceous by a great fault that runs independently of the grain of the land, and along which frequent earthquakes bear witness to crustal instability. From its steep slope the descent is abrupt to oceanic depths, 15,000 feet and more.

The main axis of the island trending NNE–SSW.—roughly parallel to the shore-line of South-East Africa—continues for over 900 miles and passes for the greater part of this distance through a plateau that rises to a mean of 4000 feet above sea-level. In consequence of the narrow and approximately elliptical form of Madagascar no part is more than 150 miles from the sea-board—the extreme width being about 350 miles near the latitude of the chief port of the eastern coast, Tamatave.

On the eastern side, where the plateau edge is most clearly defined, the coastal plain is confined to a width little more than 10 miles.[1] An almost continuous series of lagoons follows the coast, in its middle section, from the neighbourhood of Tamatave southwards, and canalization is proving a comparatively simple matter : all told, only about 30 miles of shore, mostly sandy, will require to be trenched in a distance of over 350 miles along this lagoon fringe. When complete, the Pangalanes Canal will provide the necessary facilities for coasting traffic needing shelter from the storms that frequently beset this coast. From the interior to the Mozambique Channel there are the easiest gradients in the island, though even so the western edge of the plateau, at 3000–4000 feet, forms the uppermost of a series of well-developed terraces. Although, generally, the western shore is low and shelving, the ultimate depth of the Mozambique Channel—over 200 miles across at its narrowest—descends to nearly 10,000 feet.

The irregular distribution of relict mountain ranges—carved out of the ancient crystalline platform—and of volcanic highlands divides the undulating plateau surface into a series of basins, some of them occupied by lakes[2] and by the lacustrine soils on which the first rice crops of the Island were cultivated. In the east central district, to the north of which lies the capital, Antananarivo, the plateau culminates in the great lava-covered

[1] The abrupt descent from escarpment summit to maritime lowland suggests close comparison with Eastern Natal.

[2] The most notable is Lake Alaotra.

mass—over 2000 square miles in extent—of the Ankaratra Highlands whose summits, including ancient volcanoes, attain 8000 feet
and over.[1]

Alluvial lowland of considerable expanse is limited to the
western zone, where Mesozoic strata overlie the crystalline basement rocks, and across it really great rivers flow westwards to
the Mozambique Channel from upper courses, whose descent
from the plateau is marked by falls and rapids. The most
extensive river basin is that of the Betsiboka, whose widely
separated head-streams begin their flow near or upon the nodal
plateau of the Ankaratra Highlands. In its lower course the
river meanders north-westwards across the widest plain of the
island, where land under 600 feet extends more than 100 miles
from the sea-board. During the rainy season the Betsiboka
may be used by coasting craft up to a point about 50 miles from
its maritime outlet. The river-borne soils of the western zone
of the island are frequently of high fertility, though there is
much sterile sand in places.

Climate and Vegetation

Although temperature is moderated somewhat by the prevailing South-East Trades and, in the interior, by considerable
altitude the essentially tropical situation [2] is indicated by the
very high midsummer mean, between 80° and 90° at sea-level
throughout the island. Four principal climatic régimes are
distinguished :

(1) Hot steamy conditions reach their maximum on the east
coast.[3] Although sea breezes bring some relief even the mid-
winter mean at Tamatave is as high as 68°. Rainfall is particularly heavy, usually exceeding 100 inches (Tamatave 116
inches) and is well distributed throughout the year ; indeed there
is no dry season and every month has at least 3 inches.

(2) The central plateau has a much more favourable climate
for human settlement. In contrast with the east coast, which
is, as far as possible, avoided by the most advanced peoples,
this is the most desirable region of the island, as shown by the
density of population and by the comparatively high level of
civilization. Antananarivo, standing 4600 feet above the sea,
shows a range of temperature similar to that of Nairobi in the

---

[1] Actually the highest summit of the island is found in the most
northerly highland where Amboro rises to about 9500 feet.

[2] Although the southern limit is extra-tropical, i.e. 25° 40′ S., nearly
nine-tenths of the island lies to the north of the Tropic.

[3] Mean relative humidity on many parts of the coast reaches 80 per
cent.

Kenya Highlands : no month has a higher mean than 68° and in July the figure is only 55°. In summer (December–February) the South-East Trades blow strongly and there is abundant rain-fall—not less than 10 inches in each of the three months. Comparatively high pressure over the interior of Madagascar in winter, however, repels the full strength of the Trades and there is little precipitation in this season : between May and October, inclusive, there is not as much as 1 inch in any month. Usually the annual rainfall on the central plateau is not more than half the total for the eastern littoral and the number of rainy days is only about 90, in comparison with 180 on the coast.

(3) The climate of the north-west of Madagascar resembles, in its essentials of temperature, humidity and—to a lesser degree—rainfall, that of the eastern littoral. The chief difference is the shorter season of rains. There are places where precipitation reaches 100 inches, though 60–80 inches seems to be the average. Such moist conditions would not prevail in a ' rain shadow ', and we find that in summer, when by far the greater part of the rainfall occurs, the South-East Trades are replaced by onshore north-westers. At Majunga, a port at the outlet of the Betsiboka River, precipitation is about 70 inches, most of which occurs in the period October to April. On the north-west coast there is rarely relief from torrid conditions, and if we take Majunga again as a typical station we find that even in mid-winter the mean exceeds 70°.

(4) Climatically the region of the South and South-West is the most abnormal in the island. There is an approach to semi-desert conditions, for rain occurs on only 25–30 days of the year, and the annual amount is less than 15 inches—a very low figure in view of the excessive evaporation. Meagre rainfall is explained in most parts by the ' rain shadow ' on the lee slopes of the southern extremity of the plateau; although the most southerly shore receives winds directly from the ocean, and there the ' rain-shadow ' explanation will not serve.

Rainfall, of which there are, as we have seen, several distinct régimes, is the main determinant of the three contrasted plant associations that are present on the island.

Dense rain forest with valuable cabinet-woods, including rose-wood and ebony, now covers less than one-eighth of the total area, but was formerly of much greater extent on the plains and lower slopes to the east, west and north-west, respectively, of the central plateau. The spread of cultivation to the western districts of the island in recent times has been responsible for much deforestation. It is the narrow eastern plain together with the flanking escarpment on which the largest and most luxuriant forest still remains, and mangrove is abundant on the lagoon-fringed coast.

Forest is rare on the central plateau—though woodland exists here and there—and the dominant vegetation is short grass-savanna or veld. Bush occurs intermittently, but the comparison is closer on the whole with the High Veld than with the Bush Veld of South Africa. The long period of 4–5 months of very meagre rains or actual drought is the main factor that determines the absence of forest trees.

In the south and south-west where the period of drought is longer than elsewhere in the island and, indeed, occupies the greater part of the year, xerophytic plants including aloes and cacti are characteristic, and the region is to be classed as scrubland—not unlike the Little Karroo of South Africa—rather than as savanna or veld.

Social and Economic Geography

Madagascar has been the meeting-ground for two contrasted races—one African negroid [1] the other Malayo-Polynesian—which have merged to form the commonest Malagasy type of to-day in which the negroid strain predominates. But even the most negroid of the Malagasy speak the Malayo-Polynesian language that prevails throughout the island with very little dialectic variation. From the time of earliest Malayo-Polynesian immigration—possibly from 2000 B.C. onwards—African slaves were continually introduced—many by Arab traders—and it is remarkable that their mother tongue should have left no trace in the island. If Bantu immigration had been by family groups rather than by individuals there is little doubt that the Negro language would have survived, if only in a modified form. Topographical nomenclature, whose orthography is very complex and strange to the European, is also exclusively Malayo-Polynesian.

The dominant people both numerically and culturally are the Hova who comprise one-quarter of the island's population of approximately 4,350,000 (1950). A small proportion are descended from Malay immigrants of the sixteenth century A.D. and are of purer stock than the majority : but even those of the Hova who show a strong negroid strain are fairer in their olive complexion than the other peoples of Madagascar. The Hova occupy the ' region ' [2]—formerly kingdom—of

[1] There is a division of opinion amongst ethnologists as to the place of origin of the earliest negroid immigrants. Some believe it to be African, others Melanesian : but there is common agreement that during recent centuries the Negroes introduced were Bantu.

[2] In 1946 administration, formerly in ' regions ', was re-organized in 5 provinces, each with its elected provincial assembly.

Emyrna in the east-centre of the island, and Antananarivo (1950, 174,000 inhabitants) was their capital before the arrival of the French. Within the depressions of the Emyrna Plateau density of rural settlement reaches fifty to the square mile, a much higher figure than the average for the island. By the early years of the nineteenth century the Hova had extended their authority throughout much of Eastern Madagascar, and as they were concerned to occupy only the higher and healthier plateau levels they refrained from colonizing both the western districts and the eastern coast of the island. It should perhaps be mentioned that, although the term ' Hova ' has come to be applied in a tribal or national sense to all the people of Emyrna, strictly speaking it should refer only to the middle class as distinct from the aristocracy and slaves, as they existed in the pre-French era.

To the south of the Hova dwell the more negroid Betsileo, also a plateau people and about half a million in number. Like the majority of the Malagasy they are agriculturists and show particular aptitude in the cultivation of rice. East of Emyrna and of the Betsileo province the Betsimisaraka—about 450,000 —occupy the torrid and unhealthy eastern littoral. Climate is mainly responsible for their lack of virility. Before the arrival of the French they, more than any other community, were under the domination of the Hova.

In the western districts of the island a number of related tribes, the Sakalava, are sparsely scattered and reach an aggregate of approximately 267,000. Though, culturally, the Sakalava are amongst the most primitive of the islanders they are actually closest to the Hova in respect of their high proportion of Malayo-Polynesian blood. Farther south dwell the Bara whose culture is even ruder than that of the Sakalava, a condition which is related to an inhospitable environment of which indication has been given.

Since the establishment of French authority the mobility of population has increased, and the definition of tribal boundaries is not as clear as it was at that time. A notable trend is the movement of settlers into the empty yet fertile lands of the west from the more densely-populated east-centre. Many of the Betsileo and Betsimisaraka have migrated westwards in recent years into the domain of the Sakalava, who seem to be steadily declining in numbers. It is still, however, on the side nearest to Africa that the density of population is least. With the shift of the ' centre of gravity ' of density westwards, it may be that, despite the efforts of France to confine the trade of Madagascar to her own empire, commercial interchange across the Mozambique Channel will develop. At present the island is as commercially isolated from Africa as if it were a part of that distant island world from which its culture is derived. Temperate South Africa has most to gain from trading contacts with Madagascar, for in the Union the production of tropical crops such as sugar-cane must always be very limited.

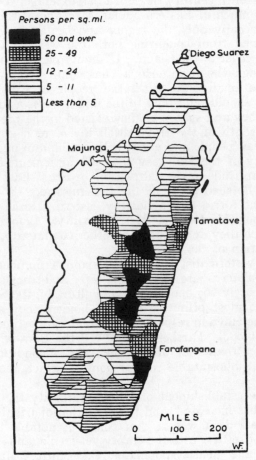

FIG. 51.—Madagascar : Density of Population (1910)

On the administrative side France has pursued a more enlightened policy in Madagascar than in the majority of her colonial possessions. The foundations laid by General Galliéni have, indeed, provided a model which has been followed elsewhere, particularly in Morocco under tne régime of Marshal Lyautey

At the outset Galliéni asserted the paramountcy of native interests and in pursuance of his policy the settlement of Europeans has not been encouraged ; so that, including officials, there are still only about 31,000 White people in the island. Galliéni was quick to realize and acknowledge the diversities—racial and cultural—that exist and was determined that the French administrative system should not be rigidly uniform, but rather adapted to particular local needs. Instead of Hova hegemony, which Galliéni destroyed,[1] there was to be a confederation of tribal communities each retaining its individuality, though accepting the suzerainty of France, and entrusted with powers of local government. In other words, Galliéni introduced ' Protectorate ' or ' indirect ' rule as it is understood, for example, in British Africa. In order to extend French authority throughout the island with a minimum of force he selected commanding centres, and from these liaison officers gained contact with native leaders, in order to devise for each of the larger communities a system of administration that should be, as far as possible, in harmony with local institutions and sentiment.

In the Hova land of Emyrna, before the French conquest, peasant proprietorship of land did not exist, and the structure of society was essentially feudal. Under the modern system of individual tenure, which has been introduced by the French throughout the greater part of the island, the social and economic standards of the new peasantry have been much improved. Moreover, experiments on the communal organization of villages are being pursued in several areas of the island. It is in keeping with the spirit of French policy that the status of the colony was changed in 1946 to that of an overseas territory.

Less than 3 per cent of the total area is cultivated, and of this proportion of the land rice occupies rather more than one-third. It is essentially the food-crop of the Hova and Betsileo, who cultivate it on the hill-slopes of the interior plateau and on the alluvial and lacustrine soils of the plain around Lake Alaotra (north of Emyrna) and of the Betsimitatatra Plain, in which the capital, Antananarivo, is situated. At the time of French occupation rice culture did not extend far beyond the plateau of the east-centre, but now more than 90 per cent of the Malagasy are concerned in its production, and the only parts of the island from which it is excluded are the south and south-west where climate is altogether unfavourable. Though formerly—early twentieth century—there was need to import rice from Indo-China the island has now a considerable surplus for export which is shipped to

---

[1] A native insurrection, led by the Hovas, was crushed in March, 1947.

Réunion and to France. Another food-crop of the Malagasy
is manioc (tapioca) which was first imported from Réunion
during the eighteenth century and quickly gained popularity.
European planters as well as native small-holders undertake
its cultivation, and within the last thirty years there has been
considerable and regular export, almost entirely to France.
Maize, the most recently introduced of the staple crops of Madagascar, has only figured in the export trade since 1911, but, as
in the cases of rice and manioc, practically all inhabited parts of
the island, except the south-west and south—where the rainfall
is too meagre—are favourable to its production on a considerable
scale.

Apart from crops grown mainly for consumption within the
island there is increasing attention on the part of native cultivators to production for export—an enterprise entirely confined
to the European population until a decade or so ago. For sugar
and rice the vast areas of alluvium in the lower basins of westward-
flowing rivers, such as the Betsiboka, are admirably suited, and
it is confidently expected that in a future not far distant Madagascar will occupy a high place amongst the sugar-producing
countries of the southern tropical belt of the world. For coffee,
already a notable crop, the best land is on the upper slopes of the
eastern escarpment, where rainfall and drainage are adequate and
where occur large areas of volcanic soil reminiscent of the coffee
lands of the East African Highlands. After the Great War the
Natives, realizing the high prices to be obtained from coffee, turned
increasingly to its cultivation, and Madagascar has supplied in
recent years one-half of the total amount imported by France.

Although the emphasis on agriculture is likely to remain,
stock-rearing may be hardly less important in the near future,
but the introduction of high-class breeds will be necessary.[1]
The native hump-backed cattle—the zebu—were until recently
treated as sacred by many of the Malagasy, but the increasing
consumption of beef reveals a dietary change due to European
influence.

Commercial agriculture will be restricted so long as France
insists on virtually monopolizing both the export and the import
trade—more than 80 per cent in each case—and in detaching
Madagascar from its natural trading associations with South-
East Africa.

Until the establishment of French authority transport was
quite primitive and native porterage was general. There were
no routes better than local trackways and consequently little

[1] The Chamber of Commerce of the French woollen centres of Roubaix
and Tourcoing early recommended the introduction of merino sheep.

internal commerce was practised; whilst the isolation of the island from the markets of the world was reflected in the absence of an import or export trade of any consequence.

With the exception of Diego-Suarez in the extreme north no port has natural shelter for shipping, and all are alike in their inadequate equipment for the handling of cargo. Diego-Suarez, described by French writers as the finest harbour in the world, is used mainly as a naval station, but now that it is linked to Antananarivo by motor-road its commercial future also is assured. At Tamatave, the port for Antananarivo and for the province

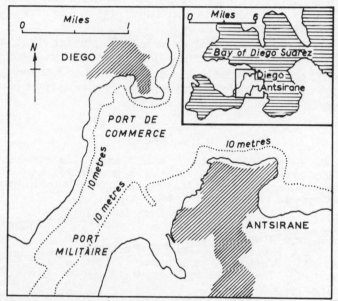

FIG. 52.—Diego-Suarez : the finest natural harbour in Madagascar
(Areas built over indicated by diagonal line shading.)

of Emyrna as a whole, extensive harbour construction has recently been undertaken. The port, 229 miles by rail from the capital, has immediate access to the Pangalanes Canal which skirts the eastern coast as far as Farafangana—nearly 400 miles to the south of Tamatave—and obviates dangerous offshore navigation.

The construction of, first, railways and, later, motor-roads has proceeded fairly vigorously during the present century. The trunk line of railway between Antananarivo and Tamatave—the 'Rice Railway', as it has been called—was planned to extend southwards across the centre of the plateau into the domain of the Betsileo and had reached Antsirabe when restrictions on further construction were imposed, shortly before the Second World War. Another railway, now completed, is from Fianarantsoa, main centre of the Betsileo, to the nearest east coast port, Mananjary—its purpose to provide an outlet for the rice, maize and manioc production of one of the most intensively farmed areas of the island. In place of additional projected railways motor-road services are now extensively developed.

The western lands are still without railways, and it seems likely that, in general, motor-roads will make them unnecessary. Already Antananarivo has become the focus of the following highways : (1) to Majunga, the port of the north-west, (2) to the southern ports, Ft. Dauphin and Tulear, (3) to Tamatave, which reinforces the existing railway.

A recent venture which may have an important effect on the island's economy was the setting up in 1951 of a state company to exploit the coal of the Sakoa district (in the south-west). It is hoped to build a railway and harbour and to extract between 300,000 and 600,000 metric tons a year.

REFERENCES

All the most valuable literature is in French. The work of Alfred Grandidier is outstanding and much of it is collected in his *Histoire naturelle, physique et politique de Madagascar* which appeared in a series of volumes between 1875 and 1921. See also :

Dandouau, A., *Géographie de Madagascar*, Paris, 1922.

Faublée, J., Falek, R., Hartweg, R., and Rouget, G., *L'Ethnographie de Madagascar*, Paris, 1946.

Galliéni, J. S., *Neuf ans à Madagascar*, Paris, 1908.

Gautier, E. F., *Madagascar*, Paris, 1902.

Gordge, J. T., ' The outlook in Madagascar ', *African Affairs*, Vol. 48 (1949), pp. 133–41.

Grandidier, A. et G., *Ethnographie de Madagascar*, 4 vols., Paris, 1901–18.

Grandidier, G., ' Madagascar ', *Geographical Review*, New York, Vol. X, 1920.

Maurette, F., *Afrique Equatoriale, Orientale et Australe*, Tome XII, Géographie Universelle, Paris, 1938.

Paulin, H., *Madagascar*, Paris, 1925.

Périer de la Bathie, *La végétation malgache*, Paris.

Roberts, S. H., *History of French Colonial Policy* (Vol. II), London, 1929.

Sarraut, A., *La mise en valeur des colonies françaises*, Paris, 1922.

CHAPTER IV

CENTRAL AFRICA

I T is difficult to define this region with even approximate precision. We are concerned with that part of the inter-tropical zone which is situated to the west of the East African Plateau and extends up to the Atlantic sea-board between limits that may be taken as the Cunene River and the Camerouns Mountain. Within this region the vast basin of the Congo, extending over one and a half million square miles, has a dominating importance : in addition, there are the land—in Angola, Gabun, and the Camerouns particularly—on the western rim of the Central African depression; and their natural orientation is Atlantic-wards, as indicated by hydrographic independence of the Congo system.

On the northern and southern extremities of the region the existing political divisions with arbitrarily-drawn frontiers greatly confuse any attempt at systematic regional classification. For example, Angola extends southwards so as to include part of the southern desert together with a large share of the semi-arid region of upper Zambezia [1]; whilst, on the northern side, French Equatorial Africa,[2] easily the most unwieldy and—on geographical grounds—least satisfactory political unit of Africa, includes the Chad Colony, the northern half of which is definitely Saharan.

Omitting the semi-arid northern, southern and south-western margins, there is, in respect of general surface conditions and of

[1] The vast depression, approximately 400,000 sq. miles, which is drained intermittently by the head-streams of the Zambezi, extends into four territories—Bechuanaland Protectorate, Northern Rhodesia, Angola and South-West Africa. It is, from the standpoint of physical geography, a distinct and indeed major region of the continent, but its present importance to man is too small to warrant separate attention in a work of this scope.

[2] For convenience the abbreviation A.E.F., for Afrique Equatoriale Française, is commonly used.

climate, a closer approximation to uniformity throughout than is to be found in any of the African regions of the first magnitude excepting the Sahara. Mean annual rainfall exceeds 40 inches and its abundance is reflected in a luxuriant vegetation varying from dense rain-forest to park-savanna and treeless savanna. Where soil distribution is concerned the feature that distinguishes the Congo Basin amongst the major regions of Africa is comparatively widespread alluvium bordering the lower courses of a large number of great tributary rivers which are in flood annually. In consequence of these natural conditions the potential agricultural resources awaiting development are on an immense scale, though, actually, the region is economically among the most primitive of the world.   The climate that promotes the luxuriance of vegetation is debilitating to native life and, except in one or two specially-favoured districts, such as the Camerouns Highlands, is an effective bar to European immigration. If the Central African agricultural output were to be withdrawn from world markets the loss would be hardly appreciable.

The direct and indirect influence of climate is not the only hindrance to enterprise.   Though the opening-up of Central Africa was rapid once it began about half a century ago, the interior is still very inaccessible, with vast areas unsurveyed.   Two of the European States—Belgium and Portugal—that hold huge territories in these latitudes are by reason of their comparatively slender resources unable to capitalize many big industrial undertakings on which, by reason of their nature, financial return would be delayed : whilst France, the other State principally concerned in the future of Central Africa, devotes more attention to dependencies in North-West and West Africa which, for a variety of reasons, including greater accessibility and superior native civilization, offer more immediate commercial advantages.

The Angola Plateau

We begin with the earliest European ' colony ' in Central Africa, namely Angola (or Portuguese West Africa), whose origins date back to the early sixteenth century. The advantage of being first in the field was neglected by the Portuguese [1], and it was not until the last quarter of the nineteenth century, when the partition of inter-tropical Africa was vigorously proceeding, that they were roused to make effective claim to a hinterland extending into the Congo and Zambezi Basins. Down to 1870 their interests were virtually confined to a few trading posts

[1] cf. similar neglected opportunities in Mozambique where the opening-up of South-East Africa was concerned.

on the coast, including Kabinda,[1] north of the Congo estuary and—south of it—the more important Loanda and Benguella.

In respect of climate and vegetation Angola is essentially transitional and its compact territory of some 480,000 sq. miles may be regarded as the area of mergence of several distinct zones which attain their fullest development outside the Colony. Structurally it represents a little-disturbed portion of the sub-continental plateau of ancient crystalline rocks partly overlaid

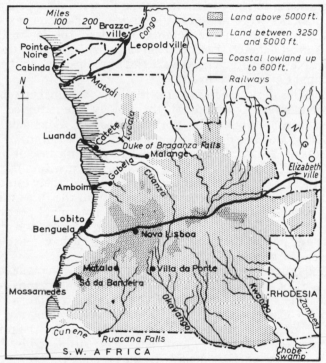

FIG. 53.—Angola: relief and drainage

by Palaeozoic sediments, with an average elevation more than 3000 feet above the Atlantic shore. The highest summits (c. 8000 ft.) occur in the west-centre, from which drainage is radial —direct to the Atlantic by the Cunene and Cuanza Rivers, to name only the most prominent, and to the Kasai (Congo) and Zambezi. From the western ramparts of the Plateau the descent is irregular by a series of terraces—in places almost precipitous—to the ocean littoral.

[1] Kabinda is administered under Angola and is officially known as the 'District of Congo'.

The coastal zone extending as far south as the Cunene (approx. lat. 17° S.) experiences a climate that is cool for its latitude and, though not properly to be described as arid in view of the high relative humidity of the atmosphere, its rainfall is particularly meagre, indicating the proximity of the south-western desert of Africa of which this coastal zone is really the northern extension. Mossamedes receives but 1 inch and even as far north as Loanda the precipitation is only 11 inches. During the rainless winter all rivers south of Benguella, except the Cunene, disappear in the sandy littoral. Vegetation is of semi-desert character, except in the extreme north, in the neighbourhood of the lower Congo. Scrub is most characteristic, though in the river valleys the flora is more luxuriant and includes varieties of palms, among them the oil-bearing *Elaeis guineensis*.

Along this desiccated coastal belt all the principal commercial and administrative centres of the Colony are situated, and, grouped in and around the ports of Loanda, Benguella (with Lobito) and Mossamedes are the majority of the European population, about 200,000 (1961), of whom by no means all are un-mixed White. Apart from the Portuguese resident within the coastal belt there is a smaller number scattered over the westernmost districts of the Plateau, though usually close to the three railways each of which climbs up the Plateau from a terminal port. It is only very recently that the more bracing climate and greater agricultural possibilities offered by the Plateau have encouraged the eastward spread of settlement.

Loanda, north of the outlet of the Cuanza River and on the widest part of the Angola coastal plain, where it expands to over 100 miles, is the headquarters of the Administration, a dignity due to its history as the earliest important Portuguese depôt south of the Congo. In earlier days Loanda was also the principal commercial outlet for the Colony, but is now surpassed by Lobito, 18 miles north of Benguella. Loanda remains, however, the largest urban centre of the Colony with a population of 232,500 in 1958, including 40,000 Europeans. It was originally intended that the Loanda–Malange railway should be extended south-eastwards into Mozambique, and there have been more recent plans to continue the line into Congo (Leopoldville). The gauge of the railway has lately been broadened from one metre to 3 ft. 6 in. and it now handles mineral (iron and manganese) in addition to agricultural produce.

Beginning about 1951, Angola has begun an ambitious programme of industrialization, based largely on hydro-electric power. Oil has been discovered on the coastal plain near Luanda, where a refinery has been operating since 1958, but the output is still modest. However, the power resources of Angola's rivers are extremely rich, and have so far been tapped at three main installations. The Cambambe Dam on the Cuanza River, which will ultimately have a capacity of 260,000 kW, supplies power to Luanda. This city is the largest manufacturing centre in Angola, with a wide range of industries, including a big cotton mill. The Benguela area receives electricity from a smaller installation at Biopic. Thirdly, the southern districts are supplied from the dam at Matala, which also serves to carry the railway over the Cuene River. Eventually a larger second dam may be built upstream on this river at the Ruacana Falls. A similar ambitious

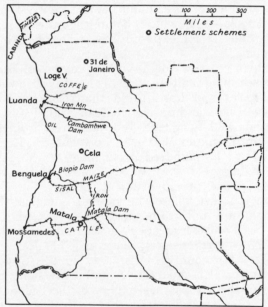

FIG. 54.—Angola : Economic Features

scheme is for a high dam at the Duke of Braganza Falls on the Lucala River. The Cambambe and Matala installations supply water for irrigation as well as for power.

On the coast as far north as Loanda the dearth of rain is sufficient to debar all agriculture for which irrigation is not available. Most prominent in commercial agriculture are coffee (a highland product) and sugar-cane. In the case of sugar output for Angola as a whole, much the greater part is produced in the low-rainfall areas of Loanda and Benguella, wherever streamwater is available. There are few parts of the world where sugar-cane is grown under such comparatively arid climatic conditions. Cacao is confined to the northernmost districts of the littoral, especially the Kabinda Enclave where irrigation is unnecessary.

Reference to this crop makes inevitable some mention of the Portuguese islands, S. Tomé and Principe, off the Central African coast, whose cacao output was formerly the largest in Africa, for their plantation labour was recruited mainly from Angola.

Nearly 300 miles to the south of Loanda, Lobito Bay, close to Benguella, is now the recognized ocean gateway not only for the Colony but also, since the completion during 1931 of the Benguella Railway, for the vast hinterland of the Upper Congo. The natural harbour is a lagoon, deep and with a wide entrance, and the growing town is still limited to the narrow sand-spit that shelters the anchorage. Benguella, until recently the main port for Central Angola—with which, before the railway, it was linked by caravan trail—is an exposed roadstead of little value for modern shipping.

The southern coast of Angola in the province of Huila, though of little account in agriculture, has the healthiest lowland climate of Angola, cooler and less humid than elsewhere. European settlement both here and on the Plateau behind was much later than at Loanda and Benguella and dates only from the arrival, in 1839, of Brazilian and Madeiran Portuguese. These colonists were followed by a few hundred Boers, many of whose descendants have since re-migrated southwards. Most of the immigrants, with the assistance of Government, sought the Plateau immediately to the east where the rainfall is higher than on the coast, though still uncertain, and often less than 25 inches in a year. Sisal and wheat succeed where maize and coffee, the commonest crops farther north, have little chance. To the east and south-east the country falls away to the Upper Zambezi and to the Etosha Pan and Lake Ngami depressions, where there is transition to the dry pastoral régime of the Kalahari.

One of the serious difficulties that confronts plantation agriculture throughout the greater part of the Angola littoral is the sparseness of native population. In order to obtain sufficient labour there was once recourse to forced recruitment, though Government finally suppressed this practice by means of a new labour law in 1962.

On the Central Plateau, in the provinces of Benguella and Bihé, the future of European colonization is much more promising than in Mossamedes farther south, as the Government now realizes. Altitude exceeds 3500 feet throughout and tempers the excessive heat of these latitudes. Rainfall is assured and comparatively abundant, varying according to locality from 40 to 60 inches, with the heaviest precipitation near the western edge of the Plateau, where altitude attains 7000 feet and more. Other advantages for the European settler or planter include a much higher density of native population—on which to draw for labour —than the average for the Colony, and the penetration of the Benguella Railway through the heart of the region. Although the railway was intended primarily as a trans-continental line its incidental and secondary function in regard to local transport is likely to be of great consequence. So assured is the future of this pivotal line that it was not surprising when the announcement to transfer the capital from Loanda to a site along the railway, 270 miles from Lobito Bay, was made in 1927. Huambo, renamed Nova Lisboa, was to be the new headquarters of the Colony : it is on the Plateau, centrally situated and much more accessible than Loanda in so far as inter-communication within the Colony is concerned. Moreover, its climate is much to be preferred. Unfortunately, the colonization project was in difficulties from the outset, and this has now been replaced by less ambitious schemes.

These have taken the form of carefully planned and relatively expensive undertakings of reclamation and settlement, catering for both European and African pioneers. The two chief centres of new European settlement are at Cela and Matala (Fig. 54). By 1962, about 400 Portuguese families from the homeland had been settled at Cela, where they concentrate on the raising of dairy and beef cattle, without the aid of any African labour. At the Matala colony, both Portuguese and African settlers have specialized in growing irrigated tobacco for export. The main areas reclaimed for purely African settlement are in the northern districts, in the Loge Valley and the district known as 31 de Janeiro. In the former colony, coffee is the main crop, in the latter, cassava. In both cases the Government has undertaken the essential preliminary clearing, ploughing and terracing.

The high western edge of the Plateau (in Benguella and Cuanza Sul Provinces) which receives copious rains is largely forest-clothed and it is here, up to about 3000 feet, that oil palms are most abundant. Physical conditions are very satisfactory for coffee culture, still the most remunerative aspect of farming in Angola, and both Natives and Europeans contribute to the output. Amongst subsistence crops maize is prominent : it is grown almost entirely by Natives, and of the large output there is a considerable proportion, usually one-third, available for export to Europe. On the open grass-lands of Central Angola, still happily free from tsetse fly, there are bright prospects for ranching, and the ready market in the industrialized parts of Katanga has already stimulated the export of cattle. Northwards, in the more tropical districts of Malange and Cuanza Norte, there are almost limitless possibilities for plantation agriculture, but the development of rubber, cacao, sugar and coffee has not passed much beyond the stage of experimentation.

The Congo border in North-Eastern Angola is a little-known region isolated from the main centres of life within the Colony and more closely associated with the interests of the Belgian Congo than with those of Angola. Its only commercial activity —diamond prospecting in Lunda—is an enterprise which produces the second most valuable of Angola's exports (after coffee). Large areas are less than 3000 feet above sea-level and experience a hot, humid climate ill-suited to White settlement. Indeed, physical conditions as a whole closely resemble those of the Congo Basin. So far as is known selva is limited to the neighbourhood of the Kasai tributaries that traverse the region in a northerly direction, and tall grass savanna is widespread.

Katanga

The incorporation of a strip of the northern margin of the sub-continental plateau within the Belgian Congo was due to the far-reaching ambitions of King Leopold who endeavoured, successfully, to extend his appanage—the Congo Free State—especially towards the south, and Belgium has inherited the enlarged domain. When, in 1908, the Congo State became a Belgian dependency certain of the great land and mining companies that had been granted vast concessions by Leopold were permitted to remain. First amongst them was the *Comité Spécial du Katanga*, which was left in possession of over 100 million acres, or much the greater part of the Province and an area about eight times that of Belgium.[1] The copper-mining operations undertaken during the last thirty years by the *Union Minière du Haut Katanga* have inaugurated a remarkable phase in the economic life of Central Africa, one which offers both good and evil possibilities for African society.[2] It is in Katanga that the greater part of Belgian enterprise has been concentrated, so that the Province, though marginal to the Belgian Congo as a whole, represents in commerce and industry the ' centre of gravity ' of the Dependency.

In respect of both physical and economic geography the orientation of Southern Katanga—richest zone of accessible ores— is towards the Republic of Zambia and Angola rather than towards the middle Congo region. The common frontier of Zambia

[1] The Belgian Government now holds two-thirds of the capital investment of the Comité Spécial.

[2] The copper of Katanga has long been worked by Natives, including the Basanga who formerly used copper implements more frequently than iron ones.

and the Belgian Province follows for several hundred miles the hardly perceptible ' divide ' of the Congo head-streams (especially the Lualaba and Lufira) and the upper Zambezi. As in the neighbouring district of Rhodesia the plateau altitude of Southern

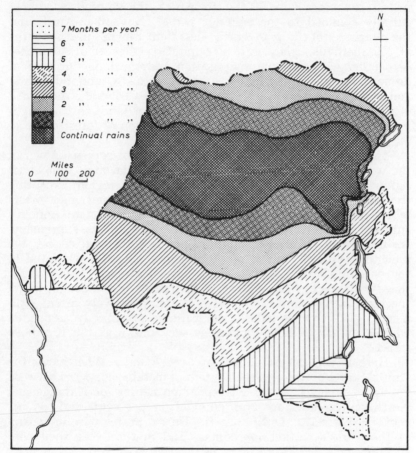

FIG. 55.—Number of months during which the dry season prevails in the Congo (Leopoldville)

Katanga exceeds an average of 3500 feet, and it is only in the extreme eastern parts of the Belgian Congo, including Ruanda-Urundi, where similar altitude is maintained over such a wide area.

The climate of southernmost Katanga, an undulating plateau comparatively high in latitude as in altitude, is of all Congo climates the most suited to European occupation. There is a greater seasonal range of temperature than is to be found in the

more equatorial Ruanda and Urundi, which together form part
of the East African Plateau. At Elisabethville, the principal
urban centre of the Province, the highest mean (October) is less
than 75°F., while the June and July figures hardly exceed 60°.
As on the grass-lands of South Africa the rainfall is almost
entirely confined to the summer period, November–April, and
the remainder of the year is arid—less than 2 inches in six months
at Elisabethville. Moderate precipitation—less than 50 inches
—together with extreme evaporation and the long duration of
drought is opposed to luxuriant forest growth, and tall grass-
and-bush savanna is most characteristic. Towards the north
of the Province, and especially on the lower lands in the neighbourhood of the Lualaba River, the proportion of forest tends to
increase.

The discovery of one of the richest fields of copper known in
the world has granted to Katanga an industrial and commercial
significance far surpassing that of any African region, excepting
the Rand. Whereas in 1900 wild rubber from the Congo forests
represented more than 80 per cent of the exports from Leopold's
entire domain, copper is now unchallenged in its supremacy.
Including gold, tin, cobalt and diamonds, in addition to copper, the
mineral wealth of the Belgian territory is generally restricted to
the outcrop of ancient rocks—Archaean and early Palaeozoic—
that surrounds the vast equatorial depression of the Congo, where
the fundamental core is concealed by comparatively recent sediments. The copper deposits of Katanga are mainly associated
with dolomitic rocks of Palaeozoic age, known as the Kambove
series.[1]

Here is the richest copper-ore yet found. Whereas in the
United States of America the content of metallic copper is between
1·0 and 1·5 per cent, the corresponding figures for Katanga and
Northern Rhodesia are approximately 7 per cent, and 3·5 per
cent, respectively. Until 1923 the United States were in control
of the world's market for copper, and in that year their contribution equalled 55 per cent of the aggregate production. By
1937 the output of the Katanga–Rhodesia field was 18 per cent
of the total world production, whilst the proportion from the
United States had fallen to 23 per cent ; by 1962, however, while
the production from the Katanga–Rhodesia area was about
295,000 tons p.a. the comparative figure for the United States
was about 1,228,000 tons.

Mining, which is completely dependent on the provision of

[1] Since the War, uranium production has been extended at Shinkolobwe.
Its output (which is kept secret), though of strategic importance, is of
insignificant value.

modern transport facilities, is still confined to the neighbourhood of the trunk railway (and its branches) that traverses Katanga diagonally from the Rhodesian border. In the early years of this century production was restricted to the vicinity of Elisabethville where the famous ' Star of the Congo ' mine was the main source of supply ; but in recent years Kambove, 100 miles to the north-west and near the junction of the Benguella Railway and the Lower Congo–Katanga line,[1] has become the main centre of activity. Mining has extended towards Bukama on the B.C.K. railway and at the head of navigation on the Lualaba

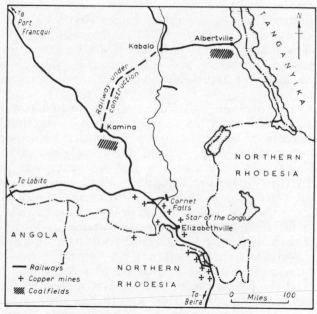

FIG. 56.—Railways serving the Katanga

—an expansion that has been dependent on the continuation of the railway north-westwards from Elisabethville. South-eastwards from the latter town the copper field continues across the frontier into Northern Rhodesia, as mentioned in an earlier chapter.

The establishment of smelting furnaces at Elisabethville and Jadotville, about 60 miles farther north-west, has widened the basis of industry in Katanga, and practically all of the metal which is exported goes out, not as ore, but as crude copper. Until very recently fuel requirements—other than timber, still

[1] Known as B.C.K.—from ' Bas Congo–Katanga '

plentifully used—were not supplied locally, and coal from the
Wankie mine of Southern Rhodesia was for long imported.
Since 1925, however, coal production from two fields within the
Belgian Congo has been on an increasing scale. The more important field, but the less accessible, is close to the River Lukuga
and not far from Albertville, the ferry-port on Lake Tanganyika.
The other, not so rich in coal, is at Luena, close to Bukama,
and its convenient position grants it special significance in the
mining and smelting industries of Kambove and Jadotville.
The annual output of the two fields does not greatly exceed 200,000
tons, but future production is not likely to be so limited. An
additional source of power is provided by a hydro-electric station
at the Cornet Falls on the upper Lufira River. The electrical
output of 45,000 H.P. is employed in the smelting industry of
Jadotville and also provides light and power for the entire copper
zone between Kambove and Elisabethville. This is only a
beginning, for other hydro-electric projects are in various stages
of completion.

In the case of a mining industry which is so far distant from
the Atlantic and Indian Ocean coasts transport becomes of very
critical importance, and the problem it poses has been approached
with commendable energy. Until the completion of the Benguella Railway in 1931 access to the sea-board was provided
mainly by the Northern and Southern Rhodesian Railways, and
so a great percentage of the copper went out by way of Beira.
As Europe is the destination of practically all the exported metal
such an indirect route as the one just mentioned soon came to be
regarded as an intolerable burden on the industry. Consequently,
another Portuguese-owned gateway to Central Africa, namely
Lobito, the most favourably situated port for traffic between
Europe and the Congo Basin, now receives a steadily increasing
proportion of the shipments from and to Katanga. Apart from
the very considerable commercial possibilities, already mentioned,
within the zone of the Benguella Railway in Angola itself, the
Belgian traffic alone is likely to make the line the most remunerative in the African continent.

The Belgian Congo has enjoyed a spectacular prosperity since
the Second World War. In the six years between 1945 and 1951,
its exports grew six-fold in value, though only 80 per cent in
tonnage—a discrepancy due partly to higher prices, and partly
to the extended local processing of produce. This boom has,
however, brought in its train problems of inflation, transport and
labour supply. The most thriving industry is the mining of
copper, which accounts for a quarter of the colony's exports ;
Union Minière is the world's second largest producer, and has

by far the richest reserves of copper ore. Not only has mining flourished, but also commercial farming, and 50 per cent by value and nearly 60 per cent by tonnage of the exports consist in crop and plantation products (mainly palm nuts and oil, cotton and coffee). The output of food crops has, however, not kept pace with local needs, and the Congo has still to import food, principally dried fish and meat from Kenya, and flour from America.

With the exception of the settlement in the Kenya Highlands the White community of Southern Katanga was the largest within the inner belt of inter-tropical Africa. Out of a total of about 112,000 Europeans (mainly Belgians) in the Belgian Congo during 1959 nearly one-half occupied the railway zone from the Rhodesian border to Bukama. Elisabethville ranks as capital of the Province as well as its principal commercial centre. For mining labour the *Union Minière du Haut Katanga* depends on immigration from a wide area of Central Africa. At the beginning of 1963, the working personnel of the *Union Minière* numbered 23,250 with 1708 staff. The density of population in the Province is low, not seven to the square mile, and of the total number of adult males about 56 per cent is already engaged in various paid employment, a proportion which the Administration admits is too high if the welfare of native society is to be upheld. In 1951 there were in the entire Belgian Congo about 1,031,000 native wage-earners, most of them in Katanga, and of these 447,000 were working at long distances from homes distributed not only in other parts of the Belgian Congo but also in Angola and East Africa.

Closely associated with Katanga so far as labour supply is concerned are the independent states of Rwanda (a republic) and Burundi (a monarchy), formerly under German sovereignty and incorporated as a province of the Congo from 1925 till 1962. In no part of Central Africa is the density of population nearly so high as in these comparatively small territories of about 20,000 sq. miles together. There are almost 5½ million Bantu, so that the average density (1960) is 243 per square mile compared with less than 10 for the Congo. One of the incentives to the Belgian claim for the control of ex-German lands lying immediately to the east of the Western Rift Valley, between Lake Kivu and the northern shores of Tanganyika, was the existence of the virile and prolific Wa-tusi and Wa-hutu stocks, regarded by the Belgian industrialists as offering a ' reservoir ' for labour, from which, down to the time of the German defeat, they had been excluded. It was once argued—strenuously by Germany—that the incorporation of Ruanda-Urundi within the Belgian Congo was a clear case of annexation and therefore a violation of the Mandate ;

to which, however, it may now be justly replied that international supervision is maintained through the United Nations Organization, a body that claims the right to criticize the Administration from the standpoint of native policy. One matter for the consideration of the United Nations is the recruitment of labour for work outside the Province and—in the case of Southern Katanga—nearly 1000 miles away. Conscious of the criticism of its labour policy the Belgian Government decided to discontinue the practice of transferring large numbers of natives from Ruanda-Urundi, and the inflow into Katanga had by 1951 almost entirely ceased. In 1952, however, shortage of labour in proportion to the rapid development of the Congo had become so acute, that the Belgian Government was again considering the import of labour on a large scale from Ruanda-Urundi. There is no doubt that, now the pernicious sytem of tribute-labour for cattle has been broken down, a transfer of population from the overcrowded trustee districts to permanent villages within or near the industrial belt would be a very beneficial step for both territories. In 1962–63 some 60,000 Wa-tusi arrived in the Congo as refugees from Rwanda.

Most affected by past recruiting of labour in Ruanda-Urundi have been the agricultural Bantu—the Wa-hutu—who represent not less than 60 per cent of the entire population and whose quick intelligence goes with industrious habits. Before the establishment of German control over this inaccessible land, i.e. prior to 1910, the Wa-hutu were under the subjection of the aristocratic and pastoral Wa-tusi.[1] The latter provide not more than 10 per cent of the population of the Province and their pride of race is too strong to permit them to accept the conditions of industrial labour that to them would mean servility. In this respect the Wa-tusi recall the Zulu, which fine stock has, however, already suffered the deterioration that accompanies urban conditions in South Africa.

THE CONGO BASIN : EQUATORIAL LANDS

Throughout this vast depression the dominating regional feature is the succession of great tributary rivers that, fan-wise, converge westwards upon the Congo before the combined outflow enters the narrow trench worn through the plateau rim. From the centre of the Basin where the altitude never descends under 1000 feet there is an irregular increase of elevation in every direction, the sides of the depression being terraced like an amphitheatre.

[1] The Wa-tusi pastoralists of Ruanda have been described as the tallest people in Africa. In them the Hamitic strain is noticeable.

The contrast between the central lowlands and the plateau-rim, unbroken save where the Congo traverses the Crystal Mountains, is strengthened by their geological dissimilarity. During the epoch extending from the Permian to the Triassic, Central Africa was near the South Pole of the world and was then entirely glaciated. The ice-sheets of this glaciation left in their retreat abundant morainic material which now appears as the conglomerates, limestones, &c., of the so-called Kundelungu beds. In

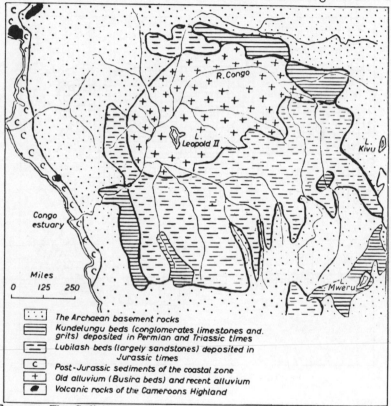

FIG. 57.—The Sedimentary Rocks of the Congo Basin, enclosed within the Archaean Plateau

Jurassic times, when Central Africa was occupied by a shallow inland sea, prolonged sedimentation occurred, producing the so-called Lubilash beds. Gradually the enclosed sea was drained away by the infant Congo River, until now the only vestiges remaining are Lakes Leopold II and Tumba. The most recent deposits of the Central Congo are the Busira alluvial beds, which provide the most fertile soils and support the richest forest in Central Africa.

A general statement concerning the climate and vegetation of the Congo lands was included in an earlier chapter (pp. 34–42), but because regional climatic differences, especially where rainfall is concerned, are so considerable it is appropriate now to grant them further consideration. Temperatures are remarkably uniform considering the immensity of the area ; and not only from place to place, but also throughout the year at a particular station.

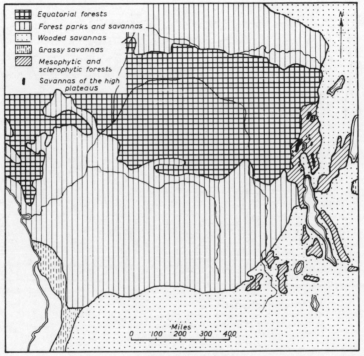

FIG. 58.—Vegetation of the Congo Basin

The only exception to a very high temperature level is in the vicinity of the Congo estuary where the Benguella Current's influence is felt. Banana records a mean annual temperature of 79° F., which is the same as for places in the interior 1000 miles farther south.

The northern half of the Congo Basin receives more than 60 inches of rainfall, whilst the western margins, well to the north of the Congo estuary, receive 80 inches and over. South of the estuary the coastal zone does not receive much more than 20 inches at any point, and farther into the interior, in the southern half of the Basin, 40 inches is generally the upward limit.

Within Central Africa the distribution and characteristics of climate, mainly on a basis of rainfall, may be classified as follows:

I. Central Congo

This type is distinguished by two seasons of particularly heavy rainfall, namely March–May and September–November ; yet the rainfall is well distributed throughout the year and the mean aggregate is about 60 inches.

II. Northern Congo (Interior) including Ubangi region

Rainfall shows only one maximum, and practically all precipitation is confined to the period May–October, with December and January virtually rainless.

III. Western Margins, typified by Gabun

Excessive heat and atmospheric humidity are unrelieved throughout the year. A particularly heavy rainfall, averaging well over 80 inches, is fairly evenly distributed seasonally, the exception being June–July, an almost rainless period.

IV. South-West Coast (Benguella type)

This zone is characterized by exceptionally low temperatures for the latitude, with little annual range ; rainfall is less than 20 inches.

V. Southern Interior Margin (Katanga type)

Here are the lowest temperatures for the Congo Basin, as a whole ; a plentiful rainfall of over 40 inches, which, however, is restricted to 7 months of the year, the ' winter ' season of May–August being virtually rainless. (Climate generally approximates to what is sometimes called the ' Rhodesia type '.)

The River System of the Congo, especially in its relation to Inland Transport

The main stream and its left-bank affluents, notably the Kasai, have two periods of low water alternating with phases of flood or high water, in contrast to the right-bank tributaries, particularly the Ubangi, where a single rise and fall is the rule.

The first maximum in the year occurs about the middle of May, in consequence of the high level of the rivers in the southern

20

part of the basin (upper Kasai and Southern Katanga).[1]   Afterwards the level of the upper Congo falls continuously until July
when, for example, there is low water at Stanleyville near Stanley
Falls.   In the same month (July), however, the lower middle
river is raised by the floods of the Ubangi and the other right-

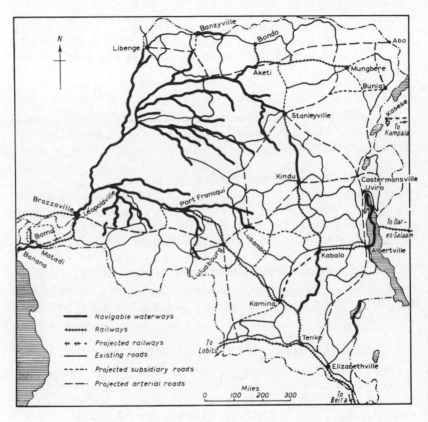

FIG. 59.—Lines of Communication in the Belgian Congo

bank tributaries.   Still farther down-stream at the mid-year the
Congo receives little water from any of its affluents—it is a time
when the Kasai is low—and at Stanley Pool the great river is at
its lowest in July and August.

The second maximum in the régime of the Congo occurs about

[1] Note that in Southern Katanga the second maximum of rainfall is
in February–March, the first—counting from the beginning of the rainy
season—being in December.

the middle of December. This is due not so much to the flood from the right-bank entrants (Ubangi, Sangha, &c.) which attain their single maximum much earlier, in October, but to the early summer floods (late November and early December) on the upper Congo system (Lualaba, &c.) that occur when there is still a considerable volume of water in the northern right-bank rivers, then beginning their winter low-level régimes.

Unlike the immense basin of the Amazon that of the Congo is debarred from wide-open access to the ocean, and the services of the railway engineer have been required to provide the outlets for its commerce. Moreover, despite an aggregate of 6000 miles of navigable waterways the middle and upper courses of the Congo and its tributary streams are interrupted at critical points by rapids, so that a railway track is necessary, as a portage past the unnavigable passages—a feature that is also characteristic of certain of the Amazon tributaries.

From Southern Katanga the Lualaba and Lufira head-streams of the Congo flow northwards, in the case of the former past the head of navigation at Bukama, to unite in Lake Kisale. The stretch between Bukama and Kongolo—about 300 miles—is navigable, but from the latter to a point about 180 miles down-stream the course of the Congo is broken by rapids, and a portage railway follows the left bank. The Lukuga River, leading from Lake Tanganyika to the Congo (or Lualaba), is not navigable, but its valley, providing easy access to the shore of the great lake, is followed by a railway. This line from Kabalo to the lake-port of Albertville (from which there is a ferry to Kigoma) has carried a considerable proportion of the copper exported from Katanga, though by this route to Dar-es-Salaam four handlings of freight used to be involved after the initial loading.[1]

On the middle Congo traffic by steamers of about 800 tons' displacement is possible right around the great loop of the river, from Stanleyville to Leopoldville, a distance of well over 1000 miles.

Of the left-bank tributaries the Kasai is the most favourable to river transport. Along it there is communication between the lower Congo centres and Katanga, the region whose traffic is most remunerative. River steamers—800-ton stern-wheelers—reach Port Francqui (Ilebo), situated well above the confluence of the Kasai and the Sankuru, whilst the latter stream, offering an east–west route over the greater part of the distance between the Lualaba and the Kasai, is navigable as far as Lusambo, more than 300 miles above the outlet to the Kasai. In order

[1] Since September 1956 there has been a continuous rail link on a gauge of 3 ft. 6 in. from the Katanga to Lake Tanganyika. (See page 299.)

to cover the unnavigable stretches of the upper Kasai and to link Katanga by way of Bukama to Port Francqui, the Bas Congo–Katanga Railway came into existence, and the 650-mile extent of the line was completed after tremendous difficulties in 1928. Not satisfied with the inconvenience involved in the transference of traffic from river to rail, and vice versa, at Port Francqui, the Belgians surveyed the cost of railway construction between this point and Leopoldville, the capital of the Dependency. The new line, 480 miles in length, in its direct approach to the lower Congo would require costly bridging to carry it over the northward-flowing affluents of the Kasai, including the Kwango River. For the present at least, therefore, this project has been abandoned, and instead, the road over the route has been improved.

The Kwango, that enters the Kasai to the south-west of Lake Leopold II, is a natural north–south avenue between North-Eastern Angola and the lower Congo. There is uninterrupted navigation as far as Senga, situated close to the Belgo-Portuguese frontier and not less than 400 miles above the outlet to the lower Kasai. More used at present is another northward-flowing tributary of the Kasai, the Chikapa, which opens the way to the diamond-fields of the upper Kasai and of the Lunda Province of Angola, though a short portage railway is needed to outflank the rapids at two points, Charleville and Djoko Punda.

Of the right-bank affluents of the Congo only the Ubangi offers an uninterrupted passage for a long distance. From its junction with the arterial river the great tributary may be followed up-stream, i.e. northwards, as far as Bangui, the head of navigation and 400 miles above the confluence with the Congo. This river-station is considered likely to provide the pivot of a vast transport system—partly rail and partly motor road—within the Equatorial Customs Union.

Transportation in the Congo Lands : a Summary

Leopold, King of the Belgians, deserves credit for an impressive scheme of rail and river communication intended to knit together the several widely-dispersed regions that, within his domain, offered abundant economic prospects. He intended that the project should be undertaken in the following stages :

(1) the opening of the lower Congo by the construction of a portage railway from Leopoldville to Matadi (Congo estuary), a distance of about 200 miles ;

(2) a combined river-and-rail route to expedite transport
between the middle Congo (e.g. Stanleyville) and the
Katanga Province which, in the earliest years of this
century, appeared to be slipping from Belgian grasp ;

(3) a direct route, railway throughout, from Katanga to the
Atlantic, either by way of Angola or along the Kasai
and lower Congo valleys.

The first of these enterprises was undertaken very early,
indeed was completed before the end of the nineteenth century :
the second was accomplished before the Great War, whilst the
third has been already completed in respect of the Angola route,
and it is unlikely that an all-Belgian line to the Atlantic will be
constructed.

The portage line between Leopoldville-Kinshasa[1] and Matadi,
flanking the gorges and rapids that characterize the course of
the lower Congo where it traverses the Crystal Mountains, had
certain serious disadvantages until a few years ago. First, it
was of narrower gauge than the railways of Southern Africa with
which sooner or later it would be bound to have contact, whilst
there were difficult gradients over long sections : again, in the
neighbourhood of Matadi the line was so narrowly confined
between the River Congo and the Portuguese frontier that projected improvements, such as widening and duplication of track,
were liable to be greatly hindered, failing a re-adjustment of
boundary between Angola and the Belgian Congo. An agreement was negotiated in 1927 whereby the Belgian zone near
Matadi was widened by the addition of 3 sq. kilometres, in
return for 3500 sq. kilometres which go to Portugal in the Dilolo
district, on the outer extremity of South-Western Katanga.[2]
This exchange clearly indicates the critical significance attached
by Belgium to the territory it has acquired. The widening of
the Matadi–Kinshasa line and the lowering of the gradient are
completed : the gauge of 3 feet 6 inches is identical with that
of other railways south of the Equator, so that when the extension
of the B.C.K. Railway is opened rolling-stock will be able to
travel from Cape Town Docks to the Congo estuary.

While the Belgians were proceeding vigorously with the
construction of the northern section of the B.C.K. Railway they
were obliged, in view of the necessity for the widening of the
Matadi zone, not only to cede the ' Dilolo Boot ' but also to agree
to provide the link between the Katanga line and the Benguella

---

[1] The two towns—one the administrative, the other the industrial
centre—stand together on the southern bank of Stanley Pool.

[2] The ceded area is often known as ' the Dilolo Boot '.

Railway within five years of the arrival of the Portuguese rail-head at the international frontier ; and so, by an inevitable compromise to assist in promoting competition with their own direct ' Atlantic ' route by railway and road or river.

The Benguella Railway will continue to possess two definite advantages over its competitor even where Belgian traffic is concerned. In the first place the distance from Elisabethville to Lobito is shorter than to Matadi, even allowing for the projected Port Francqui–Leopoldville line, by considerably more than 100 miles ; secondly, the Lobito route is a ' watershed line ', generally speaking, and consequently is immune from many of the rainy-season troubles such as ' wash-aways ' that would be likely to embarrass the completed B.C.K.

Even if the all-rail route to Matadi is built a considerable proportion of Katanga exports is likely to continue to use the river-and-rail route, that adheres to the Congo main-stream throughout, because of the relative cheapness of water transport ; and the co-ordination of river services over the entire Belgian Congo by means of a single organization, the powerful Belgian company known as the *Unatra*, is in this connexion a very marked advantage. But, whereas until the early 20th century railways merely supplemented river navigation, the relative importance of the two means of transport is now being reversed ; so that, together with motor-roads, railways are becoming the arterial lines, whilst the rivers are more and more relegated to the function of ' feeders '. An indication of this trend is perceived in the remarkable increase in the mileage of track built and in the freight carried : between 1914 and 1930 the length of railways more than doubled, from about 1000 to 2400 miles, and, during the same period, tonnage carried by rail increased to twenty times the figure before the First World War.[1]

Until 1934 the Congo lands of the French Empire were dependent on a Belgian-owned outlet provided by the Kinshasa–Matadi Railway. Herein lay one of the contributory factors in the undue congestion of traffic on that railway before the recent improvements to the track and prior to the opening of the Benguella Railway. From the French standpoint it was essential to have an independent route to the Atlantic coast, one to connect Brazzaville, the French capital on Stanley Pool, with the nearest ocean port within French territory. Although confronted with immense difficulties—including the cutting of no less than 17 tunnels through the Mayombe plateau—the engineers were able in 1934, according to schedule, to open the railway from Brazzaville to the port of Pointe Noire (the Ocean-Congo Railway, as

[1] In 1912—213,000 tons (2000 lb.) ; in 1930—4,254,000 tons.

it is known). Pointe Noire is naturally inadequate as a port, but the harbour that is being built will, it is expected, offer facilities for shipping superior to those on the lower Congo, where large vessels are not always able to reach Matadi in safety on account of the strength and irregularity of the current.[1]

With the prosperity of the whole colony during the War, the need for urgent and drastic improvements in its communications became evident, and the lesson was emphasized by the loss of quantities of perishable goods due to a bottle-neck at Leopoldville in 1948. The establishment in 1923 of Sabena (*Société aérienne belge d'exploitation de la navigation aérienne*) had made adminis-tration easier, but had done little to help with the main problem of heavy transport. In 1949, therefore, there was launched a Ten-Year Plan for the Congo, much of which is concerned with bettering communications.

To improve conditions for shipping in the Congo estuary, new dredging vessels are at work, and luminous buoys now make night navigation possible. At Matadi the deep-water quays have already been extended by 900 feet, and 1300 feet is to be added to those at Boma. Some also advocate the development of the port of Banana, outside the main estuary.

At Leopoldville, the river quays will be extended by 650 feet, and congestion in the city relieved by the construction of a new industrial suburb at Kimpolo, 18 miles to the north-east. A pipe-line is being laid to carry oil fuel from the estuary to Leopoldville. Up-river, new large 1000-ton barges are being built, diesel-driven tugs will replace the present fleet of wood-burning river steamers, and radar will make possible night nagivation.

Experience has shown that in the Congo the cost of carriage a ton-mile is higher by rail than by road up to an annual total of 400,000 tons. Consequently, plans for road construction are now taking precedence over schemes for new railways. Indeed, the short railway from Costermansville to Uvira has now been replaced by an improved road.

The rail link from Kamina to Kabalo, opened in September 1956, completes a new transcontinental crossing. It also opens up for the minerals of the Katanga a new route to the east coast at Dar-es-Salaam, alternative to and shorter than that to Beira. To avoid break of bulk at Kabalo, the line thence to Lake Tan-ganyika has been widened to a gauge of 3 ft. 6 in. The harbour equipment at Albertville has been improved, and a programme is in hand for enlarging the capacity of the line between Kigoma and Dar-es-Salaam.

[1] Above Boma, during high river, the current is often one of 5 knots ; near Noki, just below Matadi, a current of 10 knots has been reported.

The first new arterial road, from Kivu Province to the west coast, became ready in 1955 (Fig. 59).

The Political and Economic Organization of the Congo

It had been the general policy of the Belgian Administration to replace the Leopoldian concession system, with its monopolistic basis of trade and industry, by freedom of trade and the reservation of all administrative powers to the Government-General. In 1914 the Belgian Congo was divided into four Provinces—Congo-Kasai, Equator, Oriental and Katanga—to which in 1925 Ruanda-Urundi was added. A re-division, this time into seven provinces, including Ruanda-Urundi which remained unchanged, occurred in 1933 for the purpose of increasing rather than diminishing the already considerable degree of centralization of government. The old provincial names have officially disappeared—though one at least, namely Katanga, is likely long to be remembered and used—and were replaced by names of town-centres from which the new provinces were to be severally administered. These were the provinces of Leopoldville ; Coquilhatville (' capital ' of the former Equator Province and situated at the junction of the Congo and Chuapa rivers) ; Stanleyville (' capital ' of the former Oriental Province) ; Elisabethville ; Costermansville (immediately to the south of Lake Kivu and within the Western Rift Valley, yet to the west of Ruanda-Urundi) ; and finally Lusambo, within the basin of the Sankuru and south-central in position. The six provinces of the Belgian Congo became independent on June 30th, 1960, under a federal consitution. But tribal rivalries within the territory, and the very uneven distribution of its natural resources, are likely to impose a strain on such a federation. The future of Katanga Province is particularly uncertain, while there is also a possibility that the Congo Province will seek unity with the neighbouring Congo Republic.

Until the last quarter of the nineteenth century a number of native States under paramount chiefs persisted independently in the Congo : they have since disappeared as a result of inter-tribal war, slave-raiding and the oppressive régime of King Leopold II. Excepting the ' kings ' of Ruanda-Urundi and a few potentates farther north in the Rift Valley Highlands, chieftains are very rare whose tribes reach a membership of 50,000. Very little care was taken to avoid breaking the unity of individual tribal groups when the provincial system was inaugurated, though ignorance of conditions on the part of the Administration was also a factor. In consequence big tribes were divided, an example being that of the Bakusu who were divided between the Oriental and Katanga Provinces. To the credit of Belgium, however, there has been since 1921 a serious effort to re-unite groups previously dispersed or divided, and, in addition, to discover the native leaders with inherited authority and to recognize in some degree their tradition of leadership. In the latter case it has to be admitted that under the Belgian régime a native chief became a civil servant, deriving his authority not so much from popular sanction as from the European Administration : so that ' indirect rule ' as understood in British West Africa or Tanganyika is little practised in the Congo. Yet unlike French Africa where the French language was imposed and native tongues were officially discouraged, the Belgian Government encouraged the use of those vernaculars which are widely spoken. For official purposes four of the leading Bantu dialects (out of the two hundred or more in the Belgian Congo) were recognized, and because of its extensive and increasing use the Luba tongue (spoken by the Baluba who occupy country to the west of Lake Tanganyika) was recommended for recognition as the *lingua franca* of the Colony as a whole.

The ' concession ' system inherited from Leopold has an important bearing on the economic geography of the Central Congo as, we have seen, it has also on that of Katanga. One of the earliest land grants was made as compensation to the railway company which, by linking Leopoldville and Matadi, performed the service of opening up the interior to the outer world. Considerably more than two million acres, mostly forest, in the basin of the Busira River were provided. This vast tract known as the ' Bus-Bloc ' is still held by the company and by subsidiary interests, though little has been done to develop the latent agricultural and forest resources.

In 1911, just before the abandonment of the policy of wholesale concessions, the English soap-manufacturing firm of Lever Brothers, that had attempted without success both in British and in French West Africa to obtain forest concessions for oil-palm exploitation, was permitted to lease land in five separate districts, each larger than the ' Bus-Bloc ' and representing a circle 75 miles in diameter. The districts selected included some of the richest oil-bearing forests in Central Africa, although within the circles the Lever interests only actually held, on a lease which terminated in 1945, a small fraction of the land in each case, and in all an area of about 1,800,000 acres.[1] All but one of the circles are within 3° of the Equator: they are known from their centres

[1] The Lever concession company is known officially as ' Huileries du Congo Belge et Savonneries Lever Frères ' (Huilever).

as the Igende (Flandria), Bumba (Alberta), Barumbu (Eliza-
betha), Lusanga (Leverville) and Basongo (Brabanta) Circles
respectively—the bracketed name in each case being the newer,
European equivalent. In 1945 the concession was reduced to
freehold rights over an area of about 300,000 acres, not more
than 80,000 of which must be in any one of the aforementioned
circles.

At least twenty mills for the extraction and refining of palm
oil, including one at each of the centres mentioned above, are
now established and the output, which reached 171,500 tons in
the year 1949, is the mainstay of the export trade of oil from the
Belgian Congo. As the native suppliers of kernels are paid in
'spot cash' by the company the prices arranged at the mills
determine those ruling throughout the Congo as a whole. Moreover, the company is a big employer of regular labour, as many as
30,000 Natives being engaged in the mills and on the plantations.
Steadily the plantation product is increasing in output and the
company intends ultimately, indeed before very long, to be
independent of 'wild' or forest supplies. This is likely seriously to
affect those Congo Natives, a very large proportion of the total
population, whose only way of raising the amount of the government tax is by gathering palm kernels and selling them to the
mills of the *Huileries du Congo Belge*.

An important part of the Ten-Year Plan (1949–59) for
the Belgian Congo was concerned with the industrialization of the
colony. The success of this enterprise largely depended on the
development of the resources of the region in water power. In
1949, the total power available from the existing plants was
134,500 h.p., providing 547 kW., at that time about half the
country's total consumption of power. The remaining 50 per cent
had to be supplied by imports of oil and coal, as the local coal has
not yet been much exploited. It was hoped by 1959 to increase
the colony's electric power to almost four-fold what it was in 1949,
with the aid of new plants, of which the chief will be three (known
as the Bia Central) in the vicinity of Kambove, one in the Maniema
district, and others at Mwadingusha, Budana, Nia Nia, and by
the Pogge Falls on the Kasai.

With the aid of this power (which will also help agriculture by working irrigation pumps), extensive new factories will
be opened, especially for the production of margarine and cotton goods. Already oil refineries have been opened at Boyero
and Kabinda. As a result of this industrialization, textiles, shoes,
soap, edible oils, beer and sugar are already being exported to
neighbouring countries, and in Belgium concern is being expressed
about the growing competition.

From the evidence already adduced it is obvious that one of the foremost consequences of the introduction of industrialism into the Belgian Congo has been the unduly heavy demands on the part of mine and plantation owners for native labour, demands which have had a disintegrating influence on Bantu society. In 1916 the number of Natives working under European employers in the Dependency as a whole did not exceed 46,000, but it had advanced by 1951 to over a million, of whom more than 447,000 were working at long distances from their homes.

It is the opinion of many Belgians who know the Congo well that the Native population has actually decreased since the beginnings of European occupation. Such a view is held, for example, by former Governor-General Rutten.[1] Amongst the causes suggested is the spread of sleeping sickness which, until the latter part of the nineteenth century, was practically confined to the west coast of Equatorial Africa. The movements of people, either in large groups or as individuals (e.g. porters), which are incidental to the introduction of Western industrialism have been responsible for the widespread extension of the dread disease, from which, fortunately, the Province of Ruanda-Urundi is still free.

When the Congo became independent on June 30th, 1960, its prosperity was to a considerable degree bound up with that of the *Union Minière du Haut Katanga*. It is pointed out by Congolese leaders that with Katanga profits, the manufacture of palm-oil products, for example, could be doubled. So far the *Union Minière* has largely limited itself to financing undertakings connected with mining, such as the hydro-metallurgical plant at Luilu. But threat of expropriation in order to make wider use of its capital might deter further investment.

The Political and Economic Organization of French Equatorial Africa

The French acquired no responsibilities in Central Africa until about the year 1830 when they co-operated with Great Britain for the purpose of abolishing slave-trading in West African waters, and selected the Gabun coast as their special zone for operations. They obtained their first foothold on the banks of the Gabun River in 1839, but it was not until 1848, when Libreville (Gabun estuary) was founded, that the first serious effort towards settlement was made : and as its name indicates[2] the ' colony ' was intended primarily as a home for liberated slaves.

[1] v. ' Notes de demographie congolaise ' in *Congo*, Dec., 1920, p. 260.
[2] Cf. Freetown, Sierra Leone.

Between 1840 and 1875—that is up to the time of de Brazza's first great journey, mentioned in an earlier chapter—France did little to consolidate its hold on the Gabun hinterland. From Natives the inaccurate information was received that the Ogowe River offered a route right across Central Africa ; so that at first this waterway was regarded as a potential artery of commerce sufficiently important to serve a continental interior. It was not long, however, before de Brazza's explorations proved that the east-to-west course of the river is limited to the last 150 miles and that even within this distance the channel is unnavigable in places. The Ogowe valley, nevertheless, offered an indirect approach to the interior, as de Brazza discovered, for certain of its head-streams rise close to the source of a partially navigable tributary of the lower middle Congo, namely the River Alima.

The French explorer founded Franceville in the basin of the upper Ogowe and, almost immediately afterwards (1880), Brazzaville, on the western shore of Stanley Pool and over against Kinshasa which, in the first instance, was a French station. Using Brazzaville as his new base he proclaimed a protectorate for his nation over territory mainly forested and stretching north-eastwards beyond the confluence of the Congo and the Ubangi, the French zone being separated from the International State of the Congo by the course of the Ubangi-Congo.

Between 1880 and 1890 French exploration in Central Africa was mainly concerned with the discovery of the upper course of the Ubangi and with its utilization for a ' drive ' across the equatorial zone to the upper Nile. The great project failed when a military force under Marchand was obliged to withdraw from Fashoda and from the Nile Basin as a whole, at the very end of the century. Confined on their western flank by the British and German advances in Nigeria and the Camerouns, respectively, and, on their eastern side, by the British occupation of the White Nile and Bahr-el-Ghazal basins, the French were under the necessity of deflecting their ' drive ' northwards into the region east of Lake Chad, occupied by the sultanates of Kanem, Baghirmi and Wadai. Though relatively poor in their economic possibilities these Mahomedan states were, and indeed still are, regarded by the French as of high strategic significance in the imperial scheme, by reason of the contacts they provide between the equatorial ' colonies ' on the one hand and the West African and Barbary dependencies on the other. By the year 1915 the position of the French in the Chad Territories was so secure that it was then possible to substitute a civil for a military system of administration.

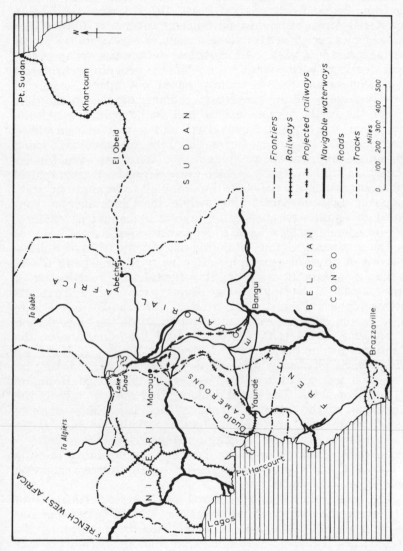

FIG. 60.—Routes of access to French Equatorial Africa

After a series of experiments in colonial government, all intended to comprehend within one organization the lands extending from Wadai to the Gabun coast, the federation of French Equatorial Africa came into existence in 1910. Its division into four colonies recognized to some extent the inevitability of decentralization in a vast territory whose extremities are so widely separated from each other,[1] whilst there is geographical interest in a delimitation that is mainly based on separate zones of river-drainage. During the great economic depression the burden of the costly administration had to be reduced, and the Federation was, in 1934, converted into a unit of centralized government (headquarters, Brazzaville), the former colonies being reorganized and known as ' regions '. There was even further subdivision into provinces, which were defined on geographical and ethnic principles, although they were all to be approximately 50,000 sq. miles in extent. Meanwhile, the Camerouns has continued to retain separate status, first as a mandated territory, and since January, 1960, as an independent republic.

The region of Gabun, the original colony, is essentially— in terms of physical geography—the basin of the Ogowe River, so that it is Atlantic-wards in its orientation. To the east of it the ' region ' of the Middle Congo drains to the Congo and extends northwards from the district between Brazzaville and Pointe Noire to the latitude, very approximately, of the river-station of Bangui. The latter centre was the head-quarters of the administration of the former Ubangi-Shari Colony (238,770 sq. miles) which physically may be described as the plateau rim, 2000–3000 feet about sea-level, enclosing the Congo Basin on its northern side. The Chad Colony (461,200 sq. miles), the fourth unit of the former Federation, included a large share of the inland drainage area of the Chad, especially the Shari Basin which it divides with the French Camerouns.

On geographical grounds the most satisfactory broad division of French Equatorial Africa is one recognizing three vegetation zones all very dissimilar.

The great rain-forest belt of the south-west, particularly of the Gabun and the greater part of the Middle Congo, extends for approximately 300,000 sq. miles (about one-third of the total area of A.E.F.). This zone, that for long barred the way to European penetration of the Ubangi-Congo interior, is still the main source of economic wealth, though even the Gabun is so undeveloped that wild-grown products, such as rubber and palm kernels, continue to exceed in importance the production

---

[1] From Pointe Noire to the northern frontier (where A.E.F., Libya and the A.E. Sudan converge) is more than 2000 miles.

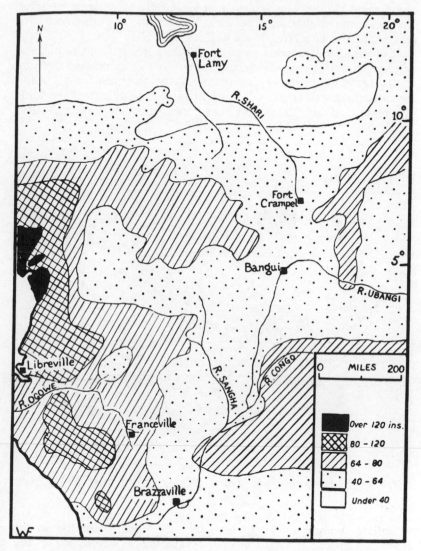

FIG. 61.—French Equatorial Africa : Average Annual Rainfall

derived from plantation agriculture. It will be remembered that the Gabun-Middle Congo forest is part only of a zone of selva that extends widely in the Belgian Congo and the southern district of the Camerouns, as well as in A.E.F.

Savanna, well wooded in parts, is characteristic of the plateau of the Ubangi-Shari. Towards the south the increasing density of tree growth indicates the transition to the rain-forest, while towards the north treeless savanna becomes increasingly evident. By reason of comparatively easy penetrability, assured and

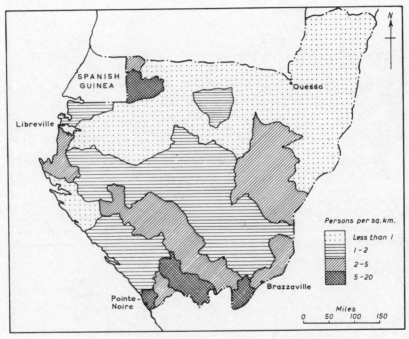

FIG. 62.—Gabun and Middle Congo: Density of Population (Oct. 1950)

abundant summer rainfall and generally healthy conditions for man and stock, the Ubangi-Shari savanna is economically the most attractive region of French Central Africa: its prospects include not only varied agriculture, embracing valuable commercial crops such as cotton and ground-nut, but also extensive cattle-ranching. Developments along these lines began only very recently, and for the first time in 1929 the Government planned cotton-growing as a leading feature of native agricultural economy. An output equal to about 44,000 bales (of

400 lb.) in 1932-3 was hailed as a striking achievement, but in more recent years (e.g. 1950) production still remains on a comparatively small scale (132,000 bales).

The southern districts of the Chad region belong to the Sudanese savanna, but going northwards there is to the east of Lake Chad definite transition to the Saharan conditions.[1] Because of the historical accident that the European penetration of this territory was undertaken from the Congo, the Saharan lands of the Chad ' region ' are still unnaturally associated for administrative purposes with the densely-forested Gabun. A more satisfactory association would appear to be with the Saharan and Sudan lands of French West Africa, notably the Niger Colony with which the Chad ' region ' is contiguous. The extension of French authority throughout the northernmost parts of A.E.F. has been completed only in the last few years ; moreover, the dry pastoral character of the territory does not attract land development companies, so that the economic life of the inhabitants is virtually unchanged.

Leaving out of account the great deserts of the continent no region comparable in area to A.E.F. has a population distributed so sparsely. For the Federation as a whole, a total of 4,407,000 (census of 1950) gives an average density of 4·5 per square mile, and the distribution over the several territories is so uniform that each is close to the average density for A.E.F. as a whole.[2]

An earlier chapter has prepared the reader for the striking contrasts noticeable in the ethnic and social types of French Equatorial Africa. The Gabun and Middle Congo forests shelter Bantu groups, some of them, like the Fang, quite primitive. One of the most important and advanced tribes is the Bateke of the Middle Congo who, during the decade 1880-90, on account of a trading monopoly they claimed, greatly hindered commercial contacts between the European traders established near Stanley Pool and the tribes of French Congo. The most numerous groups in the population of the Chad are semi-Hamitic, semi-negroid pastoralists, whose culture is much superior to that of the forest-dwellers, and whose social and political organization was strongly established before the arrival of the French. The Hamitic strain may be chiefly Fulani, but strong Tuareg,

[1] In their search for a scientific frontier the French extended the Chad Colony as far as the Tibesti Plateau.

[2] The population of each ' region ' (with density per sq. m.) was, in 1950, as follows : Gabun, 409,000 (density 4·0) ; Middle Congo, 684,000 (5·2) ; Ubangi-Shari, 1,072,000 (4·5) ; Chad, 2,242,000 (4·5). The White population is just over 20,000, and of these the majority are of temporary residence only.

21

Tibu and Kanuri traces are also present. Moslem sultanates, amongst which that of Baghirmi was the wealthiest and most powerful, existed down to the time of French conquest ; but their careers are now over, for French policy does not recognize ' protectorate rule ' as that principle is understood in the neighbouring sultanates of Northern Nigeria.

Sparseness of population is one of the chief hindrances to economic exploitation under European control : another obstacle equally serious is the deep-rooted prejudice against agricultural and industrial labour on the part of the proud pastoralists of the northern lands. It is true that recently there was recruiting in the Chad territory for the construction of the Pointe Noire–Brazzaville railway, but the labourers engaged were almost wholly negroid. It may be mentioned that working conditions on the railway construction were severely criticized because they resulted in an excessively high death-rate amongst the Chad Natives.

The Concession System of A.E.F.

Using King Leopold's régime as a model the French introduced to their Central African empire, at the very end of the nineteenth century, the principle of delegating administrative and commercial powers to a number of great land companies. Concessions were granted, in fact, as soon as the completion of the Belgian railway from Matadi to Kinshasa permitted comparatively easy access both to the French and Belgian zones of the Congo. During the year 1899 forty companies, including Belgian as well as French interests, obtained leases of thirty years' duration of areas that, in the aggregate, covered the greater part of what are now the Gabun and Middle Congo ' regions ', in addition to a very large tract in Ubangi-Shari.[1] Of the districts remaining outside the concessions in the forested lands those around Brazzaville and Libreville were the largest and most important, and the two centres mentioned have remained the bases of French activities in Central Africa.

For the period of its lease each company possessed exclusive rights of exploitation, other than mining rights, within its concession ; whilst, on the termination of the lease, all land improved by cultivation and all forest where rubber had been regularly gathered were to become the freehold property of the company. From the outset the main interest was the collection of rubber

[1] The forty concessions were distributed as follows : Gabun, 82,000 sq. kilometres ; Lower Congo, 79,000 ; Sangha Basin, 152,000 ; Lower Ubangi, 202,000 ; Upper Ubangi, 140,000 ; Basin of the Chad, 10,000.

and ivory, and output was stimulated by a head tax imposed by the companies on the Natives, a demand usually met by payment in the form of commodities, especially rubber. Outside the Gabun littoral the French Government did not insist upon the establishment of native reserves and, down to the present day, the coastal district mentioned is the only part where the Bantu have a recognized title to their land.

Pressed by enlightened opinion that was shocked by the incompetence and cruelty involved in the concession system, the French Government decided later to restrict the activities of the companies. Just before the outbreak of the First World War it was arranged that the concessions should expire not later than 1929, and that only a comparatively small proportion of the areas held under lease should remain with the companies as freehold property after that date. Greatly limited though the concessions certainly are, the system is by no means liquidated. For example, the *Compagnie Forestière Sangha-Ubangi* was empowered to hold until 1936 a monopoly of wild rubber over a vast tract in the region indicated, and, subject to the maintenance of a regular output of rubber, this concession is to be renewed indefinitely. Then, again, in the Gabun nearly 200,000 acres, of which only about 40,000 are under cultivation, are held by a group of about thirty European planters mainly interested in cocoa and oil-palm.

The ending of the worst abuses of the concession system has not yet been succeeded by forward-moving administrative and economic policies on the part of the Government. For long the Federation has been assisted by financial subsidies from France, yet stagnation rather than progress is general. Native society continues to disintegrate under the demands of rubber-exploiting and plantation companies, and forced labour which has some of the worst features of slavery has not been completely abolished. There is little or no encouragement to native agriculture where commercial crops are concerned, although the economic future of A.E.F. would seem to depend on the development of small native-owned plantations on the model of the cocoa groves of the Gold Coast. Except for the European-owned plantations of the Gabun, already mentioned, the entire emphasis is still upon the exploitation of forest resources—oil-palm, rubber (from *Funtumia elastica* and the *Landolphia* vine), cabinet woods (ebony, rosewood, mahogany) and elephant ivory. The rubber output increased regularly until 1913, but in more recent years there has been a marked decline, and the export is only some 1500 tons annually.

Apart from its shortage of communications, A.E.F. is handicapped economically by lack of coal. However, in 1948 a programme of electrification was begun. Water-power is being generated on the rivers Djoué, Loémé and Bonenza, between Brazzaville and Pointe Noire, and these installations will eventually be linked. At Port Gentil one of the world's largest ply-wood factories now uses steam-operated generating plant which burns wood, and it is hoped soon to electrify many other local industries.

The costs of construction are likely to postpone indefinitely a vast scheme of railway building, but a great arterial motor-road is already projected. Its course from Brazzaville to Fort Lamy, the administrative centre of the Chad ' region ' in the lower Shari basin, has been laid down, and feeder-roads coming in from the east and west will join it, so that the widely-separated lands of A.E.F. will in time be knitted together. In 1928 a motor-road from Bangui to Duala, chief ocean port of the French Camerouns, was completed ; its course of 600 miles direct to the Atlantic is estimated to reduce the time of travel from Bordeaux to Bangui, from eight to four weeks.

The Federal Republic of the Cameroun

As mentioned in an earlier chapter, France was obliged in 1911 to cede to Germany about 100,000 sq. miles of territory in Central Africa in order that her own ambitions in Morocco might be realized. The gain to Germany was greater even than the size of the acquired territory would suggest, for the French equatorial empire was cut right through by German zones, one of which reached the Ubangi, while another followed the Sangha valley as far as its junction with the Congo. In another direction also the strategic position of France was rendered very precarious, for a narrow strip of German territory reached the Atlantic south of the Spanish Colony of Rio Muni, at a point not much more than 10 miles from Libreville.

The division of the Camerouns between Britain and France as a prize of war was decided upon long before 1918, and, therefore, before the conception of administration by Mandate. In 1916 France took much the greater part—about 166,000 sq. miles—leaving to Great Britain, however, a valuable strip (c. 30,000 sq. miles), much of it highland, along the eastern border of Southern and Northern Nigeria. The districts ceded to Germany in 1911 were re-annexed by France and do not come under the Mandate Administration of the French Camerouns.

The Germans were preceded in the Camerouns by English missionaries and traders who settled in the districts around the ports of Duala and Victoria, which lie in the shadow of the great Camerouns Mountain. Great Britain declined a ' protectorate' offered by chiefs of the Duala tribe, whose lands are close to the present port of the same name, and in 1884 Germany was permitted to enter both here and in Togoland.

Two creditable features of German enterprise during the

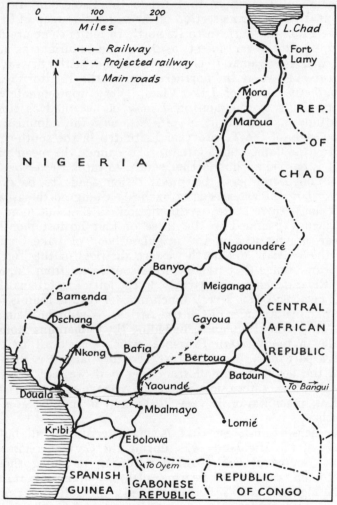

FIG. 63.—The Cameroun : Communications

brief period of occupation that ended with the Great War were overlooked by the victorious Powers at the Versailles Conference. They were, first, regard for the integrity of native society in the northern grass-lands and, secondly, vigorous and scientific application to tropical agriculture, in both of which the Germans were far in advance of their Belgian and French rivals. In her schemes of administration and economic development, it is noteworthy that Germany took account of the very varied geographic and ethnic conditions existing in the colony.

Because of its extent in latitude the Cameroun Territory offers, as it were, a cross-section of the vegetation map of Central Africa. From its southern to its northern limits there are found in turn, equatorial rain-forest, as dense and luxuriant as any in Africa, wooded savanna, treeless savanna and, lastly, dry savanna and scrub-land where the northern apex of the Territory reaches the southern shores of Lake Chad. Very approximately the northern limits of the rain-forest may be accepted as close to the latitude of Yaunde (c. 4° lat. N.), now the administrative head-quarters of the Territory and situated in the south-central district of the Camerouns Plateau. At Yaunde the mean annual rainfall is 62 inches, but farther south, towards the Gabun and Middle Congo frontiers, the precipitation tends to be greater and over large areas exceeds 70 inches. Going north-eastwards from Yaunde there is steady diminution, so that not more than 12–15 inches, confined to the three or four hottest months of the year, are received in the neighbourhood of Lake Chad.

In the western and north-western districts of the Territory the volcanic range that trends to the south-west from the upper Benue River, reaching the Atlantic in the lofty Camerouns Mountain, is responsible for a very much moister régime than is found in comparable latitudes of Central Africa. The highest summits of the Camerouns Highlands, including the Camerouns Mountain itself, lie in the Western Province, which was, until 1961, the southern part of the British Trust Territory, and it is they that receive the heaviest rainfall from the south-western monsoon ; but even on the eastern side, where the average elevation is 4000–6000 feet, precipitation is very heavy and in many places over 100 inches.

The dense rain-forest that is characteristic of all but the summits of the Highlands was, during the German régime, the principal source of wild-growing products, including those of the oil-palm and rubber-bearing plants. More important, it was the highland zone—then undivided politically—that offered the best prospects for European settlement and for the development of plantation agriculture, prospects indeed comparable to those in East Africa provided by the Kilimanjaro Highlands.

In 1901 the German Administration moved its head-quarters from Duala at the head of the Camerouns River estuary to Buea, a site on the south-eastern slope of the Camerouns Mountain and now in British Mandated Territory. By this transference was indicated the special importance attached by Germany to the highland zone. Farther to the north-east, and right into the heart of the Highlands, the way to settlement was opened by a railway leading from its ocean terminus at Bonaberi, on the Camerouns River opposite Duala, for about 100 miles as far as Bare.[1] Land alienation occurred, but not on a very extensive scale, and at the outbreak of the Great War the aggregate area under European ownership was 290,000 acres, or about 450 sq. miles, the greater part of which was in the south-western districts of the Highlands and now within the Western Province. War was declared before plantation agriculture could pass far beyond its experimental stages, and wild-grown rubber remained the principal export of the ex-German Protectorate until a few years ago. Even during the German régime, however, cultivated products—rubber, palm-oil and cocoa, particularly—made an important and ever-increasing contribution to the export trade.

It was obvious to the German Administration that the Highlands would be the scene of closest contacts between the indigenous and immigrant civilizations. That the Government was not entirely regardless of native welfare has already been indicated by the strict limitations imposed on land alienation. Native reserves, fourteen in number, were set apart in the Dschang district, one of the most densely-populated parts of the Highlands, whilst there · /as a definite tendency on the part of the Government increasingly to restrict the activities of the two great concession companies that, during the early years of this century, were permitted to exploit the forest resources in regions outside the Highlands.[2] Consequently, there was, down to 1914, comparatively little dislocation of native life. To all intents and purposes the Natives remained in possession of their lands, and where displacement occurred the population in neighbouring districts was not too congested to absorb immigrants. Throughout the Highlands the density of population is not high— taking into account the fertility of the volcanic soils—and varies from ten to forty to the square mile : yet it far exceeds the average for the southern and central zones of the Republic.

The Federal Republic of the Cameroun dates from October

---

[1] This line to the north has not been extended since the French occupation of the Camerouns.

[2] The first concession, granted in 1898, empowered a company to exploit the rubber resources of the forest in the southern districts of Yaunde, Ebolowa, &c. Though 18 million acres were at first involved, in 1905 the concession was reduced by more than three-quarters. The second concession granted in 1899 covered a vast tract between the Highlands and the Sanaga River.

1st, 1961. The Eastern Province, which was originally French Trust territory, became the independent Cameroun Republic at the beginning of 1960, and was joined the following year by the Western Province, until then the southern part of the British

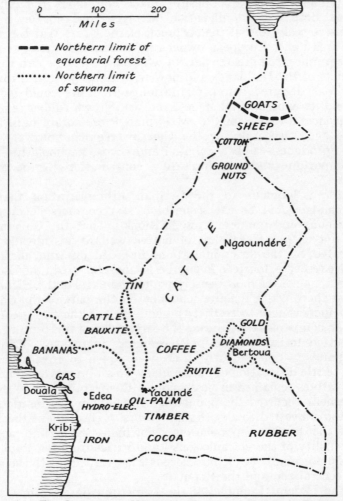

FIG. 64.—The Cameroun : Vegetation Zones and Economic Resources

Trust territory, after a referendum of the population. Although the Western Province comprises only about one-tenth of the territory of the Republic, it contains more than one-fifth of the total population of some 4,126,000 (1961).

The economy of the Republic is largely based on agriculture

which provides the bulk of its exports and raw materials for its industries. About five-sixths of the crops produced are for local consumption, millet, manioc, taro, maize and plantains being the main subsistence crops. The chief commercial crops are cocoa, coffee, bananas, oil-palm, rubber, cotton and peanuts, of which all but the last two are products of the southern half of the country (Fig. 64).

Under the five-year development plan for the years 1961–65, the Government did much to improve the standard of agriculture through the operations of some two hundred 'modernization centres' which have taught the use of fertilizers, the control of

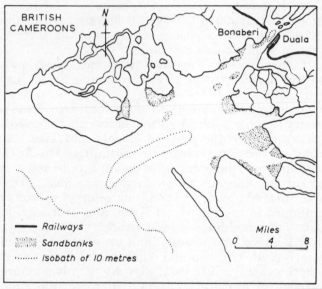

FIG. 65.—The Port of Duala : showing the Approaches to the Inner and Outer Harbours

disease, the generation of high-quality seeds, and the new techniques of food production, such as pisciculture.

Cocoa is grown over a wide area of the forests of the south and west of the Republic, and accounts for about one-third of the total value of the country's exports. In addition to helping to improve techniques of cultivation, the Government has established facilities for co-operative marketing, and for advancing credit to compensate for fluctuations in the market prices.

Coffee is a crop of the savanna plateaux of the centre, while bananas are principally grown in the western part of the great forest zone, notably in the region of black soils of Mungo. Oil palms are grown over a wide area of the forest zone and have replaced bananas in some districts.   Rubber cultivation is expanding in the Western Province.   The main commercial crop of the northern districts is cotton, which thrives particularly in the district of Lara, while groundnuts and tobacco are gaining ground in this region.

Livestock is the staple resource of wide areas of the centre and north, which are inhabited by the Foubles and other nomadic pastoralists.   The northern territories are calculated to support some 600,000 beef cattle, and over a million goats.   The commercial possibilities of the pastoral industry are being steadily realized, especially in the Adamaoua region, where a special unit at Wakwa is experimenting in the breeding of Brahma bulls. Some stock is slaughtered locally and flown frozen to the south, but most which reaches the market is driven to Douala or Yaoundé for export to neighbouring territories.

The fishing industry, marine, river and pond, provides a valuable supplement to the local diet, and a small surplus for export to Nigeria.

Forests occupy about one-third of the total area of the country, and forestry supplies a third by value of its exports.   Most of this trade passes through the ports of Douala and Tiko.   Minerals, by contrast, do not as yet contribute substantially to the country's economy, although there are extensive untapped reserves.   The most important minerals in production are gold, bauxite, tin and rutile (titarium oxide).   Promising reserves of iron ore have been confirmed in the vicinity of Kribi, and of natural gas close to Douala, but no oil has yet been struck.

Industries have been steadily built up since the Second World War, largely with the help of French enterprise.   Concentrated largely in the vicinity of Douala, they are mainly concerned with the treatment of primary products.   Of these, the large cocoa-butter factory at Douala is the most important, followed by the timber and plywood industry.

Of another nature is the aluminium industry at Edea.   This is based on the hydro-electric output of the Sanaga river, and treats some local bauxite, but mainly ore imported from France and Guinea.   With an annual output of 50,000 tons of aluminium, the Cameroun is the leading African producer, and ninth in the world.   The Eastern Province has a second hydro-electric station at Dschang, while there are smaller installations in the Western Province at Yoke, Malale and Luermanfalls.

The expansion of the economy of the Cameroun in all sectors will depend in a large measure on the improvement of its system of communications by river, road and rail (Fig. 63).   The Republic is overwhelmingly dependent for its external trade on the single port of Douala, with an annual capacity of 1,100,000 tons. It is hoped to expand this capacity to 1,850,000 tons by the 1980's. The second port, Kribi, however, can only handle 30,000 tons a year, and it is not expected to do more than double this figure. Another vital need is the extension of the Douala–Yaoundé railway. By an agreement of 1962 between the Cameroun and Chad Republics, it is planned to build this line forward through Ngaoundere to Fort Archambault to Chad, and possibly also to press forward a branch to Bangui. The effect of these measures would be not only to open up new areas of the central Cameroun, rich in agricultural and mineral wealth, but to make Douala the main outlet for the trade of the Central African and Chad Republics (Figs. 60, 63).

REFERENCES
ANGOLA

Almada Negreiros, A. L. de, *Colonies Portugaises*, 1910.

Almeida, J. de, *Sul d'Angola*, Lisbon, 1912.

Barns, T. A., ' Angola and the Isles of the Guinea Gulf ', *Geog. Jour.*, Vol. LXXII.

Boletim Geral Das Colonias (published monthly at Lisbon).

Lima Vidal, J. J. E. de, *Por Terras d'Angola*, Coimbra, 1916.

Mair, L. P., *Native Policies in Africa*, London, 1936.

Marquadsen, H., *Angola*, Berlin, 1920.

Matos, N. de, *A Provincia de Angola*, Porto, 1926.

Mello, A. B. de, *Monographie d'Angola* (Exposition Internationale Coloniale de Paris, 1931), Loanda, 1931.

Sousa e Faro, *Angola*, Lisbon, 1932.

Statham, J. C. B., *Through Angola, a Coming Colony*, London, 1922.

Varian, H. F., ' The Geography of the Benguella Railway ', *Geog. Jour.*, Vol. LXXVIII.

Vasconcelos, E. J. de, *As Colonias Portuguesas—Geografia Fisica. Economica e Politica*, Lisbon.

Whittlesey, D. S., ' Geographic Provinces of Angola ', *Geog. Review* (New York), Vol. XIV.

BELGIAN CONGO

Annuaire du Congo Belge, Brussels.

Atlas du Katanga, pub. by Comité Spécial du Katanga, 1931.

' Congo ', *Revue Générale de la Colonie Belge*, Brussels. (Many articles.)

Guide Commercial du Congo Belge, Colonial Office, Brussels.

Hailey, Lord, *An African Survey*, Oxford, Survey, 1938.

Heyse, Th., *Grandes lignes du régime des terres du Congo Belge et du Ruanda-Urundi et leurs applications (1940–46)*. Institut Royal Colonial Belge, Brussels, 1947.

Leplae, E., *Agriculture in the Belgian Congo* (Bull. Imper. Inst., Vol. XII, 1914, pp. 60–75).

Mair, L. P., *Native Policies in Africa*, London, 1936.

Malengreau, G., *Les droits coutumiers chez les indigènes du Congo Beige, Essai d'interprétation juridique*. Inst. Roy. Col. Belge, Brussels, 1947
Vers un paysannant indigène ; Les lotissements agricoles du Congo Belge, Rapport de Mission. Inst. Roy. Col. Belge, Brussels, 1949.

Maquet, J. J., ' The modern evolution of African populations in the Belgian Congo ', *Africa*, Vol. XIX, no. 4 (Oct. 1949), pp. 265–72.

Marvel, T., *The New Congo*, London, 1949.

Maurette, F., *Afrique Equatoriale, Orientale et Australe*, Tome XII, Géographie Universelle, Paris, 1938.

Philipps, T., ' The Natural Sciences in Africa, the Belgian National Parks ', *Geog. Journ.*, Vol. CXV (1950), pp. 58–62.

Robert, M., *Le Katanga Physique*, Brussels, 1927.

French Equatorial Africa

Bruel, G., *L'Afrique Equatoriale Française*, Paris, 1930.
Buell, R. L., *The Native Problem in Africa*, Vol. II, New York, 1928.
Chazelas, V., *Territoires Africains sous Mandat Français*, Paris, 1931.
Grebert, F., *Au Gabon*, Paris, 1922.
Le Commerce et la Production des Colonies Françaises (Publ. by Colonial Institute of Marseilles), 1926.
Lyautey, P., *L'Empire Colonial Français*, Paris, 1931.
Mair, L. P., *Native Policies in Africa*, London, 1936.
Paulin, H., *L'Afrique Equatoriale Française*, Paris, 1924.
Roberts, S. H., *History of French Colonial Policy*, 2 vols., London, 1929.
Sarraut, A., *La Mise en Valeur des Colonies Françaises*, Paris, 1923.
Schweitzer, A., *On the Edge of the Primeval Forest* (trans.), London, 1922.
Thillard, R., *Agriculture et Elevage au Cameroun*, Paris, 1921.
Vassal, G. M., *Life in French Congo*, London, 1925.
Vignon, L., *Un Programme de Politique Coloniale*, Paris, 1919.

CHAPTER V

WEST AFRICA

THIS tropical region, the nearest to Western Europe and the one with which the maritime Powers came first into direct trading relationship, is without prospects for permanent White settlement, if only because of climatic unsuitability. Consequently, the competitive struggle for land between native and immigrant that has dominated the life of both South and East Africa is not reproduced in the Guinea zone ; and although the cultural problem offers certain difficulties, owing largely to the sophistication of the population in and around the seaports, it is much more localized than in the two regions of East and South Africa where European settlement has taken place.

Generally it is true to say that in the region now to be treated the exploitation of forest and field for the purpose of commerce is more advanced than elsewhere in tropical Africa : yet anything approaching intensive development is confined to a few comparatively small and especially favoured districts where a single ' money crop ' is the rule. From the standpoint of the widely different stages of economic development reached in various parts of West Africa comparison is possible with another great tropical realm, namely the East Indies. There also—as in the case of Sumatra—primitive and modern, scientific agriculture exist almost side by side. In West Africa it has to be remembered, however, that agriculture is usually not of the ' plantation ' order, but is based on native-owned and native-worked plots.

In so far as emphasis is placed on the commercial geography of West Africa, it is inevitable that the British territories which, in the aggregate, are very much smaller in area than the French should nevertheless receive greater attention than the latter ; for there is a marked contrast between the two empires from the standpoint of their respective contributions to world trade.

It is impossible to relate satisfactorily the political map with its arbitrarily-drawn frontiers to the main ' natural ' divisions of the region. Accepting climate and vegetation as our principal criteria we have already seen that the zoning is latitudinal. The political boundaries run across the geographical grain, as it were, and several of the larger colonial units—Nigeria is one instance —are complete cross-sections of the vegetation map, showing the succession of (a) a humid, forested littoral, (b) wooded savanna, (c) dry treeless savanna in the far interior. The political map of the Guinea colonies has been likened to a terrace of narrow houses, some closely walled-in at the rear, others—the French colonies —opening on to a vast court, the wellnigh limitless hinterland of the Western Sudan. But however unsatisfactory the political units may be in view of their lack of correspondence with the geographical trend lines, we are obliged to take them into account : for the political and economic organization of a colony, in the course of time, provides it with a ' personality ' easily distinguishable from that of another colony, even though there should be approximate parity of potential resources between them. We may say in general terms, for example, that the natural resources of Liberia correspond to those of Sierra Leone : yet, owing to accidents of the ' partition ' phase in West African history, the contrasts between these territories in respect of political and commercial geography have become very marked.

The usually-accepted limits of West Africa are set by the Senegal River and the Niger Delta, whilst the Sahara provides an almost ideal northern boundary-zone to our region. It is acknowledged that the separation of Nigeria from the French Cameroons by allotting them to different regions in our scheme is, on the grounds of physical geography, open to certain objections, but the association of the four British colonies of Guinea on the one hand and the attachment of the Cameroons, or the greater part of this territory, to the Central African empire of France, on the other, provide strong political arguments for the division here adopted.

Taking into account both intrinsic conditions and external relationships a broad regional classification may take the following form :

I. **Western Sudan,** of which much the greater part is French territory.

II. **Western Forest Lands of Guinea,** best represented in Liberia and Sierra Leone.

III. **Mid-Guinea Forest Belt** of the Ivory Coast, Gold Coast and Dahomey.

IV. **Eastern Forest Belt,** in Southern Nigeria.

V. **Northern Nigeria.**

The Western Sudan

Apart from the two small enclaves, Portuguese Guinea and the Gambia Protectorate, the westernmost savanna lands are under French authority. This political control may be traced back to a very hesitant beginning in the middle of the seventeenth century, when the site of St. Louis near the outlet of the Senegal River was selected by the French for permanent occupation. As mentioned in an earlier chapter, there was no serious

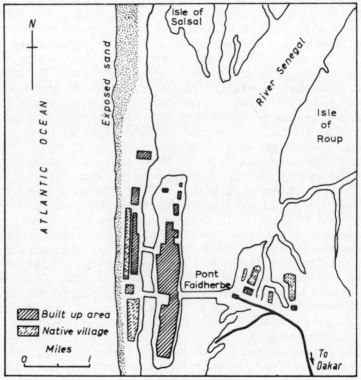

FIG. 66.—St. Louis

forward movement into the Senegal hinterland until the advance under General Faidherbe, from 1854 onwards. At the close of the Napoleonic Wars St. Louis was one of the few fragments of empire left to France, and until the early years of this century, when it was first displaced in importance by Dakar, it continued to be the principal centre of French influence in tropical Africa. Another point of vantage, seized by France in 1677, a few years later than the founding of St. Louis, was the Isle of Goree close to Cape Verde and now amalgamated, for administrative purposes, with Dakar.

The first sign of the awakening of French interest in the development of the resources within West Africa appeared after 1820 when, encouraged by the success of Dutch plantation agriculture in Java, the French Administration attempted a similar enterprise along the lower course of the Senegal River with the intention of supplying the home industrial market with certain necessary raw materials, including cotton and indigo. But the scale of operations was insignificant : indeed, stagnation or very halting progress in economic affairs were characteristic of the entire French empire in tropical Africa right down to the close of the Great War. It is a remarkable and—to the French —disconcerting fact that more than three-quarters of all tropical products imported into France are derived from colonies outside their empire.

A notable expedition by Magé in 1861, from Medina, near Kayes on the Senegal River, to Segou on the Niger, opened the way to the vast savanna zone of the upper and middle Niger Basin, where the cultivation by Natives of a number of industrial crops, including cotton, was evidence of a higher material civilization than that met with in Senegal. Shortly afterwards Binger's journey from the Niger southwards to the Guinea coast showed the French that their advance-bases in the Sudan could be reached, from the sea, by shorter land-routes than the original line from the lower Senegal. But consolidation in the region of the upper Senegal and upper Niger was not easily accomplished owing to the resistance offered by native kingdoms, many of them Moslem and remnants of the former, vast Songhai Empire. One of the most arduous tasks was the conquest of the Futa Jallon Plateau, the greater part of which is now French territory : although it was nominally annexed in 1881 desultory fighting did not cease until 1906.

It was very late in the nineteenth century before the French Ministry for the Colonies agreed to entertain with any enthusiasm the possibility of a West African empire, unified and continuous from St. Louis to Dahomey and from the Ivory Coast to Algeria. The period 1890–1900 was one of comparatively active colonial policy, as a result of which the French zone was extended to and beyond Timbuktu, with prolongations to the coasts of French Guinea (especially the neighbourhood of Konakry) and Dahomey. Because of special difficulties in the Ivory Coast dependencies— the impenetrability of the forest and the hostility of the Natives —this part of French West Africa was not fully incorporated into the general scheme until the first decade of the present century. During the coastal phase of French penetration the various groups of settlements were completely isolated from

22

each other by foreign colonies and were without inter-connexions across the Sudan hinterland. A separate administration for each group was therefore inevitable in the first instance, but before the close of the nineteenth century the effective occupation of the hinterland led to various projects for the federation of the colonies. In order to assist the process of unification railway construction was put in hand from each of the four coasts under French authority—Senegal, French Guinea, Ivory Coast and Dahomey—the plan, still far from consummated, being that the lines should converge upon a common centre somewhere within the great loop of the Niger.

The constitution of the Federation of French West Africa [1] was proclaimed in 1904. In addition to the District of Dakar

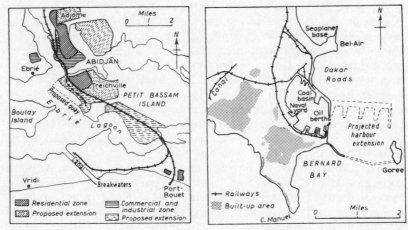

FIG. 67.—(a) Abidjan, (b) Dakar

(the federal capital) it first consisted of eight Colonies. Four of them—Senegal, French Guinea, Ivory Coast and Dahomey—were merely extensions of the original coastal settlements. The remainder included arbitrarily-defined units covering a large part of the Sahara and Western Sudan : these, the hinterland Colonies as they may be termed, were Mauritania, practically all desert and extending behind Rio de Oro from the Moroccan frontier to the Senegal River ; French Sudan, based on the middle and upper districts of the Niger Basin, but including also the critical link between Bamako (upper Niger) and Kayes (middle Senegal) as well as a vast Saharan tract between Mauritania and the

[1] Officially ' Afrique Occidentale Française ', often abbreviated to A.O.F.

outposts of the Ahaggar Plateau ; Upper Volta, a comparatively small unit to the south of French Sudan and including the country of the important Mossi group of Sudanese Negroes ; lastly, the Niger Colony whose name was rather misleading, for though one frontier coincided with the left bank of the Niger between French Sudan and Northern Nigeria, much the greater part was Saharan with its northern boundary resting on the Ahaggar and Tibesti Highlands. With the abolition of the Upper Volta Colony in 1932 its territories were attached to the neighbouring parts of French Sudan, the Niger Colony and Ivory Coast, respectively.

One of the proposed objects in the establishment of the Federation of French West Africa was the transference from the Colonial Ministry in Paris to the Government-General at Dakar of some share of legislative and financial control, though, in point of fact, the amount of initiative granted to the ' man on the spot ' continues to be small. Each of the constituent Colonies is administered by a Lieutenant-Governor, but the main lines of a common policy are made effective through the medium of the ' central ' government at Dakar. The Governor-General alone has the right of direct communication with the Home Government. He is assisted by a purely advisory Council of about forty-five members including, beside the senior French officials, a minority of Natives. With the exception of the Colonial Council of Senegal, to be discussed later, there is in French West Africa no body with powers comparable to those of the Legislative Council of a British Colony.

Senegal has a special place in the African empire of France and almost equals in status the *anciennes colonies*, namely the French West Indies and Réunion Island. It is represented by a Deputy (usually a Negro) in the French Chamber of Deputies, though the franchise that determines the election of the Senegalese representative is virtually limited to the four communes of the Colony, viz. the original settlements of St. Louis, Goree, Dakar and Rufisque. In these municipalities there are about 75,000 ' native citizens ' who are to be distinguished from the ' native subjects ' of French West Africa, whose number is 15 millions. Citizenship is reserved for Natives who adopt French culture and thus bear witness to the policy of ' assimilation ' that has been generally characteristic of French rule on the African mainland. Practically all the citizens of West Africa are resident in Senegal and, more particularly, in the four communes above mentioned.

The outstanding instance of the preferential treatment of the Senegalese is the existence of the Colonial Council of Senegal. This native parliament, endowed with considerable powers, is composed of a majority of elected native citizens and of a minority of chiefs or headmen selected from the interior of the Colony, together with a small group of Europeans who sit as equals—and no more than equals—with the Negroes.[1] Apart from its advisory functions the Colonial Council has a certain amount of control over finance, for it is able to criticize and even, on occasion, to prevent new taxation : in addition, it is empowered to initiate legislation which, however, must gain the assent of the Governor-General. As French is the only language allowed the Council is not by any means representative of the whole of Senegalese society, for the number of chiefs able to speak French is small. So long as the Wolof language is not permitted the voice of the majority of Senegal Natives will not be heard in the Council.

Nearly all the native ' states ' encountered by the French when they first entered the Sudan have been destroyed or completely emasculated. Exceptions are to be found in the desert lands of Mauritania—from the French point of view very difficult to administer—and in the two Mossi ' kingdoms ' of Yatenga and Wagaduga. Tribal boundaries are fast disappearing and hereditary chiefs are being replaced by French-speaking headmen, who are virtually civil servants of the Administration and the agents of French authority. It is the latter class from which many of the so-called ' chiefs ' are selected for membership of the Colonial Council of Senegal. Moreover, headmen are appointed over village-groups regardless of race, so that it is possible, for example—as indeed has happened—for a Wolof to be appointed over a Fulani community. In place of tribal units there are now the quite artificial administrative divisions known as ' cercles ', of which there are over 100 in French West Africa. Finally, to complete the destruction of tribal authority, since 1924 judicial powers have been withdrawn from the hereditary leaders, and French law is now administered practically throughout.

Such are the main features of the inter-related policies of ' direct rule ' and ' assimilation ' as applied to the Western Sudan and to French West Africa generally. Concessions to ' indirect rule '—the policy of ' association ' as the French term it—are more apparent than real ; they include the recent establishment of ' Councils of Notables ' in some of the ' cercles ', it being intended that the Notables should be elected from the hereditary chiefs. However valuable such bodies may be as interpreters of native ideals and needs their powers are advisory only, so that the policies they recommend may be,

[1] An indication of the absence of a colour bar in French Africa.

and actually often have been, completely disregarded by the Administration.

As in administrative policy so in economic and commercial organization assimilation to the Mother Country is attempted. By 1914 France was fully aroused to its illogical position as a great colonial Power still completely failing to supply a considerable fraction of its requirements of tropical raw materials from the overseas dependencies. At this time imported products such as ground-nuts, rubber and cotton—all of which A.O.F. should be able to furnish in quantities far exceeding French demands

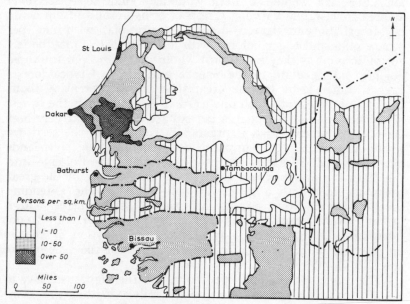

FIG. 68.—Senegal and Gambia. Density of Population
(Compilation of 1948)

—were mainly derived from non-French territories. With the appearance of M. Albert Sarraut as Minister for the Colonies after the Great War, there was the first thorough attempt to estimate and develop systematically the economic resources of A.O.F., and to determine for each constituent colony the specialization for which it was best fitted in view of the industrial requirements of France. The colonial stock-taking inaugurated by Sarraut is set out in detail in his book, *La Mise en Valeur des Colonies Françaises*.

Insufficiency of capital investment and acute shortage of labour have been the primary reasons for the relatively small commercial output of A.O.F. It was recently estimated that France has about 7,200 million francs invested in all her colonies and dependencies (African, Asiatic, &c.), and that of this total two-thirds are concentrated in North-West Africa, particularly Algeria. By way of contrast it is notable that in the Dutch East Indies the capital invested by Holland alone represents 20,000 million francs.

The low density of population which is responsible for the labour shortage is appreciated by reference to the accompanying map. An average of approximately 9·1 persons per square mile for A.O.F. as a whole is of little value as a guide to density over an area so vast, and varying in respect of habitability from dense rain-forest to unmitigated desert. Mauritania, with one per square mile, and Niger Colony, with less than three, may be left out of account as they are almost wholly Saharan. Of the three Colonies intermediate to the Sahara and to the Guinea forests French Sudan is by far the greatest in area, representing about 600,000 sq. miles (of which one-third is desert), but is the lowest in density with just over five per square mile. Relatively high density in French Sudan is practically confined to the territory within the basin of the upper Niger, including the river-lands extending from Bamako—the head-quarters of the Colony—into the Macina country, where there is annual flooding of the great river, together with a generally well-occupied zone extending south-eastwards from Segou into the Mossi country. Large urban concentrations are very few, indeed only Bamako (120,000 inhabitants in 1960) and Kayes (with a population of 28,500) on the Senegal River near the western limit of the Colony, are specially notable.

The former Colony of Upper Volta had the highest density in A.O.F., namely about 29 per square mile. Within this comparatively small unit of some 110,000 sq. miles there were over three million inhabitants, which was considerably more than one-fifth of the total for A.O.F. : yet even here there are wide areas almost uninhabited.

Senegal, after Dahomey the smallest unit of the Federation, compares with Upper Volta and has a density of twenty per square mile. Much the greater part of the western Colony is, however, very thinly settled with under ten per square mile. On the other hand, the density increases to more than 100 in three separate districts, namely (1) the hinterland of Dakar, including part of the former ' kingdom ' of Cayor, (2) the Senegal valley and (3) Casamance, which is South-Western Senegal and nearly isolated from the remainder of the Colony by the long strip of the British Protectorate of Gambia. Dakar is easily the largest township in A.O.F. Its population of 383,000 inhabitants includes 30,000 Europeans, and only St. Louis of the other old coastal settlements is at all comparable in size (48,000).

In French Guinea with its three million population the density is greatest towards the south, i.e. towards the 'Sierra Leone frontier, and its average of 30 is a much higher figure than that for the savanna lands of the Federation as a whole.

Summarizing, we may say that the only parts of the Western Sudan where occupation attains a fair density, e.g. fifty to the

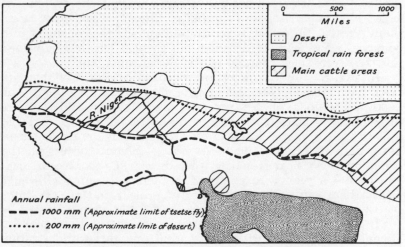

Fig. 69.—West Africa : Vegetation Zones

square mile, are (a) Western Senegal and British Gambia, (b) the river-zone of the Senegal and Upper Niger, (c) parts of Upper Volta, including wide districts in Yatenga and Mossi, (d) the southern half of French Guinea.

The Mossi people of the Upper Volta region are unable to produce for export by reason of their isolation in the far interior, at a great distance from any rail-head. Yet they have been forced to play a leading part in the commercial development of the Western Sudan. In view of the lack of outlets for their products the poll-tax weighs heavily upon them and many have been forced to emigrate for employment. In the early post-war years about 50,000 of the Mossi tribesmen were engaged on railway construction in Senegal and the Ivory Coast. Then again, thousands of Natives from the French Sudan and Upper Volta leave their homes annually for work on the harvesting of ground-nuts in Senegal and of cocoa in the (British) Gold Coast : they are engaged, not by Europeans but by native farming landowners who afford evidence of the general introduction by the French of the principle of individual land tenure. According to some estimates, more than 200,000 French Natives have made temporary or permanent homes in British territory.

Another drain on the local labour supply is the practice of conscription, introduced by the French into West Africa in 1912. The system is criticized not only for its economic effects, but also because, local garrison and frontier requirements not being large, many West African troops are drafted outside the continent into countries whose climate does not suit them. This has happened less, however, since the end of the Syrian mandate.

In French Guinea important deposits of iron and bauxite have been found. The reserves of iron ore are estimated at 2000 million tons, of 51·5 per cent concentration, and the port of Konakry is being extended to deal with an export of three million tons a year. Exports on a considerable scale began in 1952, both to Europe and to America. Bauxite occurs on the island of Kassa, near Konakry, where it was first worked in 1948. 54,000 tons a year were produced in 1960 and sent out through a special harbour. New hydro-electric projects in the Futa-Jalon plateau may treat some of this ore.

In the Western Sudan European-owned plantations play an insignificant part in agricultural output and the Administration has never seriously entertained a policy of vast concessions. With the spread of individual ownership of land native cultivation is encouraged, although individual plots are often sufficiently large to require the services of ' squatter ' labourers. The total area of alienated land in A.O.F., outside the Ivory Coast and Dahomey forests, is only about 70,000 acres of which more than one-third are in Senegal. The largest agricultural concession which the Governor-General is empowered to grant does not exceed 2000 hectares (c. 5000 acres).

Commercial agriculture in the Western Sudan is still necessarily limited to a few crops for which a climatic régime characterized by seven or eight months of drought is satisfactory. Modern irrigation works for which there are elaborate plans, to be mentioned later, are yet in too early a stage to affect very considerably the agricultural output of A.O.F., though primitive

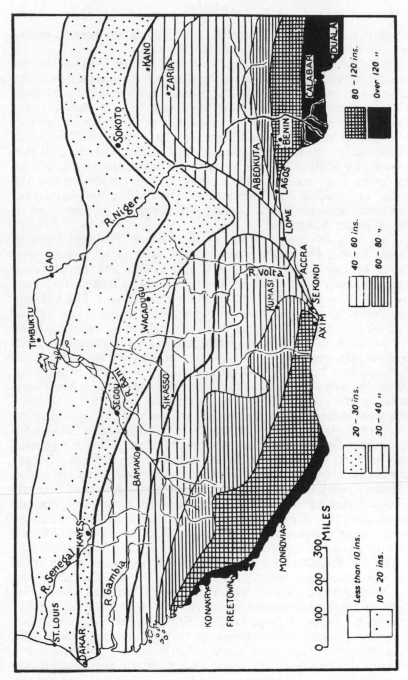

FIG. 70.—West Africa : Average Annual Rainfall

Less than 10 ins.

10 - 20 ins.

20 - 30 ins.

30 - 40 "

40 - 60 ins.

60 - 80 "

80 - 120 ins.

Over 120 "

0   100   200   300
MILES

irrigation is an important factor, especially in the regions of the middle Senegal and upper middle Niger.

Although mainly a land of savanna French Guinea—or the greater part of it—in its agricultural possibilities resembles more closely the western forest lands (Sierra Leone and Liberia) than the Western Sudan. There is no doubt that in earlier times the western and southern districts of the Colony were heavily forested, as may be inferred from the abundant rainfall received. Precipitation at Konakry exceeds 150 inches and, though this high figure is limited to the western sea-board, the area with over 55 inches is at least half the Colony. Consequently, crops like cocoa and rubber that require heavy precipitation distinguish the agriculture of French Guinea from that of the remainder of the Western Sudan.

Allowing for the exclusion of the Guinea frontage, north of Sierra Leone, the region under review still shows a very wide range of rainfall between north and south, the limits being approximately 9–10 inches on the Saharan side and 50–60 inches in the southernmost parts of the Western Sudan. The isohyets run generally east and west with very little looping—an indication of the absence of great contrasts of surface relief in West Africa north of the Guinea Highlands. In the transition from Guinea rain-forest to the Sahara two main vegetation zones are distinguished by the French geographers. One, the Sahel, over which the mean annual rainfall does not exceed 25 inches, is dry savanna or steppe: the other, the 'Sudan' proper, is tall grass and wooded savanna with a rainfall varying according to latitude from 25 to 60 inches. The northern limits of the Sahel over against the Sahara cannot be too sharply defined, but in a general way may be taken a little to the north of the latitude of Timbuktu, or along the isohyet of 9 inches approximately. The 'Sudan' vegetation zone covers the southern districts of Senegal, French Sudan and Upper Volta as well as the Futa Jallon Plateau (2500–4800 ft.) of French Guinea, and is intended by nature to be the most prosperous agricultural belt of French West Africa : here irrigation is not nearly so vital as it is in the Sahel.

As the French entered the Senegal-Upper Niger region from the west, more particularly by way of St. Louis, the Sahel was the West African zone to which they were first introduced. In spite of the precariousness of its rainfall and the strict limitation to the range of crops thereby imposed, the Sahel continues to make a bigger contribution to the export trade of A.O.F. than the other vegetation zones. Its economic life is founded on the valuable oil-bearing ground-nut that still represents much more than one-half the value of the outgoing commerce of French

West Africa as a whole. This plant, which may be cultivated without irrigation, is more suited to the Sahel environment than to the moister climate of the Sudan farther south. It prefers light sandy soil to the heavy land that is better for cotton, the second staple of Western Sudan commercial agriculture.

The centre of ground-nut marketing for export has tended to shift eastwards from the lower Senegal towards the upper Niger, with the establishment of railway communications ; but the Senegal Colony still leads easily in production, and is likely to continue to do so for long in consequence of the high costs of long-distance overland transport to the coast. With the completion of the St. Louis–Dakar railway in 1887—the first line in the Western Sudan—there followed a sharp rise in export, as the evacuation of the ground-nut from Cayor—the country of most intensive cultivation—was then made possible. In port activities St. Louis was inevitably superseded by the finer harbour of Dakar : constantly menaced by shifting sand-banks it was never satisfactory, and its early importance was due rather to Faidherbe's selection of the site as his head-quarters than to any special natural advantages it possessed.

Further impetus to ground-nut export followed the opening of the Thiès–Kayes [1] railway which avoids the great détour of the Senegal River and leads direct across the Colony—and through Cayor—from the upper Senegal to Dakar. Again, when in 1924 the great Senegal–Niger trunk line was completed as far as Bamako the navigable middle course [2] of the Niger presented a valuable connecting link in the transport of ground-nut from the potentially-rich lands in the south-western parts of the French Sudan Colony. And so by stages, each marked by an extension of railway, the ground-nut export from A.O.F. rose from an insignificant amount in 1870 to over 200,000 tons in 1950.

Since the 1914–18 War the French in West Africa have concentrated their maximum economic effort within the neighbourhood of the upper-middle Niger. Great inducement is here offered to agricultural enterprise by the vast but still uncontrolled reservoir of the Niger. Between Bamako and Timbuktu the great river floods annually an enormous delta of its own building—a ' potential Egypt ', as it has been designated prophetically. The most extensive flooding occurs down-stream from the junction of the Niger and the river Bani, that is below Segou. The river waters spread out over a maze of channels and shallow lakes, the inundation being in places over 80 miles wide, and the

[1] Thiès, close to Dakar, is the junction for the St. Louis and Niger lines.
[2] Navigable for at least five months of the year. The traffic on this section of the river increased from 4 million metric tons in 1920 to 14 million in 1935.

total area covered as much as 30,000 sq. miles in some years.
South-westwards from Timbuktu to Mopti there is a series of
vast but shallow depressions, including Lake Debo, which are
temporarily filled by the overflow of the Niger and gradually
desiccated as the level of the great river falls again. One of the
most notable features of the Niger flood régime is the very late
arrival of high water in the neighbourhood of Timbuktu and
farther downstream. The upper course has high water between
June and September, as a result of the spring and summer rains,
but the maximum in the Timbuktu district is not reached until
January owing to the retardation of the flow by dispersal throughout the intricate system of channels and lakes referred to above.

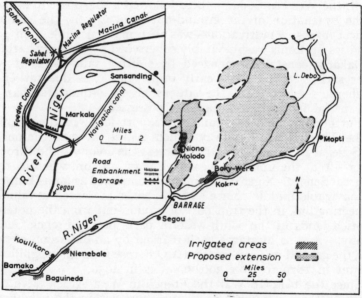

FIG. 71.—The inland delta of the Niger

Below Timbuktu the waters are again collected into one stream,
but the retardation has been so considerable that high water at
Say, in the extreme south-west of the Niger Colony, does not
occur until March, or nearly nine months after the floods in the
head-streams of the Niger.

In 1921, a French commission headed by the distinguished
engineer, M. Bélime,[1] recommended the first stage in the irrigation of the upper-middle Niger. After the railway from Dakar
was completed to Koulikoro in 1923, constructional equipment
was brought in, and small experimental schemes were tried at

[1] v. 'Report of Mission Bélime—Les Irrigations du Niger; Etudes
et Projets', 1921.

Niénébalé and Baguineda, a few miles downstream from Bamako. It was eventually decided to place the main dam at the bend of the river seven miles above Sansanding. The Sansanding barrage was accordingly started in 1934, and finished seven years later.

The barrage, which has 500 sluice-gates, is 884 yards long, and with its embankment extends to 1¾ miles. The bridge over it is one of the three which cross the Niger. This work has raised the level of the river by about 14 feet, and enables the Sahel and Macina Canals to draw off water over the inland delta region to the north and north-east. Eventually 2¼ million acres will be irrigated, and a million peasants supported on the reclaimed land. To the present, however, only 50,000 acres have been watered, and 16,000 colonists settled, from the French Sudan and Upper Volta. Each family is provided with a hut, equipment, stock, and land which has been ploughed ready. After paying his dues, the farmer is given independent tenure of his plot, and freedom to market his produce through the co-operatives or as he wishes.

The two chief areas so far settled are the Molodo and Niono districts, fed by the Sahel Canal, and the Boky-Wéré and Kokry regions, supplied from the Macina Canal. The colonists are settled in villages of between 200 and 400 inhabitants, and each farmer works a plot of about 12 acres.

One difference between the Nile and Niger floods is that the latter deposit very little silt. While this solves one engineering problem at the barrage, it also unfortunately means that the fields are not so naturally fertile, and large quantities of artificial manures are already being used.

A local problem raised by the diversions is that some of the overflow lakes have dried out, and natural pasturage receded. But it is hoped that another barrage further downstream will remedy this.

In the early days of the scheme, it was intended, in view of the needs of France's home industry, to concentrate on the production of cotton for export ; but it was soon found that the inexperienced farmers, working on an acid soil, grew a poor quality product which did not compete easily in the market after long transport. Food is much more essential in this Middle Niger country, which is so often afflicted by famine, as many early critics of the enterprise pointed out. Consequently, the *Office du Niger* has encouraged the growing of rice, which is now the chief crop in the area under its control, occupying 55 per cent of the ground, as compared with 20 per cent under cotton. In 1949, 13,000 tons of surplus rice were sold outside, and nearly 9000 tons consumed locally.

For cotton very favourable conditions of soil and climate

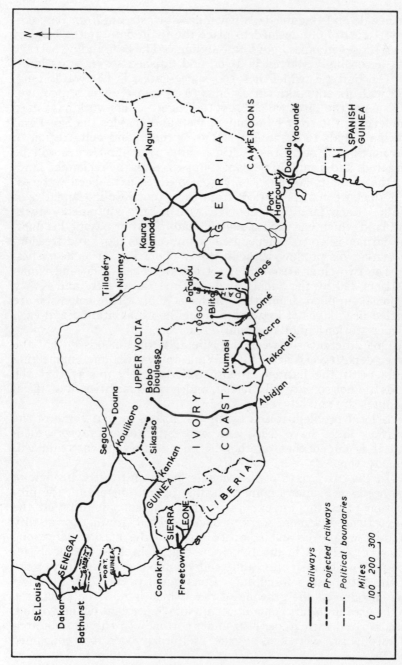

FIG. 72.—Railways of West Africa

are not confined to the Niger Basin. The irrigable riparian zone of the Senegal is a tract of admirable possibilities, conveniently situated in relation to the port of shipment. Another territory of splendid opportunities, one endowed with an assured rainfall, is divided by the converging frontiers of the four colonies —French Guinea, Ivory Coast, Upper Volta and French Sudan.

When estimating the potential resources of the Western Sudan one should not overlook the undoubted future that is offered to a ranching industry of vast dimensions, comparable that is to say to the great stock industries of the Argentine Pampas and the Australian Downs. It is remarkable that France whose woollen industry makes a big demand on the merino supplies of the southern continents should remain in this dependent position, when the Sahel of West Africa remains unutilized and yet splendidly endowed by nature as a vast sheep ranch. Though, measured by numbers, the native cattle and sheep stocks of French West Africa are by no means negligible —sheep alone are estimated at three million head—the breeds are very inferior judged by European standards.[1] For cattle the well-watered, yet generally healthy highland of Futa Jallon is considered to provide the finest possibilities, and there is the advantage that the dwarf-cattle of the region are believed to be immune from the ravages of the tsetse fly.

Of the non-French territories of the Western Sudan the Gambia Protectorate (c. 4000 sq. miles) requires more attention than Portuguese Guinea despite its much smaller area. This British enclave, associated with the longest deep water inlet of the Guinea coast, provides—if we ignore the arbitrariness of political frontiers—an obvious ocean gateway to the vast hinterland, a consideration that has led to the signing of special agreements with Senegal when Gambia became independent in 1965.

The Gambia River was the scene of the earliest English trading activity on the West Coast. The depôt of Fort James, on an island well within the estuary, was held intermittently from 1618 onwards, but another two centuries were to pass before British sovereignty over the Gambia Colony was assured by the founding of Bathurst—also on an island—at the seaward entrance to the estuary. In 1826 by the annexation of a strip of territory— the ' Ceded Mile '—on the right bank of the river and extending for about 20 miles up-stream, the British defeated the French project of acquiring this most important estuarine gateway.

A distinction is still made between the Colony and the Protectorate of Gambia. The first includes the river islands and the ' Ceded Mile ', whilst the Protectorate is a later acquisition,

---

[1] Merinos from the Cape Province have been introduced into the Upper Volta, partly as a result of the enterprise of the Chamber of Commerce of Roubaix-Tourcoing.

the result of a Franco-British bargain. By a final settlement with France, British territory is restricted to a strip approximately 12 miles wide, divided lengthwise by the river, and extending eastwards to about the 250th mile from Bathurst. The Protectorate boundaries have proved most unsatisfactory as they cut right through a number of tribal groups, including Wolof and Mandingan communities, and, in consequence, the problem of government has been greatly complicated by a continual coming and going across the international frontier.

The 250-mile zone of the Protectorate controls the entire navigable course of the Gambia, a river whose total length is about 1000 miles. Bathurst harbour is able to accept ships drawing 28 feet, whilst vessels of 17 feet draught may ascend the river for a further 150 miles.

As in the surrounding Colony of Senegal economic interests in Gambia are still dominated by the marketing and export of ground-nuts : but the Protectorate has a much larger trade in this commodity than is furnished locally, and about one-half the quantity of nuts exported from Bathurst comes across the frontier from neighbouring French territory. In 1948 the value of ground-nuts sent overseas reached £1,628,000, which was the equivalent of 98 per cent (by value) of the total exports. Since the completion of the railway from Kayes to Dakar the flow of Senegal trade through Bathurst has declined. Dakar has shared the gain from this diversion of traffic with the harbour of Kaolak. The latter, at the head of an estuary which reaches the sea about 60 miles north of Bathurst, is linked to the main Senegal railway. It taps one of the best-farmed tracts in Senegal and its trade in ground-nuts has exceeded that of Dakar in recent years.

The Western Forest Lands

It will be remembered that the coasts of Sierra Leone and Liberia first gained recognition as bases for colonial enterprise when it was decided to establish thereon colonies of freed slaves repatriated from the Americas. The excellence of the anchorage and the abundance of fresh water and other supplies available in the shelter of the Freetown peninsula were known to English captains as early as 1562, when one of the most notorious of slave traders, Sir John Hawkins, made a landing.

The Crown Colony of Sierra Leone was at first confined to the Freetown peninsula, but, though small in area, for long it ranked highest amongst British Dependencies on the West Coast, and as late as 1828 its Governor was in charge of all settlements on the Gambia and the Gold Coast. To-day its fine harbour of 7 sq. miles and 30 feet of water depth is more than the commercial outlet of a rather small Crown Colony : its commanding position gives it strategic significance as one of the finest natural harbours in Africa.

There is only one other port of any consequence in Sierra Leone, namely Sherbro, 90 miles to the south-east of Freetown and on an inshore island close to the convergence of several tidal rivers and creeks. Generally, the southern shore of the colony is bordered by sand-bars and lagoons and resembles the neighbouring littoral of Liberia, where there is no natural harbour or satisfactory anchorage. No settlement on the Liberian coast has had the natural advantages possessed by Freetown, and the freed slaves who were repatriated to this part of Guinea in 1820–1 were divided amongst a number of dispersed colonies. The chief of these, named Monrovia, after a former President of the United States, and now the capital town of Liberia, is built on the face of Cape Mesurado, which affords shelter from the south-east winds only. For long there was no harbour, and surf-boats were used for landing. After the Second World War, however, dock facilities were completed, with American aid, on Bushrod Island, which was linked to the mainland by a bridge over Stockton Creek. This new artificial harbour and free port of Monrovia was opened in July, 1948. Monrovia itself (80,000 inhabitants) is now a modern town, connected by motor-road to Ganta and beyond, and by rail to the Bomi Hill iron deposits.

More than half—or about 7000—of the descendants of freed slaves who were settled on the Liberian littoral through the efforts of the American Colonization Society [1] occupy the capital and its immediate hinterland, the St. Paul's River valley, which opens to the sea immediately to the north of Cape Mesurado. The remainder are distributed in about six townships or villages between Monrovia and Cape Palmas, the southernmost point of the Guinea sea-board. Associated with the Americo-Liberians there are about 60,000 Natives of the coast who have come under their cultural influence and no longer obey tribal discipline. However, the tribal people—estimated at over two million—still form by far the majority of the population. Their representatives now take an active share in the government of the country, and speak for the desires and needs of the tribesfolk. Thus the preponderant influence in the administration of the descendants of the settled slaves is rapidly giving place to a much more balanced representation of all sections of the population, and as a result government has become much more stable.

It will be remembered from an early chapter that two of

[1] Until 1847, the year of the proclamation of Liberian independence, the Society, acting as semi-official agent for the U.S.A., was responsible for government.

23

the great groups of West Africans—the Mandingans [1] and the Krus—inhabit the Guinea lands to the north-west of Cape Palmas. The Mandingans at a remote period made their way to the coast, possibly in search of salt, and established settlements in districts now included within North-Western Liberia and Eastern Sierra Leone. Usually classified under the Mandingan group are the Vais, one of the most intellectual communities of West Africa and the only Negroes in the continent who have invented a system of writing. The Krus—much closer than the Mandingans to the unmodified Negro type—and their very near relatives the Bassas and Grebos, are mainly confined to the coastal lands between Grand Bassam and Cape Palmas, though actually their most important village, Kru Town of 4000 inhabitants, is built on the sands at the foot of Cape Mesurado, a very convenient situation for the career of seamanship which many of the Krus prefer.

There is certainty in the minds of those intimate with Liberia that the virile Mandingans and Krus are destined to gain an increasing share of authority in the public life of the Republic, a process that is likely to be expedited by the absorption of the colonist elements into the indigenous population. Already the Krus have to be reckoned with as the claimants for supreme power. It seems not unlikely that the constitution of Liberia will evolve towards a tribal federation in which all groups will be fairly represented, and that out of this free association of peoples a coherent nationality will ultimately be born. Liberia has been an independent state since 1847, and although early in the present century she had reason to fear encroachments on her territory by her neighbours,[2] her independence and prosperity now seem assured. The success of the Liberian experiment in self-rule has doubtless been due in large measure to generous assistance from outside. The country accepted substantial loans in 1912 and again in 1927, the first mainly from British sources, the second through the Financial Corporation of America. Now Liberia is to receive assistance under President Truman's Point Four Programme, and a loan of five million dollars has been negotiated with the Import-Export Bank to finance road construction. In its day, the League of Nations undertook the responsibility of guiding the career of the Republic, and recently UNESCO has sent a team of teachers to start scientific education at Liberia College.

[1] These should not be confused with the Mendi.
[2] In 1907 France took from Liberia about 3000 sq. miles in the north-east, much of it in the upper part of the St. Paul's River basin. As late as 1925 frontier incidents led the Liberian Government to fear further aggression on the part of France.

In Sierra Leone the division of the population into colonist and indigenous Negro groups is made apparent by the nominally-accepted distinction between the original Crown Colony, essentially coastal and in all only about 4000 sq. miles, and the Protectorate (26,000 sq. miles) which was not acquired by Great Britain until 1895. In that year, by arrangement with France, the international frontier was taken up to the drainage ' divide ' on the Futa Jallon Plateau.

The density of population in Sierra Leone as a whole is over twice as high as in Liberia—approximately 78 as compared with under thirty per square mile—the closer grouping in the British dependency being in part a consequence of the much greater extent of forest clearance. Of the big communities represented in the Protectorate the Mendi are the most important and number about 570,000. Mention should also be made of the Temnes—about 475,000—in the north-west. Many of them, like the Mendi, profess the Moslem faith.

On the Freetown Peninsula live most of the 40,000 Creoles, the colonist group whose forbears were introduced as liberated slaves over a century ago. They are Europeanized to the extent that they speak a form of English, and respect no native tradition or custom. Many of them are clerks and storekeepers and, in similar capacities, a considerable number have emigrated along the Coast to the ports of the Gold Coast and Nigeria.

In 1905 the members of each tribe among the immigrants into Freetown were allowed to nominate their own tribal ruler. This experiment closely concerns the whole problem of city administration in Africa, at a stage before the complete assimilation of immigrant tribal folk. In Freetown the system, probably because it was not sufficiently closely supervised, was not completely successful, and it was modified in 1932 when the tribal rulers lost their legal powers and were reduced to the status of tribal headmen ; and in 1953 a committee of enquiry recommended further that they be elected by wards rather than by tribes.[1]

In the Protectorate the Government, always in theory and generally in practice, recognizes the administrative and judicial authority of native chiefs who hold their position by virtue of immemorial custom. The Legislative Council for the Colony and Protectorate combined includes seven persons elected to represent the electoral districts of the Colony, twelve elected by the district councils of the Protectorate, and two elected by the unofficial members of the Protectorate Assembly. All land in the Protectorate is vested in the tribal authority and may not be alienated

---

[1] M. P. Banton, ' Tribal Headmen in Freetown ', *Journal of African Administration*, Vol. VI, No. 3 (July, 1954), pp. 140–4.

unless the rarely granted assent of the Governor is forthcoming.
A further instance of the enlightened rule that has characterized
British sovereignty in Sierra Leone is the long, creditable career
of Fourah Bay College (Freetown) opened in 1827. Until the
recent establishment of Achimota College in the Gold Coast, the
Freetown institution was the only one in British West Africa
where a Negro could obtain a fairly advanced cultural training.
Many of the 'intellectuals' of Nigeria and the Gold Coast, as
well as of Sierra Leone, have graduated at Fourah Bay.

Except on the grassy slopes of the Futa Jallon Plateau,
over which the innermost parts of both Sierra Leone and Liberia
extend, physical conditions are generally suited to the rain-forest
and—in the ill-drained areas—swamp vegetation that are still
characteristic of Liberia. Although the Republic has on the
whole a heavier, more certain and better distributed rainfall
than Sierra Leone, precipitation in the British Dependency
reaches the high figure of over 70 inches except in the extreme
north-east. We find that in many parts of Sierra Leone more
than 60 inches fall in the combined months of July and August,
whilst, at the other extreme, January and February are virtually
rainless. Great patches of the primeval forest are still to be
found in the south and south-centre of the Protectorate, but in
other parts, where it formerly extended widely, its destruction
by the Natives has usually been succeeded by bush and jungle
growth.

Nowhere else in West Africa outside of Southern Nigeria is
the rain-forest so luxuriant or extensive as it is in Liberia, and
apart from comparatively small clearings, many of which are
overgrown with bush, the only open country is the park savanna
on the southernmost extension of Futa Jallon. Climatic data
for Liberia are very meagre, but from the few available records [1]
it seems certain that over much the greater part of the Republic
the mean precipitation is between 70 inches and 120 inches,
with much higher figures on or near to the coast. While for
Sierra Leone the single maximum of rainfall is generally true,
there is now sufficient evidence that parts of West-Central
Liberia experience a double maximum, in June and September :
but throughout the forested lands of the Republic between April
and November, inclusive, there appears to be no month with
less than 5 inches.

Although the two territories are contrasted in respect of their
importance in world trade, even the commercially more advanced

---

[1] The most reliable rainfall records are those kept at the Mount Barclay plantation, where the mean is over 150 inches, and at another station
in West-Central Liberia.

of the two—Sierra Leone—depends for export mainly on its
wild-grown resources rather than on cultivation. There is a
common misconception that in Sierra Leone the oil-palm grows
best in the densest rain-forest, but this is not so. As a rule the
best stands of wild-grown palms are in country that is comparatively open, save perhaps for considerable low undergrowth.
In the Protectorate the palm occurs in widely dispersed patches
wherein the density may be as high as 400–500 trees to the acre.

Since railway construction has rendered two zones of the palm
accessible from Freetown, kernels and extracted oil together have
supplied more than half the total exports (by value) of Sierra
Leone, and the Dependency ranks second to Southern Nigeria
in West African output. There are two converging railways.
The main line—of narrow gauge, $2\frac{1}{2}$ feet—leads eastwards from
Freetown for nearly 230 miles, as far as Pendembu that lies close
to the Liberian frontier and to which very considerable traffic
in palm products comes from French Guinea. This railway
traverses many of the tracts of rain-forest that still remain in
the south of the Protectorate. The second and more recently
constructed line leads north-eastwards for over 100 miles from
Boia Junction (64 miles from Freetown). In the comparatively
open country on either side of it the oil-palm is more abundant
than in the zone traversed by the main line. It may be said that
alone of West African Dependencies Sierra Leone possesses a
railway system adequate to its present needs.

Apart from the wide dispersal of the stands of oil-palm—
a disadvantage that railway and motor-road construction can
only partially remove—the Sierra Leone product has the draw-
back of inferior quality as compared with the plantation crop
of the East Indies.[1] It was recently estimated that a plantation
occupying only 1 per cent of the Protectorate could produce oil
equal in quantity and superior in quality to the present commercial output. Apart from export the big internal market for
palm-oil has to be considered : the commodity is very widely
used by the Natives in cooking and as a food.

Although a single crop dominates the outgoing trade of
Freetown, in respect of food supplies locally consumed there is
a wide variety, including rice, the most important. ' Wet land '
or ' swamp ' rice is the characteristic crop of the mangrove lands
of the coast, especially in the north ; and in other parts of the
Colony the ' upland ' variety is a staple along with millet. In

[1] The competition of the East Indies' higher-grade product is only
one factor : the price of palm-oil in world markets is governed by the
supply of a number of oils that are to some extent interchangeable—
those of the palm, ground-nut, copra and whale.

the north-eastern savanna country where both agriculturists (e.g. the Konno people) and pastoralists (e.g. the Fulani) are present the basic crops are guinea corn, millet, ground-nut and maize. On account of the prevalence of the tsetse fly throughout the forested or well-wooded lands of Guinea, cattle-rearing in both Liberia and Sierra Leone is limited to the open grass-lands of the Futa Jallon and its south-eastern extension.

Whilst it is true that throughout British West Africa as a whole the principle of selling or leasing land—alienated from tribal tenure—to concession seekers is not generally approved, we find that in Sierra Leone plantation agriculture organized by Europeans has been officially encouraged in very recent years. In 1913 the Sierra Leone and Gold Coast Governments authorized, for a term of twenty-one years, small concessions within which oil-extracting machinery might be set up and to which native collectors might bring palm fruit for sale. Later, in 1922, probably inspired by fear of severe Far Eastern competition, the Government of Sierra Leone offered, on lease, concessions individually not exceeding 5000 acres for oil-palm planting, but so far there has been little response.

The present position of Liberia in the commerce of West Africa is insignificant, but signs are not wanting that in a comparatively short space of years, largely as a result of the introduction of capital and technical equipment from the United States, the Republic will rise to a place more in keeping with the extent of its resources. Until recently the country was not even self-supporting in food and had to import rice in large quantities. With hardly a modern road,[1] no railway and no harbour Liberia was still locked away from the world. Many Natives unable to obtain wage employment had, under the pressure of taxation, migrated to neighbouring territories. Now, however, thanks to the new harbour and motor roads, and to the extension of rubber planting and the mining of iron-ore, the whole economic prospect of the Republic is changed.

Liberia, the largest continuous stretch of virgin forest in Africa west of the Niger Delta, is endowed with natural advantages of soil and climate for the production in abundance of commercial plants—such as the non-indigenous Hevea tree—that require essentially equatorial conditions. It is evident that the great industrial countries will not indefinitely permit the Republic to lie fallow, as witness the interest evinced both by the U.S.A. and France. Each of these leading industrial Powers

[1] Before 1914 there was not a proper highway in Liberia. By 1925 the first section—about 130 miles—of a trunk road leading from Monrovia into the interior was completed.

is deficient in ' Para ' (i.e. Hevea) rubber, and although the inadequacy of supply has little excuse in the case of France whose vast equatorial empire could under proper organization produce unlimited rubber, the U.S.A. have not under their control territory climatically suited to Hevea.[1]

Not until 1923 were European and American traders permitted to penetrate Liberia with comparative freedom. In that year Mr. H. S. Firestone of the large Ohio rubber firm, who shared American fears of a British and Dutch rubber monopoly, sent out a deputation which made a survey of the country from the standpoint of its rubber prospects. A disused plantation of about 2000 acres at Mount Barclay, about 30 miles north-east of Monrovia, was restored to activity, and it was proposed to the Liberian Government that the Firestone Company should be allowed to lease an aggregate of one million acres in districts suited to rubber planting and comparatively accessible.

In view of the benefits to the Republic promised by the Firestone Company, Liberia approved the lease in 1927, by which time, indeed, a start had been made towards the clearing of 24,000 acres in the hinterland of Monrovia (more particularly the neighbourhood of the Dukwia River). Two years later, six million rubber trees—many imported from Sumatra—were planted on 30,000 acres in the Dukwia region, whilst on another 11,000 acres in the extreme south-east (Maryland County) Hevea was planted at about the same time. It is intended ultimately to produce 250,000 tons annually (approximately the output of the Dutch East Indies in 1931) for which development 300,000 labourers will be required : a great stimulus was given to rubber production by the exigencies of war-time, when Liberia's output became of very great importance to the U.S.A[2]

The Firestone Plantations Company, a subsidiary of the great manufacturing corporation of Ohio, has the official encouragement of the U.S.A. Government in its enterprise. Moreover, in recent years Washington has extended loans to the hard-pressed Republic : during the decade 1950–60, the economic growth of the country was surpassed only by that of Japan. Over this period the government revenues increased eight-fold.

Under the terms of an agreement the Firestone Company guaranteed the construction of a harbour at Monrovia and a motor-road system between the plantations and the coast, in

[1] v. H. N. Whitford and A. Anthony, *Rubber Production in Africa*, U.S. Dept. of Commerce, Washington, 1926.
[2] In 1932 the export of rubber from Liberia was 150 tons and the total exports were valued at £200,000. In 1950–51, however, the exports of plantation rubber were valued at $45 millions.

addition to other works of a public nature—most of which have
already been accomplished, with great advantage to the economy
of the country as a whole. To offset these benefits, quite obviously
the introduction of the ' plantation system ' into Liberia will
involve land alienation from tribal occupancy on an extensive
and increasing scale. Furthermore, the appearance of a wage-
earning but land-less proletariat, removed from the discipline of
indigenous community life, seems equally inevitable.

So long as Hevea receives special emphasis, native-owned
plantations will be out of the question, on account of the advanced
organization that is required for the production and preparation
of rubber for market. Crude rubber in 1962 represented 43
per cent by value of the exports of the Republic. The principal
exports is iron-ore, which is likely to become increasingly important, as the reserves are rich and extensive. Native farming,
especially concerned with the basic food-crops—rice, millet and
manioc—is subject to ' shifting cultivation '. A family clears and
plants a plot within the forest, but at the end of the second or
third season the site is abandoned to overgrowing jungle, and
not reoccupied until seven or eight years have elapsed.

The Mid-Guinea Forest Belt

In each of the three political units associated here, namely
the Ivory Coast, Gold Coast and Dahomey,[1] the zone of rain-
forest is of main consequence in respect of economic geography.
The northern, or Sudanese, grass-lands of each Dependency are
still imperfectly linked by lines of transport to their natural
outlets on the Guinea Coast ; though since motor-road development, especially notable in the case of the Gold Coast, the position
is better than would appear from the railway map, which shows
four or five tracks isolated from each other and leading directly
inland, but failing to penetrate far beyond the forest at any point.

All north-south ' sections ' across the vegetation belts of
West Africa closely resemble each other, and for this the lack of
great contrasts in relief is largely responsible. Between Futa
Jallon and the Bauchi country of Nigeria areas of comparatively
high plateau are small, widely-dispersed relict masses whose
altitude does not exceed 3000 feet. Away from the coast practically all land is between 600 and 1500 feet, the only important
exception being the middle basin of the Volta. As this river—
the most considerable between the Gambia and the Niger—
flows for its entire length across country which, by Guinea

[1] Ex-German Togoland was divided into British and French trust
territories. The former was united with Ghana after a referendum of
1956 ; the latter became an independent republic in April, 1960.

standards, is one of low rainfall, its influence on soil and vegetation distributions is small, i.e. localized, when compared with that of the Niger.

The Ivory Coast Colony, whose northern confines in the Sudan are more than 300 miles from the Gulf of Guinea, is an arbitrarily-bounded political unit [1] with frontiers determined either by administrative convenience or by contact with rival colonial penetration. As the most recent addition to the Guinea empire of France the Ivory Coast is still quite primitive in respect of economic development, which may be perceived from a comparison of its potential resources and present commercial output.

Rain-forest is estimated to occupy about 40,000 sq. miles, or one-third of the total area, the widest extent being close to the Liberian border where the southernmost limit of the Colony— close to Cape Palmas—is little more than 4° from the Equator. The selva is particularly rich in cabinet woods, and abundant also are the resources of oil-palm : yet only very recently have the French fully realized the possibilities, and as late as 1917 they were purchasing from the United States mahogany grown in West Africa. As for the northern grass-lands of the Colony, they still retain their isolation from world markets, although opening-up is foreshadowed by the recent northern extension of the Ivory Coast railway, which has its terminus at Abidjan on the coast. More important is the expanding network of roads, the most complex of any of the former French West African countries, which carries five-eighths of the country's traffic, mainly coffee, cocoa and timber.

Recent economic revolution in the Gold Coast, bringing into existence a vast cocoa-growing industry, has extended farther afield, and, on a smaller scale, the agricultural and commercial developments in the British territory have been followed step by step in the Ivory Coast. Climatic and soil conditions for cocoa are very satisfactory over the greater part of the forested area of the French colony. More important for the cacao tree than particularly heavy annual rainfall are continuously high atmospheric humidity and the absence of a completely rainless period : if these conditions are satisfied the annual rainfall need not exceed 40 inches. The comparative rarity of hurricanes is another factor of first-class importance in determining the prosperity of cacao growing. Cultivation, undertaken mainly by native farmers, was not seriously begun until 1908, but so successful has the enterprise proved that in recent years cocoa has headed the list of Ivory Coast exports.

[1] For comparison, its area is almost exactly that of the British Isles, viz. *c.* 121,000 sq. miles.

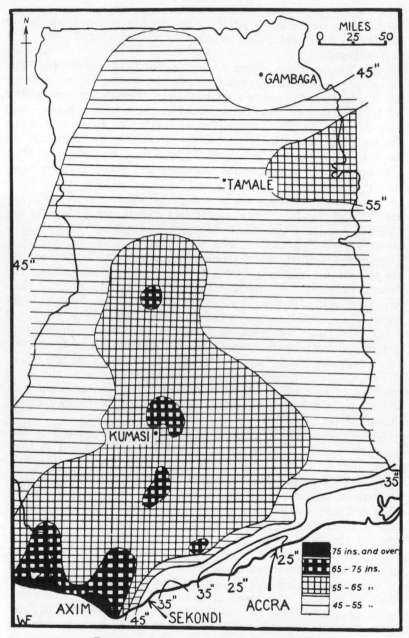

FIG. 73.—Ghana: Average Annual Rainfall

There is a growing opinion in the agricultural service of French West Africa that the introduction of plantation agriculture into the Ivory Coast is vital to its future—particularly where the palm-oil industry is concerned—on account of the severe competition imposed by high-grade East Indian and Malayan products. It has been estimated that the annual output of Ivory Coast oil could easily reach 200,000 tons from the forest resources alone. The actual export is only some 16,000 tons, but a quantity at least equal is wasted through primitive or careless methods of handling.

Along the 400 miles of the Ivory Coast there is no natural shelter for shipping. Sand-bars backed by lagoons extend continuously and render inshore navigation extremely precarious. Until recently Abidjan, the rail terminus, had to rely for its sea-trade on the open roadsteads of Port Bouet and Grand Bassam. The Vridi Canal, 3 kilometres long and 10 to 20 metres deep, now connects the lagoon of Abidjan with the sea, and on February 6th, 1951, the new port of Abidjan was officially opened. By 1961 it had grown to a population of 190,000, and in that year handled 2,300,000 tons of cargo. The efficiency of the port has been improved by connecting the Abidjan harbour with other lagoons along the coast (Fig. 67).

Unlike the majority of French West African Dependencies the Ivory Coast has comparatively few Moslems, an indication of the formidable nature of the barrier presented to southward migration by the great forest. In French West Africa as a whole, Moslems comprise just over 44 per cent of the population. In the Ivory Coast, however, the corresponding figure is approximately 6 per cent as compared with 14 in Upper Volta, 55 in French Guinea and 75 per cent in Senegal. Within the forest belt and on the grasslands distribution of population is far from uniform, and it is not only the open savannas that possess the densest settlement. Large parts of the north-west are very scantily occupied : on the other hand, some of the highest densities are found in the south-east, close to the Gold Coast, and also in northern parts of the forest.

Between the lagoons of the Ivory Coast and those of Togoland extend the 300 miles of the naturally harbourless Gold Coast, where until the building of the ports of Takoradi (1929) and Tema (1960) ocean vessels could not berth alongside. Yet this uninviting coast has been known to Europeans for 500 years and, as mentioned earlier, long remained the principal scene of commercial rivalry between the maritime Powers interested in West African trade.

As in the case of the Ivory Coast the name ' Gold Coast ' came to be applied to a hinterland extending across the Guinea forest far into the Sudan. In general use the term used to refer to a federation of three administrative divisions—the original Colony (23,500 sq. miles), Ashanti (24,500 sq. miles) and the Northern Territories (30,600 sq. miles)—to which had been added, though under trusteeship, 13,000 sq. miles of Togoland immediately to the east of the lower Volta. Excluding the trustee Territory, the units represented three separate stages in the establishment of British sovereignty. Not until 1821 were most of the coastal trading posts in the possession of the Crown, and as late as 1872 Holland still retained a footing. Owing to rivalry between the principal coastal community, the Fanti, and their northern neighbours, the Ashanti—a rivalry intensified by British encouragement to the Fanti—friction between the interior tribes and the Colony continued during the latter part of the nineteenth century. Great Britain was led, in 1901, to annex Ashanti as a Colony, not only for the above-mentioned reason but also on account of the territorial ambitions of France and Germany, operating on either side and threatening the commercial hinterland of the Gold Coast settlements. A little later the Northern Territories were proclaimed a Protectorate, and the federation of two Colonies and one Protectorate remained in force until 1957.

In 1957 the British Gold Coast Dependency became the independent country of Ghana, which in 1960 formed a provisional and indefinite union with the ex-French territory, now the Republic of Guinea, and with Mali. After referendum in 1960 Ghana adopted a republican constitution.

The easily-recognized physical divisions of Ghana include the following—to which in each case is added a brief summary of geographical conditions :

(1) The coastal lands, 20–40 miles wide and less than 250 feet in altitude, occupy the greater part of the original colony and include all the important centres of urban life—Sekondi, Takoradi, Cape Coast and Accra. The climatic and vegetational contrasts between the western and eastern districts have been mentioned but may again be emphasized. West of Cape Three Points precipitation exceeds 65 inches and rain-forest is dominant, but going eastwards from the headland there is a steady decline in rainfall to 25 inches, corresponding to passage into open country of grass and scrub. Population distribution bears a definite relationship to these phenomena. West of Cape Three Points, especially between Axim and the border, density is under sixty per square mile ; between the Cape and Sekondi it is over 150 ; and, excepting the barren sands in the extreme south-east of the country, there is no part of the north-eastward trending littoral where the figure is less than sixty. North and north-west of Accra the high densities around Sekondi

are repeated. Although much less than one-third of the territory, this region has well over half of the aggregate population.

(2) The Ashanti Plateau, averaging 500–1500 feet above sea-level, is by climate, vegetation and ethnic affinities associated with the coast-lands rather than with the Sudan. It is natural forest country, with a high rainfall usually exceeding 50 inches. Density of population is generally lower than in the littoral belt but culminates in a figure over 200 per square mile around Kumasi which, near the centre of the Plateau, is the head-quarters of the Ashanti people.

(3) The plains of the Volta and its tributary, the Black Volta, whose middle course trends eastwards to join the southward-flowing main stream, extend to the north and north-east of the Ashanti Plateau. Precipitation is much lower than in Ashanti, also more precarious and confined to a shorter rainy season. Population density is under ten, on the average, whilst large parts are almost deserted and there is little settlement based on cultivation. Tsetse fly is widespread and prevents successful stock-rearing.

(4) The northern plateau grass-lands (500–1500 ft.) merging with the plateau of the Mossi country possess a climate healthier to man and stock and more dependable in rainfall than that of the Volta plains. Consequently there is a much higher density of population—increasing to over 100 in the north-east—than in the southern, lowland districts of the Northern Territories. Light soils, well suited to guinea-corn, ground-nut, millet and cotton, support prosperous agriculture undertaken by the Dagomba and other peoples. One of the characteristic products is shea-butter derived from the fruit of a tree (*Butyrospermum Parkii*). This valuable vegetable fat is greatly in demand by Natives throughout the Central Sudan. The region is distinguished from all others of the Gold Coast by its immunity from tsetse fly and consequently is the only important cattle land of the Dependency.

The importance of the Ghanaian tribes in the life of West Africa was briefly indicated on an earlier page. Quite obviously, where frontiers take little or no account of ethnic distributions it is inevitable to find that large communities have been divided between colonies. Examples are numerous and include the Dagomba, whose lands are shared between Togoland and the Northern Territories, and the Ewe people on the eastern littoral of the territory of Ghana and in neighbouring parts of Togoland. Two big groups whose distribution is virtually confined to the Dependency are the Fanti and Ashanti, by race closely akin and belonging to the great Akan group of West African Negroes.

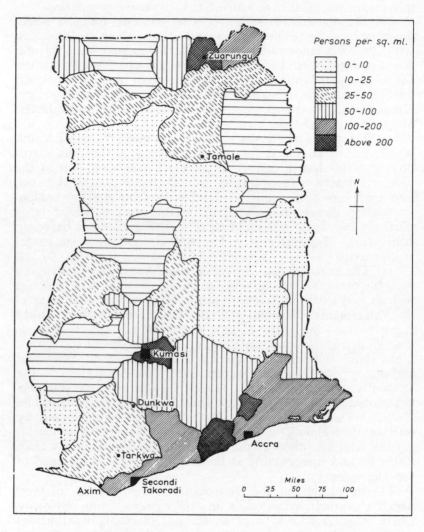

Persons per sq. ml.

0 - 10
10 - 25
25 - 50
50 - 100
100 - 200
Above 200

Fig. 74.—Ghana, showing Density of Population (1948)

354

It is believed that the Akan, originally a Sudanese group, were expelled from their lands by Hamitic invaders and took up their abode in the protecting forests, where the tsetse fly assisted in the repulse of the horse-and-cattle men.

The most urgent tasks of the Ghanaian economy are to diversify its basis, and to produce more food for the population, which is expanding at an annual rate of about $3\frac{1}{2}$ per cent. To these aims the northern territories may contribute substantially, particularly by raising more livestock. They need, however, a more assured supply of water, and easier links with the coast. It is hoped that surface dams will transform the economy of extensive districts here, by reducing the menace of seasonal famines ; self-help through the community development projects will speed progress in this direction. At the same time, a system of new roads, and notably a trunk highway through Kumasi and Tamale to Navrongo, is being set up in advance of the railways.

In the industrial life of the state of Ghana everything is subordinate to cocoa cultivation, though the age-long importance of gold is by no means terminated. Systematic gold-mining did not begin until 1879, but now is undertaken in a number of districts, mainly within the railway zone between Sekondi and Kumasi. The abundant mineral wealth may also be instanced by manganese ore which, since the Great War, has been extensively mined (434,000 tons in 1963).

The forest of the western littoral and of Ashanti is rich in its abundant resources of palm-oil, rubber and cabinet-woods, and invaluable also for the protection it affords from the southward encroachment of the Sudan climate and vegetation. Destruction of tree growth to make room for the cultivation of cocoa and other crops, as well as for mining and road construction, has already gone so far as to force the Government to undertake, on a considerable scale, the reservation of forested areas.

The cacao tree, which is not indigenous but of Central American origin, has been for a quarter of a century the dominant feature of Ghanaian agriculture. From the first shipment overseas in 1891, production for export rose quickly, especially after the Great War when it increased from 66,000 tons in 1918 to 231,000 tons in 1926 ; and to the latter total—equalling about one-third of the world's supply—output has remained close for a number of years.[1] Very little cocoa is grown within ten miles of the shore, yet the greater part of the production is from the triangular area between the Kumasi–Sekondi and Kumasi–Accra railways. It is generally believed that the crop has reached its maximum

[1] The crop for the year 1936 constituted, until 1959, a record of 311,151 tons. In 1961, 435,000 tons were produced, about one-third of the world total.

under present conditions of cultivation and that additional suitable land is scarce, except in the extreme west, i.e. between the Kumasi–Sekondi railway and the Ivory Coast frontier. In the eastern districts, which have been longest under cultivation, output has recently been declining partly in consequence of soil exhaustion. Moreover, the normal quality of Gold Coast cocoa is not high, and is excelled by the product of either Venezuela or Trinidad.

Besides being well suited to the humid forest lands of the Gold Coast, cocoa has a second advantage from the standpoint of the rather primitive cultivators who specialize in it, namely that it is easily and cheaply produced and is a lucrative crop. The spread of the swollen shoot disease has proved a great problem for the government in recent years. The recognized cure is to cut down the tree, a step which the illiterate cultivator is usually reluctant to take.

The influence of widespread commercial agriculture upon the traditional system of land tenure has been as revolutionary as in the somewhat similar circumstances of Uganda. Until half a century ago the sale of land was inconceivable, and consequently there were no landlords and tenants as at present. Cocoa-planting necessitated the abandonment of the old system of shifting agriculture which involved the hoeing of a plot and then moving on to fresh soil after two or three years. Instead of allowing that portion of his land not under cocoa to lie fallow the Native must adopt more intensive methods, such as rotation of crops and manuring, in order to furnish his family with food-stuffs. Naturally he is not satisfied with the old conception of communal occupation and desires the sole and permanent use of the plot that he has improved. Individual and family holdings now constitute much the greater part of the land under cocoa : they are usually small, and on an average sufficient for the production of one-half to a ton annually. In addition, however, are native-owned plantations which employ a wage-earning class of land-less labourers, whose numbers tend to increase, partly as a result of immigration from neighbouring French territory and from Liberia.

The untapped resources of water-power in the Volta River have been appreciated for many years, and the Volta River aluminium scheme began to be put into effect in 1962. It will involve the construction of a dam and power-station at Ajena, an aluminium smelter at Kpong (with an ultimate capacity of 210,000 tons of aluminium a year), railway extensions to the bauxite deposits at Mpraeso and Yenahin, and a new port at Tema.

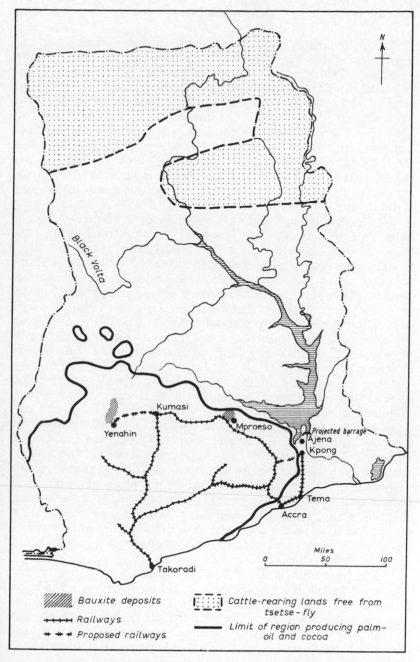

FIG. 75.—Ghana: Economic Features

Much the greater part of Togoland fell under French trustee-ship associated with Dahomey, and became an independent republic in April, 1960. Unsatisfactory as was a line of geographical division through the old Franco-British frontier, an attempt was made when defining it not to aggravate the position by weakening still further the integrity of the tribal groups. Thus a very large majority of the Ewe people are now in Ghanaian territory, and their ' nation ' would be completely re-united but for the failure of Ghana and Togo to agree on frontier adjustments. To take another instance, the Dagomba are now a re-united people, for there are scarcely any of this group to the east of the boundary.

Under the German régime Togoland—as a whole, 33,700 sq. miles—was left almost entirely to native commercial agriculture (cocoa, cotton, oil-palm) and no encouragement was given either to White settlement, for which the country's climate is quite unsuited, or to plantation agriculture under European control. Because of the isolation of Western Togoland from the Ghanaian railways, which do not penetrate east of the Volta, a large part of the outflow of commercial products (notably cocoa) from this zone continues to pass through Lome. After the plebiscite of May, 1956, British Togoland became integrated with Ghana as Trans-Volta Togoland.

As a cross-section of the selva and savanna belts of West Africa, Dahomey (with Togoland) shows clearly the succession of (a) mangrove-bounded, lagoon coast, (b) hardwood and oil-palm forest, (c) park savanna and treeless savanna, the latter in the neighbourhood of the Niger. Some of the densest and most luxuriant stands of oil-palm in Guinea are here, and the French estimate that the best oil-bearing zone covers more than 6000 sq. miles and that from it, instead of an output of about 12,000 tons of oil as at present, the figure could easily be raised to 140,000 tons. The Southern Dahomey Natives show care in their exploitation of the forest resources and actually carry out re-afforestation, whilst their methods of palm-oil collection are superior to those of most Guinea Negroes.

Apart from the neighbourhood of Lome, another district highly important in the life of Dahomey is that which lies behind the coast in the extreme east, especially between the port towns of Cotonou and Porto Novo. Here the density of population reaches its maximum for the Colony, viz. over 120 per square mile, whilst native cultivation is more intensive and more varied in its range of crops than in most parts. Porto Novo, until recently the coastal terminus of the Eastern Dahomey railway, is built on the northern shore of a lagoon whose only access to the sea is by way

of the Nigerian port of Lagos, through which indeed until a few
years ago passed one-half the overseas trade of Eastern Dahomey.
In order to divert traffic to an ocean outlet under French authority
the railway at Porto Novo has been extended to the Gulf port
of Cotonou. Until recently Dahomey was in a very undeveloped
state, but since the War its exports, particularly of its first product,
palm kernels, have shown a rapid increase. Some Dutch traders
from Indonesia have settled there.

Eastern Forest Belt (Southern Nigeria)

Nigeria, the largest state of the Guinea coast in respect of
both area (356,700 sq. miles) and population (55 millions in 1963),
grew to its present dimensions by successive stages of annexation
from the coast inwards, as in the case of the Gold Coast. Though
the most recently incorporated of our West African Dependencies,
its littoral was visited from the earliest days of British trading
in the Gulf of Guinea and, together with that of Dahomey, was
known as the Slave Coast.

After the prohibition of the slave trade (in 1807), so far
as British subjects were concerned, the lagoons which had given
Lagos its name and the creeks of the Oil Rivers [1] long remained
the haunt of slave raiders, and the region possessed no organized
government until the middle of the century. From 1850 onwards
English traders were operating on the lower Niger, and when,
in 1861, Lagos became a Crown Colony and the first British
possession on the Slave Coast, Lokoja at the junction of the Niger
and the Benue was already a well-established British trade
depôt with a commanding position in relation to the growing
commerce of the lower Niger Basin. Coming to the next stage in
annexation, we find that in order to comply with the principle
of ' effective occupation ' enunciated at the Congress of Berlin,
Great Britain declared a Protectorate over the ' Niger Coast ',
the territory concerned extending from the Lagos Colony to the
eastern limits of the Niger Delta, as well as up-stream to Lokoja
and, on the Benue, some 200 miles as far as Ibi.

The limits of the Protectorate roughly corresponded with
those of the zone in which first operated the Royal Niger Company, one of the three Chartered Companies established between
1880 and 1890 for the purpose of promoting British commercial
interests in Africa. It was through the agency of the Company
that the British sphere of influence was extended into Northern
Nigeria—as now known ; for although mainly interested in the
forest resources, especially oil-palm, of the lower Niger region
the R.N.C. foresaw the commercial advantages to be derived

[1] Proved in 1830 to be the distributaries of the Niger Delta.

from the opening-up to trade of the emirates of the Central Sudan (including Sokoto), with their ' multiculture ' embracing cereals, ground-nut, cotton, shea-nut as well as cattle. On the side of native policy, it should be added that Sir George Goldie, the founder of the Royal Niger Company, was the first West African administrator to adopt the policy of ' indirect rule ' through the medium of local chiefs. This was the policy later to be widely developed by Lugard in Northern Nigeria.

When, in 1900, the Imperial Government took over from the Niger Company, the administrative powers that it claimed ex-

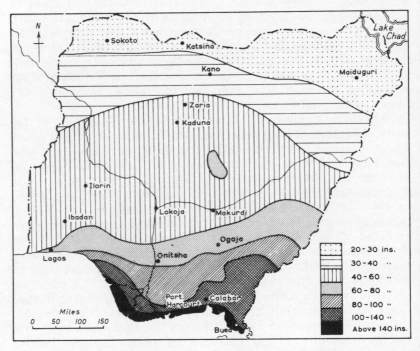

FIG. 76.—Nigeria : Average Annual Rainfall

tended as far north-westwards as Sokoto and north-eastwards as far as Bornu in the Chad region. But the work of conquest in these parts of the Sudan was by no means complete, and it was not until 1903, as a result of the military operations under Captain (later Lord) Lugard, that the Moslem rulers of Kano, the great mart, Katsina, a prominent cultural centre of the Sudan, and Sokoto, the religious capital of the Fulani, accepted British suzerainty.

From the independent existence of three closely associated units—one Crown Colony and two Protectorates—to the federation of Nigeria was a natural evolution, if only because of the mutual commercial advantages to be gained. Yet when (1906) Lugard urged the union of our Nigerian Dependencies the Home Government was reluctant to act. It actually encouraged the Northern Nigeria Protectorate to maintain its commercial independence of Lagos, by advising the construction of a railway [1] that should offer competition to the line already being built by the Southern Protectorate from Iddo (Lagos), by way of Ilorin, to Kano. In 1914, at last, the amalgamation of Northern and Southern Nigeria (with Lagos) was accomplished and Lugard, to whom unification is due, was appointed first Governor-General. The result was a federation rather than an amalgamation of regions of different geography, race, religion and political traditions, and unfortunately the differences of outlook between North and South have become recently more acute. There has been talk of secession in Northern Nigeria, and in May, 1953, the Colonial Secretary announced that the colony's constitution would have to be redrawn to provide for greater regional autonomy. The South, which is, educationally, more advanced than the North, has much to learn from the experience of the North in responsible local government. The North might lose access to Lagos, and would then have to develop an outlet by the Dahomey railway ; while interruption of the annual sale of 100,000 northern cattle in the South would harm both purchaser and supplier. The solution, reached in 1960, was an independent Federation of three self-governing Regions, Northern, Western and Eastern (a fourth, the Midwest, was to be added in 1963).

Along the coast of the Southern Provinces lies the most extensive zone of lagoons, partially-submerged mud-flats and swamps in West Africa—the width of the belt varying from about 10 miles in the neighbourhood of Lagos to over 60 in the Niger Delta. Eastwards from the many outlets of the great river,[2] deposition of alluvium by the Cross River and smaller streams reproduces similar deltaic conditions which continue up to the foot-hills of the Cameroons Highlands. The mangrove, with its stilt-like roots growing only in brackish tidal waters, is abundantly represented, whilst on the drier ground there is a particularly luxuriant and high forest in which raphia palm, the oil-palm and valuable hard woods—often 200 feet high— are characteristic. In this narrow littoral belt, especially where it extends farthest south, the double maximum of rainfall associated with the equatorial climate is well shown. From 71 inches at Lagos precipitation increases south-eastwards—in the Delta—to over 100 inches (Forcados, 147 inches; Opobo, 140 inches), and in this very low latitude there is no dry season,

[1] From Kano to Baro on the Niger, at which point transhipment to river-boats was intended.

[2] Fourteen principal distributaries of the Niger meander across the Delta which extends across 200 miles of coast.

although the rainfall in the ' winter ' period of December–February is comparatively slight. At the stations above-mentioned there is a regular increase up to June or July, followed by a few weeks' lull in the torrential onset of the rains ; after which, in September, the precipitation reaches its second maximum (at Opobo, over 23 inches).

Behind the lagoon-and-swamp belt the rain-forest continues

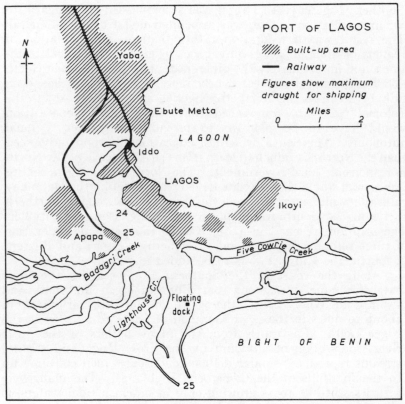

FIG. 77.—The Port of Lagos

widely, up to 50–100 miles inland. In the hinterland of Lagos altitude rises gradually to 1000–1500 feet on the Yorubaland ' plains ', and in this direction, viz. northwards, the decline in annual precipitation is more abrupt than elsewhere in Southern Nigeria : so that at Abeokuta, about 60 miles to the north of Lagos, the annual mean is but 49 inches. The formerly wooded country of Yorubaland has been completely cleared of tall forest to make way for the wasteful native system of ' shifting agriculture '. At a distance of over 100 miles from the Gulf, no part of Southern Nigeria, excepting the southward bulge of the Niger Delta, has a rainfall exceeding 70 inches, and, before the northern frontier is reached, the primitive vegetation has changed to park savanna which is also characteristic of the southernmost parts of Northern Nigeria.

Along a coast of lagoons and shifting sand-and-mud flats natural harbours with deep water are very rare, and the problem of port construction and fairway dredging has been a very formidable one in Southern Nigeria, though with vigorous attention it has been solved within a few years. To-day the Colony possesses four harbours available for ships of 20-feet draught, namely Lagos, Forcados on a western outlet of the Niger, Port Harcourt on the Bonny River outlet, and Calabar on the Cross River. The improvement of the port of Lagos has been one of the greatest engineering achievements in West African history. As recently as 1907 ships with draught greater than 11 feet were unable to enter, but by 1952 those drawing 26 feet could be accepted alongside. The new Apapa wharves on the mainland opposite Lagos are now the southern terminus of the principal Nigerian railway, and in 1951 important work was begun on their extension. In addition to sea-going traffic Lagos gains by the very busy movement of small vessels that ply along the uninterrupted chain of lagoons between Dahomey and the Niger Delta ports, especially Forcados and Port Harcourt. The latter is the terminus of the Eastern Railway through Makurdi that joins the main line at Kaduna. It owes its rank as second port in Nigeria to its contacts by rail with the richest tract of oil-palm in West Africa and with the chief mineral-bearing fields of the Colony.

For the Enugu [1] coal-field, about 1600 sq. miles in extent and to the north-east of the Niger Delta, Port Harcourt is the natural outlet. Annual production reaches about 580,000 tons, but could be greatly exceeded if the demands for coal came from a wider region than at present. As Port Harcourt is far away from an ocean trade-route coal is not needed there for bunkering, although an increasing quantity is exported to Gold Coast ports. The second mineral field, with which the Bonny River port is in direct communication, is that of the Bauchi Plateau in Northern Nigeria, where high-grade alluvial tin ore has been mined since 1902 on a very extensive scale.[2] From Forcados during high

[1] Enugu town has been selected in place of Lagos as the new capital of Southern Nigeria because of its more central position in relation to the Southern Provinces as a whole.

[2] The ' peak ' output of 15,340 tons of tin, in 1929, made Nigeria fourth producing country of the world : output was 10,513 tons in 1961.

river small sea-going boats can ascend the Niger beyond Lokoja, and the lower Benue also ; whilst at all times the main river is navigable up to Jebba—where the Kano-Lagos railway crosses the Niger—for craft not exceeding 4 feet in draught. The projects now being undertaken in French Sudan for impounding the flood waters of the middle Niger must necessarily have serious consequences for the navigation of the lower Niger which, throughout the last 700 miles of its course, flows entirely in British territory.

Excepting Yorubaland, it may be said that Southern Nigeria is a land of very primitive cultivators. The low yield in agricultural output is partly due to the lack of animal manure.[1] Much of the soil is deficient in organic matter and appears to be low in calcium and phosphates. The sands of Benin Province and of the Niger Delta are quite unsuited to a number of tropical crops on account of their acid nature and lack of mineral plant food, yet the oil-palm grows well upon them. Yams, cassava and maize are the staple food-crops, and for the first of these are reserved the best soils of the farm which, on the average, is about three acres per family. When the cultivated plot shows signs of exhaustion it is allowed to revert to bush for five to seven years and a new area is cleared. ' Shifting cultivation,' which is a commonplace of the Guinea region as well as of Central Africa, cannot, however, be practised in all parts of Southern Nigeria on account of the very high densities of population that are reached in certain districts. In the Delta Provinces of Onitsha and Owerri, where the density rises to 1700 per square mile, the period during which a given plot is cultivated must exceed that when it is left fallow, and shifting cultivation as a system has already completely broken down. In the less-congested districts of the west, e.g. Yorubaland, where the density is only 100–200 and where practically all forest has been cleared away, the period when land lies fallow exceeds that when cultivation is practised.

It is difficult to exaggerate the importance to Southern Nigeria of the oil-palm,[2] a plant requiring 60 inches of rainfall spread over not less than eight months of the year. From Benin to Calabar there are the richest stands of the palm, yet it is here that soils are amongst the poorest in West Africa and that population density attains its maximum for Southern Nigeria. The cacao tree, very sensitive to soil acidity, does not succeed on the Delta soils although vain efforts have been made to extend

[1] The tsetse fly makes stock-rearing impossible.
[2] For the year 1961 the exports of palm oil and palm kernels together were worth £30 million ; which may be compared with £2 million for Sierra Leone.

its cultivation there. In South-Western Nigeria (including a large part of Yorubaland), beginning some 10 miles from the coast and reaching 150 miles inland, there is an important cocoa belt [1] where conditions for large-scale production are at least as satisfactory as in state of Ghana. Cultivation has only been seriously undertaken since 1920—the exports growing from 3600 tons in 1913 to 121,000 tons in 1951—but the progress which these figures indicate signifies the advent of a powerful rival to

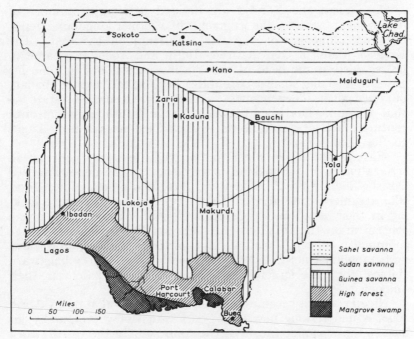

FIG. 78.—Vegetation Map of Nigeria

the older Ghanian industry. As in the case of the smaller country, cocoa is responsible for an economic revolution. Many of the cocoa farmers have ceased to grow subsistence crops, while the work on the cocoa groves is done largely by paid labourers. The growing number of Nigerians who are not self-supporting has become a menace to the country, and with the possible failure of the money crop, or a fall in its world-price, unemployment and distress would be inevitable, unless the Natives affected could return to subsistence farming as a basis of livelihood.

[1] In the Provinces of Oyo, Abeokuta, Ondo and Ijebu.

The land to the west of the lower Niger is occupied mainly by the Yoruba and their less important kinsmen. In an earlier chapter was mentioned the tendency for the Yoruba—the farmers as well as the traders—to congregate in towns that are very large by native African standards.[1] Each of ten Yoruba towns is of not less than 40,000 inhabitants, and greatest of them is Ibadan (600,000). In reality, however, much of their life is semi-rural, for townspeople commonly engage in farm-work at several miles distance.

At present the Yoruba are divided between a number of independent 'states', the fragments of a former kingdom extending from Dahomey on the west to Benin on the east. The King or Alafin of Oyo (between Ilorin and Abeokuta) came to be regarded as the head of the Yoruba nation, but in time his power waned and smaller potentates, such as the ruler of Ibadan, obtained their independence. Another great native 'state'—that of Benin—flourished between the fourteenth and nineteenth centuries, and at one time its west-east extent was from Lagos to the Bonny River.

East of the lower Niger and in the Delta the contrast in civilization with Yorubaland is marked. In the densely-settled Onitsha and Owerri Provinces live three and a half million Ibos, who are more concentrated than the Yorubas but quite lacking in their social and political cohesion. Without any urban concentration the Ibos recognize the small independent village community as the essential unit of their society, and have no paramount chiefs. Like their neighbours, the very backward Ibibios, they are largely dependent on the oil-palm for their 'money crop'.

Nigeria, which became an independent federal state in April, 1960, is undertaking new enterprises which may profoundly influence the economic future of the country. In the North, work was begun in 1959 on a branch railway from Nguru near Jos to Maiduguri, to help tap hitherto remote areas in Bauchi and Bornu. In the East and West, Israeli engineers are exploring water resources and prospects for rural electrification.

But the most revolutionary development has been the discovery of oil in the Niger delta, in a remote area of mangrove swamp and rain forest, where conditions are such that artificial islands of sand have to be built to support the derricks. In 1959 there were six producing wells in the fields at Oloibiri and Afam, whence the oil is pumped along a pipeline to a creek, where barges take it down-stream to Port Harcourt. The first shipments were made from here in February, 1958, and by

[1] No doubt the tendency was increased during slave-raiding times by the need for mutual protection.

1961 a rate of annual export of 2¼ million tons was reached. Port Harcourt is becoming a thriving oil port, and the River Bonny is being dredged to clear the obstructing bar and admit larger tankers. Offshore resources are being explored, and there are plans for using oil and natural gas for the generation of electricity for supplying new industries within Nigeria.

Northern Nigeria

The Northern or Sudanese Provinces of Nigeria cover three times the area of the forested Provinces of the south. Much the greater part is savanna, either park-like or, as in the cases of the highly important Sokoto and Kano Provinces, almost treeless : but great contrasts in vegetation are also in evidence, e.g. rain-forest in the extreme south and sandy desert where the confines of the Sahara are reached. Orographically, Northern Nigeria is a vast undulating plateau (1500–2000 ft.) diversified by occasional hills of sandstone and granite and, towards the centre, culminating in the Bauchi Plateau, averaging 4000 feet over 2000 sq. miles, which provides the drainage divide for the intermittent streams that drain north-eastwards to the Chad and for the more reliable tributaries of the Benue and middle Niger.

The dry season, dominated by the desiccating Harmattan, lasts for six or seven months—usually from October to April—except in the southernmost parts. The mean annual rainfall over the Northern Provinces as a whole is higher than the vegetation would suggest—Kaduna [1] has 54 inches and Zaria 47 inches—but north of the line Sokoto–Katsina–Hadeija there is no doubt of the meagreness of supply and the mean is considerably less than 30 inches. Practically everywhere 90 per cent of the rainfall is confined to the months when evaporation is at its maximum, and, quite obviously, one of the great problems of agriculture is concerned with the storage and utilization of the storm water, much of which is now lost through run-off and evaporation. Irrigation is in its infancy, and not even the most advanced farmers—the Hausa—knew how to store water or obtain subterranean supplies in the days before the British conquest. In addition to widespread well-sinking much could be done in the control of the flood waters of the rivers that intermittently reach the Niger from the confines of the Sahara, e.g. the Kebbi, which flows past Sokoto, and the River Kaduna. A good beginning has already been made in the vicinity of Sokoto in connexion with cotton production. The Chad region offers really great possibilities to cotton-growing under irrigation, especially as the Shuwa Arabs understand something of irrigation ; but every-

[1] The head-quarters of the Northern Nigeria Government.

thing will depend on the extension of modern lines of transport from the present rail-heads of the Nigerian system.

In the Northern as in the Southern Provinces ' shifting cultivation ' is the rule, though there are exceptional areas, e.g. around Kano, where there is continuous cultivation of rotation crops. The limitations of the rainfall régime prohibit ' permanent ' crops such as cocoa and palm-oil. Faced with a short growing season and the impossibility of producing two crops per annum on the same plot—as in the more favoured South— the aim of the northern farmer is to plant as much as possible during the wet summer. Extensive cultivation, in contrast to the ' garden ' farming of Southern Nigeria, is therefore normal. Ordinarily the farming year begins in April, as soon as sufficiently heavy rains permit the planting of millet, locally known as ' gero '. Very shortly after, guinea-corn, another staple subsistence crop, is sown,[1] while cotton is not planted until July or August, by which time the early millet is ready for harvest.

The most notable commercial products of farming are groundnuts, cotton, hides and skins. Usually an appreciation of the differences of soil texture is shown by the farmer, for light sandy soils are reserved for ground-nut, while cotton is grown on heavy land. Commercial production of both crops has depended entirely on the completion of the railway from the south as far as Kano and of a number of branch lines, including one which leads northwestwards from Zaria towards Sokoto.

Until recently the cotton of Northern Nigeria was unsuited in quality to Lancashire requirements, but in 1916 the problem of obtaining a satisfactory staple was solved by the introduction of a strain of American (' Allen ') which has become acclimatized to West African conditions and is now firmly established in Zaria, Kano and Sokoto Provinces. The Northern Provinces have one great advantage over the Southern in respect of cotton-growing in that they offer a healthier environment for the plant : nevertheless, still one of the most reliable sources of supply for export is Yorubaland, particularly Oyo and Abeokuta Provinces, where exotic types of cotton have not succeeded in competition with hardier native varieties.

The cattle industry remains largely in the hands of the Fulani herdsmen ; but the number of settled Hausa who own cattle is increasing—an indirect consequence of the *Pax Britannica*, before he establishment of which the negroid cultivators feared to possess stock on account of the inevitable raiding by the Fulani. As the Hausa fully understand the value of animal manure the

[1] Guinea-corn, a sorghum, does not succeed in the humid climate of Southern Nigeria.

way is now clear for a revolutionary advance in agriculture—
the introduction of mixed farming.

It may be said that the Hausa, the most widely-distributed
and most numerous people of Northern Nigeria, dominate the
social and economic life ; but in addition to them and other
comparatively-civilized Moslems such as the Fulani and the
Kanuri (of Bornu) there are at least 250 animist tribes, totalling
one-third of the entire population, for some of whom the Bauchi
Plateau has provided a notable refuge from the advance of
Islam. Some of the primitives of Bauchi are still in the hunting
stage of social development and others scratch the poor soil to
cultivate a cereal of their own known as ' atcha '. Density of
population in Northern Nigeria reaches its maximum in Kano
Province where a total of nearly three millions gives an average
of 160 to the square mile.

Subsequent to the Mahomedan invasions of North Africa in
the seventh-century cultural and trading contacts were established between the Mediterranean and inter-tropical Africa, and
were a factor in the foundation of formidable empires, including
those of the Mandingan and Songhai, in the Sudan. When the
Moors were expelled from the Iberian Peninsula they proceeded
to destroy the Sudanese empires and to cut the communications
between the Mediterranean and Central Africa. Then, for two
centuries, the Hausa dominated the political life of the Western
and Central Sudan. At the close of the eighteenth century a
Fulani leader (Othman dan Fodio) led a crusade, established himself at Sokoto ' city ', and sent out politically-minded priests to
rule the series of Hausa states.[1] Even at the height of its power
the Fulani empire failed to dominate the separate Mahomedan
sultanate of Bornu, and the traditional rivalry of Sokoto and
Bornu is still a notable feature of the political life of Northern
Nigeria. A few years before the close of last century Kano
revolted and chose its own emir, and about the same time an
independent emirate of Katsena was founded. Yet, in spite of
the disintegration of the Fulani empire, all the petty sultans
continued to regard the Emir of Sokoto as one endowed with
supreme spiritual authority. He remains ' Lord of the Moslems '
and ' Commander of the Faithful ', the latter title also being
held by the Sultan of Morocco and—until the dissolution of the
Ottoman Empire—by the Sultan of Turkey.

A number of highly-organized Fulani States, each with its
preponderance of negroid peoples—mainly Hausa except in the
case of Ilorin Province—provided a very favourable *milieu* for

[1] To the south the Fulani established an emirate over the Yoruba of
Ilorin, south of the Niger.

the policy of ' indirect rule ' extablished by Lugard early this
century. The experiment was extended to Yorubaland and
Benin where also there are stable and advanced native organizations upon which to build. The limitations to the independence
of the emirs which are involved in Lugard's conception of colonial
administration—including the right of the Government to depose
a ruler for misrule—are accepted with a good grace as within the
prerogative of the sovereign authority and do not produce dis-
affection. In compensation the sultans have been left not only
with the external trappings of their dignity, but also with much of
the substance of power. The Emirate of Kano, the most important of northern native administrations, covers an area of 13,000
square miles and has a population of more than two millions.

Kano, over 700 miles by rail from Lagos—its ocean port—
is in commerce and industry supreme throughout Northern
Nigeria. For 1000 years it has been a manufacturing centre,
trading its textiles and leather articles in return for raw materials.
Its sheep- and goat-skin products, skilfully treated by Hausa
tanners and dyers, became at an early time famous as ' Morocco
leather ' since they reached the commercial countries of Europe
by way of the Barbary sea-board. The city is enclosed by a mud
wall some 12 miles in circumference, within which is one of the
greatest markets in Africa. Trade is retained in the hands of
Moslems. Europeans—officials, missionaries and merchants—
are not permitted to live within the gates, but they may live
without the walls in a reservation—a most rare exception to the
usual order of things in Africa ! A town-planning scheme has
been adopted and broad streets with proper drainage are being
cut through the present congestion.

Such a vigorous commercial and industrial centre was bound
to become a focus of modern transport lines, just as formerly it
was a very important caravan depôt.[1] Actually, however, in
the railway system of Northern Nigeria, Zaria, 80 miles to the
south-west, has a greater degree of nodality : it lies on the main
line to the south, at the point where diverge two tracks—one to
the rich tin-fields of the Bauchi Plateau, the other to the promising
cotton and ground-nut lands of Sokoto Province. The city of
Sokoto is still unconnected by rail to the main artery of the Colony,
although a motor-road spans the distance to the rail-head.
Amongst other urgently required railway extensions is one, sooner
or later to be carried to the principal centres of Bornu. For this
there are three alternative routes, namely, via (a) Kano and

[1] One of the great trans-Saharan caravan routes to the Mediterranean
coast at Tripoli had its base at Kano, but there is little traffic along it at
present.

Nguru, (b) Jos, on the Bauchi Plateau, (c) Makurdi, on the Eastern Railway, and north-eastwards up the Benue valley. Unfortunately for Nigerian transport the greater part of the population and trade of Bornu are in the remote east of that Province, and more especially in the Emirate of Dikwa.

REFERENCES

The literature for both the British and French Colonies is very extensive and a short selection must suffice here, the works mentioned being listed under (a) French West Africa, (b) British West Africa, (c) other territories.

(a) Abadie, M., *La Colonie du Niger*, Paris, 1927.
Amou d'Aby, J. F., *La Côte d'Ivoire dans la Cité Africaine*, Paris, 1951.
Andre, P., *L'Islam Noir*, Paris, 1924.
L'Islam et les Races, 2 vols., Paris, 1922.
Bernard, A., *Sahara, Afrique Occidentale*, 2me partie, Tome XI, Géographie Universelle, Paris, 1939.
Buell, R. L., *The Native Problem in Africa*, 2 vols., N. York, 1928.
Chazelas, V., *Territoires Africains sous Mandat Français*, Paris, 1931.
Church, R. J. H., ' Irrigation in the inland Niger delta of the French Sudan ', *Geog. Journ.*, Vol. CXVII (1951), p. 218.
Cosnier, H., *L'Ouest Afrique Français—ses ressources agricoles*, Paris, 1921.
Delafosse, M., *Haut Sénégal-Niger*, Paris, 1912.
(The above is a standard description of the peoples of French West Africa.)
Delavignette, R., *Freedom and Authority in French West Africa*, London (O.U.P. for Intern. Afr. Inst.), 1950.
François, G., *L'Afrique Occidentale Française*, Paris, 1920.
Guy, C., *L'Afrique Occidentale Française*, Paris, 1929.
Lebeuf, J.-P., and Detourbet, A. M., *La Civilisation du Chad*, Paris, n.d.
Lhote, H., *Les Touareg du Hoggar*, Paris, 1944.
Monod, J. L., *Histoire de l'Afrique Occidentale Française*, Paris, 1926.
Pelleray, E., *L'Afrique Occidentale Française*, Paris, 1923.
Richard-Molard, J., *Afrique Occidentale Française*, Paris, 1949.
Roberts, S. H., *History of French Colonial Policy*, London, 1929.
Urvoy, Y., *Petit Atlas Ethno-Démographique du Soudan entre Sénégal et Tchad*. Mémoires de l'Institut Français d'Afrique Noire, No. 5, Paris, 1942.

(b) Ainslie, J. R., *Physiography of S. Nigeria and its Effect on the Forest Flora*, Oxford, 1926.
Buell, R. L. (as above).
Burdon, J. A., *Fulani Emirates*, London, 1909.
Burns, A. C., *A History of Nigeria*, London, 1929.
Busia, K. A., *Report on a Social Survey of Sekondi-Takoradi*, London, Crown Agents for the Colonies, for the Gold Coast Govt., 1950.
Dudgeon, G. C., *The Agricultural and Forest Products of British West Africa*, London, 1922.

Elias, T. O., *Nigerian Land Law and Custom*, London, 1951.
Falconer, J. D., *Geology and Geography of Northern Nigeria*, London, 1911.
Faulkner, O. T., and Mackie, J. R., *West African Agriculture*, Cambridge, 1933. (Useful but practically confined in its scope to Nigeria.)
Gordon, E., ' A land use map of Kantaur in the Gambia ', *Geog. Journ.*, Vol. CXVI (1950), p. 216.
Gray, Sir J., *History of Gambia*, 1940.
Grove, A. T., ' Soil Erosion and Population Problems in South-East Nigeria ', *Geog. Journ.*, Vol. CXVII (1951), p. 291.
Johnson, S., *The History of the Yorubas*, London, 1921.
Kingsley, Mary, *West African Studies*, London, 1899.
Travels in West Africa, London, 1900.
Little, K. L., *The Mende of Sierra Leone*, London, 1951.
Lugard (Lady), *A Tropical Dependency*, London, 1905.
Lugard (Lord), *The Dual Mandate in British Tropical Africa*, 3rd ed., London, 1926.
Luke, H. C., *A Bibliography of Sierra Leone*, Oxford, 1925.
MacMichael, H. A., *History of the Arabs in the Sudan*, 2 vols., Cambridge, 1922.
McPhee, A., *The Economic Revolution in British West Africa*, London, 1926.
Meek, C. K., *The Northern Tribes of Nigeria*, 2 vols., Oxford, 1925.
Nash, Dr. T. A. M., *The Anchau Rural Development and Settlement Scheme*, H.M.S.O., 1948.
Orr, C. W. J., *The Making of Northern Nigeria*, London, 1911.
Pogucki, R. J. H., *Land tenure in native customary law of the Protectorate of the Northern Territories of the Gold Coast*, Accra, Lands Dept., 1950.
Rattray, R. S., *Ashanti*, Oxford, 1923.
Southorn (Lady), *The Gambia*, London, 1952.
Steel, R. W., ' The Population of Ashanti, a geographical analysis ', *Geog. Journ.*, Vol. CXII (1949), pp. 64–77.
Talbot, P. A., *Life in Southern Nigeria*, London, 1923.
The Peoples of Southern Nigeria, 4 vols., Oxford, 1926.
The Tribes of the Niger Delta, 1932.
Unwin, A. H., *West African Forests*, London, 1920.
Ward, W. E. F., *A History of the Gold Coast*, London, 1949.

Also official handbooks of Nigeria, Gold Coast and Sierra Leone.

(*c*) Buell, R. L. (as above).
DeKeyser, P. L., and Holas, B., *Mission à l'Est Libérien*, Dakar, I.F.A.N., 1952.
Huberich, C. H., *The Political and Legislative History of Liberia*, New York, 1947.
Johnston, Sir H. H., *Liberia*, London, 1906.
Sharpe, Sir A., *The Black Republic*, London, 1923.
Strong, R. P. (editor), *The African Republic of Liberia and Belgian Congo*, 2 vols., Harvard, 1930.

CHAPTER VI

THE BARBARY STATES

'**A**FRICA begins at the Pyrenees' is a commonly-heard geographical assertion, though it would be as true to maintain that Europe terminates at the Saharan border. In its structure, climate and vegetation the Iberian Peninsula shows certain African affinities, whilst the Barbary region, both from the physical and human standpoints, is associated with the European countries of the Western Mediterranean Basin. These Atlas [1] lands forming the great north-western quadrilateral have sometimes been designated ' Africa Minor ', because their relations with the continent of which they are, as it were, the foreland recall those which have associated Asia Minor with its parent continent. To the Arab geographers the region was *Djezira-el-Maghrib*—the Western Isle—isolated by the sea and ocean and by the great desert.

In no region of Africa does *physique* play so decisive a part in the geographical environment ; and such unity as Barbary possesses is mainly derived from the Atlas ground-plan, which is dominant throughout. The emphatic east-to-west graining of the geographical pattern has favoured the migration of fauna and flora ; and, in the history of human affairs, the same routes have been followed repeatedly by communities, either in advance or in retreat. There is the route of the fertile Tell from Carthage to the Straits of Gibraltar, and the arid corridor, a continuous depression along the southern border of Barbary, all the way from the Gulf of Gabes to the Wad Draa at opposite extremities. Because of the geographical continuity from east to west, conquering powers—Phoenician, Roman, Arab and French—have been led sooner or later to extend—or attempt to extend—their domains to the farthest limits of Barbary. The Algerian Tell— the earliest base of French enterprise in North Africa—has been

[1] The name ' Atlas ' is a European gift to African topographical nomenclature and is never used by the native Berbers : it is derived from the mythical Greek god who was believed to dwell in these mountains.

373

the centre from which for over a century Gallic influence has spread both eastwards into Tunisia and westwards into Morocco. The two main phases of French expansion were signalized by the erection of Protectorates, and to-day a rigid threefold political division remains, however unnatural it may be in view of the absence of fundamental differences in social geography between east and west. And here it may be mentioned that to a majority of North African Moslems the idea of a political frontier is still either incomprehensible or repugnant.

Yet each of the Barbary States has its distinctive 'personality', partly due to the differences in orientation—as, for example, between Western Morocco and Eastern Tunisia—and partly to the complexities of the Atlas structure and relief, with their consequences for climate and vegetation and for human life.

To indicate the essential character of the ground-plan of Barbary is our first step.

THE ATLAS SYSTEM

In its physical form Barbary is to be regarded as an elongated, corrugated plateau some 1500 miles in east-west extent, with sharply-defined ramparts on north and south, and with an internal grid of lofty ranges culminating in peaks of 12,000–13,000 feet. It is Morocco (where the Atlas system is most extensive) which provides the most varied geological and geographical phenomena. The nineteenth-century explorer, de Foucauld, provided his contemporaries with an interpretative description of Moroccan geography which is still accepted, though with much modification and elaboration of detail. He distinguished the Riff Atlas (of the Betic Cordillera) from the High or Great Atlas, and also gave separate place both to the Middle Atlas and the Anti-Atlas.

The earth-storms which produced the Atlas system were not confined to one geological epoch. Both a Pre-Cambrian flexing and a Hercynian north-to-south folding have been ascertained, in addition to the Tertiary folding along axial lines extending west, south-west—east, north-east. It was in the course of the Hercynian movements that the central plateau of the Great Atlas, as well as the less elevated platform of the Moroccan Meseta farther to the west, was up-raised ; but it remained for the Pyrenean-Alpine folding, which culminated in the Eocene period of the Tertiary, to grant to the Atlas ranges their present bold relief.

The contrasts in physical geography are so well-marked as to deserve the following more elaborate statement, in which the principal physiographical elements will be distinguished.

THE REGIONS OF BARBARY

(i) The Great or High Atlas

The up-folding which produced the greatest mountain chain of Africa involved a deep-seated Hercynian plateau of Palaeozoic and earlier rocks, which now appear at lofty elevations. This greatly-disturbed Hercynian 'massif' provides some of the highest country, including the apparently impassable wall, over 12,000 feet high, which rises abruptly to the east of the southern Moroccan capital, Marrakesh ; although many of the loftiest summits of all are immense masses of andesitic lava, which has been sculptured into sharply-crested peaks, including Toubkal (13,600 ft.).[1] Throughout the short winter of these latitudes the snow remains above the 8000 ft. level, yet there is no permanent snow, and the glaciers which etched out the high intermontane valleys belonged to an earlier geological epoch. Formerly regarded as virtually impenetrable, the fastnesses of the Great Atlas are now traversed by one or two excellent motor-roads, built since and in consequence of Lyautey's pacification of the country ; one of these cuts across the chain at Tizi-n-Test [2] (7000 ft.) and leads from Marrakesh to Taroudant.

Nowhere better than in the Great Atlas is shown the juxtaposition of Mediterranean and Saharan conditions. The westward and north-westward facing slopes are well-watered, and in their deeply-trenched valleys fruit and cereal cultivation is the traditional economy of the Berber dwellers, although much of the land remains under a rich canopy of forest. The olive is widespread up to 5000 feet, and higher still is the domain of the evergreen oak. On the other hand the south-eastern flanks of the Great Atlas, excluded from humid Atlantic influences and exposed to desiccating Saharan winds, are destitute of tree-growth and cultivation : where not actually bare, they support only poor scrub. Of all Berber peoples the Chleuh of the Great Atlas are the most sedentary. Their settled agricultural life is confined to the high valleys, and it was there that the power of the Great Caids was most in evidence prior to French conquest, a decade or two ago.

(ii) The Middle Atlas

Here the terrain is folded into relatively simple anticlinal forms, although the orography suggests a plateau meeting the Great Atlas abruptly. The ancient Palaeozoic and Pre-Palaeozoic

---

[1] Many of the Atlas peaks are still unnamed, for the native Berbers seem to have no names even for the summits which provide the impressive theatre of their daily lives.

[2] In the Berber tongue ' Tizi ' signifies ' pass '.

platform is widely exposed, but in the east limestone produces a ' causse ' landscape, and, in addition, there has been igneous extrusion, as also in the case of the loftier chain.

As a determining factor in the social and economic life of Morocco the Middle Atlas possesses an importance exceeding that of the main chain, and this is due in part to an abundant and reliable rainfall (about 30 inches), augmented by snowfall, which supplies the main reservoir of Barbary ; and in part to its command of the main lines of communication between the principal centres of Morocco and Algeria. From this hydrographic ' divide ' flow the greatest rivers of North-West Africa —the Moulouya towards the Mediterranean, and the more important Sebou and Umm er R'bia, westwards directly to the Atlantic. Luxuriant forests of evergreen oak and cedar—the latter only above 4500 feet—are a notable feature, but in addition there is much mountain pasture, and stock-rearing is of greater importance in these highlands than in the Great Atlas. The Berbers here usually undertake both tillage and the care of stock, and with them transhumance is normal.

(iii) The Anti-Atlas and the Plain of Sus

Although there is clear evidence of Alpine folding in the Anti-Atlas, this highland has more the character of a ' massif ' than of a ridge. It has a broad plateau surface with a nearly-uniform altitude of about 5000 feet, and its schists and quartzites date from a very remote geological antiquity. It merges with the Great Atlas, and the attachment is provided by the volcanic mass of the Jebel Sirua, which attains 9000 feet. The triangular groove opening widely to the Atlantic, which separates the western extensions of the Great Atlas and Anti-Atlas, respectively, is the Sus, a depression resulting from the foundering and downfolding which were the counterpart of the Tertiary up-folding. The semi-Saharan climate determines a bare inhospitable landscape, where the arganier bush, resembling in appearance a spiny olive, provides, in its fruit, nourishment for the black Moroccan goats which climb amongst its branches.

(iv) The Moroccan Meseta

Western Morocco extending from the Middle and Great Atlas to the Atlantic coast, between Mogador and Rabat, is a much-denuded Archaean platform, concealed for the greater part by horizontal strata of relatively recent sediments, but exposed in places by river-action, as in the case of the valley of the Umm er R'bia. The Meseta resisted the pressure exerted by the Atlas mountain-building, and served to divert the chains which swing away from it on its northern and southern flanks, respectively. In itself it was not unaffected, and its southernmost district—the plain of Marrakesh—foundered in the Tertiary upheaval. The maritime districts form a well-farmed lowland, with wheat and barley as the usual crops. A relatively high density of population is here supported on the ' tirs ', the productive black clay soils, rich in salts of iron, which are notable in western Morocco. Since the days of earliest Portuguese navigation these coastlands have known European influence ; and Rabat, Casablanca, Mazagan, Safi and Mogador are sixteenth-century ports with a life revived in our own time by the French conquest of Morocco, a conquest which had its beginnings and its head-quarters on the Moroccan Meseta. Yet natural harbours on the straight, exposed coast are rare, and in most cases the river-outlets are hindered by sand-bars.

Farther into the interior of the Meseta, where the crystalline core is more widely uncovered, and where the climate increases in its arid severity, the land is poorer, and towards Marrakesh a rainfall of only 9 inches indicates the proximity of the desert and the necessity for irrigation, if settled life is to be maintained.

(v) The Sebou Basin and the Corridor of Taza

Immediately to the north of the Moroccan Meseta, but south of the Riff Atlas, the down-folded basin of the Sebou River has evolved from a former gulf of the sea. This alluvial lowland stands in a similar geographical relationship to the Riff Atlas and the Moroccan Meseta as the Plain of Andalusia (basin of the lower Guadalquivir) to the Sierra Nevada and the Iberian Meseta. The axial line of the Riff Atlas, with whose limits the frontiers of Spanish Morocco almost exactly correspond, is seen to approach closely the extremity of the Middle Atlas, although actually the two chains are discontinuous. The gap between—part of the ' corridor of Taza '—prolongs the Sebou Basin east-wards, and offers the only passageway between the economic heart of Morocco, with great cities of venerable antiquity like Fez and Meknes, and the well-cultivated and densely-populated lands of the Algerian Tell. Taza is the citadel guarding the defile, which at this point is about a mile and a half wide and 2000 feet above sea-level. Because the Sebou lowland opens widely to the Atlantic, maritime influences are admitted farther than is usual in Morocco. The range of temperature is small, whilst rainfall, averaging 20 inches, is generally adequate for the cereal cultivation characteristic of local farming. Formerly the cork-oak forest of Mamora in the south-west was of dense luxuriant growth, but fire and timber-felling, in order to provide pasturage, have greatly denuded it. Winter flooding of the Sebou may be very extensive when the melted Atlas snows augment the rainfall, for the gradient of the river is but slight, only 45 feet in 200 miles.

(vi) The Riff Atlas

As a series of ranges and ' massifs ' rather than as a continuous chain the Riff highland, with precipitous slopes to the Mediterranean, has proved a veritable fastness for the untamed Berber tribesmen, who have been wont to claim its protection. It is a geographical peculiarity, productive of much friction between the two Powers concerned, that whilst the French zone of Morocco was virtually deprived of Mediterranean outlets [1] the Spanish zone was cut off from its natural hinterland. The term ' Riff ' signifies ' bordering shore ', and it was this inhospitable coast (where there are, however, several useful if inadequately sheltered harbours, such as Ceuta and Melilla) which provided one of the principal bases for the Barbary pirates, who raided the shipping of the Gibraltar Straits, before the days when Great Britain and France became the guardians of Mediterranean commerce. The Riff highland offers a bare landscape, in which Jurassic limestone is prominent along with Palaeozoic exposures. Behind the westernmost part of the Riff is the Rharb (e.g. the ' west '), a well-endowed lowland of alluvium, where conditions are similar to those of the Sebou Basin.

(vii) Western Algeria

Although Algeria repeats, or continues, the structure of Morocco there is an absence of those lofty chains and extensive plains which characterize the western land. The dominant feature of its plateau geography is the series of long, narrow zones succeeding each other regularly from north to south : and the diagrammatic succession of ' tell ', dry plateau grassland (referred to as ' steppe ' by the French geographers) and desert is more complete and regular than elsewhere in Barbary. The Arabic word ' tell ' signifies ' height ' or ' eminence ', and is more particularly applied to the terraced, outer (i.e. Mediterranean) slopes of the Algerian Plateau. These terraces are characterized by well-watered fertility, and the term ' tell ' has come to embrace in a general way all cultivated lands of the Mediterranean border of North-West Africa.

The political frontiers of Algeria do not correspond, even approximately, with any natural geographic division and, as

---

[1] The Mediterranean coast of French Morocco was but 10 miles long and possessed no port.

the line of the River Moulouya most suitably defines the Moroccan border, those plateau lands which lie farther to the east should be considered as associated with the ' massif ' of the Oran Department of Algeria. Politically or administratively, Algeria is composed of three Departments—Oran, Algiers and Constantine —which divide fairly evenly the country lying between the Moroccan and Tunisian frontiers ; and it is obvious that administrative convenience has been the determining factor in their delimitation. There is no geographical or other scientific justification for this division, which since 1962, when the country became an independent Republic, has been superseded by a division into fifteen departments, including Sahara.

In the Departments of Oran and Algiers a series of disconnected and narrow plateaux, known usually as the Tell Atlas, extend behind the coast, and, intermittently between them, are the elongated lowlands and low, terraced uplands which constitute the most fertile parts of the ' tell ' of Barbary. Two of the narrow plains are those of the Shelif, longest of Algerian rivers, and the more famous Plain of Mitidja, a closed slot, 60 miles long and 9 miles wide, deeply covered with alluvium. Here are the headquarters of French farming colonization in North Africa, as witness the most magnificent vineyards to be found anywhere in the entire continent. Secluded as are these slot-like lowlands, and therefore to some extent deprived of the full advantage to be derived from the rain-bearing winds of winter, there is often the need for irrigation ; and on the Plain of Shelif a number of barrage reservoirs are projected, with one already completed.

Behind the ' tell ' of Oran and Algiers the High Plateaux, averaging more than 3500 feet, extend southwards, and in this direction there is abrupt deterioration in climate and vegetation. Intensive farming becomes impossible on the ' Hauts Plateaux ', and their dry grasslands are likely to remain the home of the nomadic pastoralist, the sheep country *par excellence*. Notable amongst the surface features are numerous shallow depressions, temporarily—i.e. during the brief rains—occupied by brackish lakes or ' shotts ', including the Shott-esh-Shergwi and others of vast extent. Although these saline lagoons are at present within separate inland-drainage basins, they were formerly connected by a river-system which flowed out to the Mediterranean —after traversing a gap in the Tell Atlas—probably by way of the Shelif valley, which provides as much as one-third of the lowland of the Oran Department. Bounding the High Plateaux on their southern side are the Saharan Atlas, which continue the line of the Anti-Atlas though at a lower elevation. Their crests are usually not more than three or four hundred feet higher than the surface of the High Plateaux.

(viii) Eastern Algeria

As we advance eastwards the High Plateaux narrow, and the relief becomes more accentuated with the intermittent occurrence of such lofty ' massifs ' as Great Kabylia [1] and Aurès. In this eastward direction the winter winds from off the Mediterranean are heavily charged with moisture, and the resultant abundant precipitation explains the luxuriance of the vegetation, and especially of the forest—a luxuriance greater than in the case of Western Algeria. Great Kabylia (also known as the Djurjura Kabylia) is one of the few remaining strongholds of Berber civilization. The local economy is concerned mainly with fruit-growing, and this highland is renowned for the cultivation of both the fig and the olive. Density of population in the Kabylia fastnesses attains in places the astonishingly-high figure of 550 persons per square mile which, even were it associated with a fertile lowland, would still suggest serious over-crowding. Actually the pressure is somewhat relieved by a constant exodus, either to the ' tell ' lands or overseas to France.

Farther east the Tell Atlas and Saharan Atlas trend-lines approach so closely to each other that the High Plateau, which is so important an element in the physique of Western Algeria, is here virtually absent, and the extent of the Barbary Quadrilateral, between the Mediterranean and the Sahara, is here at its narrowest. The complexity of the relief produced by the convergence of the Atlas folds is especially notable to the southeast of the inland town of Constantine. Here the highlands are, as it were, nucleated in the Aurès Massif whose summits are the loftiest in Algeria, attaining 6000 feet and more above sea-level. Like Kabylia the Aurès country has served as a refuge for many groups of Berber people who have, throughout a millennium of time, resisted the advance of Islam. Although supplied with a considerable rainfall, the southerly position of Aurès favours the penetration of semi-Saharan conditions, and we find that the highland is too poor to support an exclusively sedentary life, so that the village communities engage both in orchard cultivation of apricots and figs and in nomadic pastoralism. The lower plateau lands and valleys, encircling the Aurès Massif, were formerly of relatively greater importance than they are to-day. Timgad and other ancient cities of the Aurès periphery still, in their ruins, give evidence of the place of the region in the strategy of

[1] The name is derived from the Berber Kabyles (meaning ' tribes '), its inhabitants.

Imperial Rome. Here was the military centre of the Roman Province of Africa, and here the Third Legion was for a long time in garrison.

Of the lowlands of Eastern Algeria the maritime district, which has Bône as its port outlet, is the most notable. The Plain of Bône, which is about as extensive as the Plain of Mitidja, has been selected by the French as their main colonizing centre in Eastern Algeria, as the skilfully-farmed and very extensive plantations of tobacco and the vine bear witness.

(ix) Northern Tunisia

The original Protectorate of Tunisia is actually no greater than the Department of Constantine, of which, in the physical sense, it is merely the eastward prolongation.[1] Physical geography has determined that Tunisia shall turn its back upon Algeria and look eastwards : to the west, communication is made difficult by Nature, but eastwards the way to the Mediterranean is easy.

We are concerned with Tunisia north of the Shott-el-Jerid : with, that is, the geographical entity of Tunisia, as distinct from an arbitrarily-defined administrative division. Although a relatively small area, within it the geographical contrast is as profound as any in North-West Africa ; and the main distinction is between a Northern and a Southern Tunisia. It is a distinction between the cultivated ' tell ' of the rainy highlands and the arid plains of the Sahel—a term which, in French Africa, is bestowed on lands of dry grass, where rainfall is at the minimum for any form of cultivation, without irrigation, and not more than 14 inches per annum.

The Tertiary highlands of Northern Tunisia are of complicated relief, there being a series of short ranges and ' massifs ', arranged occasionally *en échelon*, and showing in their general trend the south-west—north-east alignment which we have found to be typical of the Atlas ranges. Where the highlands reach the sea they cut across the coast diagonally, so producing bold promontories—the peninsula terminating in Cape Bon being the most spectacular instance !—and naturally-protected harbours. Because of this the coast of North-Eastern Tunisia is one of age-long prominence in maritime affairs, naval as well as commercial : this was notable in the foundation of Phoenician Carthage, and is manifest to-day in the status of Bizerta. On

[1] The administrative area of Tunisia is made to include a large area of the northern Sahara, lying to the south of the vast depression, partly filled by the Shott-el-Jerid : but this has little geographical justification.

a deep, capacious and sheltered inlet, Bizerta ranked as the chief
naval base of France on the North African coast, with a remarkably advantageous position in relation to the sea-passage between
the eastern and western basins of the Mediterranean. It has
been said that France sought her Protectorate over Tunisia in
order to acquire Bizerta as a naval base.[1] After the country
became a sovereign independent republic in 1959, France continued to hold rights at Bizerta, but finally withdrew in October,
1963.

The Cape Bon Peninsula, which bounds the Bay of Tunis on
the south and east, is ribbed by a ridge which is closely associated
with a greater range, known by French geographers as the
' Tunisian Dorsal '. The latter is important not only because
it is the longest prolongation eastwards of the Atlas system,
but also because it represents the ' climatic divide ' between
Mediterranean and semi-Saharan conditions of climate and
vegetation.

North of the Tunisian Dorsal the highlands are endowed
with the most abundant rainfall (35–50 inches) in Eastern Barbary, and consequently are well-wooded. There are occasional
valleys, particularly that of the Medjerda River, where fertility
is rich, and agriculture is undertaken intensively. Without
confusing the reader with an excess of topographical detail, there
are one or two districts of special note to be mentioned. In
the extreme north-west is the Kroumirie Highland, clothed in
the richest forest of all Tunisia. The profusion of the vegetation here suggests a generous rainfall—actually over 40 inches
and the highest in Tunisia—but sparseness of settlement also
helps to explain the wealth of woodland. To the east, in sharp
contrast, are the plains behind Bizerta, where a feature of unusual
interest is prosperous orchard cultivation, dating from the time
when many of the Andalusian Moors, expelled from Spain,
settled here and employed their skill in irrigation.

The River Medjerda, whose valley provides the most easy
approach from the Tunisian ' tell ' into the interior, finally
opens out on to the Plain of Tunis, although its outflow is diverted
to the north of the Gulf of Tunis. Its extensive delta is especially
notable, for there is no other river in North-West Africa with a
deltaic outlet. Only partially settled as yet, the Medjerda delta
is still malarious over large areas, where marshes persist. On
the cultivated parts of the river valley and on the fertile Plain
of Tunis the essential farming is viticulture, but towards the

---

[1] French policy in relation to Tunisia was tersely summarized by
Jules Ferry, who said : ' C'est pour Bizerte que j'ai pris la Tunisie.'
The statesman's name is remembered in the town of Ferryville, quite
close to Bizerta.

south (i.e. towards the 'Tunisian Dorsal') the olive becomes increasingly prominent.

(x) Southern Tunisia

In the life of this region the dry plains of the Sahel have come to play the predominant rôle. The limits on north and south, respectively, are approximately set by the coast towns of Susa and Sfax. Rainfall is everywhere deficient and under 14 inches, so that cultivation without irrigation is generally impossible ; and, until half a century ago, the Sahel was left to its nomadic herdsmen. Yet the olive tree, able to offer a very prolonged resistance to drought, finds the conditions excellent, and for it irrigation is not required. Probably nowhere in the world is the planting of the olive on a larger or better organized plan than it is here, especially in the districts of Susa and Sfax. Despite the very low rainfall, atmospheric conditions are still too moist for the date-palm, which attains its maximum importance in Saharan Tunisia, to the south of the depression of the Great Shotts ; so we see that, from north to south, the succession of vine, olive and date in Tunisia follows a zoning according to rainfall. Southern Tunisia was first of the regions of Barbary to feel the impact of Islam. Here to the west of Susa is Kairuan, the earliest religious and military centre founded by the Moslems in North-West Africa. To the incoming Moslems the Sahel of Tunisia was useful as providing an easy transition from Sahara to ' tell ', where the necessary re-adjustment of life could be effected without too abrupt a change.

RAINFALL AND VEGETATION

The great contrasts in topography and altitude, which have been responsible for the difficulties experienced by France and Spain in their campaigns in Barbary, are productive of very wide differences in climate and vegetation, and consequently in social and economic life, as briefly indicated in an earlier chapter. Without unnecessary repetition, it is well to stress the importance of local differences and contrasts in annual precipitation, within a region where, excepting high mountain land, the adequate length and warmth of the growing season may be fairly assumed.

On the western sea-board of Morocco, where the Atlantic winds of winter freely penetrate, the falling-off in rainfall as we proceed southwards, from Tangier to Mogador, is represented by the difference between 32·5 and 13 inches—the decline being much more abrupt between the Gibraltar Straits and Rabat than to the south of the latter city. Heavy falls of dew, and summer temperatures, low for the latitude, are other outstanding

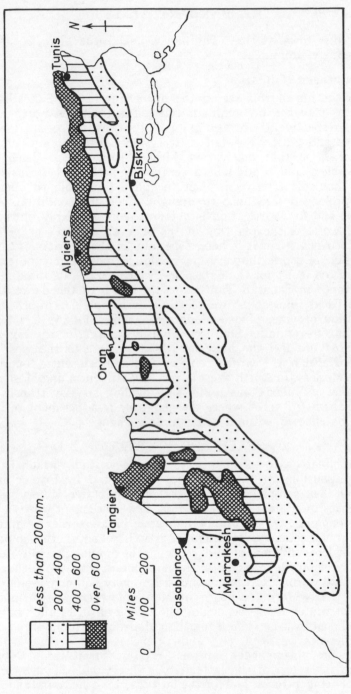

Less than 200 mm.

200 – 400

400 – 600

Over 600

Miles

0   100   200

Tunis

Biskra

Algiers

Oran

Tangier

Casablanca

Marrakesh

N

FIG. 79.—The Barbary Lands: Average Annual Rainfall

characteristics of the climate of Atlantic Morocco; and their causes have already been suggested on an earlier page (*vide* p. 57). The influence on temperature of cold surface water off-shore is greater during the summer than in winter, and there is a strange reversal of what might be expected as the normal distribution of mean summer temperature along the coast. At Tangier in the farthest north the mean for August is 76° F., whilst, for the same month at Rabat, it is 72·5° F., and at Mogador, in the south, only 68° F. These comparatively low temperatures are, from the standpoint of health, largely off-set by the high relative humidity. Because of its drier atmosphere the interior is preferred to the littoral, especially in summer.

The Jebela highlands of the Riff and the Atlantic-facing slopes of the Great and Middle Atlas are, as might be expected, the areas of highest precipitation in Morocco. In addition, the upper part of Sebou Basin is fairly well endowed with rainfall : there are 22 inches at Meknes, about the same amount at Fez, and nearly 24 inches at Taza. Elsewhere the Moroccan lowlands receive under 20 inches, and the zone with less than 16 inches extends widely around Marrakesh, and right up to the coast, south of Casablanca. The entire coastal belt between Agadir and Casablanca has under 16 inches.

On the north coast of Barbary, to the east of the Riff territory, the total amount of precipitation increases fairly regularly from Oran to Bougie, and then diminishes from Bougie to Tunis. Excepting the Department of Oran, no part of the Algerian Tell receives less than 20 inches, and Algiers with 30 and Bougie with nearly 40 are almost typical of their respective regions. The mountainous ' massifs ' between Central Algeria and the coast behind Bizerta include some of the rainiest tracts of North Africa. In the lower valley of the Medjerda and on the Plain of Tunis the deficiency becomes marked, and Tunis City itself has little more than 16 inches. On the Sahel of Susa and Sfax low precipitation is to be expected, in view of the seclusion of these coastlands from the rain-bearing cyclones of the Mediterranean. At Susa there are 13·6 inches, but at the more southerly Sfax the climate is of an almost Saharan character, and the precipitation only slightly exceeds 8 inches.

Throughout Mediterranean Algeria there is normally one rainfall maximum, occurring in December–January ; but in the Moroccan Atlas two maxima are apparent, one in November at the beginning, the other in March near the end, of the wet season. The farther we penetrate the interior of the High Plateaux the more pronounced becomes a maximum occurring in the spring time. Snowfall, especially widespread on the Great

and Middle Atlas for two or three winter months, is of particular benefit to the semi-Saharan South, and such districts as
the Plain of Sus are practically dependent on the melted snows
of the Great Atlas for such settled life as they possess.

Assuming as we may that much the greater part of the region
receiving a rainfall of over 20 inches was formerly forest-clothed,
the enormous extent of the deforestation which has occurred is
readily apparent. The Natives—if in that term we may include
both the Berbers and the Arabs—seem to show no respect for
tree-growth and to destroy it, wherever it stands in the way of
an expansion of their pastures : and when forest is cut down
it does not grow again, but is replaced by bush and scrub. So
far the control of the region by the French has not checked the
process of deforestation : indeed, their occupation has but
accelerated the cutting of timber for various uses and for land-
clearance.

In Morocco, the Middle Atlas and western slopes of the Great
Atlas ; in Algeria, the highlands of Kabylia ; and in Tunisia,
the massifs of the north-west possess large areas of rich woodland :
whilst on the lowlands, where forest is rare, the Mamora region,
to the south of the lower Sebou, still retains remnants of the
cork-oak forest which is supposed to have formerly occupied not
less than 300,000 acres. The plains of Western Morocco and the
' tell ' of Algeria and Tunisia have long been denuded of timber,
and we remember that in these parts cultivation is more intensive
than the average for Barbary. With some exaggeration beyond
the exact truth, it has been said that on a journey from Tangier
to Fez the traveller would not pass a single tree.

The most typical member of the forests of Barbary is the
cork-oak. It requires considerable moisture and, although on
the coastlands of Western Morocco, where atmospheric humidity
(relative) is high, it requires only some 16 or 17 inches, in
Algeria and Tunisia it will not grow where the precipitation is
less than 25 inches. It constitutes the remnant of the forest of
Mamora, and on high land is found up to an altitude of about
3500 feet. Amongst other types of oak the evergreen variety is
also widespread : it reaches a level of 5500 ft. on the Tell Atlas
of Algeria, and ascends even higher on the Moroccan Atlas.
The evergreen-oak mixes with the cork-oak and the aleppo-pine
in the lower areas, and with the giant cedar and juniper at high
altitudes. Of the conifers the aleppo-pine has the greatest range,
and in Algeria and Tunisia is discovered intermittently throughout the zone between the Mediterranean and the semi-Saharan
South, where rainfall diminishes from over 25 to 12 inches.
Especially characteristic of the Middle Atlas of Morocco at high

altitudes is the cedar—' the sultan of the forest ', as it has been called—which avoids land lower than 4000 feet, and is well able to endure the cold winters experienced at the 7000-ft. level.

The cultivation of fruit-bearing plants and trees, both indigenous and exotic, is—and has been for a very long time—one of the principal phases of Berber agriculture ; the vine, olive and fig are specially prominent. The date-palm will survive as far north as Tangier, but there it is out of its latitude and does not bear fruit.

Of the other plant associations represented in Barbary, namely those of steppe and desert, the second is confined to the southernmost parts of the region which more properly belong to the Saharan zone. It is notable, and of very great conse-quence in the life and history of North-West Africa, that, in response to the main trend of the Atlas system from south-west to north-east, the desert penetrates much farther northwards—actually not less than 150 miles—in Tunisia than in Morocco. On the High Plateaux of Algeria there is scrub and herbaceous vegetation, including alfa or esparto grass, which is widespread and, because of its use in the manufacture of paper, important commercially. The planting of alfa has been undertaken as one means of land reclamation in a region where ' Mediterranean agriculture ' is out of the question. Very approximately, the northward limit of the steppe in Algeria may be taken as follow-ing the isohyet of 14 inches. The steppe of Western Morocco is characterized by the arganier, a spiny, evergreen bush 20 to 25 feet high, whose range is practically confined to the extreme west of Barbary, with the basin of the Sus the centre of its distribution.

Before we proceed from this introductory statement of the physical environment to consider the ways in which the life of the resident population is adjusted to the prevailing geographical conditions, it will be convenient to interpose a study of the distribution of population, and particularly of the various elements in that population.

THE GEOGRAPHY OF POPULATION DISTRIBUTION

In the cultural sense Barbary is usually regarded without challenge as part of the Islamic world, yet many of the indigenous people do not speak Arabic, whilst along the Mediterranean fringe the Moslem veneer wears very thin. It is quite impossible to distinguish Arab from Berber by tests of physical anthro-pology, for the fundamental characters of race are the same in the two stocks. Moreover, neither group —Arab or Berber—is homogeneous, or nearly homogeneous, from an ethnic standpoint. For our purpose all that need be said on the matter of physical or racial characteristics is that about two-thirds of the population of North-West Africa possess the following features : long-headedness, brunetteness of hair and eyes and short stature. Amongst a minority of the population the occurrence of brachycephaly and of tall stature is by no means uncommon, and the individuals concerned may be either Arab or Berber. The traits which have been enumerated associate the Berber-Arab peoples with the ' Mediterranean race ', whose membership includes the principal stocks of Southern Europe, namely Spaniards, Italians and Greeks.[1]

Leaving aside the tests of racial origins, and applying those

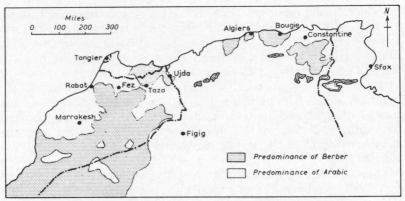

FIG. 80.—Distribution of Arabic and Berber Languages

of culture, we find that the terms ' Arab ' and ' Berber ', in certain parts of Barbary, still retain a real significance, despite the fact that the arabization of the Berbers has been proceeding for well over a thousand years and that the latter have freely borrowed—if they have not accepted, perforce—both religion and language from the men of the desert. It is, however, cultural absorption only ; for, in respect of race, the Berbers, whose numerical superiority is unchallenged, have tended rather to absorb the successive waves of Arab immigrants. The various dialects of Berber speech, which has such resemblances to Arabic as to suggest that both languages, in ancient times, derived from a common stem, are still spoken widely throughout

[1] The reader is reminded that there is an introductory reference to the Berbers and Arabs on pages 133–5.

the most mountainous parts of the region, and become more prominent as one proceeds from Tunisia towards Morocco. In Tunisia, from which the Islamic conquest was organized, there is practically no Berber spoken, whereas in Algeria about 30 per cent of the inhabitants speak it, and in Morocco about 40 per cent.

The Middle and Great Atlas remain the principal strongholds of Berber culture and language. The various Arab invasions were forced to swing round the flanks of the highland, both on the north side by way of the ' Taza Corridor ' (from which the invasion of Southern Spain took place), and on the south ; and, by both of these routes, the Atlantic plains of Morocco were reached. In recognition of the physical character of Algeria it will be realized that the highlands of Great Kabylia and Aurès provided effective refuges for the retreating Berber population. Many of the Berber highlanders, especially those of the lower Atlas slopes, are bi-lingual, and find it to their advantage to know Arabic, the language of religion and of commerce throughout Barbary.

The conquering nomads from the desert in their invasions of the seventh and later (particularly the eleventh) centuries disturbed Berber civilization most by extending the practice of nomadism. There had been nomadism in the region long before the first arrival of the Arabs, but now it was to be more universal, to the detriment of agriculture. Yet although the Berber people are not all agriculturists, including as they do many pastoral nomads also, it is equally true that the Arabs are not all wandering herdsmen, but include many sedentary farmers. Nomadism, partial nomadism and sedentary farming are all indirect responses to climate, and it is rainfall, not cultural heritage, much less ' race ', which determines whether a Berber or an Arab is a cultivator or a herdsman. The geographical transition from the sedentary life to the nomadic corresponds approximately to the transition from ' tell ' to steppe. Natives do not undertake transhumance when their land is able to support them both in summer and in winter, but outside the ' tell ' the practice is widespread. Amongst the farmers—Berber and Arab—cereal cultivation is the most general practice, although there is greater success with the rearing of fruit-trees ; and, because orchards require continuous attention, the fruit-growers of Barbary are, of necessity, sedentary. The cultivators of cereals are usually semi-nomadic pastoralists, also. After sowing, practically no attention is paid to the crop until harvest-time, for the community, with its flocks and herds, moves to the highlands, where it remains throughout the summer.

The organization of native life has been revolutionized as a

26

result of the French occupation of the region. The clan basis of society is fast disappearing even in the Berber strongholds of Morocco, which have only very recently felt the full weight of European influence, and in Algeria, as to be expected, it has entirely disappeared. The life of the Natives is becoming more and more detached from the family or clan unit, and there is an ever-increasing emphasis upon individual ownership of property. Although much of the best land has passed under European occupation—French, Italian and Spanish—the native population is growing fast, numerically, and this partly as a consequence of the benefits of civilization introduced through the French conquest. More and more of the native farmers are accepting French agricultural standards, an improvement, however, that is more apparent in fruit and cereal cultivation than in stock-rearing, which remains particularly primitive. Of all, the townspeople have been most assisted by the French occupation : they have been granted real security, for the first time in their history, whilst the normal tenor of their lives has altered comparatively little, in contrast with the nomads, to whom French penetration has meant the passing of traditional ways.

An increasingly close intercourse—if not actual fusion—between the Natives and the French colonists is promoted by the complete absence from French culture of racial and religious prejudices ; and the degree of social intimacy attained is rarely, if ever, found in any other empire of the world. There is no social, much less legal, barrier in the way of intermarriage, and the prediction of Reclus, the eminent French geographer of last century, is likely to be fulfilled. Reclus believed that an Algerian ' race ' would ultimately evolve from the mergence of the Berber-Arab stocks with the immigrant Latin elements—French, Italian and Spanish.

In respect of the distribution of native population the most pronounced change brought about, though indirectly, by the French occupation has been the tendency for the highlands to show a reduction in density, relative to the density of the lower lands. During the long centuries, when insecurity prevailed, the High and Middle Atlas, as well as the Kabylia and Aurès Massifs, became crowded refuges of the Berber folk, especially when the Arab incursions from the desert were most penetrating. Now, the flow of population is in the reverse direction, and the lands of the maritime ' tell ' and the lower lands generally—always allowing for the factor of rainfall !—show the highest densities.

Northern Algeria is the zone of greatest demographic importance. Its population numbers nearly one-half the total for

Barbary,[1] and includes much more than one-half of the European population. Yet there are very few districts where the density reaches figures which would be regarded as normal for rural averages in Western Europe. Even in the fertile areas under native farming the conditions of agriculture do not permit a high density, except where orchards are kept. A belt of relatively high density, averaging over 50 persons per square mile, and culminating at over 300 per square mile in one part of the Algerian ' tell ', extends round from Mogador (S.W. Morocco) to Sfax (E. Tunisia) ; save for two definite ' breaks ', namely :

(1) an area including the eastern part of the Riff territory,

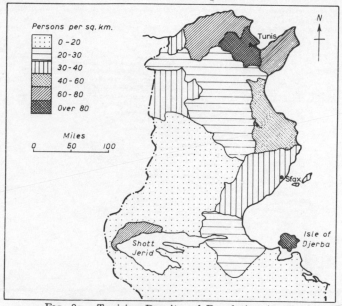

Persons per sq. km.

0 - 20
20 - 30
30 - 40
40 - 60
60 - 80
Over 80

Miles
0   50   100

N

Tunis

Sfax

Isle of Djerba

Shott Jerid

FIG. 81.—Tunisia—Density of Population (1946)

together with easternmost Morocco, where the interior semi-arid steppe reaches almost to the Mediterranean coast, north-east of Ujda. This ' rain-shadow ' area with the lowest density for a maritime district in all Barbary provides a natural frontier zone between Morocco and Algeria, and the political boundary takes account of it.

[1] In 1963 the population of Barbary was about 27 millions, as below:

Territory	Local	Expatriates	Total
Algeria (1963) .	10,323,000(?)	130,000(?)	10,453,000
Tunisia (1956) .	3,528,000	255,000	3,783,000
Morocco (1964) .	12,798,000	320,000	13,118,000

(2) a second, not so well emphasized, and less critical as a geographical factor, lies to the west of the Plain of Tunis, and detaches the relatively high densities of the eastern ' tell ' of Algeria from those in Eastern Tunisia.

The high native densities in the Algerian ' tell '—e.g. the Plain of Mitidja, where population culminates around Algiers, the largest city in North-West Africa—are partly an indirect result of European settlement, which is more concentrated here than elsewhere, and partly a consequence of immigration from less attractive parts of Algeria ; in addition there is the factor of

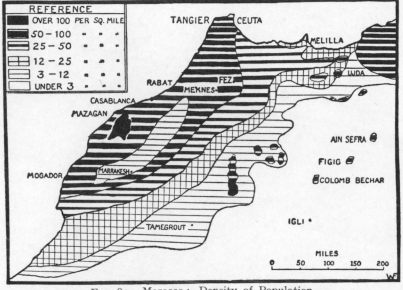

FIG. 82.—Morocco : Density of Population

rapid natural increase in the population. Since 1856 the indigenous people of Algeria have more than quadrupled in number ; from 2,328,000 to approximately 10·3 millions in 1963.

Types of Native Settlements

The tent which is characteristic of the nomadic pastoralist was introduced by the Arabs, and its use spread gradually amongst the Berbers. But, although the nomads of Barbary live in tents, all tent-dwellers are not nomads. The normal arrangement of tents is in the form of a circle (called ' douar '), the number of tents in such a settlement depending upon the character of the country and on the need for security. A more permanent dwelling is the ' gourbi ', which is a hut made usually of thatch, and

one of its varieties—cone-topped—is particularly common in
Western Morocco (e.g. in the vicinity of Casablanca). A grouping
of huts is generally surrounded by a wall of dried earth or by a
fence made up of thorn branches, both of which have been a
satisfactory defence against preying animals.

The most typical habitation of the sedentary Natives is a
rectangular house built of dried earth or clay, and consisting of
one room, without window or chimney. An especially elaborate
type of fortified house is the ' kasba ', a massive castellated
structure such as is still found commonly in the Atlas of Southern
Morocco, where, however, the need for these mountain strongholds (reminiscent of the ' keep ' of the Norman baron) no
longer exists, for the military power of the Berber chieftains
(the ' Caids ') has ceased with the pacification of the region.
In the Moroccan Atlas and in Kabylia the crowding together of
houses is such that they are actually attached to each other,
although the need for defence which caused the congestion is
no longer present. The typical Atlas village is composed of
houses attached to each other and rising in tiers on the flank of a
hill, the flat roof of one abode being level with the floor of the
one behind.

It has been said that any town in Barbary is merely an
agglomeration of such dwellings (as described above), surrounded
by a rampart and provided with a mosque. Until French
occupation brought new conceptions of town-planning, every
city was made up of the ' medina ', the native town with its
amazing congestion of dwellings ; the ' mellah ' or ' ghetto ',
reserved to the Jews, who form a very important element of
North African urban life ; and the ' kasba ', the fortified residence
of the governor, usually on the fringe of the ' medina '. All three
' elements ' of the typical town—e.g. Fez, Marrakesh—were,
and still are, surrounded by massive ramparts, built of baked
earth or clay and not of stone. Each of the great cities of
Morocco and Algeria has now a European town linked on to
it ; but this is, as might be expected, well planned and situated
a considerable distance—a mile or more—from the intolerable
congestion of ' medina ' or ' mellah '.

The vigorous trade of Barbary towns is located in the ' suk '
or market, of which there may be many in the same ' medina ',
though each specializes in some particular kind of merchandise,
e.g. leather-work, jewellery, vegetables. The ' suk ' is often in
the form of a long narrow alley, too narrow for horse traffic,
on to which open the booths—the whole being roofed in by wicker-
work, and capable of being locked at night.

Town life is relatively more important than in any other

region of the African continent, with the possible exception of the European parts of South Africa, and the urban tradition in such a city as Fez is a primary factor of social stability. Towns-people are regarded almost as a caste or race apart by the nomads and the mountain Berbers. The Moslems who, in the sixteenth and early seventeenth centuries, to the number of about two millions, retreated from Spain and established themselves mainly in the towns of Barbary, brought new vitality to urban society. The descendants of those Moslems are still known as ' Andalusians ', although ' Moors ' is the more general term. The Jewish element in the towns came mainly from Spain and from Palestine : from Spain at the time of the evacuation of that country by the Moors, and from Palestine at various times before and during the Christian epoch.

Immigration from Southern Europe

Europeans provide only a small proportion (about 2·5 per cent) of the total population, but before the emigration from Algeria the figure was about 14 per cent. Although the French predominated—they represented more than three-quarters of the non-native population of Algeria—their majority was in places challenged, either by the Spanish or by the Italian element.

These settlers from the northern shores of the Mediterranean were nearly all to be found in the zone where cultivation, because of adequate rainfall, is independent of irrigation ; and it is notable that where the density of their population was greatest the numbers of locals were comparatively small : whilst the converse was also true.[1] The Algerian towns contained 610,000 French, Spaniards and Italians, or 60 per cent of the total European population of the country. Algiers (with its suburbs) alone had 25 per cent of the European population and, as in practically every part of Africa, the towns are gaining at the expense of the rural areas.

The strong disinclination of Frenchmen to leave their home-land had long been an impediment to expansion in North Africa, and, in view of the absence of a similar conservatism on the part of Italians, it was one factor which affected the continuance of French sovereignty in Tunisia and Eastern Algeria. After 1871, when the population of France began to decline, there was little economic necessity for emigration ; indeed, the abun-

---

[1] In Algeria the Department of Oran had the largest European population—386,000 as against 1,214,000 locals : whilst the Department of Constantine had only 204,000 Europeans, out of a total population of 2,702,000.

dance and diversity of natural resources—especially those of
agriculture—required the whole of the available French man-
power for their full development. So it was that, for many
years, the only emigrants to North Africa came from comparatively poor districts of Languedoc, Provence and the neighbourhood of Marseilles, as well as from the Isle of Corsica. These
colonists had, however, the double advantage of short-distance
travel to their new home, and at least partial acclimatization
to North African conditions.

Even in Algeria to which the main stream of French colonization was directed there was doubt for a time—about the year
1880—whether the French would continue to predominate
numerically over the combined colonies of Italians and Spaniards.
By 1906 Spaniards were nearly as numerous as French in the
westernmost Department—Oran—which is closest to the Spanish
zone of Morocco ; and there to-day they slightly outnumber
the French, although a considerable proportion of them are
naturalized French citizens. The Iberian colonists, practically
all peasants, have come mainly from the south-eastern provinces
of Spain, particularly Alicante, which has provided nearly one-
half, and from Andalusia. They have not been absorbed by the
French colony, but have retained their original culture and their
associations with the homeland. On the other hand, they have not
developed a separatist political movement, and generally are well
disposed towards France ; whilst their contribution to the economic
life of Algeria, notably in stock-rearing, is very considerable.[1]

The Italians in the Department of Constantine may be
regarded as an overflow from the main centre of their colonization, which is Tunisia. Just before the establishment of the
French Protectorate in 1881 Italian settlement on the north-east
coastal plain of Tunisia was already extensive : it numbered
20,000 in 1880, when the French were still an inconsiderable
minority. Before the beginning of the present century, their
failure in viticulture caused many Italians to move across the
border into Algeria ; and, in addition, there was direct immigration into Constantine Department from Calabria, Campania and
Sicily, where, as in the case of the Midi, there is climatic similarity
to the Mediterranean lands of Barbary.

The decennial census of European population taken in Tunisia
is challenged in Italian, and even in certain French, quarters,[2]

---

[1] Oran Department includes the driest parts of the Algerian ' tell ' and
sheep-rearing by the Spaniards is notable.

[2] The publication—L'Afrique Française—investigated the relative
strengths of the Italians and French in 1911, and estimated 130,000 for
the former and only 30,000 for the latter.

it being contended that the number of Italians is greatly and
purposely underestimated.   At the census of 1931 the preponderance of Italians was officially admitted, although the French
were shown to be nearly as numerous, viz. 91,000 out of a total
non-native population of 195,000.   According to the census of
1946, by which time French and Italian were friendlier than they
were before 1939, the figures were :   French 144,000 ;   Italians
85,000.   The events of the Second World War seem to have
considerably reduced the Italian population of Tunisia.   Across
the Algerian frontier, in the Department of Constantine, Italian
colonists are fairly numerous ;   but it is almost impossible to
obtain accurate knowledge regarding them later than the year 1911,
and their mergence with the French community may be in process.
   By the terms of an agreement between the French and

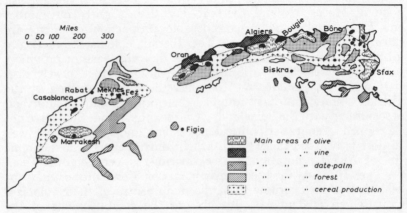

FIG. 83.—Barbary :   Agricultural Production

Italian Governments, dated 1896, the Italians of Tunisia were
guaranteed their separate identity as a community, and although,
more recently, the French Government has attempted to ensure
the ultimate absorption of the Italians the substance of the
original agreement has been preserved.   The compact and
apparently irreducible Italian *enclave*, strongly nationalistic and
established in and around the capital, Tunis, is from the French
standpoint a definite and growing danger to the political integrity
of the North African Empire ;   for it is constantly drawing support, not only from the near-by parent State, but also from the
contiguous Italian colony in Libya.   The clear division in
Tunisia between the two nationalities is emphasized in another
way by the special economic interests of the Italian settlers,
who form the greater part of the artisan and small trader classes.

Moreover, since 1912 the Italians have gained virtual control of the important wine industry of the Protectorate. The leading French authority on the geography of North-West Africa—Professor Augustin Bernard—has said that to ensure the French character of the region the proportion of French to Natives must be at least equal to that present in the Department of Oran, viz. 1 to 11,[1] whilst the proportion of French to other Europeans should be, in Tunisia and elsewhere, as high as it is in the Department mentioned.

GEOGRAPHICAL ASPECTS OF COLONIZATION AND LAND POLICY

(a) Algeria

As late as 1890 the French in Algeria actively pursued a policy of land expropriation. The Natives of the ' tell ' have been deprived of the greater part of their holdings : indeed, at first they were subjected to more than expropriation, and for a time even extermination was tried, though without success. Decade by decade the native population has increased, in spite of expulsion from many parts of the fertile ' tell ' to the semi-arid hinterland of the High Plateaux and the Saharan border.

After the disastrous war with Prussia (1870–1) the French Government looked to Algeria as a region where it might recover its lost prestige through imperial enterprise, and at the same time add to French territory in compensation for the cession of Alsace-Lorraine. To this day it is not regarded as a colony but rather as part of the political structure of France, and is controlled not by the Ministry of the Colonies but by that of the Interior. For administrative purposes it is, as we have seen, divided into Departments—Oran, Algiers and Constantine—each ᵥof which sends a senator and deputies to the National Assembly in Paris.

And so after 1870 it became the official policy to replace the Natives driven off large parts of the ' tell ', especially in the Department of Algiers, by group settlement of small-farmers from Mediterranean France. There was nothing haphazard about this colonization : it was deliberate and probably more carefully planned than any movement of people, on a large scale, overseas from Europe that has ever occurred. In many cases villages were actually constructed before their occupants-to-be arrived

---

[1] The town of Oran has a total population of 299,000, of whom three-quarters are Europeans ; which is the highest proportion of Europeans in any North African town.

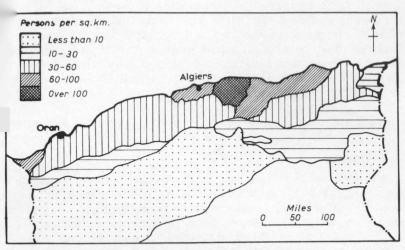

FIG. 84A.—Algeria : Density of the Native Population (Census of 1936)

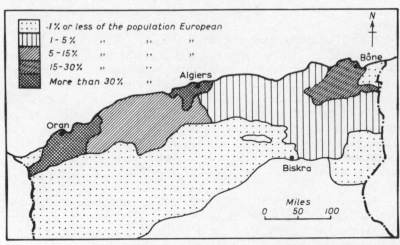

FIG. 84B.—Algeria : Relative Proportions of the Native and European
Populations (Census of 1936)

from France. The total number of villages built now exceeds 800, and they are the homes of 300,000 agriculturists.[1]

One of the factors—a quite accidental one—that helped to promote French rural settlement was the temporary destruction of the vineyards of France by the phylloxera pest in 1878. By that year the viticultural possibilities of the Plain of Mitidja were already estimated and it was hoped to build up thereon a vine industry as great as that of the lower Rhône valley. Partly in consequence of this new incentive the rural colonization of the Tell rapidly extended and as early as 1880 there were 200,000 farming settlers of whom, however, the French formed a bare majority. Before the close of last century the success of the Algerian vineyards was assured, and long prior to the Great War their output was equal to about 12 per cent of the quantity of the product of France. At present about 750,000 acres are under the vine, an area equal to about one-fifth of the French vineyards.

The French farming community is especially associated in its economic life with viticulture, which, since 1880, has been the chief interest of the country. There are nearly one million acres of vineyards—which is 20 times the acreage for the year 1879—and more than one-half are within the Department of Oran, where, as we have seen, the density of European rural population is higher than elsewhere in Barbary. The vine is essentially the crop of the lower slopes of the ' tell ', where it is protected both from frost and from the blast of the *sirocco*. French policy in placing so much land under this crop has been criticized, because very little of the wine production is consumed in the country, whose native inhabitants are mainly Moslem.

Moreover, since Algeria became independent in 1962, wine production has continued to play an important part in the country's economy, and has accounted for about half of the total value of exports, other than mineral oil. Algeria produces more wine than France, and unfortunately for her the French market on which she has been overwhelmingly reliant has become increasingly difficult to enter, because of over-production within France.

Even more serious for the economy of Algeria has been the crisis following the emigration of the bulk of the French population, and the abandonment and expropriation of the European farms. From a total of over a million, the French population of

[1] In all, the area occupied or owned by European agriculturists amounts to nearly five million acres, over 70 per cent of which total is due to ' official colonization ' and the remainder to private enterprise.

Algeria has fallen to about 130,000 in 1963, and as a consequence about 3 million acres of farmland, including some of the most fertile in the country, were deserted. The bulk of this land has been converted to a system of collective farming, and the inevitable disruption caused by this transfer resulted in a predictable decline in output.

In 1965 the economic position of the country was still insecure. Despite the high royalties from the Sahara oil, the trade balance was still unfavourable, and some 2 million of the population were unemployed. The country remained solvent only with the aid of subventions and loans from abroad, mainly from France, the U.S.A. and the U.S.S.R.

(b) Tunisia

By 1880 France was able to advance strong economic, as well as political, arguments for an extension of control eastwards from the Algerian ' tell '. It was believed that the northern lands of Tunisia exceeded those of Algeria in fertility,[1] and that, on account of the local system of tenure, they were more likely than those of the Algerian ' tell ' to be accessible to modern agricultural methods. Moreover, the Natives were known to be more docile than the Algerian Berbers, so that there was the prospect of an easy conquest.

At the time of the establishment of the Protectorate (1883) the French had forsaken—though only temporarily—their policy of assimilation and were prepared to tolerate the continuance of administration by the Bey on a basis of native law and custom. The external relations of Tunisia, however, were to be the affair of the ' protector ' Power exclusively. Until the Great War the dualism in government worked fairly well, but it became increasingly unsatisfactory and irritating to the French who have rarely shown enthusiasm for ' indirect rule '. At the same time the commerce of the towns, which contain a high percentage of the total population,[2] was generally prosperous and there was little unrest amongst the Natives.

In the last decade of the nineteenth century France had no longer serious expectation of greatly extending the area of ' official colonization ' to which reference has been made. Consequently the expropriation of native-owned land in Tunisia was on a smaller scale than previously in Algeria, and there was not

---

[1] The historical fact of Tunisia as one of the principal granaries and vineyards of the Roman Empire was recalled.

[2] The city of Tunis, with 410,000 inhabitants in 1956, has about one-ninth of the total population of Tunisia.

nearly so great a dislocation of community life as in the latter territory.

Instead of laying most emphasis on the introduction of numerous small-farming colonists the French Government preferred to encourage the establishment of large land-owning capitalists—companies and individuals—for the development of agriculture, especially vine-growing, on a scale comparable to that of Algeria. A model was provided by the company-owned Enfida estate, of more than 200,000 acres, on the 'sahel' between Tunis and Susa. It was there that experiments were made with the *métayage* system of farming which was later extended to practically the whole of the cultivated land of the Protectorate. In France and Italy *métayage* is still common. It is a system of cultivation of land for a proprietor by one who receives in return a proportion of the harvest, the proportion varying according to soil fertility and other circumstances. By arrangement the landlord and the farmer share the costs of seed, implements and other equipment.

The Enfida Company employed not French but native farmers, and by suppressing the serfdom, which was permitted by local law, it attracted immigrants from neighbouring districts. Other companies were formed on its model and by 1914 nearly two million acres had been alienated. Of this total the greater part was held by companies whose aggregate membership did not exceed 100 persons. It is true that after the year 1900 France made an attempt to foster group settlement similar to that of Algeria, but it was a belated effort as most of the productive land was already absorbed by the big companies.

No great advance in Tunisian agriculture followed the establishment of the land companies. Very early viticulture proved a disappointment,[1] and cereals were then a necessary second choice involving a considerable dependence on labour from Southern Italy. Gradually, however, the olive came to the fore as the principal product of commercial agriculture—the zone of its maximum cultivation being the southern 'sahel' between Susa and Sfax, where *métayage* was introduced about the close of last century. The oil of Sfax has a high reputation and much of it is exported to Italy.

In recent years there has been a tendency for the large estates to be divided into smaller units under the complete control of European farmers, French and—equally numerous—Italian. One of the areas of successful small-farming is the Medjerda valley that opens on to the Plain of Tunis. The Italians greatly

---

[1] In 1963, the production of wine was only 1,850,000 hectolitres ; in the same year, Algeria's output was 12,750,000 hectolitres.

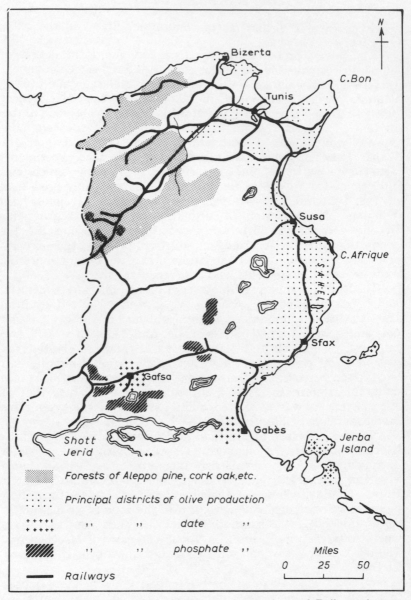

Forests of Aleppo pine, cork oak, etc.

Principal districts of olive production

   ,,   ,,   date   ,,

   ,,   ,,   phosphate ,,

Railways

Fig. 85.—Tunisia : Features of Economic Geography, and Railways in 1953

402

strengthened their hold on the land immediately after the First
World War, when, in consequence of serious Moslem unrest, there
was for a time panic amongst French proprietors, many of whom
sold their interests to Italian settlers.   Native revolt was largely
due to the attempt on the part of France to obtain control over
lands held by religious foundations in the north of the Protectorate.   Because of its relative proximity to the Senussi strongholds, Tunisia before the First World War was more directly
affected than were Algeria and Morocco by the fanaticism of
that Confederation of the desert.   The *Young Tunisians*, always
tending to be Francophobe and already influenced by Senussi
propaganda, were especially aggrieved by the attitude of France
towards the landed property of the religious foundations.   Moreover, the French were deprived of the co-operation of the party of
tradition—*Les Vieux Turbans*—and for the first time the opposing
parties of Tunisian politics joined forces.   In face of the revolt
France not only abandoned its attempt to control the lands of the
religious foundations, but also promised a measure of autonomy
to the several regions of Tunisia.   On March 20th, 1956, the
independence of Tunisia was formally recognized by France.   The
two countries will co-operate in matters of common interest,
notably in the spheres of defence and foreign policy.

(c) Morocco

Inducements to France to extend her control westwards from
Algeria were not wanting at the close of the nineteenth century.
There were the economic attractions of rich and extensive cultivable lands on the 'tell', as well as the most abundant timber
resources in North Africa.   Here was a store-house of foodstuffs
and raw materials for industrial use, still sealed to the outer world
but likely to be an easy prize to the first adventurous Power that
should appear.   Moreover, a lower density of native population
on the Moroccan lowlands than on the corresponding lands of
Algeria was encouraging to the idea of French colonization.

From a military point of view the lowlands of Morocco—
open to the ocean and exposed to the might of a Power to whom
the sea-entrance was advantageous—provided no real problem :
but, as France found to her cost, the tribesmen of the Atlas
chains were able for long to maintain a stern resistance.   The
State of Morocco whose institutions had changed little since
the sixteenth century was isolated at the western extremity
of the Moslem world, and had so declined in authority that
most of its component communities—a mosaic of tribes and
townships—had shaken off all political allegiance to the Sultan.
Even within the Sebou Basin—the heart of Morocco—the Sultan

only maintained a semblance of power by playing off one town against another or by fomenting rivalry between groups of tribes.

The anarchic condition of Western Barbary after 1894 provided France with both an excuse and an opportunity for intervention. At first, in the earliest years of the present century, military and commercial penetration proceeded from the Algerian side in the region of Ujda and, much farther south, across the western extremity of the High Plateaux, in the Figig group of oases. On account of its position in relation to trans-Saharan communications Figig, occupied by France in 1901, was of critical importance : upon it converge a series of caravan tracks including one that crosses the Sahara diagonally from the Chad region. Following immediately on the establishment of French authority at this southern outpost a railway to it was projected, and soon completed, from the Oran ' tell ', in order to tap the trans-Saharan traffic. The line now has its terminus at Colomb Bechar (some 80 miles to the south-west of Figig) which may be selected as the starting-point of the proposed trans-Saharan railway.

The advance on the Moroccan ' tell ' from the Algerian Plateau —by the back-door as it were—was obviously a most difficult route from the military point of view, as the French soon realized. In 1903 their diplomacy was preparing the way for a landing on the Atlantic coast, and the agreement with Great Britain in 1904, by which each Power withdrew opposition to the other's interests in Morocco and Egypt, respectively, made possible the launching of the new military enterprise, despite the opposition of Germany that persisted until 1911. In 1907 a force landed at Casablanca—soon to replace Tangier as the chief port of Morocco —and the military occupation of the Plain of Shawia [1] followed. The agriculturists of the Moroccan lowlands were generally friendly to the new authority, for they were now secure from the raids of desert-border Arabs and Atlas mountaineers.

General Lyautey, first Resident-General, will always be regarded as the architect of the Moroccan Protectorate, ranking, as a pro-consul, with Lugard of Nigeria and Gallièni of Madagascar. In a series of brilliant campaigns, before and during the Great War, he attached extreme importance to the control of the Taza corridor that follows the gap between the Riff Atlas and the northernmost part of the Middle Atlas, and provides the only practicable direct route from the Algerian ' tell ' to Fez and other principal centres of Morocco. From Fez and Taza Lyautey advanced into the Moulouya valley where he made contact with the earliest-occupied zone of French Morocco

[1] Usually written Chaouia on French maps.

extending westwards from Ujda; and, by the close of the Great War, had taken the preliminary steps towards the conquest of the Great Atlas by securing the road from Meknes across the Middle Atlas to the upper Moulouya River and to Tafilelt on the Saharan border.[1]

Lyautey was much impressed by the success of 'indirect rule' in Nigeria, and the native policy he adopted in Morocco bears distinct signs of resemblance to the British West African

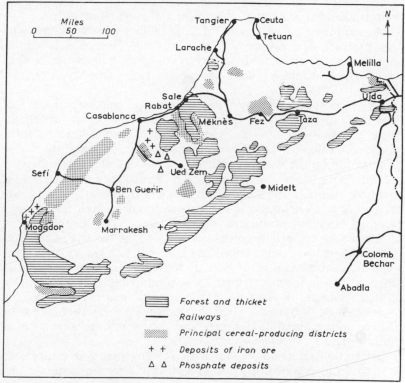

FIG. 86.—Morocco: Features of Economic Geography

model. Distinguishing French rule in Morocco from the régime in Algeria was greater flexibility, a consequence of Lyautey's departure from the normal rigid centralization characteristic of French colonial administration. In the several regions of Morocco the form of administration was adjusted to particular local conditions and was generally in harmony with popular tradition and

[1] The Meknes-Tafilelt road secured by Lyautey in order to 'contain' the Great Atlas Berbers is one of the most important north-south commercial highways of Barbary.

custom, so that there was as little interference as possible on the part of the French Government. No attempt was made to degrade the spiritual authority of the Sultan who remained ' Commander of the Faithful '. In March, 1956, France recognized the independence of the Sultan of Morocco, and the following month Spain made a similar treaty. One of the most critical of the problems facing Lyautey was the policy to be adopted towards the powerful Caids, feudal barons of the Great Atlas, in control of large confederations of hillsmen. By recognizing their traditional authority the French Government did, on the whole, gain their co-operation—though revolts were not unknown. The intention of Lyautey was to secure the Moroccan lowlands on their southern side by the creation of a friendly buffer-state, which would prevent incursions from the unconquered Sahara.

Of rural settlement by French farming colonists there has been very little since ' official colonization ' began in 1918 : nor is the prospect for such a development very bright in spite of the intention of the Government sooner or later to foster colonization on the western plains. About one and three-quarter million acres were alienated in preparation for settlement, chiefly in the Gharb, Rabat and Shawia districts : yet as late as 1927 it was estimated that there were fewer than 200 French farming families established on the land. The Europeans in Morocco were essentially town-dwellers and, at the 1947 enumeration, of their total population (325,000) not less than 40 per cent were in Casablanca alone. The increase of French population in Morocco in the inter-war years was proportionately higher than in either Algeria or Tunisia, and the total was actually trebled between 1911 and 1936. In 1963, however, only about 140,000 Europeans remained in Morocco, and their numbers were steadily diminishing.

After the independent status of the country was established in 1956, France continued to be its most important customer and supplier, taking rather more than 40 per cent of its exports and returning about the same proportion of its imports. The economic value of Morocco to France rests partly on its cereal output which is obtained mainly from the extensive plains of the west. The production of wheat in Barbary normally varies between 15 and 20 million quintals annually, which may be compared with the amount for France—approximately 90 quintals.

Although without navigable waterways Morocco has a considerable number of streams valuable for irrigation purposes— particularly the Sebou, Umm er Rbi'a and Moulouya ; and the cultivable area by utilizing the resources of the river. By 1966 about 1,000,000 acres of Moroccan land were irrigated, more than a third of them from a single dam, at Bin el Ouidiane on the Oud el Abid. This dam, the tenth largest in the world, has a hydro-electric capacity of 212,000 kW.

MINERAL EXPLOITATION IN NORTH-WEST AFRICA

Until very recently, the mineral output of North-West Africa was confined largely to phosphate of lime, the basis for a fertilizer, and iron ores of high quality. In Tunisia the phosphate rock is mined chiefly in the neighbourhood of Gafsa, north of the Shott Jerid. In Algeria the principal phosphate mines are in the district of Tebessa, on the interior plateau near the Tunisian border, and in that of Tocqueville, south of the Tell Atlas and to the north of the great Shott el Hodna. Morocco only began to produce this mineral in 1921, but now has a large export, through Casablanca, from the mines of Kourigha, 60 miles to the south-east of that port. Morocco accounts for some 19 per cent of the world's production of phosphate, Tunisia for 7 per cent, and Algeria for 3 per cent.

The Barbary iron ores, which include much haematite, find a ready market in Britain. Algeria is the largest producer, and its chief mines are on the western coast of Oran Province, in the upper Chelif valley around Miliana, and in the neighbourhood of Wenza and Bou Kadra which are close to the Tunisian border and north of the railway terminus of Tebessa. The Tunisian mines lie in the highlands of the north-west, particularly near Djerissa, while the principal centres of production in Morocco are Beni bu Ifrar and Ait Amar.

However, recent exploration in the western Sahara has proved that the desert has mineral resources far more varied and copious than those of the Atlas Mountains, though their remoteness may prove to be an obstacle in the way of their early exploitation. Tin is known at Air in Niger, and manganese in the southern foothills of the Atlas, particularly near Ougarta, while a rich coalfield has been found in Morocco conveniently near the railhead at Colomb Bechar.

But the discovery of most significance for the economy of both Algeria and metropolitan France has been that of mineral oil and natural gas in abundant quantities. Oil was first struck at the chief field, that of Hassi-Messaoud, in 1956, and in December, 1959, a pipe-line 384 miles long was opened from there to the coast at Bougie. To the south-east, successful borings have been made at Edjele, Tiguentourine, and Zarzaitine, near the

Libyan border, and oil from this area began arriving by pipeline in 1961 at the Tunisian port of Skirra. By the end of 1963, the Mediterranean terminal of the Saharan pipe-lines were exporting oil at the rate of about 24 million tons a year, enough to meet the total requirements of France. Natural gas is already being found in embarrassing quantities, particularly at In Salah, and a gas pipeline has been completed from Hassi-Messaoud to Oran and Algiers.

The economy of Mauretania appears likely to be revolutionized by the discovery, since 1952, of remarkably rich deposits of iron ore of the highest quality in the desert at Fort Gouraud. 52 separate pockets of ore have been surveyed on a 20-mile long east–west escarpment, and 2 million tons of ore, which could be marketed at a concentration of 63·5 per cent iron. Fortunately, artesian water has been tapped in the area, and there are plans for a mining town and a 400-mile railway to the coast at Port Etienne. It is hoped to export 16 million tons of ore a year.

THE CITIES OF BARBARY

To-day most of the great cities are on the sea-board, although this is more true of Algeria and Tunisia than of Morocco, where Fez, Meknes and Marrakesh dominate the urban life of the interior. The ever-increasing importance of maritime position is an inevitable consequence of the re-orientation in Barbary affairs during the last hundred years and of the removal of the isolation that formerly governed the relations of the region with the outer world. Despite the attention to mineral exploitation, to which reference has been made, mining and industrial developments dependent on it are either too immature or too dispersed geographically to have produced a great urban concentration in the interior, comparable, say, to Johannesburg. The commercial inter-dependence of France and her nearest African neighbours is now so close as to mean a great recrudescence of activity at some of the old seaports of the Barbary coast. And so we find, especially in the case of Morocco, that several cities of the interior, whose age-long functions have been those of market and road-centre, are now overshadowed by the towns of the Atlantic and Mediterranean fringe. Only one of the four former capitals of Morocco—namely the city-port of Rabat—retained its old status under the French régime.[1]

Until the beginning of this century Tangier was the first port of Western Barbary. In subsequent years it suffered from

[1] The Sultan usually resides at Rabat, though he pays occasional visits to the other old capitals, Fez, Meknes and Marrakesh.

international rivalries arising out of the Balance of Power in the Western Mediterranean that involved France, Great Britain, Spain and Germany. Its situation at the outer porch to the Mediterranean entrance was too critical for any one of the maritime Powers to be allowed to remain in sole possession. As this was the dominating consideration it follows that the interests of Tangier as a natural outlet to the Gharb were not taken into account ; and finally the port was politically detached from its hinterland. Then again, the selection by France of a port more suitably placed in relation to her own zone of Morocco meant the rise of Casablanca at the expense of Tangier. One later development that did, however, benefit the latter was the completion of a railway—a joint French and Spanish enterprise—between it and Fez ; although at that time France, as any other country in her place, was not likely to permit the diversion of traffic from Casablanca to a port not under her own control.

Prior to 1914 there were attempted agreements between France and Germany and between France and Spain in regard to the status of Tangier and of a zone extending 10 miles round it. It was not until 1923 that Tangier received its charter as a city-port, with permanently neutral international status. In 1940 Spanish Moroccan troops occupied Tangier, and Spain was virtually in control of the City and its Zone until 1945, when the Spanish Government was required to retire and international rule was restored. Tangier ceased to be international in October, 1956. It is now a province within the Kingdom of Morocco, which has, however, declared it a free port from the beginning of 1962.

The former French military base of Casablanca (the ' White House '—a name derived from its Portuguese foundation in the sixteenth century) has developed into the recognized commercial gateway of Morocco, where over 80 per cent of the overseas trade of the Moroccan kingdom is handled. There is little natural shelter for shipping, but the roadstead is deep and, unlike other Moroccan ports, is untroubled by estuarine silting. Constructional work on the artificial harbour began in 1913 and the port is now protected by two extensive breakwaters. Although in 1961 a vigorous city of 1,177,000 (four times the size of Marrakesh), as recently as 1908 Casablanca was a stagnating settlement of only 10,000 persons. The rate of growth has been so rapid that Marrakesh, recently the largest Moroccan city, has been displaced in rank ; yet, there is no real comparison between the two, for in addition to their very different functions—one an Atlantic seaport, the other an oasis on the threshold of the Sahara—Casablanca is an entirely modern town, very conscious

of its modernity; whilst, on the other hand, the centuries-old
traditions of Marrakesh still dominate its urban life.

The physical form of Morocco is such as to favour decentralization and the growth of separate political entities, each with
its capital and approximating to a physical unit, rather than
centralization and the evolution of a single great metropolitan
focus. Fez and Marrakesh are the regional centres that have
been most notable throughout Moroccan history. Each has had
the status of a capital for long periods, and during times of weak
central authority they have been the centres of the principal
rival factions in Morocco.[1]

Since its foundation early in the ninth century the prestige
of Fez in the Moslem world has surpassed that of any city of
Barbary, and this old capital still retains its function as the
western head-quarters of Islam—the ' Mecca of the West ', as it
has been called. In modern times there has been deterioration
rather than progress in most aspects of its civic life, though its
situation in the fertile Sebou Basin and, more especially, within
the easily-irrigated district where the Sebou head-streams converge, together with its position in relation to the Taza ' corridor '
from the Algerian ' tell ' by way of Ujda, are likely always to command considerable status for the city. Situated at an altitude
of 1200 feet, Fez is within a narrow valley cut into the Moroccan
platform and fed by abundant waters, which are canalized for
the benefit of the city. The water supply is more dependable
and generous than that of any other town of the interior, and
helps to account for the enduring importance of Fez at successive periods since its foundation in A.D. 806. In the thirteenth
century its population was probably about 400,000, or more
than twice that of the modern city. Apart from its vigorous
commercial and industrial life, especially associated with leather-
work and silks, which is carried on in the stifling atmosphere of
its congested ' suks ' and alleys, Fez remains the religious and
intellectual capital of Morocco. Here are the sanctuary of the
revered Moulay Idris, and the University of Karauiyine. Less
than 40 miles to the south-west is Meknes (Mequinez), also a
former capital, and the close proximity of these two cities is
evidence of the importance of the southern parts of the Sebou
Basin in the social and political as well as in the commercial
life of old Morocco.

Marrakesh [2] in the valley of the Tensift shared in the general
decay of prosperity that preceded the arrival of the French.

[1] For a valuable paper by Miss A. Garnett on the old capitals of
Morocco, v. *Scott. Geog. Magazine*, January, 1928.
[2] Sometimes erroneously known as Morocco City.

As the southern capital, founded in A.D. 1062, the city has been almost continuously concerned with the organization of the defence of settled Morocco against Saharan and Atlas tribesmen, and its relations with the lofty defiles across the Great Atlas chain have therefore been intimate. Marrakesh is 20 miles from the foot of the Great Atlas, whose snow-covered crests form the southern horizon and provide the greatest possible contrast with the desiccated, brown plain, in the midst of which the city is situated. Surrounded by palms, the town resembles a great Saharan oasis. It is a vast market, both for the Atlas mountain people and for the Saharan nomads, who there exchange skins, hides and dates for cereals and European merchandise. In size of population—264,000 in 1961—Marrakesh is superior even to Fez, but its part in the life of Morocco has not been as dominating as that of the latter.

Of the Algerian cities Algiers and Constantine are most worthy of the small space available here. Occupying a midway position along the Algerian coast the first of these cities is provided with a spacious and artificially-sheltered harbour, though the urban settlement itself is closely walled-in by the scarps of the coastal ranges, and so is limited to a narrow extension along the littoral. Apart from important bunkering activities its trade, both export and import, is mainly with Marseilles ; and these two cities that were, in a recent year, first and second respectively among French ports in amount of tonnage cleared,[1] have grown to their present eminence in close association with each other. Algiers does not monopolize the external trade of Algeria as does Casablanca in the case of Morocco and its share both of the export and of the import trade is considerably less than 50 per cent. Because of the great extent, from east to west, of the narrow ' tell ' zone and of its discontinuous character (through the interruption of ranges and ' massifs ') it may be understood why Algeria possesses a series of ports, for most of which the effective hinterland is narrowly restricted. So we have, in addition to Algiers, Oran, Philippeville, Bougie, Bône and others. Constantine with about 223,000 inhabitants is chief of the inland cities of Algeria, and lies about 50 miles from the coastal site occupied by its port of Philippeville. It is a natural fortress and when, in 1837, captured by the French its possession granted the latter virtual control of the entire eastern ' tell ' of Algeria and made possible an offensive against the unsubdued hillsmen of Kabylia.

Tunis is unapproached in size of population by any town

---

[1] Marseilles is, of course, easily of greater consequence ; and it is to be noted that a considerable proportion of the tonnage counted as cleared from Algiers is coal in bunkers.

in the same country : indeed, there is no other that equals
more than one-tenth of its 680,000 inhabitants (census of 1960).
As a port it derives great advantage from its place where the ' tell '
of North Tunisia, including the Medjerda valley, merges with the
olive-growing coastlands of the east, most notably the ' sahel '
of Susa.   But until recently Tunis was land-locked and dependent
on an out-port—Goulette.   In 1893 a sea-channel about 6 miles
long was constructed and finally deepened to 28 feet, so opening
the old port to sea-borne traffic once more.

Although the Saharan lands, that for administrative con-

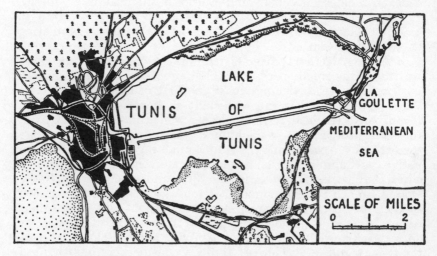

FIG. 87.—Tunis: City and Port.   The map shows the out-port—La Goulette—
and the canalized approach to the city of Tunis

venience are attached to the three French Dependencies, lie
outside the scope of this chapter, it is not inappropriate at this
point to mention that the oases of the southern territories of
Algeria have in many cases an almost urban character.   Such
are the oases of Touggourt (Souf) with 12,500 inhabitants and of
Ghardaia (Mzab) with 11,000, whose life is discussed in an admirable chapter of *Human Geography* by Professor J. Brunhes.

THE EVOLUTION OF THE MODERN SYSTEM OF COMMUNICATIONS

The introduction to Barbary of modern transport came with
the establishment of the first French colony in the Plain of
Mitidja.   Then was built a railway from Algiers to Blida, in the

extreme south of the Plain and about 30 miles from the capital. In different parts of the central ' tell ', separate lines were constructed and, by joining, provided the east-west railway axis of modern Algeria : such were the lines Algiers to Oran ; Philippeville to Constantine ; Constantine to Algiers. Tunis was the obvious choice as centre for a railway system when the French established their Protectorate over Eastern Barbary. From it the main lines are (a) to Susa, (b) to Bizerta, (c) a western line penetrating the Medjerda valley and making contact with the Algerian system. Owing to surveillance by Germany the French in Morocco were virtually prevented from undertaking railway construction until 1912, while in more recent years there has been greater attention to motor-roads than to permanent way extensions. The main lines of the Moroccan railway net include a western prolongation of the Algerian system *via* Ujda, Taza, Fez, Meknes, Rabat to Casablanca—part being widened to broad gauge as recently as 1933—and the line from Fez to Tangier. It was not until 1928 that the foremost city of the south—Marrakesh—was connected by broad-gauge railway to Casablanca and the cities of the Sebou Basin. With remarkable energy motor-road construction was undertaken during the Great War in order to make possible the thorough conquest of the Protectorate. The arterial road of Morocco follows, as one would expect, the great east-west corridor from the Algerian ' tell ' by way of Ujda, Taza and Fez, and terminates at Casablanca.

The development of communications in Barbary is closely associated with the project of one or more railways and motor-roads traversing the Sahara and having terminal points at railheads in Southern Algeria. At two places the Algerian railway system reaches the Sahara : from the Oran ' tell ' one line leads across the High Plateaux—actually traversing the Shott-esh-Shergwi—and through the Saharan Atlas by Ain Sefra to Colomb Bechar ; while another brings the important oasis-group of Touggourt into contact with the eastern centres of Algeria, especially Constantine, and follows a difficult course immediately to the west of the Aurès Massif.

In 1927 the French Government appointed the Trans-Saharan Commission to investigate possible routes for a desert railway that should link Algeria to French West Africa. The Commission finally decided to recommend a line from Colomb Bechar to Gao, on the middle Niger, from which there should be two branches, one to Niamey much lower down the Niger valley, the other to Segou in the ' delta ' of the upper middle Niger. Such a line, commercially the most promising, would naturally take advantage of the Tuat group of oases which, to the north-west of the Ahaggar Plateau, provide the most prominent converging point for caravans throughout the interior of the Sahara. Although the Commission definitely took the view that a trans-Saharan railway would be preferable to a motor-road there is a good deal of doubt if it will ever be built, in view of the inevitably high costs of construction and maintenance and of its probably precarious earning capacity. Already motor transport has proved practicable—the Sahara was first traversed by automobile about fifteen years ago—and regular services, both military and commercial, have been in operation for some years between Algeria and the Niger and Chad regions.

The caravan traffic across the Sahara has long been declining in commercial importance, and this—in part—because the economic resources of the Sudan have been tapped at many points and diverted by roads and railways to ports on the Gulf of Guinea. But it remains worthy of considerable attention and, for the student of historical geography especially, offers a particularly attractive subject for investigation. Certain of the more important caravan tracks still used, or in use until recently, are mentioned below and the accompanying map will amplify the information set out in the text. It is not unlikely, when the Sahara is crossed by a network of motor- and railway-routes, that the principal arteries will approximate fairly closely in direction to those of the days of camel transport.

During the first half of the nineteenth century two great trade routes—among the oldest in the world—gathered to themselves the main share of the traffic passing between the Western Sudan and the Barbary States. One was the ' Road of the West ', from Timbuktu to Marrakesh, by way of Taghaza and the Telouet Pass, through the Great Altas : the other lay between the ' sahel ' of Tunisia and Kano and, narrowly skirting the Ahaggar Plateau, used the oases of Air and Ghadames (where the desert territories of Italian Libya, Algeria and Tunisia converge). The journey by camel along each of these tracks usually occupied as much as eight weeks. Although proved by centuries of experience to be the most satisfactory lines of north-to-south communication in the Western and Central Sahara, respectively, these routes traverse vast stretches that are entirely waterless.[1]

Apart from the former gold traffic along the Timbuktu–Marrakesh route, salt was and still is of great consequence as a staple of long-distance trade across the Sahara. Down to the closing years of the sixteenth century the middle Niger region depended mainly on the salt-pans of Taghaza, which lies some 400 miles to the west of the Tuat oases : before the end of the

[1] In 1805, a caravan returning to Morocco from Timbuktu perished from thirst, the loss being 2000 men and about the same number of camels.

century, however, the Songhai people discovered and began to exploit the abundant salt resources of Taodeni, much nearer to the Sudan than is Taghaza. At neither of these salt-fields was there an adequate supply of water or food, and in no sense were they oases. Indeed, it may be said also of Timbuktu that this great caravan-centre likewise depended entirely upon imported provisions : its function was and is solely that of an *entrepôt*.

In the commerce of the Kano–Air–Ghadames–Tunisia ' road ' salt again was of outstanding value. Agades, in the Air country —one of the best camel pasture lands in the Sahara—retained

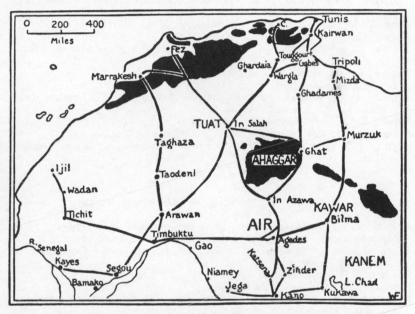

FIG. 88.—Principal Caravan Routes of the Western and Central Sahara (at the close of the nineteenth century)

(N.B.—Land over 3000 feet shown in black.)

its trading status in the nineteenth century, mainly through the organization of the immense caravan that carried salt to the Hausa States. Every autumn a vast assemblage of men and camels—the latter alone usually more than 20,000—set out from Air for Bilma, the chief centre of the Kawar oasis from which the salt was obtained. On the return a short halt was made at Agades, after which the caravan moved south to Sokoto and Kano. On the way back to Air corn and textiles, received in exchange for salt, provided the cargoes.

REFERENCES

In French the literature is abundant and much of it very scholarly, the name of Augustin Bernard being especially prominent. In English there are many works of travel, but from the standpoint of the systematic geographer the bibliography in our language is quite inadequate. For this reason practically all the works listed in the selected bibliography below are of French authorship. A good work of reference for the physical geography, history, ethnology and colonization of French North Africa is:

Despois, J., *L'Afrique Blanche Française, Tome I, L'Afrique du Nord*, Paris, 1949.

MOROCCO

Bernard, A., *Le Maroc*, 6th ed., Paris, 1922.
Afrique septentrionale, Tome XI, La Géographie Universelle, Paris, 1937.
Célérier, J., *Le Maroc*, Paris, 1931.
Fogg, W., ' The Sebou Basin ', *Scott. Geog. Mag.*, March, 1931.
Gentil, L., *Le Maroc physique*, Paris, 1912.
Hardy, J., et Célérier, J., *Les grandes lignes de la géographie du Maroc*, Paris, 1922.
Piquet, V., *Le Maroc*, 3rd ed., Paris, 1920.
Les peuples marocaines, Paris, 1925.
Roberts, S. H., *History of French Colonial Policy*, Vol. II, London, 1929. (Also for Algeria and Tunisia.)
Russo, P., *La terre marocaine*, Ujda, 1921.
Stuart, G. H., *The International City of Tangier*, London, 1931.
Torres, J.-M. Cordero, *Tratado elemental de derecho colonial español*, 1941.

ALGERIA

Bernard, A., *L'Algérie*, Paris, 1931.
Bernard, A., et Ficheur, E., ' Les régions naturelles de l'Algérie ', *Annales de Géographie*, Vol. XI, 1902.
Demontes, V., *L'Algérie industrielle et commerçante*, Paris, 1930.
Renseignements sur l'Algérie économique, 2 vols., Paris, 1922.
Franc, J., *La colonisation de la Mitidja*, Collection du Centenaire de l'Algérie, Paris, 1929.
Gautier, E. F., *Structure de l'Algérie*, Paris, 1922.
Larnaude, M., *L'Algérie*, Paris, 1950.
Peyerimhoff, H. de, *Enquête sur les résultats de la colonisation officielle*, 2 vols., Algiers, 1906 (republ. Paris, 1928).
Piquet, V., *La colonisation française dans l'Afrique du nord*, Paris, 1912.
L'Algérie française ; un siècle de colonisation, Paris, 1930.
Saint-Hilaire, H. G., *L'Elèvage dans l'Afrique du nord*, Paris, 1919.

TUNISIA

Bernard et Flotte-Roquevaire, *Atlas d'Algérie et de Tunisie* (Gouvernement-Général de l'Algérie).
Bernard, A., *L'habitation rurale des indigènes de la Tunisie*, Tunis, 1924.
de Lanessan, *La Tunisie*, Paris, 1917.
Monchicourt, C., *La région du Haut Tell tunisien*, Paris, 1913.
Saurin, J., *Le peuplement français en Tunisie*, Paris, 1918.
Solignac, M., *Etude géologique de la Tunisie septentrionale*, Paris, 1927.

For each of the three French territories see also the sheets, on various scales, published by the ' Service Géographique de l'Armée '.

As reference has been made to trans-Saharan traffic one or two works on the great desert are given below.

Gautier, E. F., *Le Sahara*, Paris, 1928.
  La Conquête du Sahara, 3rd ed., Paris, 1922.
Augiéeras, *Le Sahara occidental*, Paris, 1919.
Bovill, E. W., *Caravans of the Old Sahara*, London, 1933.

CHAPTER VII

THE NILE VALLEY

(WITH SPECIAL REFERENCE TO EGYPT)

AMONGST African lands Egypt is exceptional, not only by reason of the great antiquity and high achievements of its former civilization, but also on account of the many centuries during which its territory, great river and the life of its people have been familiar to the civilized world. According to the principles of regional geography Egypt is to be associated with the lands of similar environmental conditions in South-West Asia—especially the flood plains of the Tigris and Euphrates —which, like the Nile Valley, served as the stage for the evolution and decay of advanced civilizations in the ancient world.

In its cultural, commercial and political contacts of days prior to the late nineteenth century Egypt represented an Asiatic rather than an African territory.[1] Its restricted relations with the remainder of the African continent have been due to its position as a river-land inset within a vast, encircling desert, and detached from the civilizations of the Sudan, except where the fertile riparian strip of the Nile leads to the Negro domain. The Asiatic orientation of Egypt is an instance where the popularly-accepted division of the world into continents should not be allowed to obscure the natural association of the constituent parts of a major region, whose limits surmount conventional boundaries.

The Nile whose length, measured from a source near Lake Tanganyika, is estimated as 4060 miles was easily the greatest river of the world known to the ancients. To the early Egyptians its vast volume, flowing northwards through the rainless desert, was an unsolved mystery, and to the Greeks also, though it is true that the latter propounded a variety of theories concerning the origins of the mighty stream. In the words of Diodorus (i. 36) who travelled in Egypt between 60 and 57 B.C.—' The rising of the Nile is a phenomenon which astounds those who see it and appears quite incredible to those who hear of it. For,

[1] As recently as 1914 Egypt was a vassal state of the Turkish Empire.

418

whereas other rivers shrink about the summer solstice and grow smaller and smaller from that point onwards, the Nile alone begins to swell, and its waters rise day by day until in the end they overflow almost the whole of Egypt '. The salient features of its régime were not known until late in the nineteenth century, and were then described by E. Lombardini in his *Essai sur l'hydrologie du Nil*. Not before the beginning of the present century, however, was it learned that the autumn floods of Egypt are due almost entirely to the contribution of the Blue Nile : down to that time the highest levels were believed to be due as much to the White Nile as to the afore-mentioned river, whose source is on the Abyssinian Plateau.

PHYSICAL CHARACTER OF THE NILE VALLEY

If a longitudinal section of the main valley be taken from the foot of the Equatorial Plateau to the Mediterranean coast, three reaches, distinct in their respective gradients, are apparent. The first, about 900 miles in length, extends from Bor, below Mongalla, to beyond Khartoum, and a very low gradient nowhere exceeding 1 : 19,000 is maintained throughout, rapids being absent. Then from the Shabluka gorge, about 50 miles below Khartoum, as far as the First Cataract (immediately above Aswan) there is a stretch of nearly 1200 miles, where the bed is alternately, (*a*) of low gradient, usually with sandstone as the surface rock, and (*b*) of comparatively abrupt, broken descent over outcropping crystalline rocks that provide the famous five ' cataracts ', or series of rapids.[1] Below Aswan, the third reach is, like the first, of low uninterrupted gradient, approximately 1 : 14,000, over a distance of about 700 miles.

The Nile enters Egypt a little to the north of the Second Cataract, which is above Wadi Halfa, and for about 250 miles— save at Aswan where resistant igneous and metamorphic rocks appear in the rapids of the First Cataract—flows over sandstone in a narrow valley, on the average less than 2 miles across.[2] Northwards again, for about 500 miles, the valley is a level-floored groove, averaging 10–14 miles in width, in a limestone plateau, and is enclosed by scarps rising in places to 1500 feet above the river level. From Nag Hammadi to Cairo, the width of cultivated land is about 10 miles, outside of which there is a border of unfarmed land, sandy or stony in character. It is very noticeable on a fairly large-scaled map that for the last 200 miles of its course,

---

[1] The aggregate drop in the river-bed over this section of 1200 miles is about 800 feet.

[2] At one point the valley is only about 220 yards wide.

before Cairo is reached, the Nile shows a strong tendency to hug the eastern edge of the valley-floor, so that much the greater part of the cultivated land is to the west (i.e. on the left bank) of the river.

The walls of the plateau that define the Nile valley become lower in altitude in a down-stream direction ; and below Cairo, which is at the head of the alluvial plain of Lower Egypt,[1] they are so low and ill-defined as to be almost imperceptible, and diverge from each other, leaving in between a triangular lowland

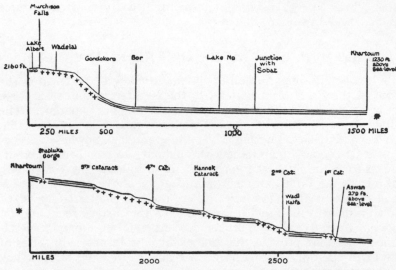

FIG. 89.—Longitudinal Section of the Nile Valley from Lake Albert to Aswan
(N.B.—Crystalline rocks at surface shown by crosses. Sandstone at surface shown by parallel lines. Distances, in miles, reckoned from Ripon Falls. Height greatly exaggerated.)

that is entirely deltaic. The term ' delta ', one of the oldest in the vocabulary of the geographer, appears in Herodotus (ii. 15) and is explained by Diodorus as the triangle, formed between the outermost distributaries of the Nile, that resembles the Greek letter.

Away from the immediate neighbourhood of the Nile valley there are comparatively few strong contrasts in relief throughout, not only Egypt, but the country of the Sudan also. Gently-sloping plains, averaging 600–1800 feet above sea-level, are characteristic. The region most exceptional in its structure and surface

---

[1] The traditional as well as the geographical division between Lower and Upper Egypt—' the Two lands ' of the early Egyptians—occurs at the apex of the Delta.

form is in the extreme east where highly resistant crystalline rocks (gneiss, granite, &c.) and metamorphosed sediments (slate and schist) rise to over 5000 feet and represent a northerly extension of the ancient plateau of Abyssinia. These eastern highlands of Egypt and the Sudan have been much affected by folding and fracturing, as well as by age-long erosive action, as witness the deep and widespread dissection of their. surface. Elsewhere the continental core is not widely exposed, but is generally overlaid by limestone or sandstone, which sediments are of either Cretaceous or early Tertiary origin. Other districts in which the crystalline basis is exposed include part of the Gezira— the tract between the lower White and lower Blue Niles—and large areas in the province of Kordofan.

From Khartoum northwards to the Egypt-Sudan frontier widely-developed horizontal beds of sandstone have weathered into flat or slightly undulating plains, relieved by flat-topped tabular hills. Northwards across Egypt the sedimentary rocks are of successively younger strata, a consequence of their dip being more abrupt than the decline of the surface of the country towards the Mediterranean. Within the Mediterranean fringe of Egypt, but outside the Delta, the altitude is low—less than 600 feet from sea-level—and much of this northern plain is composed of easily-weathered Miocene limestone.

The alluvium of the outer part of the Nile Delta is increasing only at a very slow rate, owing to the river depositing much the greater part of its load of silt before approaching the sea-board— a condition of things to which the artificial control of the river, especially marked in recent years, has contributed. It is conceivable that at a not-too-distant date, as a result of ever-increasing demands for water on the part of expanding agriculture, there will not be, even during time of flood, any discharge from the Nile into the Mediterranean. As it is, during the low season of the Nile none of its water is permitted to run to waste into the sea.

The Delta is a monotonous plain with its greatest width— 155 miles—between Alexandria and Port Said, and extends 100 miles from north to south. Its alluvium, including the débris of Abyssinian basalt and the most fertile soil in Africa, varies in depth from 50 to 75 feet. Towards the seaward border there is a considerable amount of salt-marsh and a number of extensive lagoons, one of the latter—Lake Menzala—bounded on the east by the Suez Canal, having an area of nearly 800 sq. miles. The reclamation of this water-logged part of the Delta will ultimately be undertaken by pumping operations, made necessary by the very slight elevation above sea-level.

28

THE NILE WATERS

In the earliest years of this century, when the modern phase of vast irrigation projects was initiated, the investigation and recording of the rise and fall of the Nile floods throughout the valley were undertaken with the utmost possible scientific accuracy. Nowadays, the discharges of the main stream and of its several great tributaries are regularly measured at all points critical in irrigation ; and certainly there is no river in the world of comparable size whose régime is so well known. This is not to say that our geographical and hydrographical knowledge of the Nile and its valley is now complete. To take but two instances of still deficient information : as yet very little is known of the régime of Lake Edward and of its Nile outlet, the Semliki River ; whilst owing to recent difficulties associated with reconnaissance work in Abyssinia, the same may be said of the upper Blue Nile, which provides a very large proportion of the autumn flood-waters of Egypt.

Although the late summer and autumn floods of the Blue Nile are very much more abundant than those of the White Nile [1] it is the latter that provides the most regular supply all through the year : without it there would be very little water in the lower Nile during April and May, when 85 per cent of the volume is of White Nile origin. It draws from two main sources : first, the Equatorial Plateau, where the reservoirs are Lakes Victoria, Albert and Edward ; secondly, South-Western Abyssinia, drained by the Sobat which enters the main stream more than 80 miles below the latter's junction with the Bahr-el-Ghazal. Estimates show that, on the average of the year, Abyssinia and the Great Lakes Plateau share approximately equally in their contributions to the White Nile. Yet the régimes of the Sobat and of the Bahr-el-Jebel are widely different from each other.

After the final stage in its descent from the Equatorial Plateau the Bahr-el-Jebel enters upon a course of some 400 miles, crossing the level plains of the Sudan to its junction (in Lake No) with the Bahr-el-Ghazal. From Bor (about 90 miles below Mongalla) to Khartoum—a distance of well over 800 miles—the fall in the bed of the Nile is only 135 feet. For the first half of this distance the Nile percolates through vast swamps of papyrus and reeds : here is the region of the ' Sudd ', a term that refers to drifting vegetation, torn from its place of growth and carried down-stream, to impede not only navigation but the course of

---

[1] This name, or the native ' Bahr-el-Abiad ', is strictly applied only to the river between the junction of the Bahr-el-Jebel and Bahr-el-Ghazal and the junction with the Blue Nile—a distance of over 500 miles.

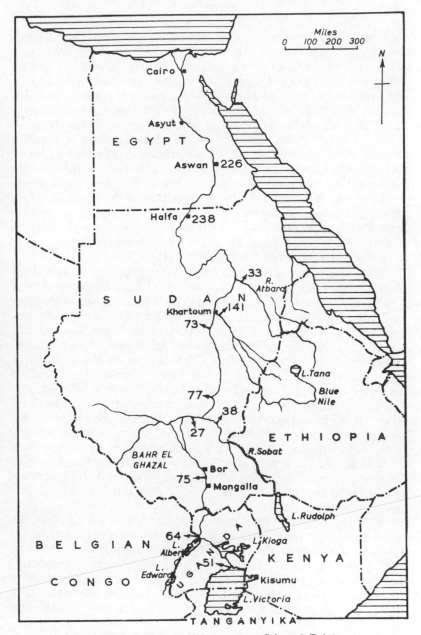

FIG. 90.—The Nile : Discharge at Selected Points

Numbers, e.g. **75,** indicate average daily discharge of water in millions of cubic metres.

423

the river itself. Since 1903, however, a navigable channel has been kept comparatively free from 'sudd'. Through spreading out over a vast area in this region the Bahr-el-Jebel loses half its volume by means of evaporation.[1] At the same time, the swamps and lagoons, by their great absorptive capacity, regulate the outflow, so that there is a relatively small variation in the discharge into the White Nile. Deepening of the channel of the Bahr-el-Jebel, to prevent the dispersal of the river through a maze of swamps and lagoons, would be an immense enterprise, but a diversionary canal, the Jonglei Cut, is planned to by-pass the main part of the Sudd and to save much loss by evaporation.

The Bahr-el-Ghazal, the most negligible of the big Nile tributaries in respect of amount of discharge, suffers to a greater extent than the Bahr-el-Jebel from dispersal through swamps and, in consequence, from excessive evaporation. Very little of its water, in fact, ever reaches the White Nile.

The proportions of Bahr-el-Jebel water supplied by the three plateau reservoirs, respectively—namely Lakes Victoria, Albert and Edward—are fairly accurately known in the cases of the first two only. The last-named is still an obscure factor in the hydrology of the equatorial Nile. Down-stream from Mongalla as far as Lake No the river receives no tributary of importance, and even as far away from the Great Lakes as Mongalla (over 300 miles from the northern end of Lake Albert) 80 per cent of the river water is derived from Lakes Victoria and Albert together.[2] On account of its low ratio of area to volume, Lake Albert is an ideal natural reservoir : moreover, its volume could be greatly increased artificially, without adding correspondingly to the area exposed to evaporation, by reason of the steepness of its shores. And it is generally held by irrigation authorities that, for the maximum development of Egypt's agricultural resources, the water of this lake must be utilized to a much greater extent than at present.

The reader will recall that the shallow Victoria Nyanza, itself occupying the centre of a wide, shallow depression in the Equatorial Plateau, is within a region of rather indecisive drainage—a circumstance largely due to the encumbering vegetation and to the swamps in the valleys of the basin. Only a small fraction of the rain that falls over the basin reaches the lake, whilst the outflow (Victoria Nile) represents only about one-

[1] The discharge into the White Nile is only 12,000–14,000 cubic feet per second compared with 21,000–28,000 cubic feet at low water at Gondokoro near the Uganda frontier.
[2] It is to be remembered that the Victoria Nyanza supplies more than half the water that drains into Lake Albert.

quarter of the rain that falls directly upon the surface of Victoria Nyanza. So that as a feeder of the Sudan Nile the widest African lake is greatly restricted in its usefulness, taking into account its magnitude and the abundant precipitation over its basin.

Annual flooding of the Sobat, to which is due much the greater part of the variation in level of the White Nile, is a consequence of the Abyssinian summer monsoon. In its lower and middle courses, especially down-stream from the junction of its principal affluents, the Baro and Pibor, the Sobat crosses plains where its inundations are widespread. Slow percolation of the flood waters through the lagoons and swamps of the inundated zone delays for as much as three months the occurrence of high level at the outlet to the White Nile. The rains that swell the Sobat commence over its upper valley in April, and fade away in October : yet, in the lower reaches of the river, the greatest volume is delayed until November–December, after which the fall of level is rapid. Up-stream to Lake No, and even farther, the Sobat floods pond up the White Nile, and this temporary damming of the main stream is an important contributory cause of the formation of 'sudd'.

Of the three great Abyssinian affluents of the Nile the Bahr-el-Azrak (Blue Nile) is easily of first importance. Unfortunately for Egypt and the Sudan, practically the entire catchment area of this great river is in Ethiopia, where British and Egyptian approaches, for the purpose of water-control, have not been welcome, and where no sympathetic interest in the irrigation of Egypt can be expected. The need for a vast reservoir on the upper Blue Nile is urgent, and for it an enlarged Lake Tana—the source of the river at an altitude of 5800 feet—seems the obvious choice. In its régime the Blue Nile somewhat resembles the Sobat, the main distinction being the more rapid passage of its flood waters into the main stream. River level begins to rise in June, and at Khartoum the maximum is reached about the first week in September, a period when the Abyssinian river is bearing fifteen times the volume of water in the White Nile. Further resembling the Sobat, the Blue Nile, when in flood, ponds up the White Nile— in this case for about 280 miles above Khartoum.[1] In August and September much the greater part of the water from which Egypt benefits is of Blue Nile origin, for then the lower White Nile is virtually a lake which, until the subsidence of the Blue Nile torrent, is obstructed in its outflow. One other factor of special note concerning the floods of the Blue Nile is the vast amount of silt carried down from the Abyssinian Plateau and

[1] Above Khartoum for about 500 miles the gradient of the bed of the White Nile is only 0·6 inch per mile.

deposited in the narrow trench of the Nile : it has been the great fertilizing agency in the agriculture of Egypt for thousands of years.

During the autumn floods the maximum volume of the Nile is measured immediately below the confluence of the main stream and the Atbara, i.e. about 1700 miles from the Mediterranean coast. The Atbara's torrential flow, like that of the Blue Nile, is limited to summer and early autumn, and a chain of pools replaces the stream during the low season. Farther towards the sea, without further addition to its volume, the Nile is progressively reduced by means of evaporation, seepage and the demands of irrigation. The small winter rainfall of the Mediterranean fringe is either absorbed by the soil or evaporated, and none of it affects the Nile volume.

One of the most critical periods in the Egyptian year is early January, when the Blue Nile has practically exhausted its contribution. At this time, however, the Sobat is still furnishing a considerable supply—for reasons mentioned earlier—while the two natural but very temporary reservoirs of the White Nile, above the confluences of, respectively, the Blue Nile and Sobat with the main stream, are now draining away to extend the period of flood in the lower Nile valley. By the end of January the temporary lakes of the White Nile have disappeared, whilst the Abyssinian supplies from all three great tributaries are of little account ; and, from this time until June, Egypt has depended mainly—before the very modern practice of water-storage—upon the comparatively regular volume brought by the Bahr-el-Jebel from the Great Lakes Plateau.

The Owen Falls Dam at Jinja in Uganda, opened by H.M. the Queen on 29th April, 1954, is founded on a rocky spur which, in the lowest section of the Owen Falls, constricts the Victoria Nile into a channel only 500 feet wide. The dam is 2500 feet long and carries a main road, will cause the Owen and Ripon Falls to disappear, though the Jinja–Kampala rail bridge which crosses the river between them will remain above water-level.

Though the main purpose of the dam is to generate hydro-electric power for Uganda, it has been constructed, at the request and cost of the Egyptian Government, one metre higher than was necessary for hydro-electric purposes, in order to help control the irrigation waters of the Nile.

With the intention of further conserving irrigation water, it is proposed to construct a regulator at Atura, between Jinja and Mutir, which will prevent the loss of water by evaporation in Lake Kioga.

Lower down the Nile valley a dam will be built at Mutir, below Lake Albert, to provide a balancing reservoir. In the

Sudd region of the Sudan, where half the volume of the White Nile is lost by evaporation and the transpiration of plants, it is proposed to cut a diversionary canal near Jonglei, to carry the storage water without so much loss in flow.

Egypt's construction of the High Dam at Aswan, and the building in the Sudan of a storage dam at Roseires on the Blue Nile, have made necessary a revision of the agreement of 1929 on the division of the Nile waters. From 1966 the Roseires Dam will supply the Sudan with more than her present due of water (one-twelfth that of Egypt), while the Aswan High Dam will flood the Nile valley 100 miles into the Sudan, and dispossess 50,000 Sudanese in the region of Wadi Halfa.

In November, 1959, the Sudan and Egypt agreed to share the Nile discharge in the proportion of 1 : 3; and the Sudan agreed, with financial help from Egypt, to resettle the population from the area of the Aswan Lake in the plains of the Atbara, irrigated from a new dam at Kheshon el Girba.[1]

IRRIGATION IN EGYPT

The use of irrigation as an aid to cultivation began almost certainly in Egypt, where there is clear evidence that prior to 2000 B.C. the inhabitants were accustomed to baling water from the river on to their farmed plots. The ' shaduf ', a simple contrivance for lifting water by bucket, has been employed from very early times down to the present day, and other devices for raising water from river or canal to the land that have been long in use are the ' sakia ' and the ' Archimedean screw '.

Canal construction for widespread irrigation during time of flood is also a practice of long standing in Egypt, where it is associated with the system of ' basin ' irrigation—as distinct from perennial irrigation, a very much more recent innovation. According to this old method, a canal, leading from the river and filled only during floods, serves a series of plots, each surrounded by embankments and known as a ' basin '. Some of the ' basins ' are large units, as much as 50,000 acres each. When the land has been saturated for several weeks and the river level has fallen

[1] The ' Lake Victoria Project ' and its implications are described by E. B. Worthington in an article on ' Geography and the development of East Africa ', in the Geographical Journal, Vol. CXVI (1950), pp. 29-48. Further information is given by J. W. Wright in ' The White Nile Flood Plain, and the effect of the proposed control scheme ' (Geog. Journ., Vol. CXIV (1949), pp. 173-90). Basic information is to be found in The Nile Basin, by Hurst, H. E., Phillips, P., and Black, R. P. (7 vols., Cairo, 1931-46). H. E. Hurst gives a general account in The Nile (London, 1952). For the Aswan project, see H. Addison, Sun and Shadow at Aswan (London, 1959).

sufficiently after flood, the water—usually 3 to 5 feet deep—in
the basin is drained away, and the sowing of crops begins on the
soil that is renewed by the annual silt deposit. Parts of Upper
Egypt are still irrigated in this way, but the High Dam will permit
perennial watering here. The system is suited to the cultivation
of cereals and green crops that grow during the period from
November to April, but for cotton that is planted in March and
picked in September ' basin ' irrigation is obviously useless.

The perennial system in Egypt depends on two principles of
water utilization : one, the artificial damming of the Nile during
flood, in order to permit the filling of high-level canals; the
other, the storage of water in reservoirs for use during the low
Nile, making possible two and, more rarely, even three crops per
annum from the same plot of land.

In the early part of the nineteenth century Mehemet Ali, the
' founder of modern Egypt ', introduced cotton cultivation into
the Nile Delta, and thereby initiated a revolution in the agricultural economy of the country. The crop requires an assured
water supply just when the Nile is at its lowest, from April to
June, and the Egyptian ruler was advised to deepen the canals
of Lower Egypt to enable them to carry water at this time. But
the work proved to be a fruitless undertaking, for the channels
filled with silt at the first subsequent flood, so that re-excavation
had to be repeated year by year.

A partial solution of the problem facing cotton cultivation,
and the first big step to perennial irrigation, came much later,
in 1861, with the completion of a series of weirs across the apex
of the Delta, about 12 miles north of Cairo. This undertaking
had the desired effect of raising the level of the water up-
stream, and thereby enabled the filling of irrigation canals for a
considerable time before high flood. Subsequently, during the
early years of the British occupation, the Delta Barrage was
extended and improved, and in 1901 another weir was ready at
Zifta, which is nearly halfway along the Damietta branch of the
deltaic Nile.

One year later, perennial irrigation was introduced to Upper
Egypt by the completion of a barrage, half a mile long, at Assiut
(over 200 miles up-stream from Cairo), the purpose being to raise
the level, so that a previously-built canal might carry water during
the summer months as well as during the autumn floods. The
great success of the Assiut scheme was an encouragement to
similar construction elsewhere in Upper Egypt, notably at Esna
(or Isna) where a barrage was completed in 1909. Like its Assiut
model it irrigates a large neighbouring district—in this case
much of the Kena (Qena) Province—even during an autumn of
low flood, and also makes possible the watering of land in summer

before the arrival of the flood. Most recent of all but essentially of the same order is the barrage at Nag Hammadi (about 159 miles above Assiut), which was completed in 1930 and assures the irrigation of Sohag Province, regardless of low floods. So that to-day Egypt is independent of variations in Nile volume, year by year, and, even during a low year, water is carried to all the cultivated land : though, for the irrigation of still unreclaimed but potentially useful soil in the northern parts of the Nile Delta, there is need for more water than is supplied to Egypt in summer.

The demands which an increasing population in Egypt will make upon Nile water that is at present running to waste in the Sudan and Abyssinia are likely to conflict with local interests. Every new barrage affects the régime of the river farther downstream, and since the introduction of modern irrigation into the Sudan the Egyptian Government has expressed its anxiety lest any project on the middle Nile should interfere with the vital supplies farther down-stream. There is no region in Africa where geography suggests more clearly than in the Nile Basin the need for economic and political co-operation between States.

Water shortage during the late spring and early summer raised a very serious problem in every year between 1890 and 1902, and yet during this period there was no reservoir for storing flood water and distributing supplies throughout the low season. One of the practical difficulties of conserving Nile flood water arises from the abundance of silt in suspension, much of which would be deposited in a reservoir and likely to render it useless after a number of years. On investigation, however, it was discovered that by the second or third week of November the river is comparatively free from silt, and this time was considered possible for filling the projected reservoir, without depriving agriculture of its immediate requirements. As designed, the dam was to be provided with sluices large enough, when open, to discharge the entire volume of the river at maximum flood.

For the dam of the reservoir the site selected was at the head of the First Cataract, above Aswan. Here a dyke of very resistant igneous rock traverses the valley and was used as the foundation for the masonry. The original structure, completed in 1903 at a cost of three millions sterling, was later—between 1907 and 1912—raised in height by 23 feet, and its capacity was increased in 1933 to 176,500 million cubic feet. The completed Aswan High Dam will be still bigger.

In late November, when the Nile level is falling and Egypt is well supplied, the sluice gates of the Aswan Dam are partially closed, and the valley up-stream is gradually filled. Three or four months later, when there is insufficient water in the Nile

for irrigation, the stored supplies are released and distributed
with the utmost economy ; for it is upon them that the cotton
crop depends.

In the country of the Sudan large-scale irrigation really
began with the completion of the combined dam and barrage
near Sennar, on the Blue Nile, in 1925. One of the largest
areas of the Sudan, within reach of irrigation from the Nile, is
the Gezira, a tract that has a frontage of about 200 miles both
on the White and on the Blue Nile, and is enclosed by these two
streams. Its area is estimated as approximately five million
acres, and about three millions are capable of cultivation with
the aid of Nile water. Quite close to Khartoum there is a
considerable amount of land within the Gezira incapable of
utilization, by reason of its sandy nature.

Although the latitude is low—the greater part of the Gezira
is south of lat. 15° N.—and the region lies outside the desert,
its rainfall is meagre and very uncertain, so that famines were
frequent until the building of the Sennar Dam. At Sennar the
average rainfall—for the last thirty years—is about 17 inches,
but this station lies towards the south of the Gezira and has a
much greater precipitation than more northerly places, e.g. El
Dueim (13° 59′ N.) with 10·6 inches and Geteima (14° 49′ N.)
with 7·2 inches. At Khartoum, on the very edge of the desert
and at the apex of the Gezira, the rainfall is only 5·7 inches.

One of the main objects of the irrigation of the Gezira is the
cultivation of cotton on a very large scale, although on a four-
year rotation only a fraction of the irrigated land will be under
cotton, in any one year. The terrific heat of summer proved too
exacting, and it was decided to experiment with a mid-July sowing,
the crop to be picked during the following spring. The results
were highly successful and, on the average, 400 lb. per acre—the
normal output in Egypt—were picked. Apart from the climatic
advantage of a winter growing season the Gezira crop is produced
when there is an abundance of water, especially in the Blue Nile.

But where Blue Nile water is concerned the Gezira cannot live
to itself alone. The needs of Egypt at the time when the Sudan
cotton is receiving its last waterings have had to be taken into
account. Usually the Gezira cotton has received its last supply
by April 1, but before this date—indeed between January and
March—Egypt, though drawing on the Aswan Reservoir, requires
in a low year all that the Blue Nile can provide. It was necessary, therefore, to build for the Gezira a reservoir in which to store
flood water against the critical period of January to March, when
the prior claim of Egypt on the Blue Nile has to be recognized.

The site selected for the construction of the dam was at a
point 5 miles above Sennar—actually at Makwar—where a narrow
band of highly-resistant rock crosses the valley. Serving the
reservoir is a newly-constructed canal-system, including a main

channel that extends for 36 miles, before branching into sub-sidiary canals.

Following those at Aswan and Sennar, a third reservoir was completed in 1937 at Gebel Aulia on the White Nile. Two further ' annual storage ' works are planned in the Sudan, one near Meroe, the Fourth Cataract Dam, designed primarily for flood control, and the other at El Roseires on the Blue Nile, near the Ethiopian border.

More ambitious are the plans for ' over-year storage ' or ' century-storage ' dams which will enable Nile water in abundant years to be saved for lean years. The vast reservoirs required must be closely associated—if not identical—with one or other of the Great Lakes, and the first of these has been impounded just below Victoria Nyanza by the dam across the Victoria Nile at Owen Falls near Jinja, which was opened in April, 1954. Unfortunately, the capacity of the White Nile to carry the stored water of Victoria will be limited by the swamps of the Sudd below Mongalla : so great is the loss of water here from evaporation and other causes that out of every 100 cubic feet which pass Mongalla only 62 reach Aswan. A White Nile canal to by-pass the Sudd is therefore proposed. Other dams are planned to impound and store the waters of Lake Albert and of Lake Tana.

COMMERCIAL AGRICULTURE IN EGYPT

Concentration almost entirely upon one crop for market—namely good-quality cotton—has persisted in Egypt since the middle of last century, when the American Civil War had the effect of greatly improving the country's prospects in the Lanca-shire market. Cotton requires for its favourable growth from six to seven months of sunny weather without frost, relieved by short showers of rain, and terminating in a dry period which checks vegetative growth when the boll is reaching maturity. In Egypt, where a sufficiently long frost-free and sunny period is assured, the weather is not a factor that causes anxiety and as, even in Lower Egypt, practically all moisture is derived from the Nile, the watering of the crop can be regulated with precision. From a survey of the most important cotton lands of the world it is apparent that, given a favourable climate, the plant will grow on a variety of soils ranging from light sandy types to fairly heavy clay. The Nile Delta soils, from which the greater part of the Egyptian crop is gathered, are in two groups—(a) sandy, known as ' safra ', and (b) black clays. The latter give the better yields, both of quality and quantity. On the heavy clay admixture of sand is beneficial, and this occurs naturally in Upper Egypt where, however, on the whole sandy soils pre-dominate.

Of a total cropped area (in 1960) of approximately 10·37

million feddans,[1] the proportion under cotton cultivation was 18 per cent. So extensive is now the range of perennial irrigation that it serves about 80 per cent of the agricultural land of Egypt. It was mentioned earlier that two, and sometimes three, crops per annum are harvested on the perennially-irrigated soil. Normally the agricultural year is divided into three seasons—winter, summer and ' Nili ', which is the period when the Nile overflows its banks. Clover, or wheat, or beans is the usual choice for the winter crop, whilst in summer cotton is all but universal. On good Delta soils a three-year rotation is common, and careful landowners insist that it be followed. His three staples—cotton, wheat and clover (useful as fodder and also in supplying the nitrogen that is deficient in the soil)—make the Egyptian farmer virtually self-supporting.

Mehemet Ali was responsible for introducing a number of varieties of cotton into Egypt. In time, hybrid types developed, and from these the Ashmouni plant, as it is known, was isolated to become, and long remain, the standard crop of the country. As indicated by its name, it was discovered at Ashmoun, in the Delta : this was in 1860, and from then onwards it spread throughout the Delta, eventually penetrating Upper Egypt also. Until 1882 Ashmouni, or ' Old Brown Egyptian ' as it is sometimes known, offered the best quality of any variety grown in Africa, but in that year a new type appeared, namely Mitafifi, which quickly displaced Ashmouni in the Delta. The older variety continued to prove, however, the more satisfactory under the conditions of greater heat and aridity in Upper Egypt. In 1921 Ashmouni was grown on more than 80 per cent of the cotton land of Upper Egypt, on 58 per cent of that of Middle Egypt (the valley between Assiut and Cairo) and on about 13 per cent of that of the Delta. It remains after the fluctuations of 80 years one of the most important of the standard cottons of Egypt, though in length of staple it is excelled by many newer varieties.

Mitafifi, a variety discovered in a field of an Ashmouni crop, was cultivated on a commercial scale from 1887 onwards. Its advantages over Ashmouni include a longer lint—$1\frac{1}{2}$ inches, as against $1\frac{1}{4}$ in the case of the older type—as well as a finer and softer quality. So rapidly did it jump into favour with Lancashire spinners that in the early years of this century it constituted much more than half the Egyptian crop, and in 1906 as much as 77 per cent ; but after 1910 it declined in favour, and was largely replaced by a new-comer, the renowned Sakellarides variety. The latter—usually abbreviated to ' Sakel '—was the standard high-

[1] The feddan may be considered equivalent to an acre, the actual figure being 1·04 acre.

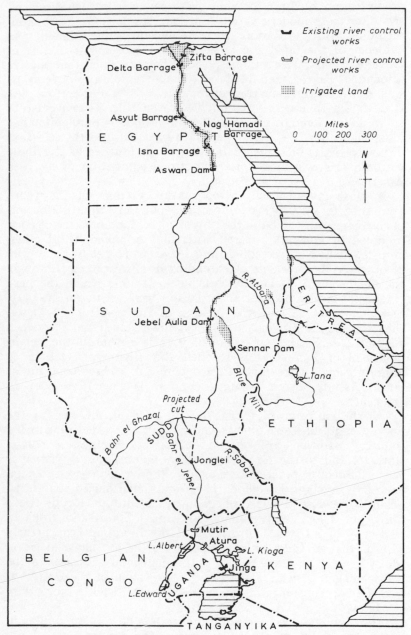

FIG. 91.—River Control Works on the Nile

grade Egyptian cotton for some years, but was in turn displaced by other more modern varieties of long staple (over 1⅜ inches), including Giza 7, Karnak and the incomparable Malaki. As evidence of the rapid rise to favour and subsequent decline of particular long-staple varieties, it may be mentioned that shortly after 1920 ' Sakel ', then the standard long-staple Egyptian cotton, was grown on three-quarters of the total area under cotton. At that time a zone across the middle of the Nile Delta from east to west was foremost in ' Sakel ' cultivation. Complaints that its splendid qualities were deteriorating encouraged the selection of new varieties including Malaki, which is regarded as the finest cotton ever grown in Egypt and a strong competitor of the best American ' Sea Islands ' cotton.

A close investigation, based on an average of the years from 1922 to 1925 inclusive, indicates not only the distribution of cotton-growing, but also the proportion of land in every district occupied by cotton, compared with that occupied by all other crops combined. Proceeding from Lower to Upper Egypt, it will be observed that a wide zone extending from west to east through the north-centre of the Delta includes districts where the percentage of cultivated land under cotton varies between the very high figures of 44 and 52. Nearer to the apex of the Delta, the corresponding figures are much lower, and range between 18 and 40. Farther up the valley it is not until the neighbourhood of Beni Suef is reached that there is a return to uniformly high percentages (from 30 to 40). These continue as far as Assiut, beyond which the figure is generally under 10 per cent.

As the entire crop is irrigated by Government, and as the Survey and Tax Departments know every cultivated plot in the country, conditions are very favourable to exactness in cotton statistics and to the forecasting of the harvest for a particular year. Moreover, practically the entire production passes through one port—Alexandria—which is an additional aid to the statistician. Amongst the leading countries of output Egypt ranks third, but a long way behind the United States and India in respect of quantity. The quality of the Egyptian crop greatly exceeds that of India and is superior to the average American, whilst it must be remembered that, whereas in the cases of the two leading producers a very large proportion of the output is retained for consumption at home, Egypt disposes abroad of nearly two-thirds of its production.

Although modern agricultural technique is spreading in Egypt, especially on the large estates, the greater part of the cultivation is in the hands of the fellahin, the majority of whom are comparatively primitive farmers. After the clover or wheat has been gathered in February, ploughing, preparatory to the sowing of cotton, takes place. The plough of traditional usage consists of a wooden pole, pointed with metal and drawn by yoked oxen. As a result of ploughing, ridges are formed, about 30 inches apart from each other, and on these the seed is sown, usually in March. During June, July and August the crop is watered about once a fortnight. Each watering requires approximately 350 tons of water per feddan, and as, during the growth of the plant, nine or ten are given, the amount supplied per feddan aggregates over 3000 tons, which is reckoned as the equivalent of 30 inches of rainfall.

In 1910 a commission was appointed to investigate the causes of deterioration in the quality of the cotton crop. It stated that they included over-cropping and the substitution of a two-year for a three-year rotation, insect pests and water-logged soil. A further reason may be added, namely the inadequate use of artificial fertilizers. In addition to deterioration in quality, there has been—for similar reasons—a decline in the yield per feddan : the highest yield was 5·8 kantars in 1897 and by 1921 the output had fallen off to 3·4 kantars.

LAND TENURE AND POPULATION DISTRIBUTION

The extent to which modern Egypt is a country of small land-owning agriculturists is due in great measure to Mehemet Ali, the early nineteenth-century ruler who, claiming that to the State belonged all land, proceeded to allocate to every adult peasant from 3 to 4 feddans, secured to him by title-deed for life. To-day, however, a very large proportion of cultivated Egypt remains outside the ownership of small-holders, as will be seen from figures supplied later. Between 1896 and 1926 the average size of holdings decreased from 6½ to under 3 feddans, a development due in part to the Islamic law that determines the equal division of inherited property.

At the close of 1945 more than 70 per cent of the landowners (about 1,850,000 persons, representing nearly as many families) possessed plots of 1 feddan or less ; whilst the proportion with holdings of less than 50 feddans was over 99 per cent. Of the total area of cultivated land (5,882,000 feddans) about 2,400,000 feddans were in units of more than 50 feddans; moreover, this very large proportion—nearly 40 per cent—was the property of 12,000 persons, or much less than 1 per cent of the total land-owning class. An average of 200 feddans per landlord covering two-fifths of the cultivated land of Egypt should be

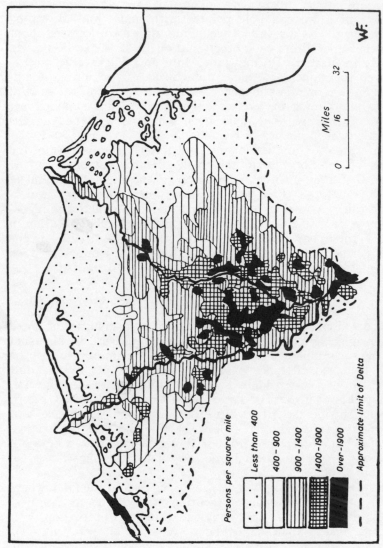

Persons per square mile

Less than 400
400 – 900
900 – 1400
1400 – 1900
Over – 1900

Approximate limit of Delta

Miles
0   16   32

W.F.

FIG. 92.—Density of Population in the Nile Delta

borne in mind to qualify the impression that Egypt is a land of very small cultivators. The table, simplified from more elaborate data, that is included below may be of service as a statistical indication of the position.[1] Not all the fellahin are small-holders : many are labourers in receipt of a daily wage : others receive from the landlord right to cultivate a small piece of land, usually from 1 to 3 feddans. One of the consequences of the phenomenal rise in land values since the introduction of perennial irrigation has been the leasing of land by many large landlords, who find this to be more profitable than undertaking cultivation for themselves. It should be remembered, when studying the land-tenure of cultivated Egypt, that of the total area of the country, viz. 383,000 sq. miles, all but 13,600 are desert and may be left out of account. This occupied area is approximately equal to the area of Belgium, which, though the most crowded country of Europe, has less than one-half the population of Egypt.

The pressure of population on the land may be realized when the following facts are presented : first, in the last century, the population has increased five-fold—from about 4½ millions in 1846 to 25 millions in 1958 ; secondly, the average density on the cultivated territory is now considerably in excess of 1000 to the square mile ; thirdly, the only hope of increasing the cultivable area significantly is by means of new large irrigation works such as the Aswan High Dam.

In Upper Egypt the general distribution of density is briefly as follows. Above Cairo as far as Beni Suef the valley belt of cultivated land averages about 6 miles in width, and there the density, nowhere under 750, generally exceeds 1000 per square mile. From Beni Suef to Assiut the edges of the desert, bordering the valley on either side, are separated by some 10 miles throughout, and within these limits the average approaches 1000 per square mile, whilst close to the Nile—which keeps to the eastern side of the

[1]

Extent of Individual Holdings in Feddans	Foreigners		Egyptians		Total of Landowners	
	Area in Feddans	Land-owners	Area in Feddans	Land-owners	Number	Per-centage
1 or less . .	662	1528	753,000	1,843,000	1,844,212	70·8
From 1 to 5 .	2,206	883	1,214,000	602,000	602,741	23·1
From 5 to 50	25,064	1433	1,749,000	145,574	147,007	5·6
Over 50 . .	354,000	746	1,784,000	11,200	11,960	0·5
Total . . .	381,932	4590	5,500,000	2,601,774	2,605,920	100·0

29

valley—much of the territory carries a density of over 1500. Above Luxor, as far as Aswan, the sedentary population is limited to a valley strip with a mean width not exceeding 3 miles, though similar high densities are maintained. Above the great reservoir, as far as the Sudan frontier, the groove of cultivated land is of even narrower dimensions. The density of population in the Faiyum oasis which lies close to the Nile valley (in the neighbourhood of Beni Suef) will be considered later.

In the Delta the salient features of the population map— leaving the towns out of account for the time being—are

(a) the very high densities, averaging 1200–1500 per square mile, throughout the territory lying between the upper reaches of the Damietta and Rosetta branches of the Nile ;

(b) the narrow belts of high density that follow the two chief distributaries almost to the Mediterranean sea- board ;

(c) the comparatively low densities within two extensive outer tracts where marsh and lagoon are widespread : the first, and larger, of the two stretching for some 70 miles between Rosetta and Damietta ; the second in the north-east of the Delta, between the Damietta branch of the Nile and the Suez Canal.

THE CITIES OF EGYPT

The distribution of towns indicates the overwhelming import- ance of the Delta in Egyptian urban life. Of the major of Egypt's cities only one, namely Assiut, is situated in Upper Egypt though Aswan is growing rapidly and in 1965 exceeded 60,000. The other large towns—with the exceptions of the Faiyum Oasis and the two Suez Canal terminal ports of Port Said and Suez—are within either the lower Nile Valley or the Delta. Cairo, easily most populous city of Egypt, grew greatly in numbers after the First World War ; and especially since 1937 (from 1,312,000 to 3,346,000 in 1960). Alexandria has grown substan- tially although less dramatically, and in 1960 held 1,513,000. In view of the urgent need for all available cultivable land the towns must not extend territorially more than is absolutely necessary ; and hence, almost without exception, they are cramped and congested. The mass of the Egyptian population remains rural, and despite recent progress in industrialization, is likely to remain so.

Monuments of the illustrious antiquity of Egypt include the ruins of cities long derelict, as well as vestiges of early occupation, in the cases of a number of towns that have retained or increased their importance with the passage of time. Three ancient cities, now in complete ruin, were Memphis, the Pharaonic capital, situated on the left bank of the Nile about 14 miles above Cairo ; Heliopolis, some 5 miles to the north of Cairo ; and Thebes in Upper Egypt, close to, and succeeded by, Luxor.

Cairo, though the greatest African city judged by size of population (3,346,000 in 1960), occupies only 8 sq. miles,[1] which affords an illustration of the congestion that characterizes many Egyptian towns. It is situated on the right bank of the Nile along which the town spreads for 5 miles, northwards from an old Roman fortress. This citadel, on a spur of the Mokattam Hills, that are included within the south-eastern angle of Cairo, was occupied by one of the three legions stationed in Egypt. Before Roman occupation there was, however, a Greek settlement close by—an outer suburb, as it were, of Heliopolis. From the Mokattam Hills, rising to 550 feet above the banks of the Nile, Cairo extends on to the alluvial plain, especially in a northerly direction.

The eastern half of the city suggests an outpost of Semitic Asia, and includes the Mahomedan, the Coptic (Christian) and the Jewish quarters. Modern Cairo lies towards the west and close to the river, where are the Government offices and other public buildings, as well as the residential districts of Europeans. Very varied are the elements in the city's population : in addition to groups already indicated, there are the native Cairenes, usually tradesmen and artisans, who differ from the fellahin, in ethnic character, mainly by their larger proportion of Semitic blood ; also there are Arabs, Armenians, Syrians and other Levantine types, as well as Negroes or half-Negroes who are mostly labourers and domestic servants.

Although pre-eminent to-day amongst Egyptian cities, Cairo became the national capital only as recently as 1863. Long before that time, however, its importance in the life of the country had made inevitable, sooner or later, the grant of metropolitan status. The greatest artery of traffic must always be the one that binds together the Lower and Upper Provinces and has its most critical point where the converging routes of the Delta combine and penetrate the corridor of the Nile Valley. Another route of first-class importance, in days prior to railway construction, was a caravan track leading between the Libyan Desert

[1] Cf. Johannesburg, with 1,152,000 inhabitants and a municipal area of not less than 30 square miles, of which more than one-half may be classed as urban.

oases (e.g. Siwa), Cyrenaica and even the Barbary States, on the west, and, on the east, Palestine and North-Western Arabia. This desert highway, that passed through both Cairo and Suez was determined in its alignment, not only by the northward-extending Gulf of Suez, but also by the physical nature of the Delta, whose innumerable drainage channels, including the Nile distributaries, together with the annual flooding, provided an impassable barrier to east-west communication, forcing it southwards as far as the apex of the triangular plain.

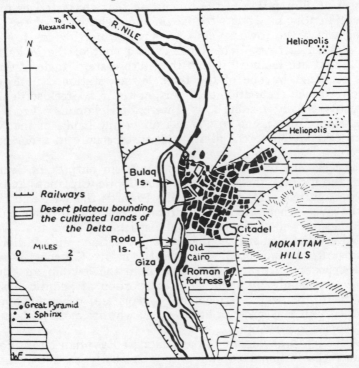

FIG. 93.—The City of Cairo

For the greater part of two thousand years Alexandria (1960, pop. 1,513,000) was the capital city of Egypt. Situated nearly 130 miles from Cairo and at the extreme westerly point of the maritime edge of the Delta, the port was founded by Alexander in 332 B.C. and by him was intended to be both a naval base for projected operations against the Persian Empire and an outlet for the agricultural wealth of the Nile Valley. The site had two obvious advantages : it was outside the range of the silt-depositing Nile, and was protected from Mediterranean storms by the Island of Pharos which, in modern times, was linked to the mainland, first by a mole and later by an isthmus of silt, half a mile wide. Pharos, now a T-shaped peninsula, provides the two harbours—eastern and western—of Alexandria, but the main part of the city is upon the narrow strip that separates Lake Mareotis from the sea.

The early commerce of Alexandria was exceedingly prosperous and included much that formerly passed through Tyre, on the Syrian coast. Indeed, the port rose to commercial pre-eminence in the Eastern Mediterranean through its development as an *entrepôt*, in a newly-grown stream of traffic, between the Levant and the Indian and Arabian coasts. In its social life it was not Egyptian but cosmopolitan : apart from being a centre of Hellenism it was for long the principal Jewish city of the ancient world.

In late medieval times the fortunes of Alexandria generally declined, whilst the building of Cairo in 969 introduced a formidable commercial competitor. The most serious threat to the port's trading supremacy came, however, in 1498, when the sea-route to India via the Cape of Good Hope was opened. From that date until the early years of the nineteenth century, when it was reduced to only 4000 inhabitants, Alexandria had only a local importance as one of the ports of Lower Egypt.

Mehemet Ali is to be credited with restoring its greatness. Alexandria had suffered much through the silting of the canal that supplied it with fresh water from the Nile. By the construction of the Mahmudiya Canal, completed in 1820, the water supply was restored and at the same time inland navigation was promoted between the port and the Rosetta branch of the Nile. Mehemet maintained a palace at Alexandria and used it especially during the summer, when the heat at the coast is less trying than at Cairo ; and to-day also it is the custom of the Egyptian court and ministers to leave the capital for Alexandria, during the period of greatest heat.

The other ports—Port Said and Suez—because of their special functions in relation to the Suez Canal—have but a small share of the commerce of Egypt. This is seen particularly well from the export returns of Egypt—not less than three-quarters passing through Alexandria.

Of the fifteen Egyptian towns, whose populations in each case exceed 50,000 inhabitants, Faiyum, or more properly Madinet-el-Faiyum, is an oasis city just within the Libyan Desert. The other large oases of Egypt—namely Siwa, Baharia, Farafra, Dakhla and Kharga—are far more distant than is Faiyum from the Nile Valley and more isolated from its life, though they were known to and occupied by the Egyptians as early as 1600 B.C.

The Faiyum oasis, about 670 sq. miles in extent, lies within a vast depression of the Libyan Desert. A gravelly ridge separates it from the Nile valley but is trenched by the channel of the Bahr Yusef, which is connected to the great river. To the north-west of the town and cultivated area, and in the deepest part of the depression, is the lake—Birket Kar Qarun—which, with a surface at present about 140 feet below Mediterranean level, is shrinking steadily. The origin of this lake is traced back to very early times, when the flow of the Nile into the Faiyum was much more free and considerable than it is to-day.

During the periods of Arab and Turkish rule the Faiyum became increasingly derelict, but revived in the later part of the nineteenth century when Egypt passed under British control. Each autumn the Nile floods enter the Bahr Yusef, from which water is conveyed through a system of canals to the cultivated lands of the oasis. Although the area farmed has extended rapidly since 1882 there is still much that has not been reclaimed from a derelict condition. In intensity of cultivation and value of agricultural output the Faiyum compares favourably with the average lands of the Delta. Density of population reaches the high figure of 850 per square mile. From 201,000 in 1882 the number of inhabitants rose, in 1947, to 672,000, of which total 72,000 were in the oasis city, Madinet-el-Faiyum.

EGYPT'S RECENT POLITICAL HISTORY

There has been, throughout the vast range of Egyptian history, a marked tendency, assisted by the geographical conditions, for the community of the lower Nile Valley to split up politically into small independent states. Political cohesion and stability are naturally difficult in a country whose inhabitants are distributed throughout a zone, generally very narrow but not less than 700 miles in extent from north to south. It is inevitable that the people of the Delta, with their Mediterranean and West Asiatic associations, should be conscious of interests in some ways different from those of the fellahin of southernmost Egypt, where the proximity of the Sudan has necessarily a dominating significance. On the other hand, approximate ethnic uniformity, a common religious faith and age-long social traditions throughout practically the entire agricultural community, are factors that, from the standpoint of the development of nationality, tend towards unification. So that, when the conception of nationality as fostered in Western Europe was introduced into Egypt towards

FIG. 94.—The Sudan : Economic Features

443

the end of last century, there were those who believed it would prove acceptable to Egyptian civilization and, in time, rouse the backward peasantry from a passive to an active rôle in Mediterranean and North African affairs.

The Suez Canal was built by French enterprise, while Britain showed not only disinterest, but even public opposition. It was opened with great ceremony in December, 1869. Although at first slow to perceive the advantages likely to accrue to herself and her Empire from the construction of the waterway, Great Britain soon gained a leading position in the finances of the Canal Company by acquiring a large block of the shares. In 1881, an insurgent, Arabi Pasha, caused riots which resulted in the death of a number of Europeans in Alexandria. In the following year, Lord Wolseley put down the rising at the battle of Tel el-kebir, and restored the constitution and nominal Turkish suzerainty. However, so weak was the ruler, and so lax the Ottoman administration, that from this time Great Britain found herself in virtual control of the country and canal.

The birth of Egyptian nationalism may be said to date from the period between the completion of the Suez Canal in 1869 and the occupation of the Nile Valley by Great Britain in 1882. At first it was rather an anti-foreign movement than one inspired by constructive political ideals : moreover, it hardly affected the fellahin at all, being confined to a section of the middle class only. After 1882 the position of Egypt as, virtually, a Protectorate of Great Britain and the despotism, however benevolent, of Lord Cromer's long rule were used as strong arguments by nationalists against British imperialism. The revolt spread to an ever-widening circle, and even brought into intermittent co-operation the Moslems and Copts. All this time, and indeed down to the outbreak of the Great War, Egypt was officially recognized in the chancelleries of Europe as being under Turkish sovereignty ; but this fiction had no significance for the actual political situation.

As an offset to the extreme nationalists' programme, Lord Cromer tried to rally Egyptian moderates to the support of the Administration. With his encouragement they formed in 1907 the ' Party of the Nation ', to which belonged one who became the most prominent figure in recent Egyptian history, Zaghlul Pasha. Although Cromer's régime is rightly credited with much that was beneficial to Egypt—including security and economic prosperity—by its neglect of popular education and by withholding facilities for training in self-government it failed to assist directly the evolution of an Egyptian nation, properly equipped for its career : and to Egyptians the British Administration, without popular sanction but backed by military force, came to be regarded as a barrier to the fulfilment of nationhood.

By the close of the Great War, during which Egypt was officially a Protectorate of Great Britain, the progress of nationalism was so considerable that the fellahin were awakened to political consciousness. At a time when the 'self-determination of small nations' was a guiding principle in the political re-shaping of shattered empires the Egyptian claims were too vociferous to be overlooked. In 1922 Great Britain terminated her Protectorate of Egypt, at the same time announcing four very important reservations : they were that Britain was to remain responsible for (1) the safety of imperial communications (referring particularly to the Suez Canal), (2) the defence of Egypt against foreign attack, (3) the protection of minorities and foreign interests in Egypt. A fourth reservation applied to the Sudan which was to remain a Condominium. Egypt became a sovereign state by the Anglo-Egyptian treaty of 1936, under which military occupation outside the Canal Zone was ended, and Britain defended the Canal and the frontiers of Egypt in the battles of 1940–42, as the treaty required. After the War, Egypt demanded the revision of the treaty, and after protracted negotiations an agreement was reached which provided for the withdrawal of British troops from the Canal Zone by June, 1956, leaving Egypt responsible for the security of the base and for its equipment, which was to be maintained by civilians. This pact was broken by Egypt's seizure of the Canal in July, 1956, since when there has been discrimination against Israeli ships and cargoes.

A convention between the British and Egyptian Governments, signed in 1899, provided for the administration of the territory of the Anglo-Egyptian Sudan by a Governor-General, appointed by Egypt, with the assent of Great Britain. The status of the territory as a Condominium was re-affirmed in 1936. For purposes of administration, the Sudan is divided into eight provinces (*mudirias*), which are further divided into Districts.

By the provisions of the Self-Government Statute of March, 1953, the Sudanese were entrusted with a gradually increasing share in the government, and on January 1st, 1956, the country was proclaimed a sovereign independent republic.

THE SUEZ CANAL AND OTHER LINES OF COMMUNICATION

However views may vary on the importance to British imperial communications of the Suez Canal, there is no doubt that, in the opinion of every British ministry of the last half-century, the waterway has been considered vital to the defence of the most critical and exposed to attack of all our sea-routes, namely the direct line to the Far East via the Mediterranean and Red Sea.

The project of a canal across the Isthmus of Suez was considered as early as the eighth century A.D., and, after the opening of the Cape route to India at the close of the fifteenth century,

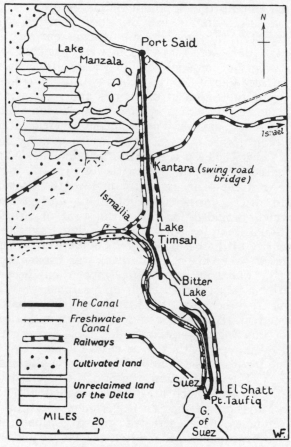

FIG. 95.—The Suez Canal

Venice indicated to Egypt the commercial value of such an undertaking. In 1854, Ferdinand de Lesseps appeared as the champion of canal construction, and proposed for it a fairly direct line from the Gulf of Suez to the Mediterranean coast, in order to utilize the depressions of the Bitter Lakes, Lakes Timsah and Menzala. By a strange irony, de Lesseps met the greatest opposition to his scheme from the British Government, although nowadays Great Britain claims that the Canal is of much greater consequence to her than to all other Powers.

As originally constructed (in 1869), the waterway had a depth of 26¼ feet, with a bottom width of 72 feet ; to-day it is 42 feet deep and 390 feet wide. As a result of the repeated enlargement of the Canal it is now possible for vessels of over 30 feet draught to pass each other throughout the greater part of its length of 100 miles, the practice being for one ship to stop while the other proceeds on her way. At present, however, the largest ships can cross other traffic in the Great Bitter Lake only. The average passage through the Canal occupies 15 hours, and, by using search-lights, vessels are able to proceed by night as well as day, which was not possible in earlier days. The growth of traffic has been enormous : from 436,000 tons of shipping in 1870 to 80 million tons in 1951 (with individual vessels of 45,000 tons).

From the outset there were certain obvious advantages in using the Canal. The voyage from Europe to India was shortened by 4000–5000 miles, according to the situation of the particular European port—those on the Mediterranean gaining more advantage than those on the western sea-board. Consequently, there was a considerable impetus to trade with India on the part of France, Italy and Austria after 1869. The Canal was also an attraction to fast Australian traffic, especially shipments of wool and meat to the London market and the movement of passengers and mails in both directions, all of which were diverted from the Cape route. To the latter remains, however, Australia-bound cargo traffic for which a quick passage is not urgently needed. In this last case the Suez Canal tolls prove too high and outweigh the advantage of a voyage 1000 miles shorter, between London and Melbourne, which the Canal provides.[1]

The opening of the Panama Canal has not greatly affected the trend of traffic between Europe and the Far East, or even between Europe and Western and South-Eastern Australia. Taking distance alone into consideration, the only regions where the Panama Canal can compete with Suez are the Pacific coast of Soviet Russia, Eastern Australia, New Zealand and the Pacific coasts of the Americas. Since the Central American Canal was

[1] As the intensity of traffic on the Canal continues to mount, the World Bank in December, 1959 approved a loan of about £20 million to the United Arab Republic to widen and deepen the passage. In addition, there is a commercial scheme for an oil pipe-line to run the length of the Canal, by which a tanker at Suez could transfer its load to another at Port Said.

opened in 1914 the net tonnage at Suez has exceeded that at Panama in every year except 1923, when to the phenomenal rise in the export of Californian petroleum was due the temporary traffic-bearing priority of the newer waterway. The preeminence of British shipping in Suez Canal traffic has been in evidence from the start, and, although in recent years the proportion of the total net tonnage that is British-owned has declined, it is still in excess of one-third.

For the commerce of Egypt itself the Canal has little significance and, in conclusion, it is necessary to refer—though very briefly—to the development of modern transport within the Nile Valley.

In Upper Egypt, the river still competes as a carrier with the railway, but in the Delta rail-transport is unchallenged by inland navigation, even though there are in Lower Egypt eight main canals that still have a small traffic. The Nile is navigable throughout its course in Egypt ; and above Shellal, very close to Aswan, it is still the only means of communication, apart from desert caravans. Before the existence of railways in the Sudan —referring particularly to the trunk lines from Khartoum to Wadi Halfa and to Port Sudan, respectively—Aswan at the head of the long navigable section of the Egyptian Nile was a place of mercantile importance, an *entrepôt* for cargoes passing between either the Central or Eastern Sudan and the Lower Nile Valley. From this town regular caravan communication was maintained, across the Nubian Desert, with Berber, on the great eastward loop of the Nile, and—along the line of the present railway— with Suakin on the Red Sea coast. As a caravan-centre Aswan was, however, subordinate in importance to Cairo which, especially before the suppression of the slave trade and the opening of the Suez Canal, had intimate and valuable trans-desert trade relations with the Central and Eastern Sudan, Tripolitania, Arabia and Syria.

By the use of sails, river-boats are able to proceed up-stream through the agency of the prevailing north and north-east winds— the Trades. On the return voyage, when sails are lowered, the vessels drift with the current. A typical native vessel is the *dahabiya*, whose build somewhat resembles the house-boat on an English river.

The main railways of Lower Egypt converge upon Cairo, from Alexandria and Port Said respectively. From the capital southwards a line is continued as far as Shellal, nearly 690 miles from Alexandria, and keeps close to the river throughout, crossing from the left to the right bank at Nag Hammadi. Between the termini of the systems of the Sudan and Egypt, respectively, there are about 160 miles—from Shellal to Wadi Halfa—which are still unprovided with a railway. Here is one of the biggest gaps in the slowly-evolving Cape-to-Cairo railway system. Important extensions or projected extensions of the Egyptian system include (a) the one built during the Great War from Kantara on the Suez Canal across Northern Sinai to connect with the main line of Palestine, (b) a railway, already started, that will connect Alexandria and Tripoli and form part of a North African system, with its western terminus at Casablanca.

The railway system of the country of the Sudan has already been mentioned indirectly. Its trunk lines extend from Wadi Halfa across the Nubian Desert to Abu Hamed and Berber, near which is the junction of the route to Suakin and Port Sudan ; and farther south, to Khartoum, where the Blue Nile is bridged, and from which there is an extension through the Gezira to Sennar. There are branches from the latter to Nyala in Kordofan and to Kassala, close to the Abyssinian frontier and a newly developed cotton-growing centre. Until 1906, when the railway to the Red Sea was opened, the external trade of the Sudan was much hindered by the heavy costs and delays involved in transit through Egypt. Port Sudan has developed a vigorous commerce, and is now a principal outlet for the staple commercial products of its hinterland, namely cotton and gum arabic.

THE SUDAN

The middle Nile valley has always been the main route by which regions further north have made contact with negro Africa. From the middle Nile, the line of migration divides and leads westwards across the savanna lands of French Sudan, or south by the East African grasslands. These highways have been followed in the past one or two thousand years by Hamitic-speaking folk of Eurafrican stock. It is to their wide spread, and influence as ruling aristocracies, that we must attribute, for example, the well-known similarities between systems of kingship, or techniques of iron-working, over the greater part of Africa south of the Sahara. These customs and techniques can often also be paralleled in ancient Egypt. Doubtless, Hellenistic states of the middle Nile, like those of Napata or Meroe, were the intermediaries.

In the last century, there was still regular contact by way of the middle Nile between the Mediterranean world and negro Africa, largely for the purpose of trading in gold, ivory, feathers, and, above all, slaves. It was in a frustrated effort to stop this vicious traffic that Baker, and later Gordon, accepted the governorship of the Equatorial Provinces of the Sudan, under Egyptian suzerainty. General Gordon's noble and tragic failure in 1885 to control the Sudanese nationalist uprising under the Mahdi led to joint Egyptian and British conquest of the territory, and proclamation in 1899 of the Condominium, a form of government which persisted until the end of 1955.

In the last half-century, the Sudan has been making a slow recovery from the devastation wrought during the brief rule of the Mahdi and Khalifa. Excluding Darfur, the population of the country before the Mahdist rule was estimated at 8,500,000. In 1905, this had fallen as low as 1,853,000. By 1961, however, the figure had risen to an estimated 12,100,000.

As the population grows, more water must be obtained for the Maragil area of the Gezira. But the first task of the Sudanese Republic is to develop its three southern provinces, which contrast abruptly with the others in both topography and culture.

The north, from about 16° of latitude, is open mimosa scrub country, an extension of the Sahara : the south is fertile, well watered, and over wide areas covered with mahogany forest or papyrus swamp. The population of the north is of Eurafrican race, Moslem, and Arabic-speaking : that of the south is predominantly negro and pagan, and speaks Sudanic tongues. Commercial agriculture, especially of irrigated cotton, is largely confined to the northern provinces : in the south, most of the people lead a semi-nomadic existence, depending on cattle or on the shifting cultivation of millet on burnt-over bush country. Finally, the inhabitants of the northern provinces are much more educated than their southern neighbours, most of whom live in self-contained tribal communities.

Especially since the inauguration of the Ten-Year Development Plan in 1961, much attention has been paid to improving the economy of the southern provinces. Attempts have been made to improve the efficiency of shifting agriculture, and to make possible the marketing of its produce, notably in the Zande area around Vambio near the Congo border. At the same time, the quality of the cattle has been improved and the construction of numerous new wells and reservoirs, along with extensions of the railway to Nyala (1959) and Wau (1962), have made markets for livestock more accessible.

The Sudan owes it present economic welfare to two enterprises : the building in 1906 of the Port Sudan railway, which short-circuited the long export route through Egypt ; and the installation of the large irrigation canals for growing long-staple cotton, principally in the Gezira, but also on the inland deltas of the Gash and Baraba. The history of the Gezira project has already been related (p. 430). The land there is worked on the basis of a partnership between the Government, the Sudan Plantations syndicate, and the Sudanese cultivators. The syndicate breaks up new land, provides villages and cultivating plant, and collects the produce. The cultivator gets the whole of the rotation food crops, 40 per cent of the value of the cotton, and free land and water. In the irrigated region of the inland delta

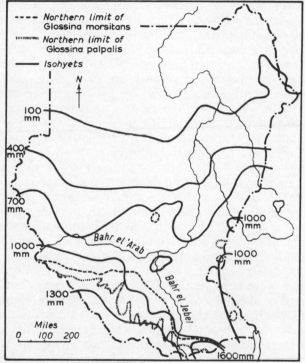

FIG. 96.—The Sudan : Average Annual Rainfall, and Range of the Tsetse Fly

of the Gash, the Kassala Cotton company operates under a similar arrangement.

As the Gezira plains have specialized so much in cotton production, the burden of growing grain for the country's increasing population has fallen more heavily on the upper Blue Nile country and the sandy plains of Kordofan. In these regions, experiments have been made in improving the traditional system of burning off carefully husbanded grass prior to cultivation, and some mechanized farming has been started near Gedaref.

Further south, some American cotton is grown as a rain-crop, especially in the Nuba mountains, but agriculture is still generally primitive. A research experimental station at Kagelu in Equatoria has, however, already done much to introduce pest-resisting crops. All the Equatoria Province, especially up the Bahr-el-Ghazal, which is only passable in some seasons after laborious cutting of the Sudd, is likely for long to remain economically remote. The most enlightened and immediate way of improving the conditions of life here is to diminish the harm done to man and beast by the tsetse fly.

There are two main species of this fly which cause sleeping-sickness, *Glossina palpalis*, which attacks humans, and *Glossina morsitans*, which is primarily a menace to cattle. The *morsitans* is found in a wide horse-shoe shaped region round the Nile swamps, in an area far enough south to have sufficient rain and high enough to be above the swamp land near the river (Fig. 96). It has caused great hardship to the Zande, by preventing them from keeping cattle. Moreover, the biggest and most important belt of *morsitans* country is that lying immediately south of the big swamps, and this effectively shuts off the cattle-owning tribes of the northern part of Equatoria Province from the agricultural tribes of the south. This belt of fly country is thus a barrier to what might well be a lucrative intertribal trade. The diet of the vegetarian agricultural tribes would be improved by regular supplies of meat, while their crops would be acceptable to the cattle-owning tribes of the north. What is more alarming is that there is much evidence to show that, despite all precautions, the fly is extending its range northwards in places, and is limiting the number of cattle that the Dinka can keep. The Moru around Amadi had quite large herds within living memory, but are now almost purely agriculturalists. Much the same is happening to the Latuka. It seems that movements of wild game are largely to blame for the spread of the fly. The remedy often causes as much distress as the pestilence itself. To move out the cattle may result in overgrazing and famine in neighbouring territories. To cut or burn vegetation may rid a district of fly, but at the expense of eroded soil and dried-out streams, which leave a desert where formerly there was good pasture. So far there has been some success from an opposite approach, to protect a barrier belt against fire until the vegetation becomes so thick that the fly cannot penetrate it.

Glossina palpalis, which carries the most serious form of sleeping-sickness which attacks humans, is more restricted in its habitat, keeping to riverain districts within the main *morsitans* area. In its case, countermeasures include controlling the movements of the population, and restricting the range of the fly by means of clearings and screens.

Manifestly, the southern provinces have their own particular problems, such as this of the tsetse fly, and for the administration present a problem quite different from that of the northern districts.   In view of this, the requests from the south for a federal status are understandable.

The external economy of the Sudan is largely dependent on cotton, which, along with cotton-seed, makes up 60 per cent of the total exports.   For the rest, gum arabic from the acacia woods of Kordofan (with almost a world monopoly) is next in importance, while cattle, oilseeds, groundnuts and hides account for most of the remainder of the export trade of the country.

REFERENCES

There is an extensive literature, in English alone, on various aspects of the territory and people of Egypt.   The following selection will, it is hoped, prove useful :

Atlas of Egypt, Survey of Egypt, Giza, 1928.
Ball, J., ' Contributions to the Geography of Egypt ', Survey and Mines Dept., Cairo, 1939.
Bonné, A., *The Economic Development of the Middle East*, London, 1945.
' Climatological Normals for Egypt and the Sudan ', Ministry of Public Works, Physical Dept., Cairo, 1938.
Colvin, Sir A., *The Making of Modern Egypt*, London, 1906.
Craig, J. J.*, The Rains of the Nile Basin*, Cairo, 1913.
Cromer, Earl of, *Modern Egypt*, 2 vols., London, 1908.
Hallberg, C. W., *The Suez Canal*, Columbia University Press, 1931.
Hoskins, H. L., *British Routes to India*, London, 1928.
Hume, W. F., *Geology of Egypt*, Vol. I, The Surface Features, Cairo, 1925.
Hurst, H. E., ' Progress in the Study of the Hydrology of the Nile in the last 20 years ', *Geog. Jour.*, Vol. LXX, 1927.
Hurst, H. E., Phillips, P., and Black, R. P., *The Nile Basin*, 7 vols., Cairo, 1931–46.
Issawi, C., *Egypt : an Economic and Social Analysis*, London, 1947.
Lorin, H., *L'Egypte d'aujourd'hui : le pays et les hommes*, Cairo, 1926.
Lozach, J., *Le Delta du Nil*, Cairo, 1935.
Lozach, J., and Hug, G., *L'Habitat rural en Egypte*, Cairo, 1930.
Macdonald, Sir M., *Nile Control*, Cairo, 1920.
Maurette, F., *Afrique Equatoriale, Orientale et Australe*, Tome XII, Géographie Universelle, Paris, 1938.
Mosséri, V. M., *Du sol égyptien sous le régime de l'arrosage par inondation*, Bull. Inst. Egypt., 1922–3.
La fertilité de l'Egypte, Compte rendu, Congrès Inter. de Géog., Cairo, 1926.
M. Travers Symons, *Britain and Egypt : the Rise of Egyptian Nationalism*, London, 1925.
Murray, G. W. (ed.), *The Survey of Egypt, 1848–1948*, Surv. of Egypt, Departmental Paper No. 50 (1950).
Report, International Cotton Congress, held in Egypt, 1927.
Report, The Nile Projects Commission, Cairo, 1920.
Schmidt, A., *Cotton-Growing in Egypt*, Manchester, 1912.
Semple, E. C., *The Geography of the Mediterranean Region*, London, 1932.

' The Nile Waters Agreement ', Cmd. 3348 H.M. Stat. Off., 1929.

Toussoun (Prince), *Mémoire sur l'Histoire du Nil*, Mémoires de l'Institut d'Egypte, Cairo, 1925.

' La Géographie de l'Egypte a l'Epoque Arabe ' (*Mem. Soc. Roy. d'Egypte*, Tome VIII, 1), 1926.

Toynbee, A. J., *Survey of International Affairs*, 1925, Vol. I, The Islamic World since the Peace Settlement, 1925.

Willcocks, W., and Craig, J., *Egyptian Irrigation*, 3rd ed., London, 1913.

SUDAN

Allen, R. W., ' The Gezira Irrigation Scheme ', *Journal of the African Society*, Vol. 25, 1926.

Bloss, J. F. E., ' The Tsetse Fly in the Sudan ', *Sudan Notes and Records*, Vol. XXVI, Pt. I, 1945, pp. 139–56.

Evans-Pritchard, E. E., *The Nuer*, Oxford, 1940.

' Nilotic Studies ', *Journ. Roy. Anthrop. Inst.*, Vol. LXXX (1950), pp. 1–6.

Gaitskell, A., ' The Sudan Gezira Scheme ', *African Affairs*, vol. 51 (1952), pp. 306–13.

Hamilton, J. A., *The Anglo-Egyptian Sudan from Within*, London, 1935.

Hill, R. L., *A Bibliography of the Anglo-Egyptian Sudan*, Oxford, 1939.

Lewis, D. J., ' The Ṭsetse Fly Problem in the Anglo-Egyptian Sudan ', *Sudan Notes and Records*, Vol. XXX, Pt. II (1949), pp. 179–211.

Nadel, S. F., *The Nuba*, London, 1947.

Newhouse, F., ' The Draining of the Upper Nile ', London, 1939.

Tothill, Dr. J. D. (ed.), *Agriculture in the Sudan*, Oxford, 1948.

CHAPTER VIII

ABYSSINIA AND ITS BORDERLANDS

SEPARATE attention to the high plateaux (and their maritime borderlands) of North-East Africa is justified mainly by the characteristics of a civilization which is almost completely separated from the Bantu world of East and Central Africa. Geographical detachment from the lands of the lower Nile has been much more complete than from Arabia, and Abyssinia, together with the drier lands which limit it on the east, was the first African zone to experience the influence of the Semitic world; and this at a time which, by innumerable centuries, antedated the coming of Islam to East and North-East Africa.

The virtual isolation from Egypt, promoted by the forbidding ramparts of the Ethiopian Massif, has its counterpart on the southern margin of the region, where the intervention of an arid, sparsely-populated zone, extending both north-westwards and south-eastwards of Lake Rudolf, isolates Abyssinia from the main mass of the East African Plateau. This southern zone of separation extends between the basin of the River Sobat and the Jubaland coast, with an average width of considerably more than one hundred miles; and its torrid aridity, hostile to life, suggests a 'marcher' zone, alike in a cultural and in a political sense. The Bantu have not been entirely excluded by it, but their penetration northwards has been in small, easily-absorbed numbers. There can be no doubt that this arid depression, between the East African Plateau and the Abyssinian Massifs, provides one of the most complete ethnological 'divides' of the entire continent. The zone of drought which laps around Abyssinia on north, west and south is continued in the Eritrean and Somaliland coastlands, which complete the encirclement of our region.

Until the middle years of the 1930–40 decade, the territorial holdings by European Powers were confined to the Somaliland

and Eritrean coasts, whose ports—especially Assab (Italian), Massowah (Italian), Jibuti (French) and Zeila (British)—were of special consequence, though more because of their relationships with the navigation of the narrow Straits of Bab-el-Mandeb than because of their possibilities as starting-points for the commercial or political penetration of the hinterland.

THE PHYSICAL ENVIRONMENT

Our region is one of impressive physical diversity, wherein attention is inevitably directed towards the Highlands, which

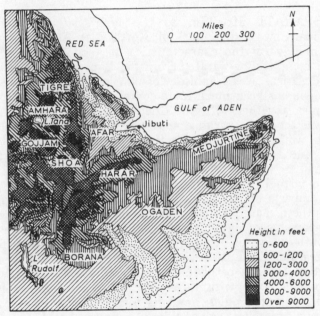

FIG. 97.—Orography of Abyssinia and the ' Horn '

at many points ascend to levels of 13,000 feet and more above sea-level. These vast spaces of lofty plateaux owe their origin and present physical character to the series of great crustal dislocations and eruptions which, beginning in Upper Jurassic times, continued through the Cretaceous and Tertiary Ages. For these tectonic events the extensive outpouring of lava and the existence of the Great Rift Valley, traversing Abyssinia diagonally, provide the most obvious evidence.

From the south of the region, in the neighbourhood of Lake Rudolf, the Rift Valley can be traced along its two bifurcations.

The less important branch leads north-westwards from Lake
Rudolf to the lower basin of the River Sobat, but its line is not
easily visible, except on a large-scale map : the other, deeper
and more continuous, is directed north-eastwards towards the
Red Sea, and is, in part, occupied by a chain of lakes, some of
which—notably Lake Margherita, 50 miles long—are of considerable magnitude. This, the main branch of the Rift Valley,

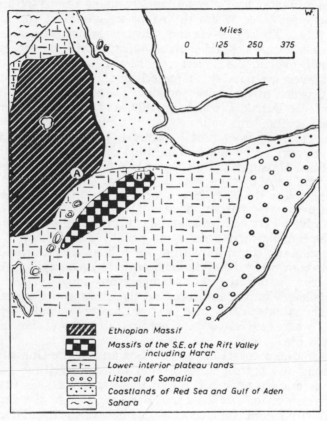

Fig. 98.—Climatic Provinces of North-East Africa

divides the Abyssinian Highlands into two geographically unequal
parts, namely :

   (a) the Ethiopian Massif proper, including the provinces of
Tigre, Amhara, Shoa and Kaffa ;

   (b) the narrow zone of high plateaux, extending from Harar
province south-westwards, along the eastern flank of the Rift
Valley.

Over each region igneous rocks, mainly basalts and trachytes, are widely developed, and their great thickness—as much as 6000 feet in parts of the province of Shoa—bears impressive witness to the scale of the crustal events which produced them.

Farther east, and outside of Ethiopia proper (though controlled until recently by Abyssinian rulers), are found less elevated and more arid plateau lands, ranging from 1500 to 5000 feet above sea-level, where the Archaean basement rocks occur extensively. Their gneisses and schists weather, as a rule, into poor, sandy soils, which, taken in conjunction with the meagreness of rainfall, explain the poverty of the vegetation. These lower plateau levels are notably characteristic of the great province of Ogaden, which merges with Somaliland, and also of the ' plains of Afar ' (or Danakil), which provide, as it were, the northern vestibule to the Rift Valley.

The greatest orographical contrast throughout the entire region is provided by the juxtaposition of the immense rampart of the Shoa Massif, attaining abruptly a height of 9000 feet, and the plateau of Afar, some 5000 feet below. In the recent Italo-Abyssinian war the Natives tended to regard this great wall as an insurmountable barrier, lying in the way of the main line of Italian advance from Eritrea, and its impregnability had certainly been dependable in days of more primitive armament.

The climatic contrasts within North-East Africa are perhaps the least-known features of its much-neglected geography. Aridity and torrid characteristics of temperature have tended to be over-emphasized, probably because the European Powers have had their contacts mainly with the coastal lands, outside Abyssinia proper, where excessive temperature and desert-like aridity dominate life.

The southern coasts of the Red Sea and of the Gulf of Aden are among the hottest lands of the world. Maritime position brings practically no relief, for in these enclosed seas the land areas predominate. At Zeila and Berbera,[1] two of the very few stations with records for a considerable period, the mean temperatures for June, July and August exceed 90° F. in each month, and, as usual on these coasts, the annual as well as the diurnal range is very moderate. Farther into the interior, owing to ' continentality ' and to relatively high altitude, the diurnal range in ' winter ' is very wide—as it is in other desert lands at this season.

On the Ethiopian Massif, where contrasts of altitude are

---

[1] Mean temperatures at Berbera are as follows :

Jan.	Feb.	Mar.	Apr.	May	June	July	Aug.	Sept.	Oct.	Nov.	Dec.	Range
76°	76°	78°	82°	87°	96°	97°	97°	91°	83°	79°	77°	21°

marked, three zones are distinguished by the inhabitants ; they are :

(a) the *kolla*, extending up to approximately 5500 feet, where mean monthly temperatures exceed 68° F. It is indeed doubtful if the thermometer ever registers under 68° F. ;

(b) the *woina-dega*, between the upward limit of the *kolla* and 8000 feet. Cool nights (41°–50° F.) are common in winter, and the temperature range is similar to that of the Kenya Highlands. Like Nairobi, Addis Ababa (at 8000 feet above sea-level) has no monthly mean under 58° F. or over 66° F.—the annual range in the case of each town being 7 degrees. Within this zone there is the greatest concentration of population to be found in Abyssinia ;

(c) above 8000 feet, the *dega* zone, where it is always cool and the mean of the three hottest months—March, April and May—is only slightly more than 60° F. It is to be noted that May has the highest temperatures of the year, as also in the North-West of India, whose monsoonal climate has certain similarities to that of North-East Africa. The later months— June, July and August—are cooled by the cloud cover, and by the rains which accompany the onset of the summer monsoon. The comparatively low temperatures of the *dega* would seem to be an advantage to human settlement, but this advantage is considerably offset by atmospheric rarefaction, which makes work, or even residence, rather exhausting for the settler.

On the plateaux of Harar, Shoa, Amhara and Tigre the rainfall of summer is regular and in fair abundance. The Harar Highlands receive from 20 to 35 inches in the year, and, as evaporation is not excessive at over 6000 feet, the rains are sufficient for permanent agriculture. On the Ethiopian Massif rain occurs in each month of the year, so that there is no completely dry season. Addis Ababa, the only station with records for a considerable period, may be regarded as typical of the Massif's rainfall régime. Its main season of rains is from June to October, with 11 inches in July and 12 inches in August—the annual amount being considerably more than 45 inches. Again, as on the Harar Highlands, lofty elevation increases the value of the precipitation by reducing evaporation.

By way of systematizing our knowledge of the climates of North-East Africa, we may distinguish the following ' climatic provinces ' :

(1) The Ethiopian Massif

Temperatures vary greatly according to altitude, but generally the coolest conditions in North-East Africa are found here. The rainfall is abundant, and better distributed than elsewhere, although the emphasis on midsummer precipitation is strongly marked.   Torrid conditions prevail in the deep and narrow valleys which dissect the Massif.

(2) The Massifs to the South-East of the Rift Valley, including Harar

Many of the conditions of (1) are repeated, but there are the following important differences : with lower average altitude, temperatures are higher, though in the valleys, which are wider and less sunken than those of Ethiopia proper, conditions are actually less torrid.   The summer rainfall is regular in occurrence, but less plentiful than that of (1).

(3) Lower Interior Plateau Lands

Temperatures are excessively high, but there is a wide diurnal range.   Rainfall confined to ' summer ' is precarious, and averages about 15 inches.

(4) Littoral of Somalia

The principal difference from (3) is an even lower and more precarious rainfall, which averages less than 10 inches.

(5) Coastlands of the Red Sea and Gulf of Aden

The torrid conditions of (3) and (4) are here still more intensified.   There is a meagre rainfall of not more than 5 inches (Berbera, 2·5 ins.) brought by the north-east monsoon of ' winter ', and deposited mainly on the hills behind the coast.

The meteorological problem concerned with the origin of the rains which reach western districts of the Ethiopian Massif is still unsolved, and it is not yet known to what extent this precipitation is dependent on winds drawn in from the Indian Ocean, or on winds which originate over the Southern Atlantic and thereafter cross Central Africa as south-westerlies.   Certainly, the summer rainfall of Eastern Somalia and of eastern parts of Ogaden province is due to the prevailing monsoon of March–September, which blows as a south-wester along the Somaliland coast.   On the other hand, little or nothing is known of the strength, humidity or direction of the air currents over vast areas of Western Abyssinia, and statements concerning the climatic peculiarities of this region must be accepted with reserve.

The zoning of vegetation closely reflects the climatic distinctions which we have noted.   On the high plateaux it varies according to altitude in the following manner :

(a) Luxuriant forest occupies the western districts of the

Ethiopian Massif, although occasionally interrupted by stretches of park savanna.

(*b*) Over the remainder of the Ethiopian Massif, and on the highlands to the south-east of the Rift Valley (e.g. Harar), at elevations from 6000 to 9000 feet, woodland savanna is widely developed, with tree-growth more and more noticeable towards the west.

(*c*) Over the extreme eastern districts of the high plateaux, where the rains become unreliable, the savanna deteriorates, and gives place to scrubby steppe.

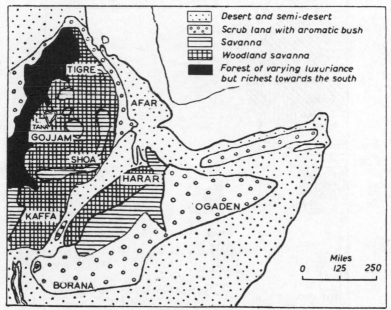

FIG. 99 —The Zones of Vegetation : North-East Africa

(*d*) On the lowlands and low plateaux—e.g. Afar, Eastern Somalia, Eastern Ogaden and the lands adjoining Lake Rudolf—semi-desert or actual desert prevails. In the hills behind the Gulf of Aden coast there is much thorn-bush, and here are found the small bushes, still valued for their aromatic resins, which, in Biblical times, were much sought by traders.

The zoning of vegetation is shown again in the geographical range of cultivated plants. Within the *kolla* of Ethiopia tropical and sub-tropical cultivation includes the banana and cotton, although, as this zone is neglected by agriculturists, the output is on an insignificant scale. In the *woina-dega*, the main zone of agriculture and of sedentary settlement, the highly fertile soils of its woodland savanna could be widely used for coffee, which is here indigenous ; whilst the *dega* is specially associated with maize and millet cultivation. Above 10,000 feet, there is much grass, short and lush, which has a closer resemblance to Alpine pastures than to the normal dry grass cover of the African veld.

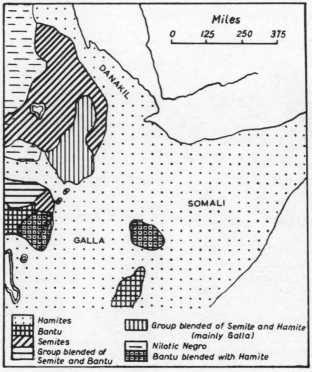

FIG. 100.—Distribution of Ethnic Groups in North-East Africa

Very hot and humid, with a considerable extent of dense forest, the *kolla* zone is generally avoided as unhealthy, whereas the *woina-dega*, without excessive temperatures, has the additional advantage of a reliable and well-distributed rainfall. The greater part of the southern half of the Ethiopian Massif is devoted to tillage, but farther north, where the country is drier as well as cooler, stock-rearing becomes the dominant interest.

From this study of climatic and vegetation zones it emerges that, economically, the most desirable region of Abyssinia comprises the western districts which, from both the Red Sea and Indian Ocean coasts, are the most inaccessible parts of the entire country.

On the Highlands, where agriculture is practised, such husbandry is mainly the work of the Galla people, who are of Hamitic stock ; but in the extreme south of the Highlands—especially parts south-east of the Rift Valley—both Galla and Bantu people are engaged in tillage. The Abyssinians proper are rarely farmers, yet they are the proprietors, and represent a social caste rather than a race apart. (We shall refer later to their ethnic affinities.) Farming by the Galla and Bantu is a very primitive art, although, considering the equipment, the practice is reasonably efficient. Their irrigation equipment is that of the Egyptians of past millennia, and their ploughs are of wood. The staple crops are for subsistence, as foreign trade, or even inter-regional exchange, is on a very small scale.

EXTERNAL RELATIONS AND THE PROGRESS OF SETTLEMENT

The small dimensions of foreign trade in recent times are an index of the geographical isolation of the region and of the difficulty of access from one part of the country to another.

The most ancient commerce of Ethiopia was carried on with the Egypt of the Pharaohs, and two main routes were then employed : one passed up the Nile to Khartoum and penetrated Ethiopia by way of the Blue Nile, while the other—a maritime route—was used by the Pharaohs as far as Assab (which some suppose to be the original Sheba). The Arab invasions cut the Sudan route, and this highway for caravans was not re-opened until Kitchener's conquest of the Eastern Sudan, late in the nineteenth century.

During the eighteenth century Massowah was the port terminus of a caravan track from Ethiopia to the Red Sea, and it was from here that the Scottish explorer, Bruce, started on his search for the source of the Blue Nile. The Negus, Menelik II, greatly encouraged trade between Abyssinia and the Red Sea coast, and Massowah continued to be the chief outlet for merchandise. A less important, but continuously-used, route (from the sixteenth to the nineteenth century) led from the town of Harar to the Benadir coast, in what is now the south of Italian Somaliland.

Addis Ababa became the chief market in Abyssinia, when, in the late years of the nineteenth century, the Negus, Menelik II, selected its site—at a height of 8000 feet above sea-level—as his new capital: and its dominating importance in the commercial life of the country was confirmed, when the railway from Jibuti (Fr. Somaliland) was extended to it in 1929. Tracing the course of the ' Jibuti Railway ', it will be noted that it utilizes the groove of the Rift Valley for about 100 miles, in its approach to Addis Ababa. This town is in the very heart of Shoa, the most central province of Abyssinia ; and it was from here that Menelik II extended his authority over the eastern provinces of Harar and Ogaden. Until very recent times, the old town of Harar was the principal market of the entire region, and, in particular, it controlled the trade in *mocha* coffee, which was brought by caravan from various parts of the Ethiopian Massif (especially Kaffa Province), and from Harar Province itself. Much of this trade persists, although the town of Harar inevitably loses by the distance which separates it from the Jibuti Railway, which passes to the north, in the valley below. Under the heights of the plateau, on which Harar town stands, there is the newly-created town of Addis Harar, which, situated on the Jibuti Railway and developing in response to the commerce of that highway, has largely replaced the older town above it. The cosmopolitan character of old Harar, and the range of its former commercial contacts, are indicated by the large number of Indian and Arab traders in its population of 40,000, all told. In the Moslem world the prestige of no town in Abyssinia is as high as that of Harar : for it is regarded as the headquarters of Islam, in this region of Africa.

As late as 1935, apart from the Jibuti Railway, 487 miles in length, which is French-owned and French-controlled, Ethiopia had no railway, and no roads fit for motor traffic outside the immediate vicinity of the two largest towns—Addis Ababa and Harar.

The geographical diversity of the regions of Abyssinia largely determines the separate existence of a number of communities, each with ethnic individuality. From the most remote antiquity of which there is any record, people of Semitic stock, traditionally regarded as the ancestors of the Amhara Abyssinians, have occupied the high plateaux both to the north and south of the Rift Valley. At the southern extremity of the region, especially in the neighbourhood of Lake Rudolf, there was, at a very early time, a tendency for Bantu negro people to penetrate northwards ; but the geographical limits of this movement may be regarded as falling short of the province of Shoa. It should be remembered that, in their earliest migrations, the Bantu of East Africa pressed southwards from the ' Horn ' into Kenya and Uganda : and it is possible, as an alternative theory explaining the presence of the Bantu in southern Ethiopia, that these groups were left behind in the first southward migrations of the Bantu family of peoples.

A third element of first-class importance in the population of Abyssinia and the ' Horn ' is that which predominates within the eastern plateau lands, including Harar and Ogaden, as well as the maritime borders along the Indian Ocean, Gulf of Aden and Red Sea. Here is the Hamitic zone, in which the Galla and Somali are the characteristic groups. These people are supposed to have entered North-East Africa from Southern Arabia at a very remote time, though subsequent to the southward migration of the Bantu from the ' Horn '. Because of the precarious and scanty rainfall of these parts, the Hamites, unlike their Galla brethren of Ethiopia proper, are pastoral nomads, whose nomadism is, however, increasingly restricted, with the extension of European authority.

During the sixteenth century the Hamites of the ' Horn ' began a prolonged movement of widespread expansion : this was associated with the religious influence of Islam, to which they had been converted by contacts with the Arabs of Oman, who traded on the East African coast, from Cape Guardafui as far south as the Zambezi delta. The Danakil and Somali Hamites made a series of assaults on the high plateaux occupied by the Abyssinians, who, although Semitic, had long accepted Christianity. They found it impossible to scale the great eastern ramparts of Shoa and Tigre, but they were more successful in obtaining a foothold in Harar Province. The Hamitic Galla were pushed forward by the advance of the Somali and Danakil (who are now confined to Eritrea and Afar), and of all Hamitic peoples they have the closest contacts with the Semitic Abyssinians, as well as with the Bantu. It has been estimated that the Galla, both the relatively pure and the mixed types, number more than one-half of the total population of Abyssinia, which has been put at $21\frac{1}{2}$ millions (1962).

Because of long-continued intermixture with Semitic and Bantu strains, there are very few of the Galla who may, even approximately, be described as ' pure '. The Semitic strain is not nearly so easily perceived as the Bantu, owing to the fundamental resemblances between Hamite and Semite. Like the Somali and the Danakil, the very few Galla tribesmen who resemble the ideal type are fairly tall, of thin build and with long face and aquiline nose. More detached from the Bantu zone, the Somali and Danakil show more frequently the characteristic Hamitic features, though even amongst these communities there is a tendency towards negroid woolliness of hair.

The modern Abyssinians, who claim purity of Semitic descent, are themselves mixed with Hamitic, Bantu and Nilotic blood ; and these strains appear even amongst the Amhara Abyssinians, who regard themselves as racially exclusive.

During the nineteenth century the Semitic Abyssinians, from their bases in Amhara, Tigre and Shoa, began the re-conquest of the southern and eastern plateau lands ; and their expansion culminated in 1880–1900, during the reign of the Negus, Menelik II. It was in this period—actually in the year 1896—that an Italian force, invading from the Red Sea coast, was annihilated at Adowa. This defeat rankled for long in the minds of imperialistic Italians, who have found in its memory an incentive to the recovery of their lost military prestige. Although successful in their conquest of the Hamitic groups, the Abyssinians were not able to displace them from occupancy of the land. Yet they exerted an overlordship, and especially over the Galla, who, though pastoralists by tradition, readily applied themselves to agriculture in their settlement of southern parts of the Ethiopian Massif, including, most notably, Shoa.

We have seen that the first attempts made by a European Power to penetrate Abyssinia were frustrated by the strength of Menelik II, who, after the conquest of his empire, established his headquarters at Addis Ababa, in the province of Shoa. In 1906, an agreement between Abyssinia and the three European Powers—Great Britain, France and Italy—all with special interests on the Red Sea and Gulf of Aden littoral, confirmed the Abyssinian Emperor in his conquests, although nowhere was his authority permitted to reach the sea-board. By this time, the entire shore-line, from the northern limit of Eritrea round to Jubaland, was claimed by one or other of the three Powers already named.

In 1867, France had obtained a title to the harbour of Obok, at the entrance to the Gulf of Tadjura—the largest inlet on the North-East African coast—and within 50 miles of the Straits of Bab-el-Mandeb. This first-class strategic position was greatly improved by France, when Jibuti, at the opposite side of the entrance to the Gulf of Tadjura, was preferred to Obok as the French Somaliland naval base, and as the terminus of the railway from Addis Ababa. Jibuti was annexed by France in 1884, and within a decade the Negus, Menelik II, was co-operating in the construction of the railway which, passing by way of Addis Harar, reached the Abyssinian capital, in 1926.

Italy was almost equally early in the field, for in 1869 a commercial company of Italians was established at Assab, the port which had been, throughout a large part of the history of Ethiopia, the principal maritime outlet. From the foundation of this trading interest on the Eritrean coast may be traced the increasingly-menacing competition between Italy and France for strategic supremacy, in those waters and along those coasts that lead from the Eastern Mediterranean to the Indian Ocean. After proclaiming sovereignty over Assab in 1882, Italy proceeded to annex the sister-port of Massowah, also on the Eritrean coast, but 300 miles farther to the north ; and then, in 1890, to occupy the territory between these two port bases. In such ways began the history of the Italian Empire in Africa.

Annexation of the eastern coast of the Somaliland ' Horn ' was carried, stage by stage, in a similar way. In 1889, by arrangement with the Sultan of Obbia (approximately midway along the Somaliland coast), Italy obtained a concession which meant, in effect, full sovereignty of rights. And so the Italians were brought into uneasy territorial contact with the Negus, Menelik II, who, at this time, was extending his authority east-wards across Ogaden towards the Somaliland littoral. In 1901, a treaty with another Moslem chief, the Sultan of Medjurtine, gained for Italy the hinterland of Cape Guardafui and an extent of coast along the Gulf of Aden of not less than 150 miles. Here, Italian Somaliland marches with the British Protectorate, which covers the greater part of the Gulf of Aden shore on the African side. This British zone had been acquired in 1882, in the same series of events which had established Great Britain in Egypt and in the dependencies of Egypt, including the Eastern Sudan: for Britain came to regard herself as responsible for the commitments of the Khedive of Egypt, who had interests on the Gulf of Aden coast, especially in the neighbourhood of Zeila and Berbera.

Subsequently, Italy added to her territory of Somaliland the Benadir coast, with the port of Mogadishu, acquired from the Sultan of Zanzibar, and Jubaland, part of which was transferred from Abyssinia in 1908, and part from Kenya after the First World War. By the Tripartite Agreement of 1906, France, Great Britain and Italy respected one another's interests in Abyssinia, which were, briefly, to prolong the Jibuti railway, to build a barrage at Lake Tana, and to construct a railroad through Abyssinia from Italian Somaliland to Eritrea. According to the Hoare-Laval Agreement of 1935, Italy was to be given portions of Abyssinian territory near the Eritrean and Somaliland borders, and rights to develop the southern part of the country, in exchange for an Abyssinian corridor to the port of Assab. This agreement aroused wide opposition and was never applied. By 1936 Italy had annexed the whole of Abyssinia ; colonization was begun immediately, especially in Eastern Amhara, in the southern highlands of Sidamo, and near the towns of Addis Ababa and Harar.

The settlement of Italians on the land, an enterprise from which much was expected and for which extravagant prophecies were made, occurred in two principal ways.

First, the establishment of peasant proprietors, with freehold titles to their plots, such as the settlement at Oletta, a few miles to the west of Addis Ababa, where 200 demobilized soldiers and their families were accommodated on land which formerly belonged to the estates of the Negus. The altitude at Oletta varies from 6500 to 7500 feet, and the soil of the colony's 30,000 acres is all of high fertility. Each family was allotted about 120 acres, an area obviously too large for cultivation by a single family, without other aid.

Another type of settlement was that of the *métayer* tenant, who paid with part of the produce of his labour for his occupation of the land and for the assistance which he received in the form of seeds and farming equipment. This system of land-tenure is common enough in Southern Italy, and it was from that region the *métayer* peasants were recruited. Two land-development companies, in the districts of Asmara and Harar, respectively, engaged and were dependent on such labour.

Despite declarations to the contrary, Italian policy accepted, perforce, the principle that European settlement in Abyssinia should be, at least partially, dependent on native manual labour; and there can be no possible doubt that this change in the official attitude was mainly due to difficulties of acclimatization encountered by those Italians who were " planted " at altitudes exceeding 6000 feet. With special advantages of soil and rainfall, much of the best land on the Ethiopian Massif ranges from 7500 to 10,000 feet, and sojourn at such altitudes is quite outside the experience of the Italians, as a people. Atmospheric rarefaction, rather than low latitude, will remain the insuperable barrier to the effective colonization of Ethiopia, as it has also in the cases of the Kenya Highlands and the Andean Plateau of Spanish South America. By 1939 there were signs that some of the Italian settlers who had entered Abyssinia immediately after the conquest had difficulty in maintaining their health at high altitudes. Members of the Italian administrative services in Addis Ababa demanded frequent leave of absence in order to obtain the relief which descent to sea-level alone can bring. On the other hand, those parts of Abyssinia which are below 5000 feet, and therefore more tolerable because of higher atmospheric density, are generally characterized by deficiency and variability of rainfall, and so are of low agricultural value.

It is difficult to estimate what might have been the economic prospects for Italian enterprise in Abyssinia, for most of the available statements on this subject are prejudiced by the point of view of the writer. Much depended on the pacification of the country and on the extent of native co-operation with the Italians. It has to be admitted that, after the Italo-Abyssinian War, many of the Natives showed a friendly disposition towards their masters who, on their part, acted more leniently than one could have foretold from the brutalities of the war. Racial segregation was not demanded by Italy, and the absence of colour prejudice on the part of the conquerors seemed likely to improve their relations with the Abyssinians.

Without the aid of accurate and detailed surveys—geological, climatological, &c.—which will take many laborious years to complete—it is not possible to obtain even an approximate picture of the future lines of agricultural and mining development. There is, however, sufficient to show that the available resources are at least as attractive to would-be settlers as those of Kenya Colony have proved to be ; and it may be noted in this con-nexion that, by the middle of 1939, the European residents of the town of Addis Ababa—almost all of them Italians—were already in numerical excess of the entire White population of Kenya Colony.[1]

The western lands of Abyssinia are, as we have seen, possessed of a climate which produces a luxuriant vegetation, and in these parts the possibilities for coffee in particular, cotton, cereals and stock-animals at various altitudes, would seem to be more favourable than in most areas of corresponding size in tropical Africa.

The mineral wealth of Abyssinia is perhaps the least-known factor, and on this subject speculation is quite worthless. In-vestigations made by Italian men of science over a period of more than three years suggest that there are no dramatic sur-prises in store. Platinum is present in quantities which were regarded as adequate for the requirements of Italy,[2] but the most sanguine of Italian prospectors had little hope of discovering considerable quantities of petroleum, which was more needed by the Italians than any other mineral resource.

The failure to discover petroleum was a particularly severe

---

[1] On May 1st, 1939, there were in Addis Ababa 30,200 Europeans, of whom 3800 were women. The White population had quickly risen from 5200 in 1937, and from 23,000 in 1938. In Kenya Colony, as a whole, the White settlers in 1948 did not exceed 30,000—after a period of colonization lasting over half a century.

[2] v. F. Quaranta, *Ethiopia : an empire in the making*, London, 1939.

disappointment, and soon had a sobering effect on the highly-ambitious programme of motor-road building which was begun in 1935. Large imports of petrol were virtually impracticable, on account of prohibitive costs. The aeroplane, which played an all-important part in the short-lived Italian conquest, is not designed for the economical transport of heavy freights—neither the raw materials which Abyssinia is to produce, nor the agricultural and other machinery which will be a normal import. Moreover, air services, like road transport, will be restricted by the high costs of fuel.

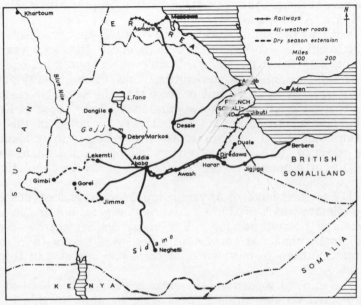

FIG. 101.—Ethiopia—Communications

For a very long time, therefore, the French-owned Jibuti Railway is likely to constitute one of the main arteries between the heart of the country and the outer lands. It is a narrow-gauge, single-track line whose carrying capacity, though increased to 250 tons a day, was quite incapable of transporting more than a small fraction of the traffic which resulted from the Italian occupation. Double-tracking is projected, indeed is long overdue ; and other improvements in the organization of the railway are likely to be undertaken. At the time of her annexation of Abyssinia, Italy obtained a proportion of the shares of the company owning the Jibuti Railway. With the elimination of Italy from Africa, however, the Railway came under British military management. The other railway of Italian East Africa was built to serve the needs of Eritrea : its construction represents a triumph of engineering, for, leading inland from the port of Massowah, it scales the plateau escarpment at a height of nearly 8000 feet before reaching Asmara and Keren, the terminus north-west of Asmara.

In May, 1941, the reconquest of Abyssinia was complete, and the Negus was able to return to his Kingdom of Ethiopia. The 40,000 Italian civilians still living there were evacuated shortly afterwards. One valuable legacy of five years of Italian occupation was 4,300 miles of all-weather roads, of which 3,000 miles were macadamized or asphalted. The six chief highways were :

1. Addis Ababa to Asmara, via Dessie. (Asmara is the railhead for Massowah. Ethiopia has been guaranteed the free use of the ports of Massowah and Assab.)
2. Addis Ababa to Jimma (and forward to Gorei in the dry season).
3. Addis Ababa to Neghelli, via Shashmanna.
4. Addis Ababa to Dire Dawa, via Awash (with an extension to Duale in the dry season).
5. Addis Ababa to Assab, via Dessie, and to Lekemti (with an extension to Gimbi in dry weather).
6. Dire Dawa to British Somaliland, via Harar and Jigjiga.

Unfortunately, these roads have not been properly maintained, and in 1951 it appears that communications were poor and the outer provinces uncontrolled. However, some progress has been made since the International Bank for Reconstruction and Development made a loan in 1950–57 of 20 million dollars for road construction and maintenance, 3 millions for a new development bank, and 1½ millions for telecommunications. As a result, an imperial highways authority has been set up, which has rebuilt the bridge over the Gibbe on the Jimma road, and replaced by an all-season bridge the low-water pontoon structure over the Blue Nile on the road from the capital to Gojjam Province.

Recent efforts to improve the country's economy have included widespread inoculation of cattle against rinderpest and other diseases (with the help of the Food and Agricultural Organization of the United Nations), and the extension of cotton growing. Oil prospectors, too, have been at work, although the first wells sunk in Ogaden have proved dry.

Small quantities of gold, platinum and copper (at Ankober) are being mined, and there are factories at Dire Dawa for cement and cotton (established by the Emperor before the Italian occupation). At Addis Ababa the Italians began the manufacture of sacks, shoes, biscuits and flour, and these are still being made.

Other industries may be started after the Blue Nile source in Lake Tana has been harnessed to produce electricity, but this scheme, which will involve the collaboration of Egypt and the Sudan, is still in a tentative state.

The economy of Ethiopia is indeed still based almost entirely on agriculture. In 1963, coffee represented about 50 per cent of the country's exports, followed by pulses, oilseeds, hides, goat and sheep skins. Among the main imports were cotton goods (40 per cent) and salt (7 per cent). It is clear that Ethiopia, with a population estimated in 1962 at only 21½ millions, is still a very underdeveloped country, and her future will depend to a large degree on the success of her present efforts to attract capital investment.

The future of the former Italian colonies was determined by the General Assembly of the United Nations in a resolution of November 21st, 1949, and subsequent subsidiary resolutions. Italian authority was restored only in Somalia, and this merged with British Somaliland in July 1960 to become the independent republic of Somalia. Eritrea now constitutes an autonomous unit federated with Ethiopia under the Ethiopian crown, and on December 24th, 1951, the United Kingdom of Libya became the first independent state to be created by the United Nations. The ephemeral Empire of Italian East Africa has thus vanished. But both in the East and the North, the Italian colonists have proved both their industry and their need, and, under proper guidance, they may have a valuable part to play in the development of Africa.

An unresolved frontier dispute of long standing in the Horn of Africa arises from the irredentist claims of the Somali peoples. The Republic of Somalia, with a population of some 1,870,000, claims territory in the Ethiopian districts of Ogaden and Haud occupied by 750,000 Somalis, and parts of Northern Kenya where live a further 200,000. Somalia is diversifying its traditional pastoral economy by developing the growing of cotton, sorghum, and, in the hinterland of the expanding port of Kismayu near the southern frontier, plantation bananas.

REFERENCES

(*From the standpoint of the geographer the literature in English is particularly meagre.*)

Badoglio, P., *La Guerra d'Etiopia*, Milan, 1936. English edition, London, 1937.

Bruce, J., *Travels to discover the Source of the Nile* (ed. C. F. Beckingham), Edinburgh, 1964.

Buxton, David, *Travels in Ethiopia*, London, 1949.
' The Shoan plateau and its people : an essay in local geography ',
   Geog. Journ., Vol. CXIV (1949), pp. 157–172.
Cheesman, R. E., *Lake Tana and the Blue Nile*, London, 1936.
   Handbook of Ethiopia, Khartoum, 1940.
Dainelli, G., ' Italian Colonies ', *Geographical Review*, Vol. XIX, 1919.
Doresse, J., *Ethiopia*, London, 1960.
Dower, K. Gandar, *Abyssinian Patchwork*, London, 1949.
Grabham, G. W., and Black, R. P., *Report on the Mission to Lake Tana,
   1920–1*, Cairo, 1925.
Jones, A. H. M., and Monroe, E., *A History of Abyssinia*, Oxford, 1935.

Lipsky, G. A. (ed.), *Ethiopia, its people, its society, its culture*, New Haven,
   Conn., 1962.
Luther, E. W., *Ethiopia Today*, Stanford Univ. Press., 1958.

Trevankis, G. K. N., *Eritrea*, London, 1960.

Ullendorf, E., *The Ethiopians*, O.U.P. 1960.

APPENDIX A

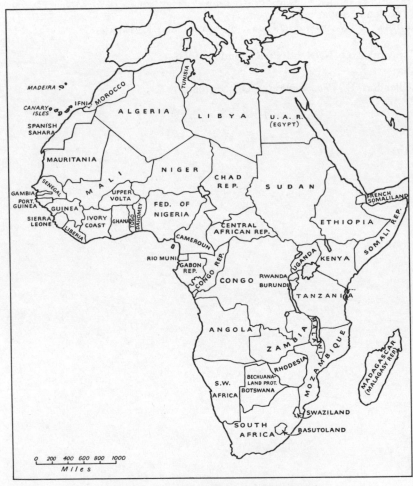

FIG. 102.—Political Map of Africa (1965)

APPENDIX B

WATER-POWER IN AFRICA

IN the Belgian Congo, the *Union Minière* had by 1957 harnessed the Lufina and Lualaba rivers. On this latter stream, the Le Marinal plant has an installed capacity of 248,000 kw., half that of the whole Upper Katanga. A transit line therefrom to Kitwe has been constructed as part of a general scheme of rural electrification in the Northern and Luapula provinces of Northern Rhodesia. In this same area there was opened, in April, 1960, the Kasama power station, linked to the Chishimba Falls. Ultimately the whole district should draw from Kariba.

By May, 1960, Ethiopia opened at Koka on the Awash river, a dam and station with a capacity of 43,000 kw.

On a much larger scale are the Owen Falls Dam in Uganda and the Kariba Dam in Southern Rhodesia (see pages 220–1), of which the first stage was opened in May, 1960. The second stage will cost £40 million, and will increase its capacity from 600 to 1500 megawatts.

The following major schemes have yet to be completed:

1. The Aswan High Dam, which will supply power to Egypt. It was begun in December, 1959, and will be completed in 1968.

2. A dam at Bujagali in Uganda, 4½ miles downstream from the Owen Falls Dam, and with twice its capacity.

3. The Ajena Dam on the Volta in Ghana (see page 356 and Fig. 75). It is now planned to produce power for general purposes as well as for smelting aluminium.

4. The Konkouré River and nearby Fria projects in Guinea, to produce 150,000 tons of aluminium annually from the vast bauxite deposits about Conakry. The cost will be about £215 million, to be raised internationally.

5. The Inga scheme, which will involve damming the Congo. It would be the largest hydro-electric station in the world, and would make of Leopoldville province 'an African Ruhr'. The cost would exceed £1000 million.

6. The Shiré River hydro-electric scheme in Nyasaland, which is expected to encourage aluminium, wood-pulp, fertilizer, ethyl-alcohol, and cotton industries in that country, and to provide power for Southern Rhodesia, including much which will be needed for drying tea and tobacco.

APPENDIX C

LIBYA

ON December 24th, 1951, the provinces of the former *Libia
Italiana* became the United Kingdom of Libya, the first
independent state to be created by the United Nations.
The Italian colonization of Libya began shortly after Italy took
over the country from Turkey in 1912, and continued till the Second
World War ; it won, over this period, considerable prestige, due largely
to the successful struggle of a hardworking peasantry in winning a
livelihood from the North African desert.

Under the term ' Libya ' there are the two separate provinces of
Tripolitania and Cyrenaica, the first much more extensive though less
habitable than the second. Cyrenaica recalls the ancient Greek
colony of Cyrene and is a peninsula detached to some extent from the
Libyan wilderness. Here is a plateau ridge—the Jebel el Akdar, or
Green Mountain—rising to over 2700 feet from the Mediterranean
coast. Save only the short-lived conquest of Ethiopia, of all former
Italian possessions in Africa this fragment of Cyrenaica was unique
in its comparative abundance of rainfall—20 inches covering 60 days
of the winter season—though on the coastal plain aridity is severe.
Even the capital—Benghazi—has only 8 inches per annum. Further
advantages to the settlement of Jebel el Akdar are the reduced summer
temperatures and the richer soils, whose humus recalls the former
forest (juniper, cypress, &c.) of this Mediterranean fringe.

Early in their colonization of northern Cyrenaica the Italians
appreciated that rainfall was adequate for olive cultivation and, except
in years of unusually long drought, for wheat also. By Government
order these two crops—both for subsistence use—were to be grown,
if necessary, to the exclusion of all others. In 1932 measures were
taken to drive the pastoral Arabs, to the number of 80,000, from the
Jebel el Akdar into the desert, and the brutality then shown will always
be associated with the name of General Graziani. The more humane
Balbo succeeded Graziani and in his day a meagre compensation of
10s. per acre was paid to the dispossessed Arabs. It was Balbo's
intention over a period of 10 years from 1938 onwards to instal 40,000
Italian settlers as farmers on the Jebel el Akdar. The outbreak of
the Second World War in 1939 seems to have cut short the most
promising plan of European settlement in Africa which has been tried
in modern times. From the most depressed areas of Italy in 1938

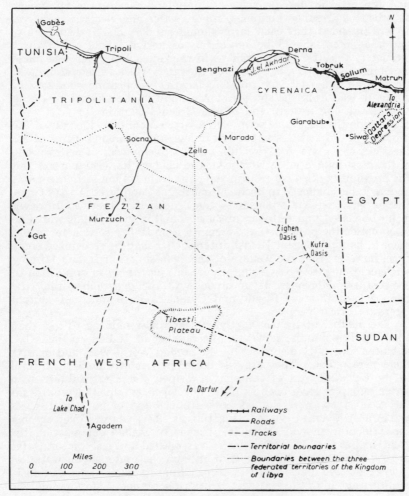

FIG. 103.—The Kingdom of Libya

a fleet of 16 ships brought combined families, with their social organization intact. The State provided not only land but also the equipment of private and public buildings, roads, water and electrical services. It was intended that each farm should support one Italian family, and that there should be no hiring of native labour. A project ultimately to settle 40,000 Italians in the Green Mountain area made inevitable the tapping of underground water, which is here abundant. In 1939 an aqueduct, 100 miles in length, was nearing completion : it was to lead from the springs of Ain Mara in the vicinity of Derna to Barce at the western end of the Green Mountain.

Outside the cultivable strip of the Green Mountain, the rest of the province of Cyrenaica is virtually rainless, and its main centres of life the oases of Kufara and Jaghlub. The Moslem order of Senussi, one of the most influential in North Africa, has here its headquarters and the proximity of Senussi resistance to the main Italian settlement was an inevitable challenge to both. First in 1943 and later in 1945 Great Britain gave explicit promises to the Senussi that they would never again be placed under Italian authority, and in view of this war-time intervention the protection of Cyrenaica from Italian settlement would seem to be a permanent British interest. It may be recognized some time, however, that the welfare of the Senussi and of Italian farming settlement on the Green Mountain are not inevitably in opposition to each other. Moreover, it is obvious to the geographer that the boundary contacts of Egypt and Cyrenaica have much of mutual interest to their peoples.

The number of Italians in Cyrenaica is now reduced to less than 200. In Tripolitania, however, the number of Italian colonists has not been so greatly disturbed by the Second World War, and in 1951 there were 45,800. They are distributed particularly along the littoral to the east and west of the city of Tripoli where the subterranean water resources have been skilfully developed. Tripoli city is by far the greatest concentration of both Italians and of natives (Berbers and Arabs). With a view to knitting as closely as possible together the Tripolitanian and Cyrenaican nuclei of Italian colonization the great highway—' La Littoranea '—was opened for fast motor traffic in 1937. To the south of the Gulf of Sidra the route is over waterless country for 450 miles, and the project from its outset was obviously as important from the strategic as from the economic standpoint. In addition to Tripolitania and Cyrenaica, there has been included in the new United Kingdom of Libya a third province, Fezzan, which had been under French administration since 1945. It is a desert area occupied by the Tibu people, whose affinities are with the Chad Colony and not with the coastal communities in the vicinity of Tripoli.

The circumstances of the rise of Arab national consciousness in this area, and the relations between Bedouin and Italians are fully described by Professor E. E. Evans-Pritchard in *The Sanusi of Cyrenaica* (Oxford, 1949).

APPENDIX D

OLD AND NEW ROUTES IN EAST AFRICA

RAILWAYS in these parts of Africa have never been planned continentally, nor even on a regional plan—if we exclude Cecil J. Rhodes' concept of a ' Cape-to-Cairo railway ' which would have depended in any case for its fulfilment on British domination throughout Africa. The existing lines were laid down piecemeal, from time to time, in isolation from each other and for some local purpose— defensive or economic ; and, far from assisting each other in the development of a region which they territorially shared, the competitive colonial Powers usually frustrated each other as much as possible in their railway enterprises ; as the British and French in West Africa, and the British and Germans in East Africa prior to 1919.

(a) The Mombasa–Kasese line—originally the Uganda Railway. The westward extension from Kampala to Kasese was opened in November 1956. The annual traffic carried (2 million tons) includes almost the entire Uganda cotton crop, one of the largest grown in the sterling area.

(b) Tanga–Arusha Railway (270 miles) of N.E. Tanganyika. The line (German built) climbs from the coast into the Usambara highlands, thence to Moshi below Mt. Kilimanjaro and on to Arusha below Mt. Meru (14,900 ft.). Here the main traffic is in sisal.

(c) Central Tanganyika Railway (also German built at the beginning of the century—to compete with the Uganda railway). These lines are being amalgamated with the Kenya–Uganda system, under the authority of the East African High Commission.

(d) Beira to Salima (Lake Nyasa).

(e) Beira to the Southern Rhodesian centres. Coal from Wankie and coffee from the coffee zone of both Katanga and N. Rhodesia are the main goods traffic (Fig. 38).

The most pressing of the new railway links required are :

(1) A short-circuiting of the last-named line between Salisbury and Lusaka ; it would save a detour of 500 miles.

(2) A line—about 80 miles—to link the Union system with the Rhodesian railways by way of Beit Bridge (across the Limpopo) north-west to West Nicholson or Fort Victoria (Fig. 38).

(3) A connexion between the two lines of Tanganyika would enable Mombasa to relieve these lines. Similarly Dar-es-Salaam would be able to serve Kenya in a reversal of need.

(4) Oldest perhaps amongst suggested links is one between the Rhodesian and Union lines on the one hand and those of British East Africa on the other. For this the unification of two distinct gauges would be a prerequisite.

(5) Not a link, but an entirely new line is directed towards the head of Lake Nyasa, near which the Njombi highlands are attractive for future White settlement.

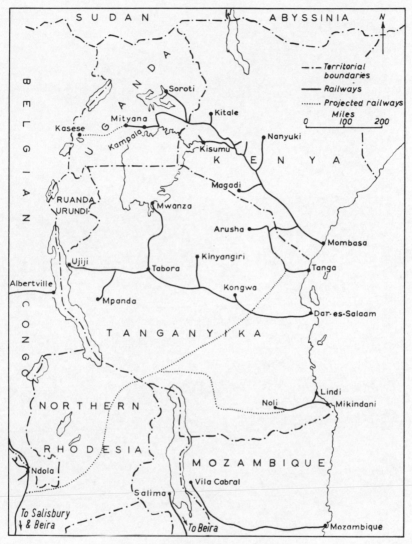

FIG. 104.—The Railways of East Africa

INDEX

ABEOKUTA, town and province, 117,
362, 365, 368
Abercorn, 217
Aberdare Plateau, 253
Abidjan, map, 326; 349, 351
Abu Hamed, 21, 449
Abyssinia, 5, 6, 10; physical, 21-2,
452-4; climate, 32, 33, 44,
50, 454-9; vegetation, 55,
454-9; exploration, 86;
population, etc., 106, 109,
110, 130, 425, **455-73**
Acacia bush, 53, 54, 55, 60, 61, 69,
154
Acclimatization of Europeans, 28,
43, 139, 141, 188, 199-200,
229, 283, 468
Accra, 37, 352, 355
Achimota College, 344
Achowa tribe, 218
Adamawa, 132, 316
Addis Ababa, 51, 459, 463, 466, 468,
469, 471
Addis Harar (see also Harar), 464,
466
Aden, 22; Gulf of, 22, 58, 458, 460,
467
Adowa, 103, 466
Afar plains, 21, 458, 461
Africa, origin of name, 75
African Association of London, 86
African Land Utilization and Settle-
ment Organization, 260
Afrikander cattle, 190
Agades, 415, 416
Agadir, 373
Agulhas, Bank, 12; Cape, 12, 63,
150
Ahaggar, 17, 18, 32, 56, 60, 129, 131,
327, 414
Ain Sefra, 413
Air, oases of, 414, 415, 416
Air services, 299, 300, 470, 480-1

Ajena, 356
Akabah, Gulf of, 4
Akamba, 121, 128, 256, 261
Akan, the, 353, 355
Akassa, rainfall, 38
Akida system, 241, 247
Alaotra, Lake, 267, 273
Albert, Lake, 6, 15, 39, 92, 121, 242,
422, 424, 431, 483
Albertville, 288, 295
Aleppo pine, 386
Alexander the Great, 76, 440
Alexandria, 67, 76, 100, 109, 434,
438, **440-1,** 444, 448, 449
Alfa (see Esparto)
Algeria, 18, 19, 60, 62, 89, 101,
132-4; **Part III, Chapter
VI (Barbary States)**
Algiers, 62, 64, 379, 385, 392, 394,
397, **411,** 413
Algoa Bay (see also Port Elizabeth),
80, 85, 192, 196
Aloe, the, 69, 154
Alpine mountain-building, 7; map,
18; 374, 376
Alluvium (see Soils)
Amadi, 452
Amani Institute, 233
Amazon Basin, 14; comparison
with Congo, 35, 36, 39, 42,
295
Amboro, Mt., 268
Amhara, the, 464, 466
Amhara Province, 457, 459, 467
Amin, 134
Anglo-Egyptian Sudan, see Sudan
(political state)
Angola, 3, 23, 24, 52, 80, 92, 125,
126, 185, 277, **278-84,** 289,
297, 476
Angoni, 124, 218, 223, 238
Angora goat, 169
Ankaratra Mts., 268

483